Augmented Reality

What is Augmented Reality?

Depiction of a 3D object being superimposed on top of a book using augmented reality FIG. 1

Augmented Reality is a technology that superimposes a computer-generated image onto a user's view of the real world in real-time. The augmented reality software that comes with this book, AR Engineering, helps you learn 3D visualization skills by combining virtual 3D models with real-time video. The result is a unique experience; an interactive world that makes the learning process faster and more engaging. This book represents a new way of adapting traditional engineering graphics materials to modern times.

About the AR Engineering Software

This textbook comes with augmented reality computer software and apps, called AR Engineering. AR Engineering is designed to be used while you progress through the text. The AR Engineering software and apps, in conjunction with the book, allow you to visualize the models described in the text in full 3D. Versions of the AR Engineering software are available for both the Mac and PC operating systems. AR Engineering apps are available for both Apple® iOS and Android® smartphones and tablets.

After you install the AR Engineering software or app onto your device, place the markers located throughout the book along with the large primary marker found at the front of this book, so they are both visible to your device's camera. A 3D model will appear on your screen, superimposed on top of the large marker. As you rotate and move the marker the 3D model will follow your movements, allowing you to manipulate the 3D model in real time.

AR Engineering Logo FIG. 2

Installation

Installing the AR Engineering Software

Load the CD, packaged with this book, into your computer. If your computer does not have a disc drive you can download the software from the publisher's website at www.SDCpublications.com. Locate the version of the software that matches your operating system and double click the software installer. A software installer will appear that will walk you through a series of steps to complete the installation.

Installing the AR Engineering Apps

Fig. 3 AR Engineering app QR code

AR Engineering for Apple® iOS devices can be downloaded from the Apple® App Store. AR Engineering for Android devices is available from the Google® Play Store. If your device has an app installed that can read QR codes you can use it to scan the QR code to the left (see Figure 3) and you will be redirected to the correct app for your device. Otherwise, visit your device's corresponding app store and search for AR Engineering. AR Engineering was developed by Bienetec.

Using the 3D models

In addition to the AR Engineering software and Apps, SolidWorks® files of the models used throughout the book are available. These files are included on the CD or are available for download from the publisher's website at www.SDCpublications.com. In addition, STL files have been provided so the models can be opened using your solid modeling CAD package of choice or printed using a 3D printer.

Using AR Engineering

1. Launch AR Engineering

Once you have the AR Engineering software or app installed on your device you will need to start the application. To start the software, locate and select the AR Engineering icon. If you are using the AR Engineering software on a Mac or PC you will need to have a webcam connected for the software to work correctly. The webcam can be a built-in or an external webcam.

If you are using the AR Engineering App, you will be given two viewing choices when the software loads. The app will ask you if you want to view the 3D models 'Without AR' or 'With AR'. Choosing 'Without AR' will allow you to view the 3D models without augmented reality. Choosing 'With AR' will allow you view the 3D models using augmented reality.

2. Scan the markers in the book

Starting in chapter two, at the top of many of the pages will be two black squares with white shapes inside of them. These are called markers. Place the book so your device's camera can see and detect the markers on the page. Green boxes will outline the markers when the software has successfully detected them. This tells the software what page you are on so it knows what 3D model to load. The chapter and section title will also now appear at the top of screen.

3. Manipulate the 3D model

Place the large marker located at the front of this book so that it is visible to your device's camera. A 3D model will appear on your screen superimposed on top of the marker. You can now interact with the 3D model. As you rotate and move the marker the 3D model will also follow your movements, allowing you to manipulate the 3D model in real time. (see Figure 4)

Depiction of the AR Engineering software in use FIG. 4

Troubleshooting

If you have trouble getting the software to recognize the markers, review the following tips:

- Be sure the marker is flat. If the marker is curved or bent the software might not correctly recognize its shape.
- Make sure your device's camera can "see" the entire marker. If the markers are even slightly covered, or not entirely visible to the camera, the virtual content will not display. Additionally, it is necessary to keep a small white margin around the marker.
- You may need to adjust your camera's distance from the marker. Try moving the marker closer or farther away from your device's camera. In some cases moving the marker farther away may make it easier for the software to detect it.
- Try adjusting the angle of the marker to the camera. Adjust the marker so that the camera points perpendicular to the marker.
- Make sure your device's camera is focused on the marker. If the camera is out of focus the marker will appear blurry and the software will not be able to recognize it.
- Check the lighting. If the lighting is too bright or too dark the software will have a hard time recognizing the marker. You may be able to adjust your camera's settings or the lighting in your room to correct this.

System Requirements

Mac and PC

- Intel Dual Core or higher
- 1 GB RAM (2 GB recommended)
- A computer with a webcam (built-in or external)

iOS and Android

- A smartphone or tablet with built-in camera

AR Engineering has been tested on Windows XP SP3 / Vista / Windows 7 / Windows 8 / iOS and Android Devices. The Mac version has been tested on Mountain Lion 10.8.2

Visualization and Engineering Design Graphics with Augmented Reality

Designed by:
Bienetec
www.bienetec.com

Cover Image:
The 3D model used on the front was provided courtesy of Steen Winther.

Published by:
Stephen Schroff
SDC Publications
P.O. Box 1334
Mission KS 66222
(913) 262-2664
www.SDCpublications.com

ISBN:
ISBN: 978-1-58503-905-0

Visualization and Engineering Design Graphics with Augmented Reality

Jorge Dorribo Camba
Jeffrey Otey
Manuel Contero
Mariano Alcañiz

Table of Contents

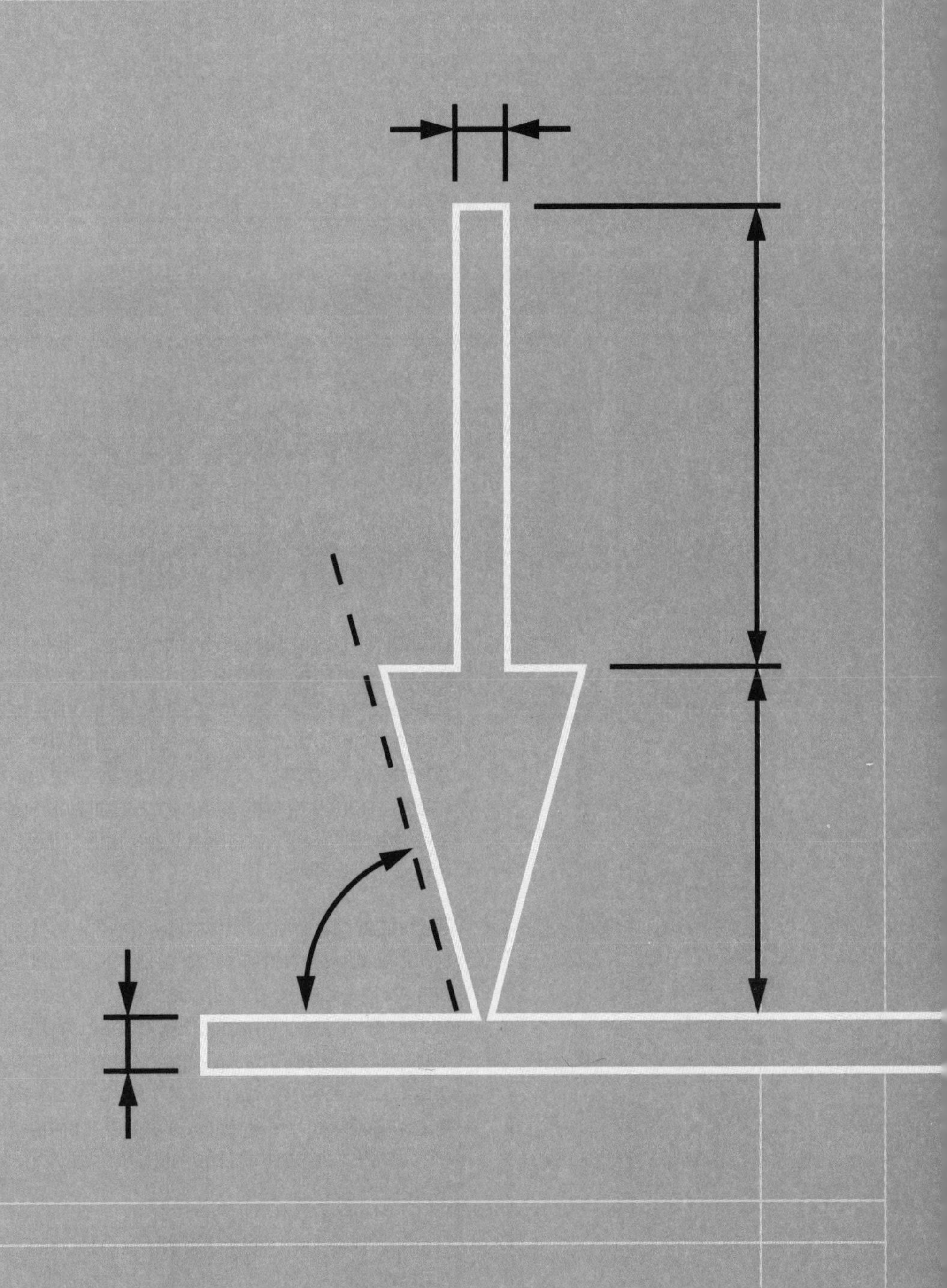

Introduction

10

Introduction

Graphical communication has been used for hundreds of years to document ideas and designs. From prehistoric paintings, to architectural drawings in ancient Greece and Rome, to Da Vinci's famous illustrations during the Renaissance, to the development of descriptive geometry and projection techniques, to computer graphics and parametric modeling software, to virtual and augmented reality, drawings and graphical information have been used with the purpose of communicating ideas.

Technical communication is a useful tool to transfer knowledge in a collaborative environment, and to convince others of the quality of a design in order to obtain permits, patents, or funding. Communication in engineering happens verbally, in the form of meetings, presentations, discussions, or conversations; and in writing, in the form of proposals, reports, technical memorandums, notes, emails, and other documents. However, many engineering ideas are simply too complex to be communicated with words and require the use of graphic representations.

Traditionally, engineering communication has primarily taken the form of drawings, which can be reproduced and shared at low cost. Currently, drawings can be converted to electronic formats and delivered to others almost instantaneously regardless of their location. These drawings can then be utilized by other members of the team to construct or manufacture the final product.

Engineering drawings are used in all engineering fields and will follow industry or organizational guidelines in their creation and application. As an example, mechanical engineers will use drawings to document an improved design for brake pads, while structural engineers will use a set of house plans, drawn by architects, to properly design beams and joists. Regardless of the technical field, various rules govern many facets of graphical communication.

1

STANDARDS VS. CONVENTIONS

Technical communication is driven by rules that ensure all parties understand a message clearly and unambiguously. The terms "standards" and "conventions" are commonly used interchangeably, but they have very explicit definitions. Standards are official rules that govern an activity. They are manifestations of various governmental and industrial organizations. Examples include the distance from the free throw line to the front of the rim in basketball (defined by FIBA), the asphalt content in roof shingles (defined by ASTM, formerly the American Society for Testing and Materials), or the viscosity of 10W-30 motor oil (Society of Automotive Engineers). Conventions, on the other hand, are practices or methods used so frequently and extensively that they become the most common approach used to accomplish certain tasks. In this case, there is not a formal document that defines the activity, but a general consensus about how the activity is performed. Conventions are also known as "industry standards" or "de facto standards." Examples of conventions include shaking with a right hand when meeting someone, or common file formats used for engineering drawings.

The Engineering Design Process

The Engineering Design Process is a problem analysis mechanism that incorporates creativity, the scientific method, mathematics, and engineering principles in order to solve a particular problem. It is normally represented as a cycle, in which each step can move the project forward, or revert to a previous stage (if problems need to be corrected) before further, and more expensive, design steps are taken. Variations of the design process are found across different industries, companies, and even problems. Some traditional design processes are linear, moving sequentially from one step to next. Others are concurrent, where multiple steps are performed in parallel.

The common stages of the engineering design process include defining the problem, brainstorming possible solutions, selecting preliminary designs, development and analysis, refinement, and implementation (see Figure 1).

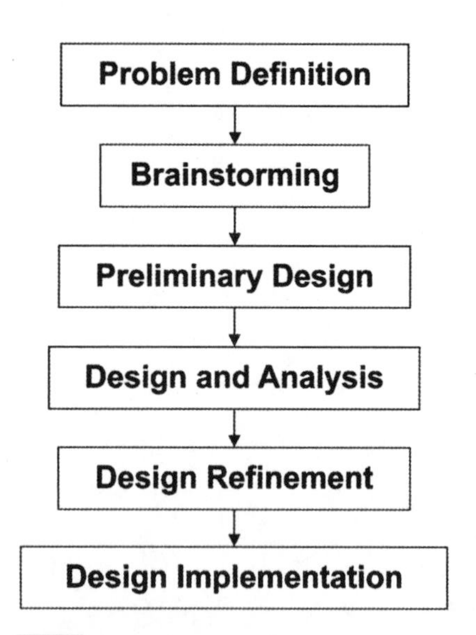

FIG. 1 Linear engineering design process

DEFINE THE PROBLEM

Defining or recognizing the problem is the first step of the design process. The problem must be clearly articulated, criteria and constraints must be identified, and decisions must be made as to what results will determine a successful outcome. At this stage, much information is graphical in nature; sketches, preliminary calculations, tables, charts, etc. Oftentimes, technical information is more easily understood and visualized, when communicated in graphical form.

BRAINSTORMING

In this stage of the design process, preliminary ideas and solutions are listed. The amount of ideas is more important than the quality of each suggestion. To ensure successful brainstorming sessions in group settings, it is important that any value judgment with regard to the quality of any idea is withheld. Quality discernment will occur in later stages, after a sufficient amount of ideas has been proposed. Ideas are typically accompanied with sketches (often with dimensions and notes) in order to fully grasp their appeal and applicability. Ideas can be original or refinements of previous designs.

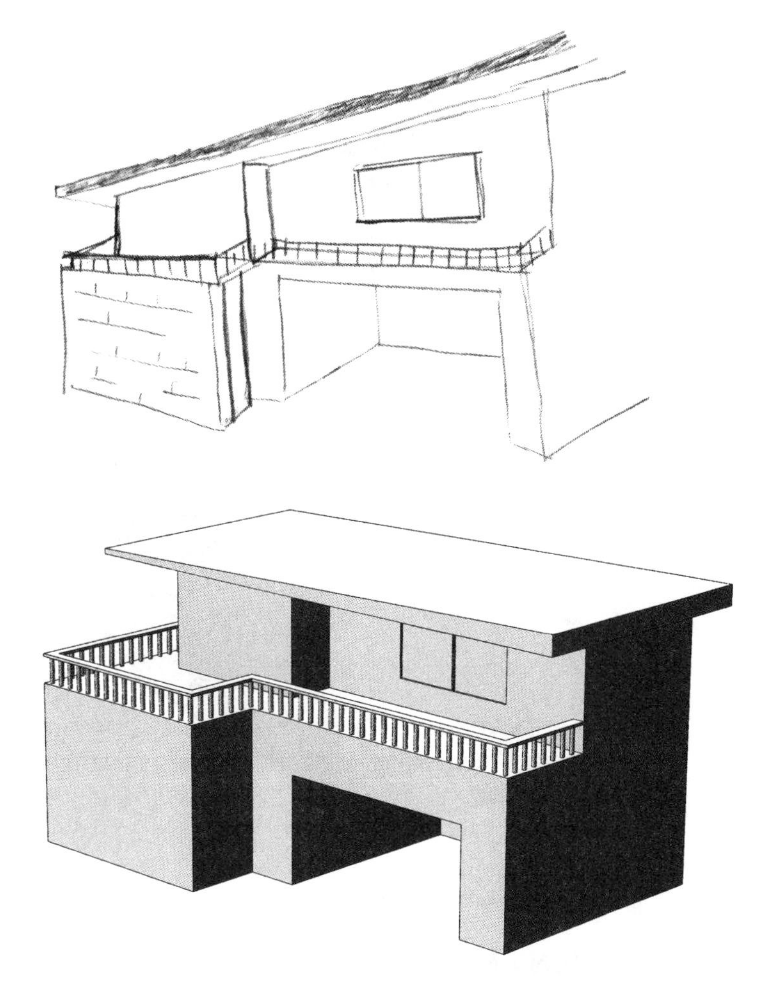

Refined sketch and CAD model FIG. 2

Preliminary Design

After completion of the brainstorming stage, all ideas are evaluated. Similar or complementary ideas are combined, ideas that do not seem promising are discarded, refined sketches are produced, and the functional relationships among the various components of an idea are illustrated.

The best ideas are further developed, sketches are turned into drawings using CAD (see Figure 2), and preliminary analysis may be performed in order to separate the best ideas from those that fail to meet the objectives established in the problem definition stage. Prototypes can be produced, for increased visualization, and possibly shown to potential clients or focus groups in order to obtain important feedback.

Thought must be given to issues such as how various components will be assembled, what materials should be used to build different parts, estimated production costs, and other specific details. The purpose of this stage is to consider several alternatives and develop them to a sufficient point that an informed decision can be made.

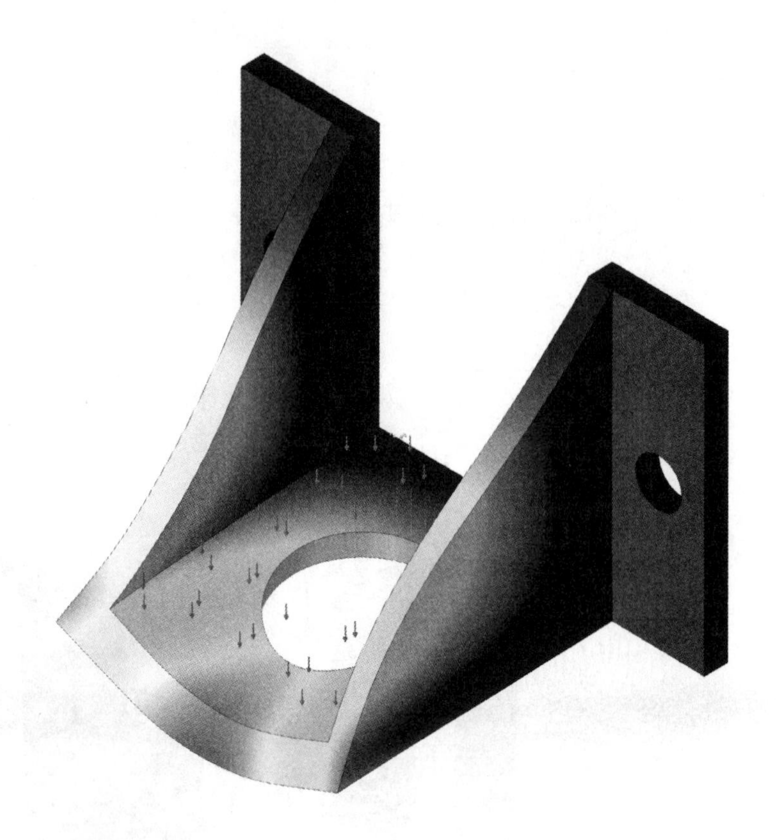

FIG. 3 Finite Element Analysis

Design and Analysis

When the field is narrowed to one design, parametric computer models are typically constructed and analyzed. The solution is revised and subjected to increased scrutiny, using mathematics, engineering, materials science, technology, and simulation tools. Forces, stresses, flow, thermal conductivity, and other physical properties are considered and evaluated (see Figure 3). The design is examined in terms of functionality, manufacturability, strength, safety, and cost. Various standards organizations or governmental bodies may define exactly which methods must be used to analyze certain aspects of the design. CAD software is especially crucial in assisting with these determinations, with certain packages being almost considered industry standards.

Design Refinement

Additional testing of your designs may show weaknesses or oversights. These drawbacks may not invalidate a possible solution, but instead can be improved and optimized before the next design iteration. Prototypes are often manufactured, and depending upon their material, could even be physically tested. Recent advances in computer aided manufacturing and additive manufacturing are popularizing rapid prototyping technologies, which allow the creation of physical parts directly from 3D computer models (see Figure 4).

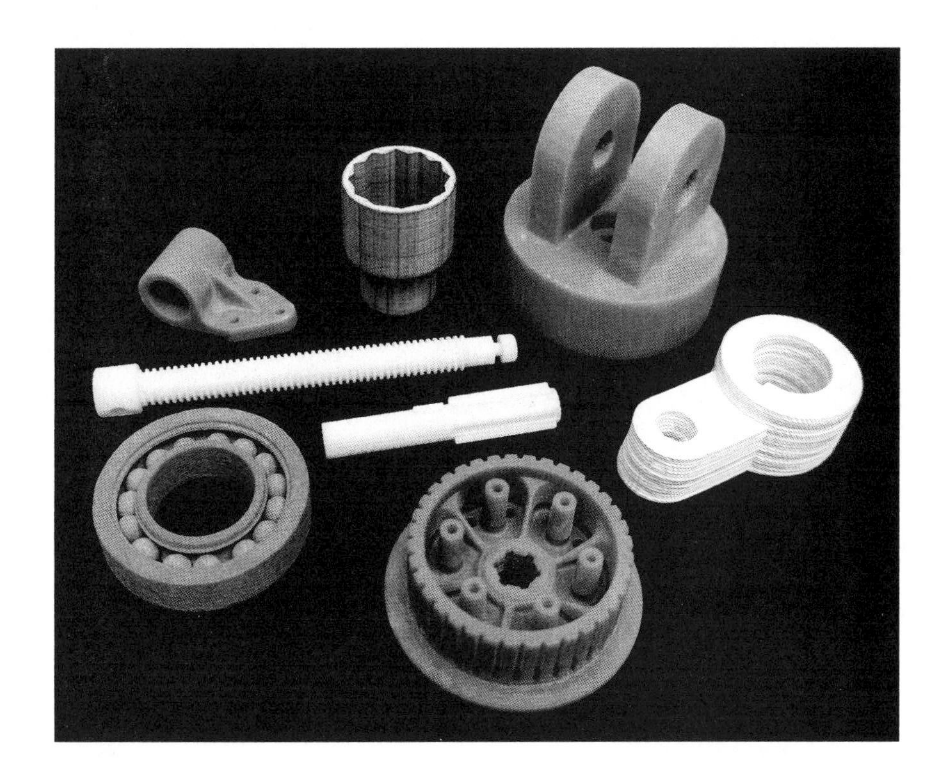

Rapid prototypes FIG. 4

Design Implementation

Once the final design has been properly tested and analyzed, the implementation step completes the engineering design process. At this stage, construction of the design begins, facilitated by a full set of engineering documents detailing the specific steps needed to ensure proper manufacturing. This documentation does not only include dimensioned drawings, but may also incorporate animations, physical simulations, rendered photo-realistic images, and augmented reality.

Documentation

Documentation is a complementary step performed at every stage of the engineering design process. It involves recording and reporting the functionality and details of a design. Technical manuals, user guides, handbooks, instruction booklets, test results, presentation materials, charts, graphs, technical reports, and packing and shipping instructions are examples of documents developed throughout the product life cycle.

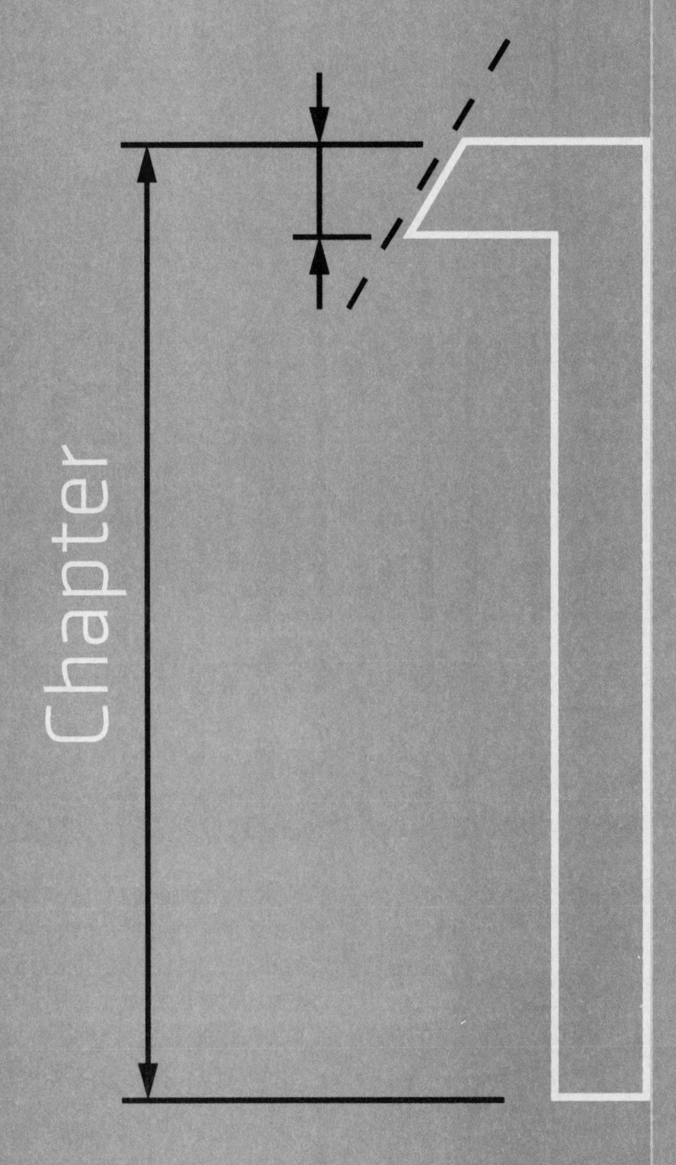

Sketching and Lettering

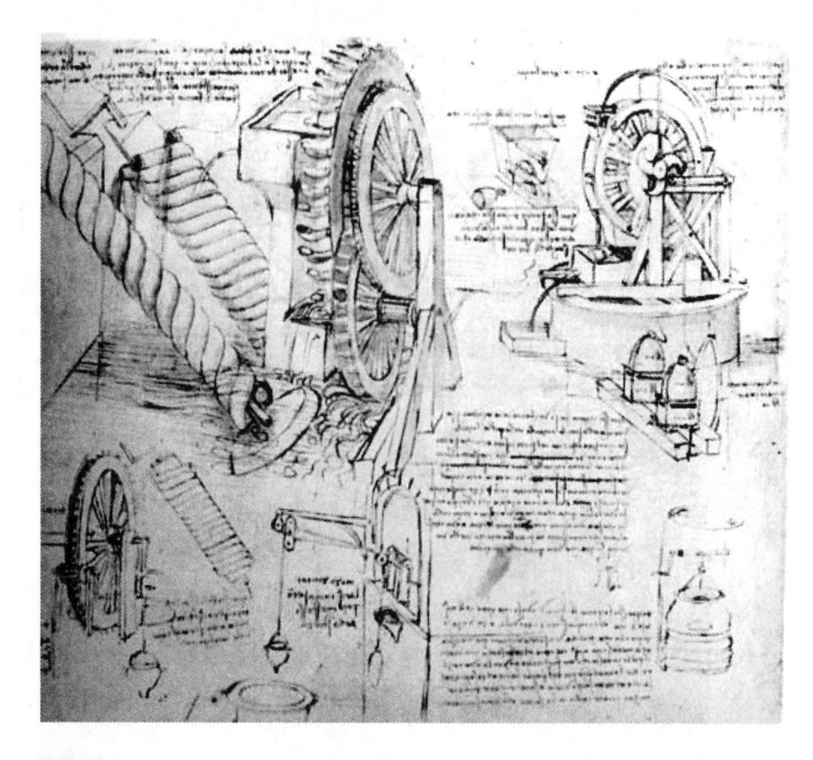

FIG. 1.1 "Water Lifting Devices" by Leonardo Da Vinci (between 1480 and 1482)

Introduction

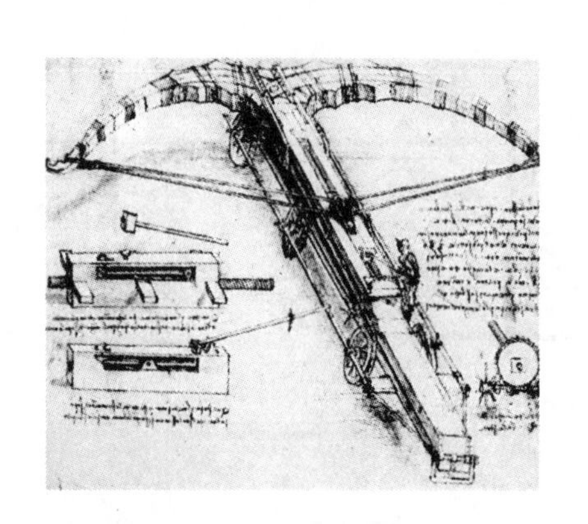

FIG. 1.1 "Crossbow", by Leonardo Da Vinci (between 1480 and 1482)

As an engineer, you will need to produce, revise, and interpret drawings and models of designs, structures, and systems. Graphic communication is, and has been for centuries (see Figure 1.1), the universal language that allows you to express and share technical ideas, and a tool capable of storing a great amount of information in a very small space. After all, "a picture is worth a thousand words."

The connection between engineering and graphic communication is undeniable. The ability to visualize objects three dimensionally and create good quality graphics is a necessity for today's designers, architects, engineers, and anyone working in technical fields. Graphic communication facilitates the design process by helping ideas take shape on paper.

In this chapter, we introduce the traditional method of design: sketching. We present sketching not only as an illustration tool, but also as an essential part of the design methodology. Despite the computer graphics tools available today, the ability to sketch ideas quickly on paper is the only practical way to evaluate them and see which ones are worth exploring further. You will learn about the importance of freehand sketching, particularly in the early stages of the design process, and familiarize yourself with the most common drawing techniques and practices. Lettering is discussed as an instrument to provide textual information to drawings.

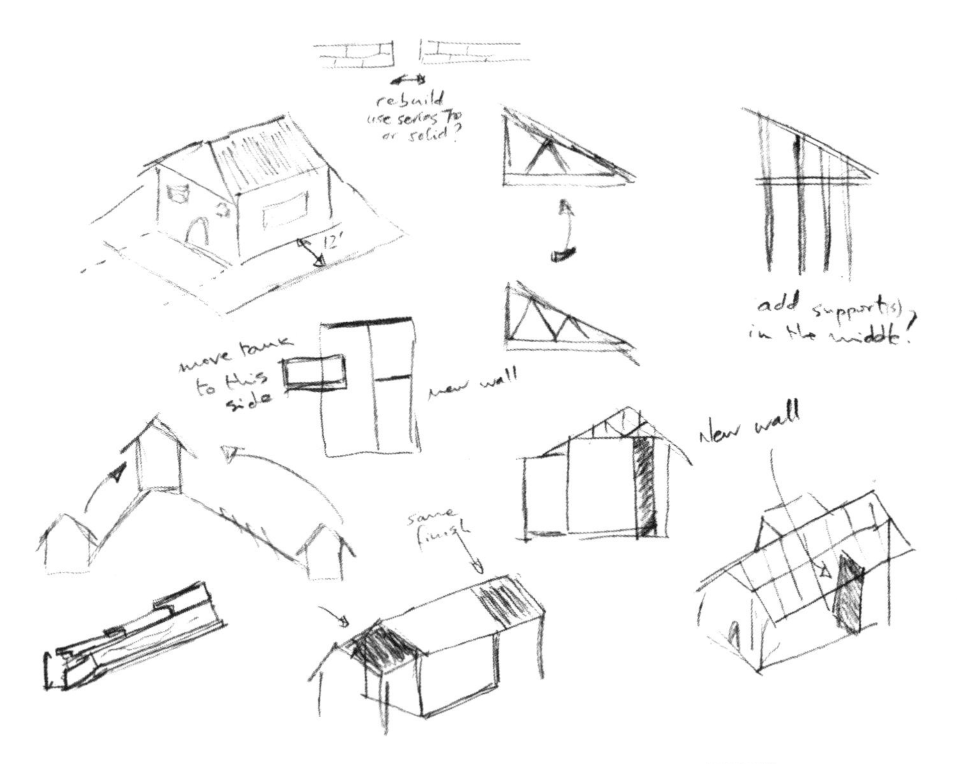

Freehand Sketches as means to communicate ideas  FIG. 1.2

Sketching

A sketch is a rough graphic representation of an idea or concept (see Figure 1.2). They are quick, black and white drawings that communicate the shape and size of an object without excessive attention to accuracy or details. Sketches are typically created freehand, without the aid of drawing instruments.

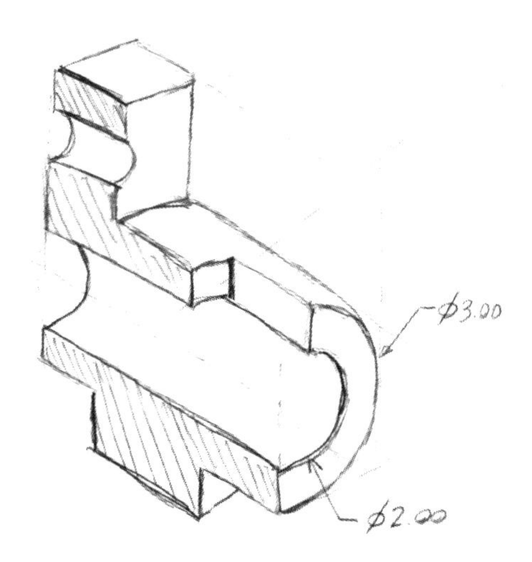

Freehand Sketches as means to communicate ideas FIG. 1.2

Sketches are used in a variety of situations:

- As a thinking process, to quickly communicate ideas and visualize concepts. To brainstorm and explore design alternatives creatively.
- To record information in the field.
- As reminders to help engineers reconstruct ideas and details that may otherwise forget.
- As a starting point for refined models and final designs.

Unlike artistic sketches, which are primarily focused on color, composition, texture, and aesthetics, technical sketches communicate practical details and ideas, and they are constantly subject to changes and revisions.

Engineering sketches are generally presented in a 2D format, although pictorial drawings that show a 3D view of the object are often used for clarity. In future chapters, you will study the different projection

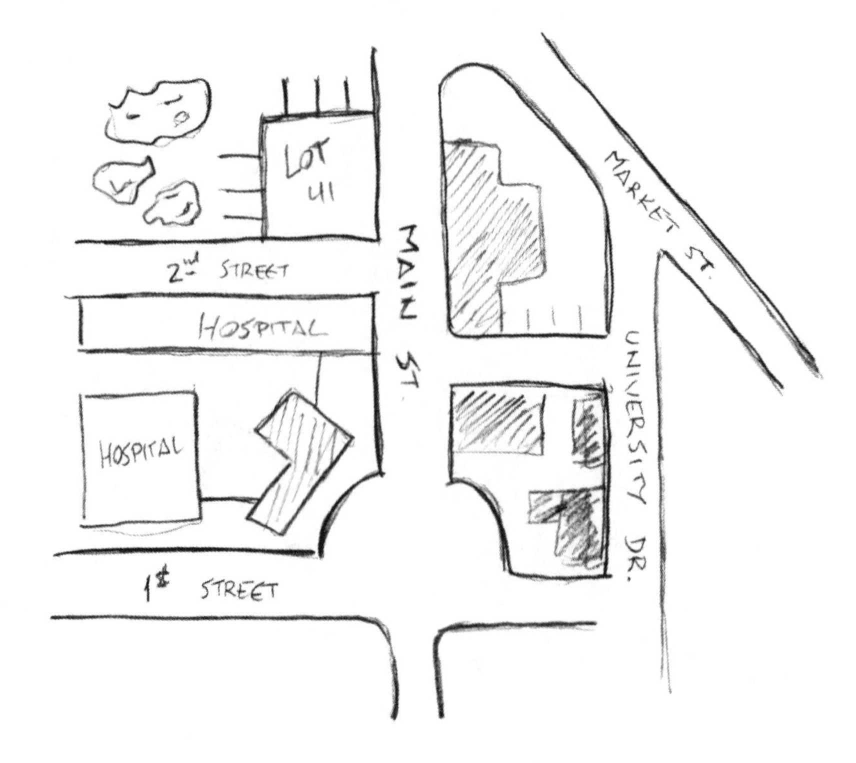

FIG. 1.3 Different uses of sketching

methods used in engineering drawing. Sketching will certainly help you improve your visualization skills, which will have an immediate effect on the quality of your drawings.

Sketches must be clear, concise, and dark enough to stand out from the page so they can be faxed and scanned properly. In some cases, shading or hatching elements may be included to emphasize volumes and shapes or to mimic the appearance and textures of some materials. Textual annotations are also common as they provide additional information to a sketch, such as dimensions, assembly instructions, or manufacturing details.

It is important that you sign and date your sketches to verify ownership. Use copies of your sketches for distribution and keep the originals in your archives. Sketches are considered historical and legal documents and can be presented as evidence in cases of lawsuits that are brought before court.

Although many people do not feel confident about their own drawing abilities, engineering sketching is a technical skill, which means that it can be acquired and improved with practice and dedication. Common excuses such as "I am not an artist" or "I have no artistic eye" have no place in this type of sketching. In fact, many situations will only require the use of basic shapes, arrows, and stick figures to communicate your ideas to others. Doodling is also good practice for sketching. Some sketching examples are shown in Figure 1.3.

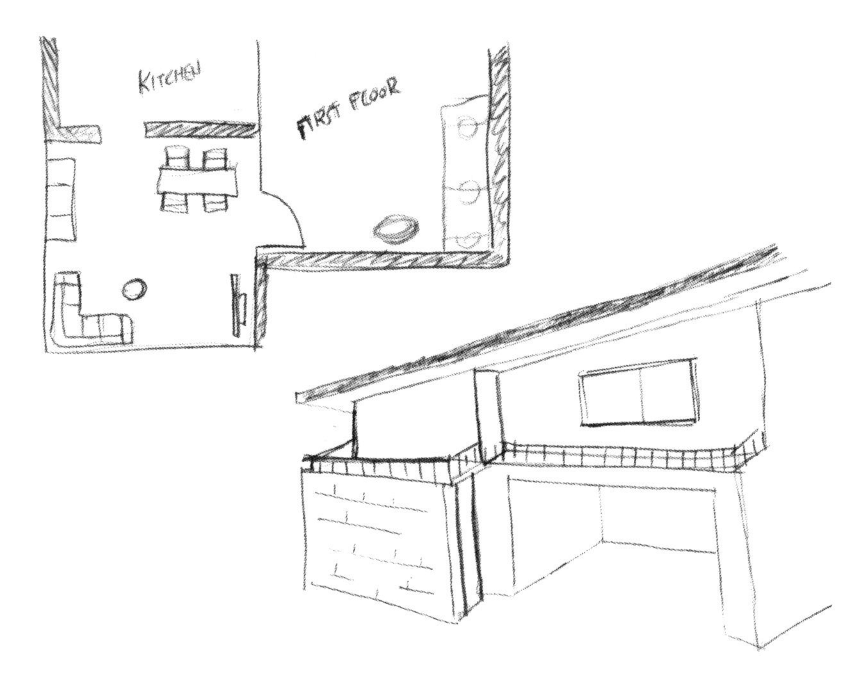

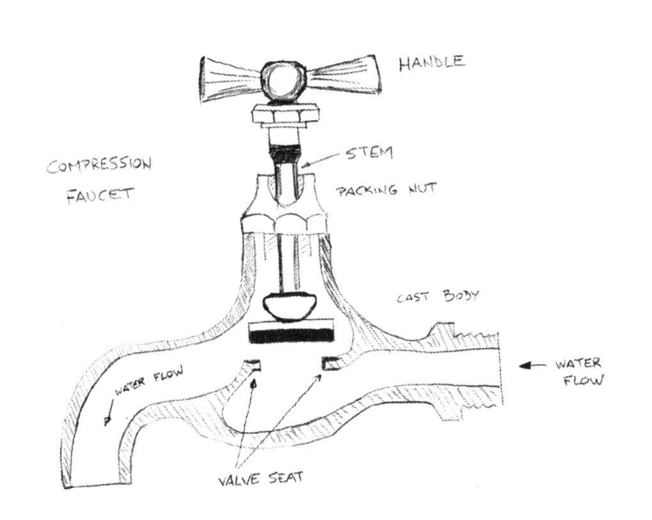

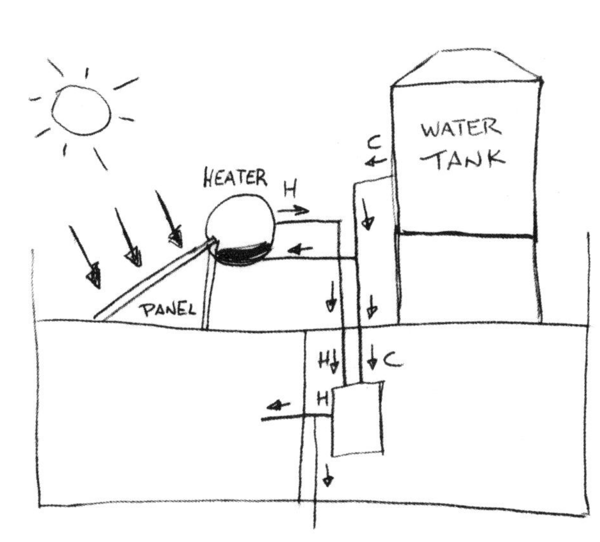

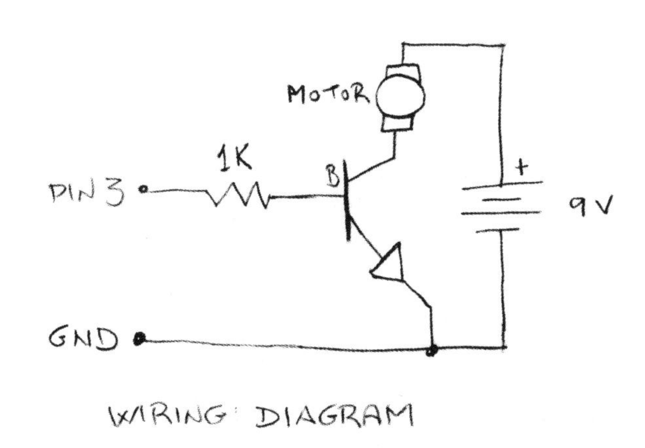

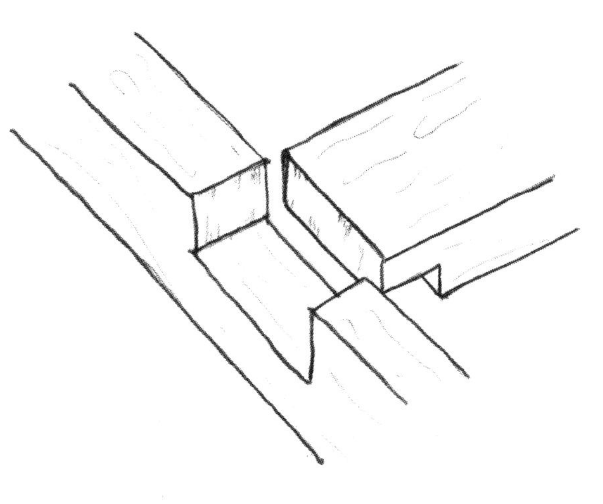

Different uses of sketching FIG. 1.3

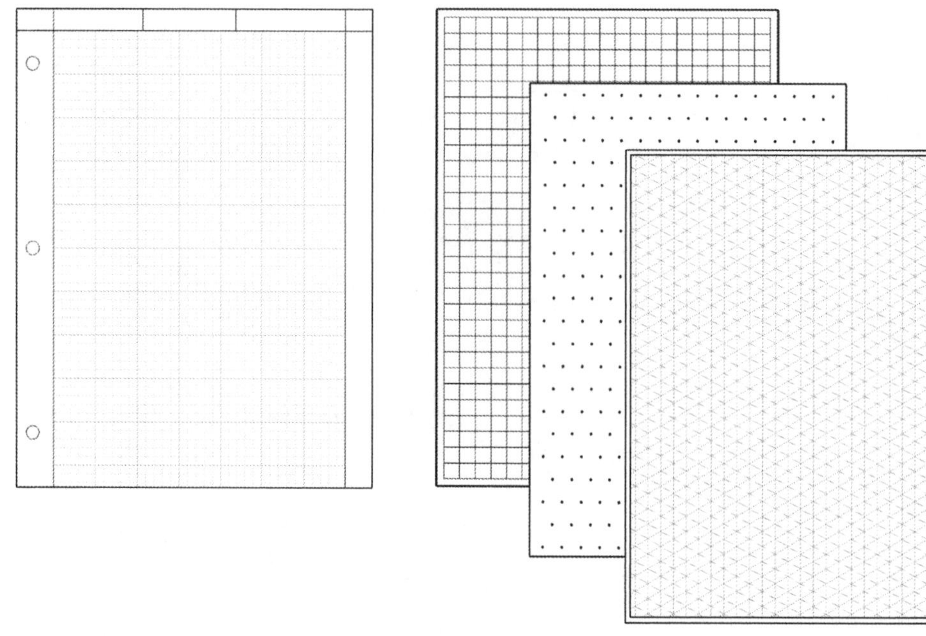

Fig. 1.4 Engineering Paper

Fig. 1.5 Grid Papers

Sketching Tools

There is a wide variety of tools available for sketching. However, since sketches may be needed quickly, only pencil, paper, and eraser are essential. Rulers, T-squares, triangles, templates, and other technical instruments can only slow you down during the early stages of a design and restrict the type of forms and shapes explored. In addition, there are many situations where these tools are not available, such as when sketches are created in the field or during lunch meetings. Consequently, it is important for a designer to be able to sketch without any supporting tools. You can master this craft with adequate practice.

Paper is the primary medium where you will create your sketches, but you may also find yourself sketching on dry-erase boards, smartphones, chalkboards, etc. There is a wide variety of paper choices in the market. Although good quality paper is preferred, the selection normally depends on availability. If you are at home or at the office you will likely use plain or engineering paper (see Figure 1.4) or a sketch pad. Grid paper is also useful if you need guidance with alignment and proportions (see Figure 1.5). If nothing else is on hand, improvise and use what you have. Paper napkins or the back of an envelope are some examples you probably have heard before. Any type of paper is acceptable for quickly sketching your ideas.

Find a pencil that suits your style and particular uses. Both mechanical and wooden pencils work well for sketching. Lead thickness for mechanical pencils ranges from .2 mm to .9mm, with .5 and .7 mm

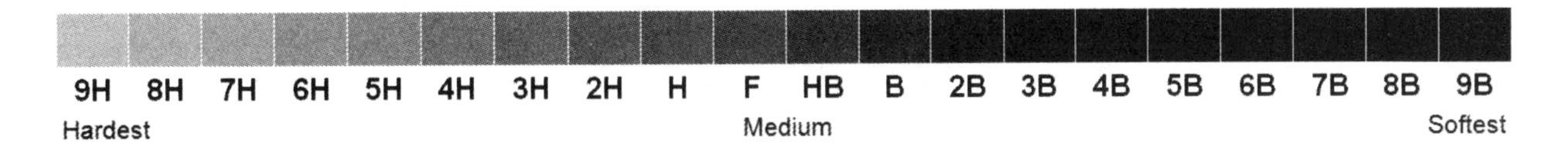

Lead grades for pencils FIG. 1.6

being the most popular. Leads over .9 mm thick are not suitable for sketching.

Most wooden pencils are graded on a system that uses a scale from "H" (for hardness) to "B" (for blackness), as well as "F", an arbitrary letter that indicates the midpoint of the range (see Figure 1.6). Medium grades (HB and F) are best for sketching. Harder leads (9H – 3H) have some uses in engineering drawings, but the lines tend to be too light. Soft leads (2B – 9B) are mostly used by artists.

In the United States there is an alternative system to designate pencil grades that uses numbers from 1 to 4 (you are probably familiar with the popular #2 pencil). The equivalence with the previous scale is shown in Figure 1.7.

If you are using a wooden pencil, keep it sharpened and hold it at an angle of about 60 degrees to the paper. Rotate the pencil frequently as you sketch to keep the wear of the lead even. Chisel shaped leads can create fuzzy lines with unexpected thicknesses.

Erasing lines with the purpose of making changes to a design is not recommended. Erasers should be used almost exclusively to correct inaccuracies or mistakes in lines. In general, soft vinyl or gum-like erasers are preferred as they leave less residue when used and they are less likely to damage the surface of the paper.

US	#4	#3	#2 ½	#2	#1
World	2H	H	F	HB	B

Alternative scale of lead grades for pencils FIG. 1.7

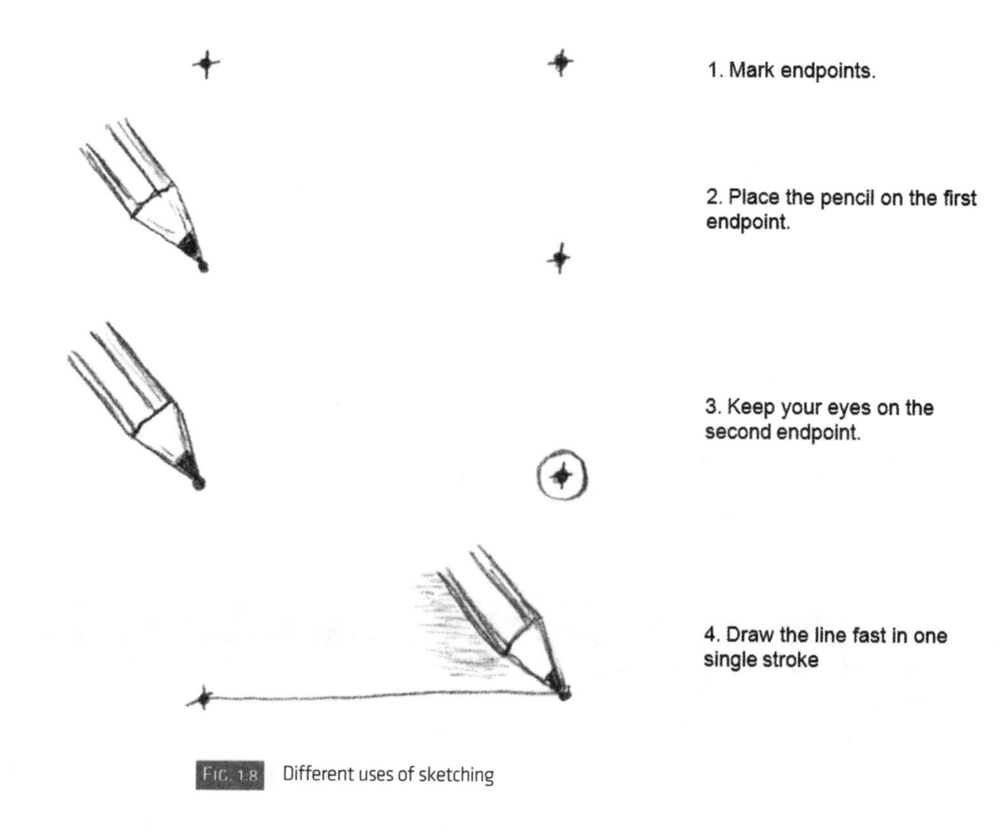

FIG. 1.8 Different uses of sketching

Sketching Techniques

STRAIGHT LINES

Lines are the most basic elements of sketching. They represent the edges of objects. Lines used in sketching should be dark, consistent, and have a uniform thickness. Construction lines can be used as references and guidelines to help you during the sketching process. They are significantly lighter in thickness, and they are generally erased when the sketch is finalized.

A good method to sketch straight lines freehand is to keep your eyes fixed on the endpoint of your line and draw the line in one fast stroke (See Figure 1.8). Do not stare and follow the tip of the pencil while you draw the line. To prepare for the gesture, you can initially move your pencil between the two endpoints a few times without drawing. For a particularly long line you can use a combination of shorter strokes, breaking the long line into shorter segments. Do not be afraid to rotate the paper as you sketch to find your most efficient angle.

You can practice by creating two points on a paper and trying to connect them with one straight line. Place the two points close together first and gradually move them farther apart as you feel more comfortable sketching. Practice sketching lines at different angles too.

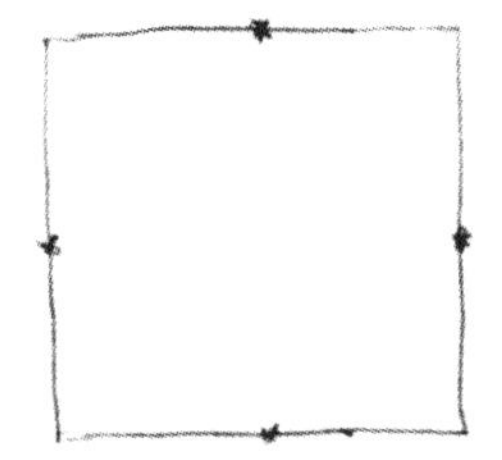

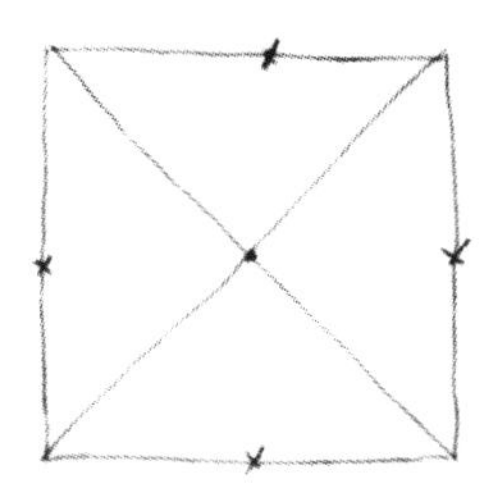

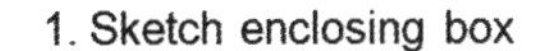

1. Sketch enclosing box
2. Locate midpoints
3. Draw diagonals

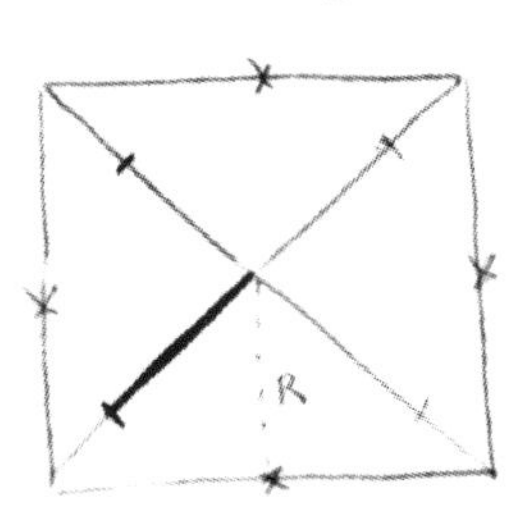

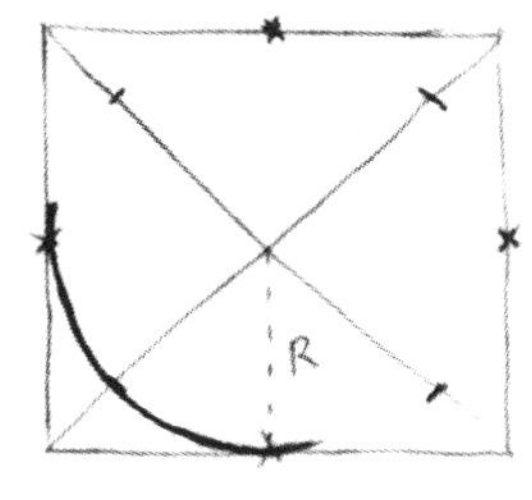

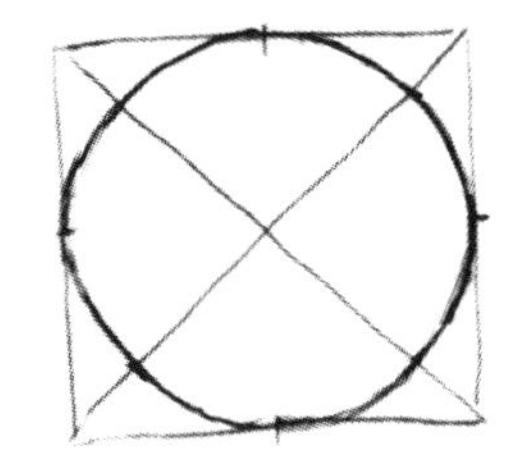

4. By eye mark radius on diagonals
5. Trace quadrants
6. Complete circle

Sketching circles  FIG. 1.9

CIRCLES, ELLIPSES, AND CURVES

Sketching circles and ellipses is considerably more challenging than straight lines. The most common method uses squares and rectangles as construction elements that enclose the circles and ellipses. The midpoints of the sides of the enclosing rectangle will be the four points of connection with the circle or ellipse. The diagonals of the square or rectangle will give you the center point of the circle or ellipse. Next, by eye, mark the radius of the circle on the diagonals to get additional points on the circumference. The sketching process is shown in Figure 1.9.

Construction boxes can also be used to sketch arcs and curves. By combining multiple boxes together, data points on the curve can be obtained. See Figure 1.10 for some examples.

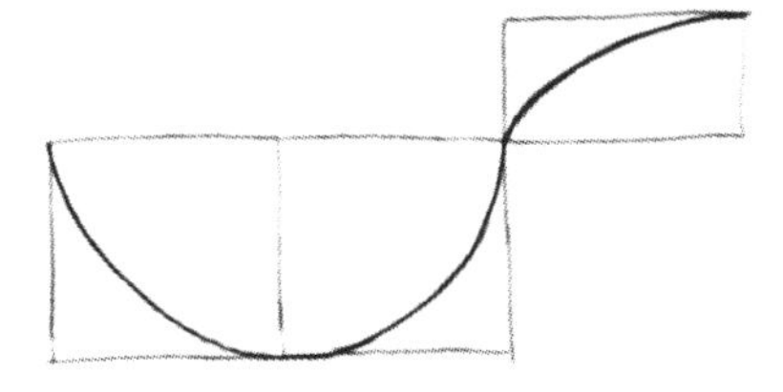

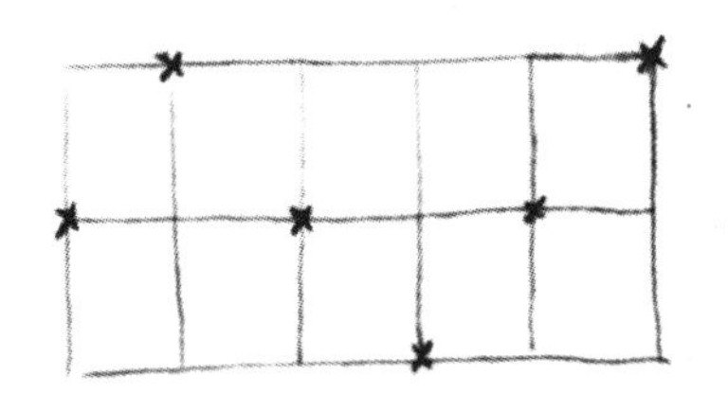

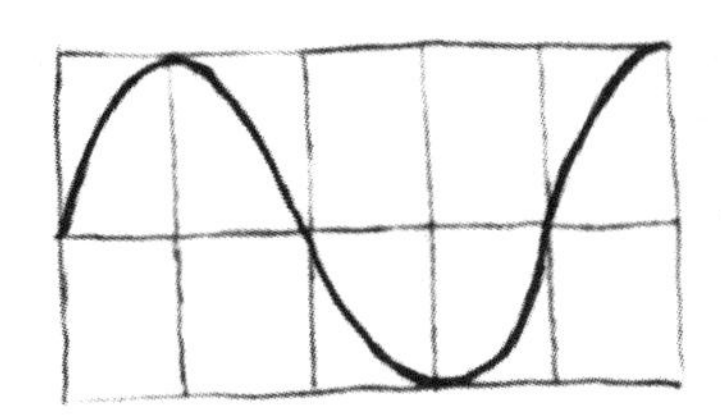

Sketching curves FIG. 1.10

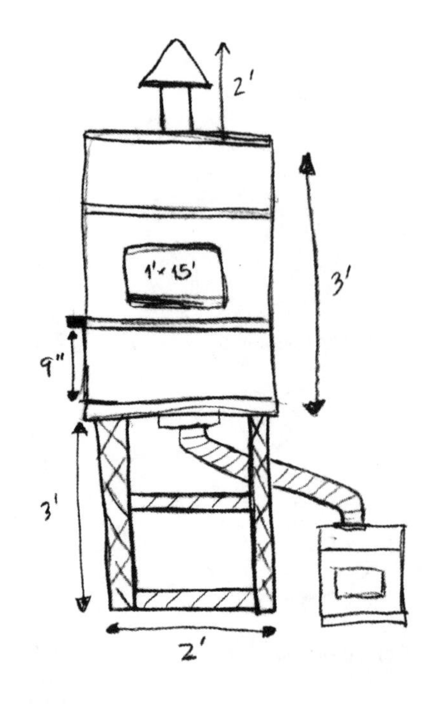

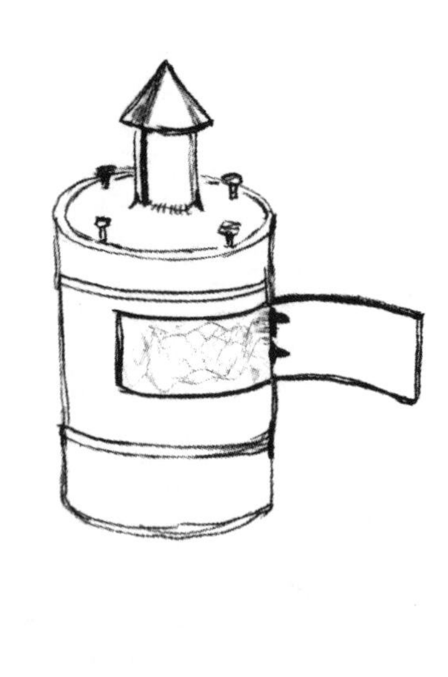

Fig. 1.11 Building blocks

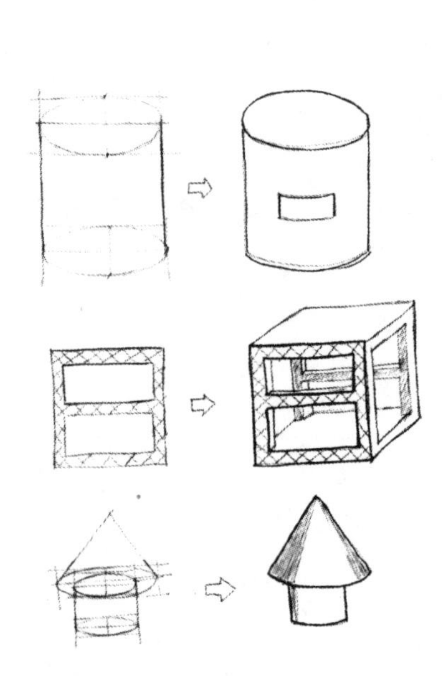

Fig. 1.11 Building blocks

Complex Objects

Virtually any object can be broken down into basic elements. Straight lines can be combined into rectangles and triangles. Circles can be used to create arcs and curves. These shapes constitute the basic building blocks of the objects you see every day. Basic shapes combine to form more elaborate drawings. With practice, you will be able to visualize and break objects down into their individual blocks, which will help you during the sketching process (see Figure 1.11).

Basic shapes are also the foundation for human characters (see Figure 1.12). Quick sketches of people can help communicate proportions and relative sizes in your drawings. In addition, the human figure is an essential aspect in most designs in terms of usability and performance.

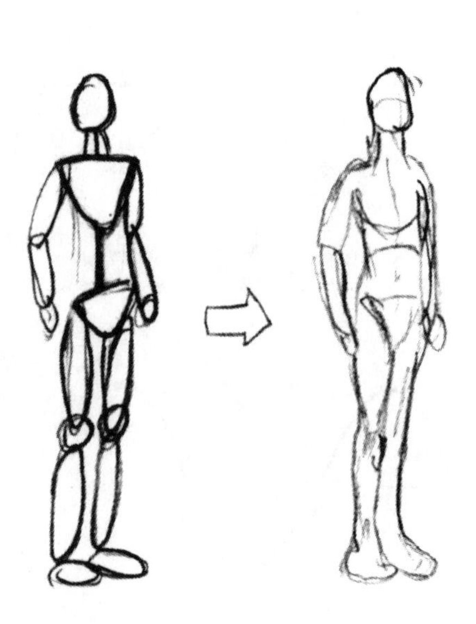

Fig. 1.12 Sketching people

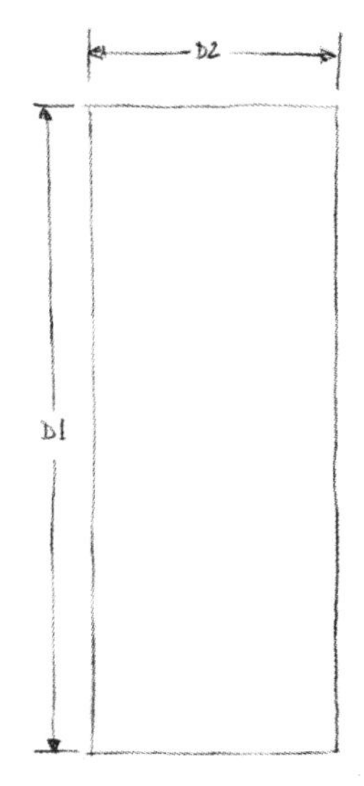

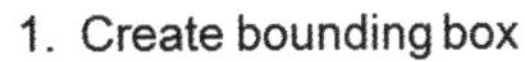
1. Create bounding box

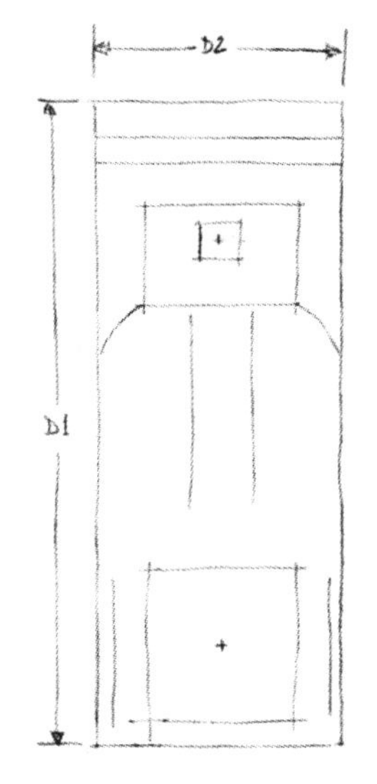

2. Estimate features with respect to bounding box

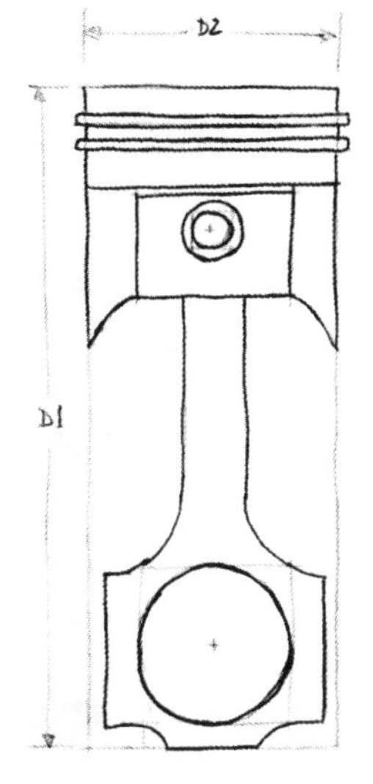

3. Complete features with previous estimations

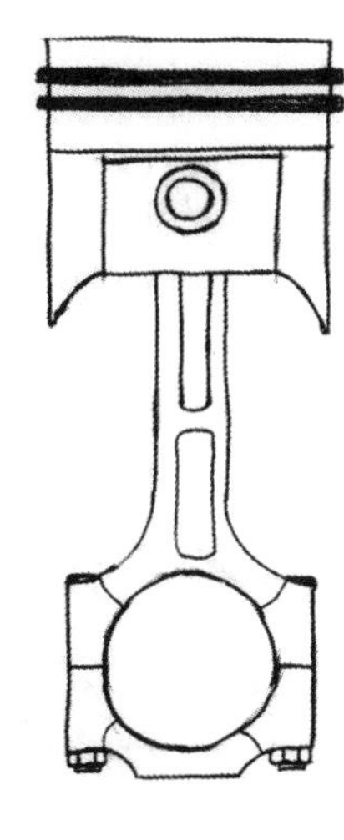

4. Finished sketch

Working with proportion  FIG. 1.13

PROPORTION

Although sketches are not usually drawn to scale, it is important that they are proportional. If proportions are not correct, your sketch will never look realistic, regardless of the quality of the lines or the level of detail you put in it.

Proportion refers to the relationships between elements of a sketch. As a designer, concentrate on the relative sizes and shapes of all the elements of the sketch with respect to the whole, as well as symmetries, patterns, and other visual indicators.

A simple way to maintain proportions in your drawings is by using the overall dimensions of the object you want to sketch. Start by sketching a bounding box defined by these dimensions. Next, create the remaining features, estimating their sizes and locations with respect to this bounding box. An example of this method is shown in Figure 1.13.

Oftentimes, the pencil can be used as a measuring tool. In this case, the different features of the object that is being sketched are visually compared to the length of the pencil. This information is then used to estimate and judge proportions.

ABCDEFGHIJKLM
NOPQRSTUVWXYZ
0123456789

ABCDEFGHIJKLM
NOPQRSTUVWXYZ
0123456789

FIG. 1.15 Single-Stroke Gothic Lettering. Vertical (top) and Inclined (bottom)

LETTERING

Dimensions, notes, labels, remarks, and technical specifications are bits of textual information used to supplement drawings. Text is always necessary, as not all information can be communicated graphically.

Lettering refers to forming letters and numbers to accompany drawings. There are many lettering styles used for different purposes. "Old-fashioned" and artistic styles like Classic German and Old-English (see Figure 1.14), for example, are used in old manuscripts and documents that are artistic in nature such as diplomas and certificates.

This is Old English Lettering
This is Classic German Lettering

FIG. 1.14 Some lettering styles are not appropriate for engineering drawings

Engineering drawings require a clear and unambiguous type of lettering to ensure readability. For this reason, many industries have adopted their own lettering guidelines that are typically based on national and international standards. The lettering style shown in Figure 1.15 is known as Single Stroke Gothic and is almost universally accepted in engineering drawings.

CORRECT SPACING
INCORRECT SPACING

Incorrect spacing makes text unbalanced FIG. 1.16

Single Stroke Gothic lettering is simple, easily read, and any letter can be made with a series of single strokes. There are no flourishes or double lines. Letters can be vertical or inclined (italic) and, with only few exceptions, only capital letters are used.

All letters have the same height, typically 3 mm (1/8 of an inch), although height may vary among different industries. If fractions are needed, they take up twice the height of standard letters.

Spacing between letters in a word must be consistent. However, because some letters are wider than others, the spacing between some letters needs to be adjusted to avoid making the text unbalanced. This adjustment is known as "kerning."

Spacing between words in a sentence must be approximately equal to the width of a full letter, such as "O" or "H". Spacing between lines of text is normally half the standard lettering height. See Figure 1.16 for an example.

In final engineering drawings, lettering is done exclusively by software. Most parameters such as font, spacing, and letter height are managed automatically by the computer. During the sketching process, it is not unusual to see annotations spread over a drawing as ideas flow and concepts take shape. In fact, this practice is encouraged; as it is usually necessary to explain or clarify certain parts of the sketch. In these cases, proper engineering lettering should be done by hand.

Exercises

Sketch a map that provides directions from your house/apartment to your school. Don't forget to label the streets and the most relevant landmarks.

Create a sketch of your house or apartment. Include a floor plan with the layout of the furniture. Include basic dimensions for walls.

Exercise 01

Name:

Date:

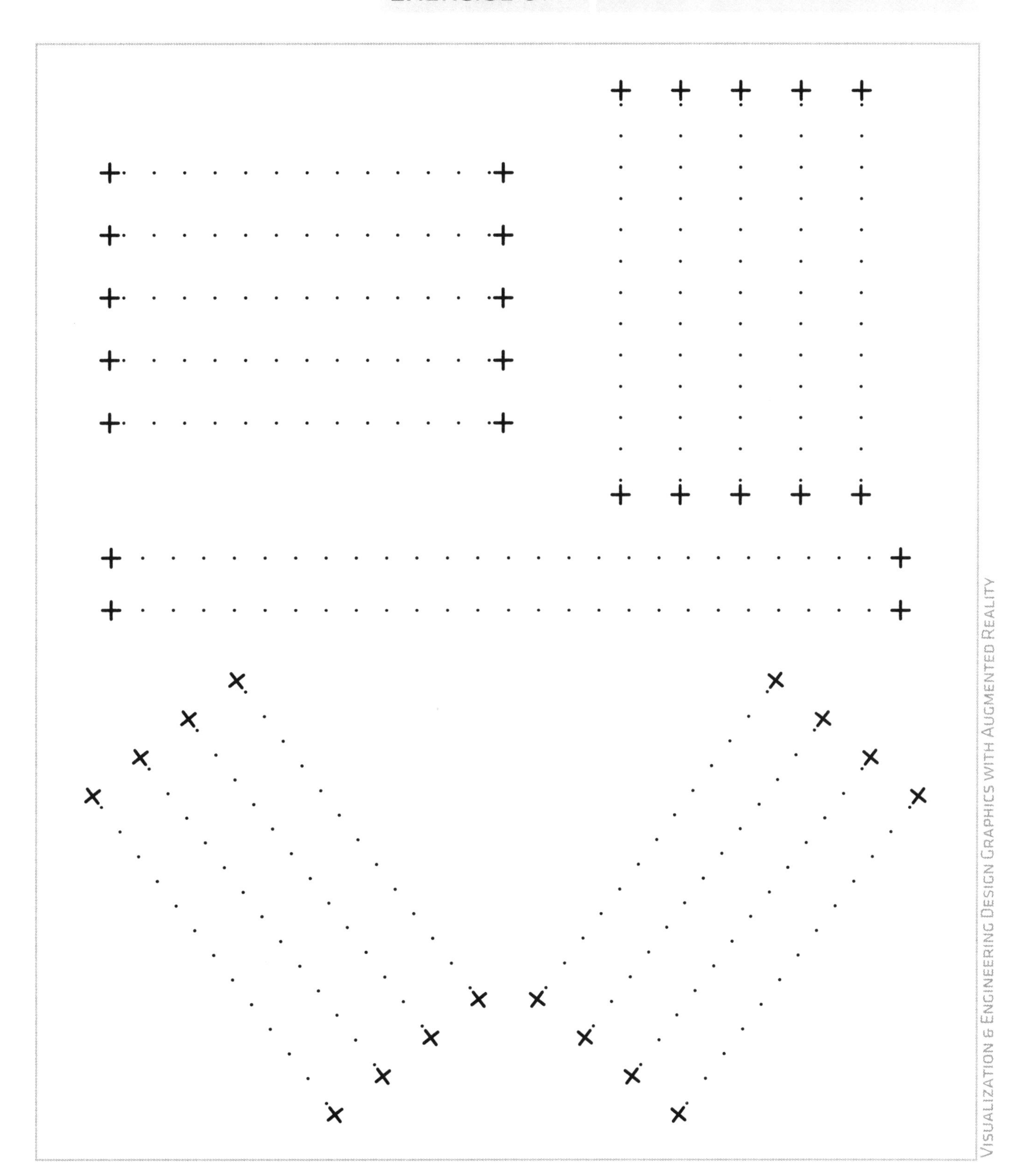

Sketch the straight lines above using the guidelines.

Sketching and Lettering

Chapter 01

Exercise 02

Name:

Date:

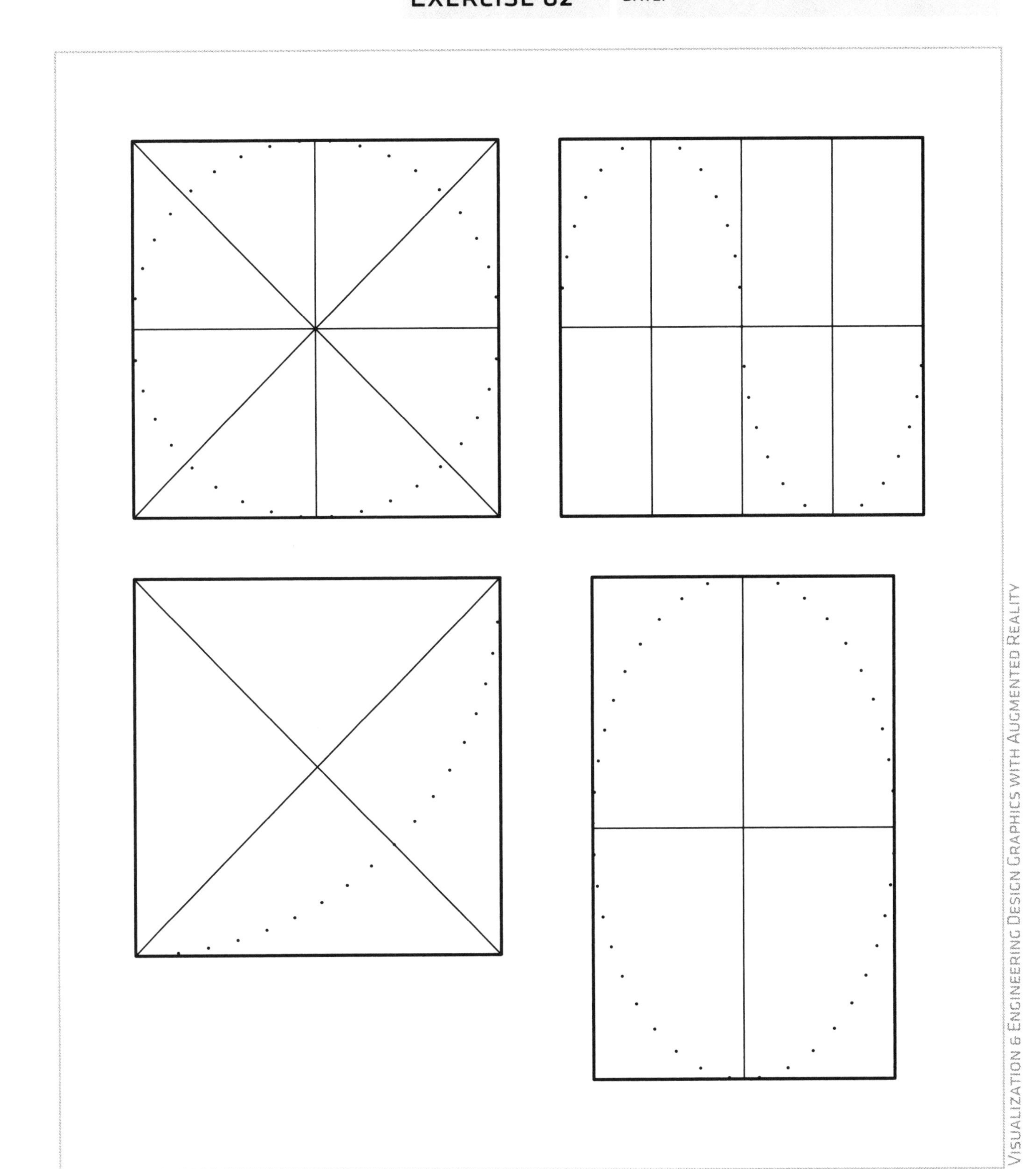

Sketch the circles, ellipses, and arcs above using the guidelines.

SKETCHING AND LETTERING

CHAPTER 01

EXERCISE 03

NAME:

DATE:

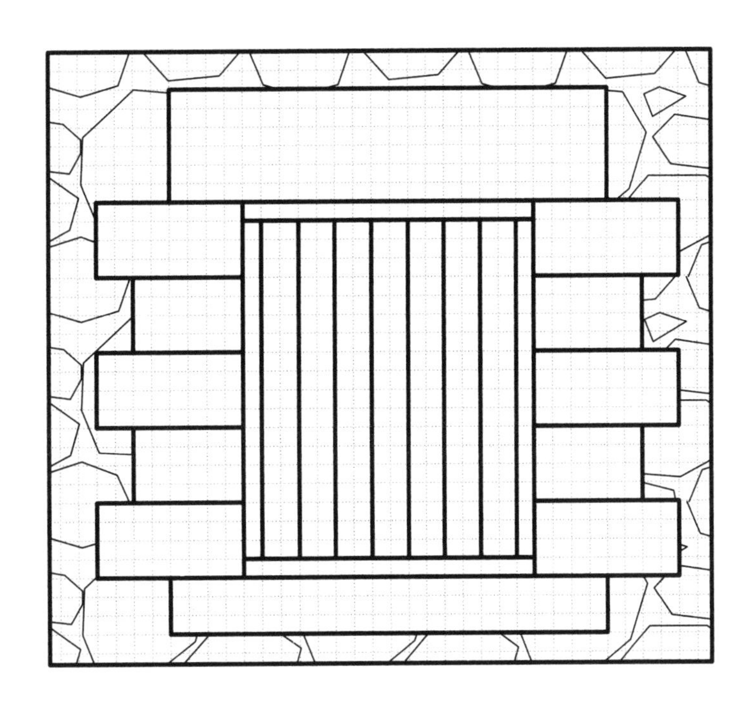

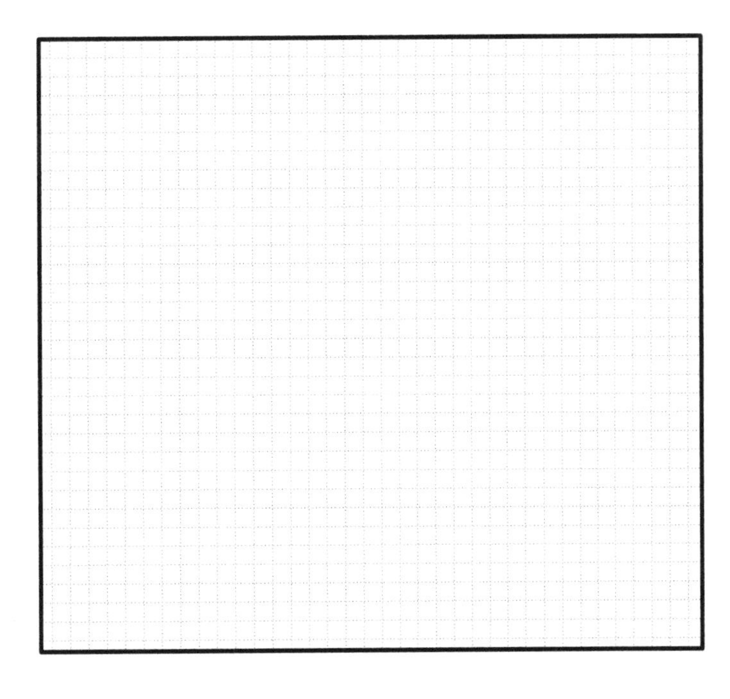

SKETCH THE CIRCLES, ELLIPSES, AND ARCS ABOVE USING THE GUIDELINES.

Exercise 04

Name:

Date:

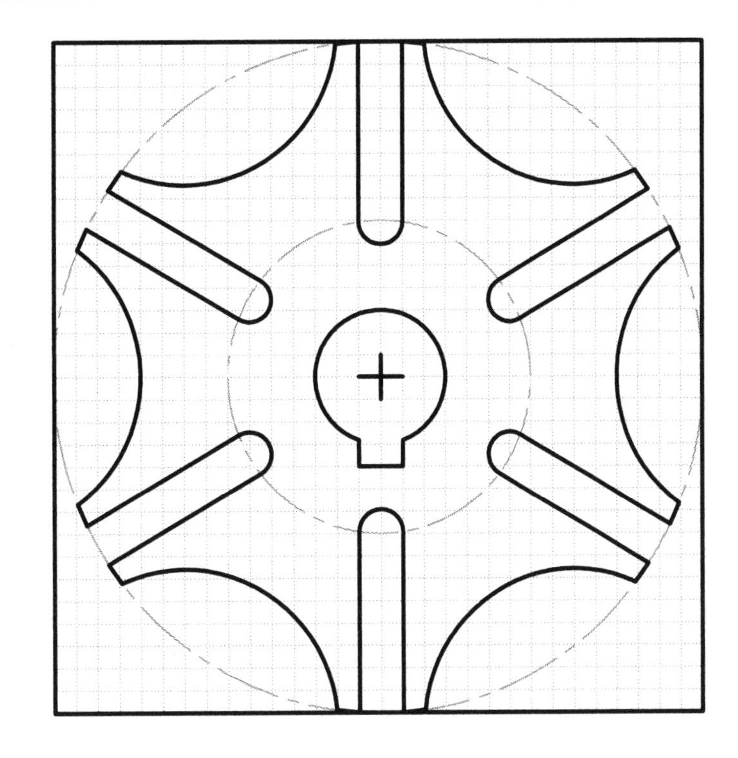

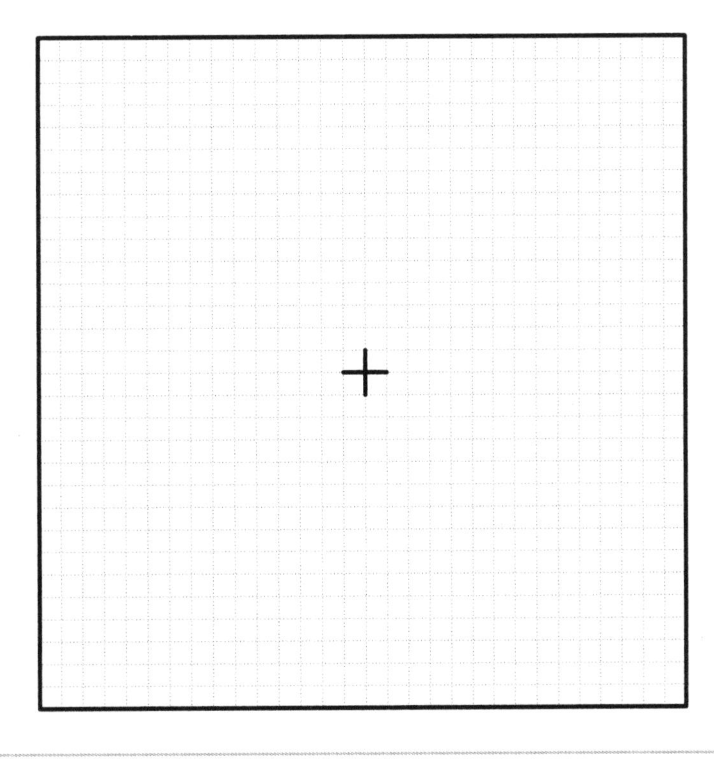

Create a freehand sketch of the Geneva cam using the space provided.

Sketching and Lettering

Name:

Chapter 01
Exercise 05

Date:

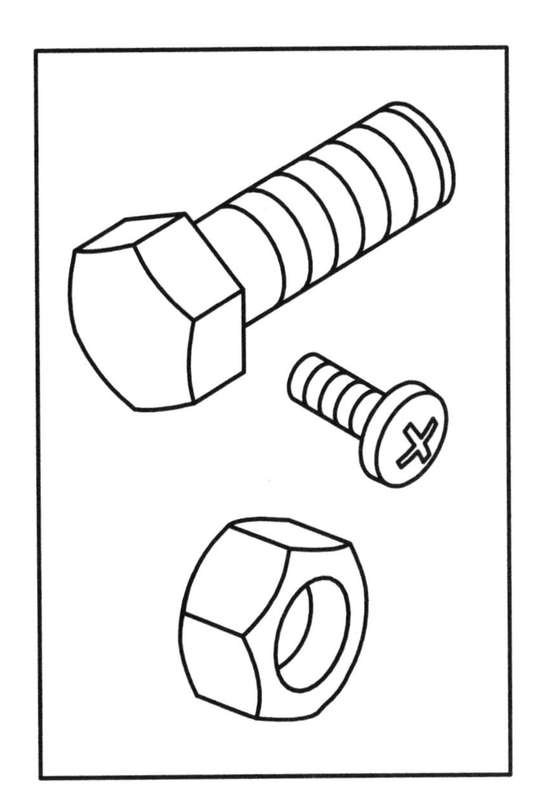

Create a freehand sketch of the fasteners shown using the space provided.

Sketching and Lettering

Chapter 01

Exercise 06

Name:

Date:

A ..... B ..... C ..... D ..... E ..... F .....

G ..... H ..... I ..... J ..... K ..... L .....

M ..... N ..... O ..... P ..... Q ..... R .....

S ..... T ..... U ..... V ..... W ..... X .....

Y ..... Z .....

0 ..... 1 ..... 2 ..... 3 ..... 4 .....

5 ..... 6 ..... 7 ..... 8 ..... 9 .....

THE STANDARD LETTERING FOR ENGINEERING DRAWINGS IS SINGLE STROKE GOTHIC.

THE

THE

ONLY CAPITAL LETTERS ARE USED IN ENGINEERING DRAWINGS.

ONLY

ONLY

STANDARD LETTERING IS USED FOR CLARITY, SIMPLICITY AND READABILITY.

STANDARD

STANDARD

Repeat the letters and sentences above.

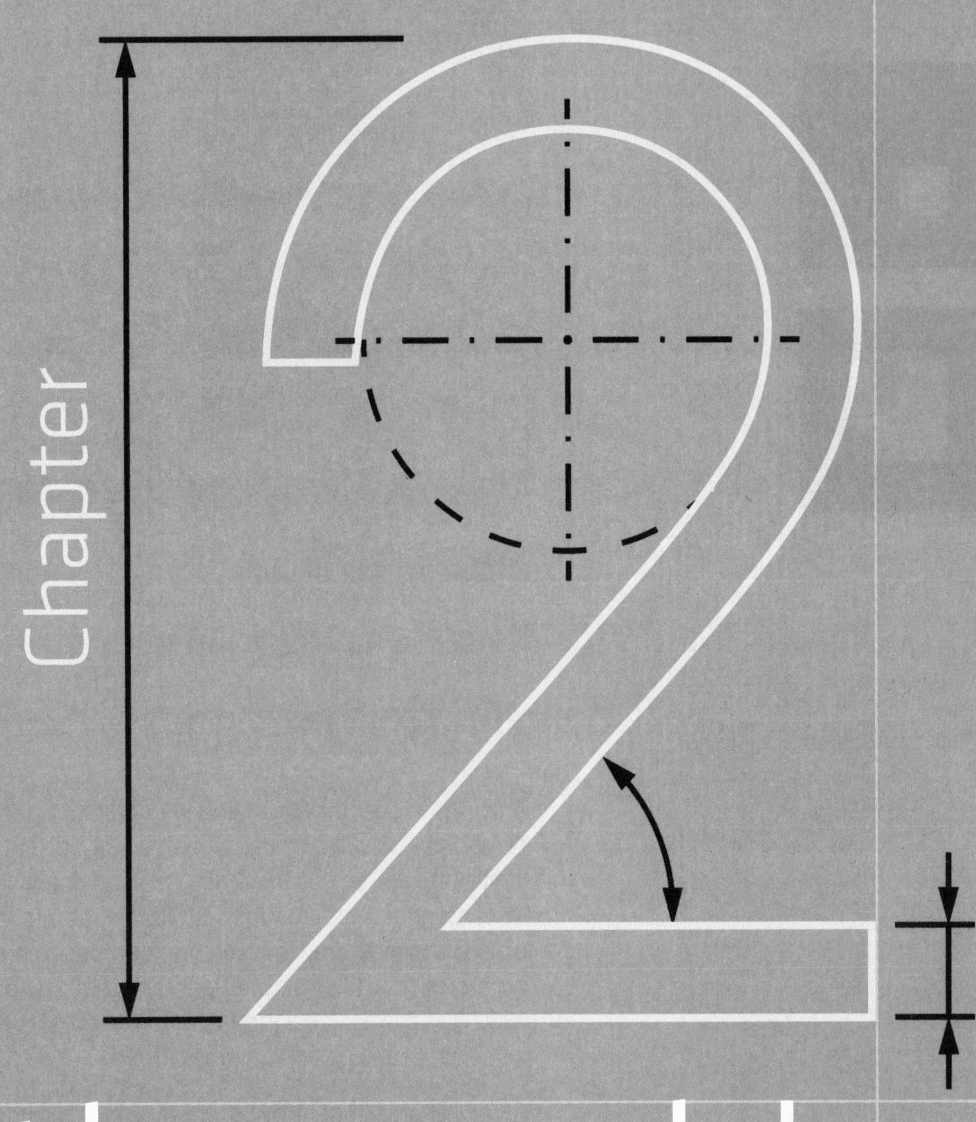

Orthographic Projection

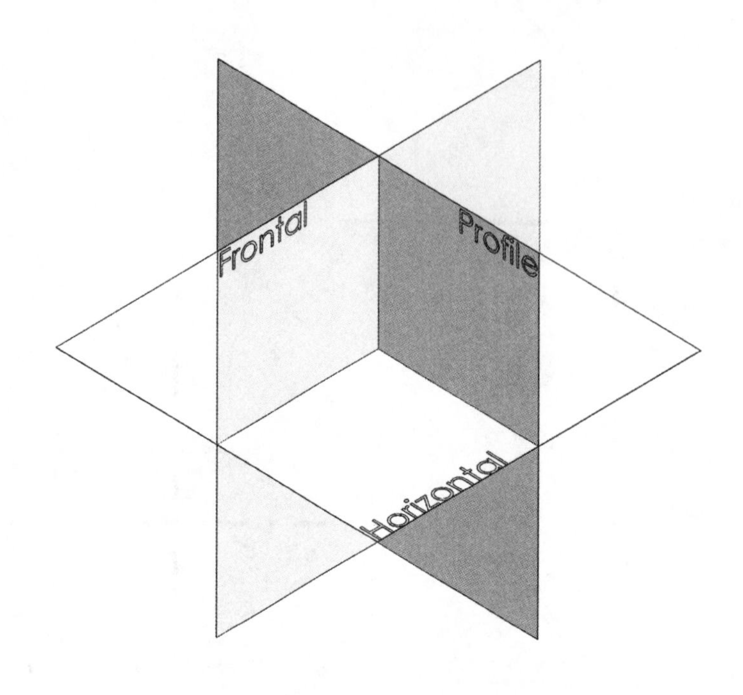

FIG. 2.1 Principal projection planes

Introduction

A common dilemma in engineering graphics presents itself when attempting to portray three-dimensional objects in two-dimensional space (a piece of paper). Unlike artistic drawings, which are primarily concerned with creating visually appealing representations of an object, technical drawings require methods to precisely specify its geometry, size, and structure to ensure that an object is manufactured exactly as the designer intended it. The most fundamental technique involved is called graphical projection.

Graphical projection is a system by which a three dimensional object is represented on a planar surface. There are different graphical projection methods that are used in technical graphics: orthographics, obliques, axonometrics, and perspectives. While obliques, perspectives, and axonometrics attempt to represent multiple faces of an object in a single drawing, orthographic projection uses a series of two-dimensional views, arranged in a standard manner, in order to fully document the object's geometry. This chapter introduces the primary method used in engineering: orthographic projection. The remaining techniques will be discussed in detail in subsequent chapters.

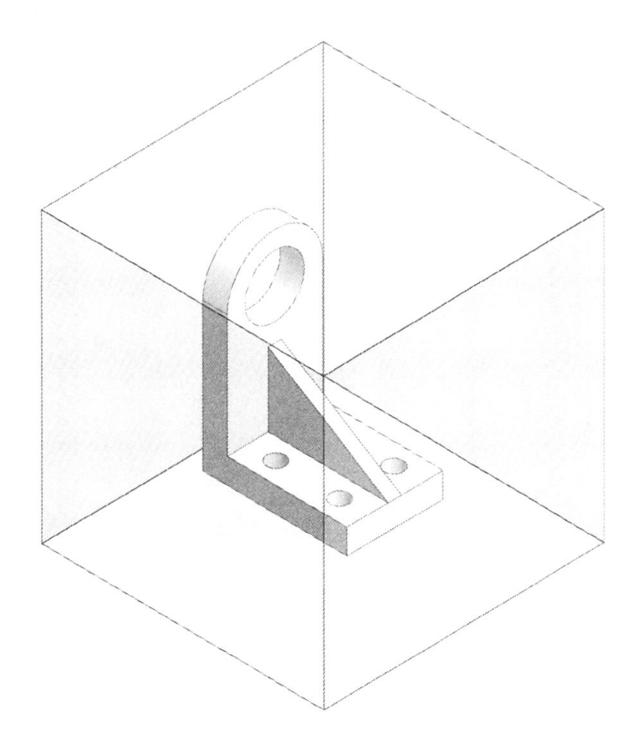

Bracket inside glass box FIG. 2.2

Orthographic Projection

Orthographic projection is a graphic representation method based on the creation of a group of two-dimensional views using three mutually perpendicular planes called frontal, horizontal, and profile. These planes intersect each other at 90° angles (see Figure 2.1).

To understand how orthographic projection works, visualize an object displayed inside an imaginary cube or glass box, like the bracket shown in Figure 2.2.

The edges of the bracket are projected normally onto the planes of this imaginary glass box. You can think of this concept as an observer located outside the box looking at the object inside (see Figure 2.3). The process is then repeated for the six faces of the glass box, as shown in Figure 2.4.

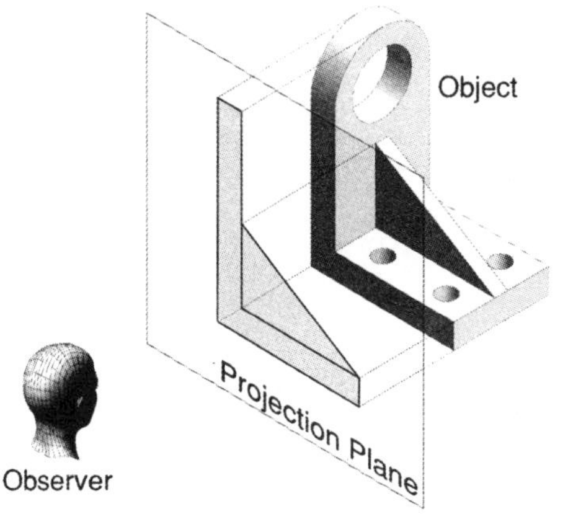

Projection on the glass plane FIG. 2.3

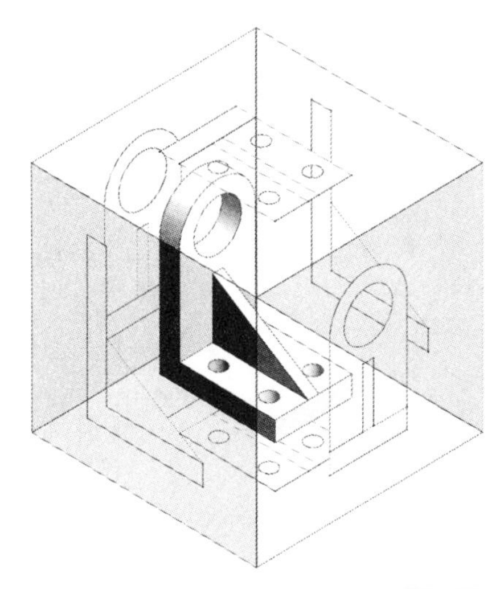
Views projected onto the faces of the box FIG. 2.4

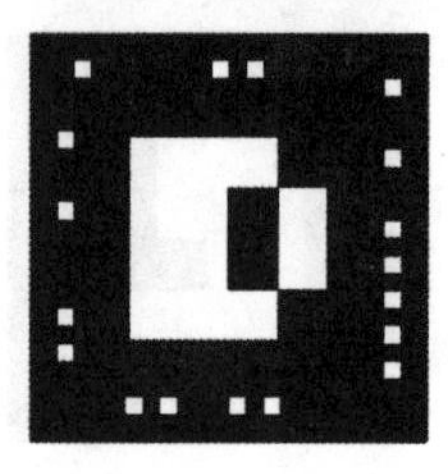

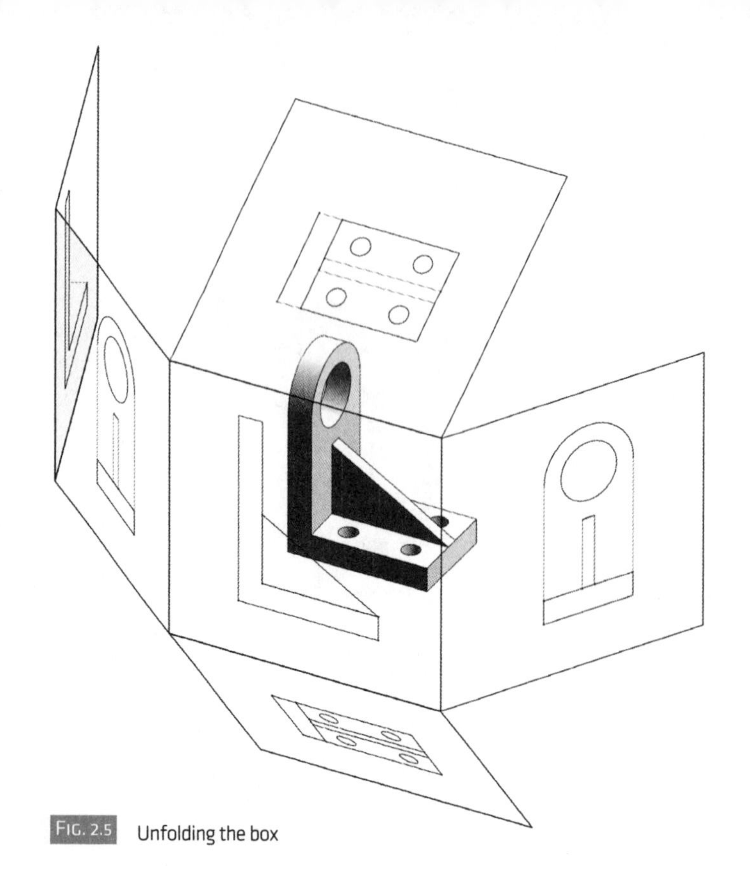

FIG. 2.5 Unfolding the box

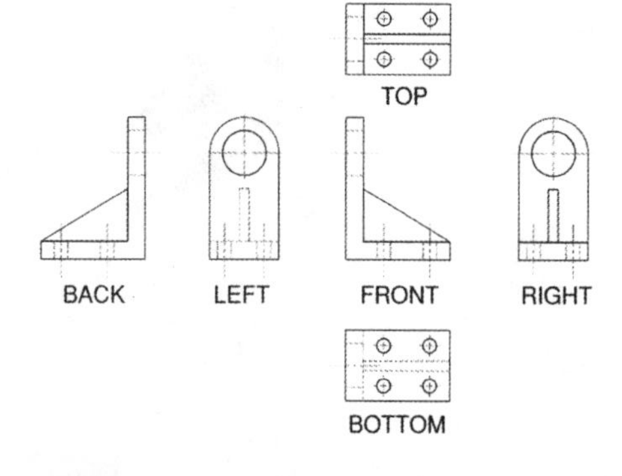

FIG. 2.6 Complete orthographic representation of the bracket

The six faces of the box are then unfolded in a standard manner so that the top view is shown directly above the front and the side view is placed directly to the side of the front view (see Figure 2.5). The six views generated are called the principal views and they constitute the complete orthographic representation of the object (see Figure 2.6).

Each orthographic view shows only two dimensions of the object, which means that more than one view is necessary to fully describe the object. For this reason, orthographic drawings are also called multiview drawings.

Orthographic views must be aligned and sufficiently spaced to allow for dimensions. Each view shares at least one dimension (width, height, and depth) with another view (see Figure 2.7). The front and back views correspond to the frontal plane, the top and bottom views correspond to the horizontal plane, and the left and right side views correspond to the profile plane. While the views associated with each plane are similar in appearance, they are mirror images of each other.

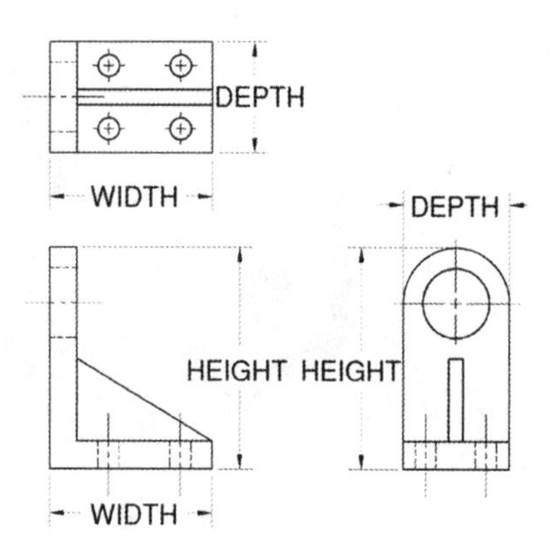

FIG. 2.7 Shared dimensions

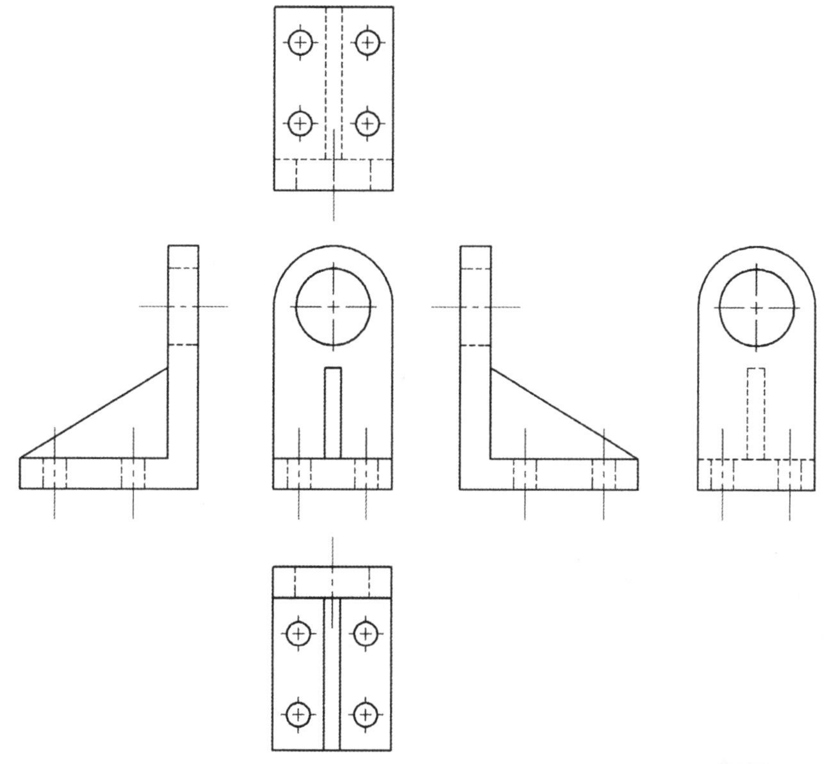

Complete orthographic representation of the bracket in First Angle Projection FIG. 2.10

Projection Methods

There are two major methods in which an object's views are projected onto the enclosing glass box. In the United States, Third Angle Projection is used, which can be understood as viewing the object from outside the glass box. The examples shown in previous figures use Third Angle Projection. In other countries, however, the preferred method is First Angle Projection, in which the viewer is looking at the object from inside the box and the images are projected onto the planes behind the object. (see Figure 2.8 and Figure 2.9).

The complete orthographic representation of the bracket in First Angle Projection is shown in Figure 2.10.

Both First and Third Angle Projection methods are valid as they result in the same six views. The difference is the arrangement of these views around the glass box. To avoid confusion, the type of projection must be clearly indicated with a symbol on the drawing. The projection symbol for both projection methods consists on a truncated cone (see Figure 2.11).

Third Angle Projection is the default projection system used in the United States according to the standard ASME Y14.3-2003, which regulates multiview drawings. For this reason, all the examples and exercises in this book will use Third Angle Projection.

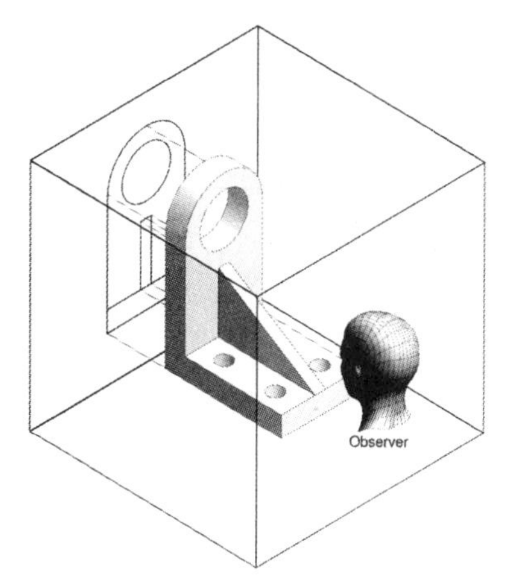

Observer located inside the box  FIG. 2.8

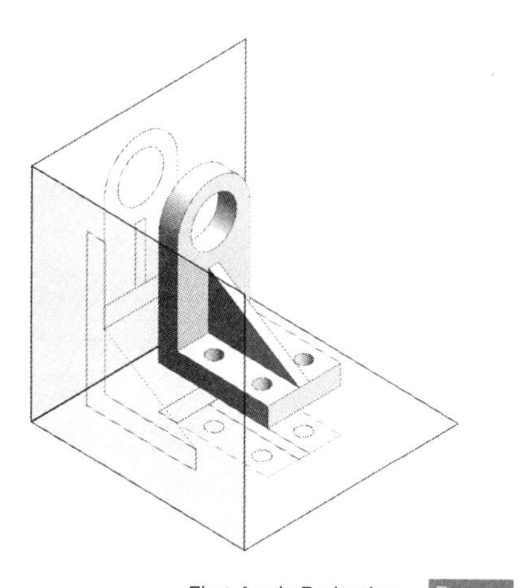

First Angle Projection  FIG. 2.9

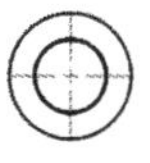 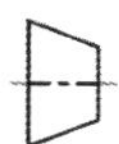 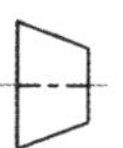 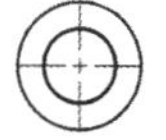

Left: 1st Angle Projection symbol
Right: 3rd Angle Projection symbol  FIG. 2.11

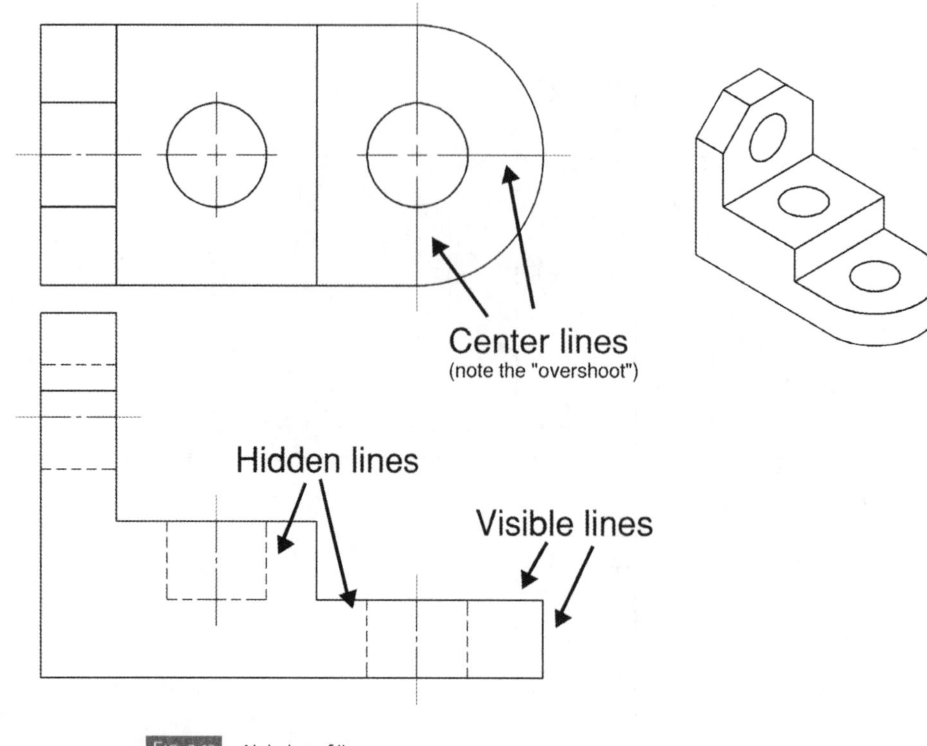

FIG. 2.13 Alphabet of lines

Alphabet of Lines

VISIBLE
HIDDEN
CENTER

FIG. 2.12 Standard line types

In orthographic projection, different line types are utilized to show various geometric features. While standard line types have different patterns and thicknesses, they are all equally dark. Visible lines are thick, continuous lines used to portray edges and visible features. Hidden lines are thin, dashed lines used to illustrate features that are hidden behind visible surfaces. Center lines are thin lines, with alternating long and short dashes, used to indicate the centers of holes, cylinders, and arcs. The different line types are illustrated in Figure 2.12.

Center lines are drawn equidistant from the edge of each edge in the rectangular view of a hole or cylinder and cross each other in the circular view. Center lines also extend a short distance past the visible edge see Figure 2.13). Construction lines are light lines, noticeable if the paper is held at arm's length, used as guidelines to make construction of other features easier. Construction lines are represented by a series of dots, but they are typically erased after the drawing is finished.

When lines happen to overlap, because various geometric features coincide, only one line is shown over the others. The rule is that visible lines take precedence over hidden lines and hidden lines take precedence over center lines. The precedence of lines is illustrated in Figure 2.14.

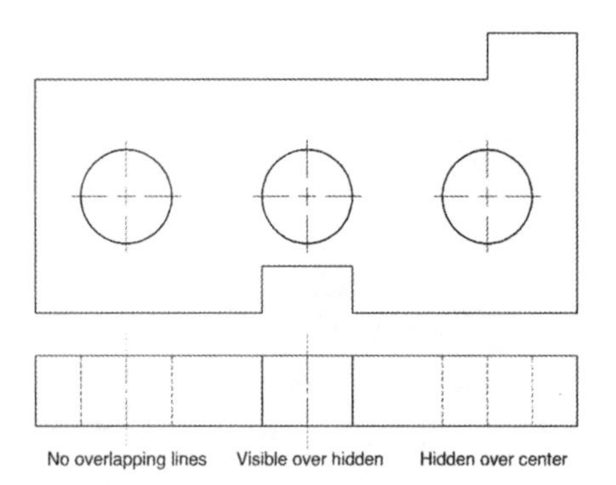

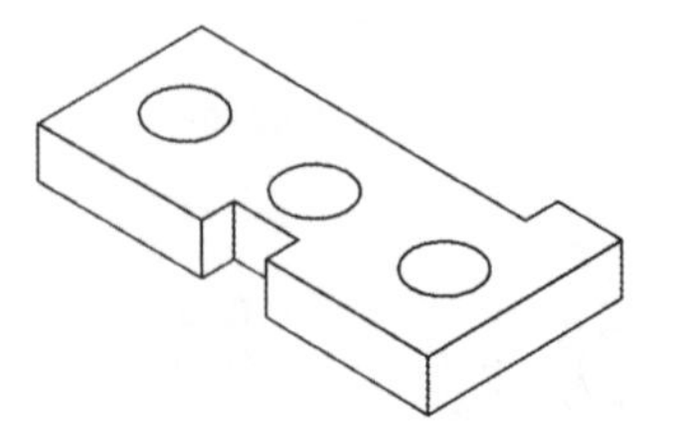

FIG. 2.14 Precedence of lines

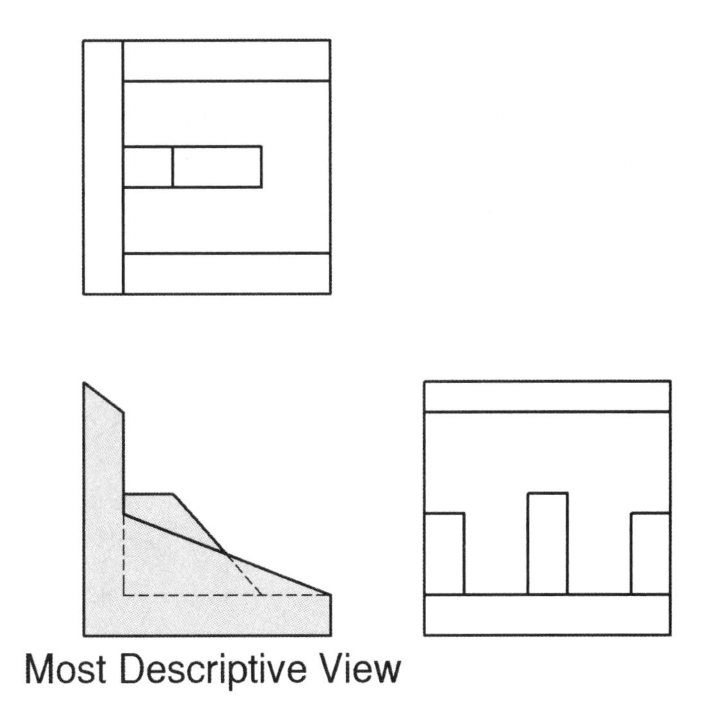

Choosing the most descriptive view as front view FIG. 2.15A

View Selection

Although there are six principal orthographic views generated by unfolding the imaginary glass box discussed previously, not all views are necessary to fully describe an object. Three of the views provide essentially the same information as the other three, except that they are viewed from the opposite direction.

In general, the number of orthographic views in a drawing must be kept to a minimum. For very simple objects with uniform thickness, a single view supplemented by a note is sufficient. Other objects may need two views, while more complex objects may need three or more. Conventionally for most objects, front, top, and right side views are used. Additionally, decisions must be made about which views should be selected as front, top, and side views. The following list provides guidelines to help make these determinations.

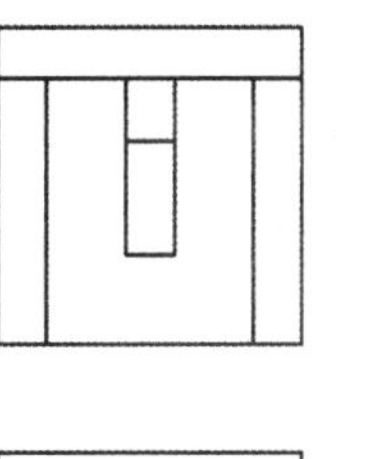

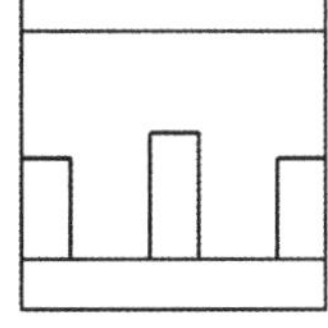

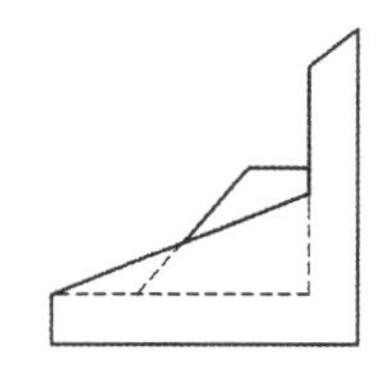

Not Most Descriptive View FIG. 2.15B

1. The most descriptive view should be selected as the front view. This view will usually have more curved or sloping lines, and reflect most of an object's distinguishing features. See Figure 2.15.

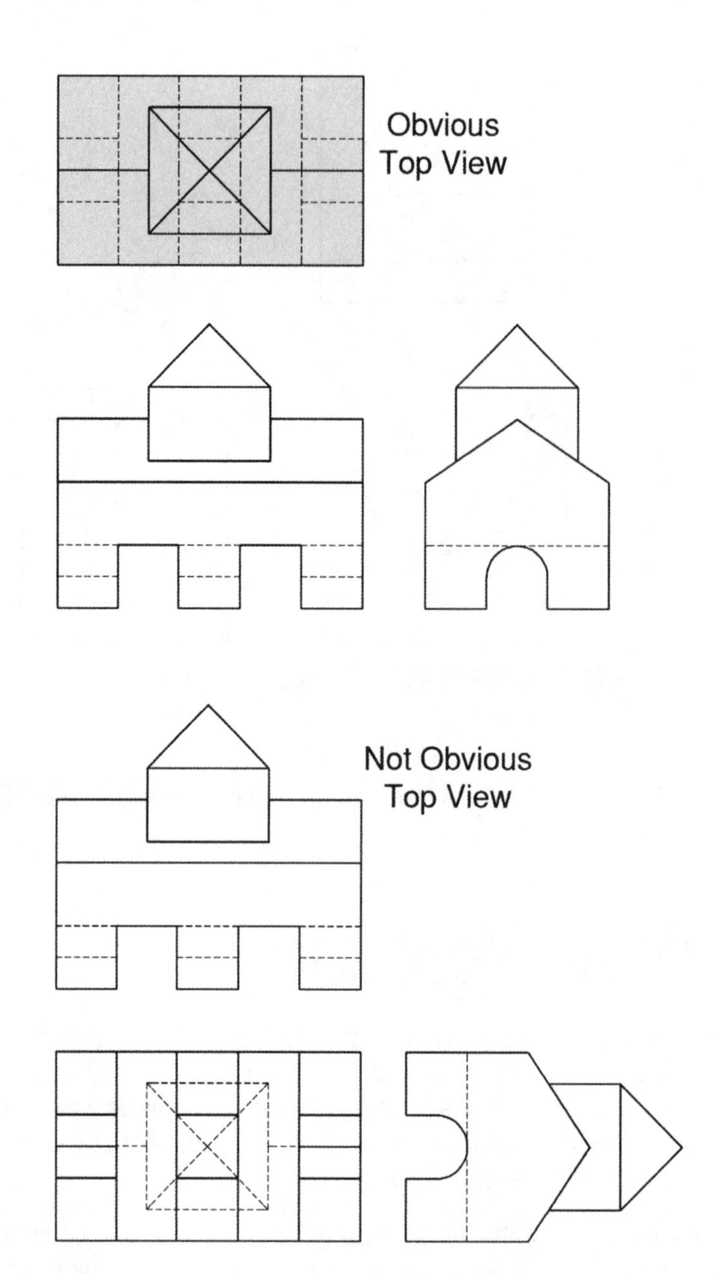

Fig. 2.16 Choosing the obvious top view

2. If an object has an obvious top, then that view should be selected as the top view. See Figure 2.16

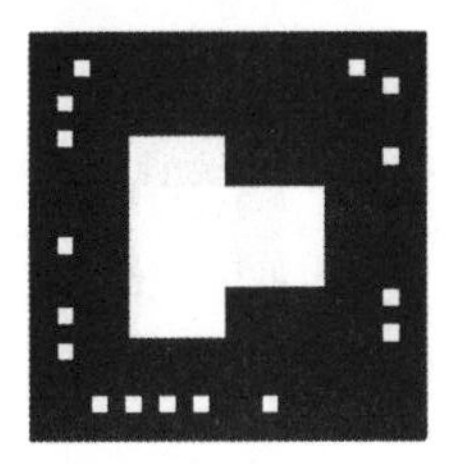

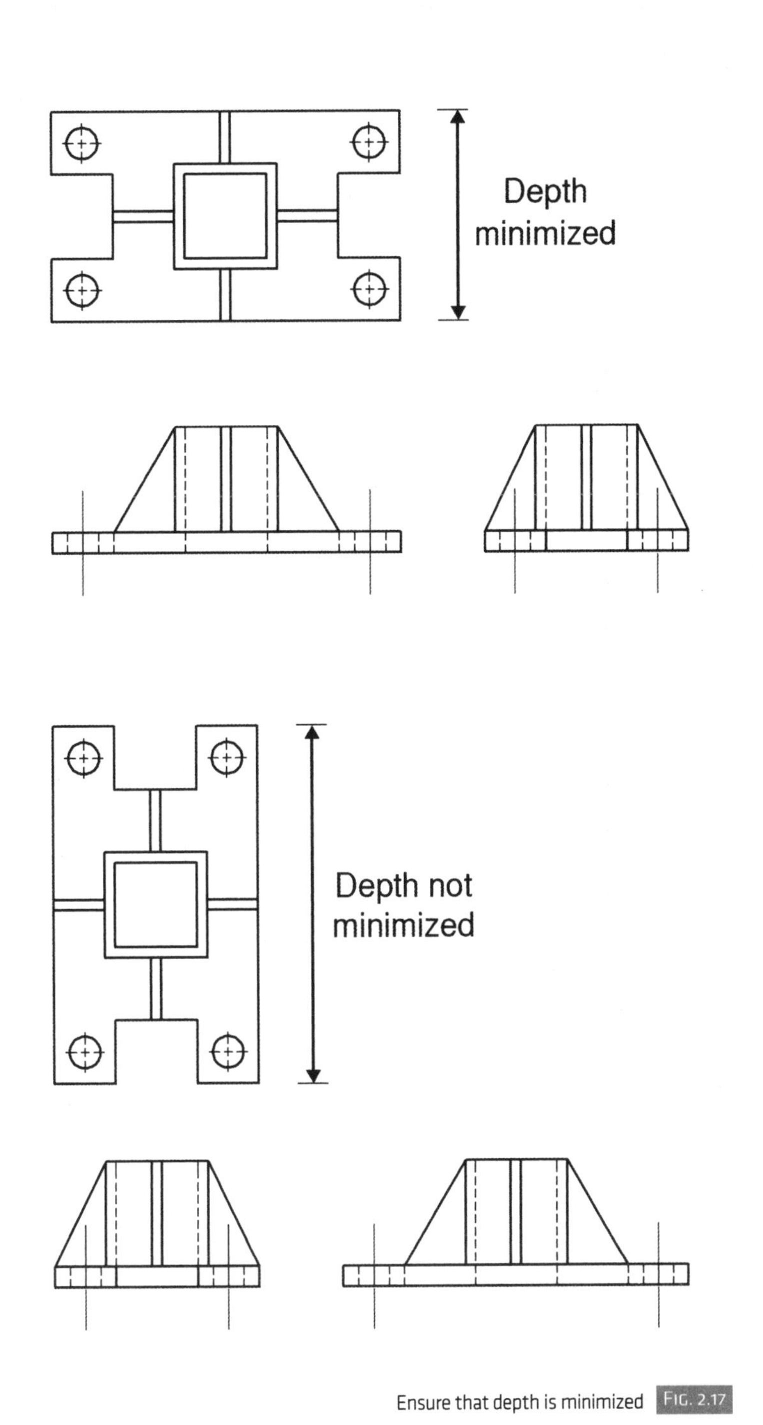

Ensure that depth is minimized FIG. 2.17

3. The depth dimension should be minimized in order to conserve space and provide adequate room for orthographic views of other objects on the same page. See Figure 2.17.

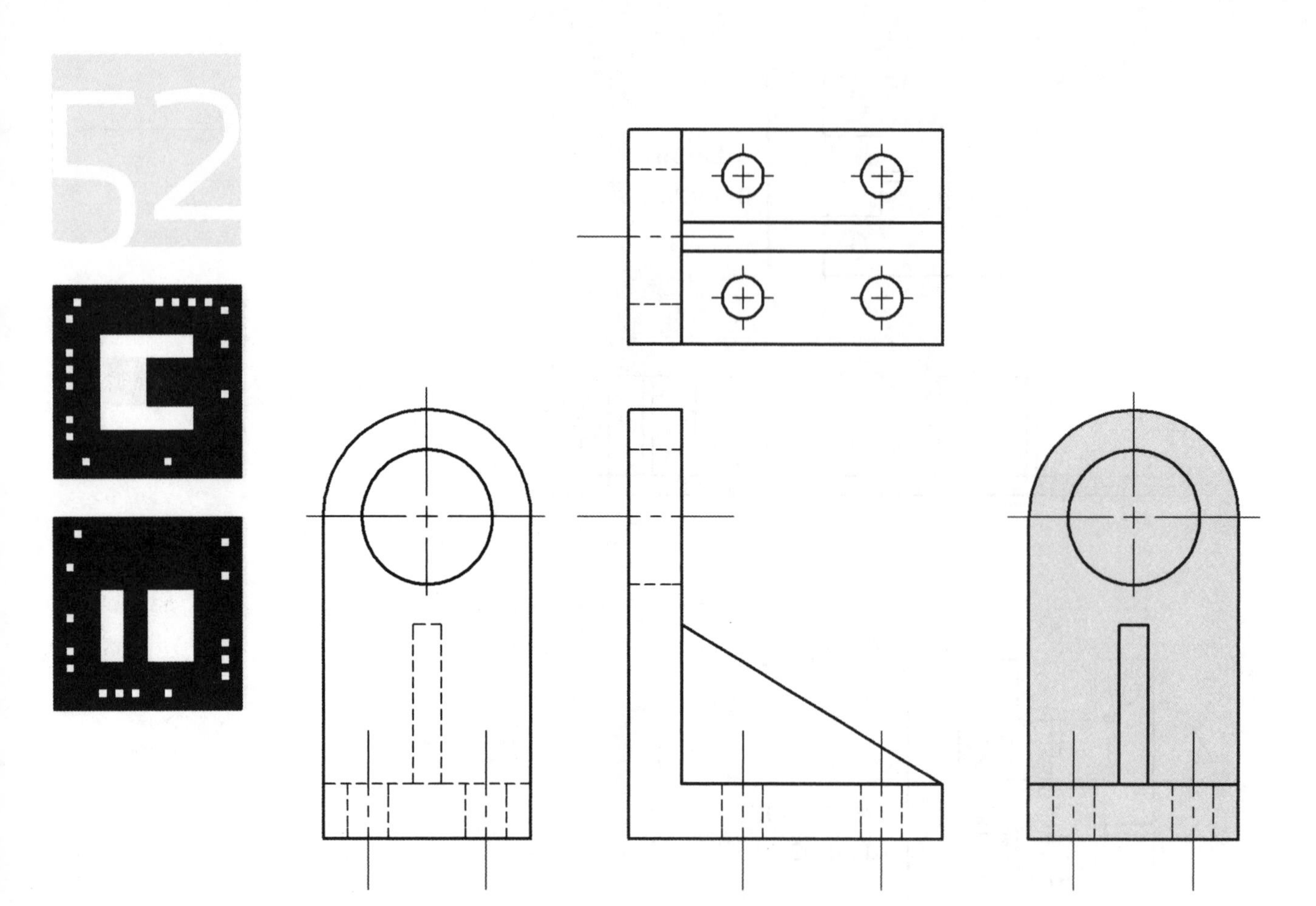

FIG. 2.18 Minimize the number of hidden lines

4. Views should be selected so that the total number of hidden lines in the drawing is minimized. See Figure 2.18.

5. Both the left and right side views are acceptable in a drawing. However, if both views describe the object's geometry equally well, the right side view is conventionally preferred.

While the previous guidelines are recommended, there are situations where no clear cut case presents itself, such as when the obvious top view also maximizes depth. In such cases, experience and good judgment should be your guide.

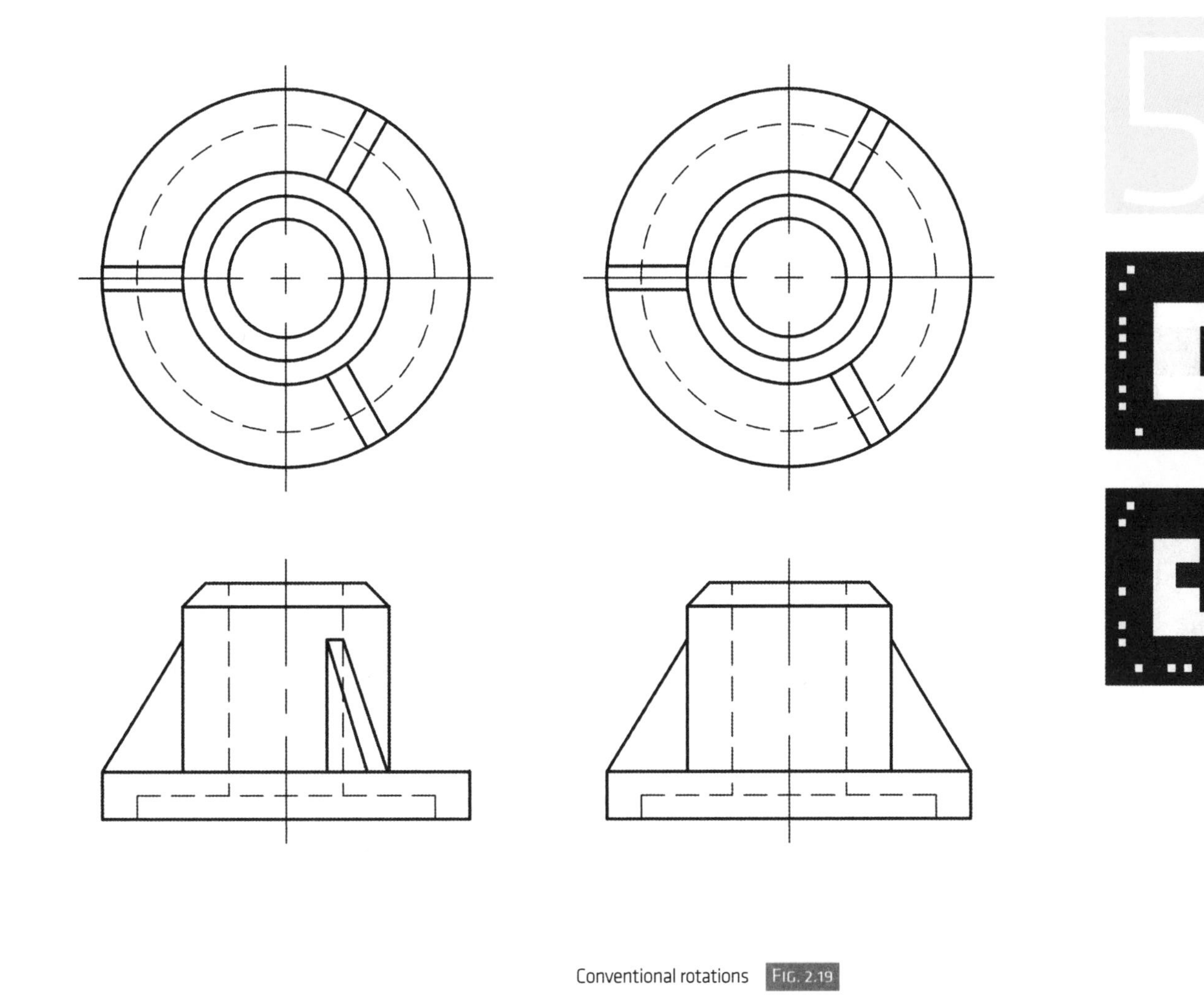

Conventional rotations FIG. 2.19

Conventional Practices

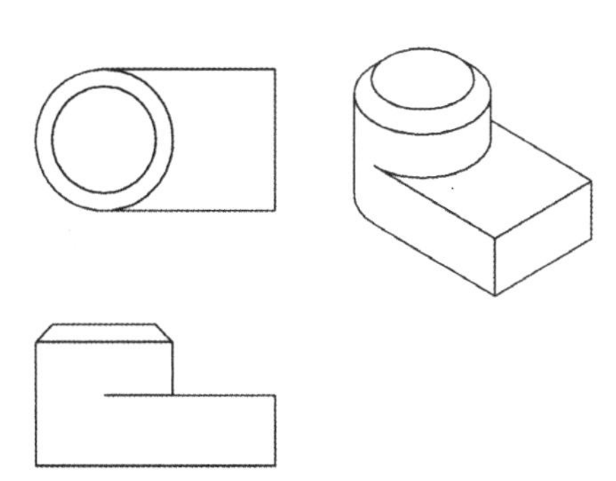

Occasionally, it may be necessary to break standard orthographic projection rules in order to illustrate an object more clearly. A common example is when a cylindrical object has equally spaced features. In this case, the general orthographic views are correct, but confusing. In order to provide a more aesthetically pleasing view, while also increasing clarity, it may be useful to show the features spaced at 180°, even if the spacing is actually 60°. See Figure 2.19.

Runouts are displayed when cylindrical features intersect rectangular features. A visible line is drawn to represent where this intersection occurs. See Figure 2.20.

Proper representation of runouts 

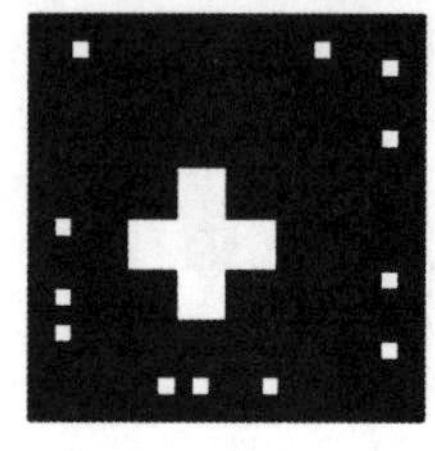

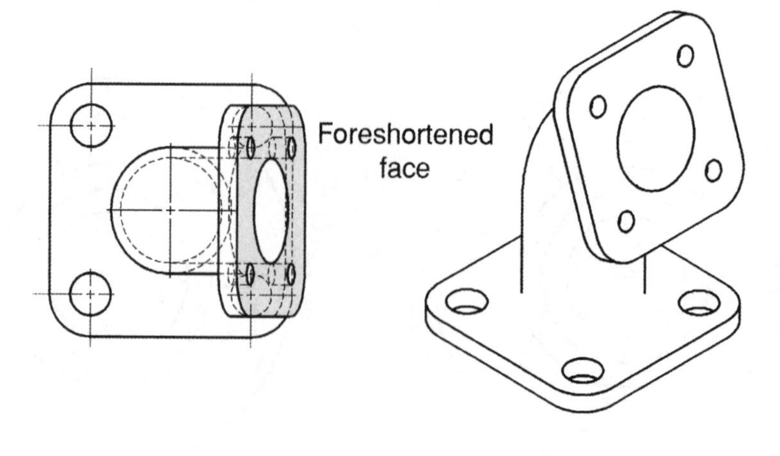

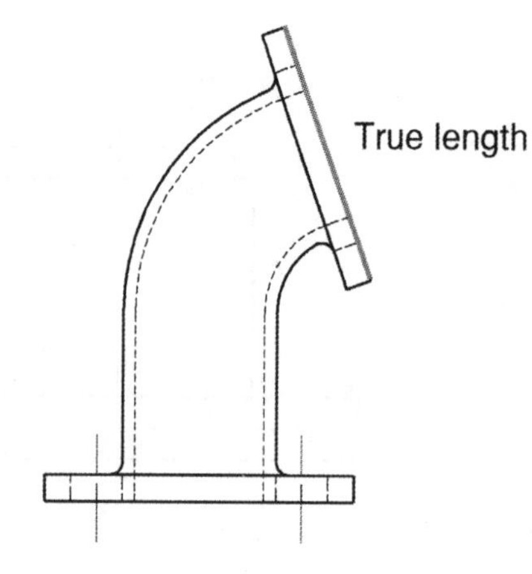

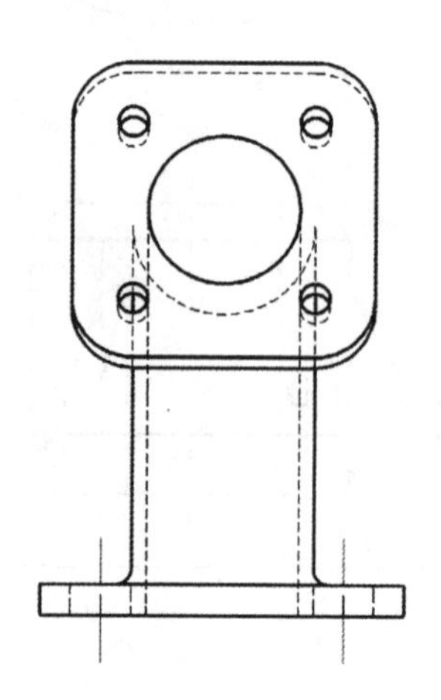

FIG. 2.21 Foreshortened distance

Foreshortening

Foreshortening occurs when a feature appears to be shorter than its true length because it extends away from the viewer. This concept appears oftentimes in orthographic projection since each view only portrays two dimensions. This situation can be alleviated with the use of auxiliary views, as you will study in future chapters. SeeFigure 2.21 .

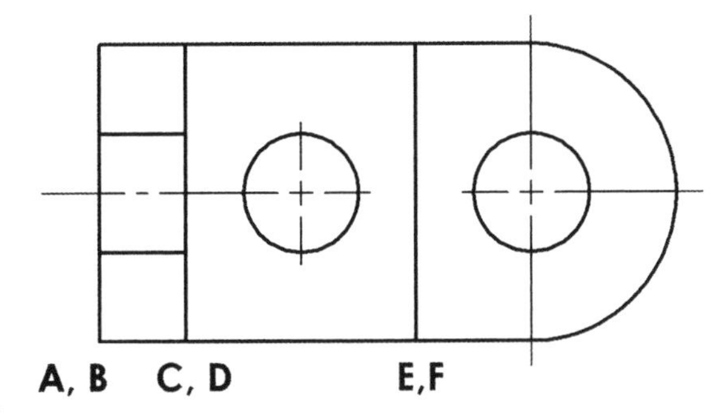

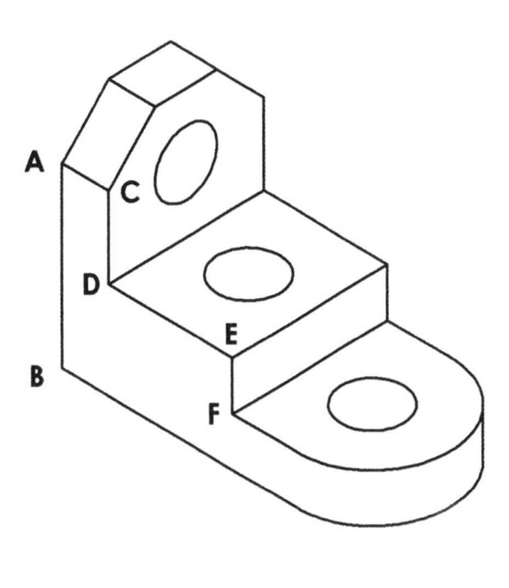

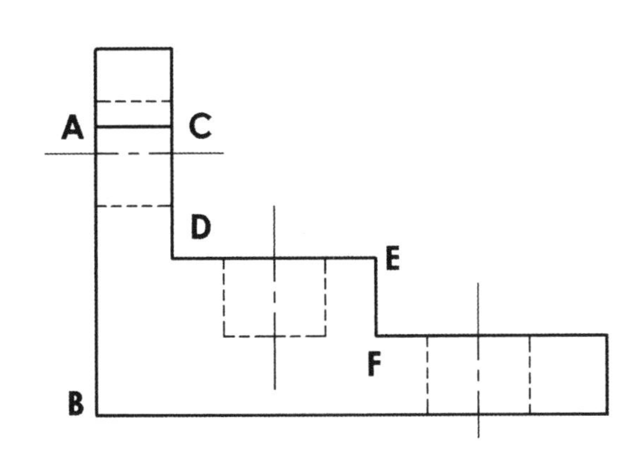

Scheme for labeling edges and points FIG. 2.22

Orthographic Projection Aids

When working with orthographic projection, it may be helpful to label features on an object, such as lines, faces, and points. Depending on which orthographic view is considered, each feature could be shown as an edge or a face. Notice that no one orthographic view contains all the geometric information about an object. An important fact to consider is that a corner in one view is frequently shown as an edge in another. See Figure 2.22 for an example of this process.

Orthographic Projection

Chapter 02
Exercise 01

Name:

Date:

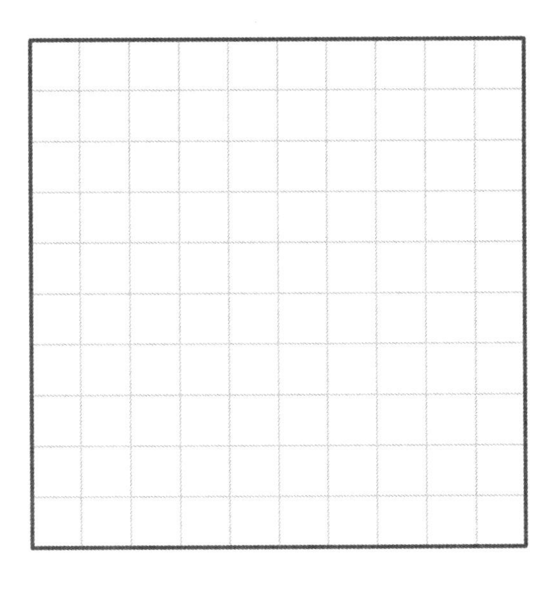

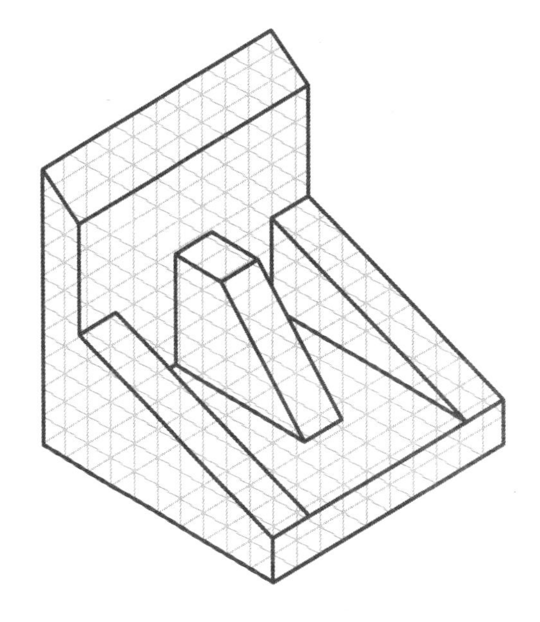

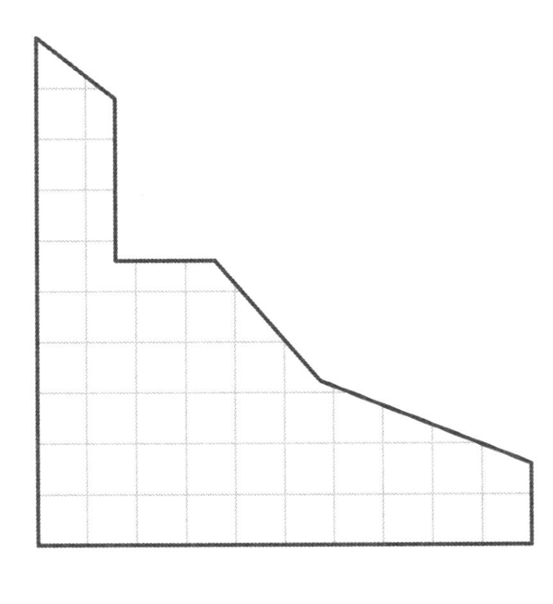

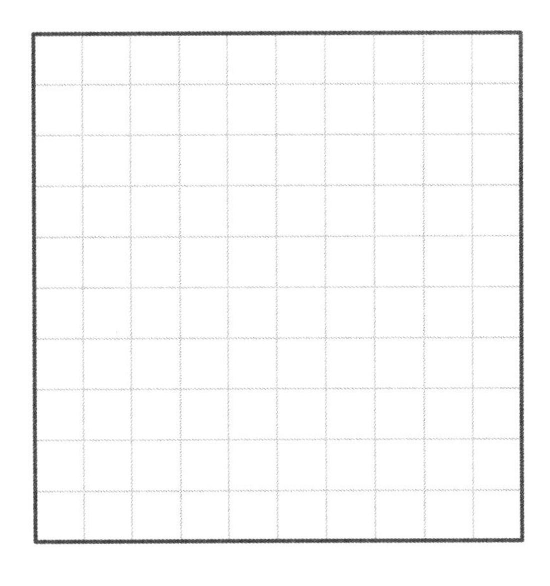

Add the missing lines to the orthographic views provided. All lines must fit inside the existing boundaries. Round up to the nearest grid square.

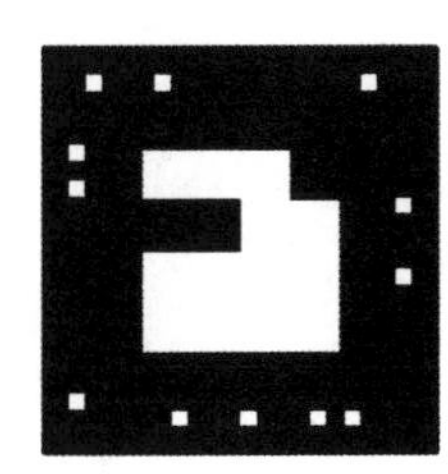

Orthographic Projection

Chapter 02
Exercise 02

Name:

Date:

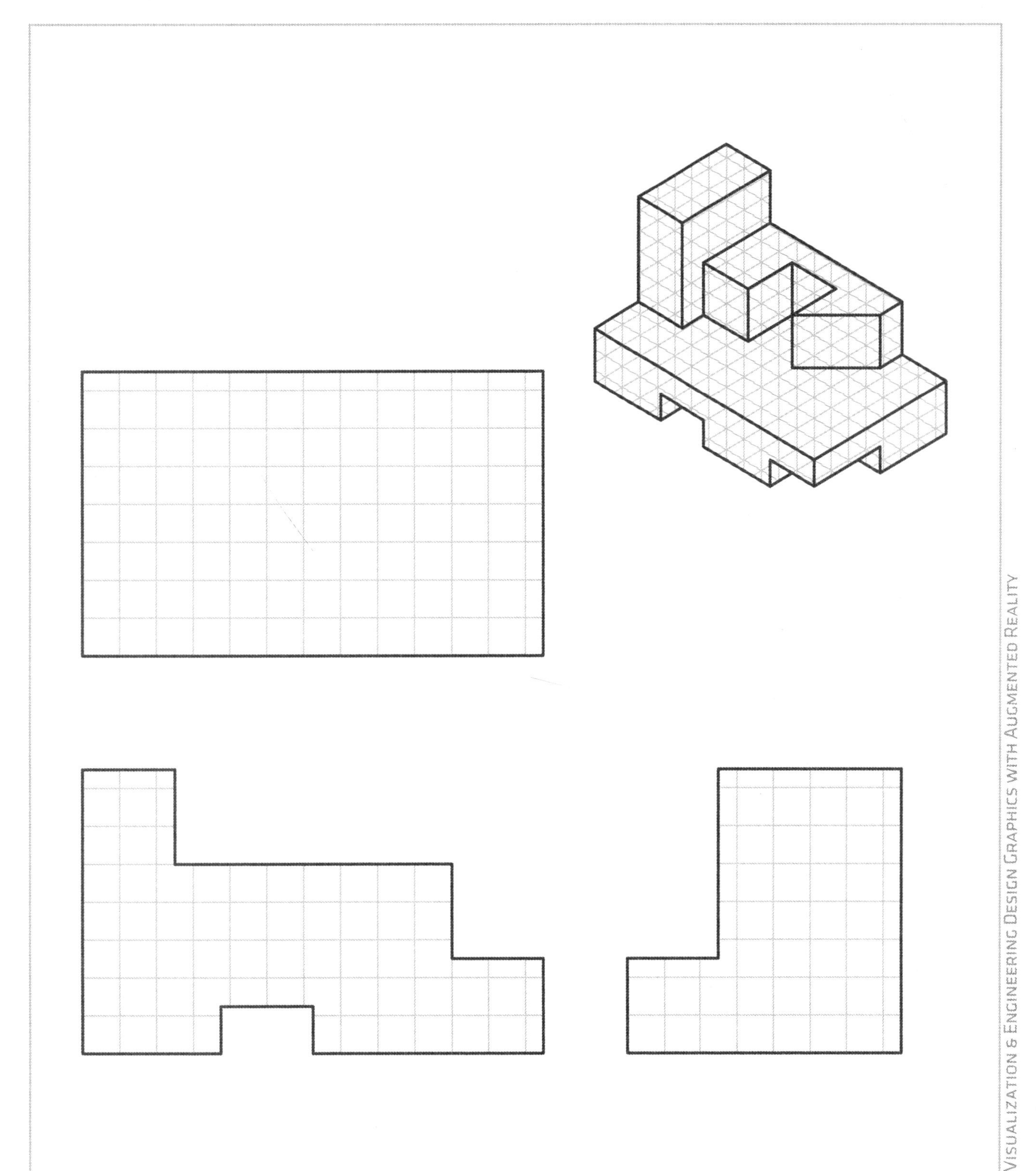

Add the missing lines to the orthographic views provided. All lines must fit inside the existing boundaries. Round up to the nearest grid square.

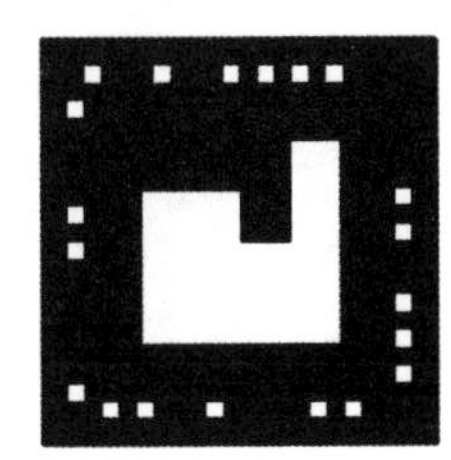

ORTHOGRAPHIC PROJECTION

CHAPTER 02
EXERCISE 03

NAME:

DATE:

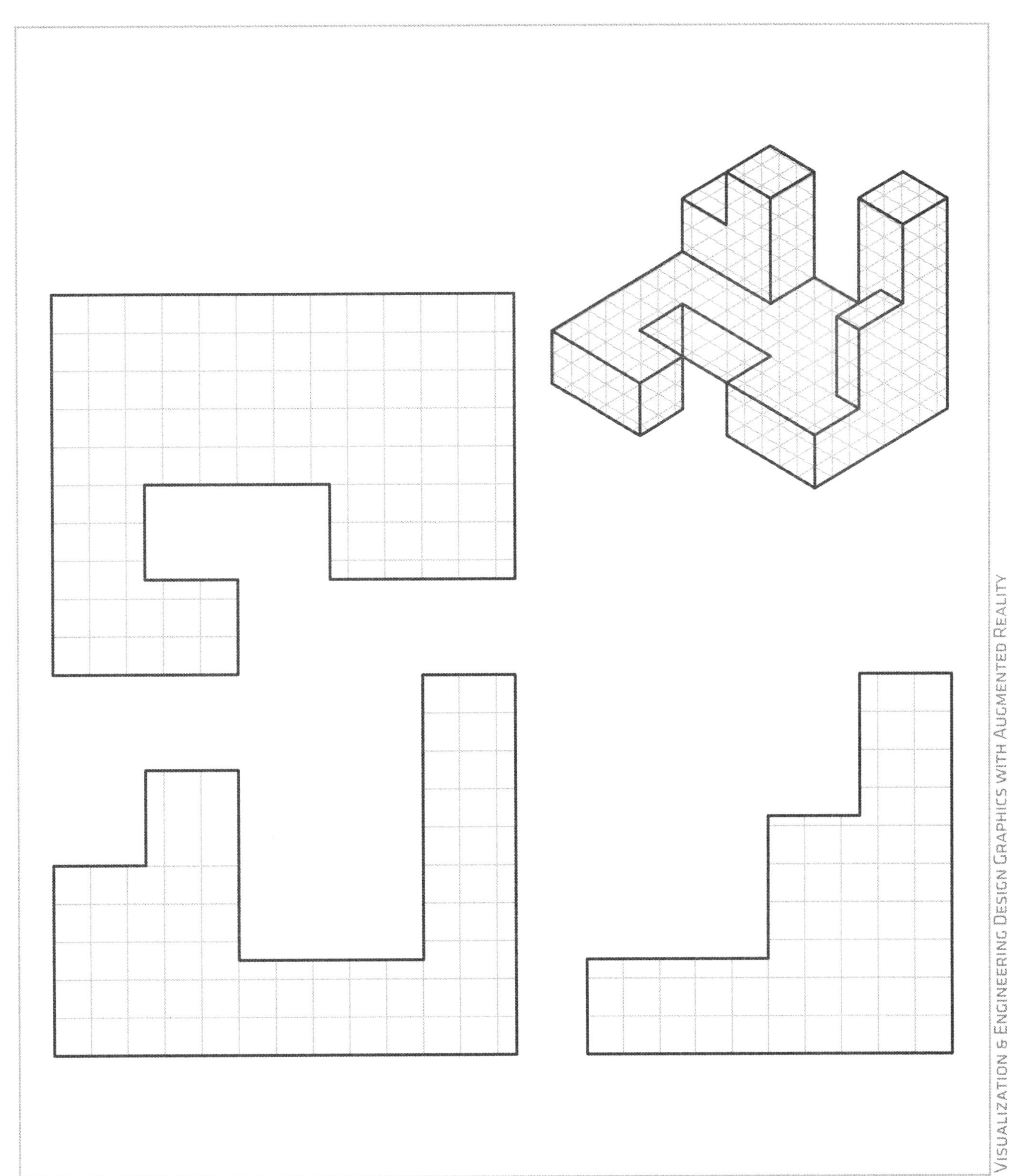

ADD THE MISSING LINES TO THE ORTHOGRAPHIC VIEWS PROVIDED. ALL LINES MUST FIT INSIDE THE EXISTING BOUNDARIES. ROUND UP TO THE NEAREST GRID SQUARE.

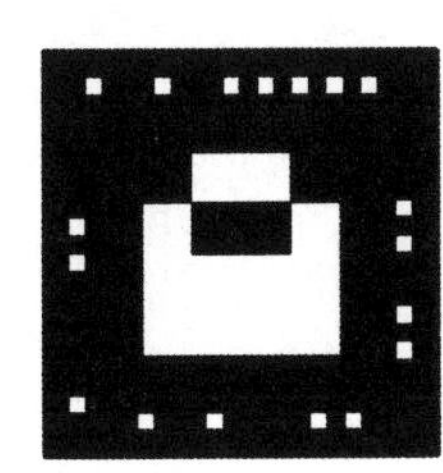

ORTHOGRAPHIC PROJECTION

CHAPTER 02
EXERCISE 04

NAME:

DATE:

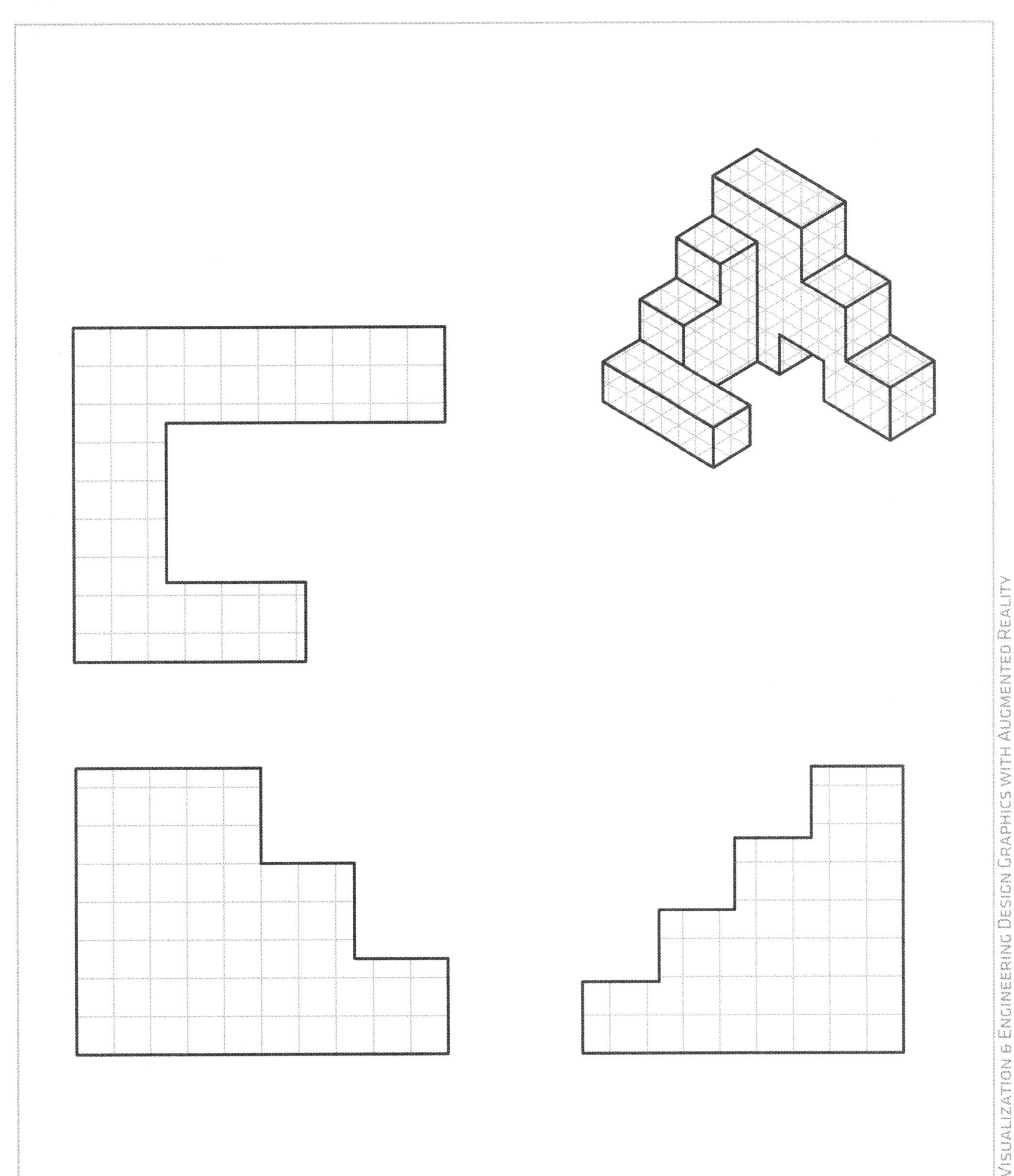

ADD THE MISSING LINES TO THE ORTHOGRAPHIC VIEWS PROVIDED. ALL LINES MUST FIT INSIDE THE EXISTING BOUNDARIES. ROUND UP TO THE NEAREST GRID SQUARE.

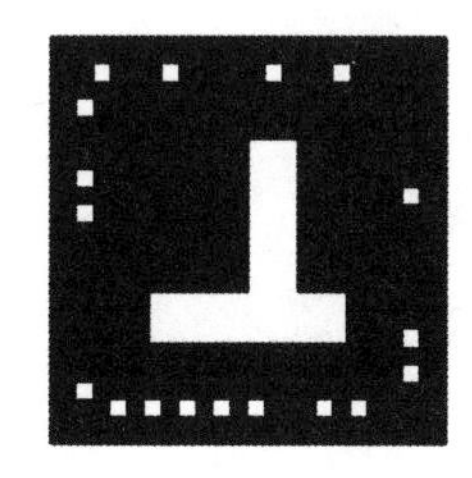
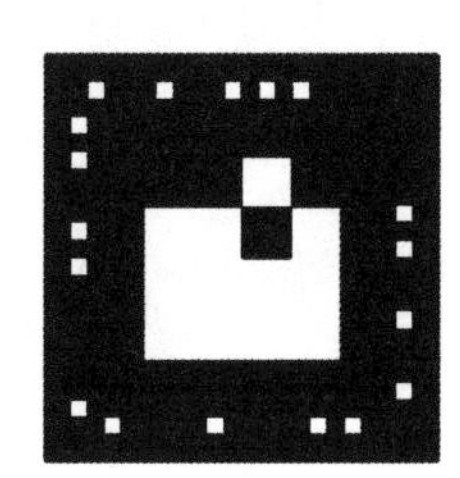

ORTHOGRAPHIC PROJECTION

CHAPTER 02
EXERCISE 05

NAME:

DATE:

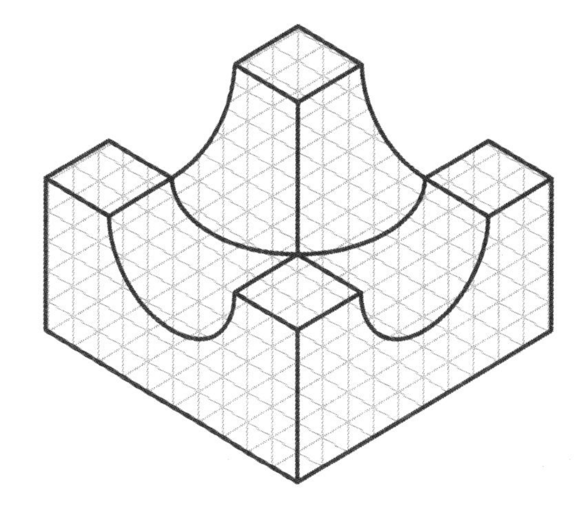
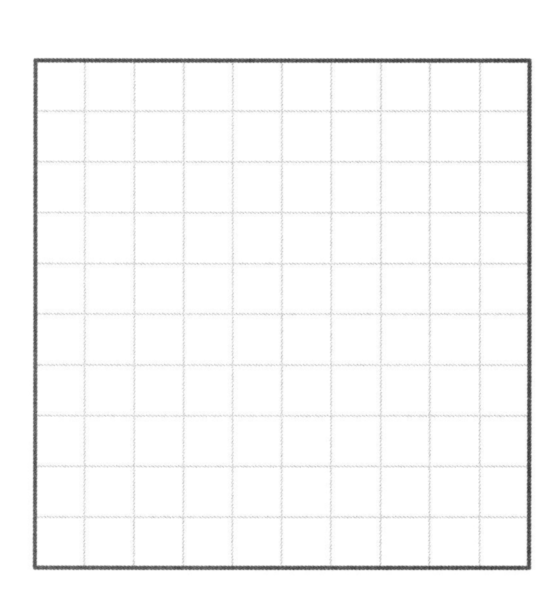
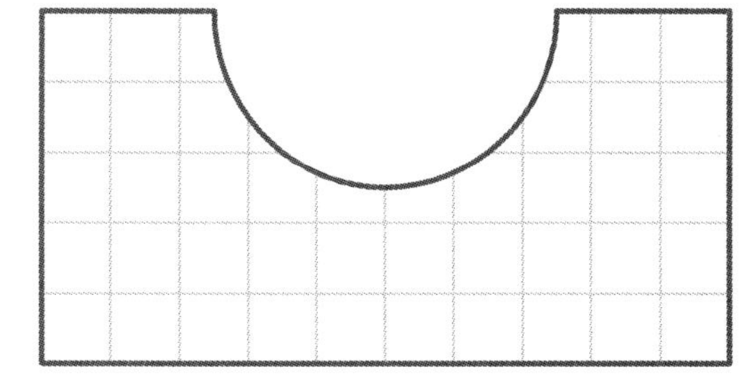

ADD THE MISSING LINES TO THE ORTHOGRAPHIC VIEWS PROVIDED. ALL LINES MUST FIT INSIDE THE EXISTING BOUNDARIES. ROUND UP TO THE NEAREST GRID SQUARE.

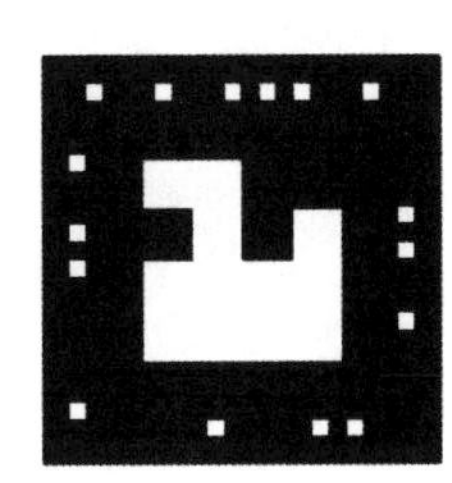

ORTHOGRAPHIC PROJECTION

CHAPTER 02

EXERCISE 06

NAME:

DATE:

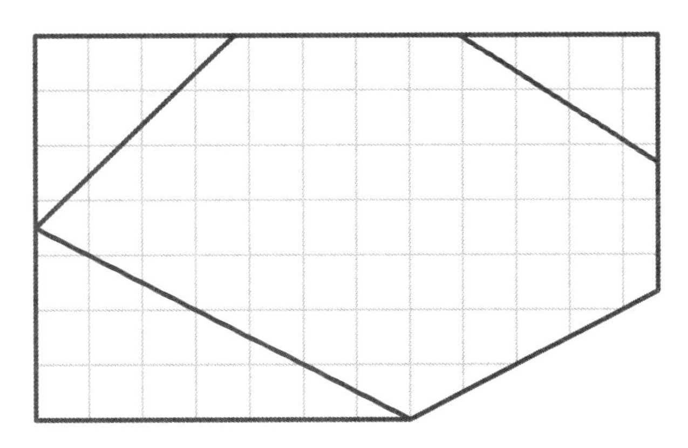

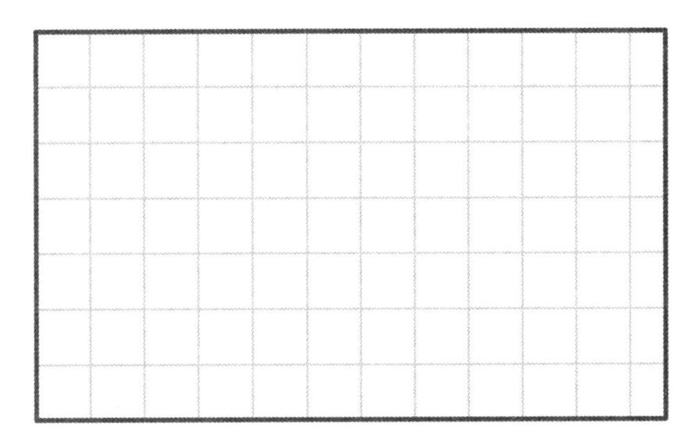

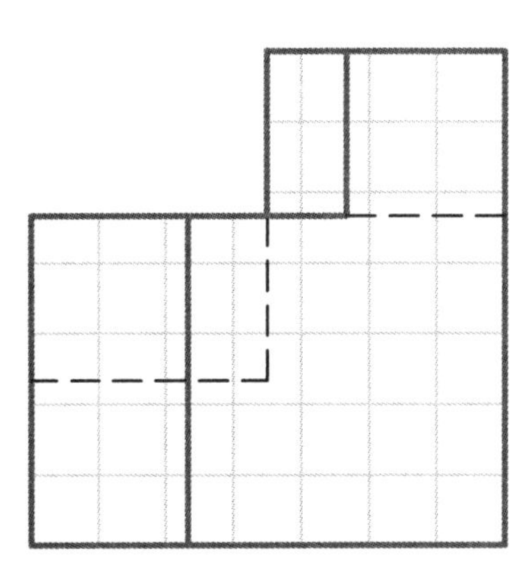

SKETCH THE MISSING VIEW. ALL LINES MUST FIT INSIDE THE EXISTING BOUNDARIES.
ROUND UP TO THE NEAREST GRID SQUARE.

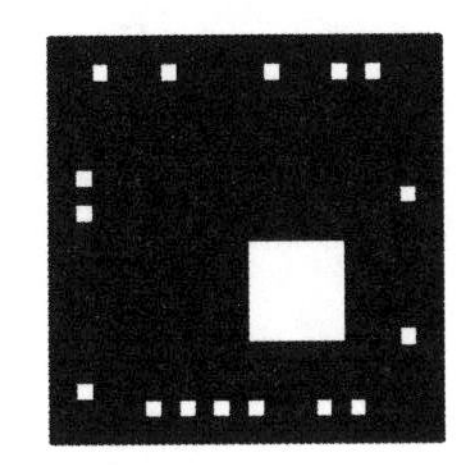
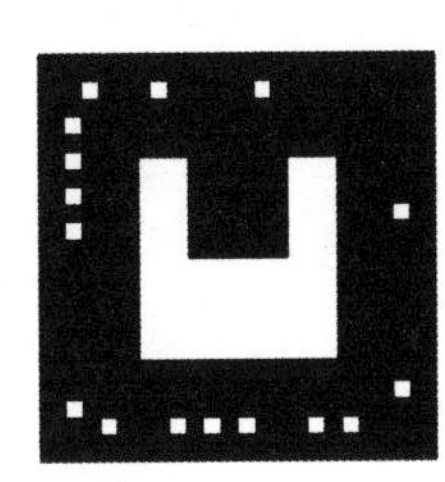

Orthographic Projection

Chapter 02

Exercise 07

Name:

Date:

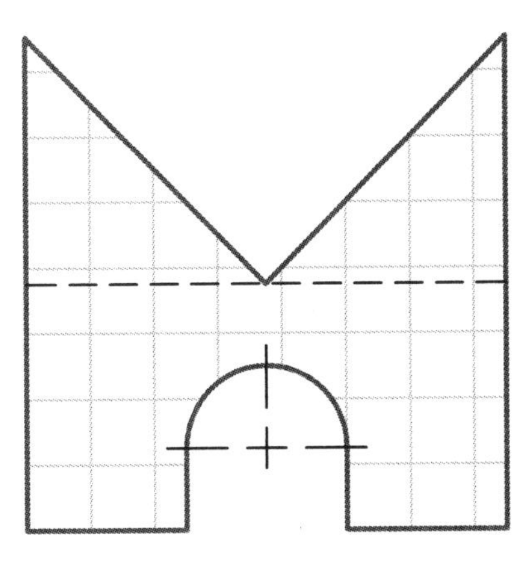

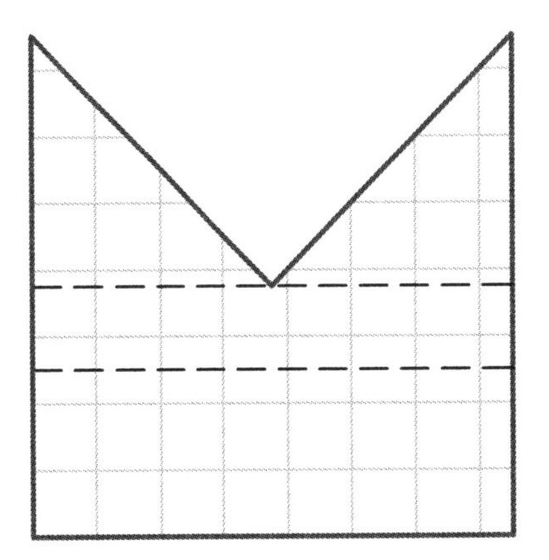

Sketch the missing view. All lines must fit inside the existing boundaries.
Round up to the nearest grid square.

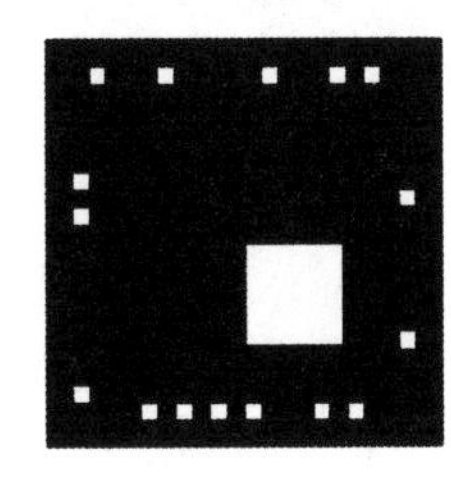
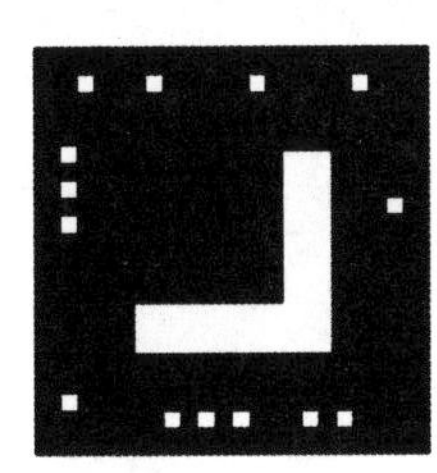

ORTHOGRAPHIC PROJECTION

CHAPTER 02
EXERCISE 08

NAME:

DATE:

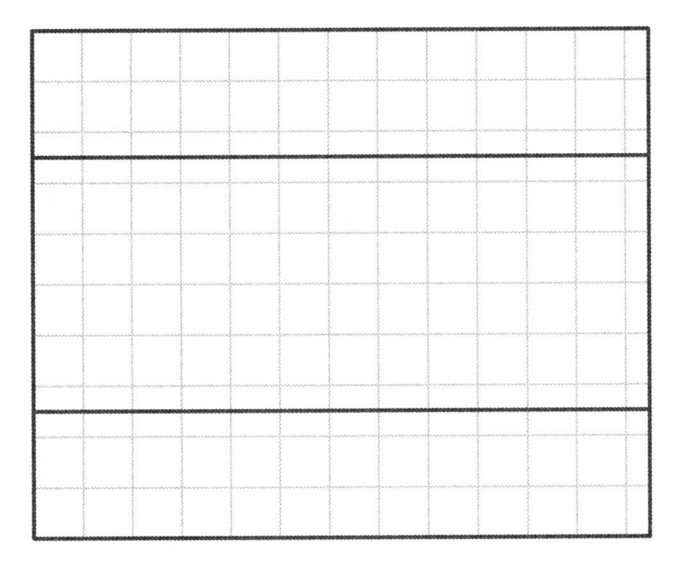

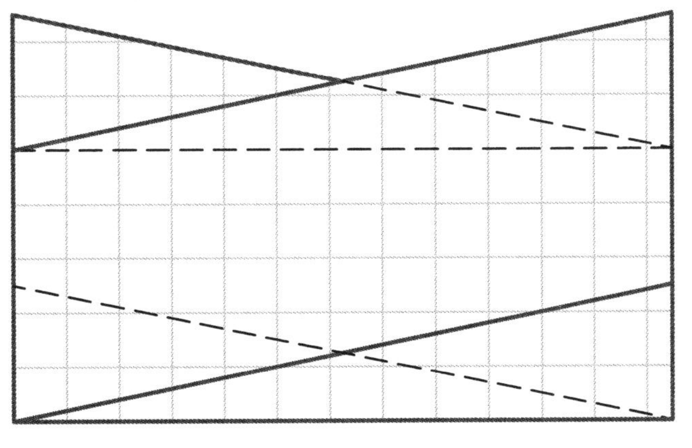

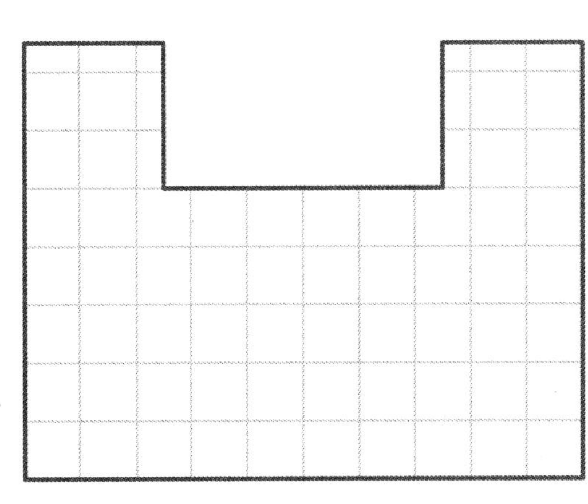

SKETCH THE MISSING VIEW. ALL LINES MUST FIT INSIDE THE EXISTING BOUNDARIES.
ROUND UP TO THE NEAREST GRID SQUARE.

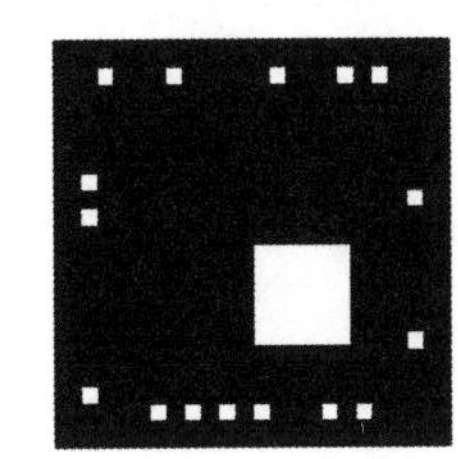
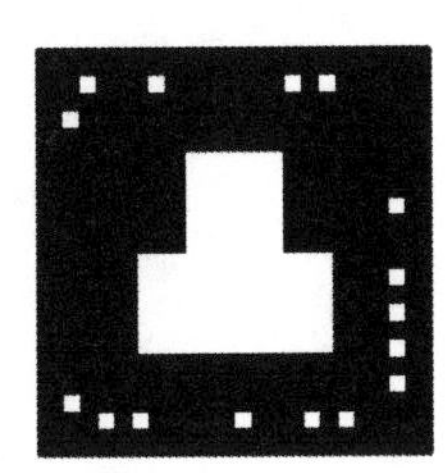

ORTHOGRAPHIC PROJECTION

CHAPTER 02

EXERCISE 09

NAME:

DATE:

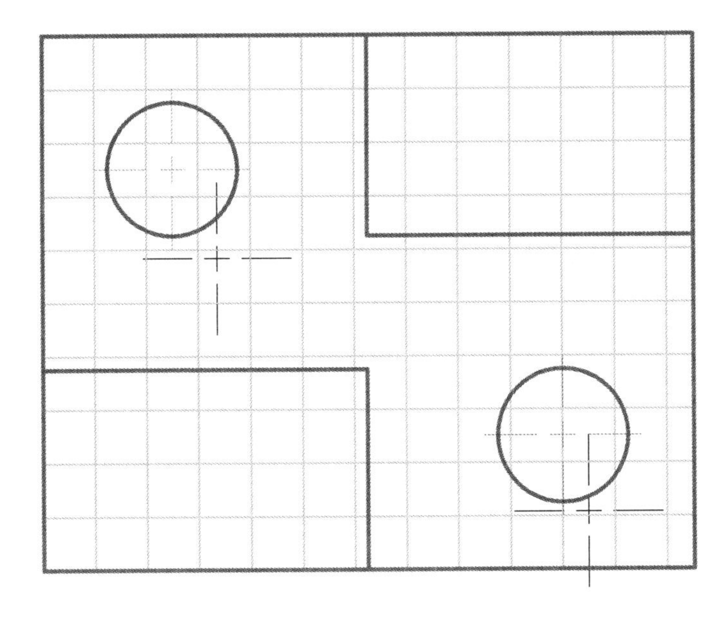

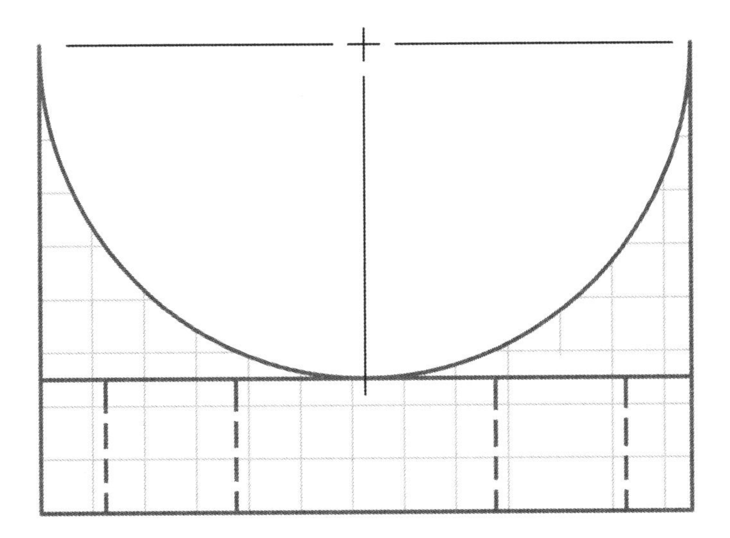

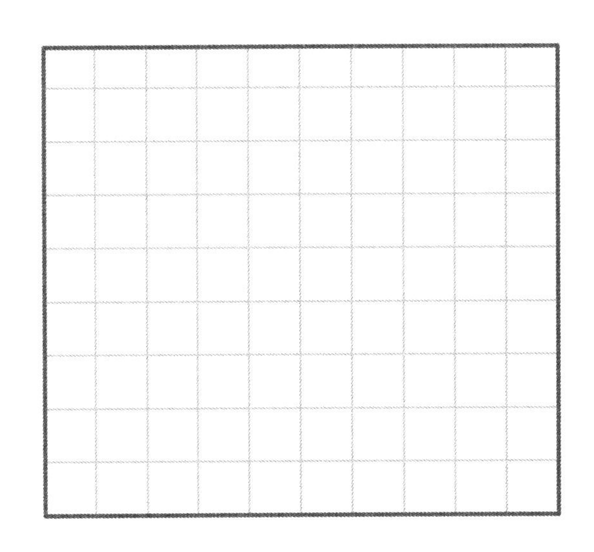

SKETCH THE MISSING VIEW. ALL LINES MUST FIT INSIDE THE EXISTING BOUNDARIES.
ROUND UP TO THE NEAREST GRID SQUARE.

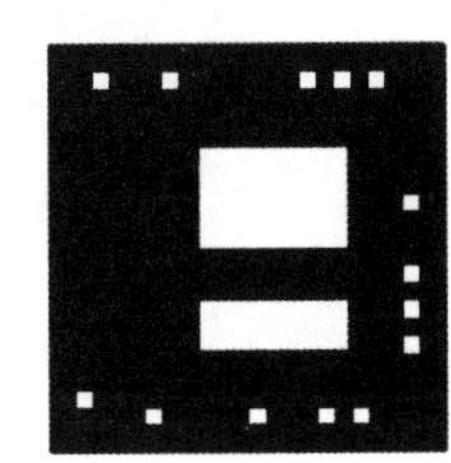

Orthographic Projection

Chapter 02

Exercise 10

Name:

Date:

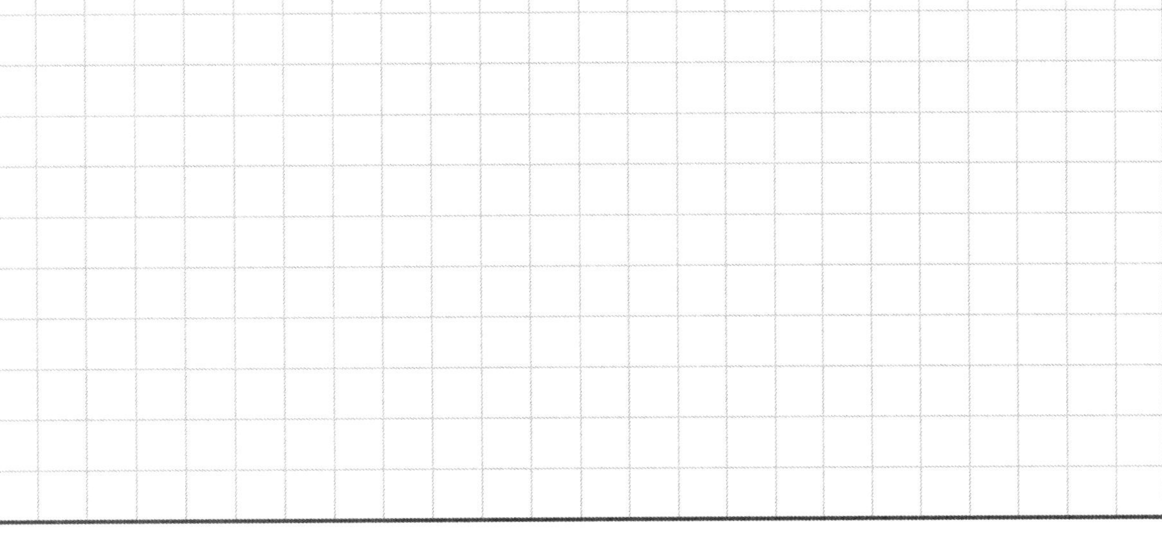

Sketch all necessary views to completely describe the object.
Round up to the nearest grid square.

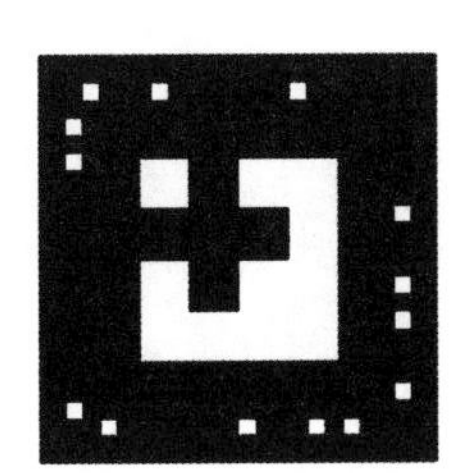

Orthographic Projection

Chapter 02

Exercise 11

Name:

Date:

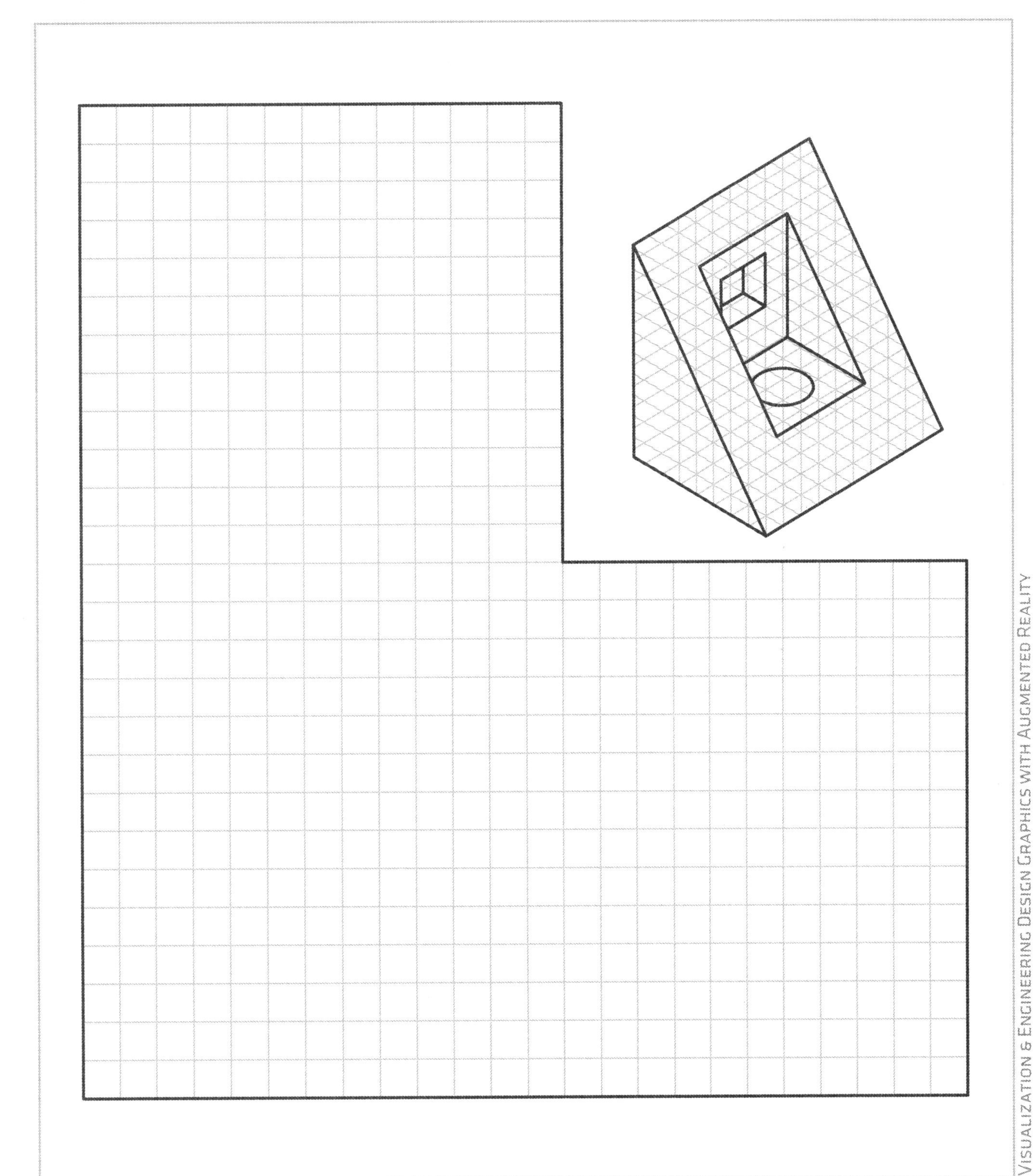

Sketch all necessary views to completely describe the object.
Round up to the nearest grid square.

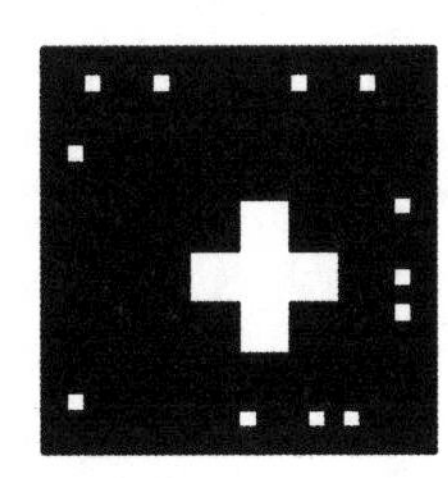

Orthographic Projection

Chapter 02
Exercise 12

Name:

Date:

Sketch all necessary views to completely describe the object.
Round up to the nearest grid square.

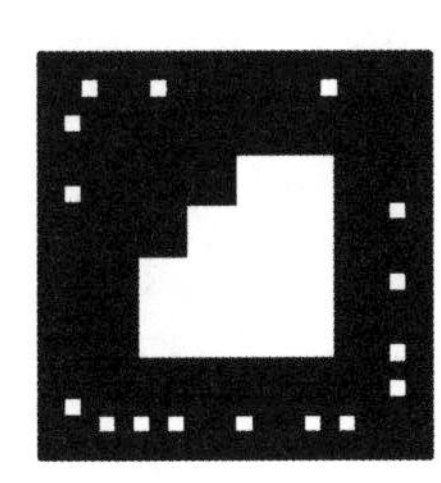

Orthographic Projection

Chapter 02
Exercise 13

Name:

Date:

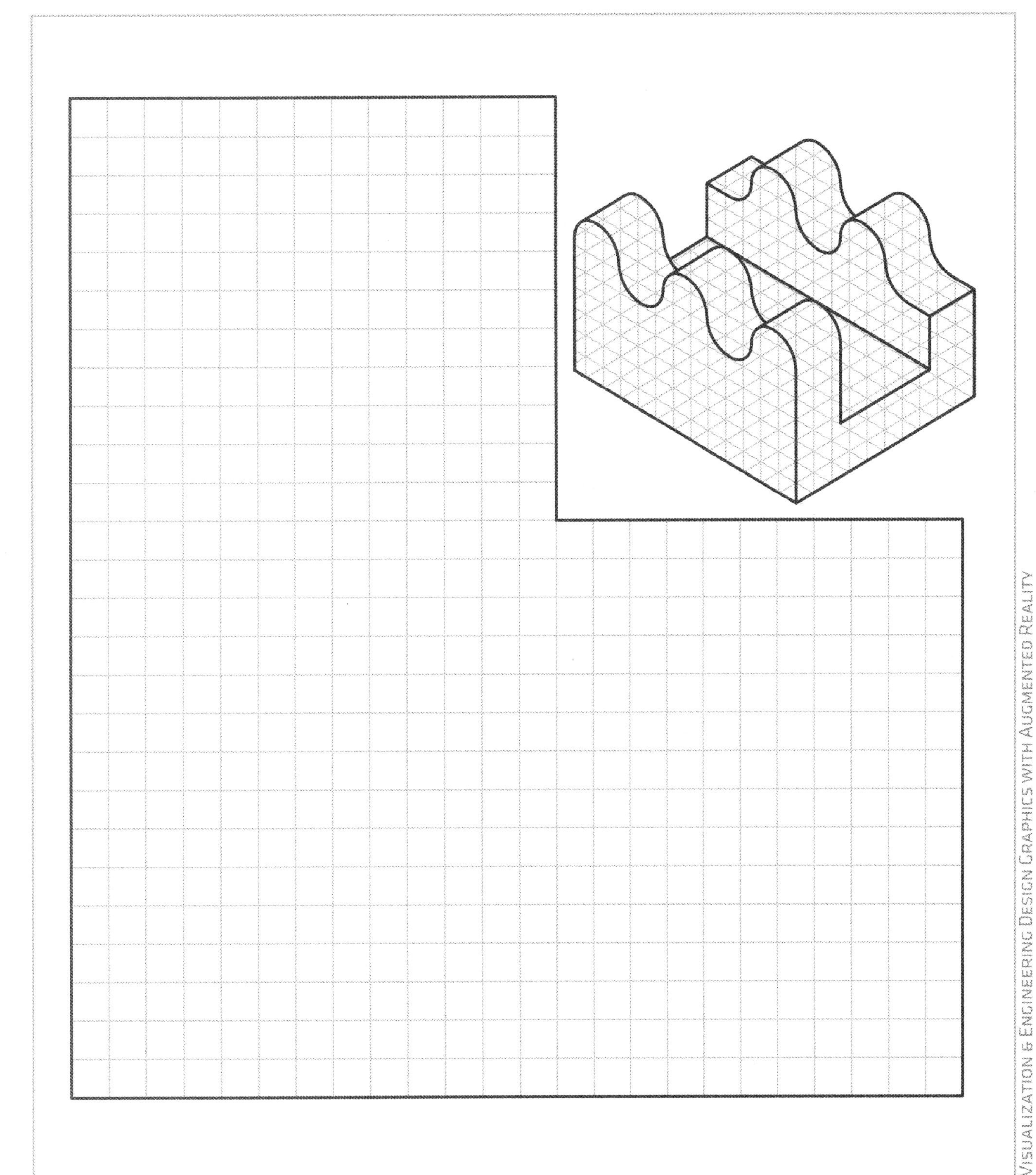

Sketch all necessary views to completely describe the object.
Round up to the nearest grid square.

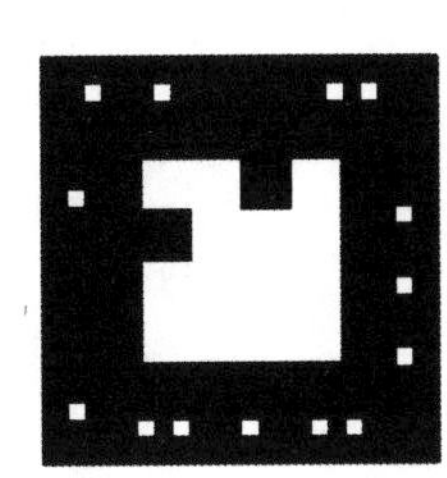

Orthographic Projection

Chapter 02
Exercise 14

Name:

Date:

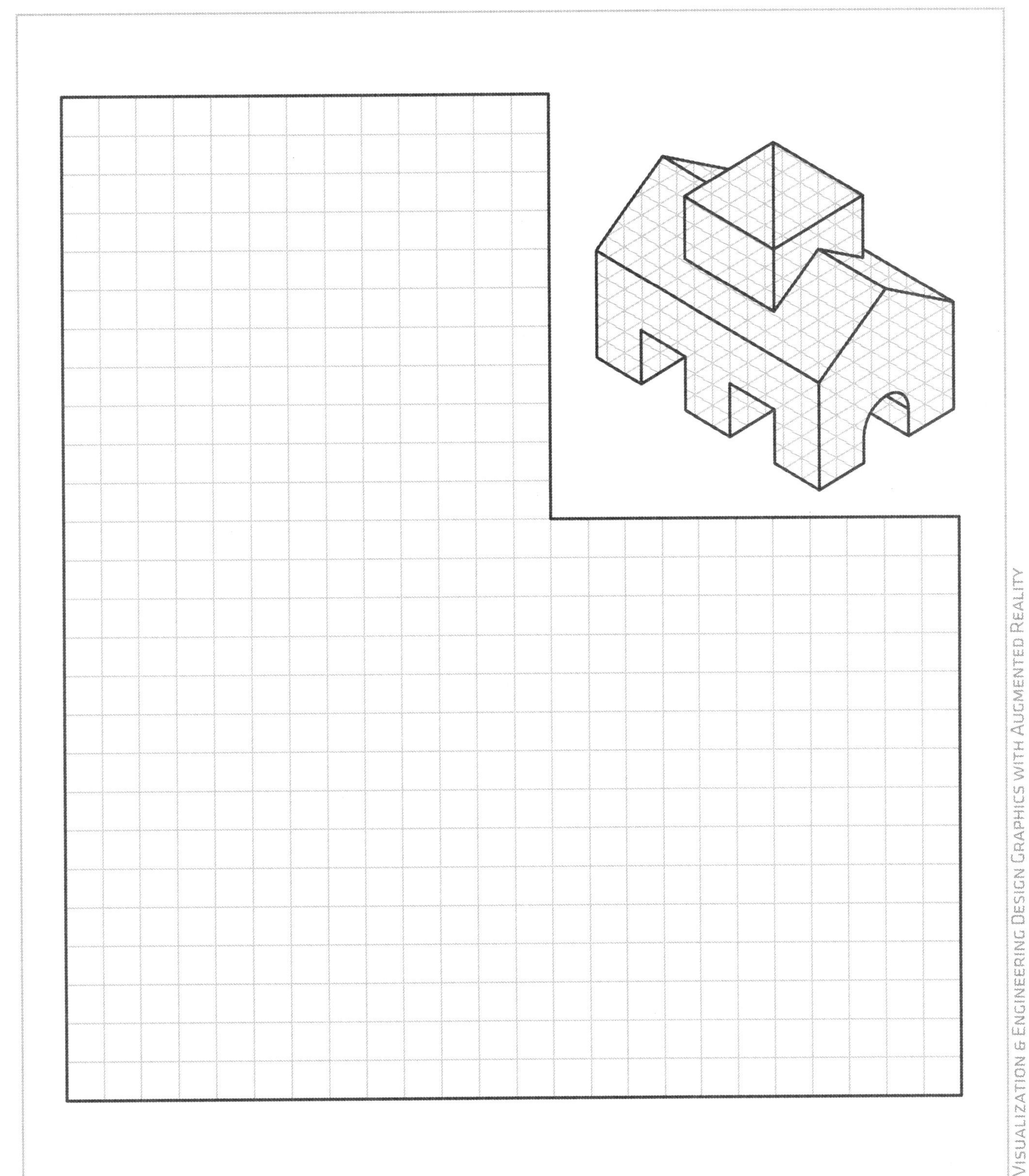

Sketch all necessary views to completely describe the object.
Round up to the nearest grid square.

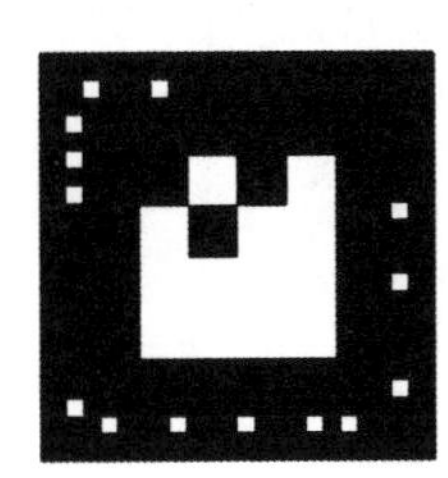

Orthographic Projection

Name:

Chapter 02
Exercise 15

Date:

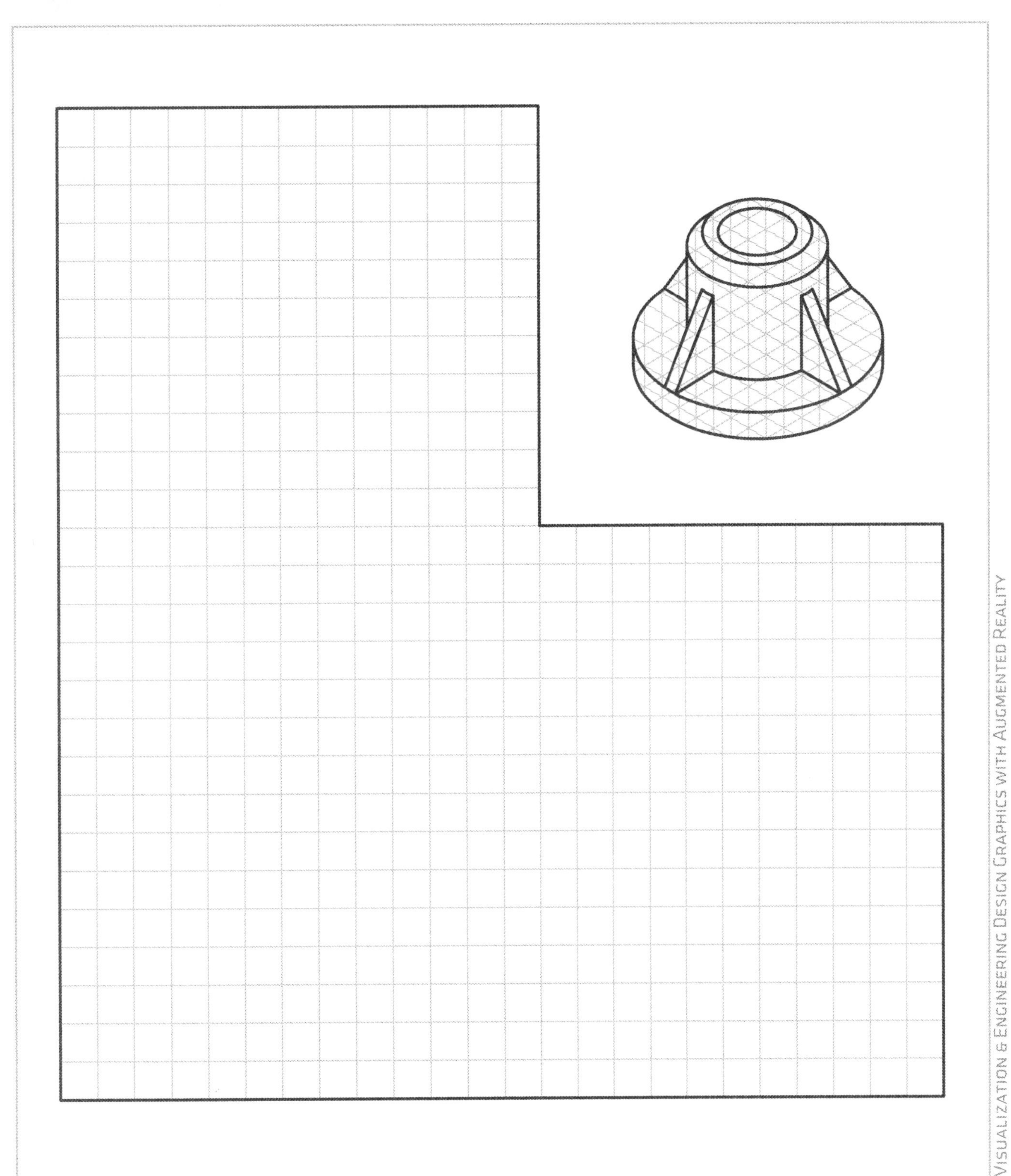

Sketch all necessary views to completely describe the object.
Round up to the nearest grid square.

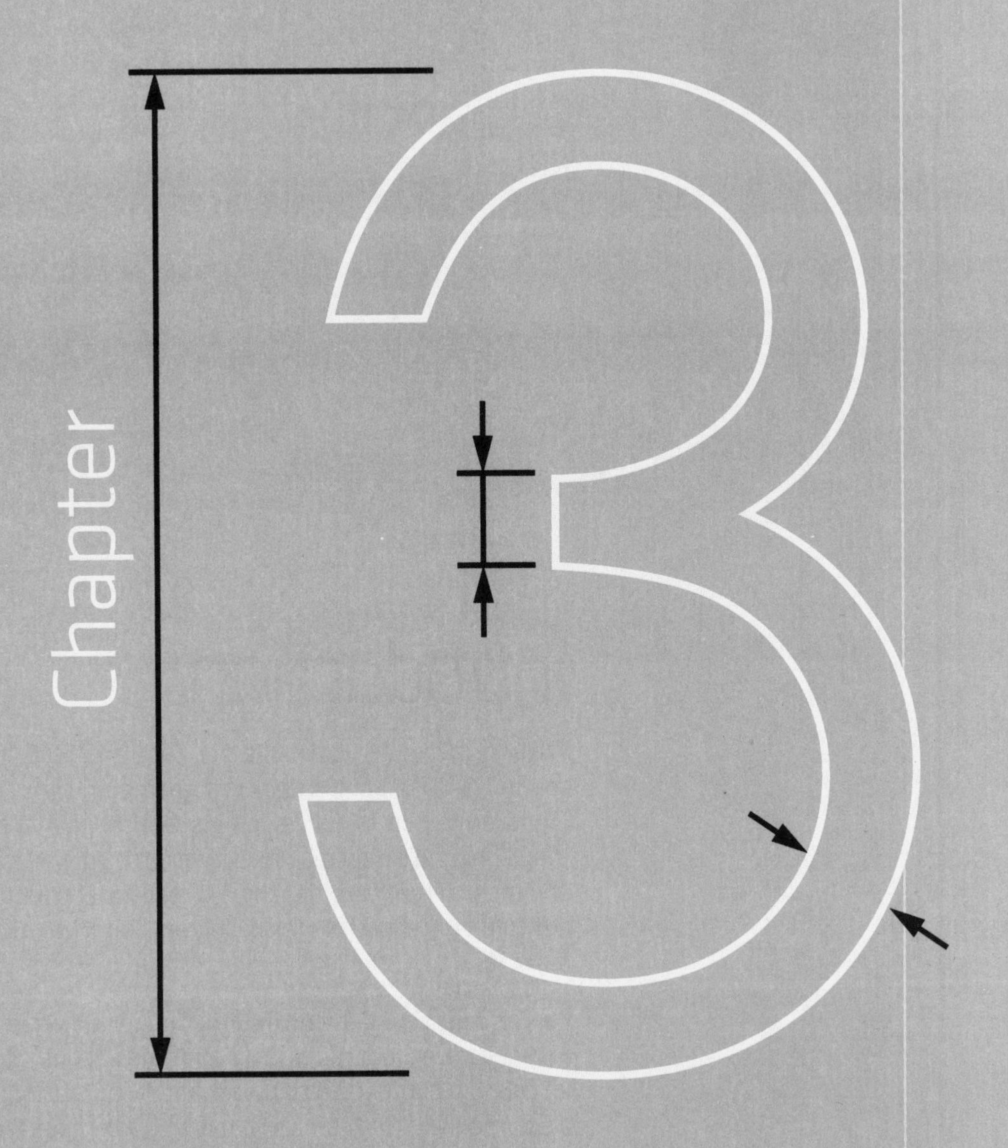

Pictorials

Introduction

While orthographic drawings are excellent tools to communicate specific details about an object's geometry, they are not the most intuitive method to convey its general shape and appearance. Orthographic projection requires viewers to combine multiple drawings and mentally recreate the three dimensional object, which can be a difficult task, especially for people not familiar with these types of drawings.

For communicating design information to non-technical audiences or other engineers not necessarily concerned about the exact details of an object, a photograph could accurately represent the object in a realistic manner. Unfortunately, this solution is not always viable. The object may be difficult to isolate, either because it is hidden within some mechanism or is otherwise inaccessible; or it may not yet exist in physical form, since its creation is the goal of the design process.

Pictorials are types of technical drawings used to illustrate objects in a way that is similar to how they appear in a photograph. Objects are drawn so that they approach what our eyes perceive in reality. Unlike orthographic drawings, in which each view of an object displays only two dimensions, pictorial drawings depict all three dimensions in a single drawing.

Pictorial sketching is used extensive during the design process to quickly communicate ideas. Pictorial drawings are used to illustrate assemblies, structures, machine design, technical manuals, and many other aspects of a design. In this chapter, you will study the different types of pictorial projections and the common techniques used to produce technical illustrations.

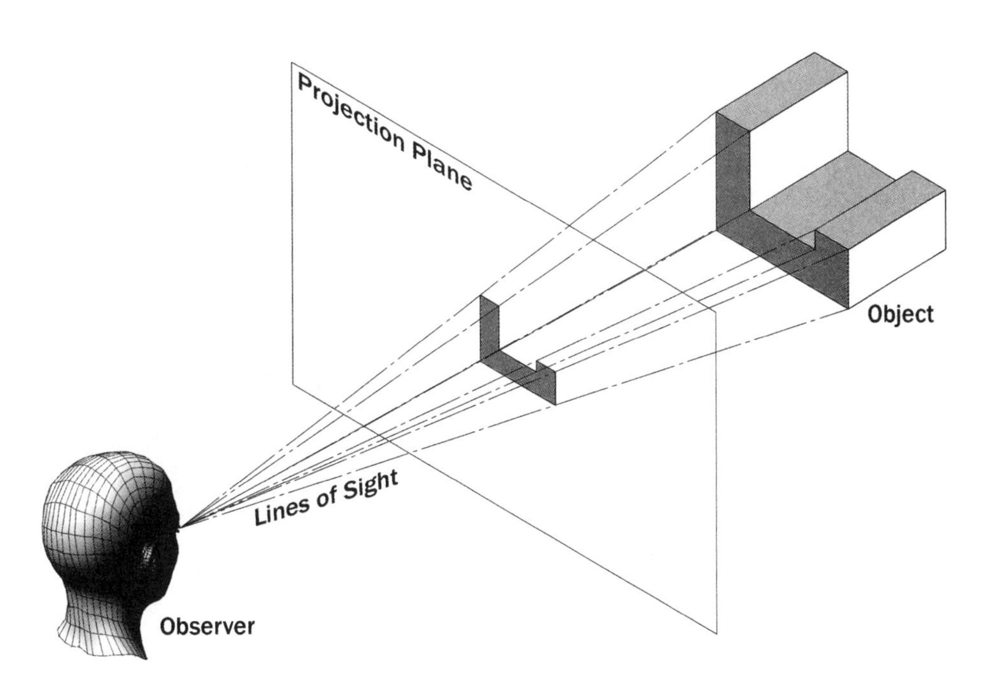

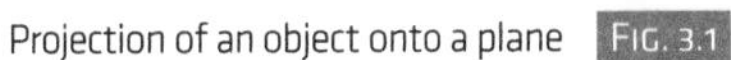
Projection of an object onto a plane FIG. 3.1

Projections

Projection techniques are methods used to represent a three dimensional object on two dimensional media, such as a sheet of paper. Although it is impossible to truly depict 3D reality on a 2D plane without distortion, projection techniques allow for a fairly accurate representation.

The projection of an object onto a plane is determined by the location of the observer with respect to the object, the location of the projection plane (placed between the observer and the object), and the orientation of the object. The projection plane can be understood as the sheet of paper where the drawing will be created. The lines of the drawing are produced by the lines of sight, traveling from the observer's position toward the object, intersecting the projection plane (see Figure 3.1).

Creating the true projection of an object is a laborious task. Instead, alternative methods exist that simplify the process. There are four major projection methods used in engineering drawing: orthographic, axonometric, oblique, and perspective.

Orthographic, Axonometric, and Oblique projections are parallel projections, in which the observer is theoretically located at an infinite distance from the object. In this case, a practical simplification can be made, by considering all lines of sight to be parallel and traveling perpendicularly to the projection plane. This process also causes all lines

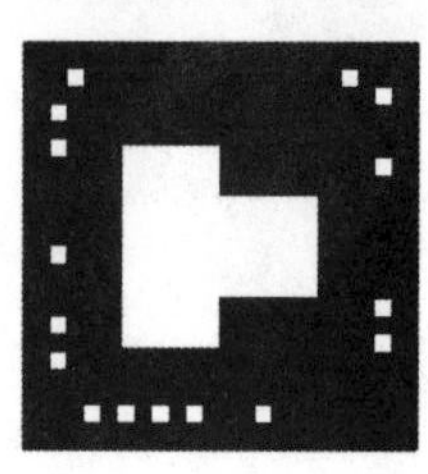

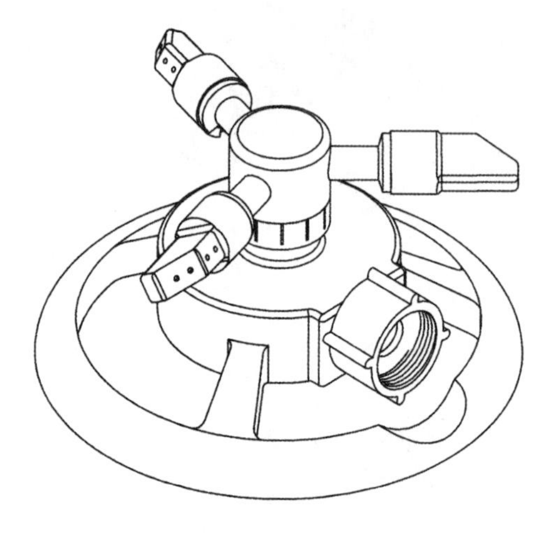

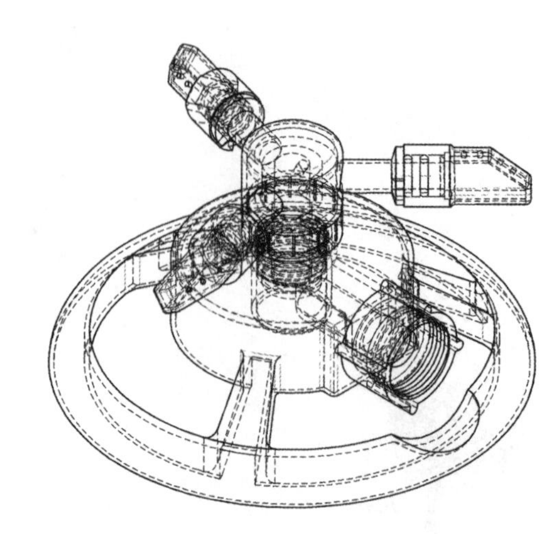

FIG. 3.6 Effect of hidden lines in pictorial drawings

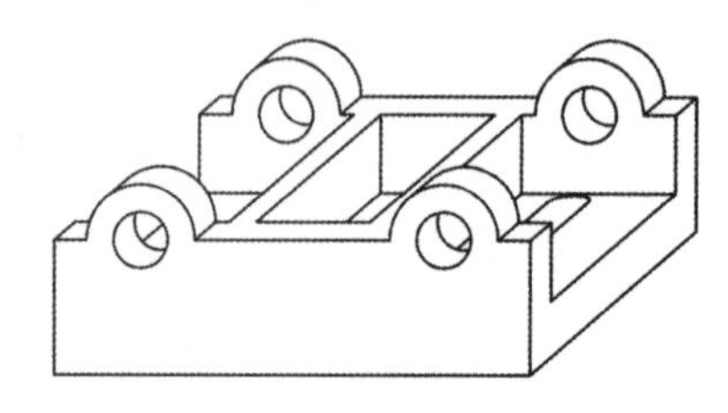

FIG. 3.3 Oblique pictorial

that are parallel in the real object to appear parallel in the drawing as well. Although this simplification is, in part, the cause of distortion in the drawing and a partial loss of visual realism, parallel projections have the advantage of providing actual dimensions that can be measured directly in the drawing when the scale is known. For this reason, they are extremely useful in technical fields.

Perspective projections are used to mimic how our eyes perceive the real world. They are more accurate than parallel projections, reproducing visual effects such as objects appearing smaller in size as their distance from the observer increases, or depicting parallel lines converging to a single point (called a vanishing point). In perspective projection, the observer is located at a finite distance from the object. A classification of projection techniques is shown below.

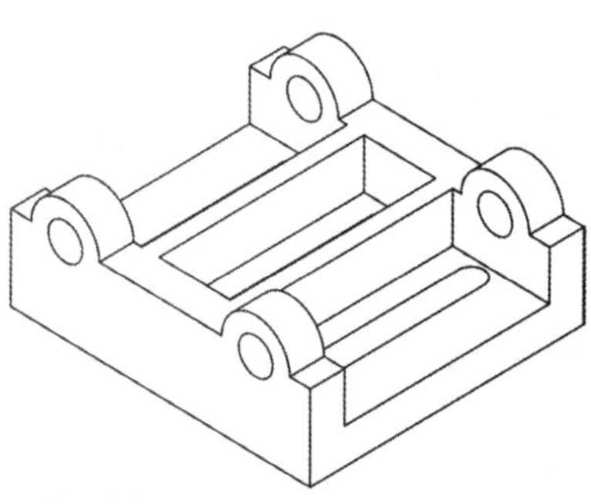

FIG. 3.4 Axonometric pictorial

Parallel Projections			
ORTHOGRAPHIC	**OBLIQUE**	**AXONOMETRIC**	**PERSPECTIVE**
	Pictorials		

In the previous chapter, you studied orthographic projection, which is a method that requires multiple projection planes and views (each view showing only two dimensions) to fully represent an object. Pictorial drawings, on the other hand, depict all dimensions in a single view. In the following sections, the different types of pictorials, shown in Figure 3.3 ,Figure 3.4 , andFigure 3.5 , will be examined.

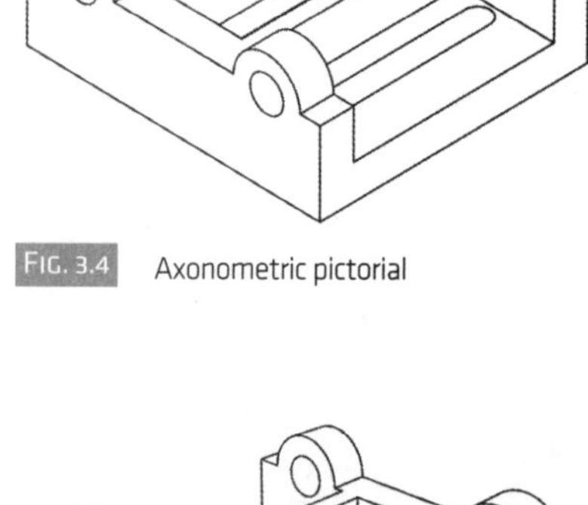

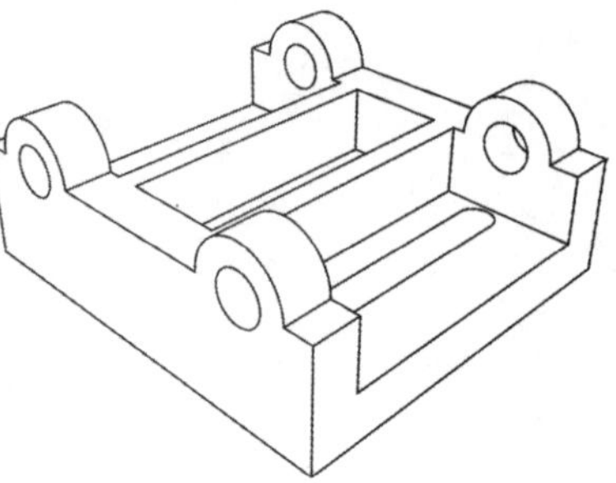

FIG. 3.5 Perspective pictorial

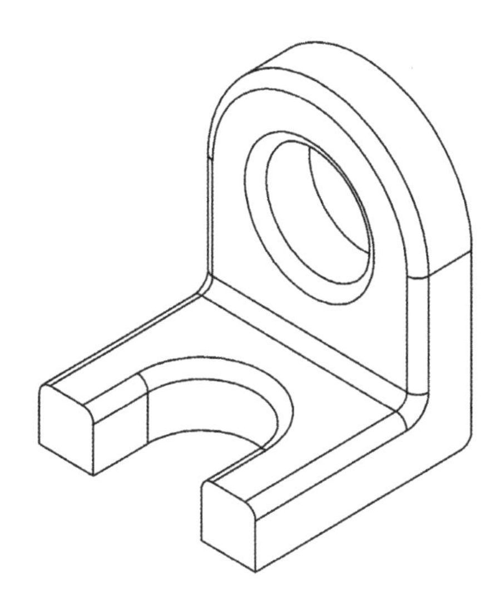

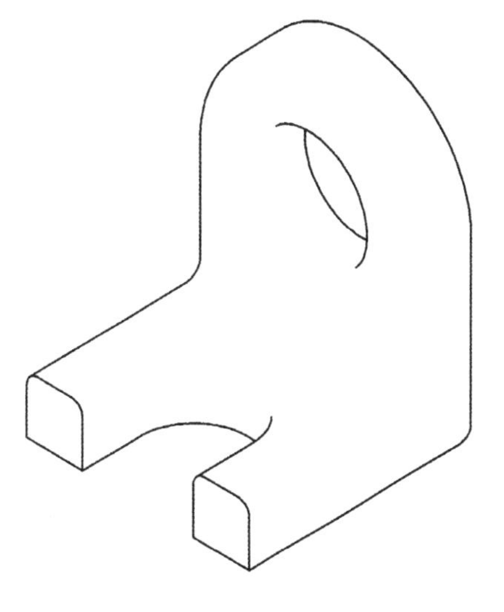

Pictorial with tangent edges (left) and tangent edges removed (right) FIG. 3.7

General Practices for Pictorial Drawings

It is common practice to include pictorials in a set of production drawings in order to accompany and clarify the orthographic views of a part or an assembly. As a general rule, hidden and center lines are excluded from pictorial drawings, since they generally do not add any useful information to the drawing and may create confusion in the viewer (see the rotary sprinkler shown in Figure 3.6). Exceptions exist, however, that may require hidden lines to be provided to add clarity to a particular feature of the drawing. Likewise, when additional clarity is required to indicate concentricity, centerlines may be shown.

While tangent edges (lines indicating tangent transitions between features) are never shown in orthographic drawings, they are sometimes needed in pictorials. Omitting tangent edges on a pictorial may severely affect its quality, leaving out important visual information from the drawing (see Figure 3.7). In general, tangent edges are excluded, but the geometry of the object will determine if they need to be provided.

Dimensions are usually not included in pictorial drawings. For production, only orthographic views are dimensioned. In recent years, however, new standards have been developed that regulate model-based definitions. These standards dictate guidelines used to dimension pictorial drawings when orthographic views are not available. Dimensioning practices will be discussed in future chapters.

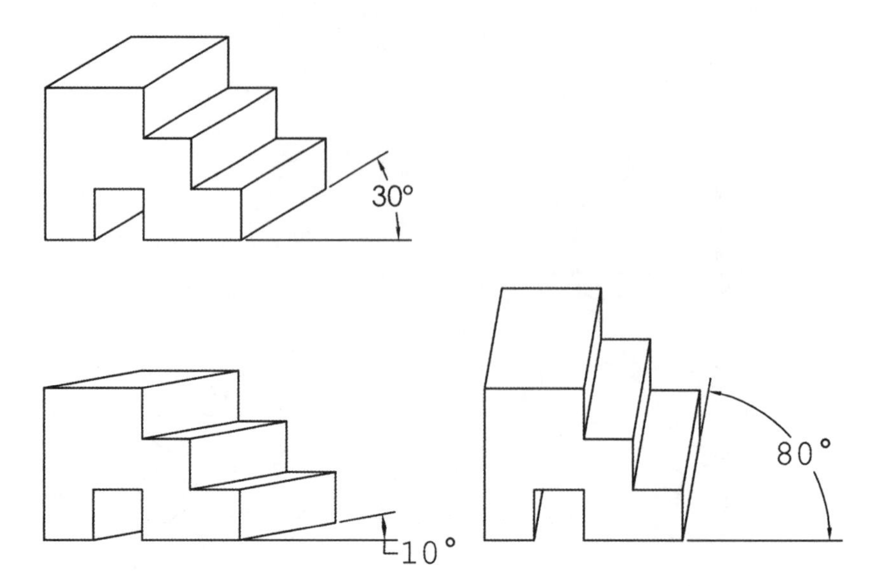

FIG. 3.8 Receding angles on oblique pictorials

Oblique Projections

Oblique projections are created by locating the projection plane parallel to the most descriptive view of the object, causing this view to appear true size. Depth is represented by angled parallel lines taken from every point of the front view. In reality, oblique projection is a system where a two dimensional view is given the illusion of depth by creating receding axis lines at a specific angle.

Oblique pictorials are easy to master, but they are rarely used in production environments. The amount of distortion that occurs, even in simple parts, makes oblique pictorials unrealistic and unconvincing to the eye. Their use is normally limited to parts where the focus is on frontal surfaces with little detail on the depth dimension. On the other hand, their simplicity makes them useful in the early stages of the design process, where ideas and designs need to be quickly sketched and communicated.

In oblique drawings, depth can be represented at any receding angle. For practical purposes, the range is reduced to angles between 15 and 75 degrees, since excessive angular measurements make the drawing appear extremely distorted. See Figure 3.8 for an example.

Depending on the length of the depth dimension, three types of oblique projections can be produced. If depth is represented true size along the receding axis, the pictorial is called a Cavalier oblique. In this type of projection, true measurements can be taken directly from the drawing, but the practical result is a drawing with great amounts of

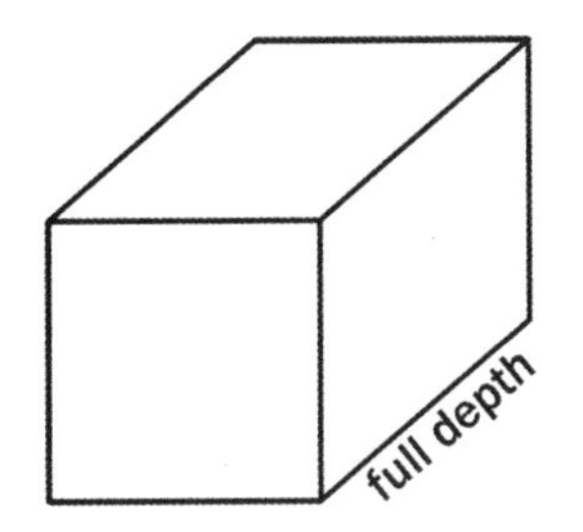

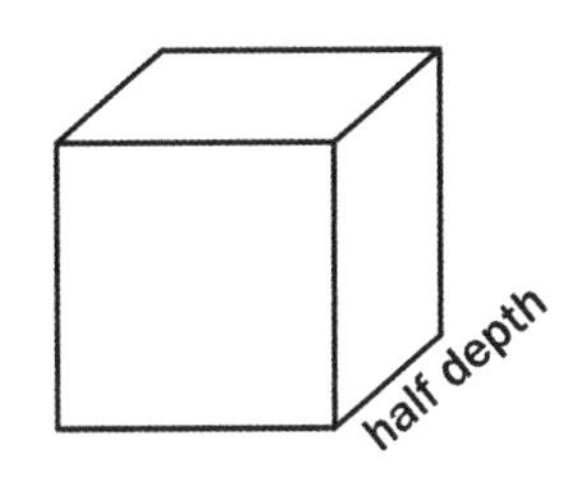

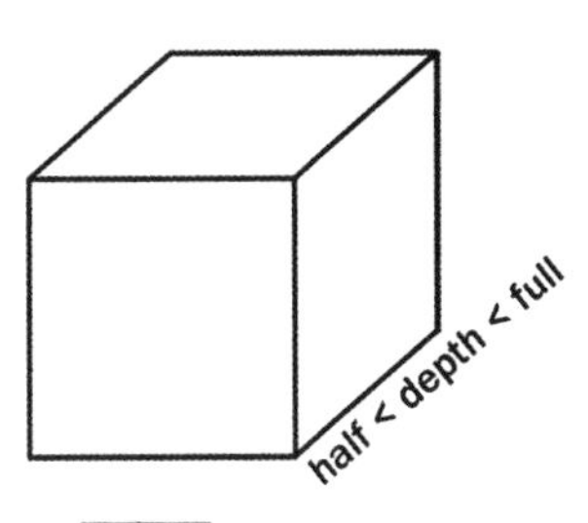

Cavalier (left), Cabinet (center), and General (right) oblique projections  FIG. 3.9

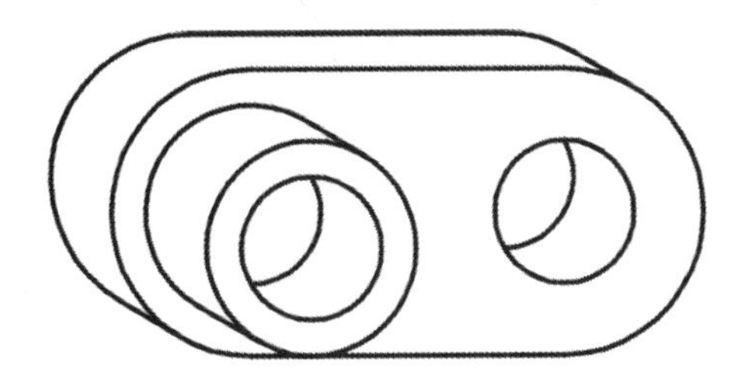

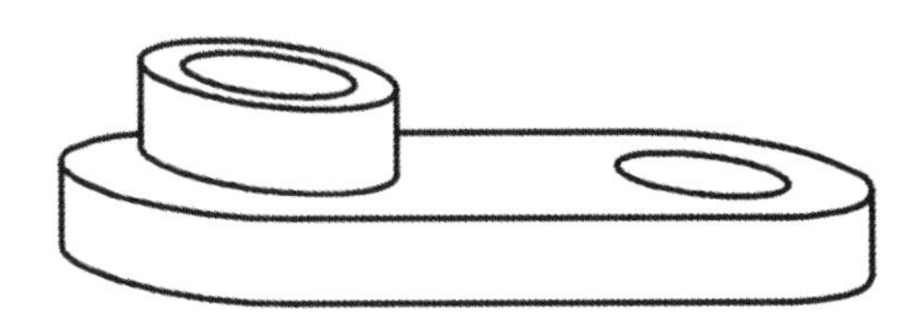

Circular features on the front face (left) look less distorted than on the receding face (right)  FIG. 3.10

distortion. Cavalier obliques are typically used for parts with a depth dimension that is significantly shorter that the width and height, so distortion is not accentuated. If the depth dimension is represented at half the actual size, a Cabinet oblique is produced. This scale reduction lessens the distortion effect, which results in a more visually accurate drawing. Finally, General oblique projections are created when the depth dimension is scaled down to a value other than one half. General obliques are drawn by selecting the depth percentage that most favorably depicts the object when both cavalier and cabinet projections do not succeed.

The example shown in Figure 3.9illustrates the three types of oblique projections. In all cases, a regular cube (width, height, and depth dimensions are equal) is portrayed. Notice the evident distortion that occurs in the case of the Cavalier oblique.

To minimize distortion, it is essential to select the most descriptive view of the object as the oblique's front view. This determination is especially important in objects with curved and circular features, since these features cause more visual distortion than rectangular shapes (see Figure 3.10). Angular features also need to be represented in the oblique front view, whenever possible. When angles and irregular curves are represented in receding faces, they are created by plotting multiple points along the path of the receding lines of the oblique projection. The more points utilized, the more accurate your sketch, but the longer it takes to complete the drawing.

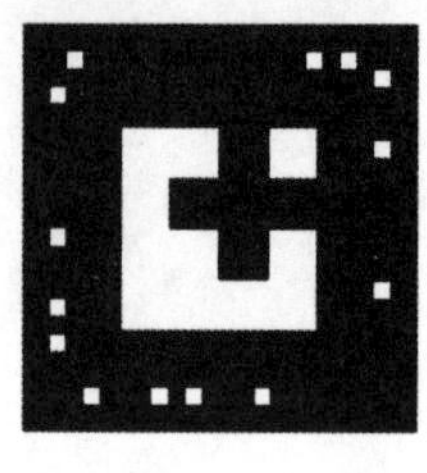

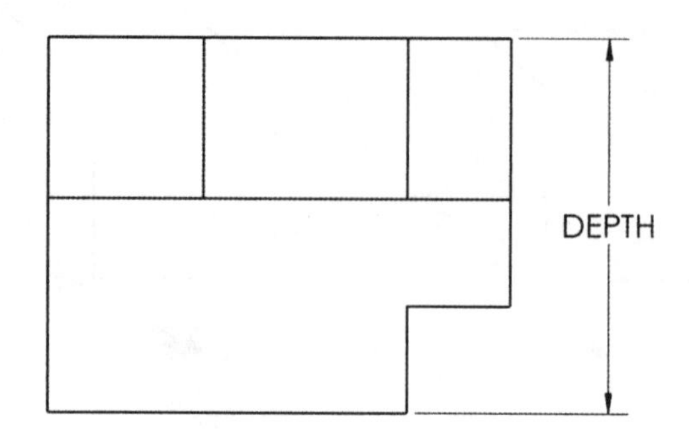

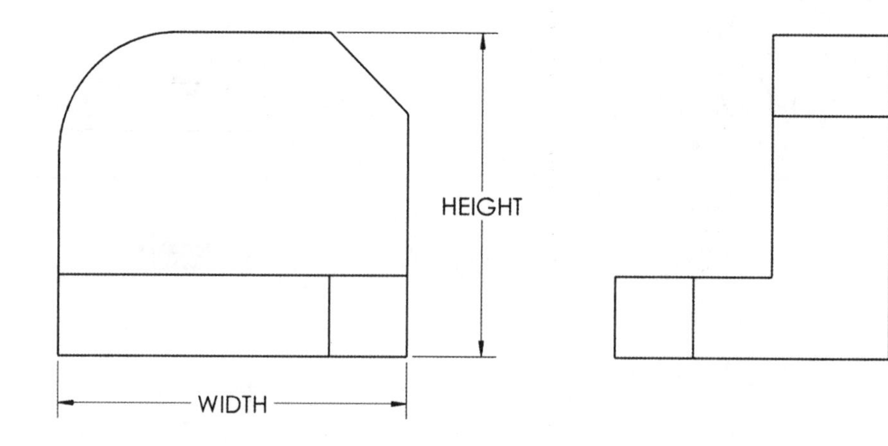

FIG. 3.11 Orthographic views of the object used for construction of an oblique pictorial

Sketching Oblique Drawings

To sketch an oblique pictorial of an object, it is necessary to determine the receding axis angle that will be used, which face will be shown as the front view, and the format (cavalier, cabinet, or general). The process begins by measuring the overall height, width, and depth of the object and sketching a construction box with these dimensions. Remember that the depth dimension must be halved if a cabinet oblique is drawn.

The orthographic views of the object that will be used as an example of this process are shown in Figure 3.11. The example will describe the basic steps required to draw a cavalier oblique using a 40° receding axis angle on the right side of the object.

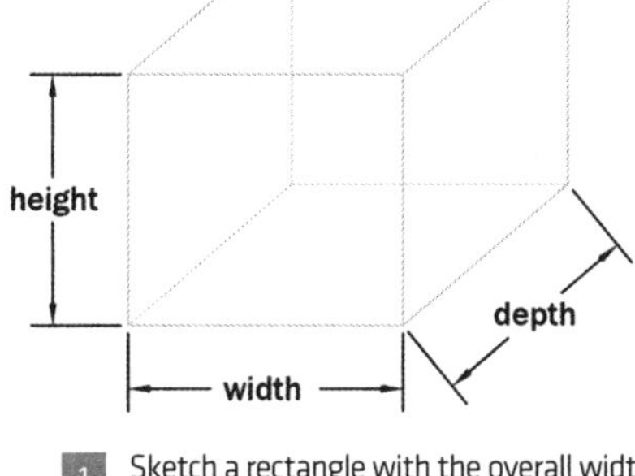

1 Sketch a rectangle with the overall width and height dimensions of the object. From each corner, create lines at a 40° angles. This box will be the envelope that will contain the oblique projection of the object.

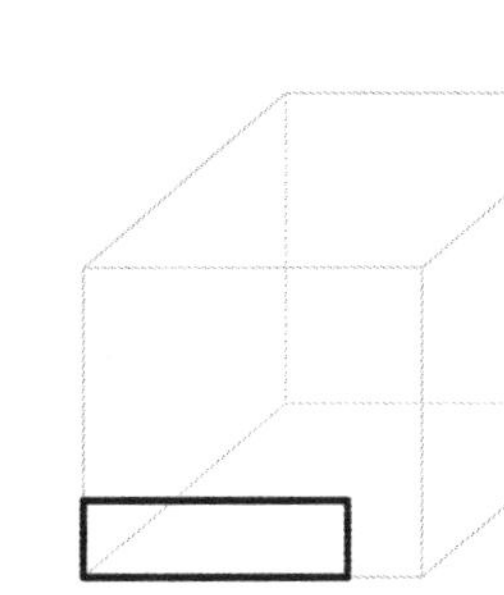

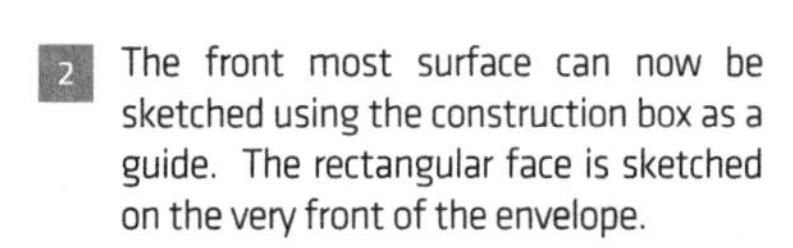

2 The front most surface can now be sketched using the construction box as a guide. The rectangular face is sketched on the very front of the envelope.

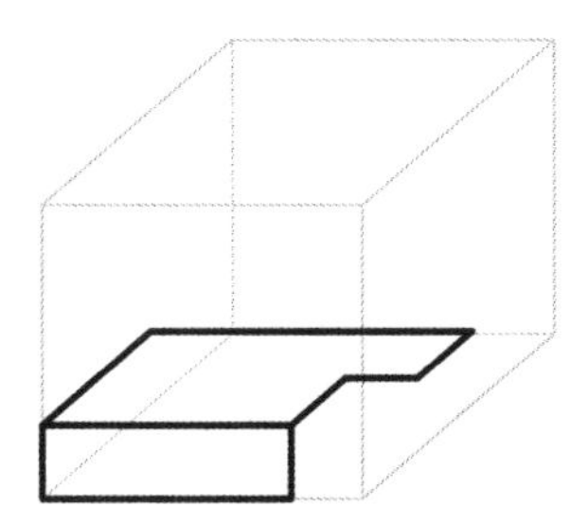

3 Additional surfaces can be added, building from the initial rectangle. The horizontal surface needs to have the receding depth measured along the 40° direction.

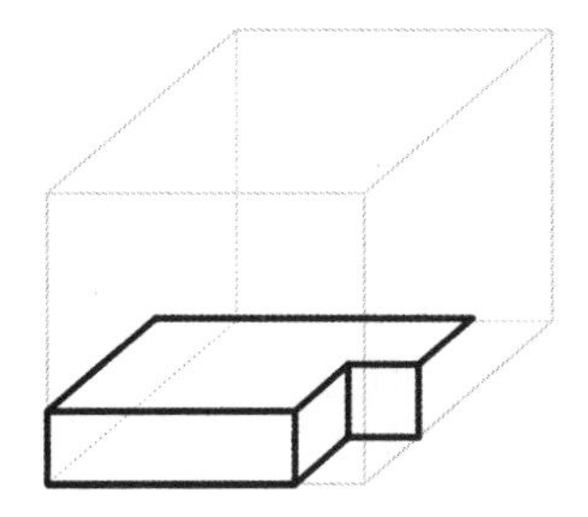

4 The notch in the front corner can be completed by sketching parallel to the lines surrounding it.

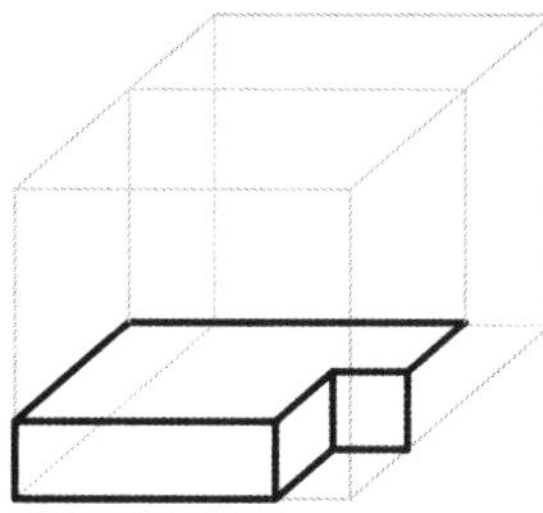

5 The frontal surface with the arc and the angled line rises directly from the back edge of the horizontal surface. Initially, the bounding rectangle must be sketched.

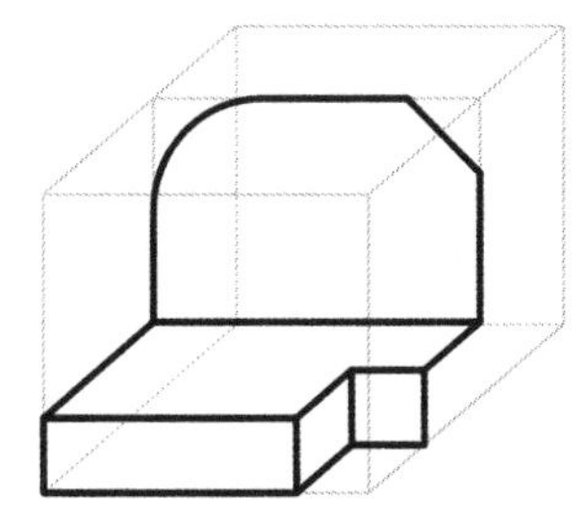

6 The arc and the dog-eared corner can be added to the drawing using the bounding rectangle as reference.

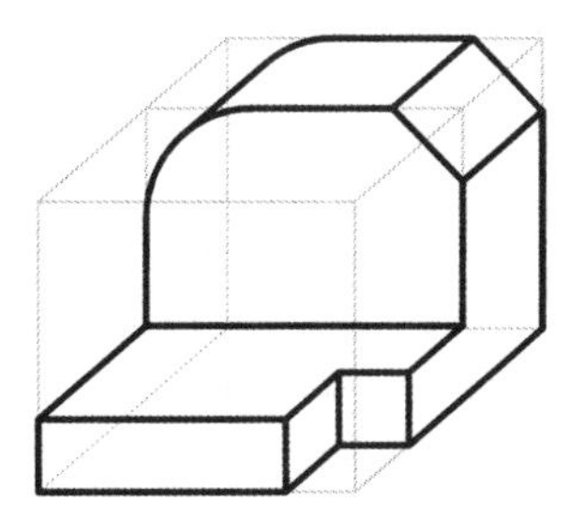

7 The back most surface can be sketched by extending the recent frontal surface back, making sure to include a tangent line across the two arcs and any other receding axis lines necessary to complete the sketch.

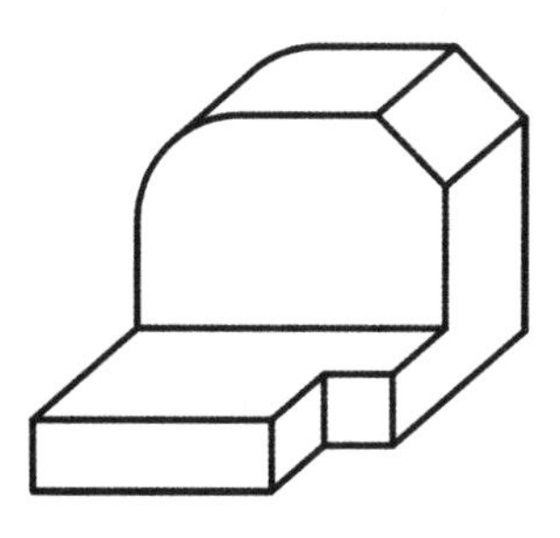

8 The process is finished by erasing the construction box.

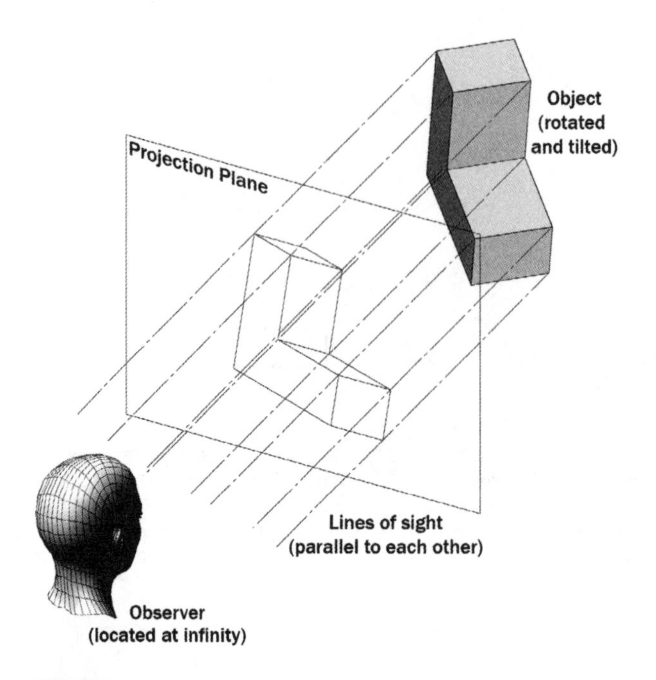

FIG. 3.12 Axonometric projection

Axonometric Projections

Axonometric projections are parallel projections where the principle views of the object are not parallel to the projection plane. They are technically a type of orthographic projection in which the object is rotated and tilted relative to the projection plane in order to reveal all three dimensions (see Figure 3.12). The angles of rotation and tilt of the object determine the amount of foreshortening (and thus, distortion) for the lines and angles along each dimension in the drawing. The closer a face of the object comes to being perpendicular to the projection plane, the shorter the corresponding lines become in the drawing.

Axonometric projections are classified into three categories: isometric, diametric, and trimetric. The determining factor used to categorize them is the orientation of the primary axes of the object with respect to the projection plane. Using a basic cube as an example, the primary axes are defined by the edges of the cube that meet at the corner nearest to the projection plane. If the three angles between the primary axes are equal (all axes are equally foreshortened), the axonometric projection is called isometric. If only two of the angles are equal (two axes equally foreshortened), the projection is called diametric. If all angles are different (all axes foreshortened differently), the projection is called trimetric. See Figure 3.13 and Figure 3.14 for examples of the three types of axonometric projection.

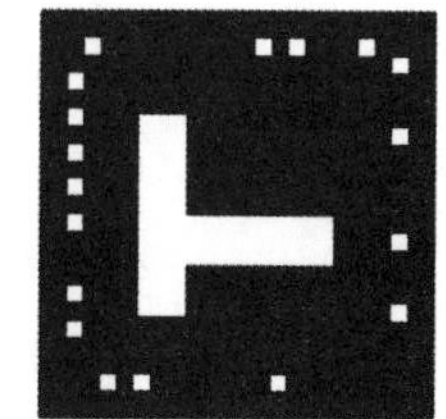

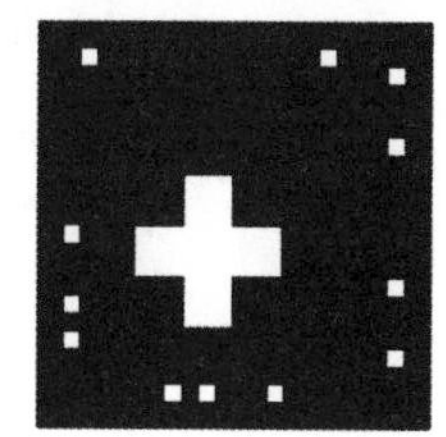

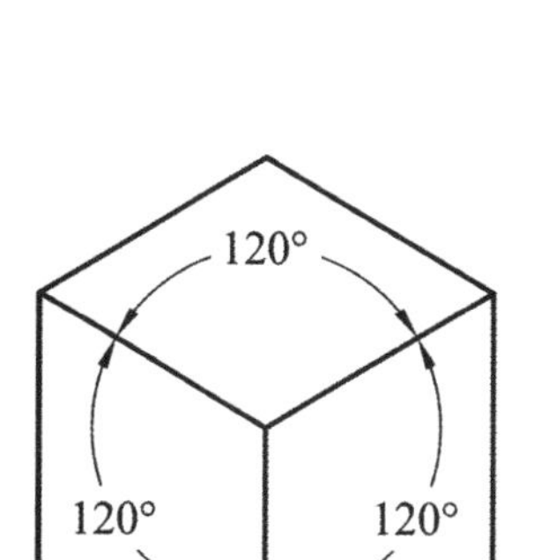

ISOMETRIC

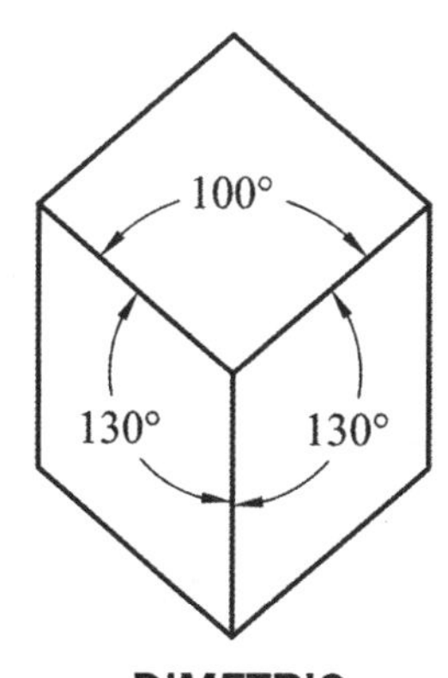

DIMETRIC

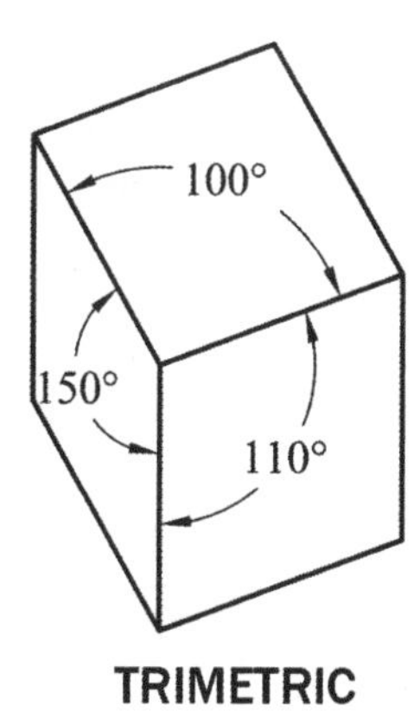

TRIMETRIC

Types of axonometric projections FIG. 3.13

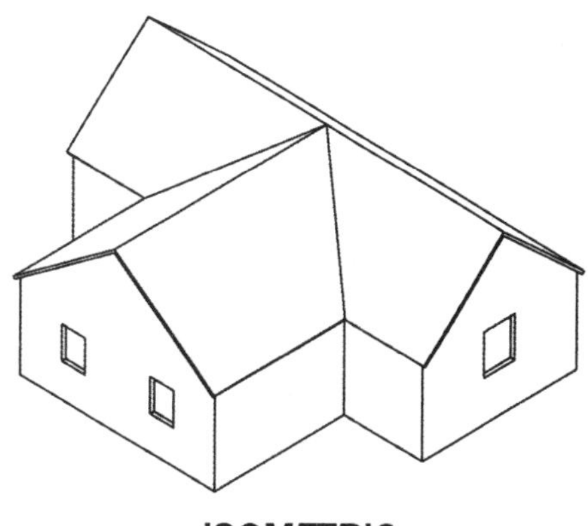

ISOMETRIC

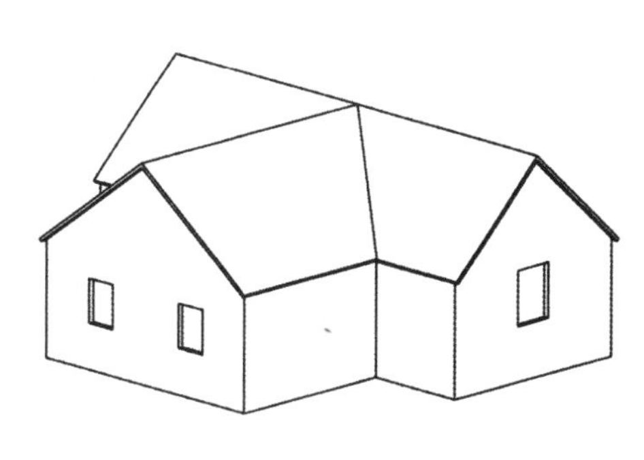

DIMETRIC

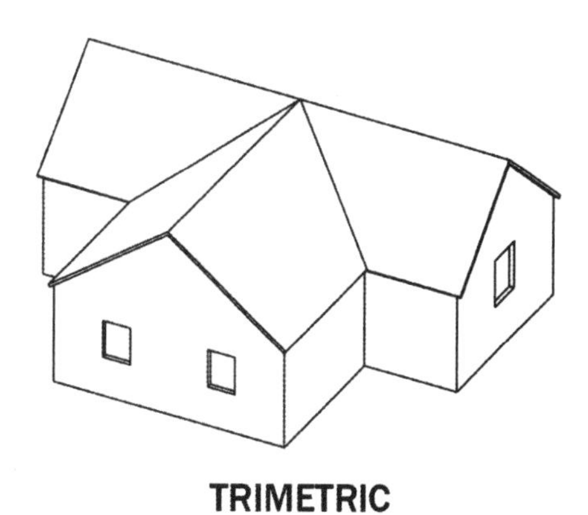

TRIMETRIC

Example of axonometric projections  FIG. 3.14

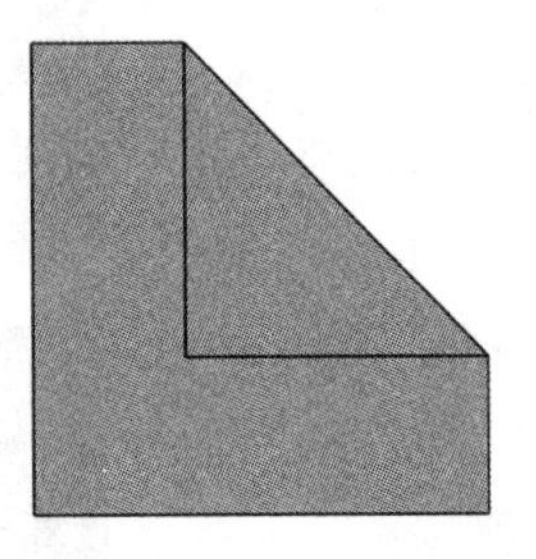

Initial View

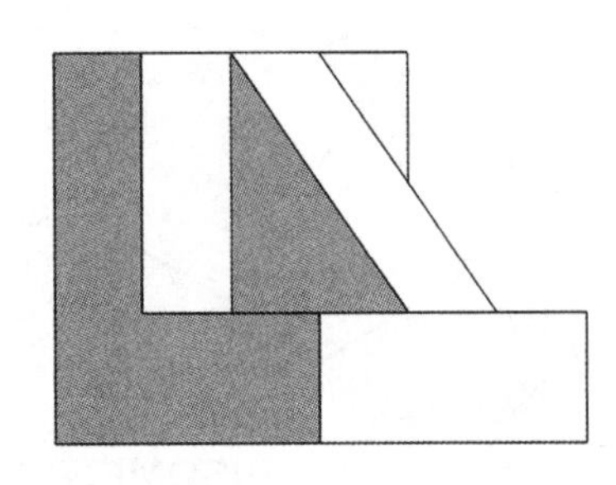

45° rotation about vertical axis

35.264° tilt about horizontal axis

Fig. 3.15 Creation of an isometric projection

Isometric Projection

Isometric projection is the most common type of pictorial used in engineering and technical fields. It is produced by rotating the object 45° about its vertical axis, and tilting it forward approximately 35.264° (precisely arcsin(tan 30°)), as shown in Figure 3.15 These rotation angles cause the object to be oriented with respect to the projection plane in such a way that the three primary axes form 120° angles among themselves, and a 30° angle with the horizontal. This particular orientation of the primary axes ensures that all three axes are equally foreshortened, while maintaining the drawing proportional in size (see Figure 3.16).

The rotations performed to the object in order to produce an isometric have a direct effect on the scale of the drawing projected onto the projection plane. Specifically, there is a scale reduction of approximately 0.815 with respect to the object. For practical purposes, the scale of the isometric drawing is typically adjusted back to 1, so accurate measurements can be taken directly from the drawing.

An important consideration when creating isometric drawings is the orientation of the primary axes. In general, a proper orientation must be selected to ensure the isometric drawing provides a natural and intuitive view of the object, without the need for hidden lines or additional views (see Figure 3.17).

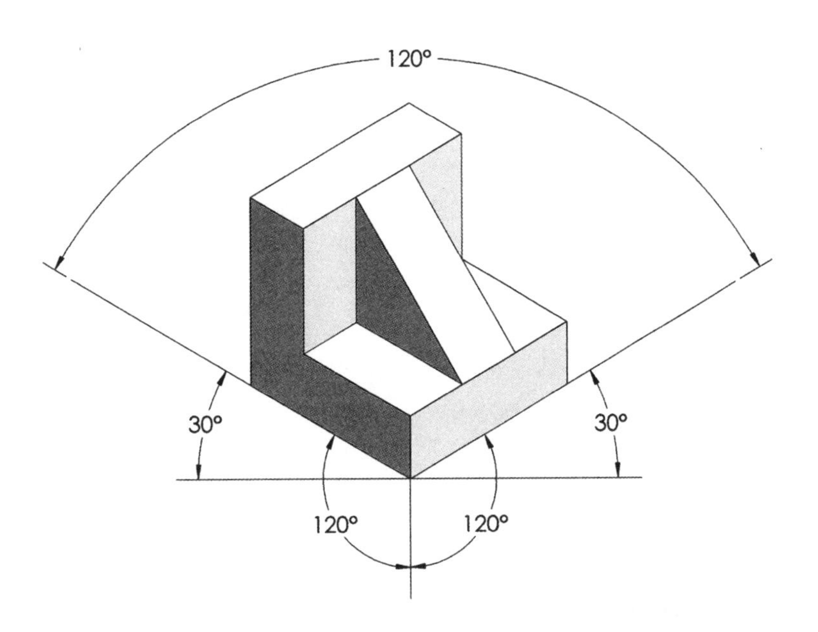

Angles on isometric axes FIG. 3.16

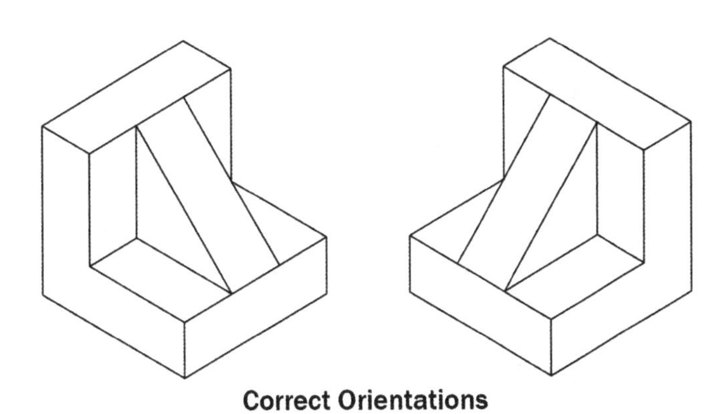

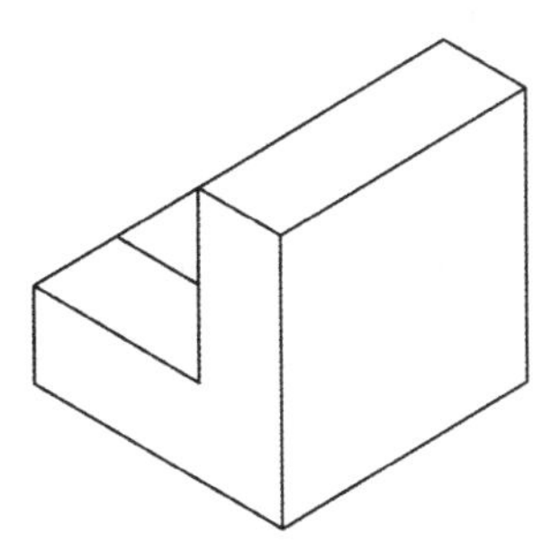
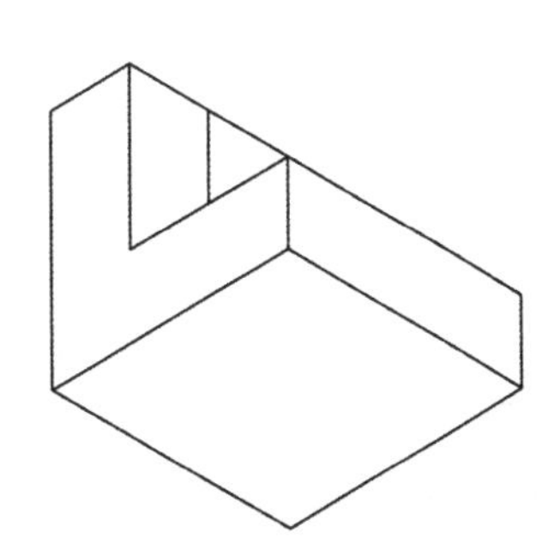
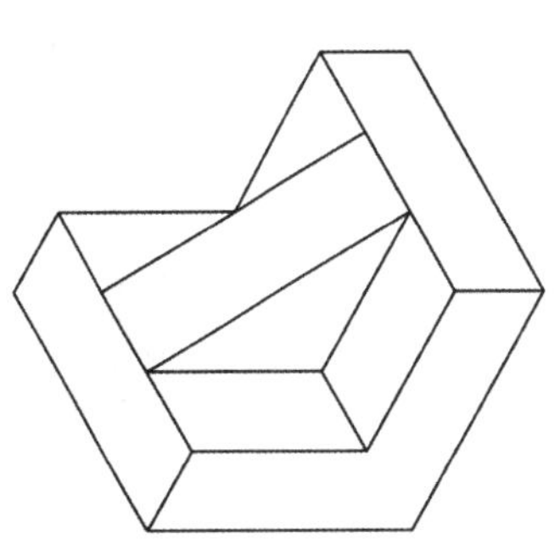

Incorrect Orientations

Isometric orientations FIG. 3.17

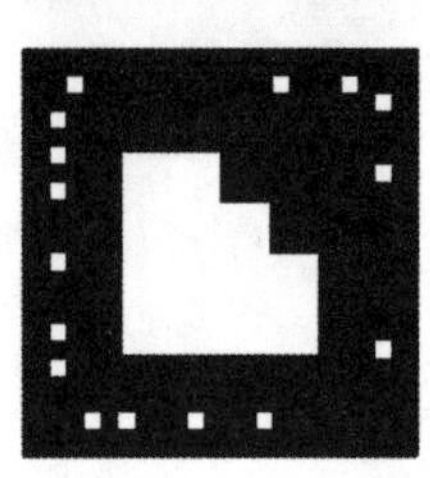

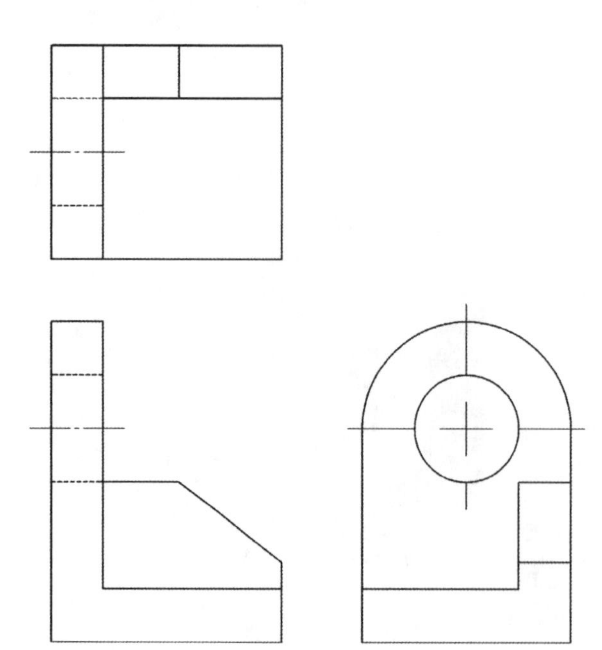

FIG. 3.18 Orthographic views of object used for isometric pictorial construction

Sketching Isometric Drawings

Isometric drawings for professional purposes are typically produced with Computer Assisted Design (CAD) software packages. Using these programs, precise and detailed isometric drawings can be created with relative ease, compared to hand drawn approaches. Nevertheless, freehand isometric sketching is still used to quickly illustrate and communicate ideas, particularly in the early stages of the engineering design process.

Although a wide variety of drafting tools are available to assist in the creation of accurate isometric drawings by hand, proper practice will allow you to sketch isometrics freehand. Isometric paper, however, may be useful when creating your first sketches. Isometric paper is a type of graph paper that provides a grid comprised of three sets of parallel lines forming a triangular pattern. The lines correspond to the three dimensions of space: width, height, and depth. Height is aligned along the vertical direction with depth and width aligning at 30° with the horizontal.

Similar to oblique drawings, isometric sketching is typically performed using construction boxes as visual guides. The orthographic views of the object that will be used to illustrate the process are shown in Figure 3.18.

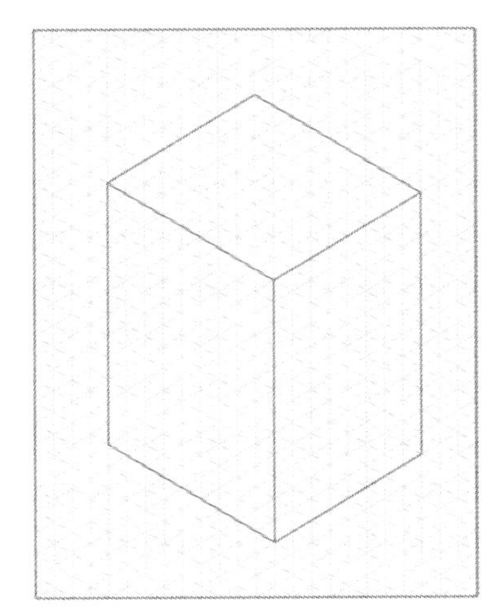

1 Determine the overall size of the object and sketch the outline of the bounding box that will contain it. This step is done as light construction lines.

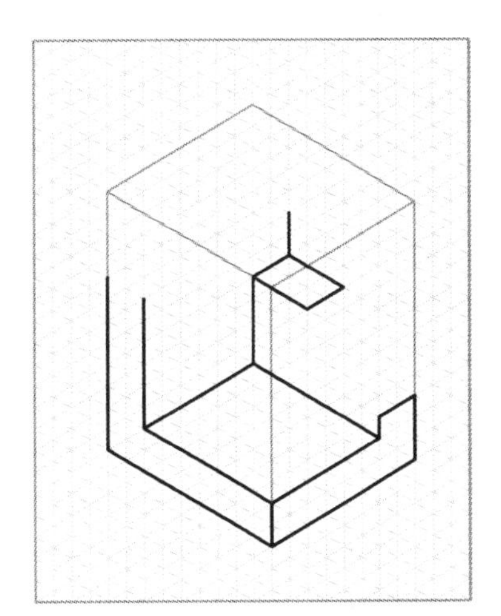

2 Add the interior features to the faces of the box by simply counting the grid and sketching the lines that follow the grid lines. Continue this process for all the isometric lines.

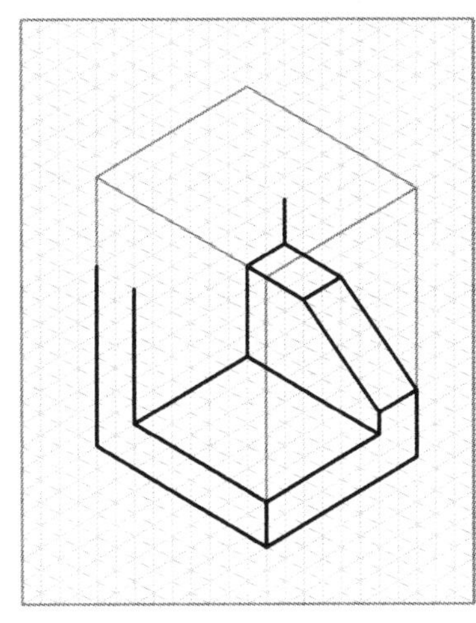

3 The angled corner is now obvious as it can be simply sketched by connecting the lines that already exist.

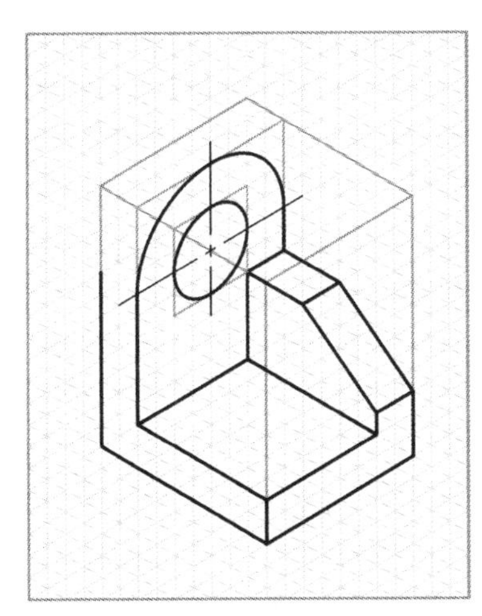

4 The remaining features are circular. While centerlines are optional in pictorial drawings, they tend to be helpful when preparing isometric sketches, especially when you have concentric features. Add the center lines and mark the radius of both the arc and circle. With these marked, the bounding square can be drawn to frame the resulting ellipse.

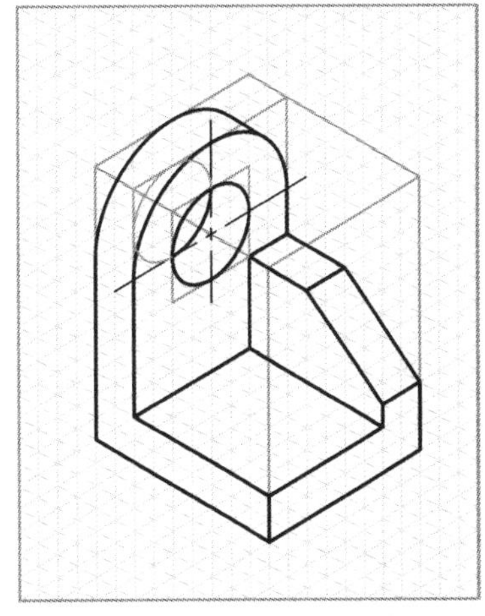

5 The ellipses on the back side must be added along with any tangent lines that may be necessary. In this case, a portion of the ellipse on the back of the object must be shown to represent the part of the round edge that is visible through the opening.

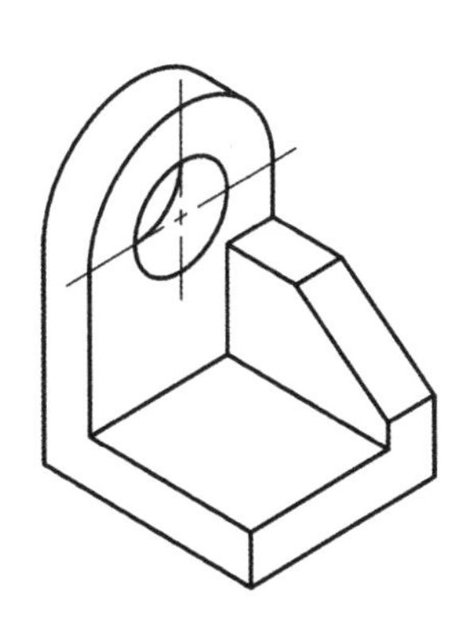

6 The process is finished by erasing the construction box.

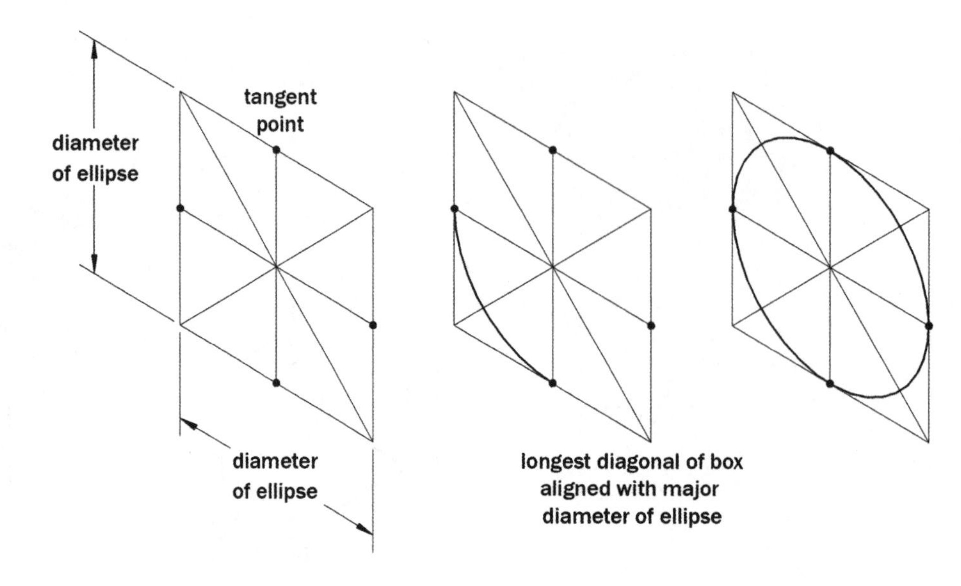

FIG. 3.20 Sketching ellipses inside the bounding box

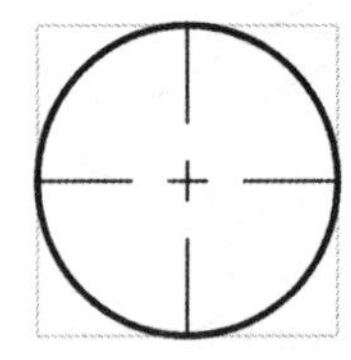

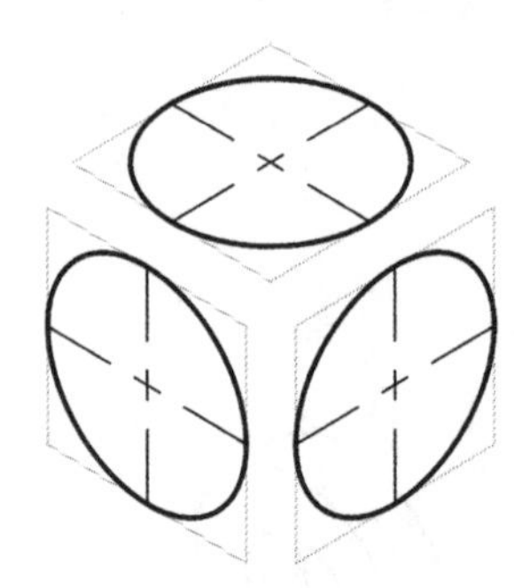

FIG. 3.19 Circles in isometric projection

In an isometric drawing, all lines that are parallel to the primary axes are known as isometric lines, and they can be measured true size. Lines that are not parallel to any isometric lines, however, will not appear true size, making them more difficult to sketch.

Circular features require special attention, since they will always appear as ellipses due to the effects of foreshortening (seeFigure 3.19). Despite the wide variety of isometric templates and tools available, ellipses are difficult to draw and orient correctly. A simple construction box can be used, such as the length of each side equals the diameter of the desired circle. The ellipse can be oriented using the longest diagonal of the construction box, since it is always aligned with the major diameter of the ellipse. The midpoints of each side of the construction box are tangent to the ellipse (seeFigure 3.20).

Irregular curves are sketched by defining a grid in the orthographic view where the curved feature is shown. The intersections of the curve with the lines on the grid provide a set of points that can be used to plot the curves on the isometric face (seeFigure 3.21).

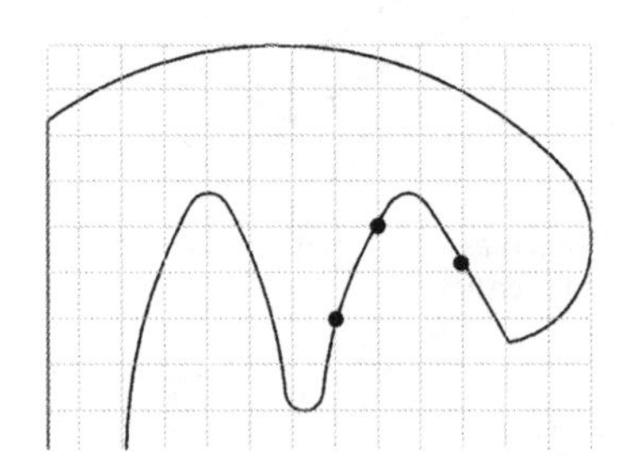

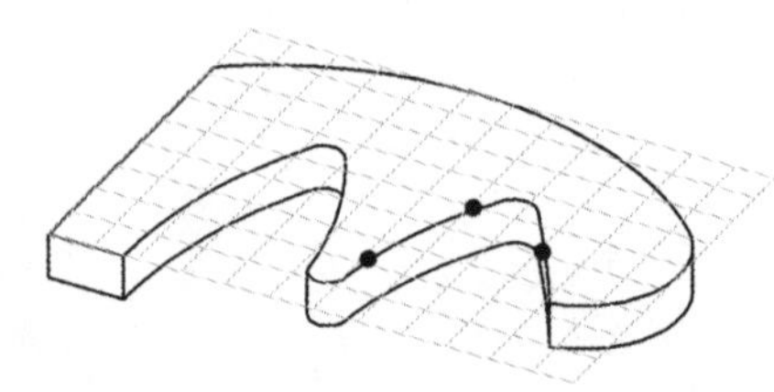

FIG. 3.21 Sketching irregular curves in isometric

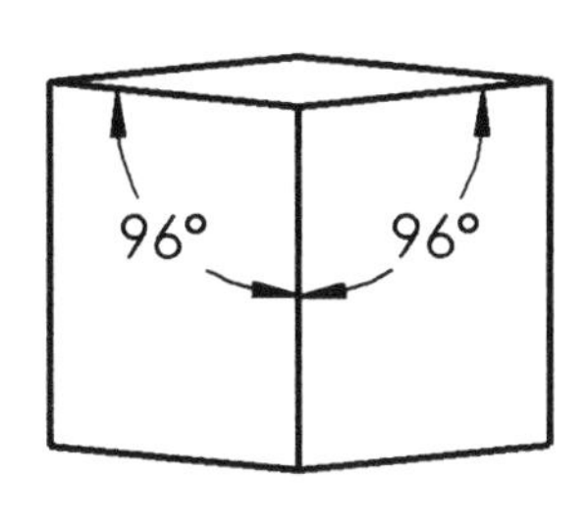

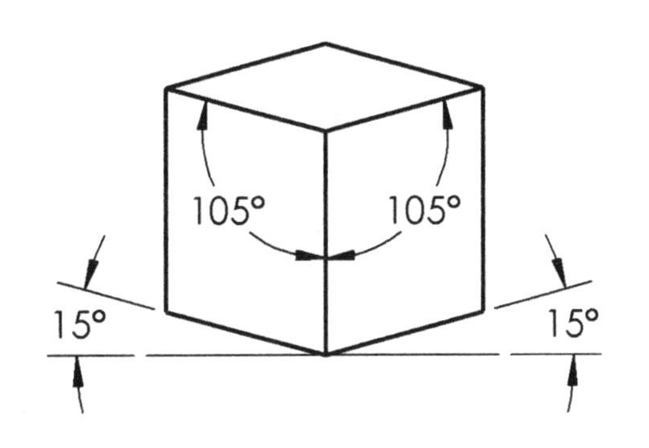

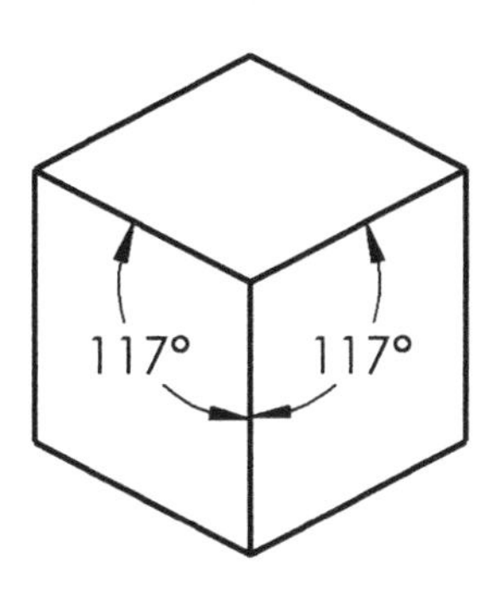

Dimetric projections at different angles FIG. 3.22

Dimetric Projection

Dimetric projections are a type of axonometric projection constructed by rotating the object 45° about its vertical axis, and then tilting it horizontally at an angle other than 35.264° (which would otherwise produce an isometric projection) with respect to the projection plane. The result is a pictorial where two primary axes are equally foreshortened and one is foreshortened at a different scale. In terms of orientation, only two of the angles formed among the primary axes are equal.

The tilt angle can be adjusted to produce different dimetric configurations. Common configurations for the equal angles include 105° (thus, 150° for the unequal angle, and 15° for the angle with the horizontal) and 130° (thus, 100° for the unequal angle). See Figure 3.22 for some dimetric projection examples.

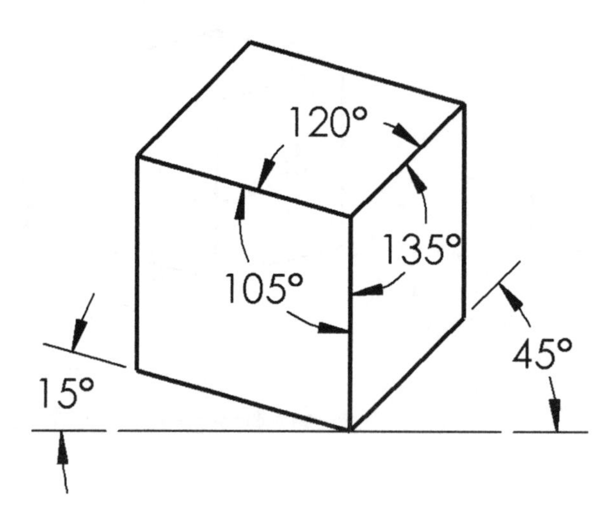

FIG. 3.23 Trimetric projection

Trimetric Projection

Trimetric projections are a type of axonometric projection constructed by rotating the object at an angle other than 45° (which would produce an isometric or a dimetric projection) about its vertical axis, and then tilting it horizontally with respect to the projection plane. The result is a pictorial with the three primary axes foreshortened at a different scale, causing the angles formed by the three axes to be different.

Similar to dimetric projections, the rotation and tilt angles for trimetric drawings can be adjusted to produce different configurations. The most popular configuration uses 105°, 120°, and 135° angles for the axes and 15° and 45° for the angle with the horizontal (see Figure 3.23).

Although trimetric projection is popular in architecture to help focus attention on one side of a building, they are not frequently used in engineering (at least hand drawn trimetric sketches) because of the difficulties involved in working with three different scales.

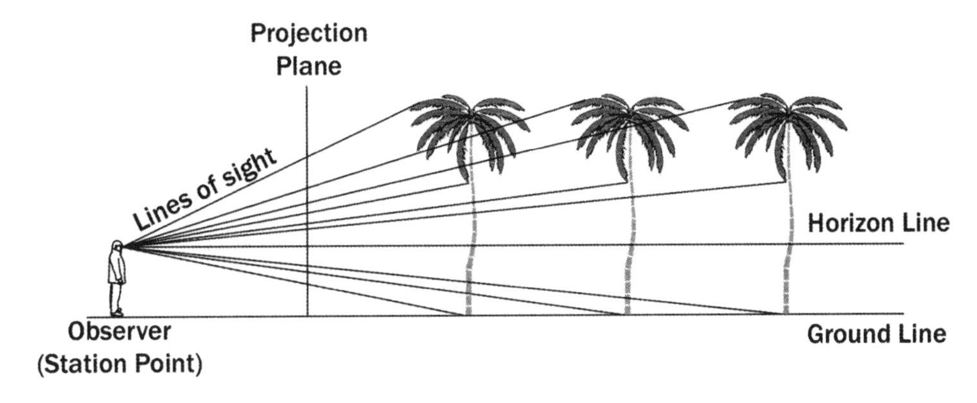

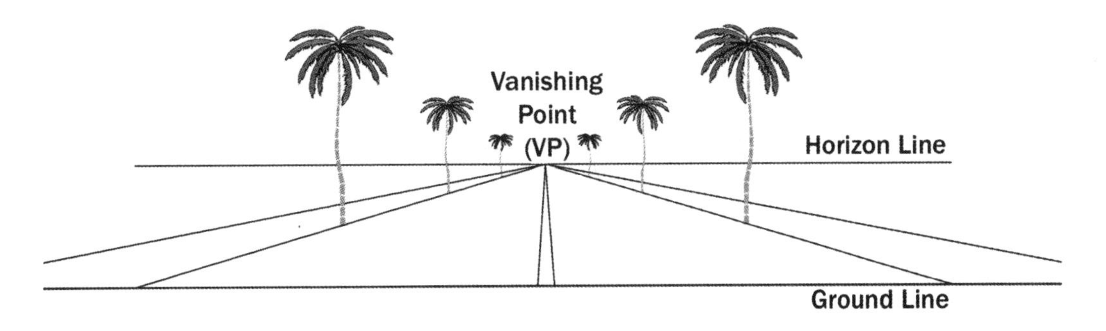

Location of the observer (top) and view from observer's standpoint (bottom) FIG. 3.24

Perspective Projection

Perspective projections are the most realistic method used for illustrations, as they portray objects as seen by the human eye. Unlike parallel projections, where the observer is theoretically located at infinity (causing the lines of sight to travel parallel to each other toward the object), perspective projections require the viewer to be at a finite distance from the projection plane. As a result, visual rays emanate from a single point, called the station point (the eye), and diverge while passing through the projection plane prior to striking the object. Unlike axonometric projection, parallel lines in perspectives appear to converge at single point (known as the vanishing point), producing a visual effect in which objects that are further away from the observer appear smaller than those that are closer (see Figure 3.24).

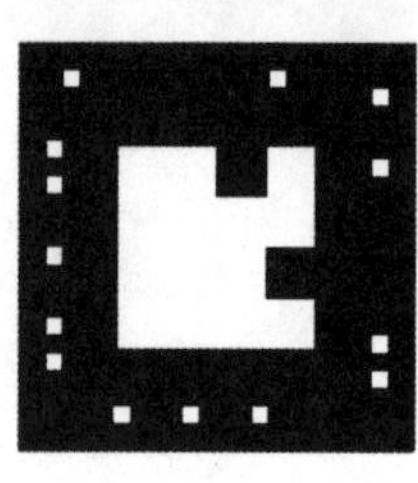

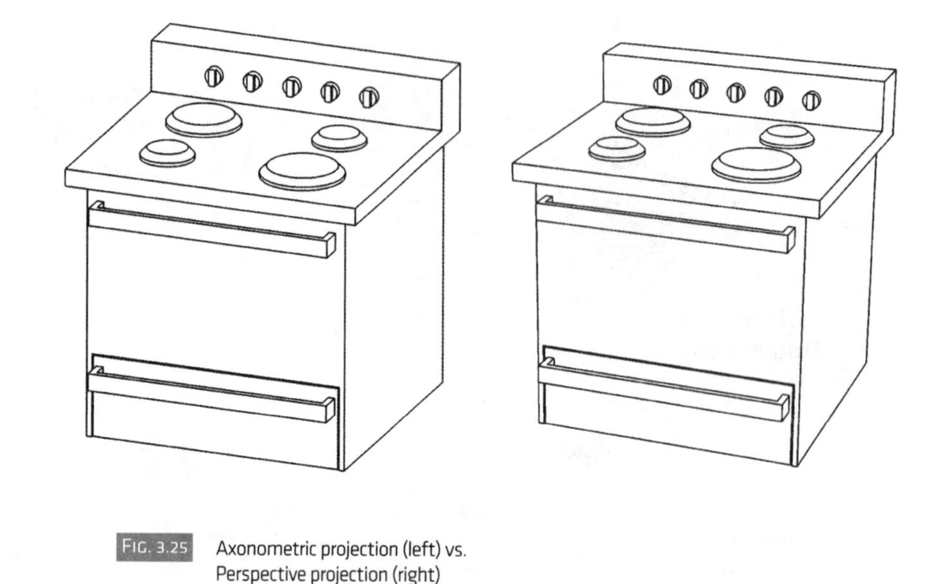

FIG. 3.25 Axonometric projection (left) vs. Perspective projection (right)

The realism of perspective projections makes them suitable for visualization, presentations, and technical illustration purposes (see Figure 3.25). Perspective drawings are in used in product and industrial design, architectural visualizations, and engineering illustrations. Creating perspective drawings by hand is a difficult and time consuming process, depending on the complexity of the drawing. However, modern Computer Aided Design (CAD) packages provide tools to automatically generate perspective drawings from 3D models.

Perspective drawings are classified according to the number of vanishing points, which are determined by the orientation of the object with respect to the projection plane. If one face of the object is parallel to the projection plane, only one vanishing point is required to represent depth. This projection is called One-Point Perspective. If the object is rotated a certain angle relative to the projection plane, but keeping vertical edges parallel to the projection plane (such as looking at the corner of a house, for example), then two vanishing points are required, thus producing a Two-Point Perspective. Three-Point Perspective is used almost exclusively to represent buildings as seen from a higher or lower position. In this case, the object is rotated relative to the projection plane (as with Two-Point Perspectives) and the vertical edges converge toward a third vanishing point. The basic steps used to create One-Point and Two-Point perspective drawings are shown in the following illustrations:

Sketching Perspective Drawings

One-Point Perspective

Horizon Line VP

1 Sketch the front view of the object true size. Define the horizon line and a point on that line. This point will be the vanishing point.

Horizon Line VP

2 From every point on the font view, trace the receding lines toward the vanishing point.

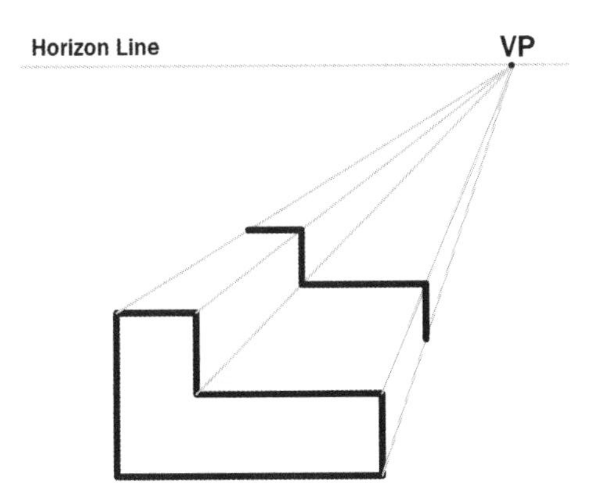

3 Estimate the depth of the sketch and create the lines that represent the back side of the object.

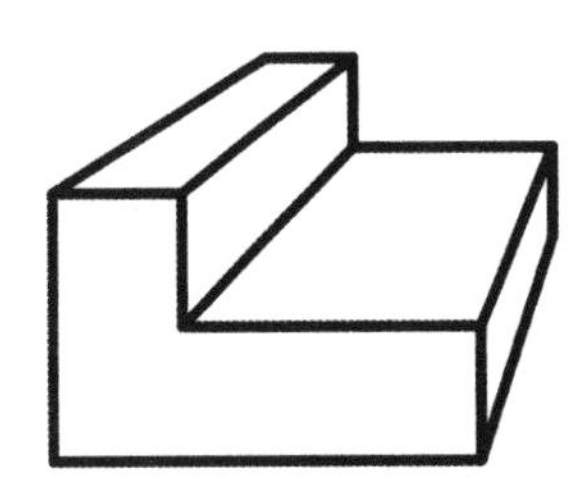

4 Darken the lines that are part of the object and erase construction lines.

Two-Point Perspective

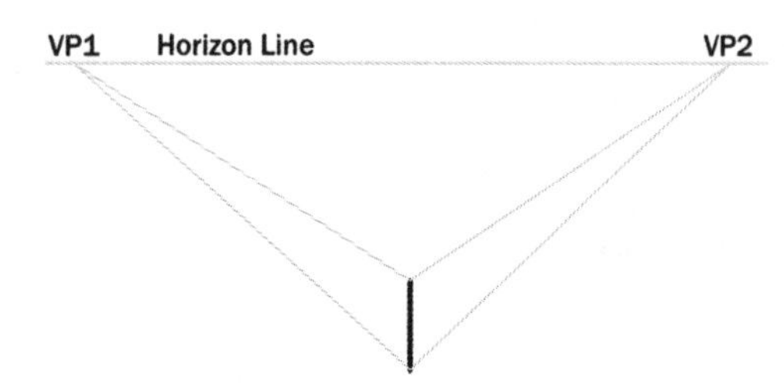

1 Sketch the front corner of the object true height. Define the horizon line and two vanishing points on that line. From each endpoint, trace receding lines toward both vanishing points.

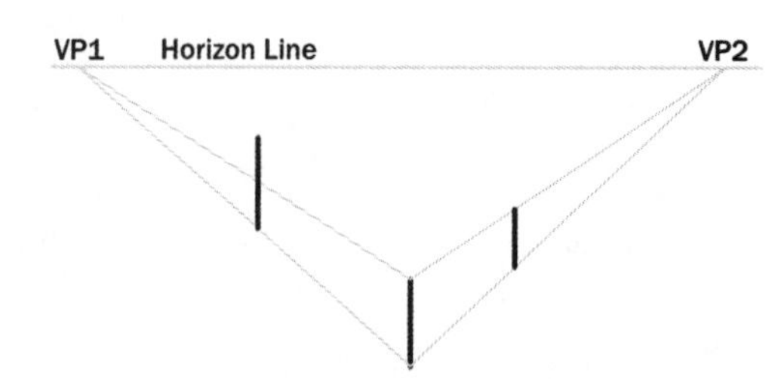

2 Estimate the width and depth of the object and create vertical lines to define the overall size of the object.

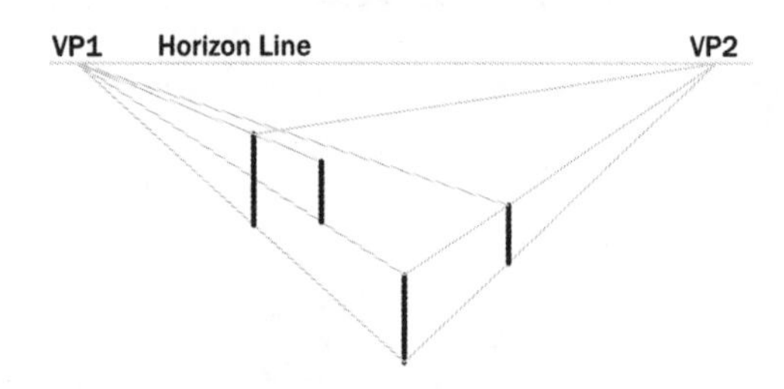

3 Receding lines toward the vanishing points are used to define edges along the width and depth dimensions.

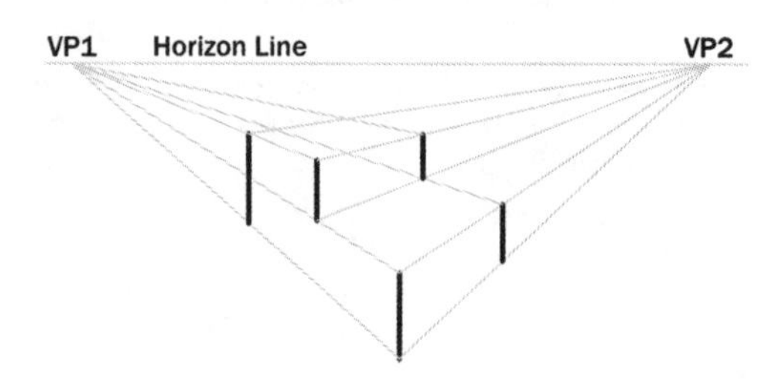

4 From the endpoints of each vertical line, trace receding lines toward both vanishing points.

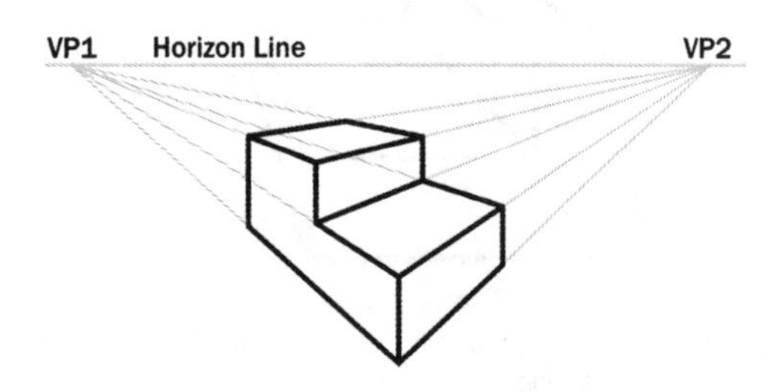

5 Block in the outline by darkening the lines that are part of the object.

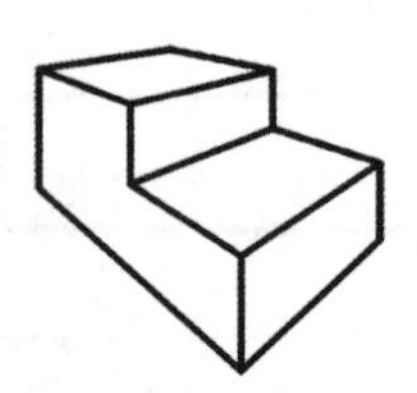

6 Erase construction lines. Finish drawing.

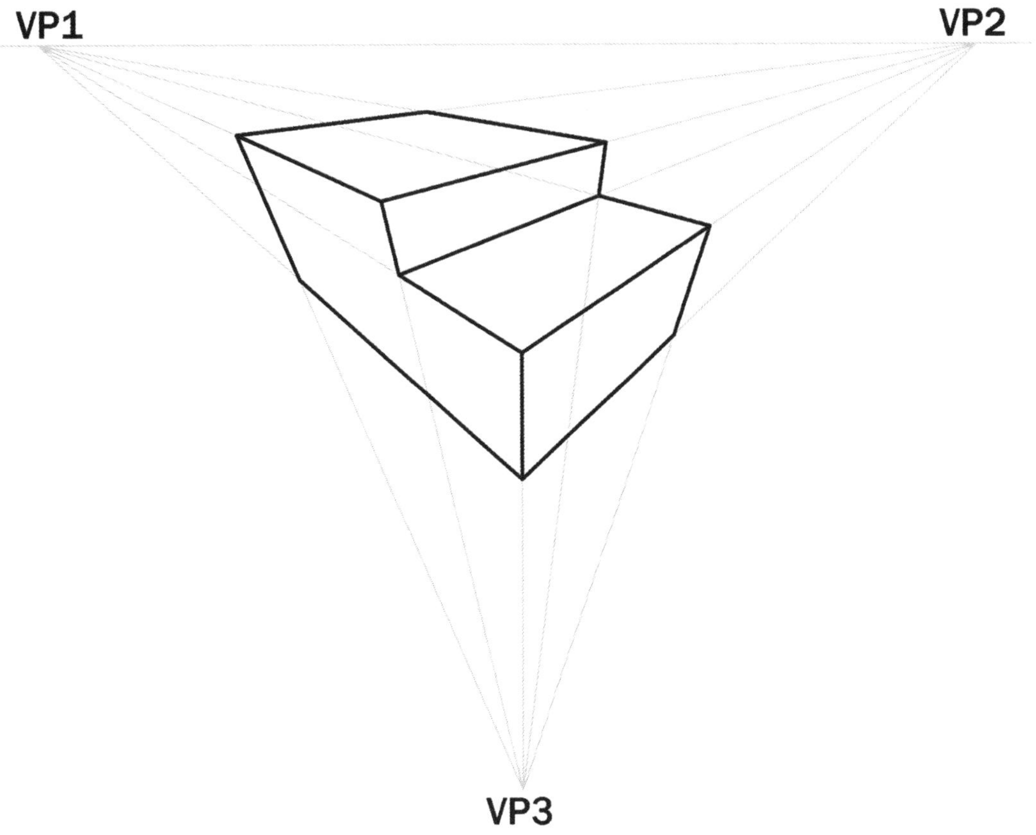

VP1 VP2 VP3

Three-point perspective FIG. 3.26

Three-Point Perspective

To create a three-point perspective sketch, the basic process for two-point perspectives can be used. WIn this case, however, vertical lines will not be parallel. Instead, they will converge toward a third vanishing point located above or below the horizon line, as shown in Figure 3.26

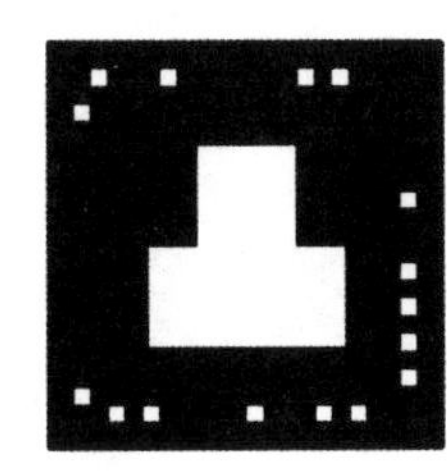

Pictorials

Name:

Chapter 03

Exercise 01

Date:

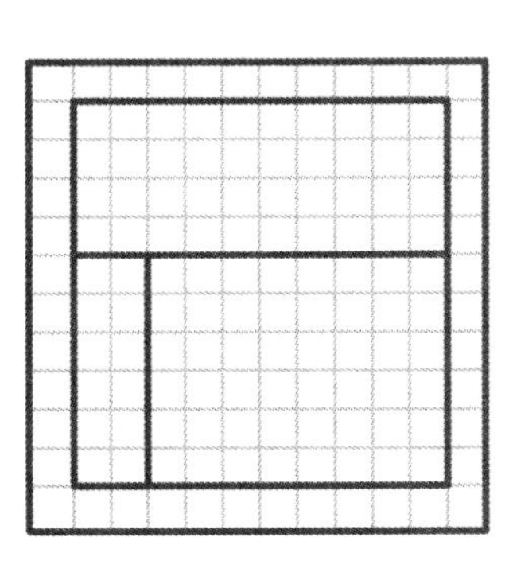

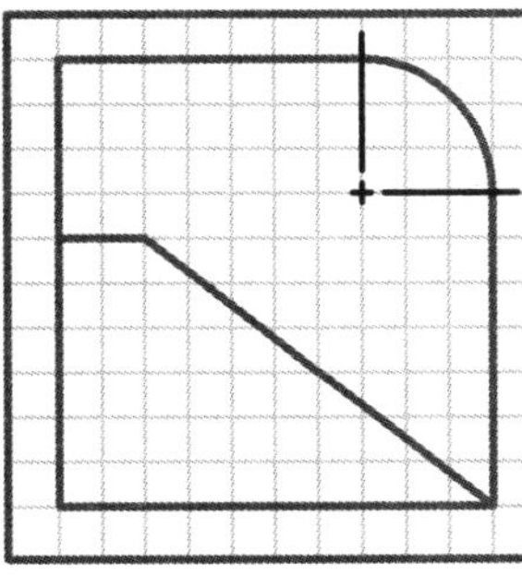

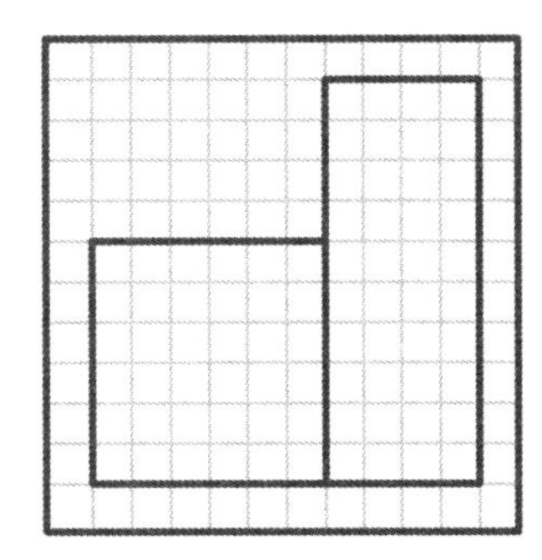

Given the orthographic views, create an isometric sketch of the following object.

EXERCISE 02

NAME:

DATE:

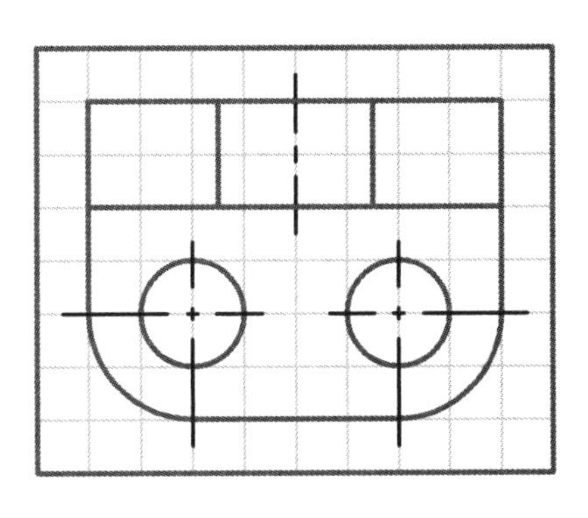

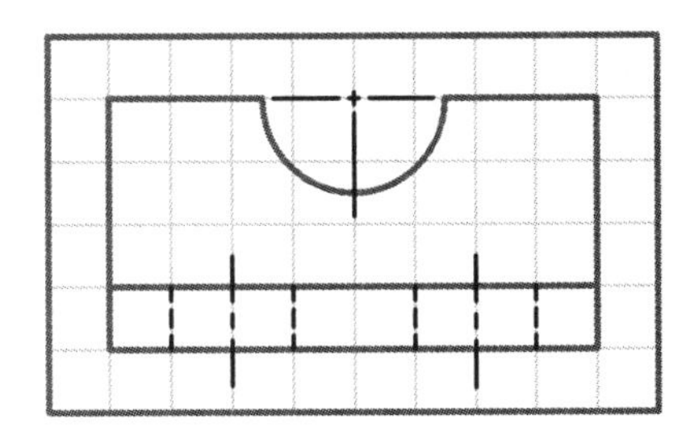

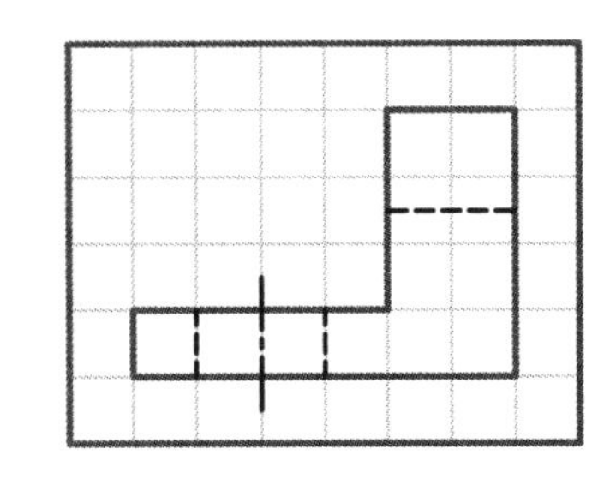

GIVEN THE ORTHOGRAPHIC VIEWS, CREATE AN ISOMETRIC SKETCH OF THE FOLLOWING OBJECT.

PICTORIALS

CHAPTER 03

EXERCISE 03

NAME:

DATE:

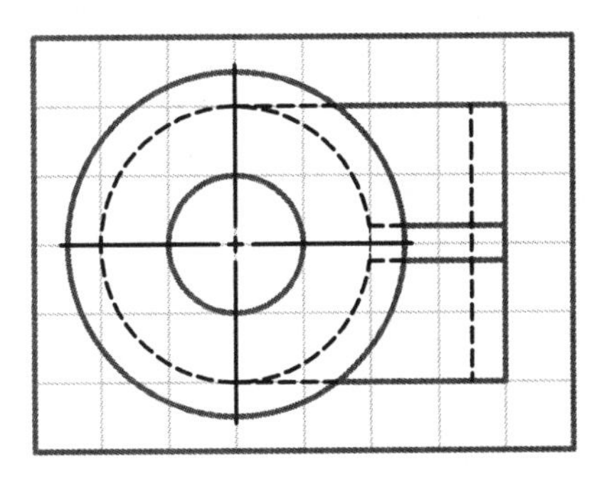

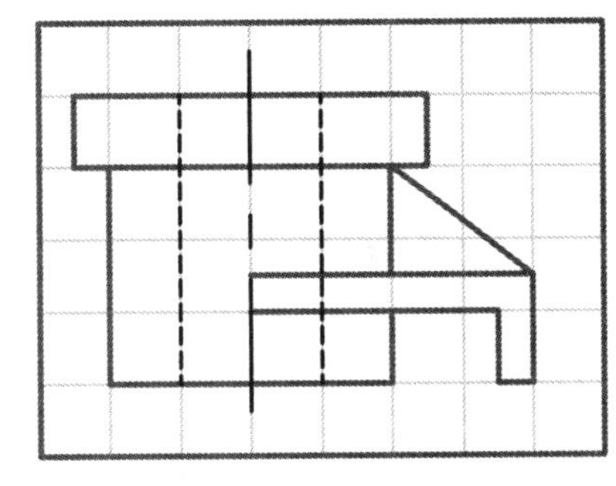

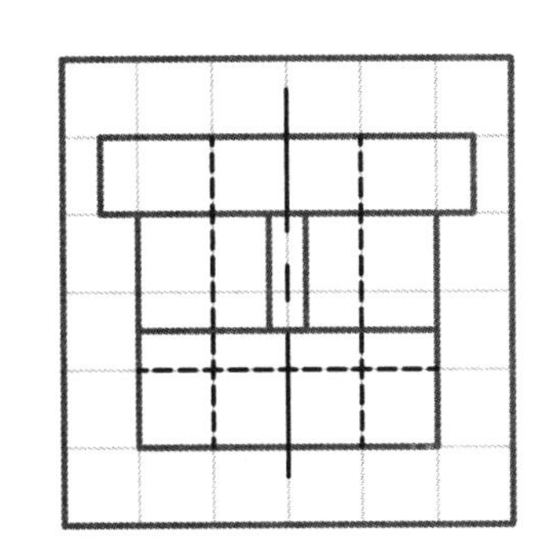

GIVEN THE ORTHOGRAPHIC VIEWS, CREATE AN ISOMETRIC SKETCH OF THE FOLLOWING OBJECT.

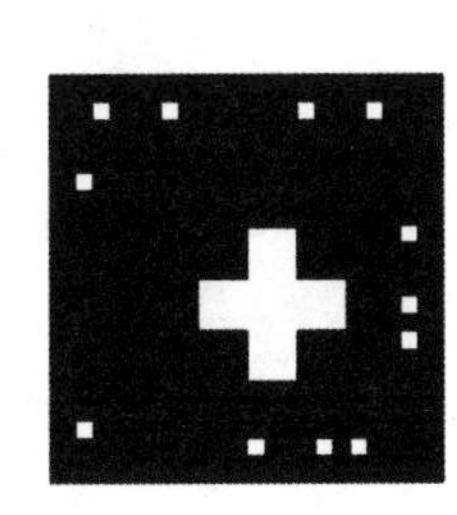

PICTORIALS

NAME:

CHAPTER 03
EXERCISE 04

DATE:

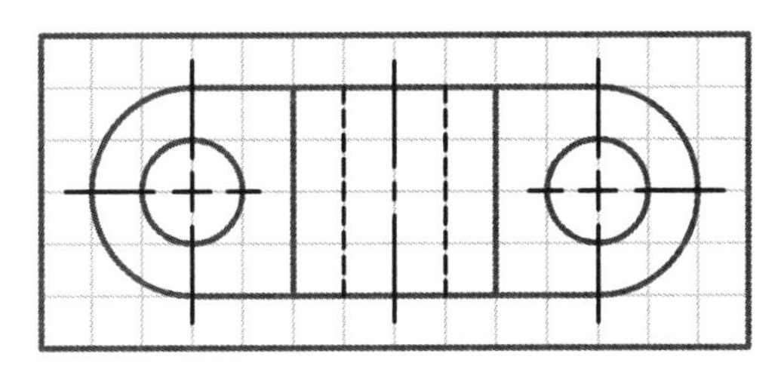

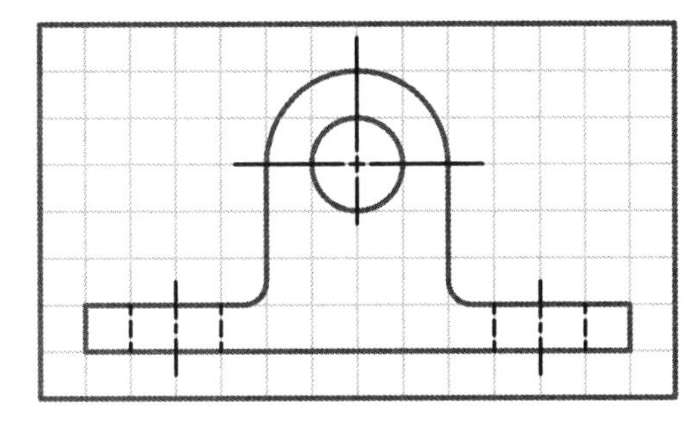

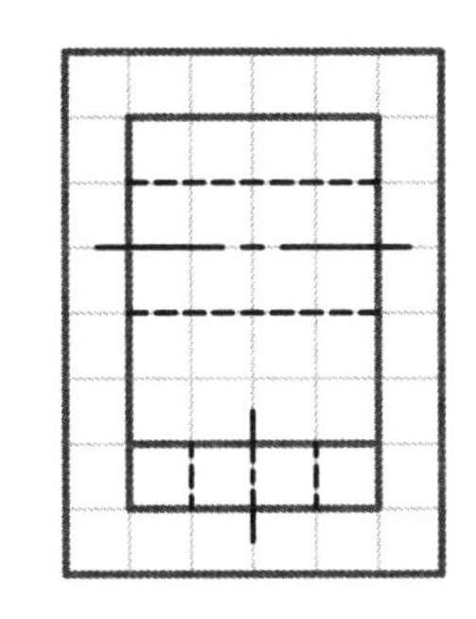

GIVEN THE ORTHOGRAPHIC VIEWS, CREATE AN ISOMETRIC SKETCH OF THE FOLLOWING OBJECT.

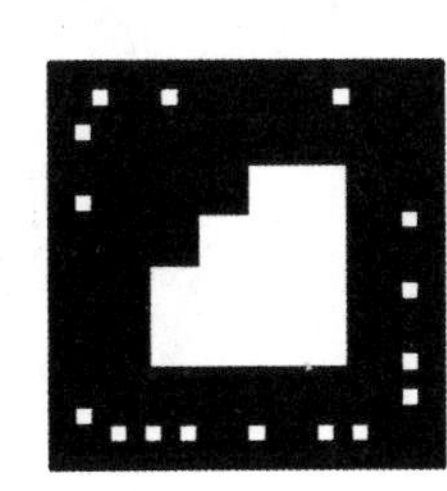

Pictorials

Name:

Chapter 03
Exercise 05

Date:

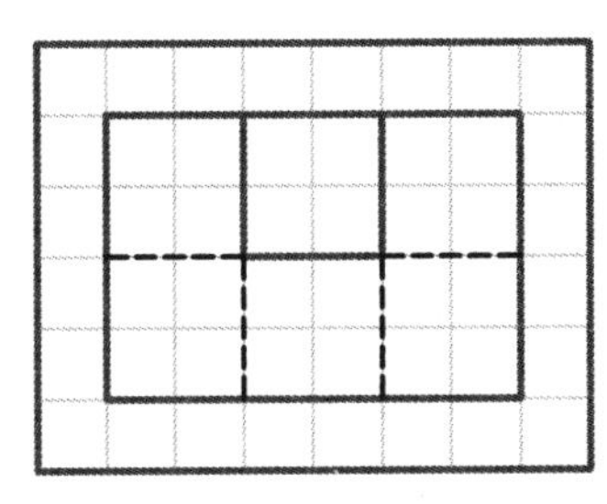

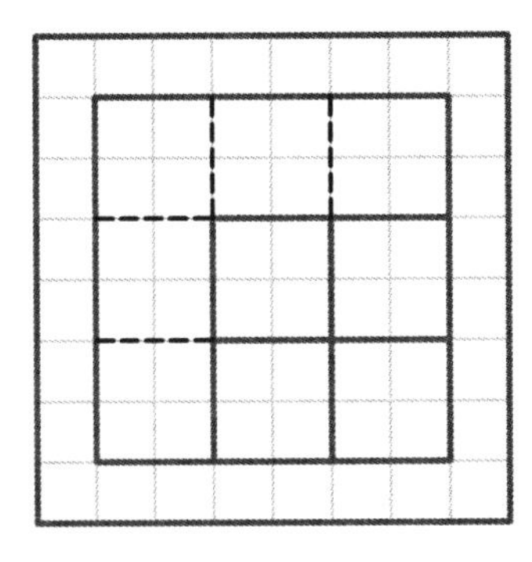
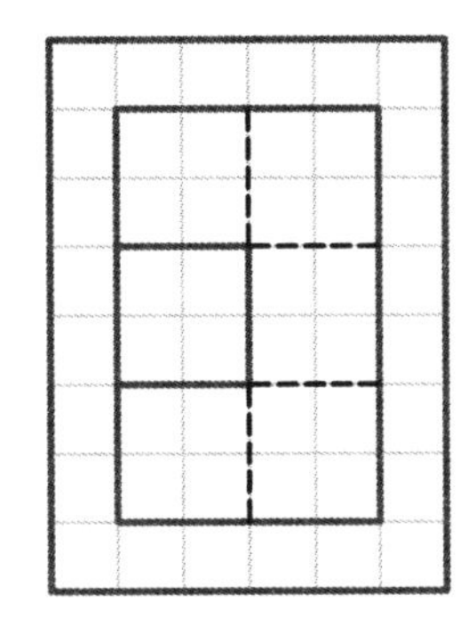

Given the orthographic views, create an isometric sketch of the following object.

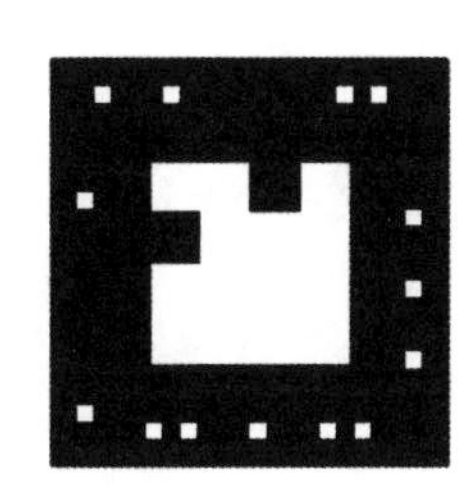

PICTORIALS

CHAPTER 03
EXERCISE 06

NAME:

DATE:

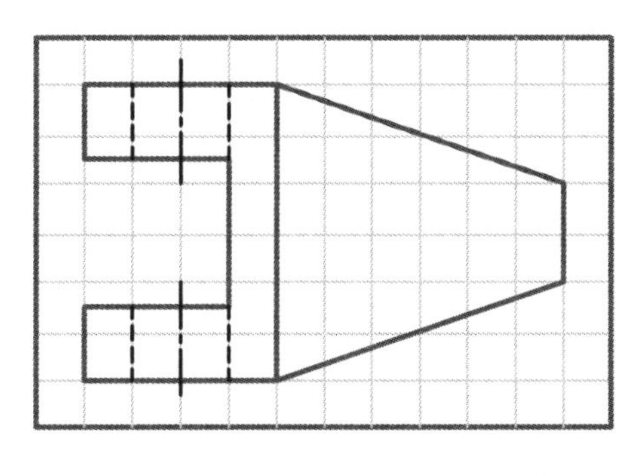

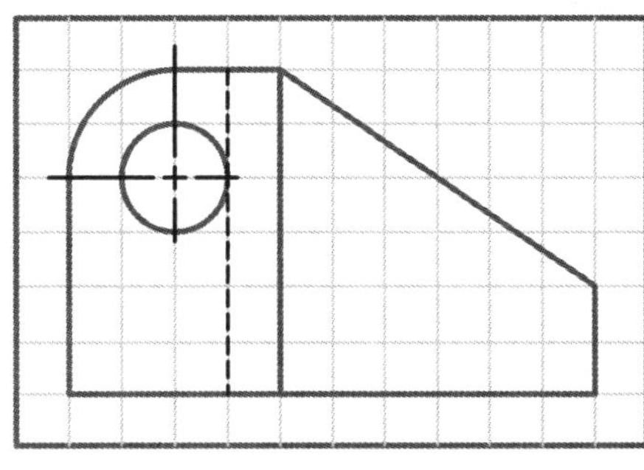

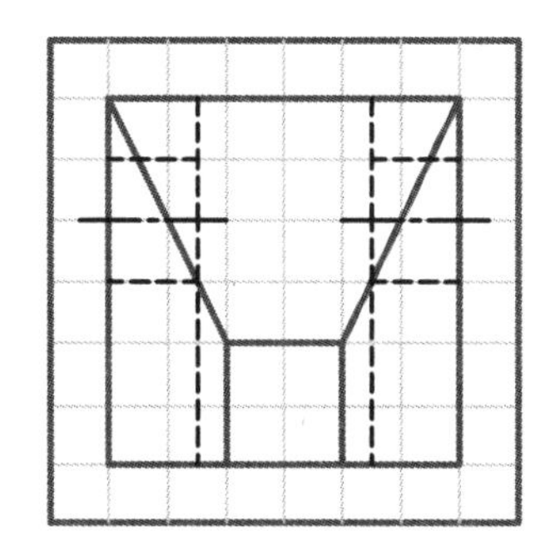

GIVEN THE ORTHOGRAPHIC VIEWS, CREATE AN ISOMETRIC SKETCH OF THE FOLLOWING OBJECT.

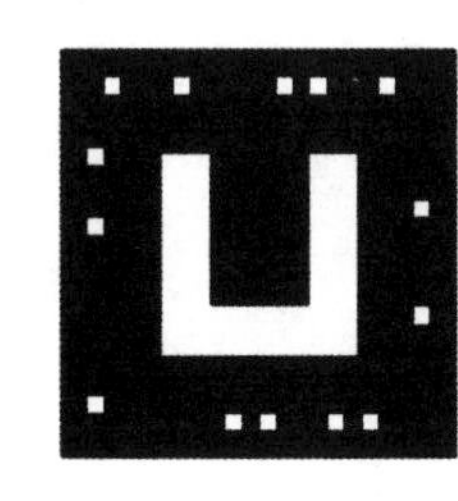

Pictorials

Chapter 03
Exercise 07

Name:

Date:

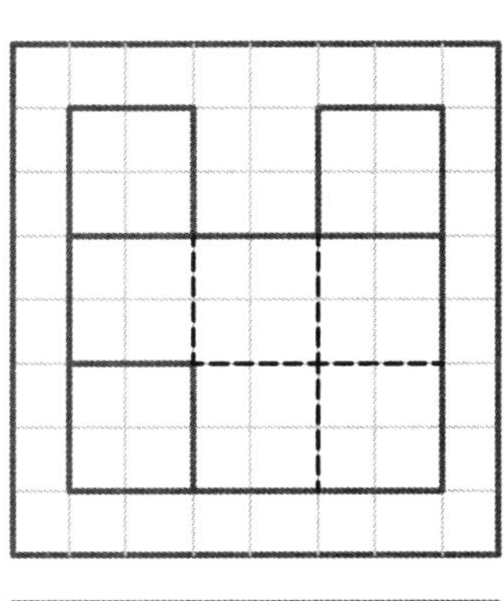

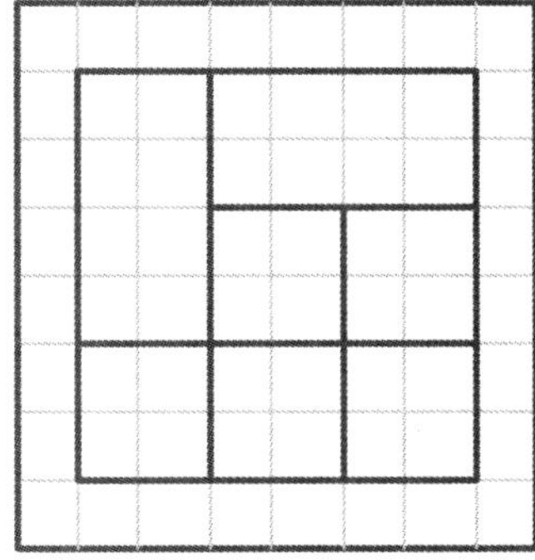

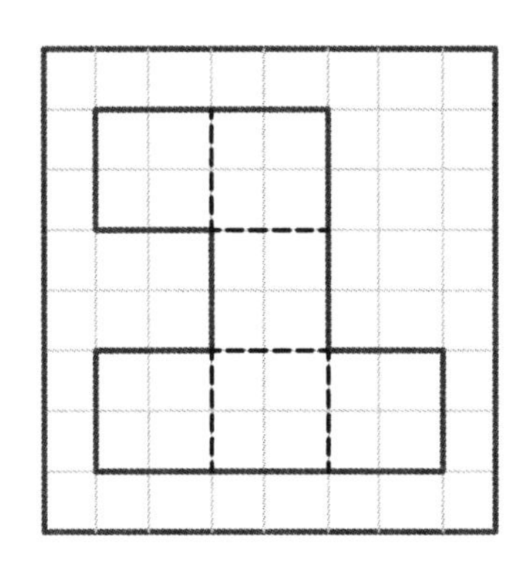

Given the orthographic views, create an isometric sketch of the following object.

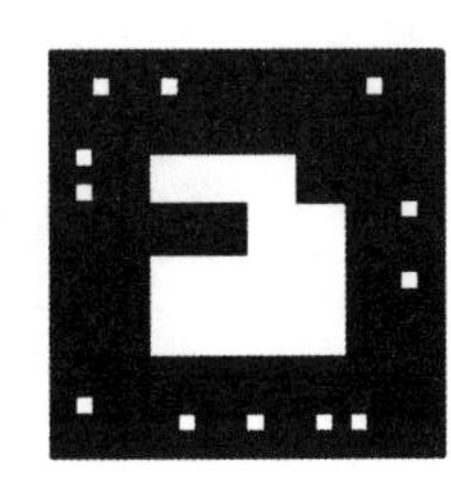

PICTORIALS

NAME:

CHAPTER 03
EXERCISE 08

DATE:

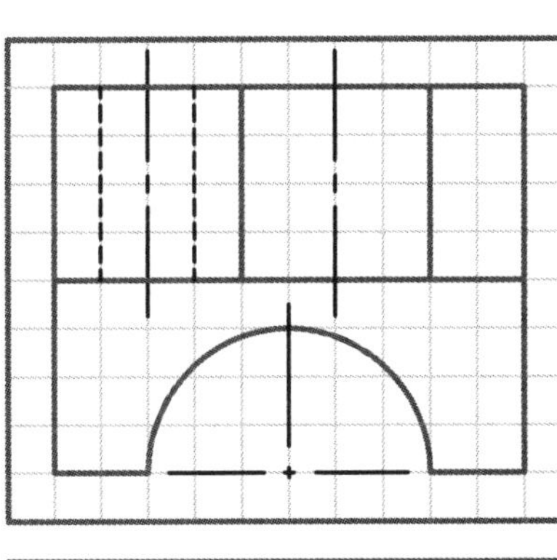

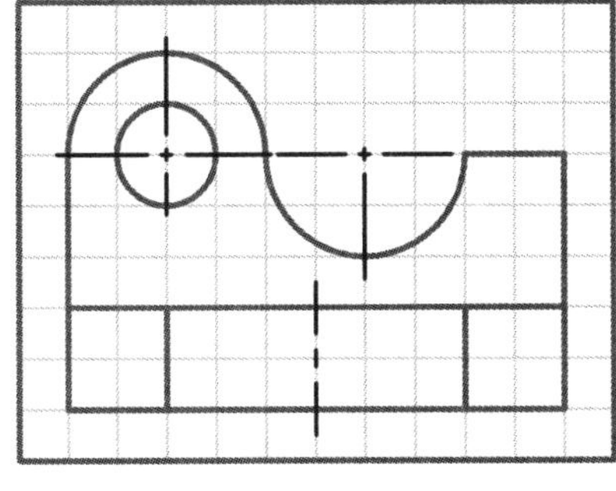

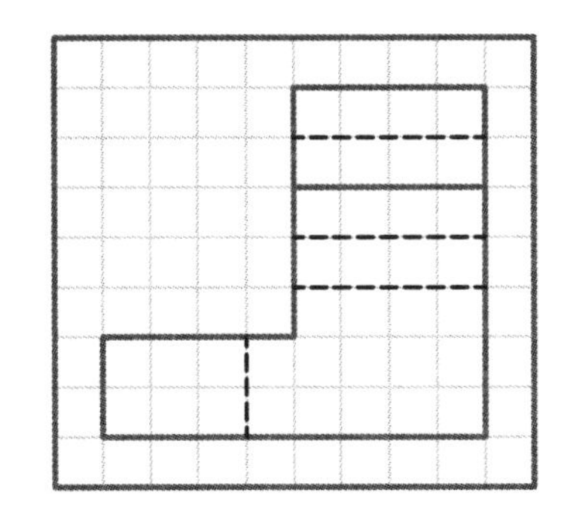

GIVEN THE ORTHOGRAPHIC VIEWS, CREATE AN ISOMETRIC SKETCH OF THE FOLLOWING OBJECT.

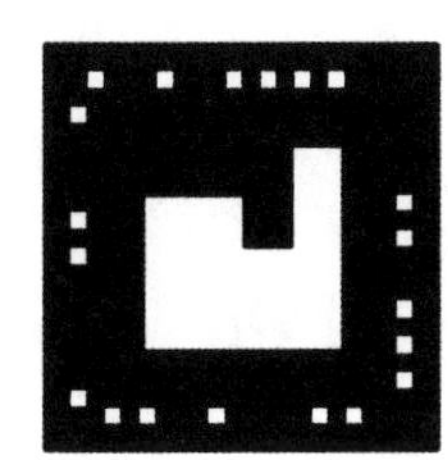

EXERCISE 09

NAME:

DATE:

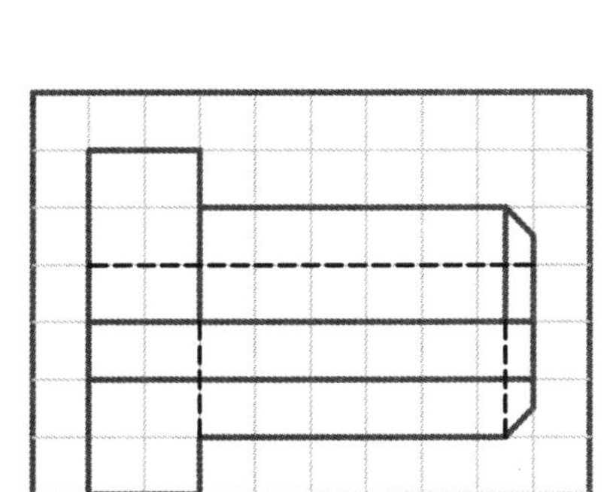

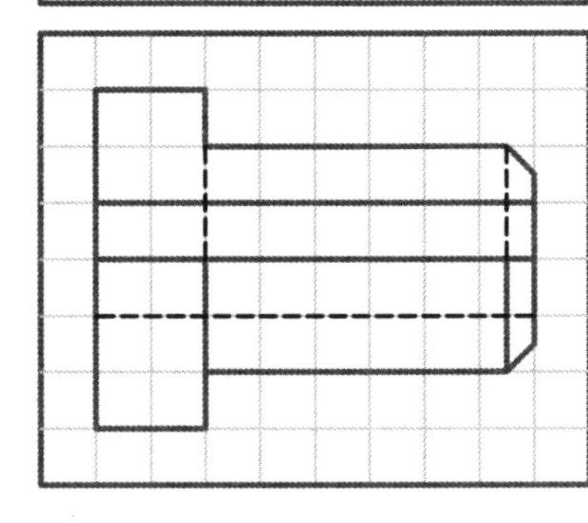

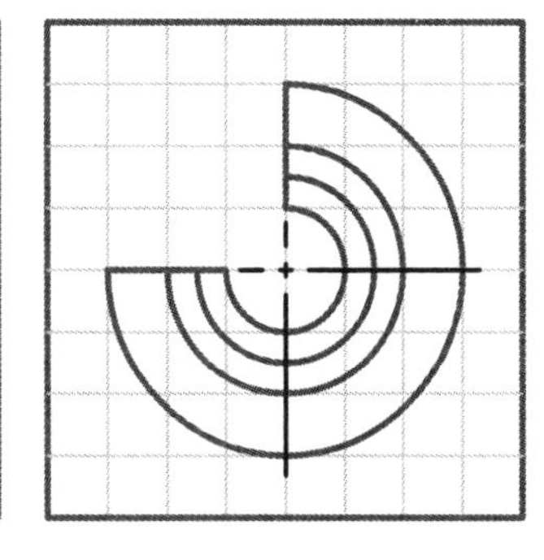

GIVEN THE ORTHOGRAPHIC VIEWS, CREATE AN ISOMETRIC SKETCH OF THE FOLLOWING OBJECT.

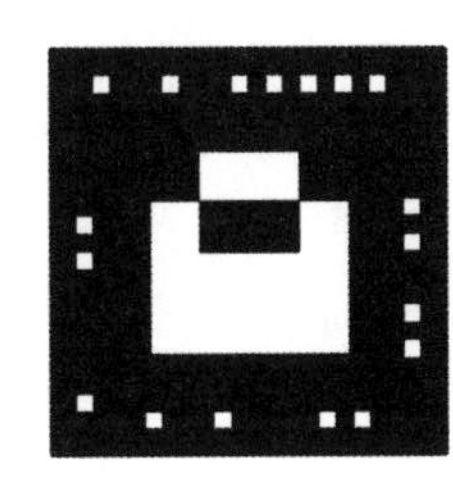

PICTORIALS

CHAPTER 03
EXERCISE 10

NAME:

DATE:

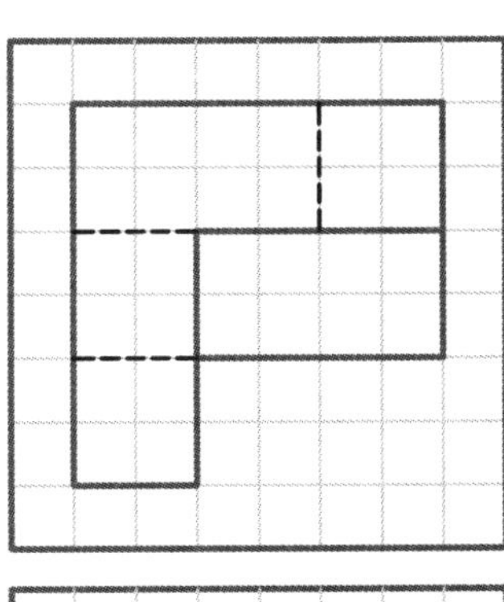

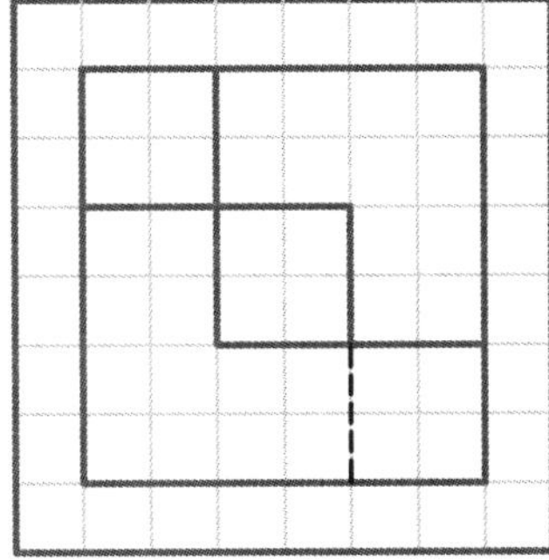

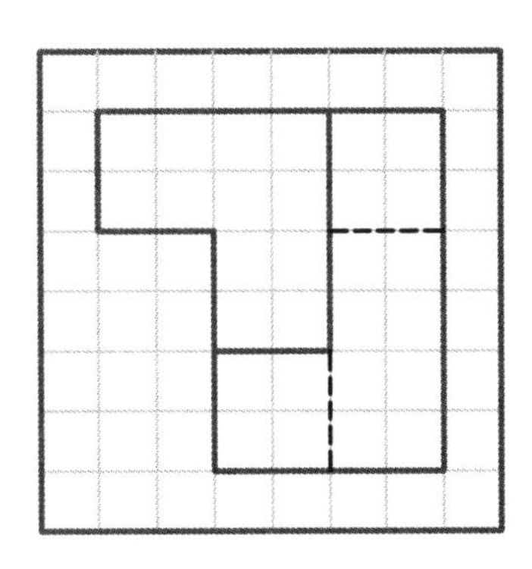

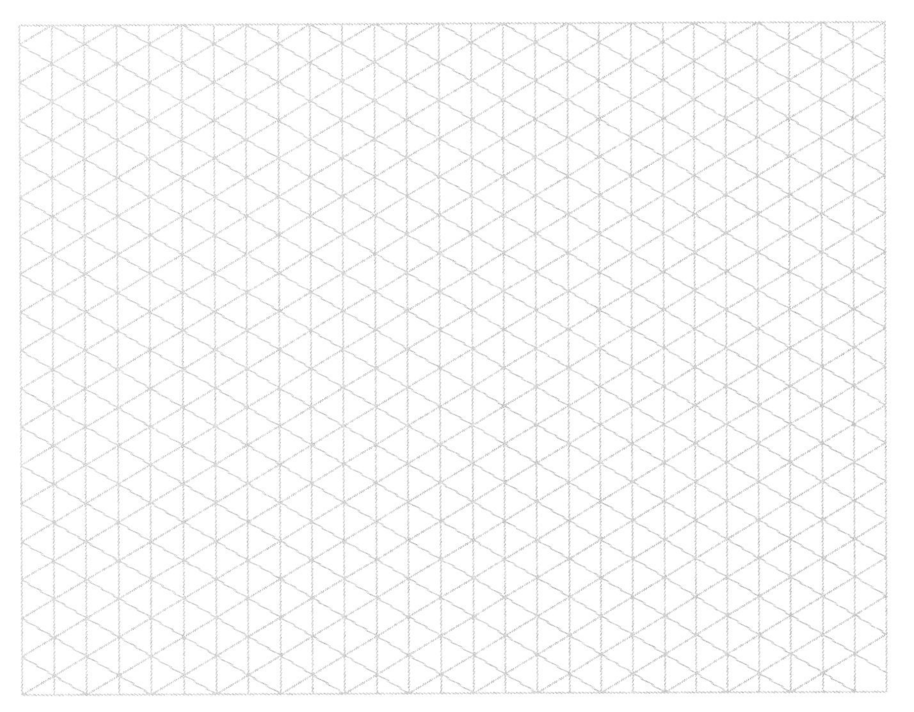

GIVEN THE ORTHOGRAPHIC VIEWS, CREATE AN ISOMETRIC SKETCH OF THE FOLLOWING OBJECT.

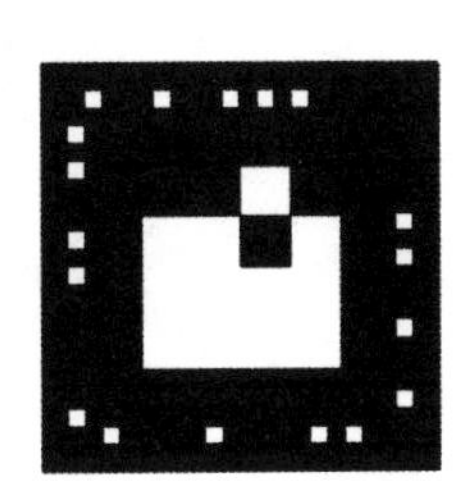

Pictorials

Name:

Chapter 03
Exercise 11

Date:

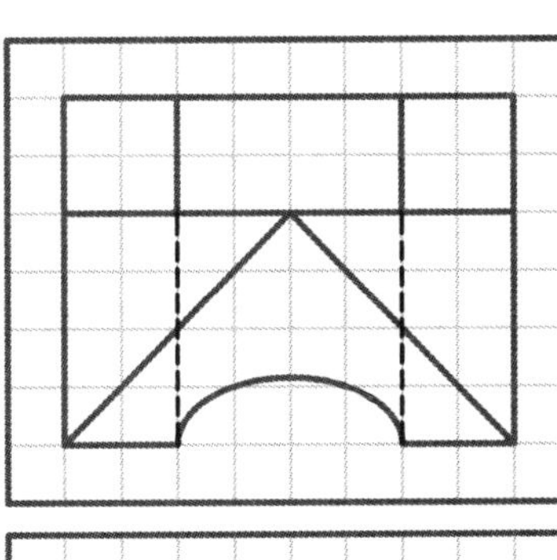

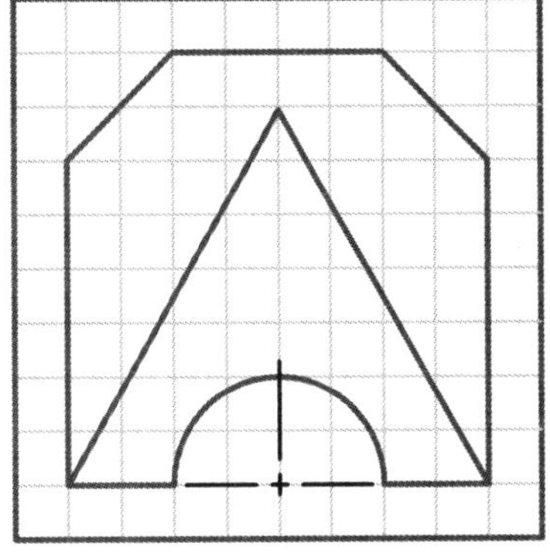

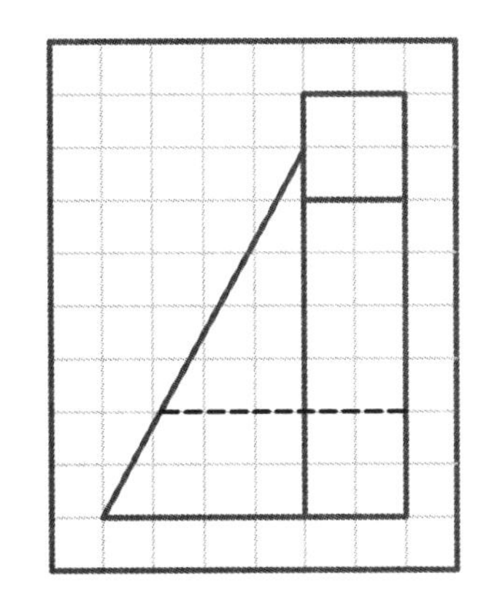

Given the orthographic views, create an isometric sketch of the following object.

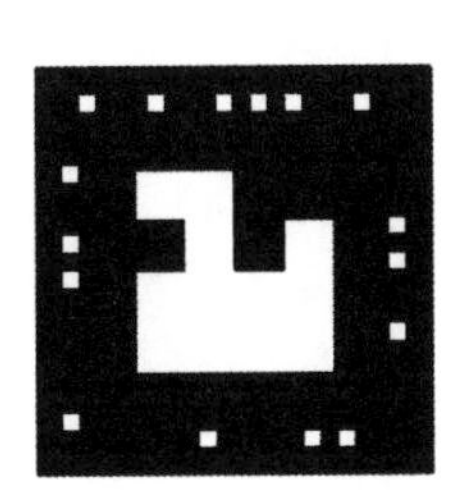

Exercise 12

Name:

Date:

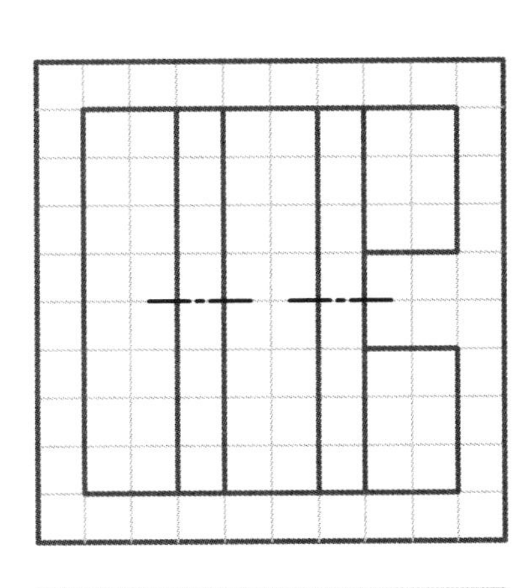

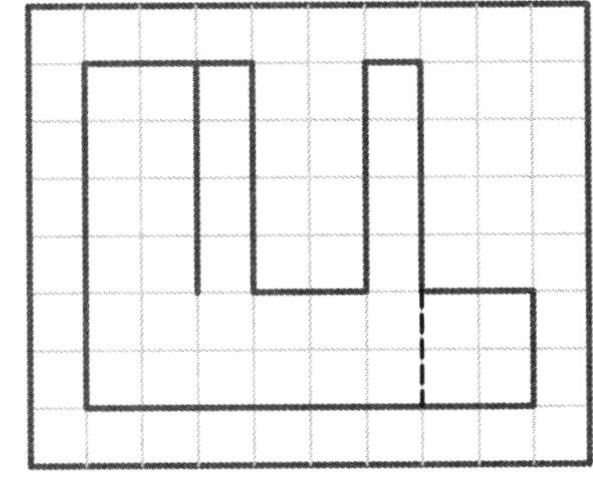

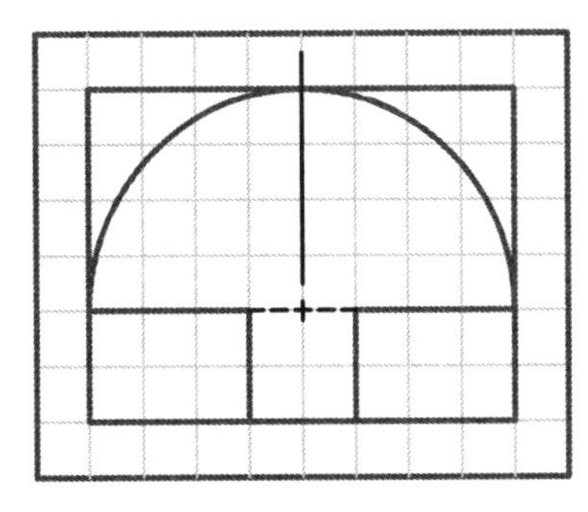

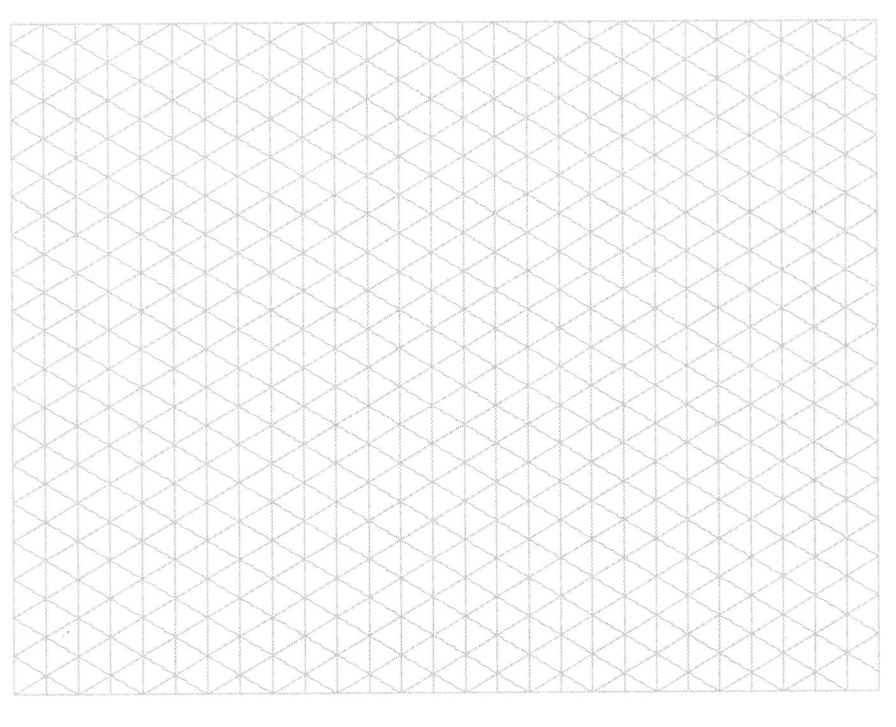

Given the orthographic views, create an isometric sketch of the following object.

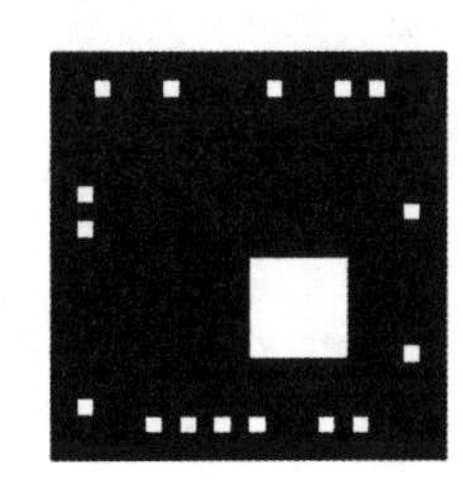

PICTORIALS

CHAPTER 03

EXERCISE 13

NAME:

DATE:

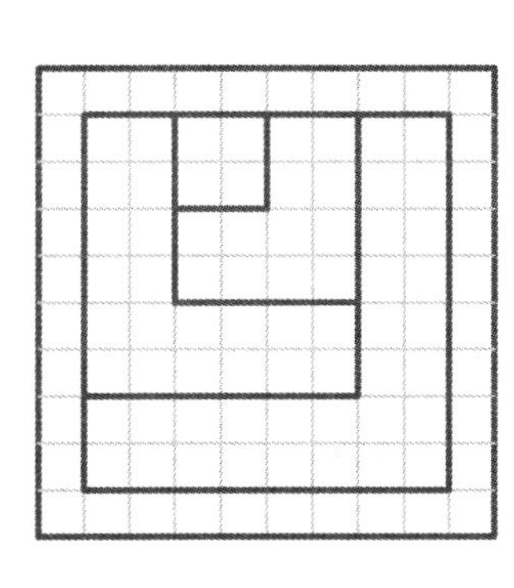

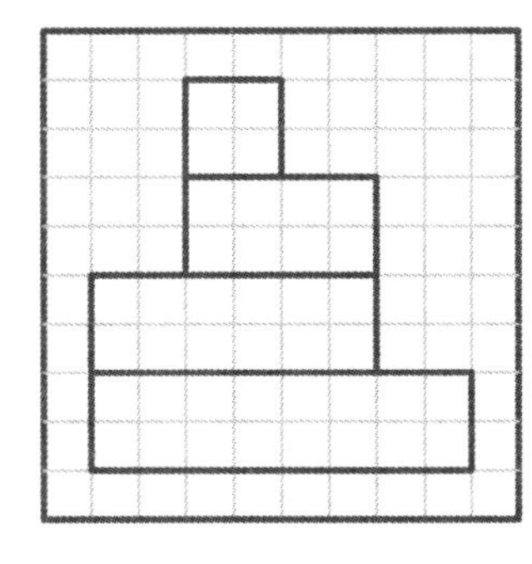

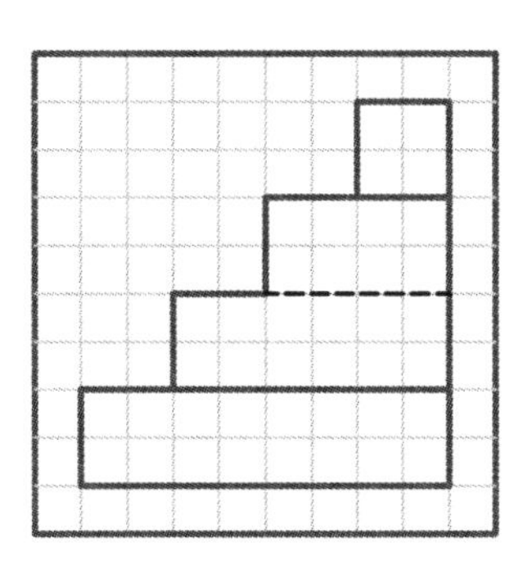

GIVEN THE ORTHOGRAPHIC VIEWS, CREATE AN ISOMETRIC SKETCH OF THE FOLLOWING OBJECT.

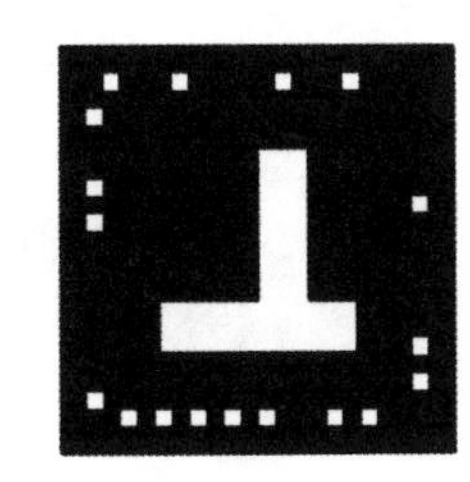
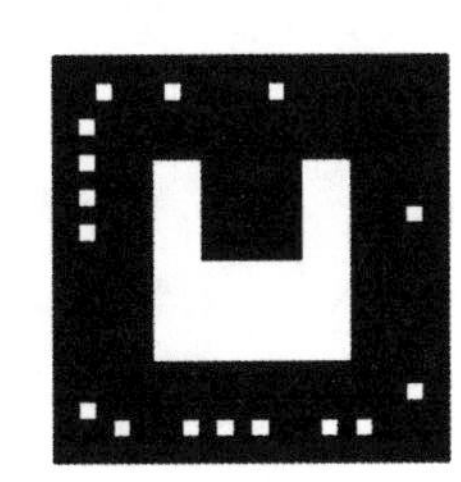

PICTORIALS

CHAPTER 03

EXERCISE 14

NAME:

DATE:

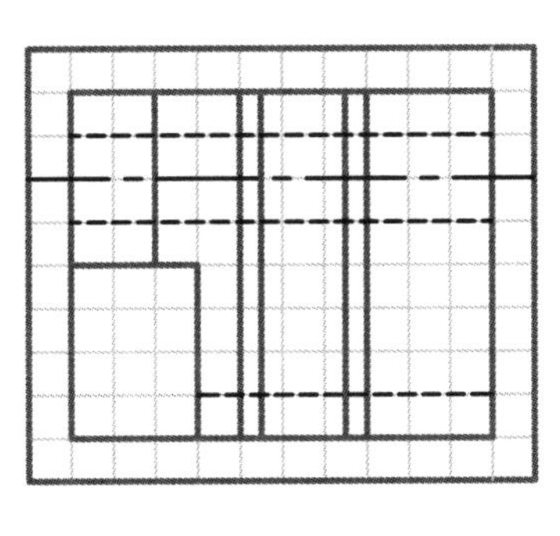

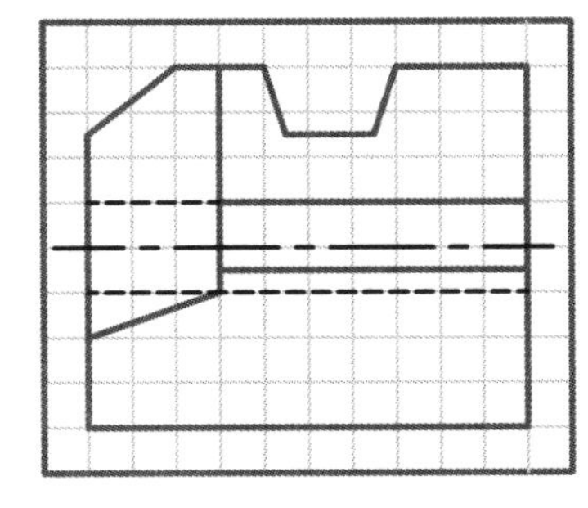

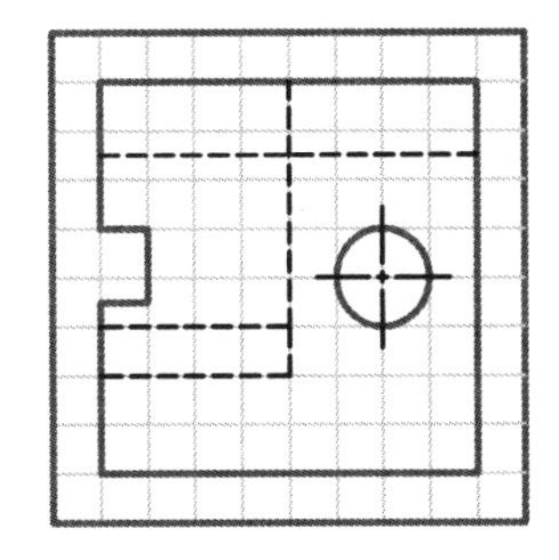

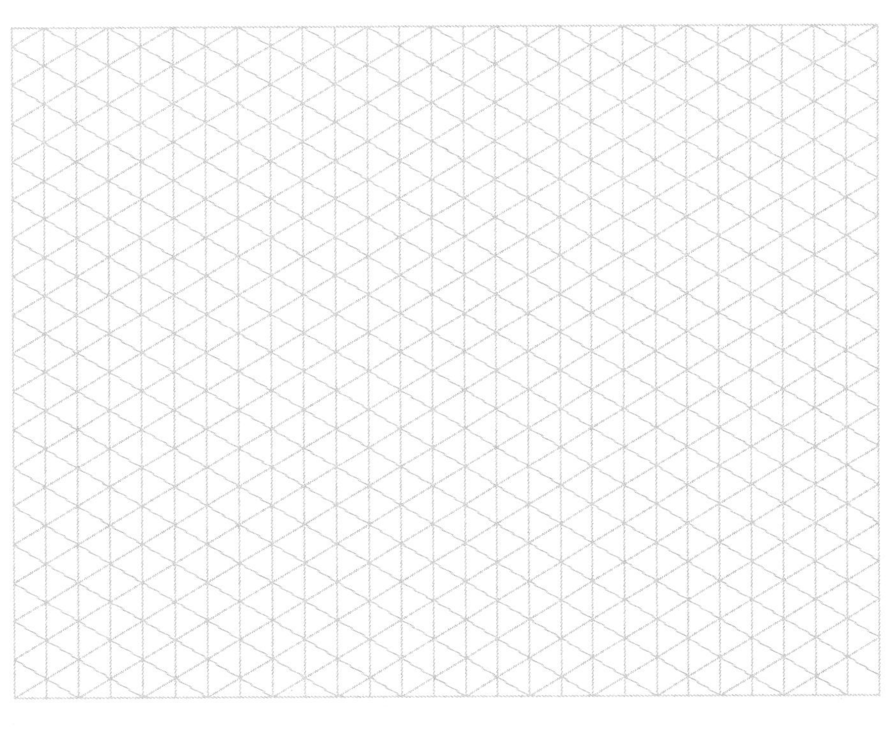

GIVEN THE ORTHOGRAPHIC VIEWS, CREATE AN ISOMETRIC SKETCH OF THE FOLLOWING OBJECT.

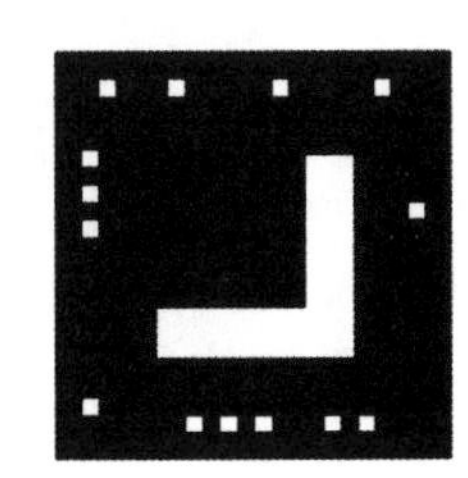

PICTORIALS

CHAPTER 03
EXERCISE 15

NAME:

DATE:

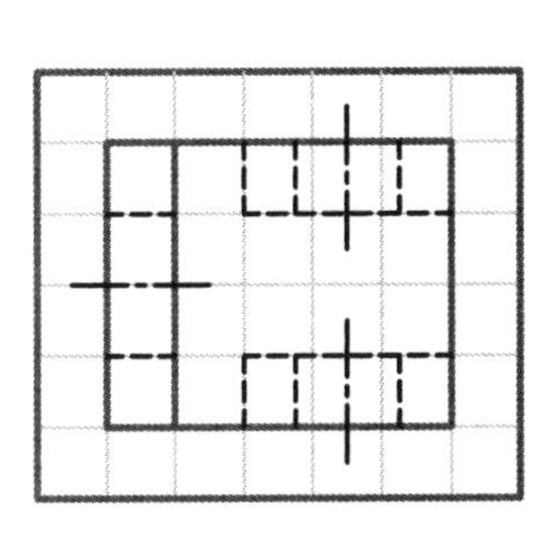

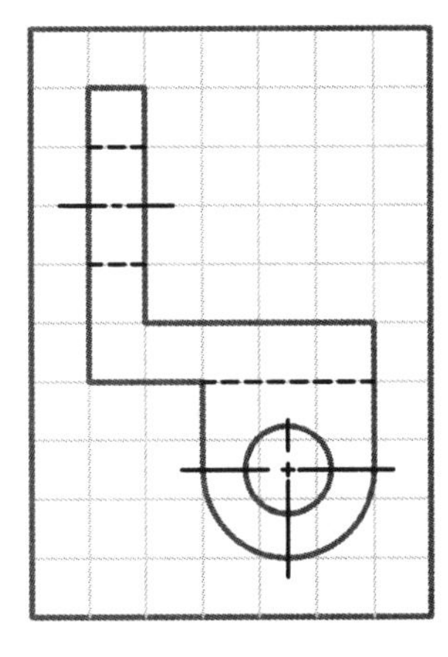

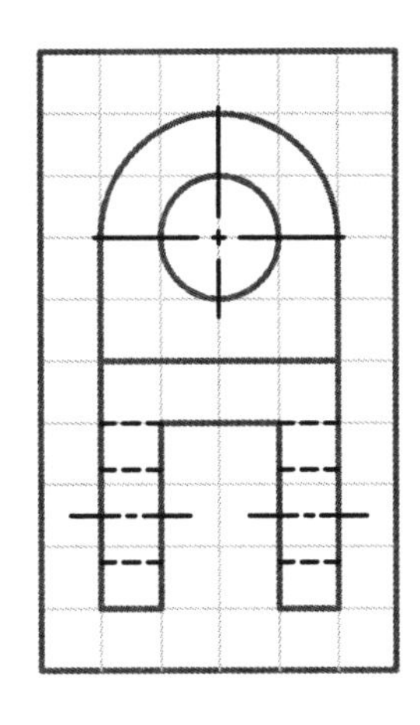

GIVEN THE ORTHOGRAPHIC VIEWS, CREATE AN ISOMETRIC SKETCH OF THE FOLLOWING OBJECT.

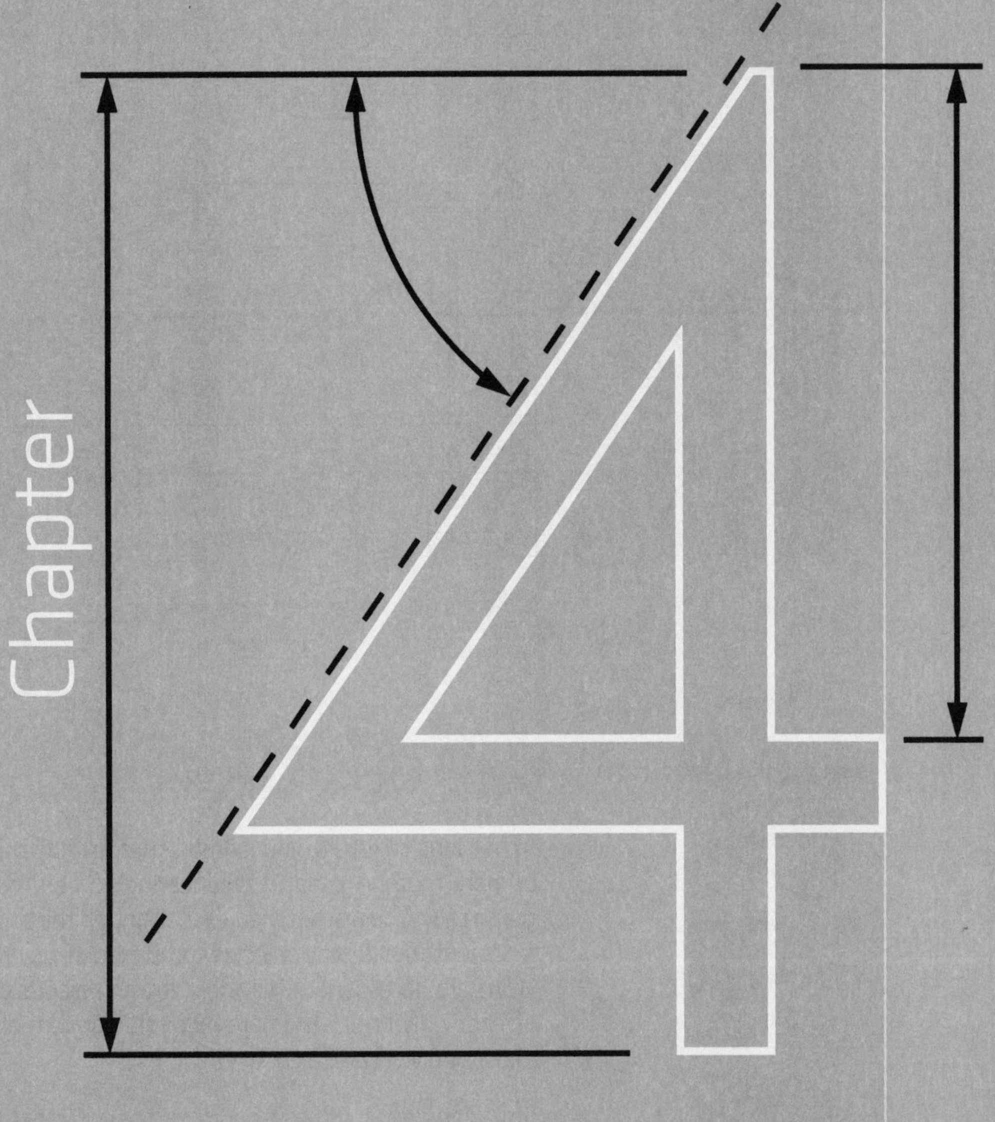

Sectional Views

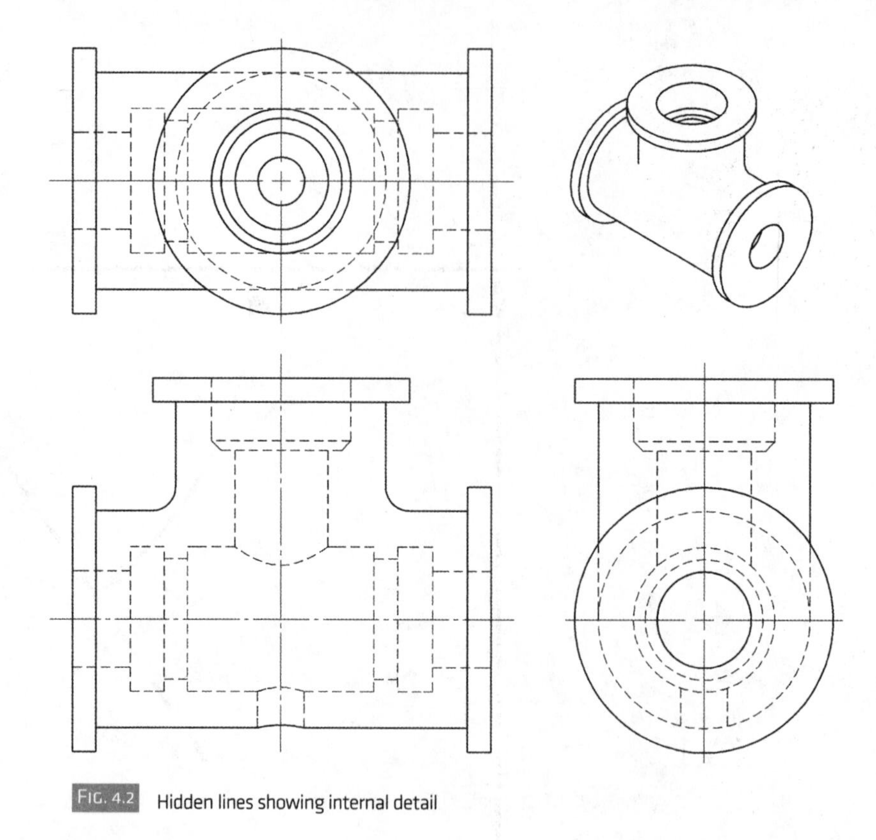

FIG. 4.2 Hidden lines showing internal detail

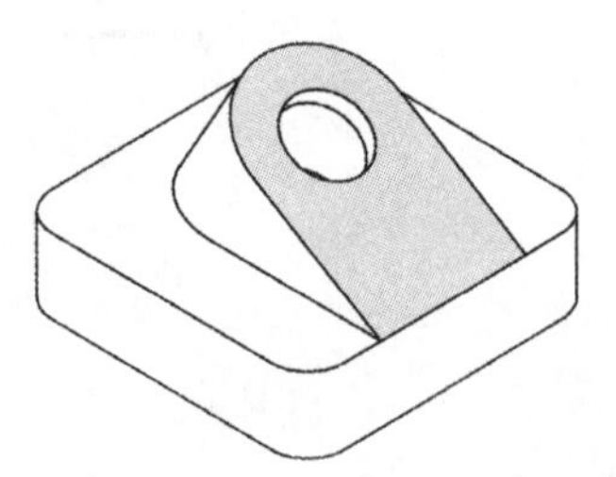

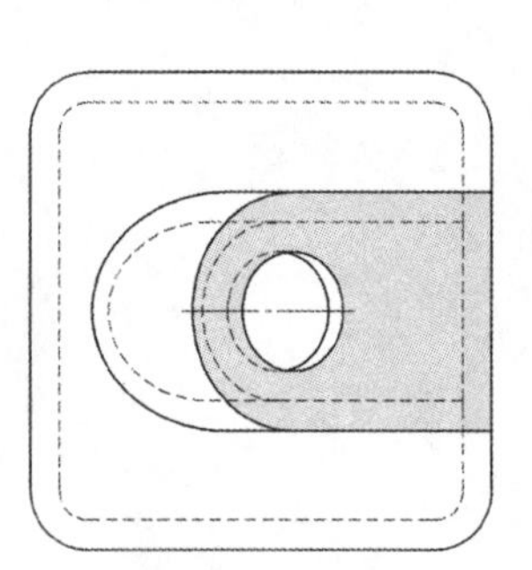

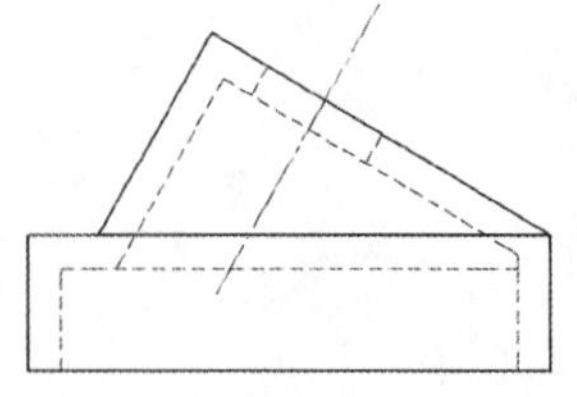

FIG. 4.1 True size of sloped surfaces is unclear

Introduction

In previous chapters, you learned that orthographic projection is the primary method used in engineering to communicate information graphically. You also learned that although the complete orthographic representation of any object is comprised of six principal views, not all views are necessary to fully describe an object's geometry. For most objects, only three views are required. Conventionally, the front, top, and a side view are used.

Situations exist, however, where the principal orthographic views may provide an unclear or confusing representation of an object. Illustrating objects with slanted surfaces or abundant internal detail, for example, may produce views that are difficult to interpret because of the effects of foreshortening or the amount of hidden lines that need to be included, which ultimately makes drawings difficult to comprehend (see Figure 4.1 and Figure 4.2). In these cases, special techniques such as auxiliary and sectional views are used to ensure that all aspects in the drawing are clear.

In this chapter, you will study the proper use of special views (and when they are needed) and the techniques and conventions employed in their construction.

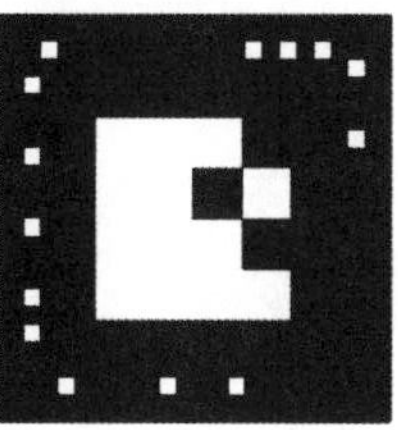

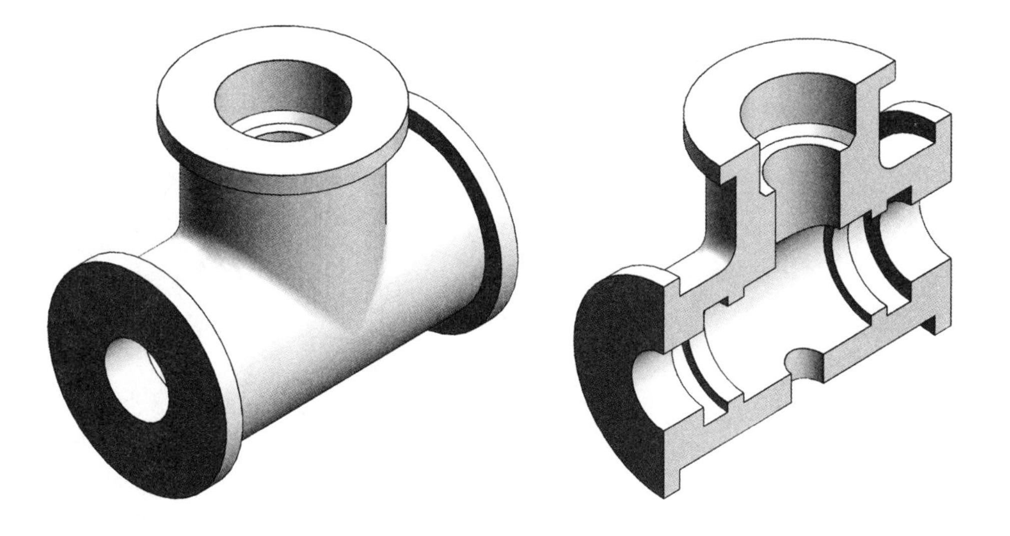

Fitting (left) and sectioned fitting (right) exposing internal details FIG. 4.3

Sectional Views

Sectional views, or simply sections, are special types of views created by visually removing a portion of an object in order to expose its internal detail (see Figure 4.3), thus reducing the number of hidden lines in a drawing. Although acceptable, the use of hidden lines is not effective when there is great amount of internal detail in the object. Instead, sectional views are used to maintain the drawing clear, simple, and easy to dimension (since it is unacceptable to dimension to hidden lines). Additionally, sections can be used to describe an object or assembly's material.

In general, sectional views replace one of the standard orthographic views. Occasionally, however, sections are used as supplemental views to support a standard set of multiview drawings. Certain rules and guidelines must be followed in order to use sectional views effectively and unambiguously.

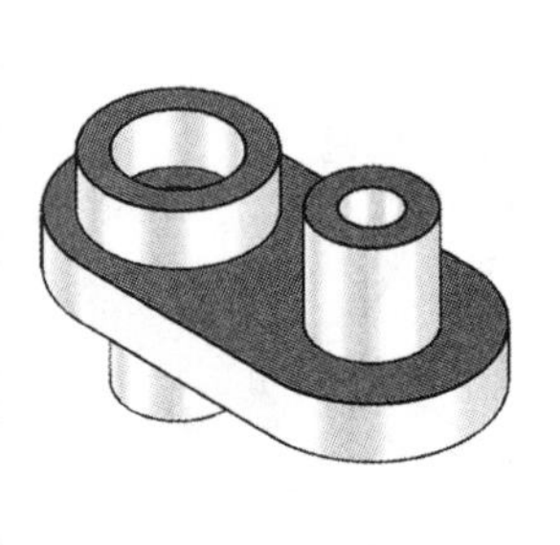

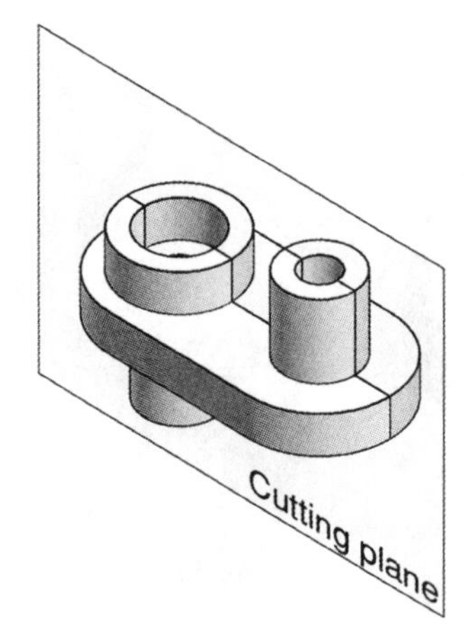

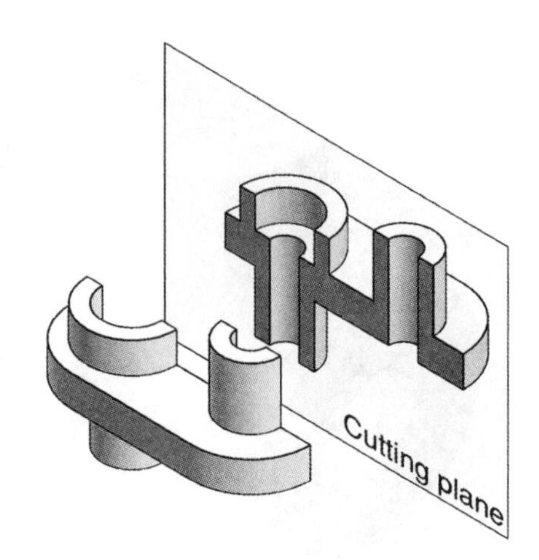

FIG. 4.4 The cutting plane is the imaginary plane used to visually slice the object

The cutting plane

The first step when creating a sectional view is the position of the cutting plane. The cutting plane can be understood as an imaginary blade used to slice an object in order to expose its internal structure. The position of the cutting plane will determine what type of section will be created and what part of the object will be shown or omitted.

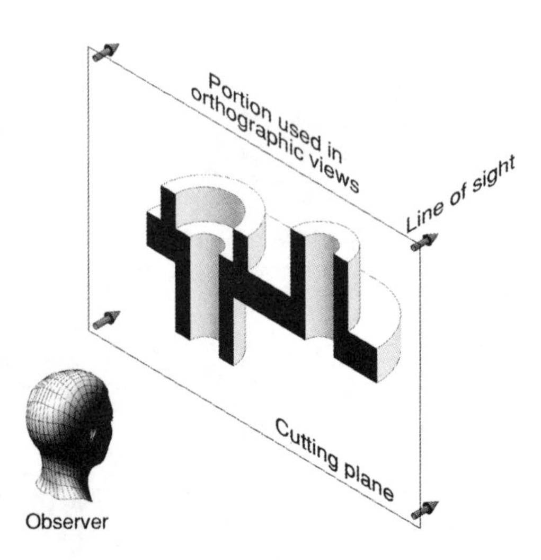

FIG. 4.5 The portion behind the cutting plane is used in the orthographic drawing

Although any plane can be used to perform an imaginary cut on an object, the cutting plane is typically parallel to one of the three orthographic planes (frontal, horizontal, and profile) and bisects the features that need to be exposed. Obviously, the position of the cutting plane depends on the shape of the object.

Once the imaginary cut is performed, the portion of the object that is in front of the cutting plane (closer to the observer) is discarded. The remaining portion is used to create an orthographic view (see Figure 4.5 and Figure 4.6).

Notice that the only view where a portion of the object (the portion in front of the cutting plane) is discarded is the sectional view itself. The remaing orthographic views still show the entire object (ex. the other views are not altered to show the imaginary cut made in the sectioned view).

In the example shown in Figure 4.6, a sectional view is used to replace the standard front view. The cutting plane is shown in a view where it appears as an edge (the top view, in the example). Cutting plane lines have the same thickness as visible lines, but consist of alternating long

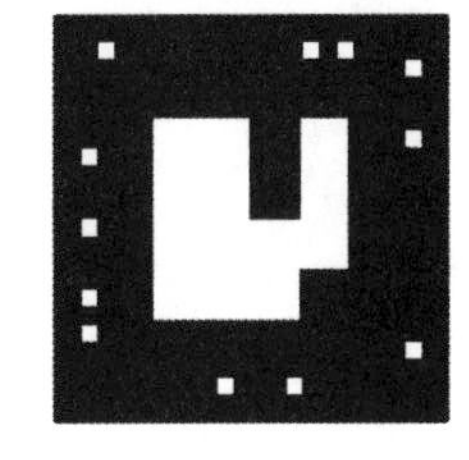

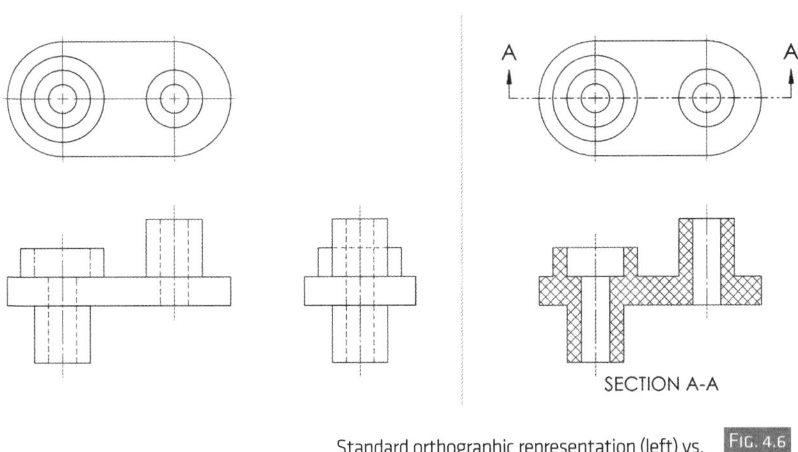

Standard orthographic representation (left) vs. Orthographic representation with sectional view (right) FIG. 4.6

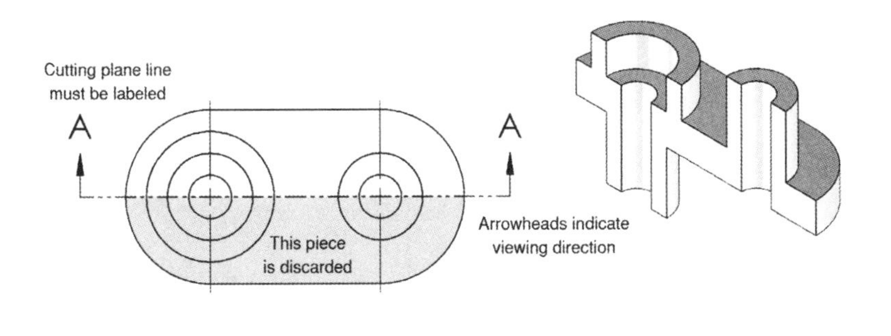

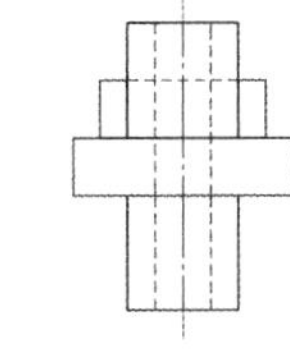

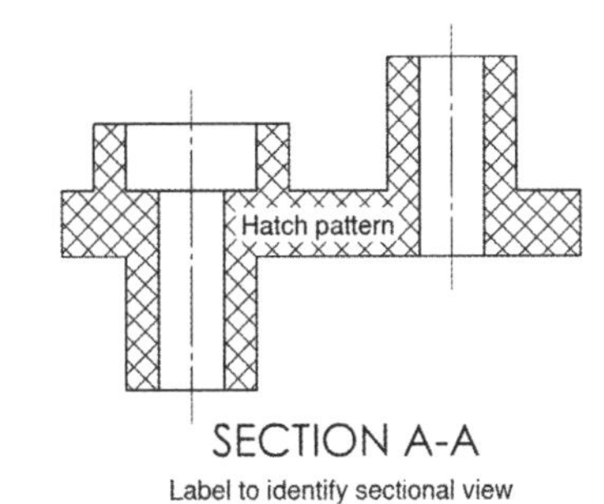

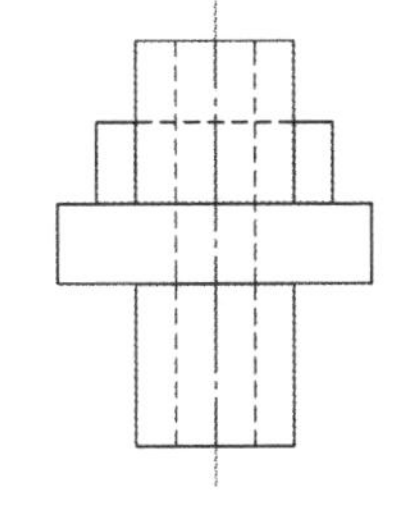

Elements of a sectional view FIG. 4.7

lines and pairs of short dashes. Cutting plane lines take precedence over other lines, if there is overlap. It is important to add two arrowheads at both ends of the cutting plane line to indicate the direction of sight, so it is clear which portion of the object is removed. Additionally, cutting plane lines can be labeled with two letters located at both ends, so the sectional view can be correctly identified. Labeling is especially important in drawings with multiple sectional views. Finally, the surfaces that intersect the cutting plane must be shaded or marked with a series of lines called hatch patterns. The example shown in Figure 4.7 illustrates the different elements of a sectional view drawing. The pictorial view is shown for illustration purposes only.

Many of the hidden lines in the original object will become exposed, and thus visible, when the cut is performed. However, lines that are still hidden after the part is cut must be omitted (see Figure 4.8).

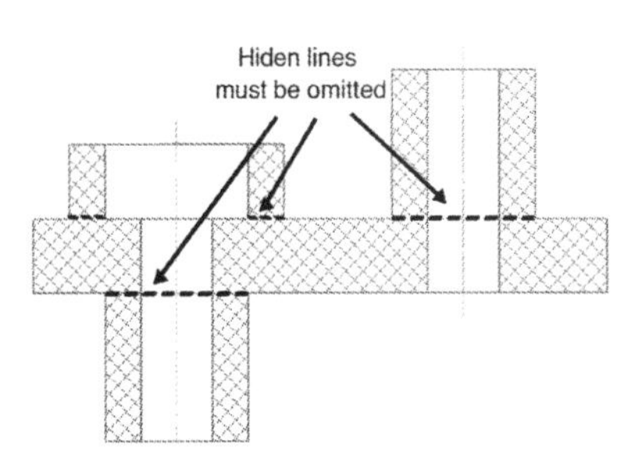

Incorrect sectional view with hidden lines

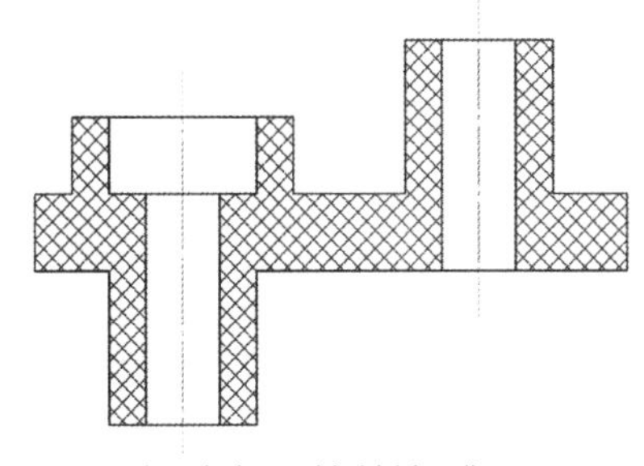

Correct sectional view with hidden lines removed

Remove hidden lines in sectional views FIG. 4.8

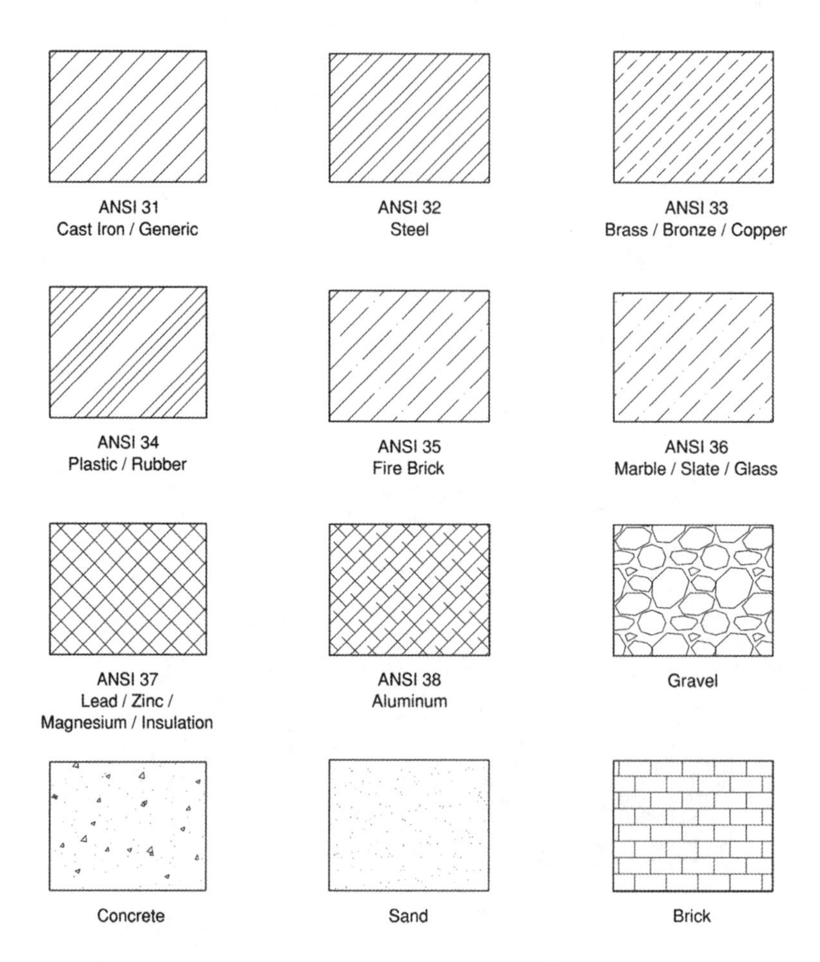

FIG. 4.9 Common hatch patterns

Hatching

Hatching, or section lining, refers to the application of line patterns to the areas where the solid surfaces of the object are directly sliced by the cutting plane. In addition, the configuration of this pattern communicates the object's material.

Drawing standards, such as ANSI and ISO, define hatch patterns for commonly used materials. Patterns for more specific materials used in different engineering sectors are dictated by industry codes or company practices. Common standard hatch patterns are shown in Figure 4.9.

There are several rules that must be considered to avoid confusion when applying hatch patterns to certain areas in the drawing. In general, hatch lines must be parallel, properly spaced, oriented at an angle that is not parallel or perpendicular to any existed visible line (typically 30°, 45°, or 60°), and slightly thinner that visible lines. Some examples of good and bad hatching practices are illustrated in Figure 4.10.

In sectional views where the cutting plane slices through more than one component, it is important that each component is hatched at a different angle. This practice creates contrast and makes it easy to differentiate each individual component (see Figure 4.11).

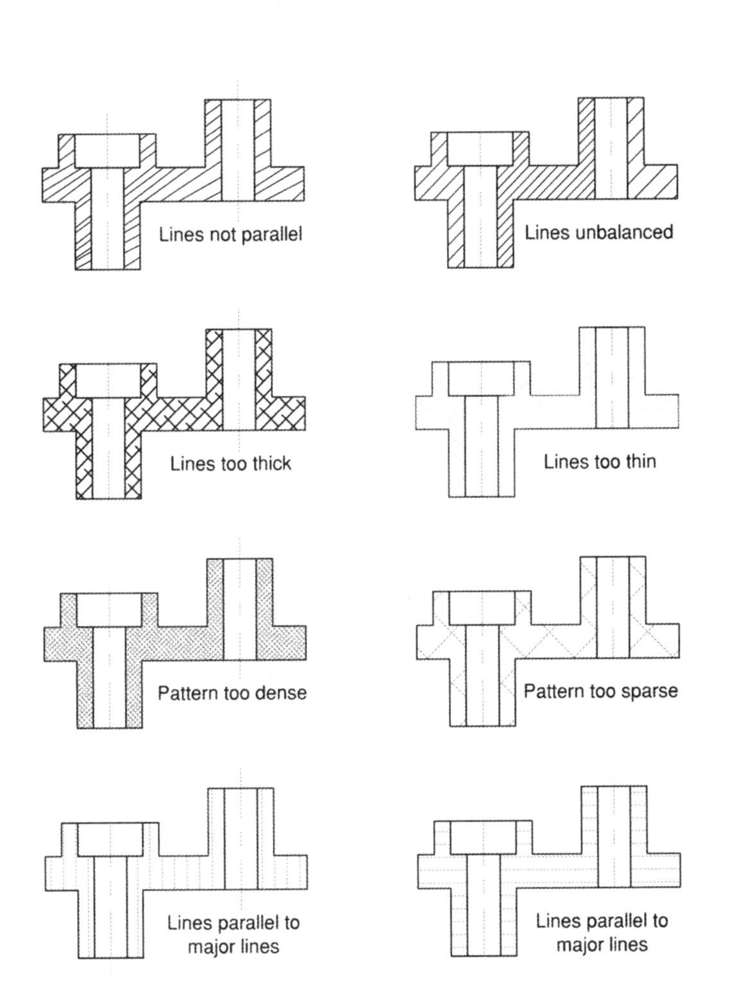

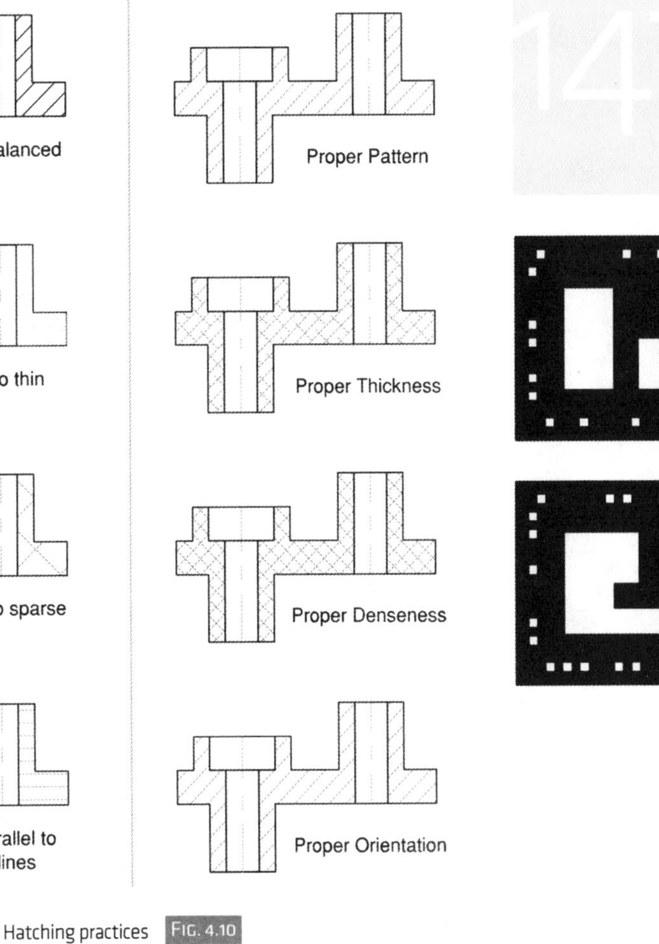

Hatching practices FIG. 4.10

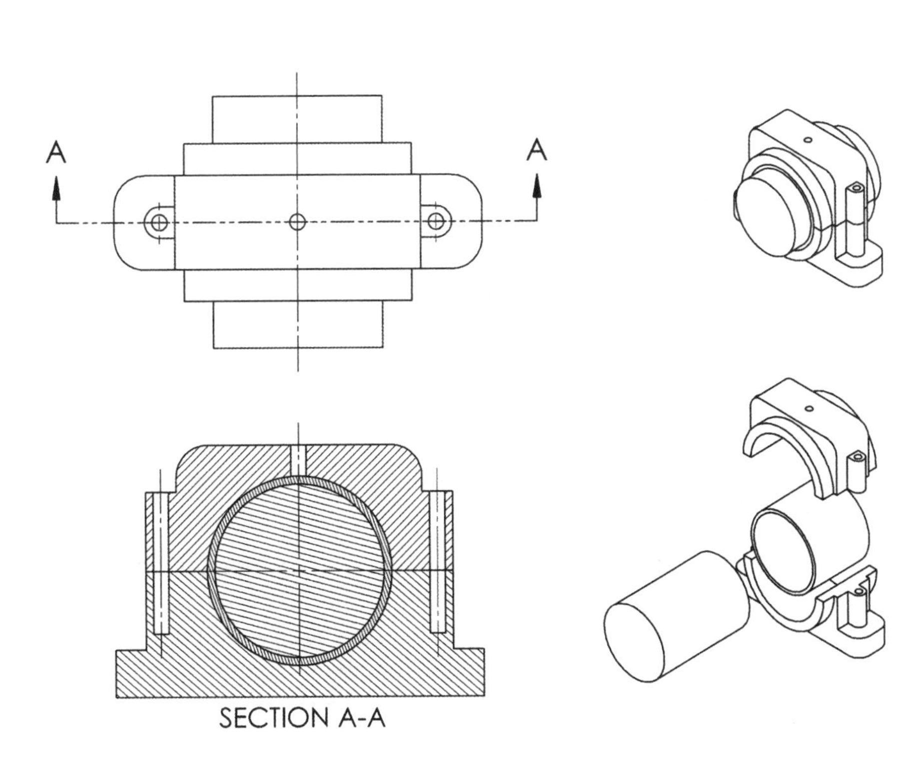

Hatch different components at different angles FIG. 4.11

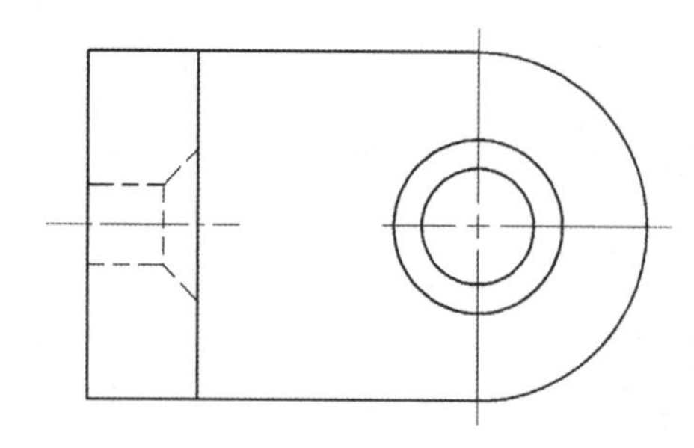

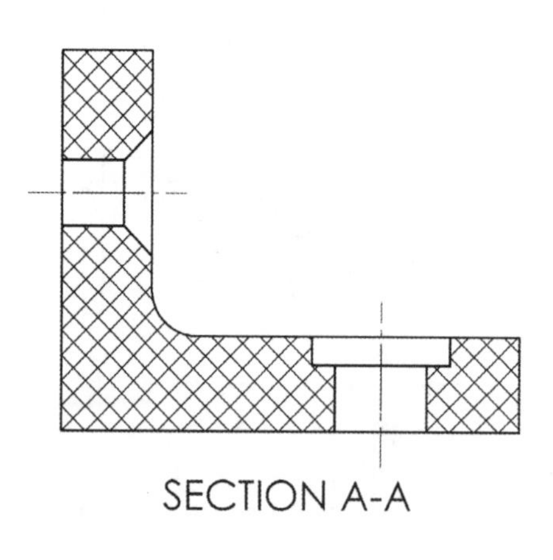

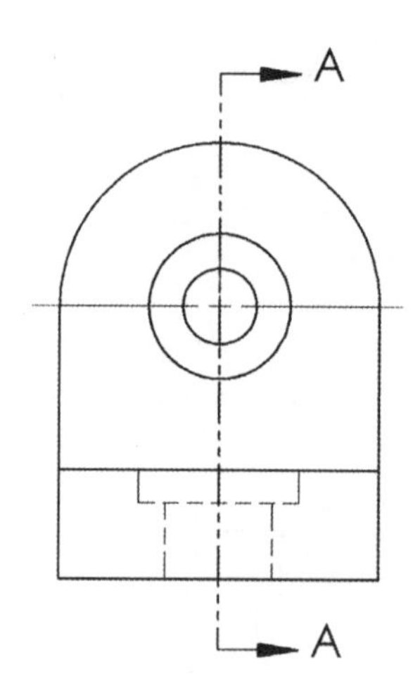

FIG. 4.13 Full section

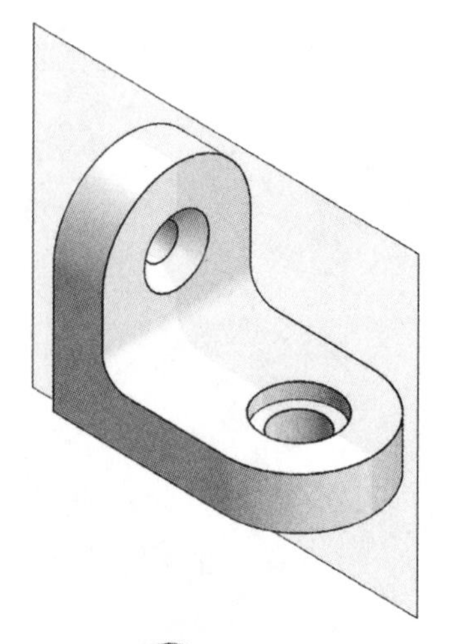

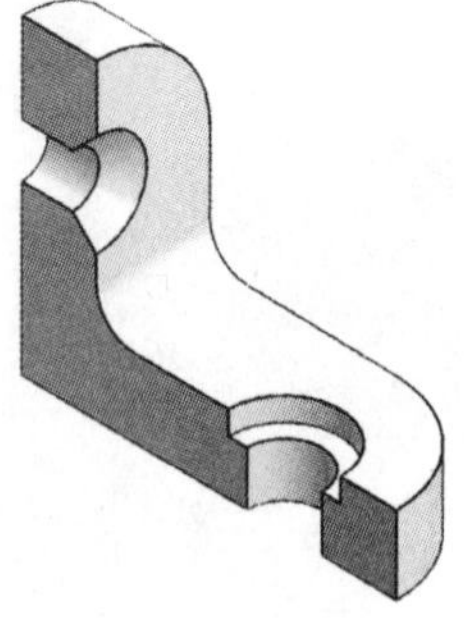

FIG. 4.12 Creation of a full section

Types of Sectional Views

Depending on the type of cut and how the cutting plane is manipulated, different types of sectional views can be generated. Some are more specific than others, but it is important for engineers to understand the different uses and applications of sectioned orthographic views.

Full Sections

Full sections are created when the cutting plane passes entirely through the object, slicing it in two pieces. Depending on the shape of the object, the cutting plane may pass exactly through the middle, making two identical halves, or it may be offset from the middle to cut through specific features of the object. See Figure 4.12 and Figure 4.13 for an example of a full section.

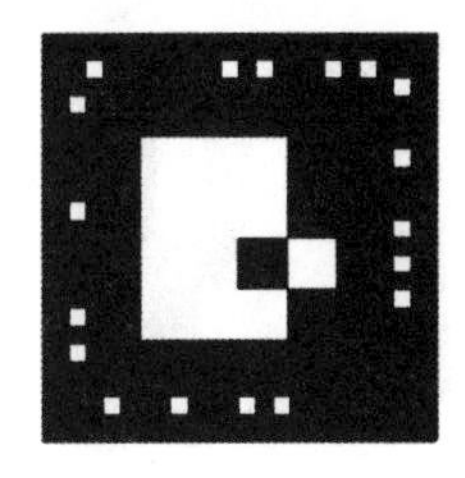

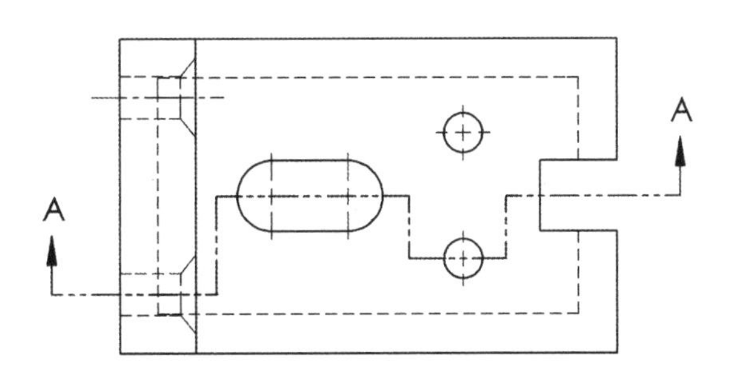

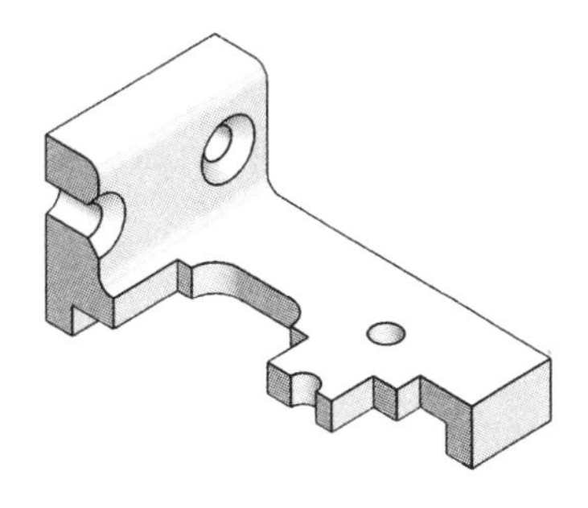

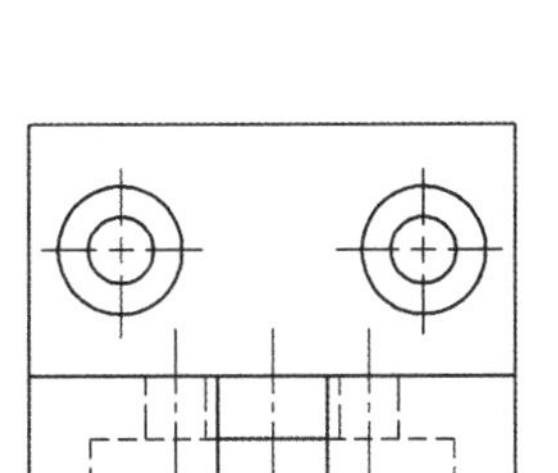

SECTION A-A

Offset section. The pictorial drawing is shown for illustration purposes only  FIG. 4.15

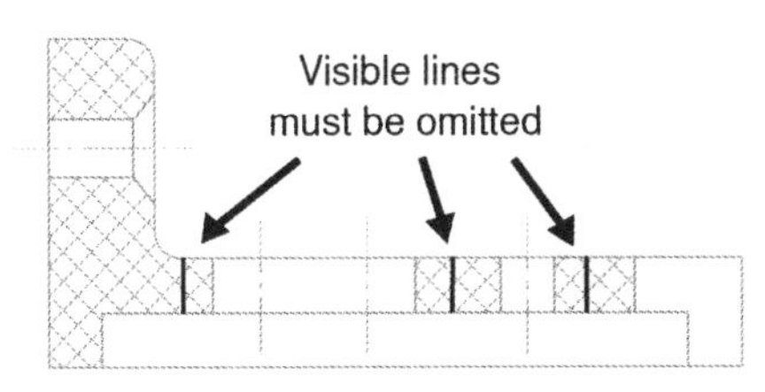

Incorrect sectional view with visible lines

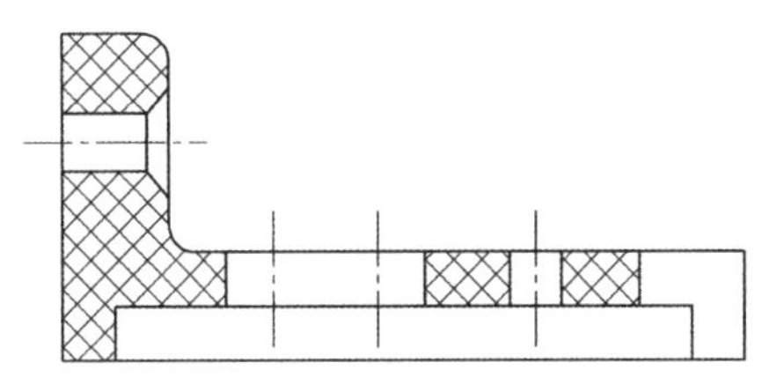

Correct sectional view with visible lines removed

Remove visible lines representing bends in the cutting plane FIG. 4.16

Offset Sections

An offset section is a modified version of a full section, typically used for objects with features that are not aligned and specific features would be missed by the continuous section created by a flat plane (see Figure 4.14). In this type of section, the cutting plane line is manipulated and bent at 90° to make a more efficient cut that passes through the important details of the object. See Figure 4.14 and Figure 4.15.

Although the edges where the cutting plane is bent theoretically should be represented with visible lines in the sectional view, they are conventionally omitted to keep the drawing clear and simple (see Figure 4.16).

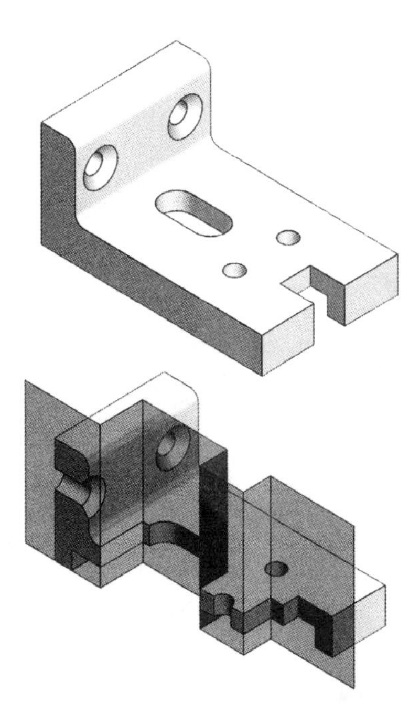

An object unsuitable for a full section (top) can be sectioned by a bent cutting plane (bottom) FIG. 4.14

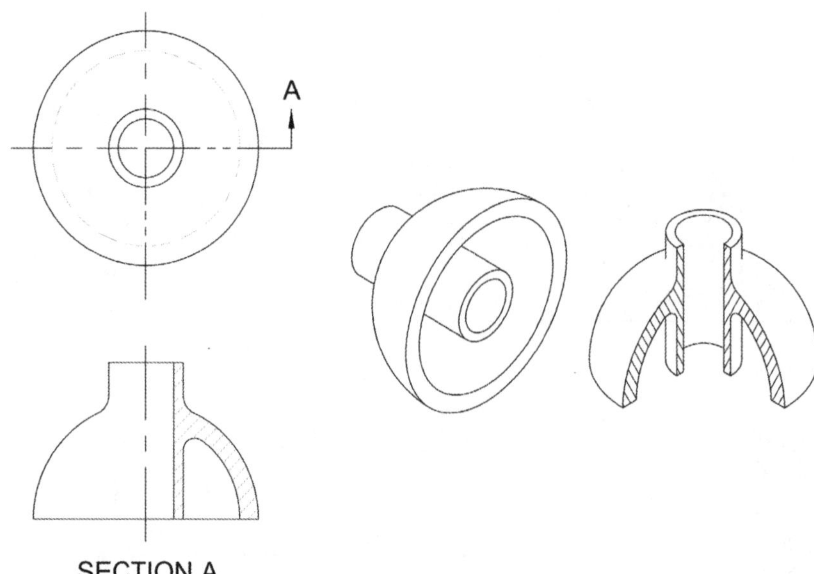

FIG. 4.18 Orthographic views with half section

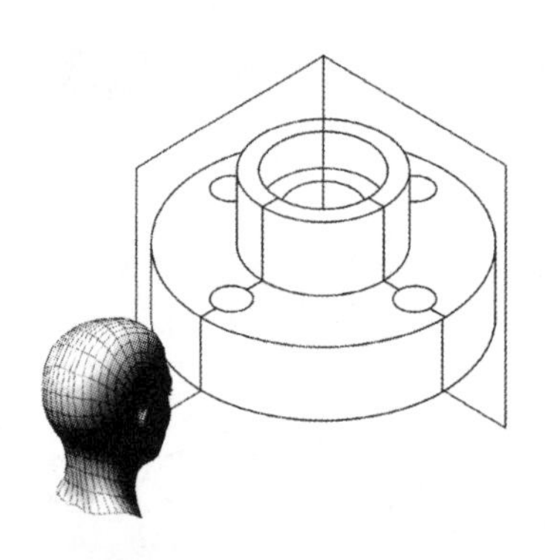

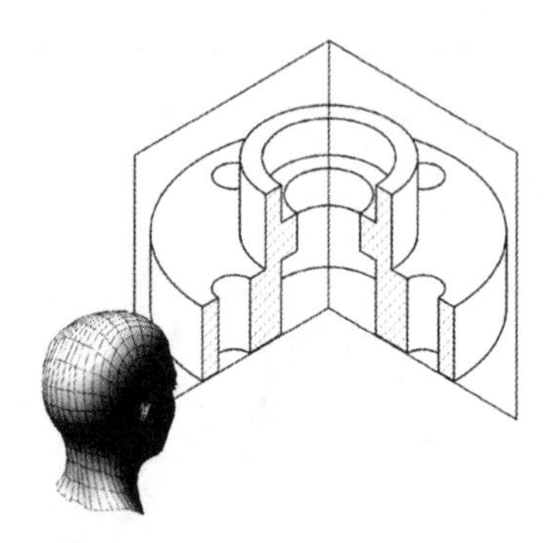

FIG. 4.17A Creation of half sections

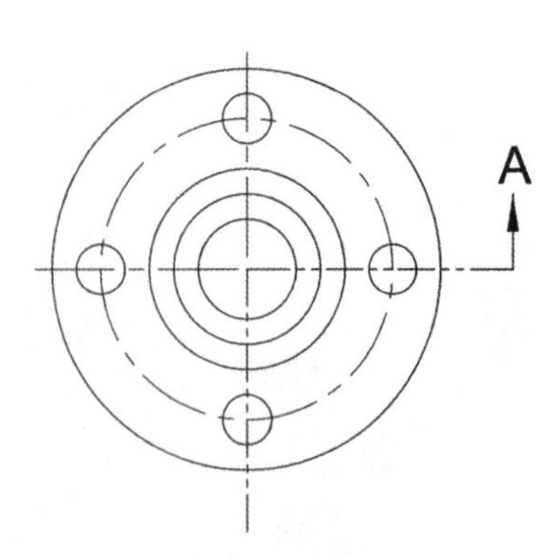

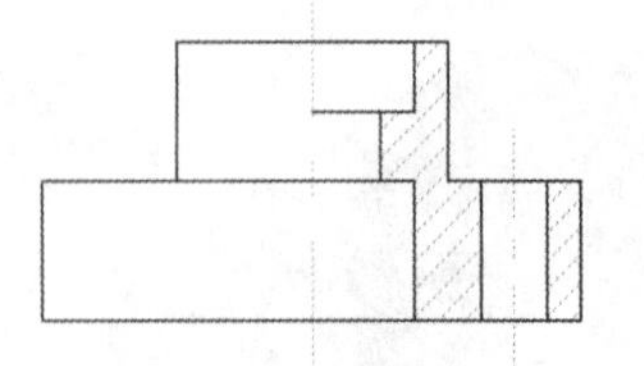

FIG. 4.17B Creation of half sections

Half Sections

Half sections are typically used with cylindrical and symmetric objects. They are created by bending the cutting plane at a 90° angle so that a quarter of the object is removed. The viewing direction is always parallel to one part of the cutting plane and perpendicular to the other.

The following conventions are used when working with half sections:

- A center line is used to divide the sectioned half of the object from the unsectioned half.
- The cutting plane line is shown with only one arrowhead and labeled with one letter. The sectional view is identified with the same letter.
- All hidden lines are omitted, including those in the unsectioned half of the object.

The drawing shown in Figure 4.18 illustrates a half section. The pictorial illustrations are provided for clarification purposes.

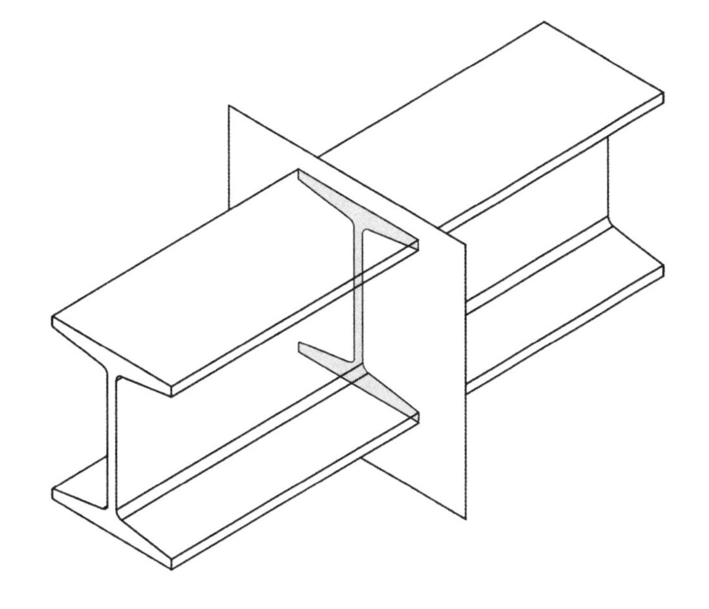

Creation of revolved and removed sections  FIG. 4.19

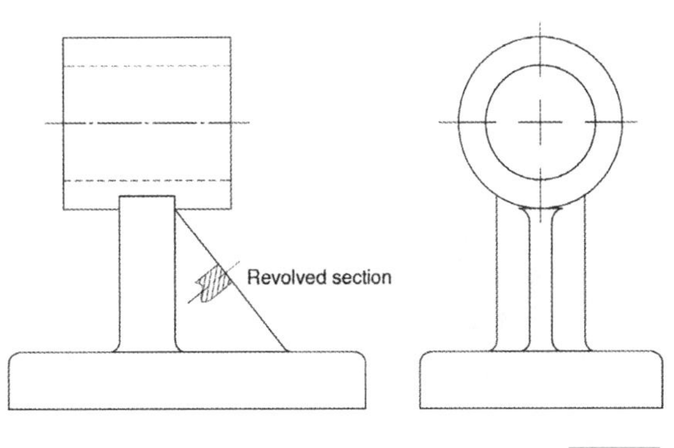

Revolved section FIG. 4.20

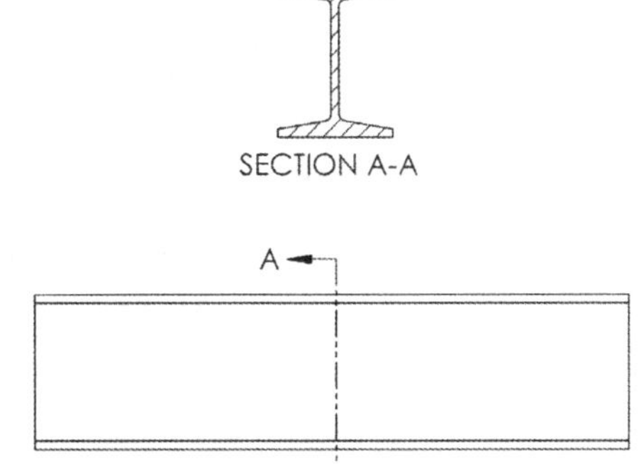

Removed section  FIG. 4.21

Revolved and Removed Sections

Revolved and Removed sectional views result from a cut that takes a very thin slice of an object and rotates it 90° around the center axis toward the plane of projection (see Figure 4.19). These types of sectional views are used to provide contour (cross-section) and material information of objects without the complexity of adding additional orthographic views.

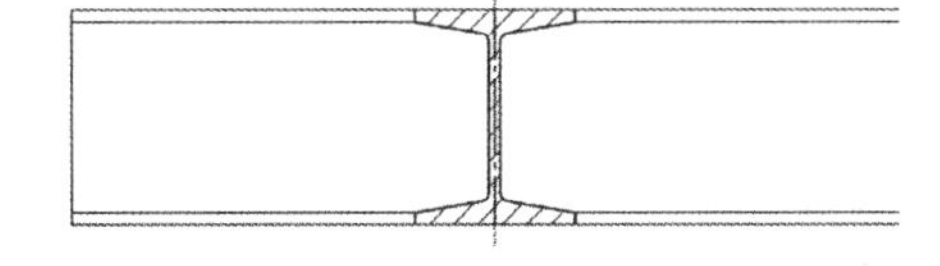

Revolved section superimposed onto view FIG. 4.22

The process of creating revolved and removed sections is identical. The difference between the two is that revolved sections are drawn superimposed over an existing orthographic view (see Figure 4.20), whereas removed sections are offset a certain distance from the view (see Figure 4.21). In revolved sections, a center line is shown to indicate the axis of revolution.

Revolved sections are sometimes represented between break lines to give the view focus and make it stand out from the drawing (see Figure 4.22 and Figure 4.23).

Revolved section between break lines FIG. 4.23

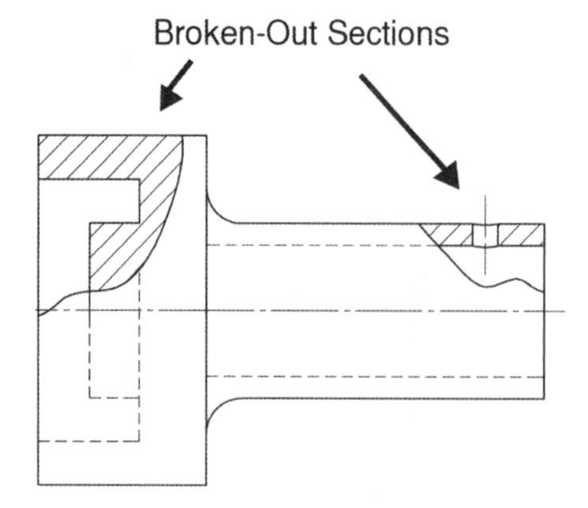

Fig. 4.24 Broken-out section

Fig. 4.25 2007 Saturn Vue GreenLine with exposed hybrid components at the Washington Auto Show (public domain)

Broken-Out Sections

Broken-out sections are created by taking a small portion away from an object to reveal part of its internal detail. In this type of sectional view, the broken-out portion is part of the original view. Also, the cutting plane line is replaced by an irregular line that is typically sketched freehand. This break line separates the exposed part of the object from the unexposed. Unlike the other types of sections, broken-out views retain their hidden lines, if any. See Figure 4.24 for an example of broken-out sections.

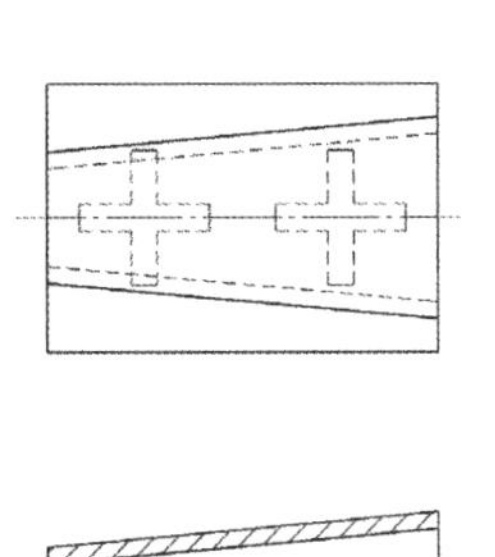

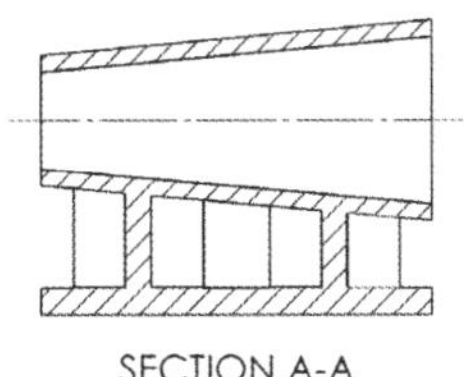

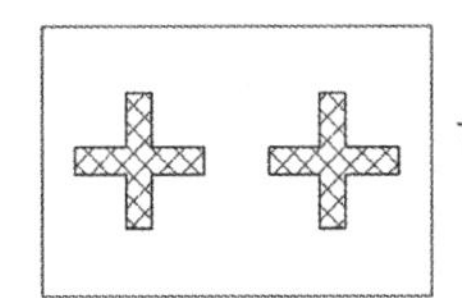

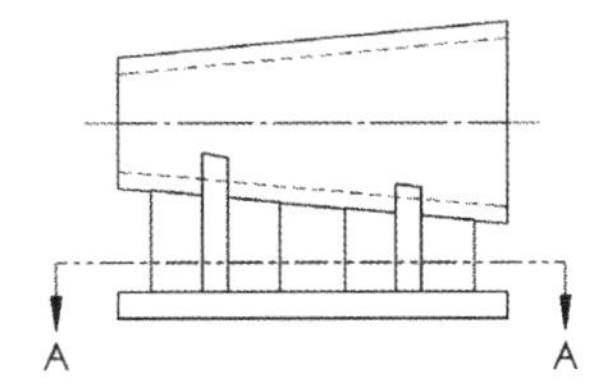

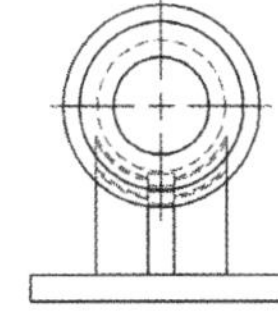

Sectioning webs FIG. 4.29

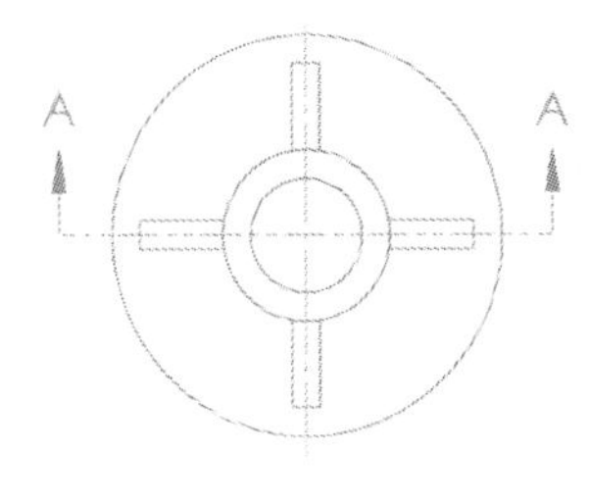

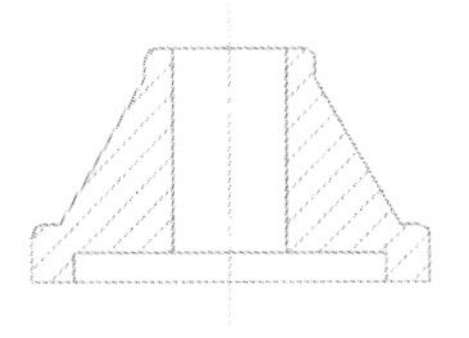

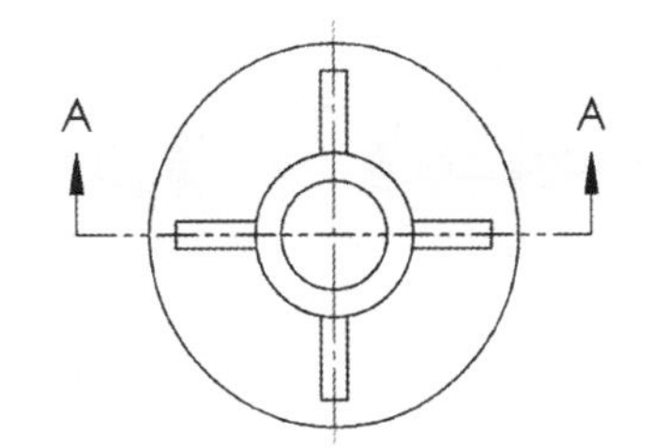

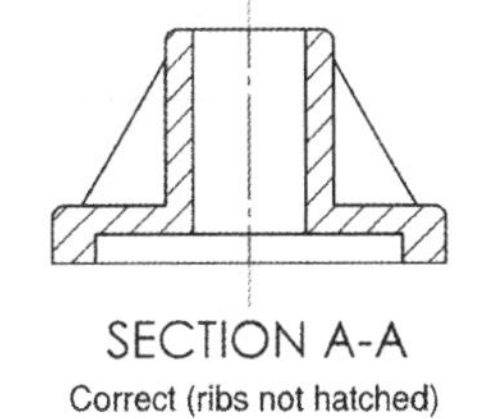

Sectioning ribs FIG. 4.28

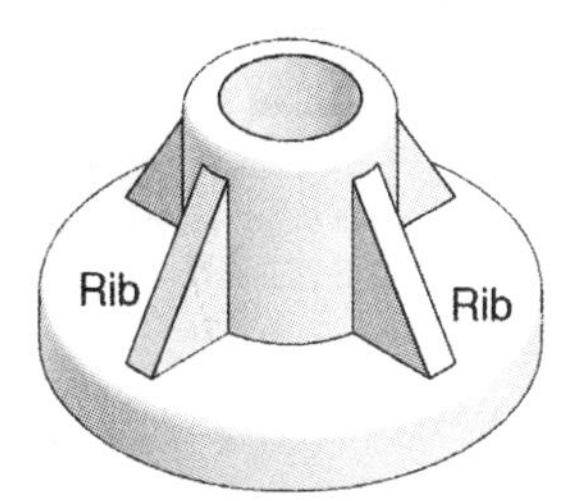

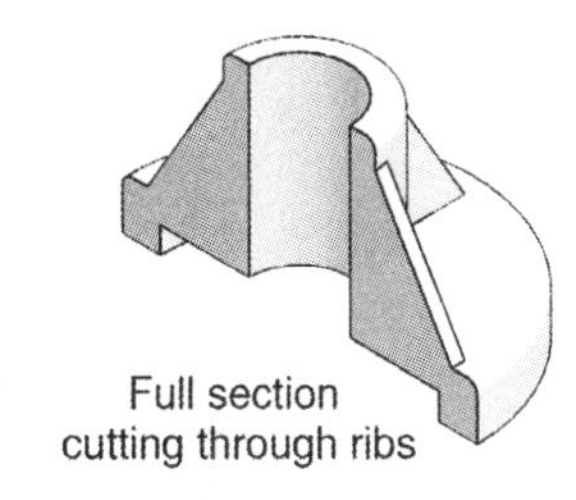

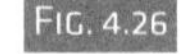

Object with ribs (top) and full sectional view (bottom) FIG. 4.26

General and Conventional Sectioning Practices

Unhatched Features

There are certain design features that are normally left unhatched when the cutting plane cuts through them in any type of sectional view. This practice is used to avoid misinterpretations of a drawing due to false impressions of material thicknesses. The most common features include:

- Ribs and webs: thin features added to objects for structural support. See Figure 4.26 to Figure 4.29.

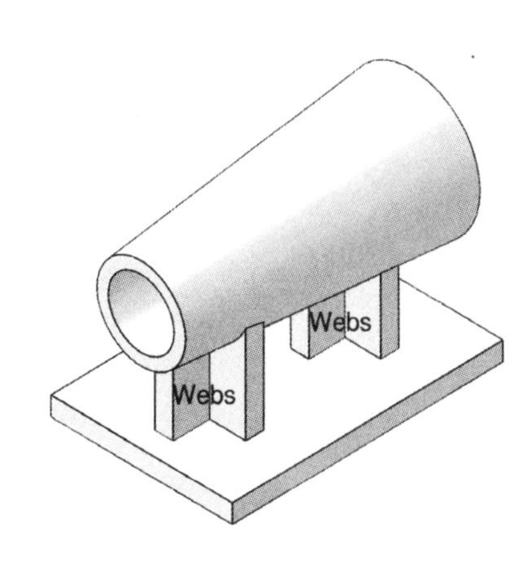

Pictorial view of object with webs FIG. 4.27

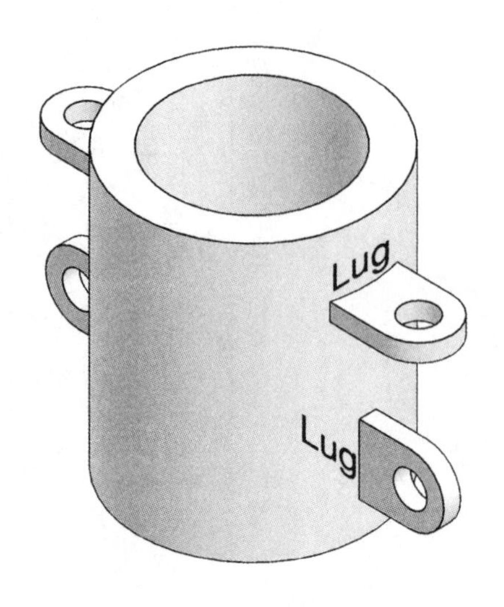

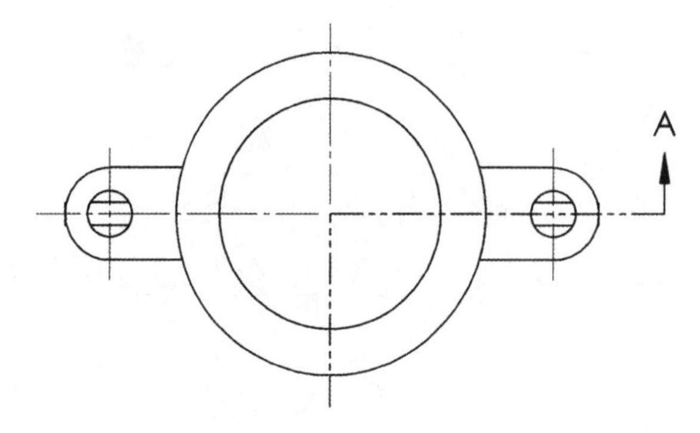

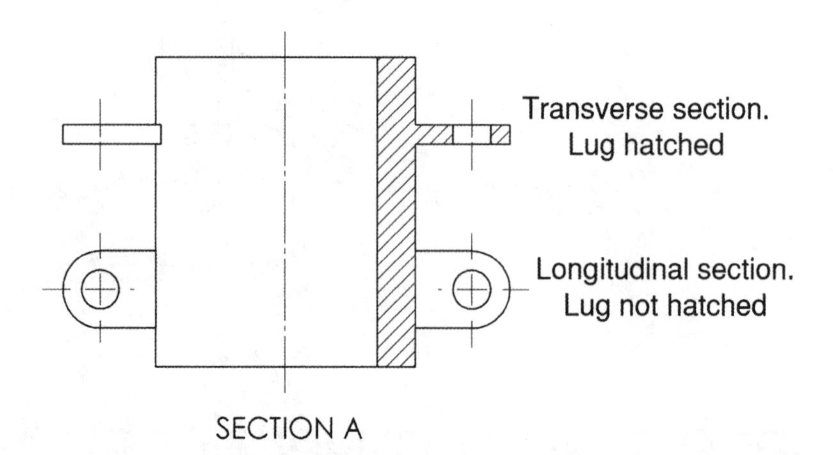

FIG. 4.30 Sectioning lugs

- Lugs: protrusions added to an object for attachment to other objects. See Figure 4.30.

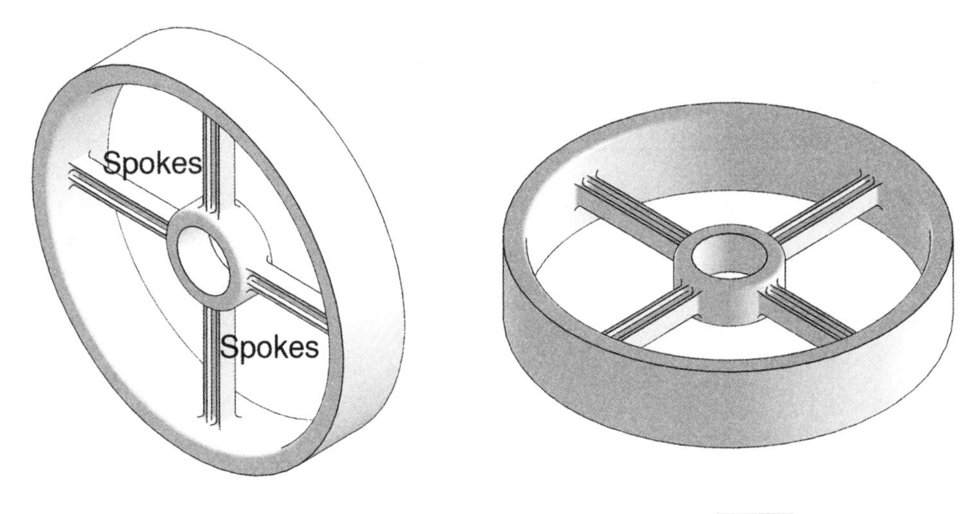

Pictorial views of wheel with four spokes FIG. 4.31

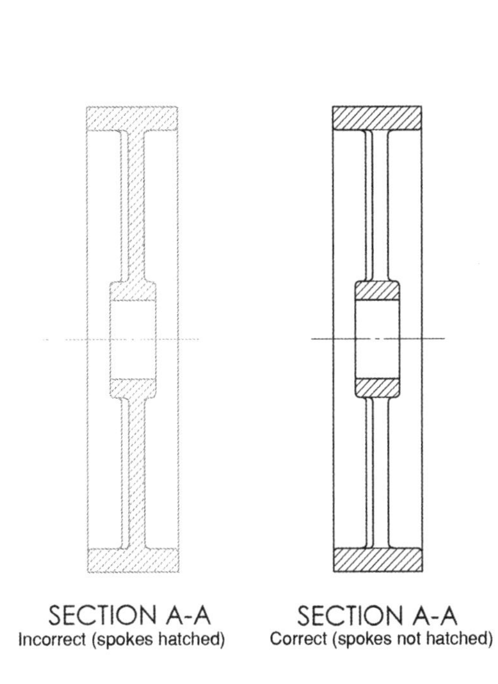

Sectioning spokes FIG. 4.32

- Spokes: rods radiating from the center to the rim of a wheel. See Figure 4.31 and Figure 4.32.

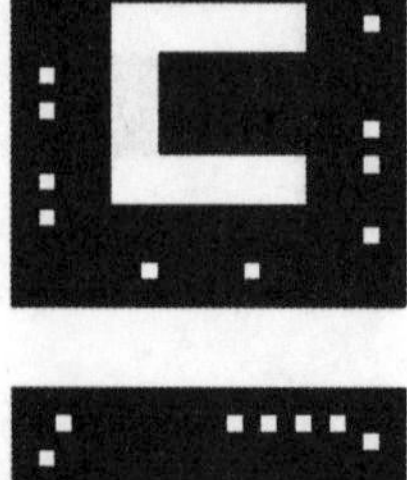

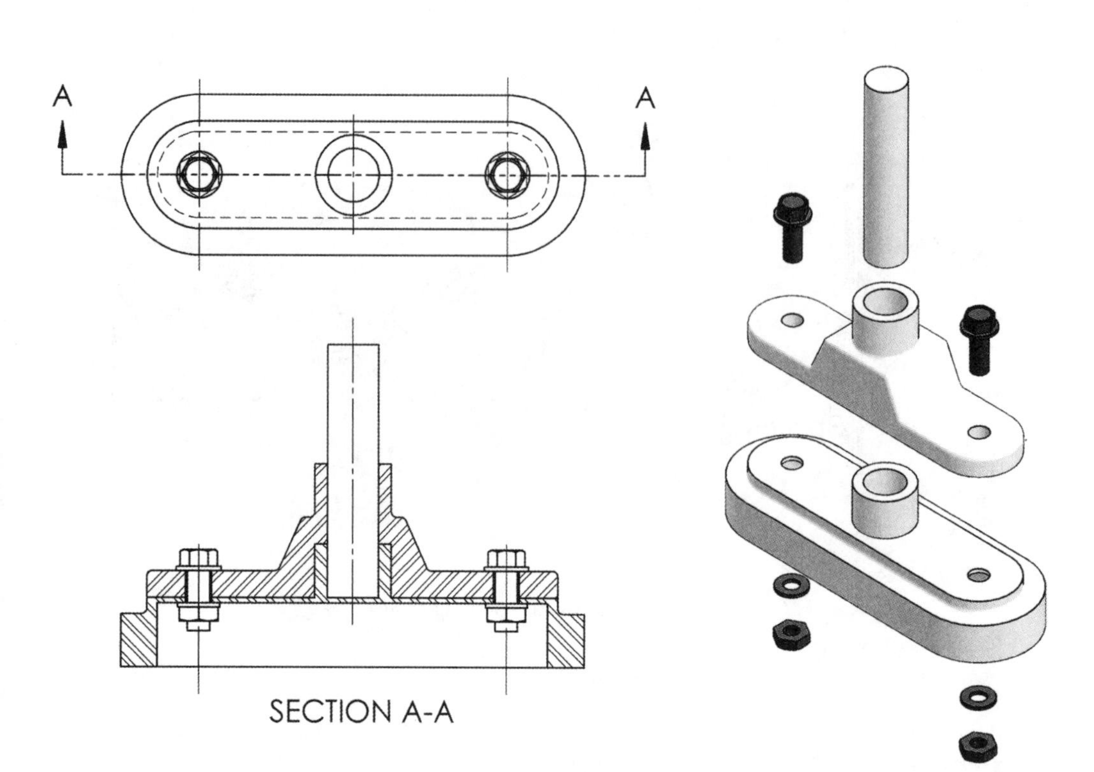

FIG. 4.33 Assembly section with parts not hatched

Additionally, there are certain components that are usually not hatched when an entire assembly is sectioned. These components include fasteners, gaskets, rings, gears, springs, bearings, axles, and shafts.

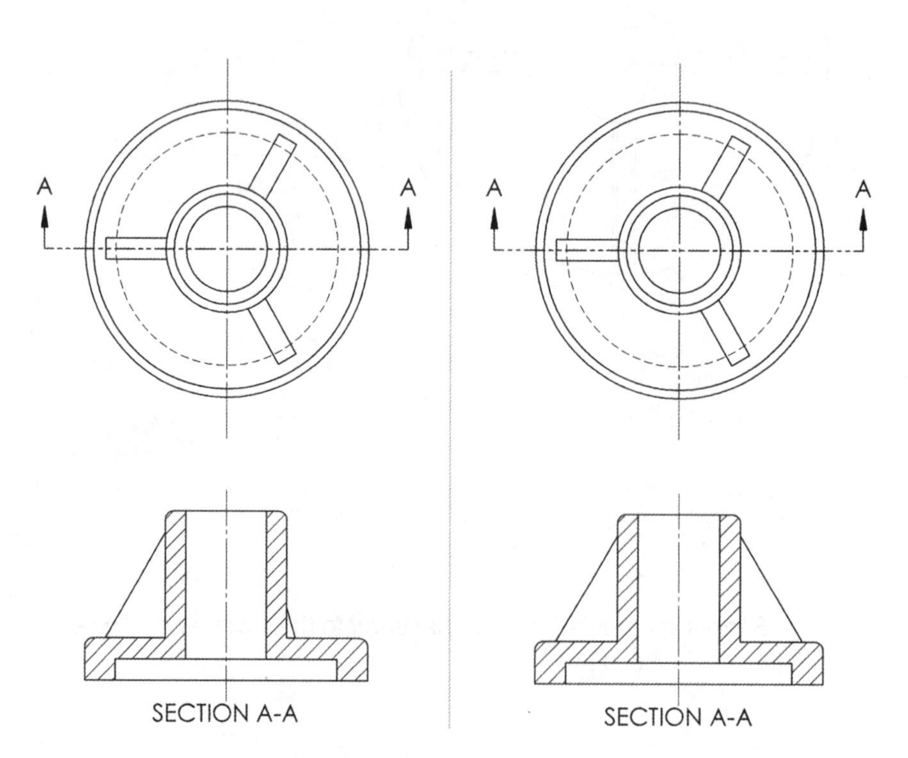

FIG. 4.34 Conventional rotations

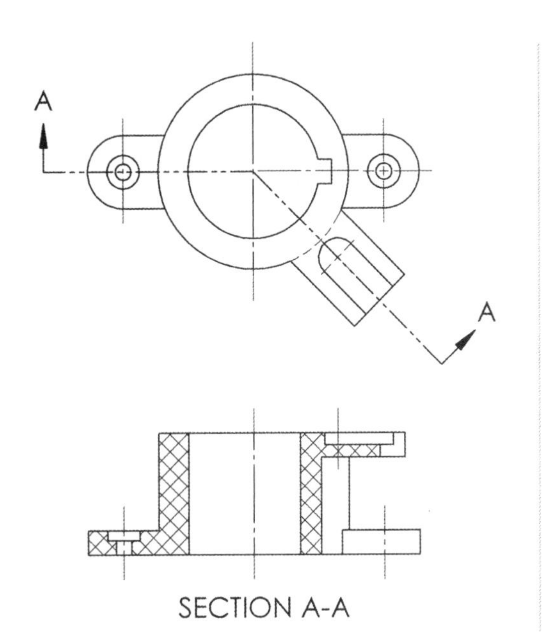

True sectional view.

Notice the effects of foreshortening on the angled surface, missing hole information on the right lug, and confusing hatch pattern hiding keyway lines

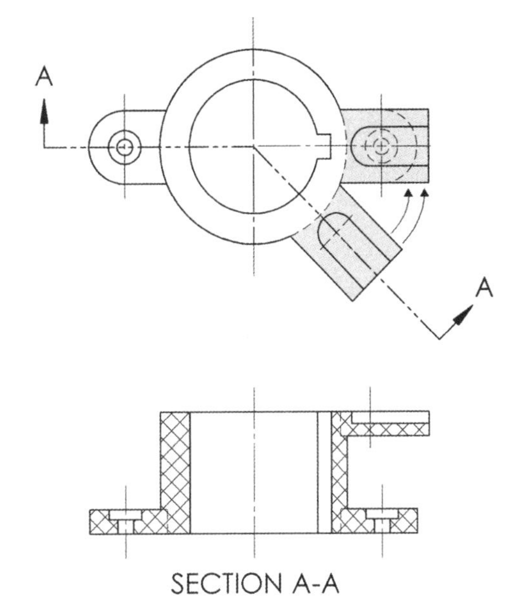

Aligned section.

The angled feature is adjusted so complete information can be provided in a more descriptive sectional view

Aligned section FIG. 4.36

Conventional Rotations

Conventional rotations are violations of the general rules of orthographic projection, in order to simplify a drawing and provide increased clarity of the object. The conventional practices studied in the orthographic projection chapter also apply to sectional views.

Cylindrical objects with equally spaced features but unclear orthographic views, such as the one shown in Figure 4.34, are typically adjusted by changing the angle between the features to present a view that can be more easily understood.

Objects with angled features, such as the lug shown in Figure 4.35, also produce orthographic views that are confusing. Although the cutting plane must be bent to pass through the angled features, the effects of foreshortening and the nature of the cut do not provide a clear picture of the geometry of the object.

To solve this problem, the angled feature is aligned to a vertical or horizontal position, providing complete information about the object (see Figure 4.36).

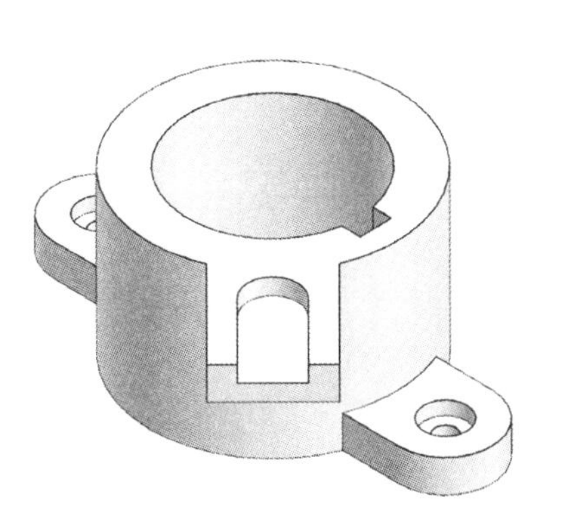

Angled features FIG. 4.35

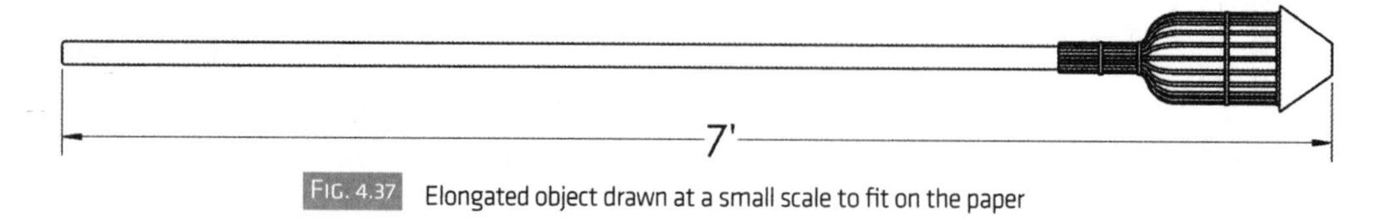

FIG. 4.37 Elongated object drawn at a small scale to fit on the paper

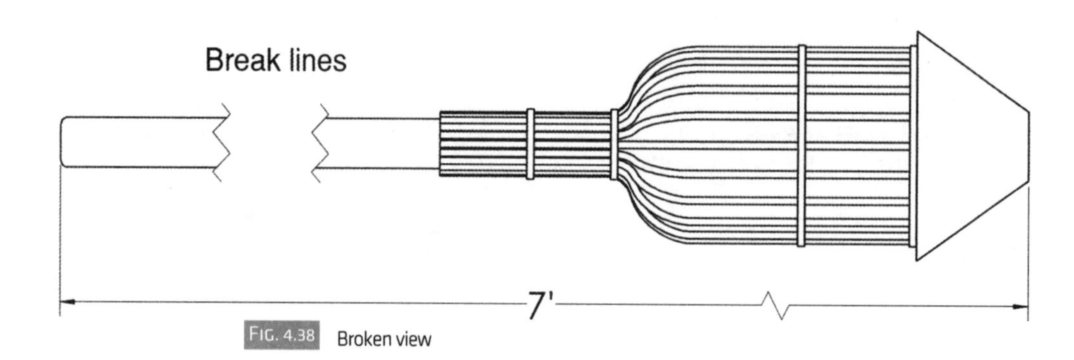

FIG. 4.38 Broken view

Broken Views and Conventional Breaks

Broken views are used to illustrate objects with uniform elongated features in such a manner that the object can be drawn at a larger scale on the paper and the features can be seen and dimensioned more easily. The example shown in Figure 4.37 illustrates a tiki torch drawn at a small scale so it can be accommodated on the paper. The details at the end of the torch are hard to see (and are of most interest) because of the scale used. In addition, there is inadequate space for proper dimensioning.

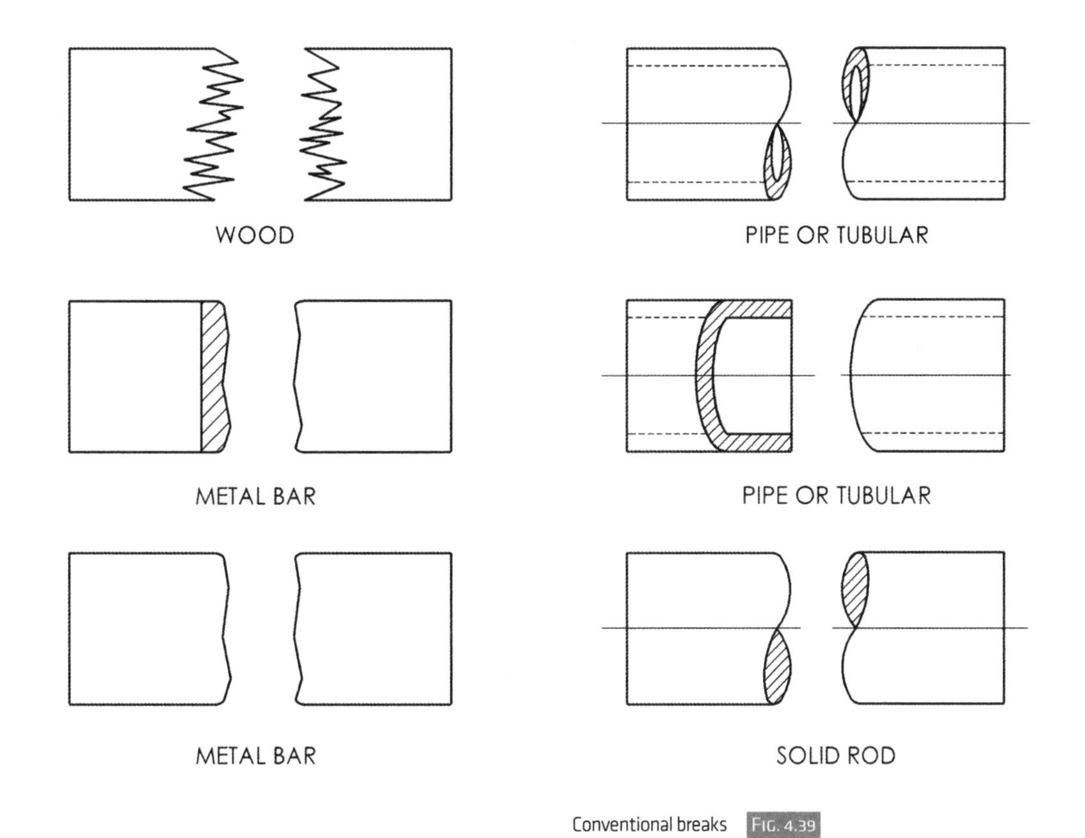

Conventional breaks FIG. 4.39

Since the long portion of the object is fairly uniform and contains no essential information, it can be shortened, which allows the use of a larger scale (see Figure 4.38). Although the portion between the break lines is removed from the drawing, the full-length dimension needs to be provided, just as if the entire torch was drawn. Notice the break line added to the dimension line to indicate the overall dimension.

Different symbols can be used to represent break lines. Zig-zags, curves, and straight lines are common, although some conventional symbols can provide additional material information. Standard breaks are shown in Figure 4.39.

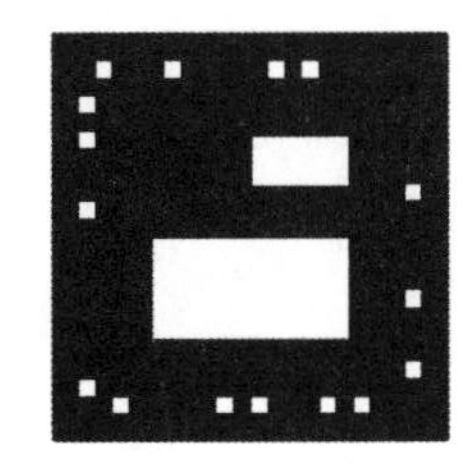

SECTIONAL VIEWS

NAME: Solomon Victoriano

CHAPTER 04
EXERCISE 01

DATE: 5/2/18

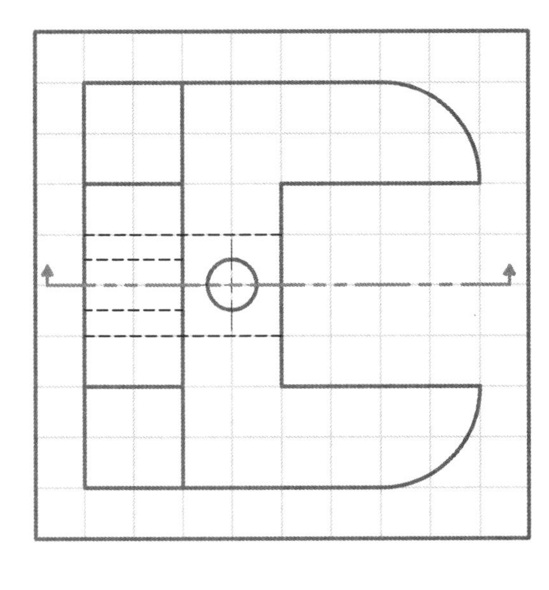

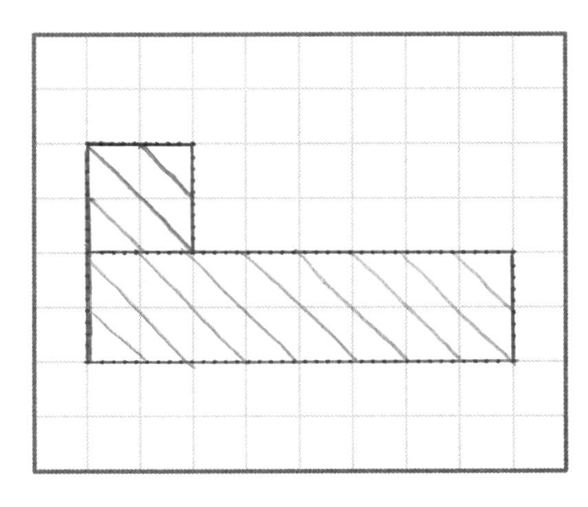

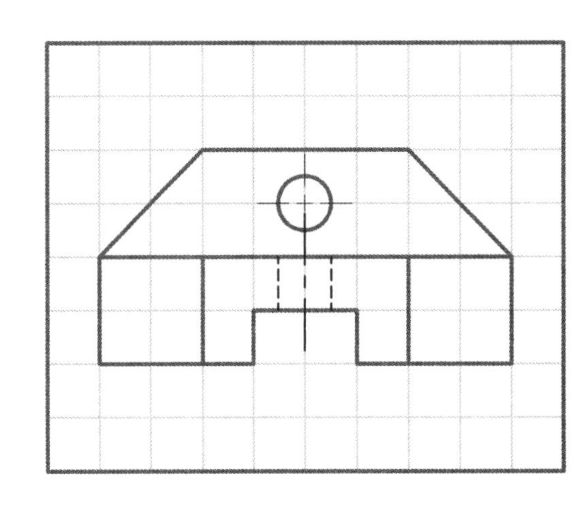

SKETCH THE APPROPRIATE SECTIONAL VIEW.
OBJECT IS MADE OF CAST IRON.

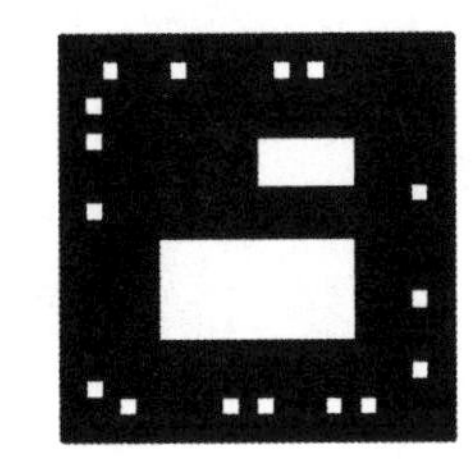

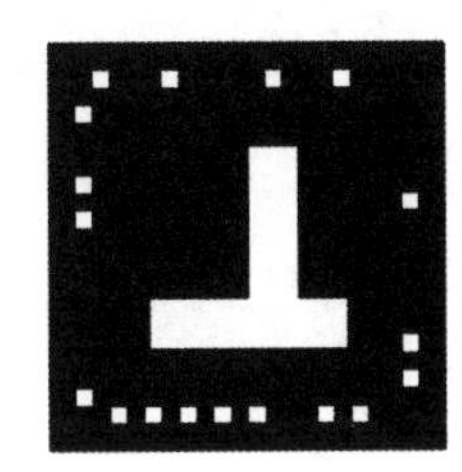

EXERCISE 02

NAME:

DATE:

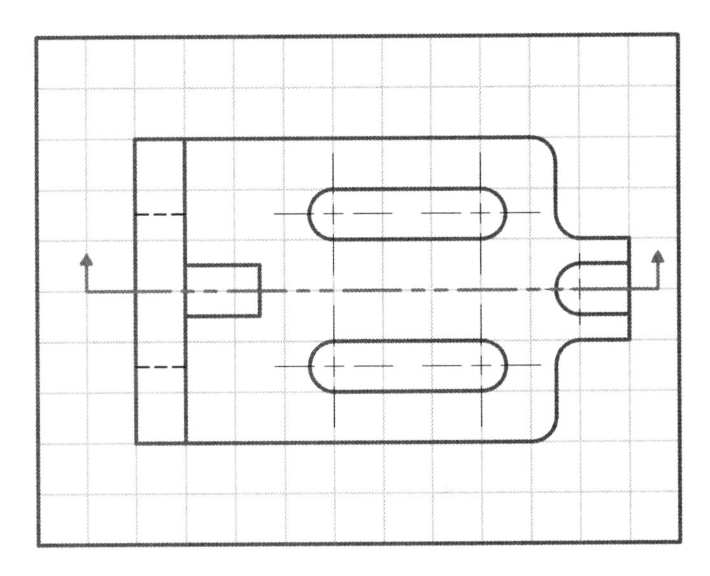

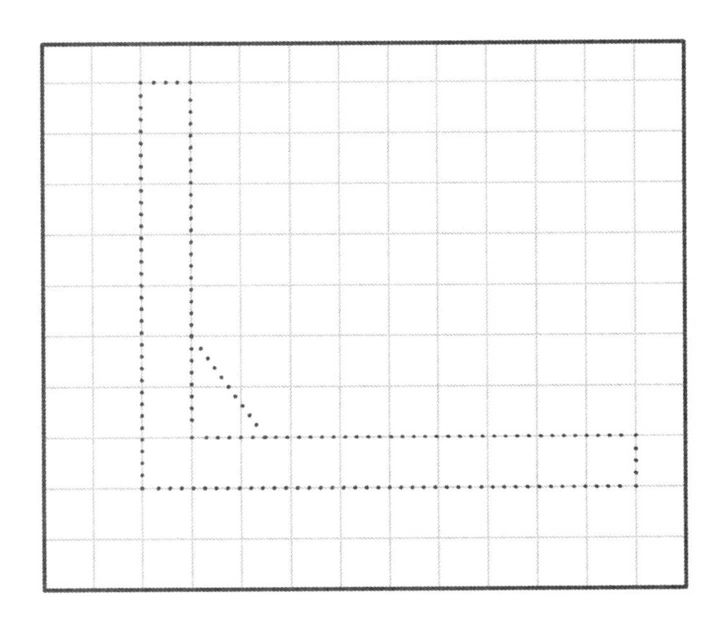

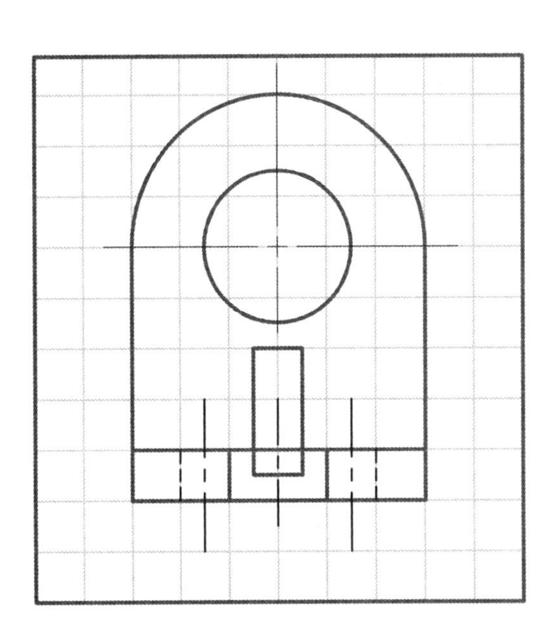

SKETCH THE APPROPRIATE SECTIONAL VIEW.
OBJECT IS MADE OF STEEL.

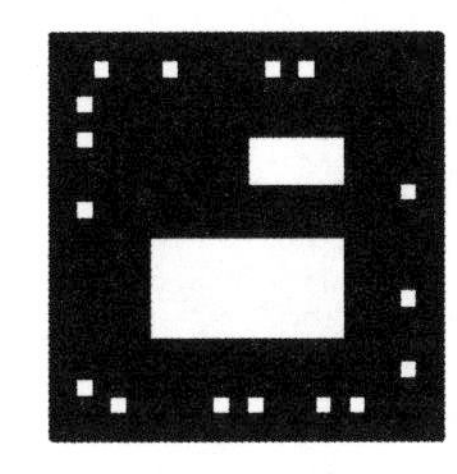
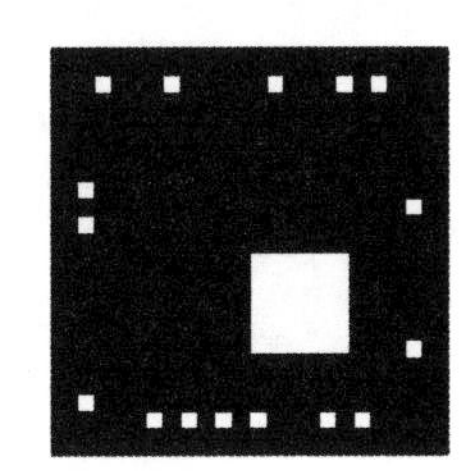

Sectional Views

Chapter 04
Exercise 03

Name: Solomon V

Date: 5/2/18

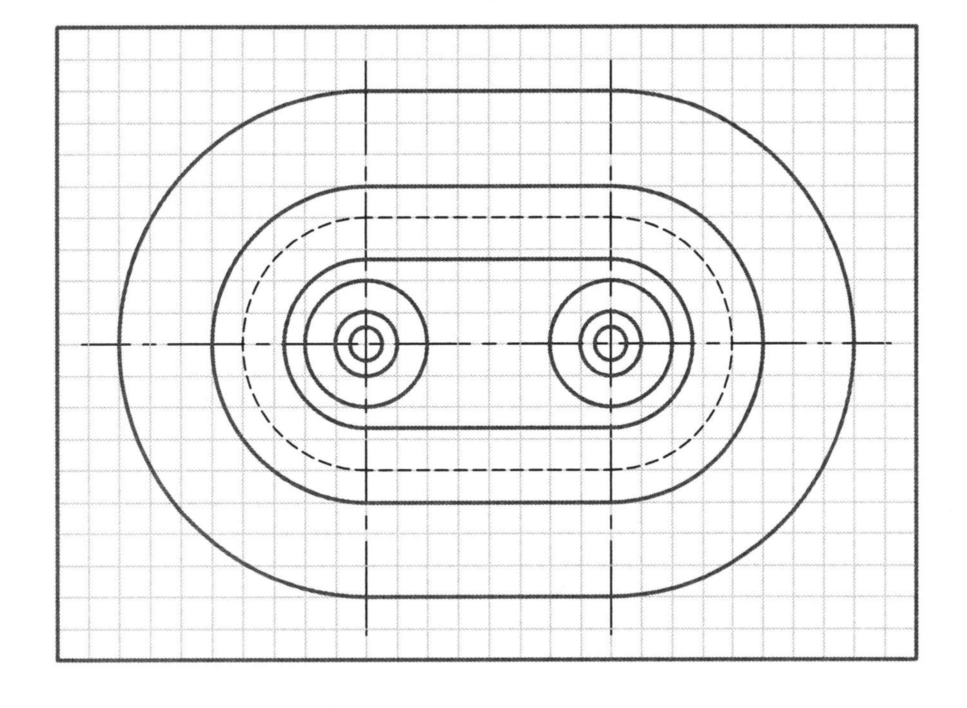

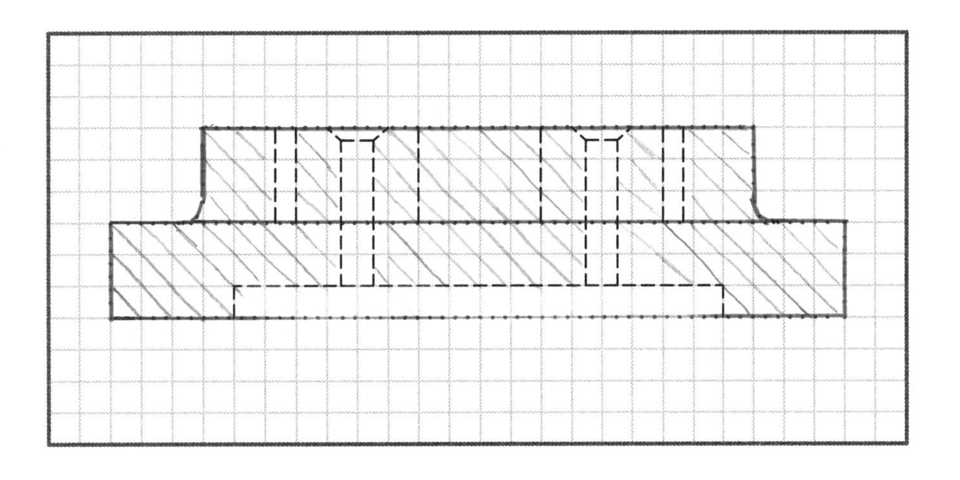

Sketch a half sectional view.
Object is made of aluminum.

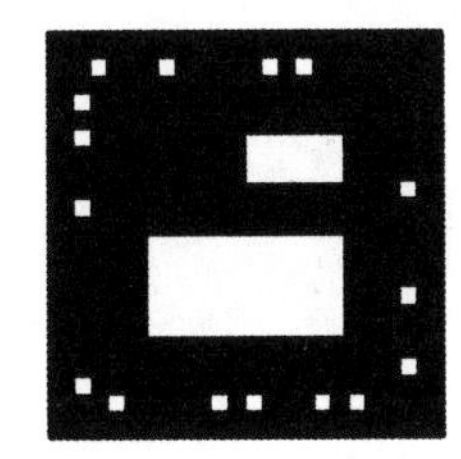
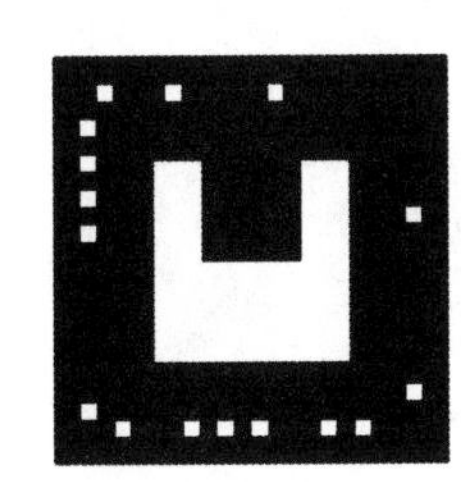

Exercise 04

Name:

Date:

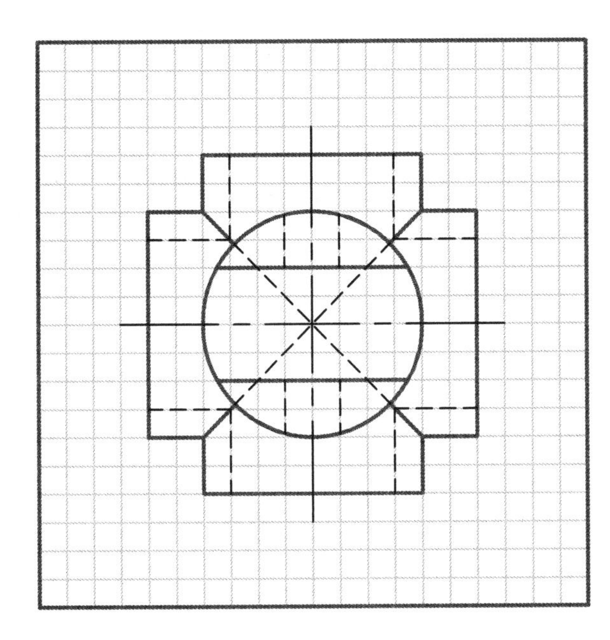

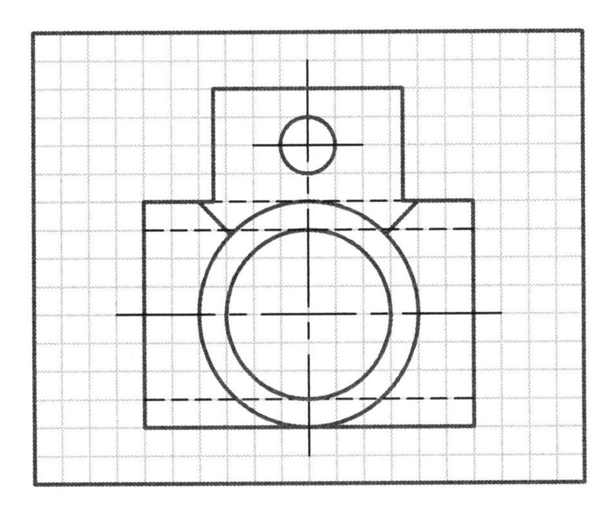

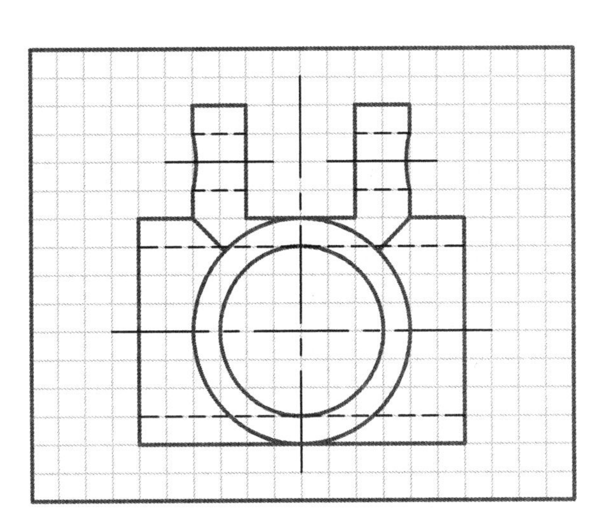

Sketch the appropriate sectional view.
Object is made of plastic.

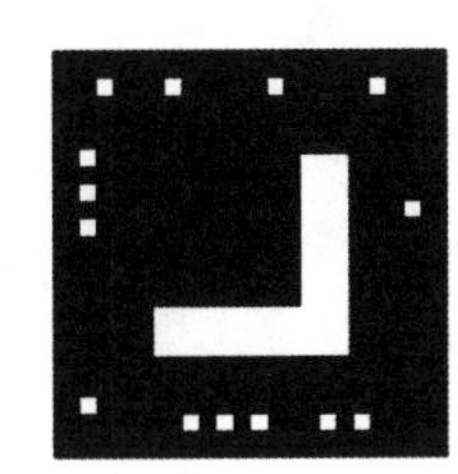

EXERCISE 05

NAME:

DATE:

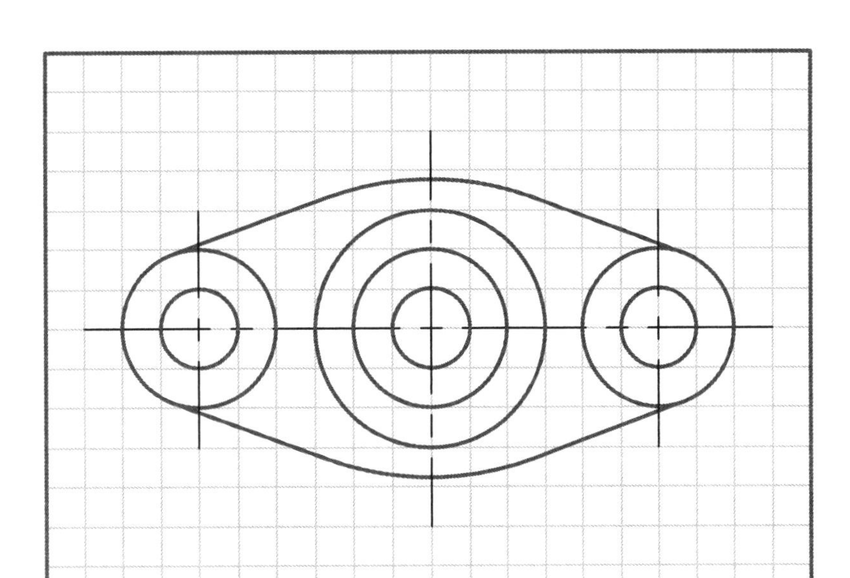

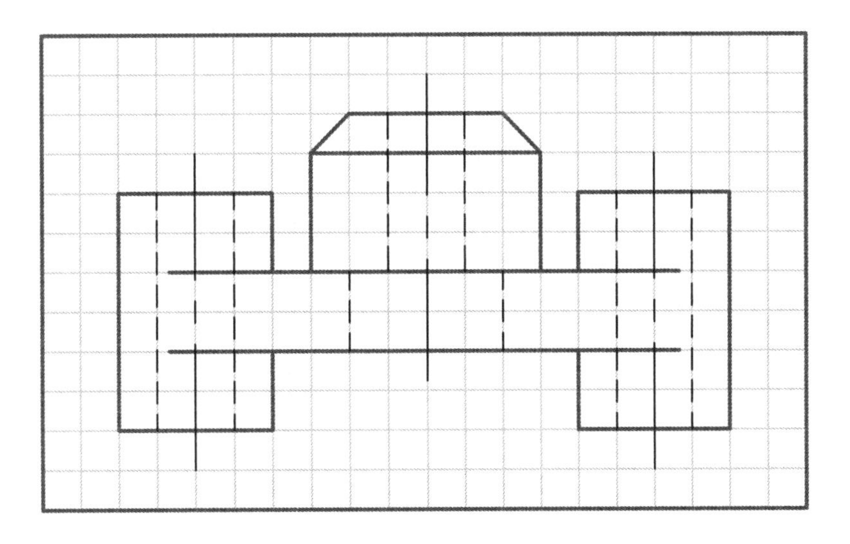

SKETCH THE APPROPRIATE SECTIONAL VIEW.
OBJECT IS MADE OF BRASS.

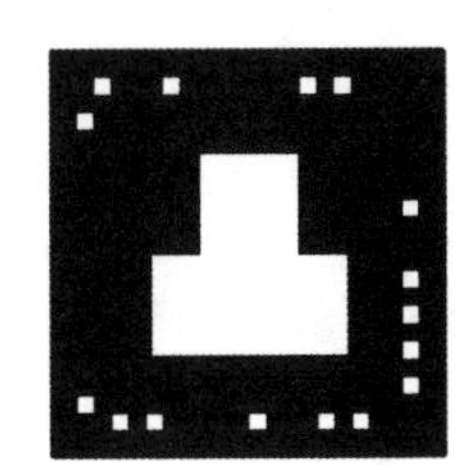

Sectional Views

Chapter 04
Exercise 06

Name:

Date:

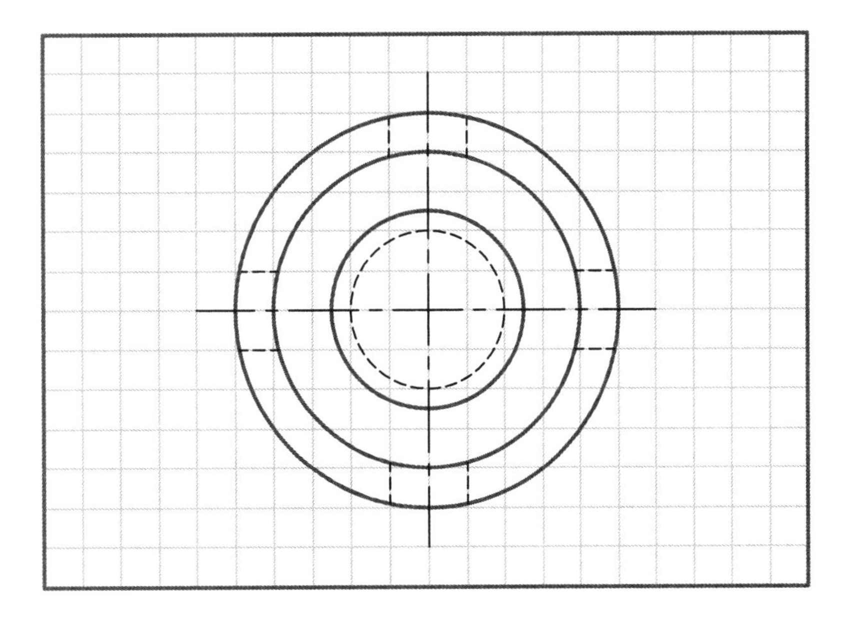

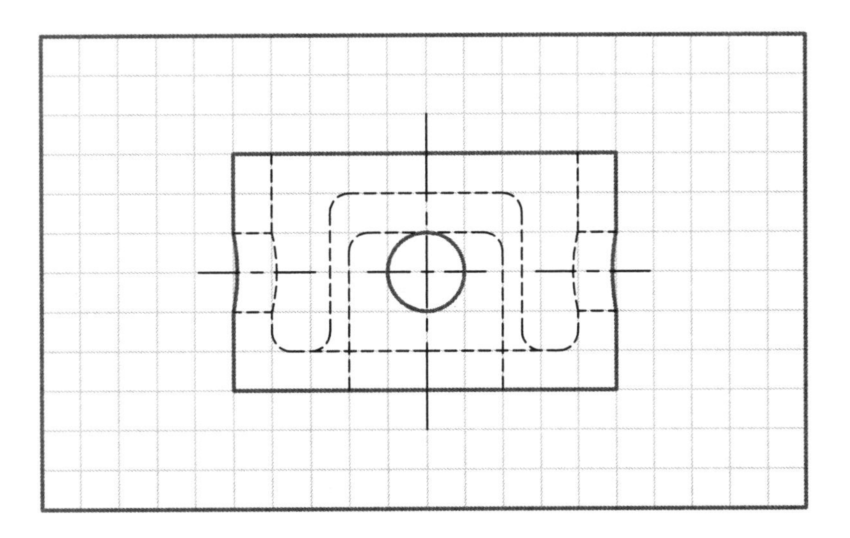

Sketch the appropriate sectional view.
Object is made of lead.

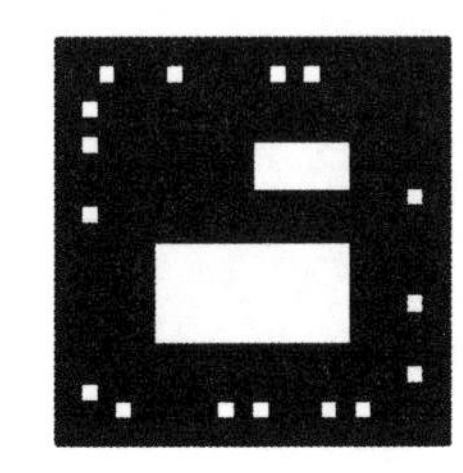
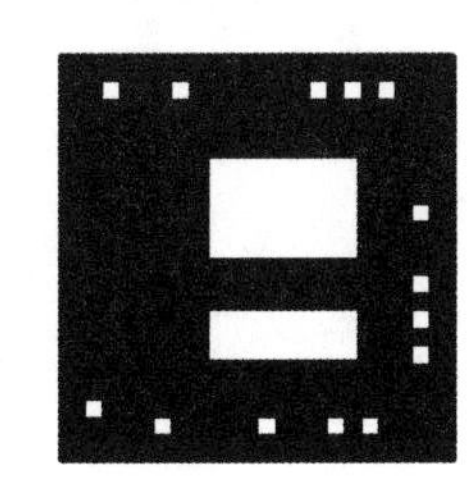

NAME:

CHAPTER 04
EXERCISE 07

DATE:

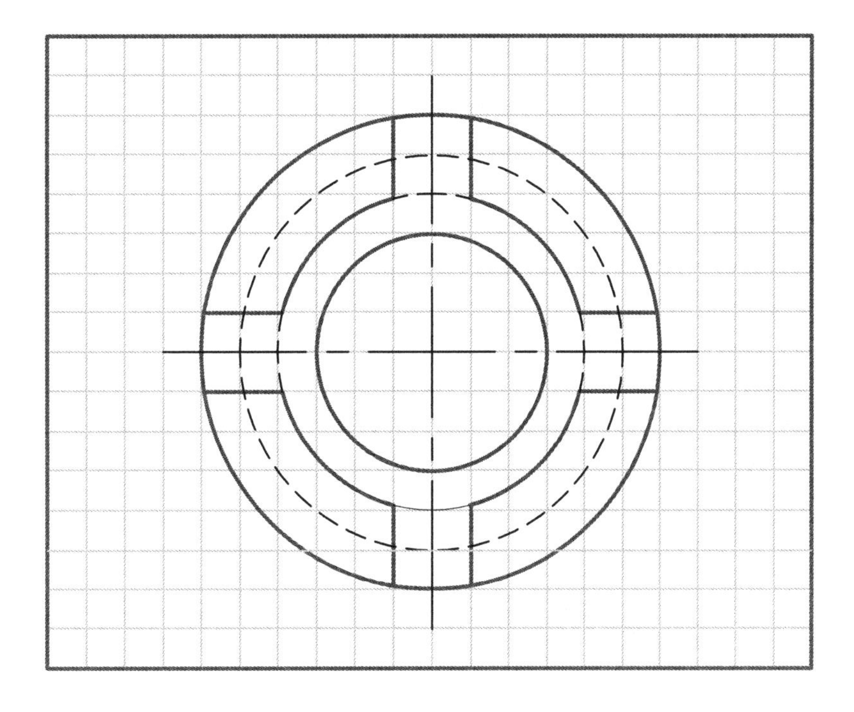

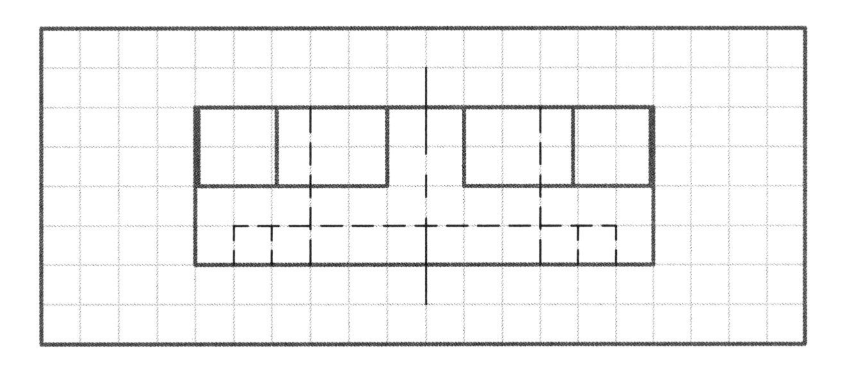

SKETCH THE APPROPRIATE SECTIONAL VIEW.
OBJECT IS MADE OF BRONZE.

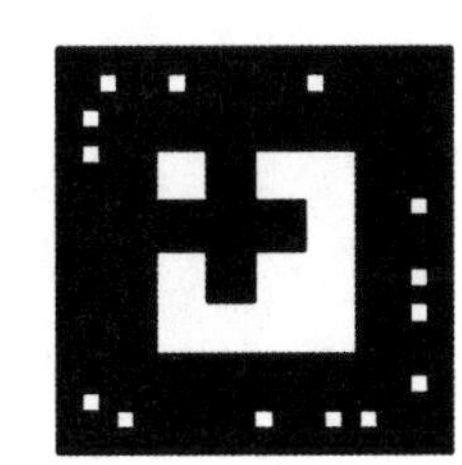

Name:

Exercise 08

Date:

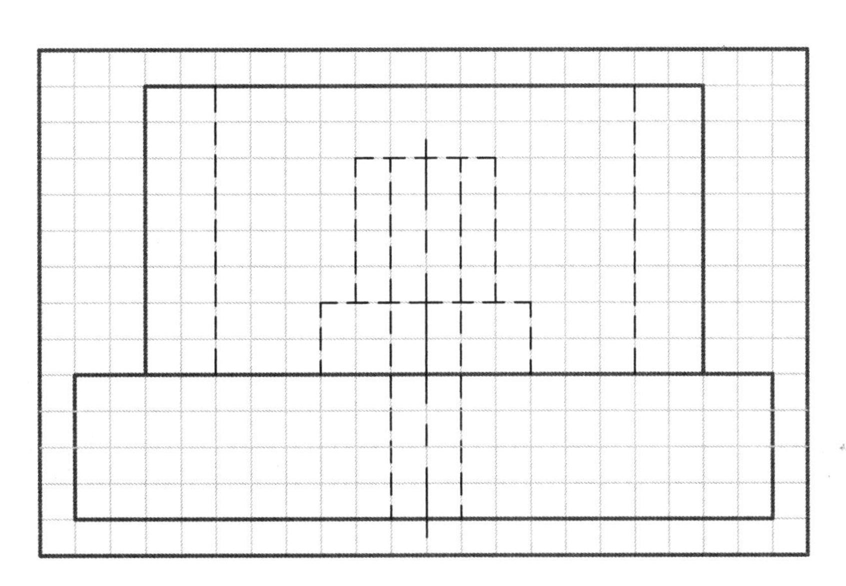

Sketch the appropriate sectional view.
Object is made of rubber.

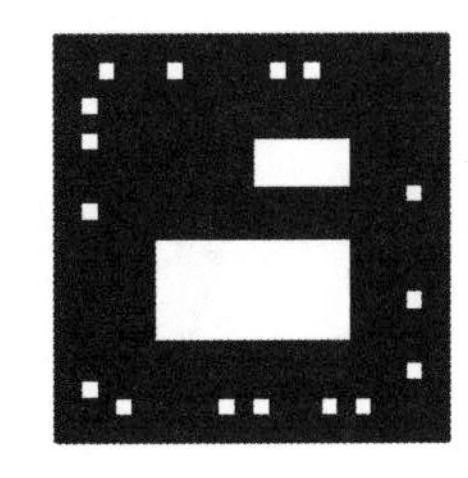
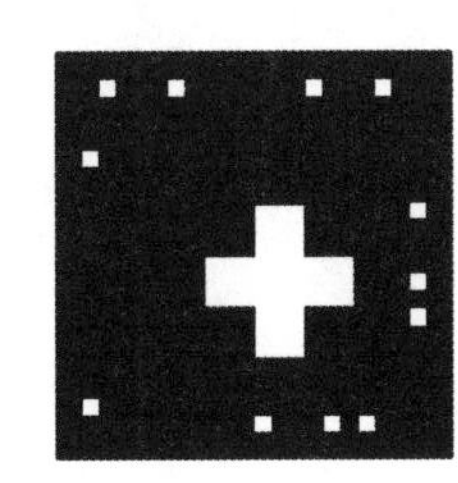

SECTIONAL VIEWS

CHAPTER 04
EXERCISE 09

NAME: Soloman V

DATE: 5/2/18

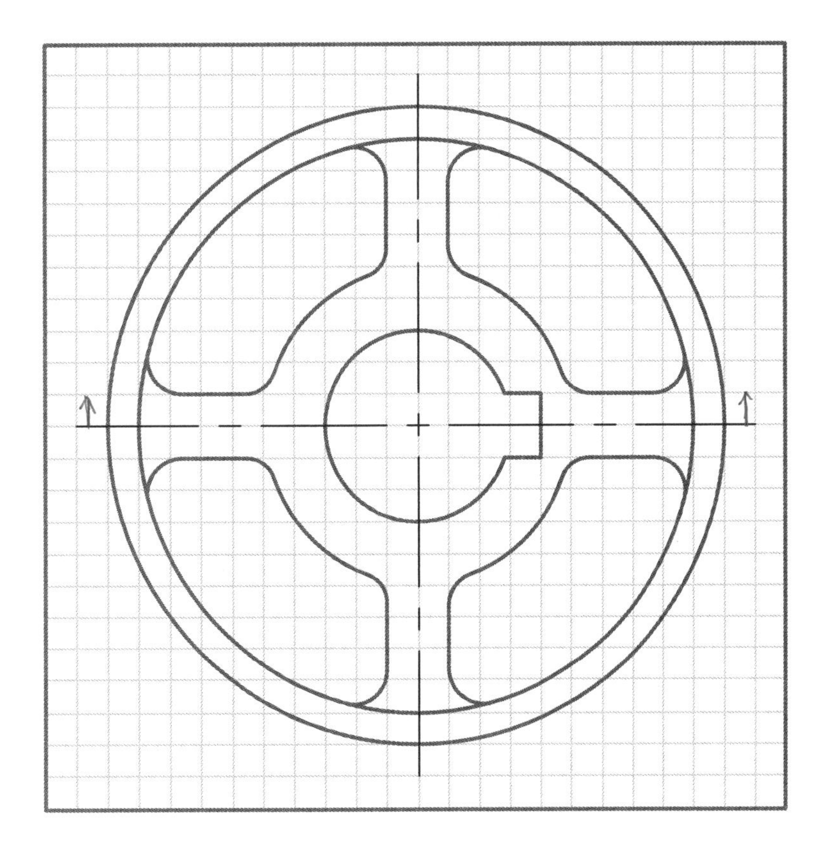

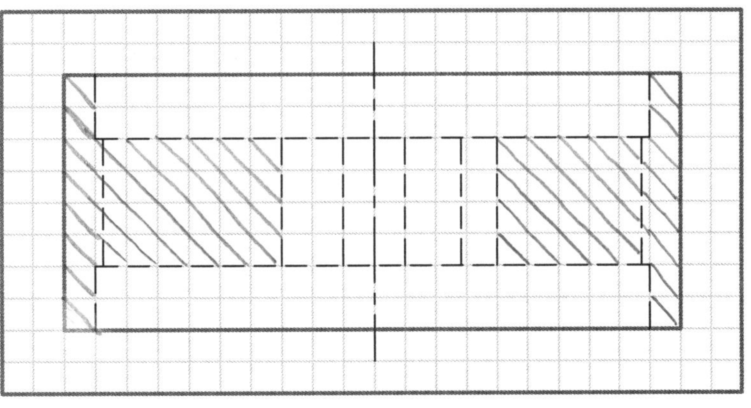

SKETCH THE APPROPRIATE SECTIONAL VIEW.
OBJECT IS MADE OF CAST IRON.

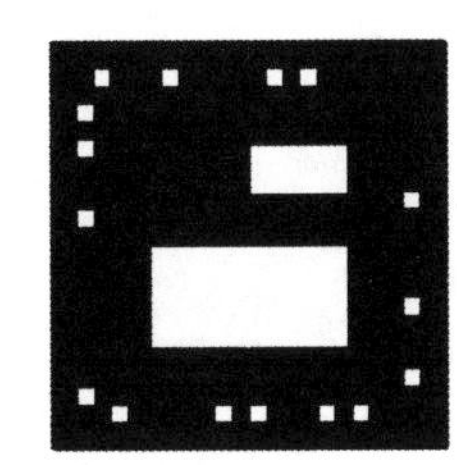
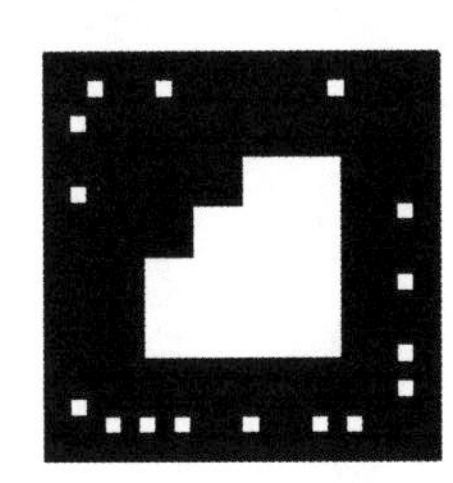

SECTIONAL VIEWS

NAME:

CHAPTER 04

EXERCISE 10

DATE:

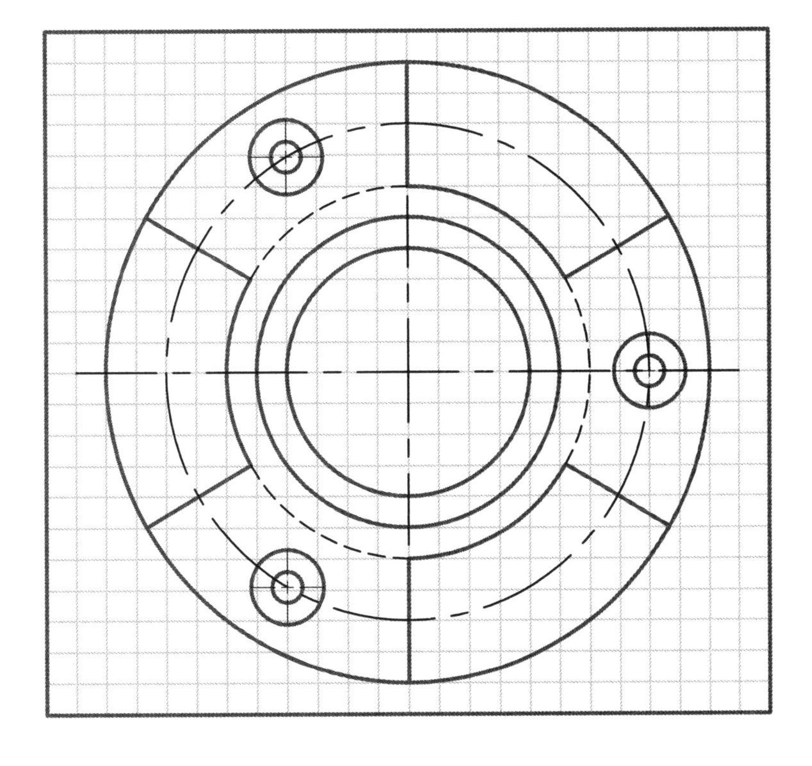
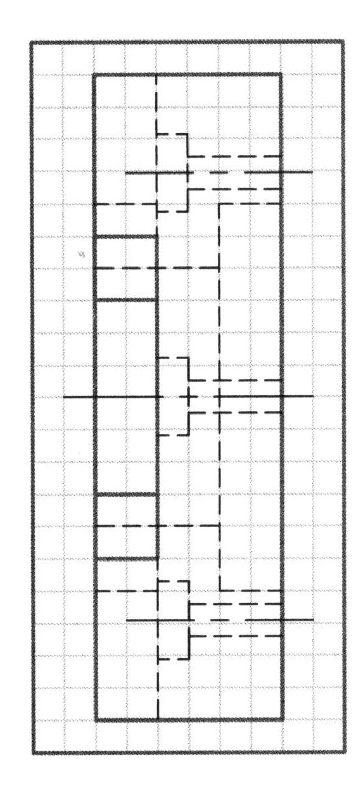

SKETCH THE APPROPRIATE SECTIONAL VIEW.
OBJECT IS MADE OF BRONZE.

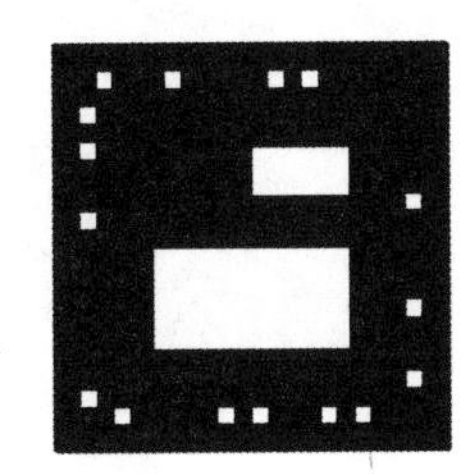

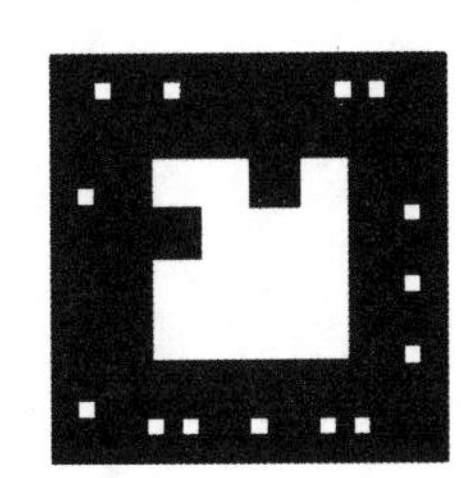

EXERCISE 11

NAME:

DATE:

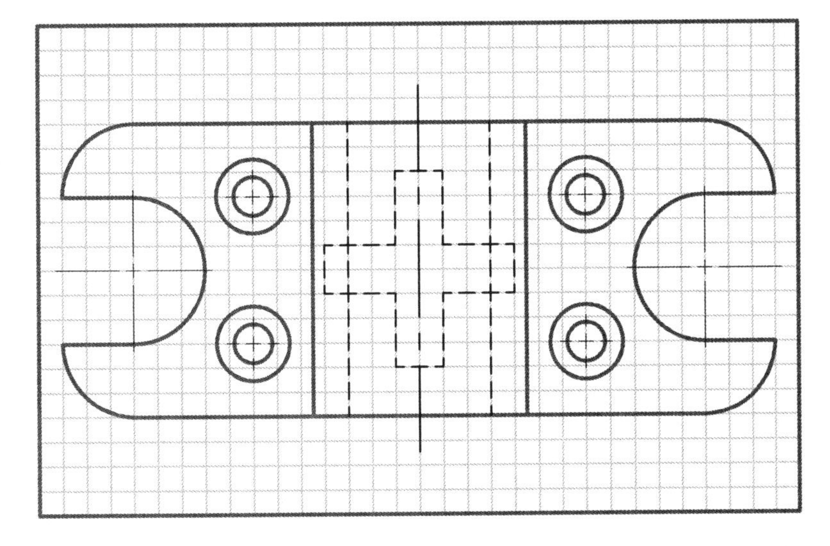

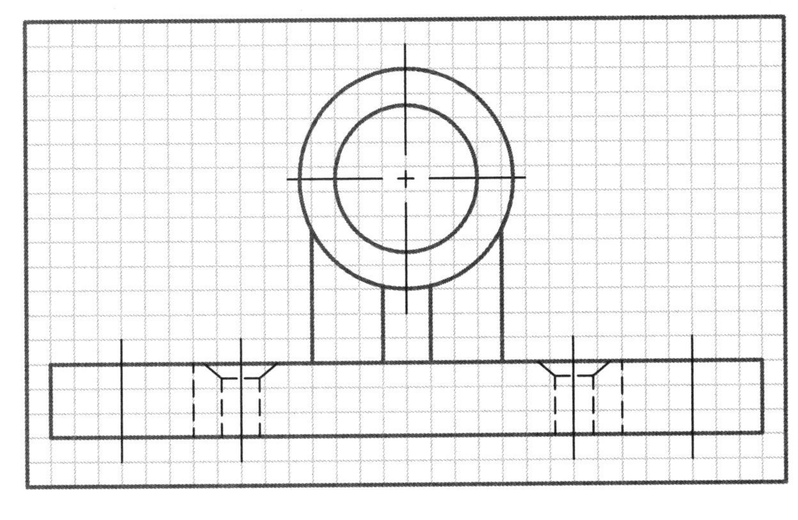

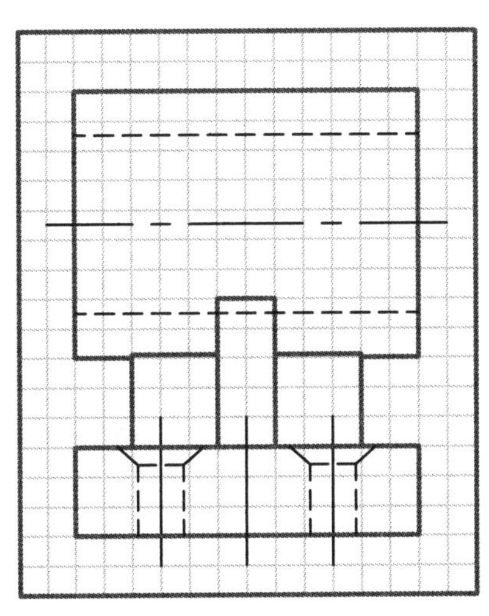

SKETCH THE APPROPRIATE SECTIONAL VIEW.
OBJECT IS MADE OF PLASTIC.

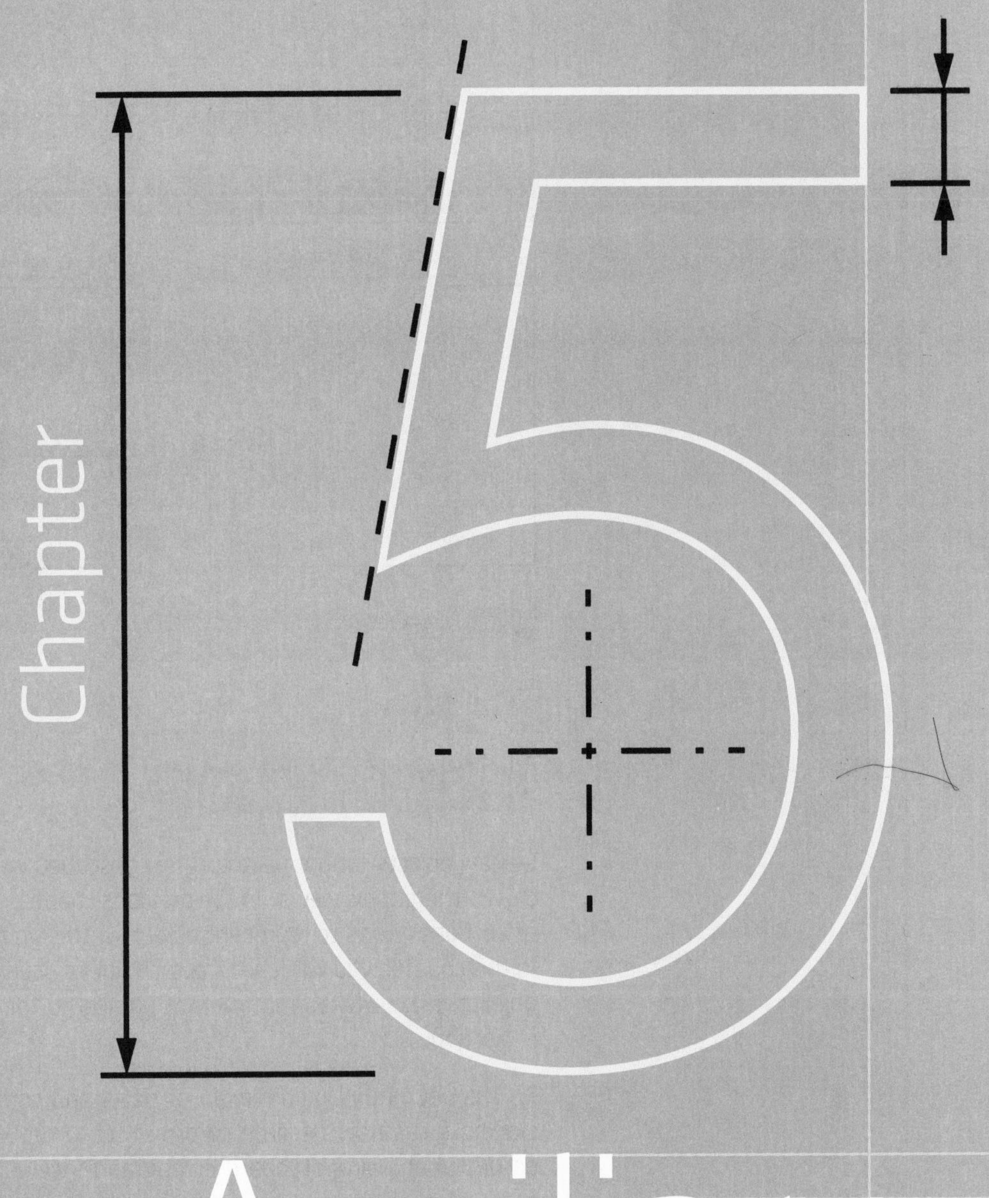

Chapter 5 Auxiliary Views

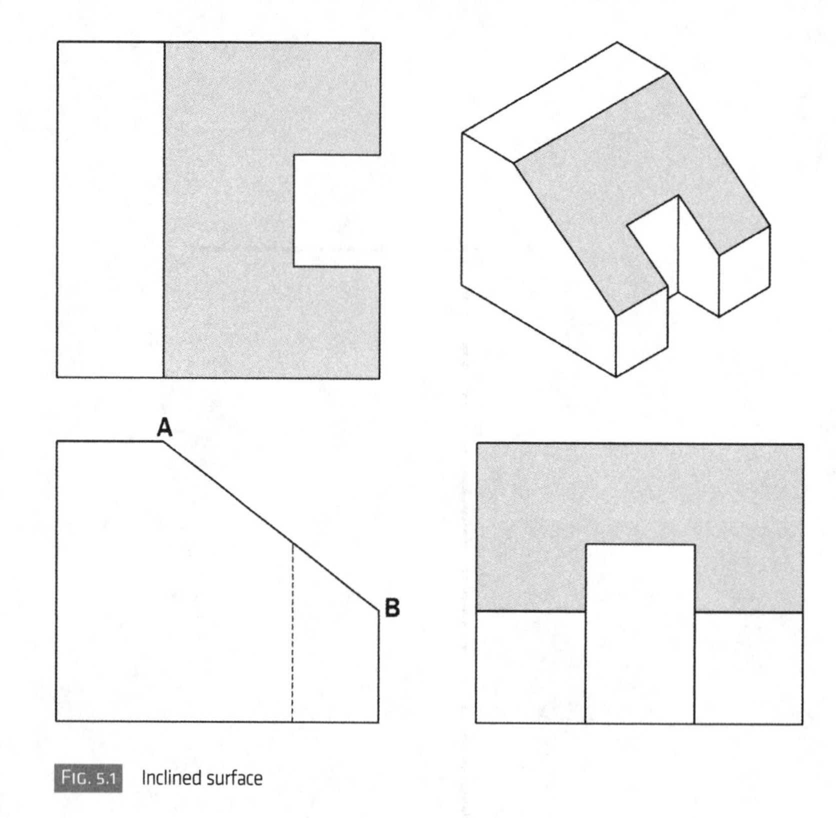

FIG. 5.1 Inclined surface

Introduction

Certain objects cannot be accurately described with the primary principal orthographic views. In the previous chapter, you studied the use of sectional views to represent objects with significantinternal detail. In this chapter, you will learn the techniques used to properly describe objects with surfaces that are not parallel to the standard planes of projection.

As the geometrical complexity of parts and components increases, sloping faces may become common features. However, distortion occurs when using standard orthographic views to represent these faces because the sloping surface is not parallel to the line of sight. In the object shown in Figure 5.1, the inclined surface (in gray) appears distorted (shorter than actual size) in the top and side views and as edge AB (true length) in the front view, making the surface difficult to visualize.

In orthographic projection, visual distortion is caused by foreshortening effects (discussed in previous chapters). Lines, angles, and features never appear true shape and size in any standard orthographic view if they are located on slanted or inclined surfaces. This problem affects the perception of the object. To correct the effects of distortion, and provide a more realistic representation, additional orthographic views are required. These additional views are created by projecting the inclined surfaces of the object onto auxiliary planes.

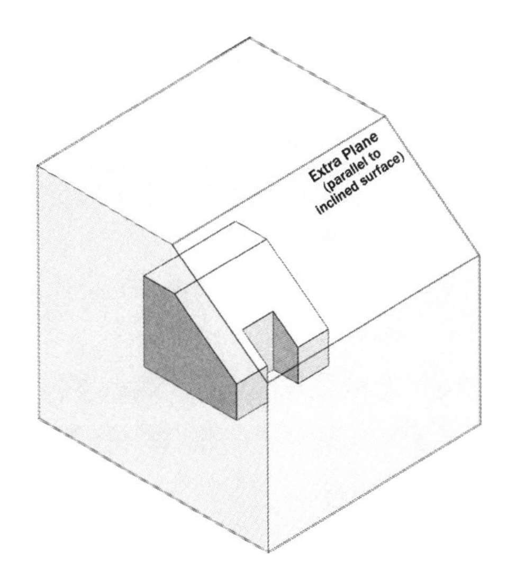

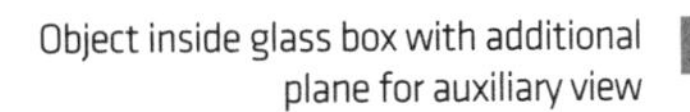
Object inside glass box with additional plane for auxiliary view FIG. 5.2

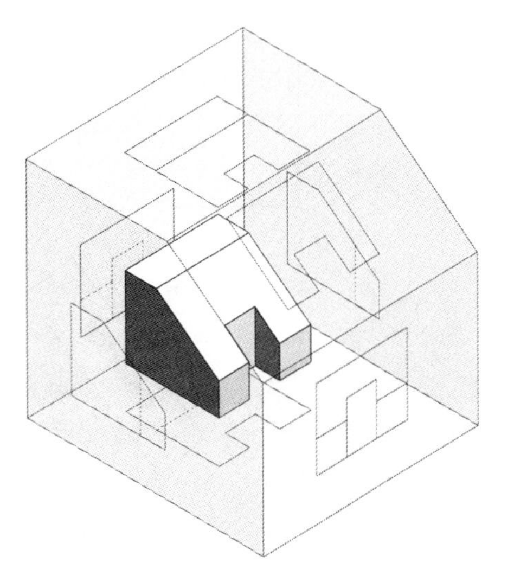

Faces projected onto the planes of the box FIG. 5.3

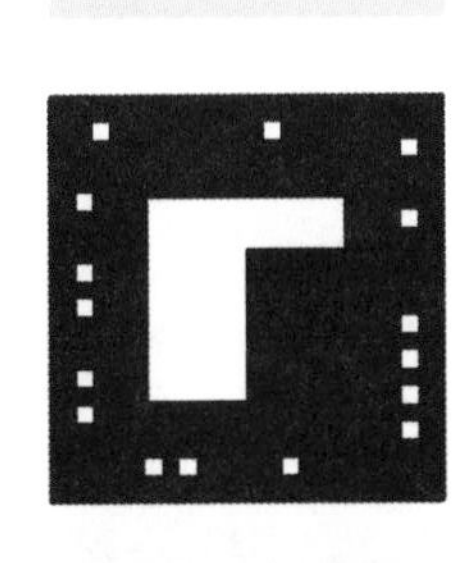

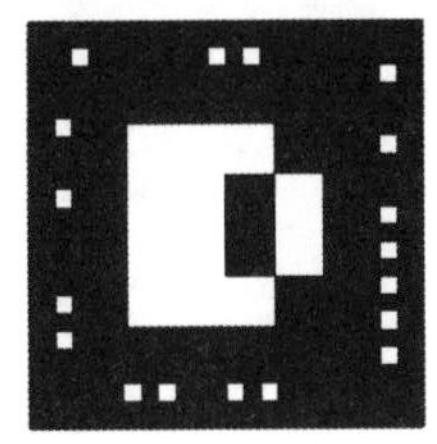

Auxiliary Views and Planes

An auxiliary view is projected onto a plane other than the three standard planes of projection (horizontal, frontal, and profile). Auxiliary planes can be visualized as additional planes on the imaginary "glass box" model used in previous chapters to illustrate the creation of the principal orthographic views. These extra planes are created parallel to the inclined surfaces (see Figure 5.2) so that the true shape and size of the surface can be depicted.

Similarly to the process followed to create the standard orthographic views, the sloping faces of the object are projected perpendicularly onto extra planes parallel to the surfaces of the "modified" glass box (see Figure 5.3).

The faces of the box are then unfolded to create the orthographic views (see Figure 5.4). The edges or joints between the faces of the glass box act as "hinges" (typically referred to as folding lines). The planes of the modified box are presented using the same scheme employed for the standard box. The auxiliary view is unfolded using the line between the auxiliary plane and the standard plane where the inclined surface appears as an edge (the front view, in the example).

The resulting drawing with the auxiliary view is shown in Figure 5.5.

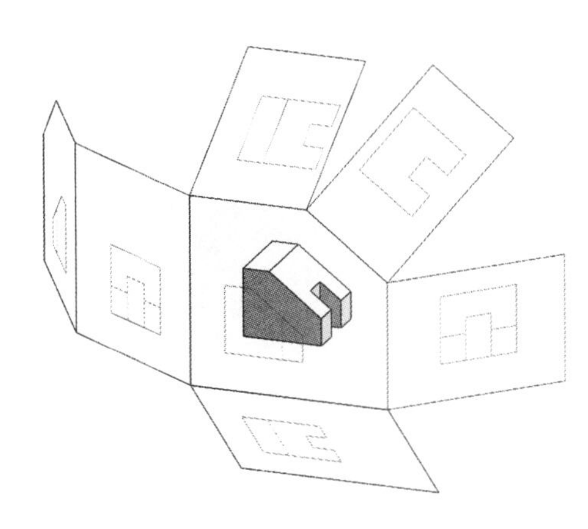

Unfolding the box with auxiliary plane  FIG. 5.4

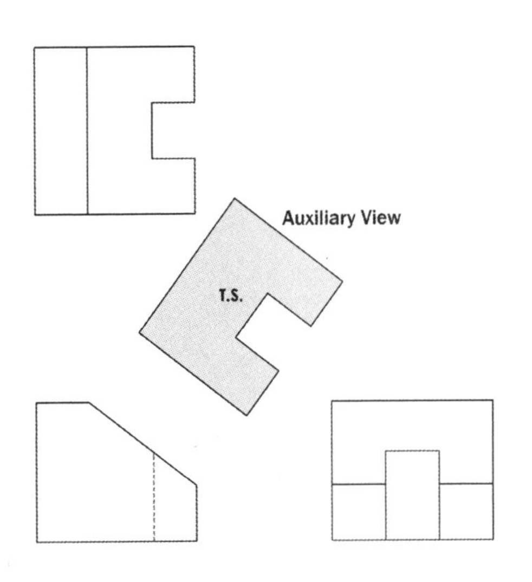

Orthographic views with auxiliary view FIG. 5.5

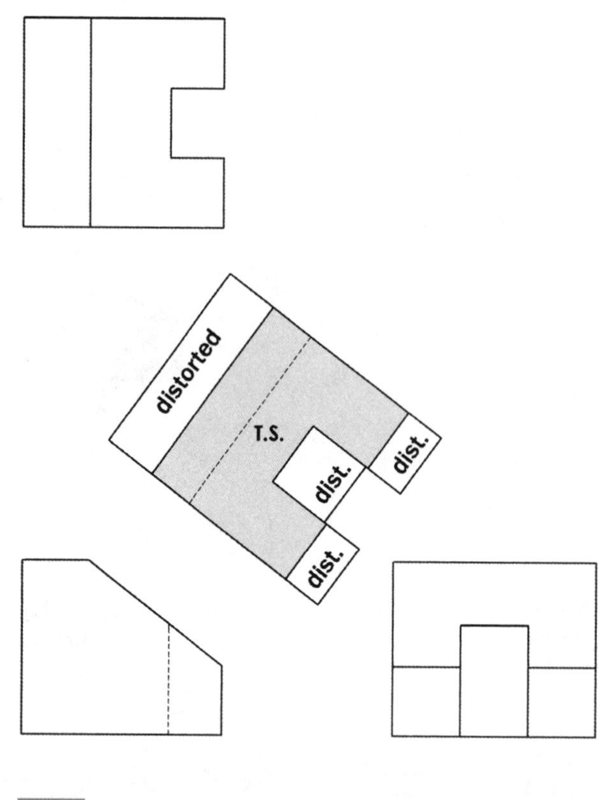

FIG. 5.6 Full auxiliary view

General Practices For Auxiliary Views

If all surfaces of the object are projected onto the auxiliary plane, the view generated is referred to as a full auxiliary view (see Figure 5.6). If only the inclined surface is projected, the view is called a partial auxiliary view. Partial auxiliary views are more common than full auxiliary views. In a full auxiliary view, all surfaces other than the inclined one will appear distorted, providing little value to the drawing, if any, and may create confusion in the viewer.

Hidden lines are normally omitted in auxiliary views unless required for clarity. Additionally, the capital letters "T.S", indicating that the geometry in the view is shown "True Size," must be included in the auxiliary view.

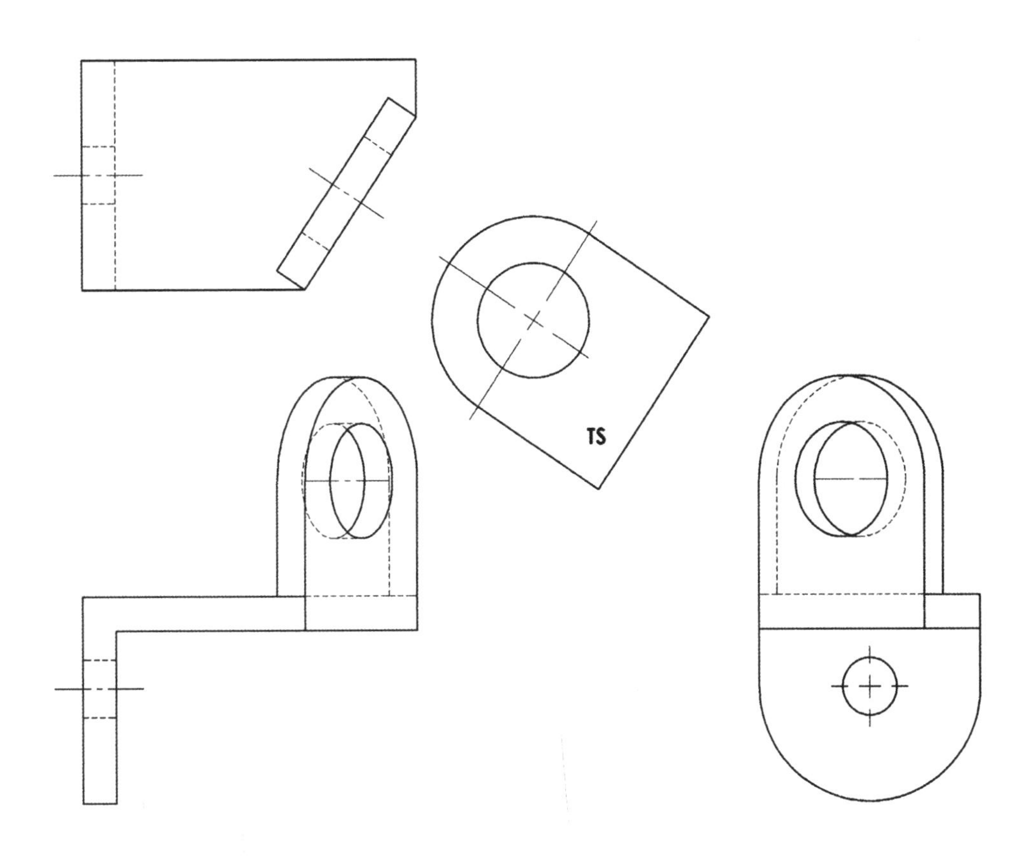

Auxiliary view projected from the top view FIG. 5.7

Auxiliary views can be constructed from any view in a drawing, but it depends on the view where the inclined surface appears as an edge. For this reason, some authors will refer to auxiliary views as front auxiliary view, top auxiliary view, or side auxiliary view, based on the view from which they originate. Other authors use the terms depth auxiliary view (if projected from the front view), height auxiliary view (if projected from the top view), and width auxiliary view (if projected from the side view), to identify the dimension that is shown true size.

Auxiliary views can also be constructed from other auxiliary views. An auxiliary view that is projected from one of the principal views is referred to as primary auxiliary view. From a primary auxiliary view, a secondary auxiliary view can be projected; then from it, a third auxiliary view, and so on. Although an unlimited number of successive auxiliary views can be created, most objects can be adequately described with primary or secondary auxiliary views. See Figure 5.7 for an example of auxiliary view projected from the top view.

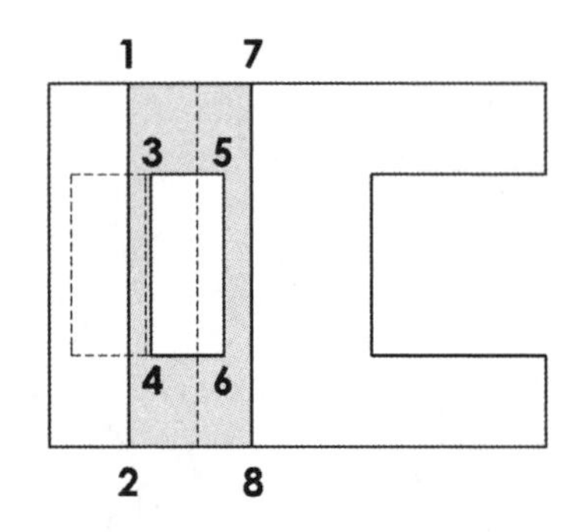

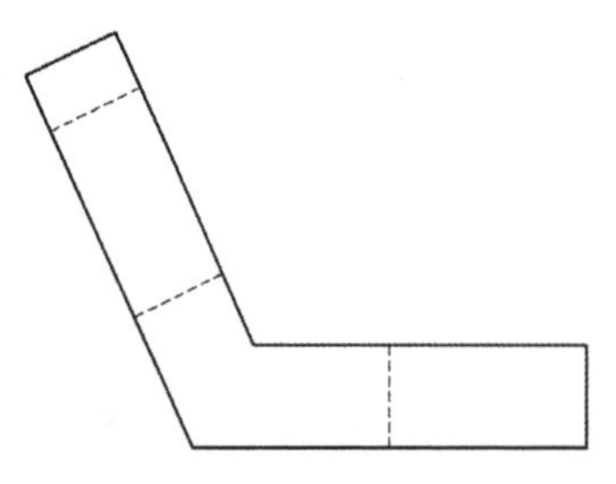

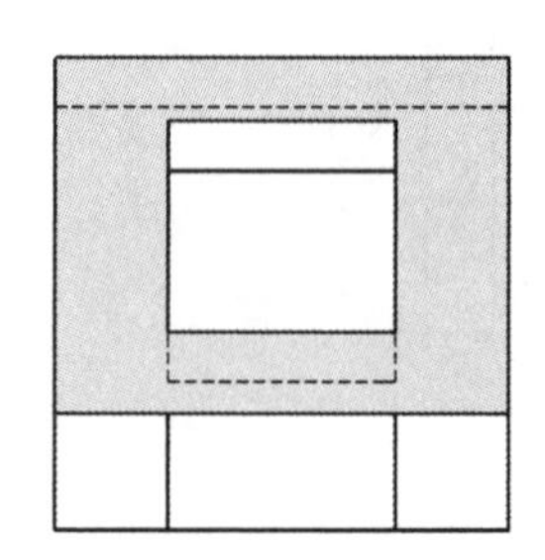

FIG. 5.8A Number corners of the inclined surface in a view where it appears as a surface, not an edge

Construction of Auxiliary Views

While most parametric CAD packages will easily create auxiliary views, the following steps illustrate the method used to create them by hand. Label the corners of the inclined surface in an orthographic view where the inclined surface appears as a face, not as an edge. Although you may be able to easily identify the corners mentally, it is good practice to label them. In the example shown in Figure 5.8A, the top view is used to create the auxiliary view, although the right side view is also acceptable since the inclined surface also appears as a face in this view.

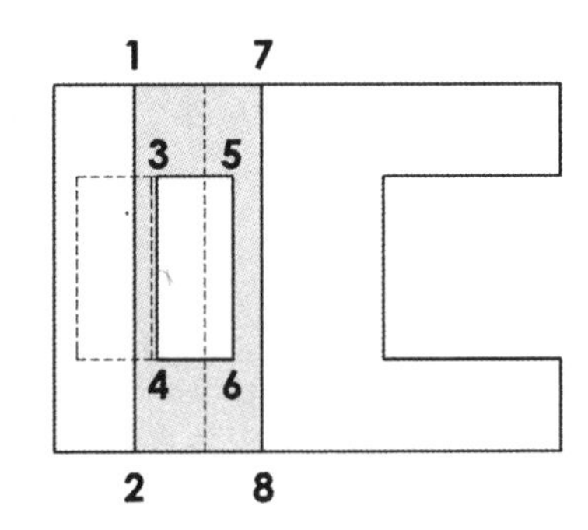

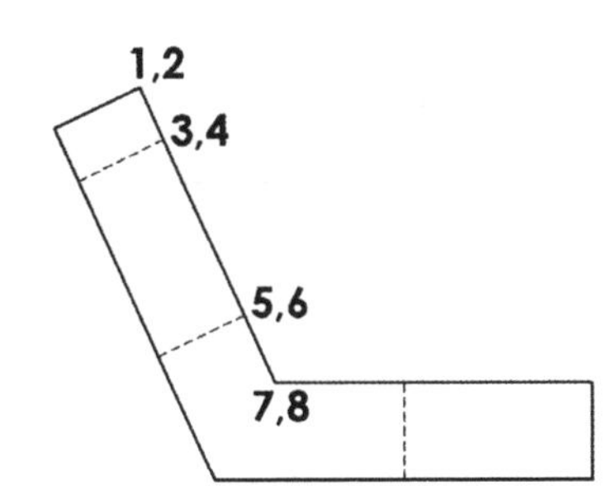

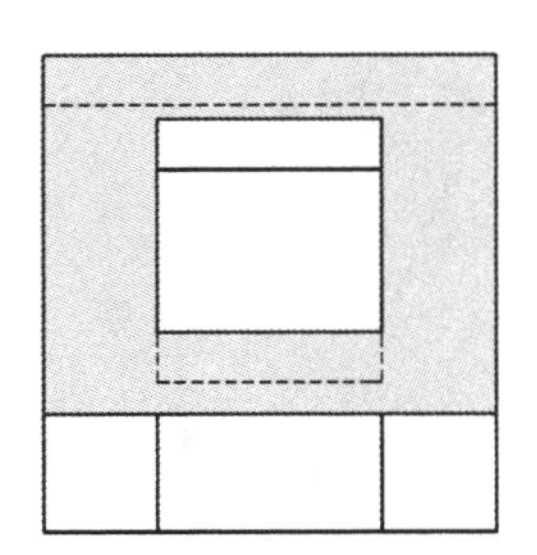

Transfer numbers to the view where the surface appears as an edge

FIG. 5.8B

Next, transfer the numbers from the previous view to the view where the inclined surface appears as an edge (see Figure 5.8B). Notice that there is the possibility that some points will represent two or more corners of the inclined surface.

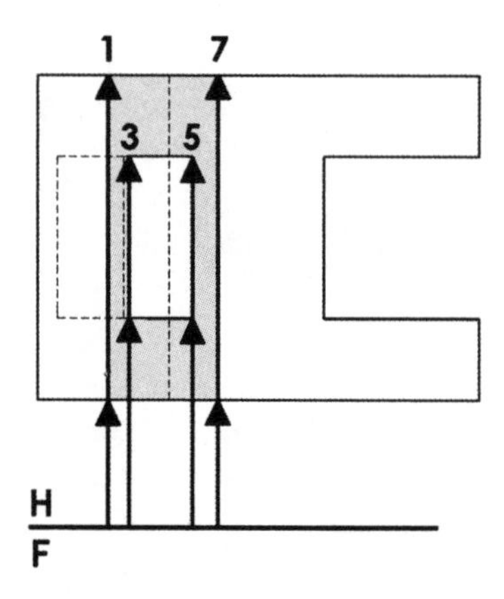

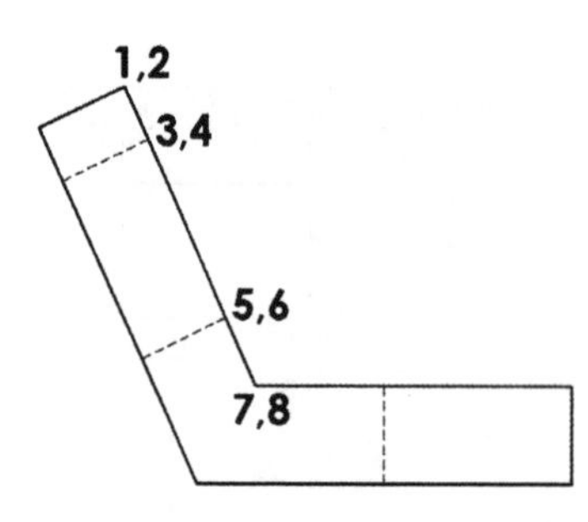

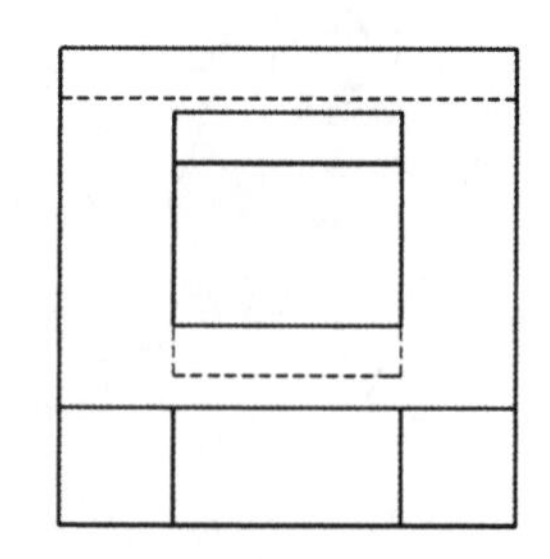

FIG. 5.8C Define folding line between views and measure perpendicular distances from the folding to each numbered corner

Define the folding line between the two orthographic views so that measurements can be taken. The folding line is a straight line that represents the edge or "hinge" of the glass box model used to unfold the views. The distance from the folding line to the orthographic view is inconsequential, as it just represents the location of the object inside the glass box; it does not affect the auxiliary view. Folding lines must be labeled according to the planes they connect. The folding line between the horizontal (H) and frontal (F) planes, for example, is labeled HF. The folding line FP connects the frontal (F) and profile (P) planes.

From the folding line, take perpendicular measurements to each numbered corner of the surface in the view where it appears as a face. The process is illustrated in Figure 5.8C.

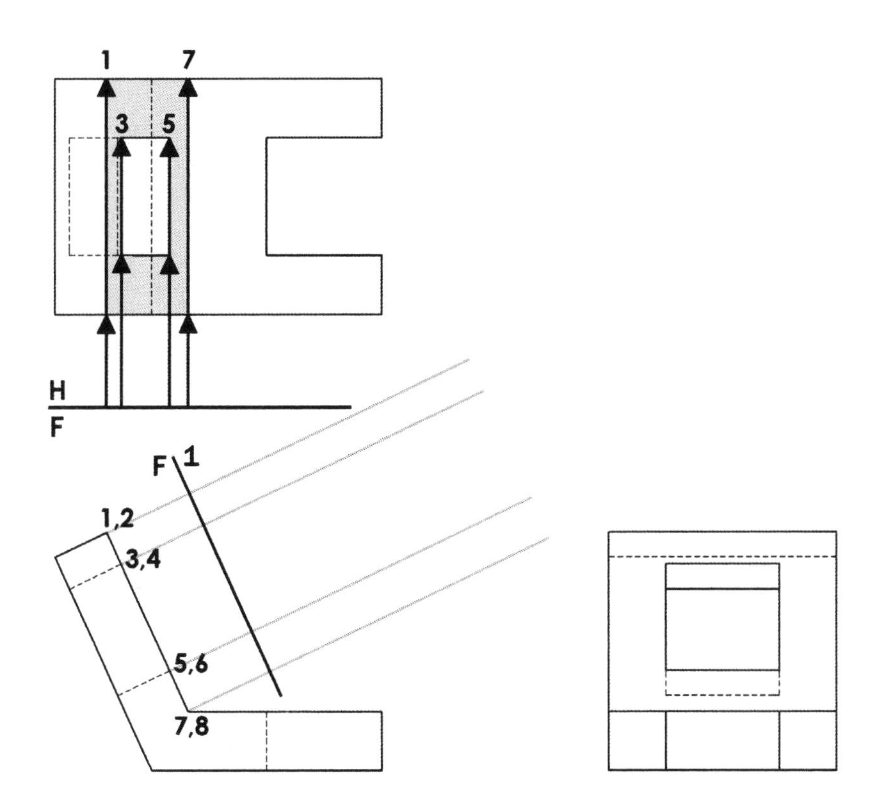

Define auxiliary folding line and establish direction of sight perpendicular to surface from each number corner

FIG. 5.8D

Next, the auxiliary folding line needs to be defined. This line represents the edge along which the auxiliary plane is unfolded. It is drawn parallel to the edge that represents the inclined surface at a convenient distance. Folding lines for auxiliary views are labeled with the initial of the plane they connect (Horizontal, Frontal, or Profile) followed by a number that indicates the auxiliary view constructed.

From every numbered corner of the edge representing the inclined surface, draw perpendicular construction lines to indicate the line of sight. These lines will be used later to transfer distances. This step is illustrated in Figure 5.8D.

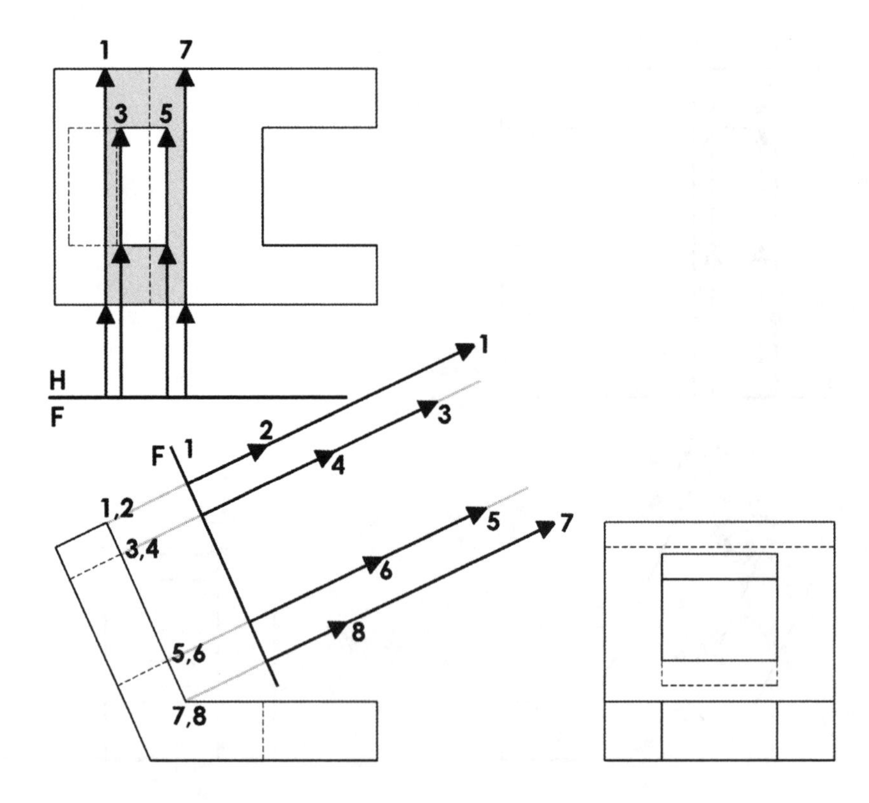

Fig. 5.8E Define folding line between views and measure perpendicular distances from the folding to each numbered corner

The distances located from the orthographic folding line (H/F in the example) to the points on the surface need to be transferred to the auxiliary folding line following the direction of sight defined in the previous step (see Figure 5.8E).

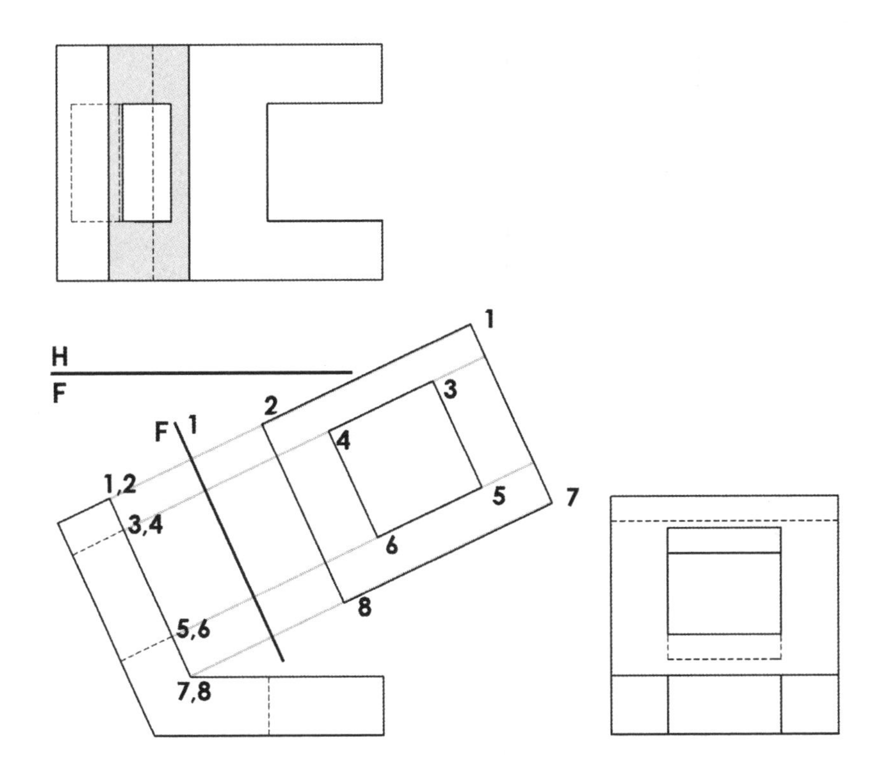

Define auxiliary folding line and establish direction of sight perpendicular to surface from each number corner

FIG. 5.8F

Finally, connect the points using the numbering sequence defined in the first step (see Figure 5.8F).

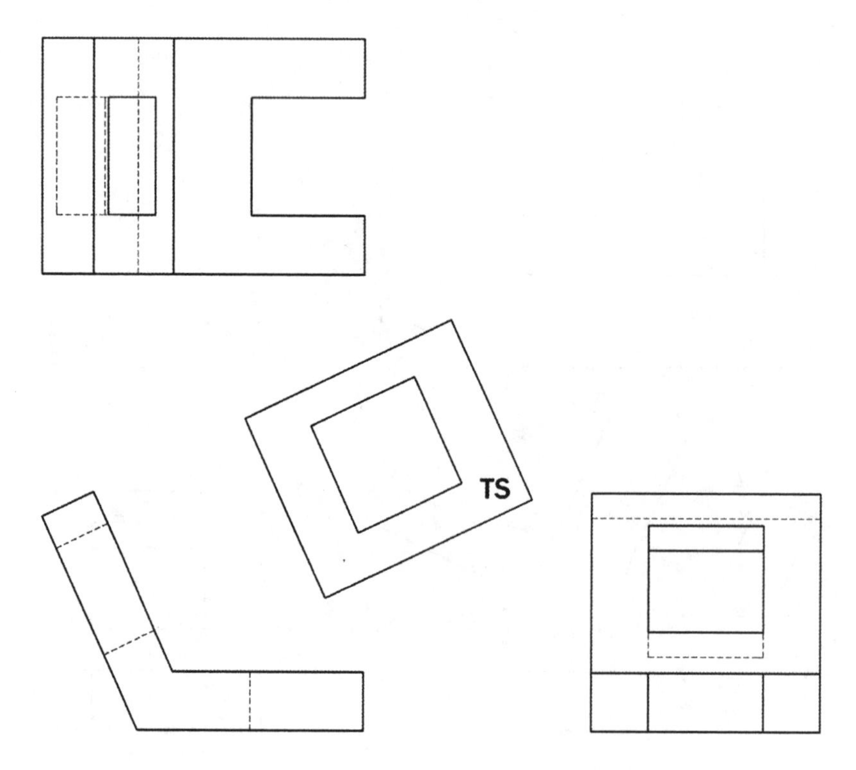

FIG. 5.9 Define folding line between views and measure perpendicular distances from the folding to each numbered corner

The completed drawing is shown in Figure 5.9. Notice that the construction lines and numbers have been erased, as well as the folding lines. Although folding lines are acceptable in a drawing, they are usually deleted for clarity. The label "TS" must be placed in the auxiliary view, indicating that the view is "True Size".

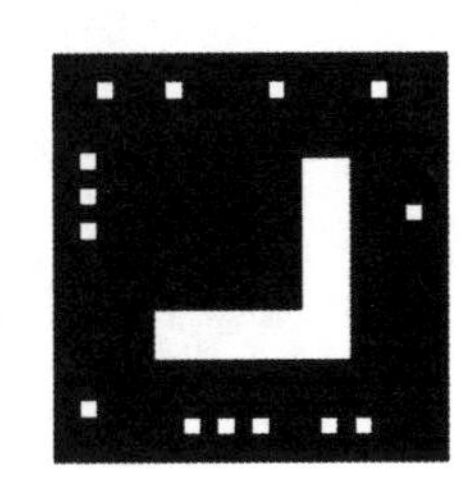

Auxiliary Views

Name:

Chapter 05
Exercise 01

Date:

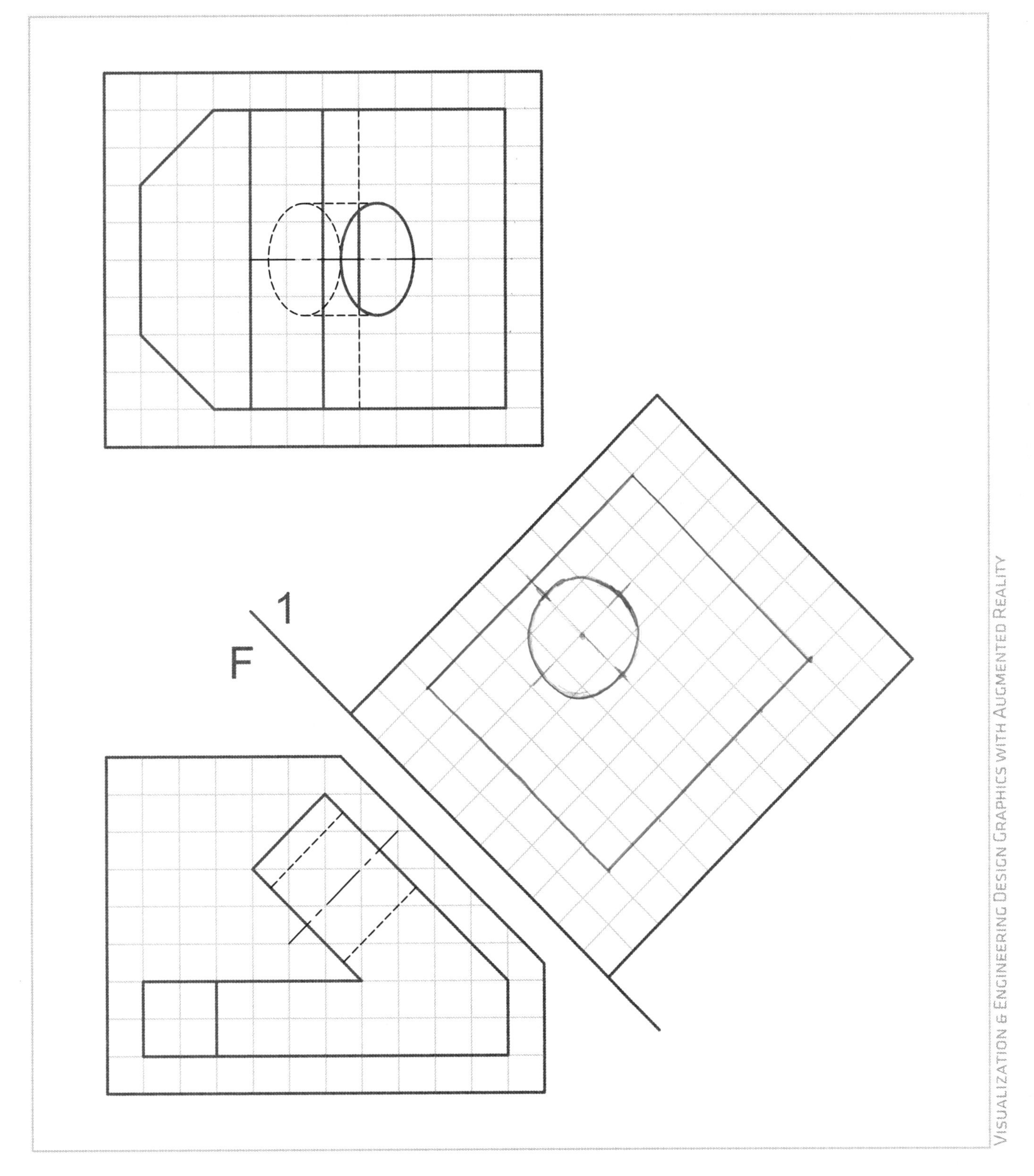

Sketch the appropriate auxiliary view.

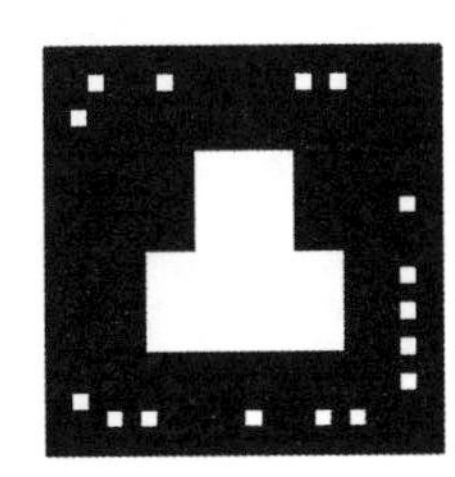

Exercise 02

Name:

Date:

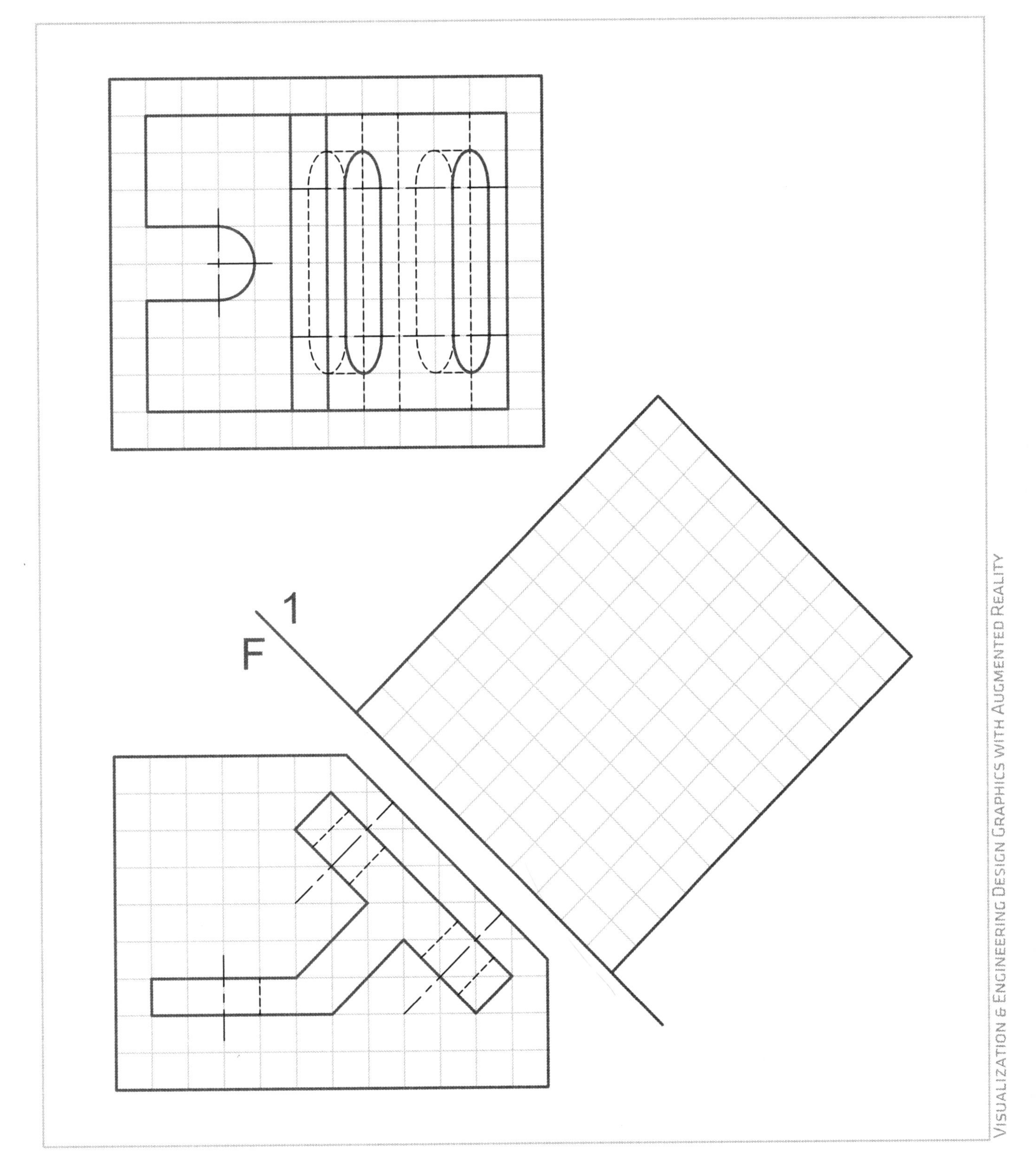

Sketch the appropriate auxiliary view.

Auxiliary Views

Name:

Chapter 05
Exercise 03

Date:

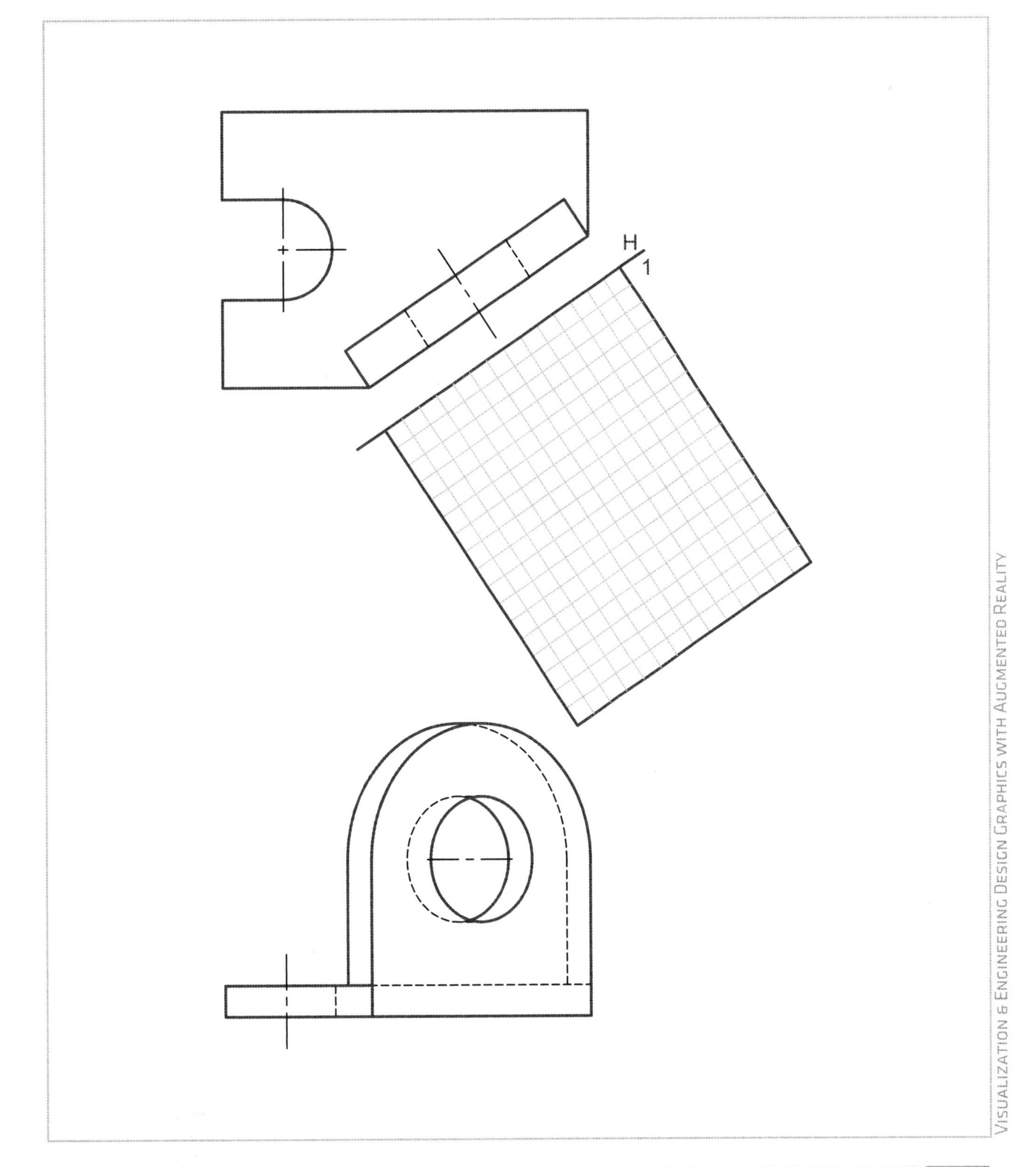

Sketch the appropriate auxiliary view.

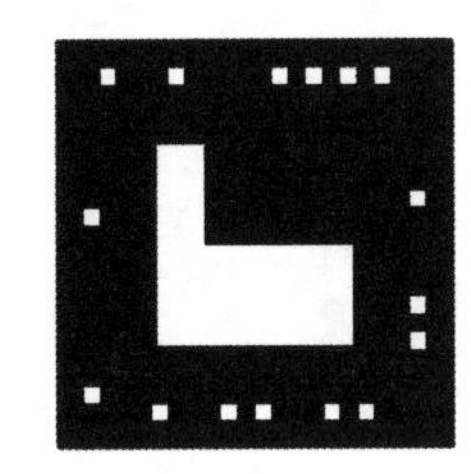
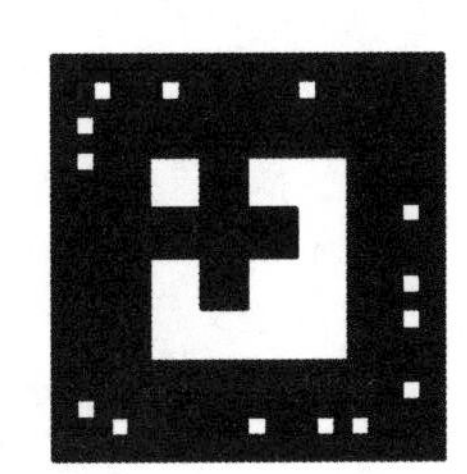

EXERCISE 04

NAME:

DATE:

SKETCH THE APPROPRIATE AUXILIARY VIEW.

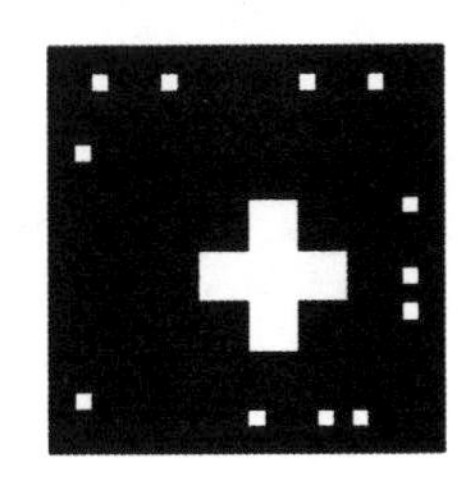

AUXILIARY VIEWS

CHAPTER 05

EXERCISE 05

NAME:

DATE:

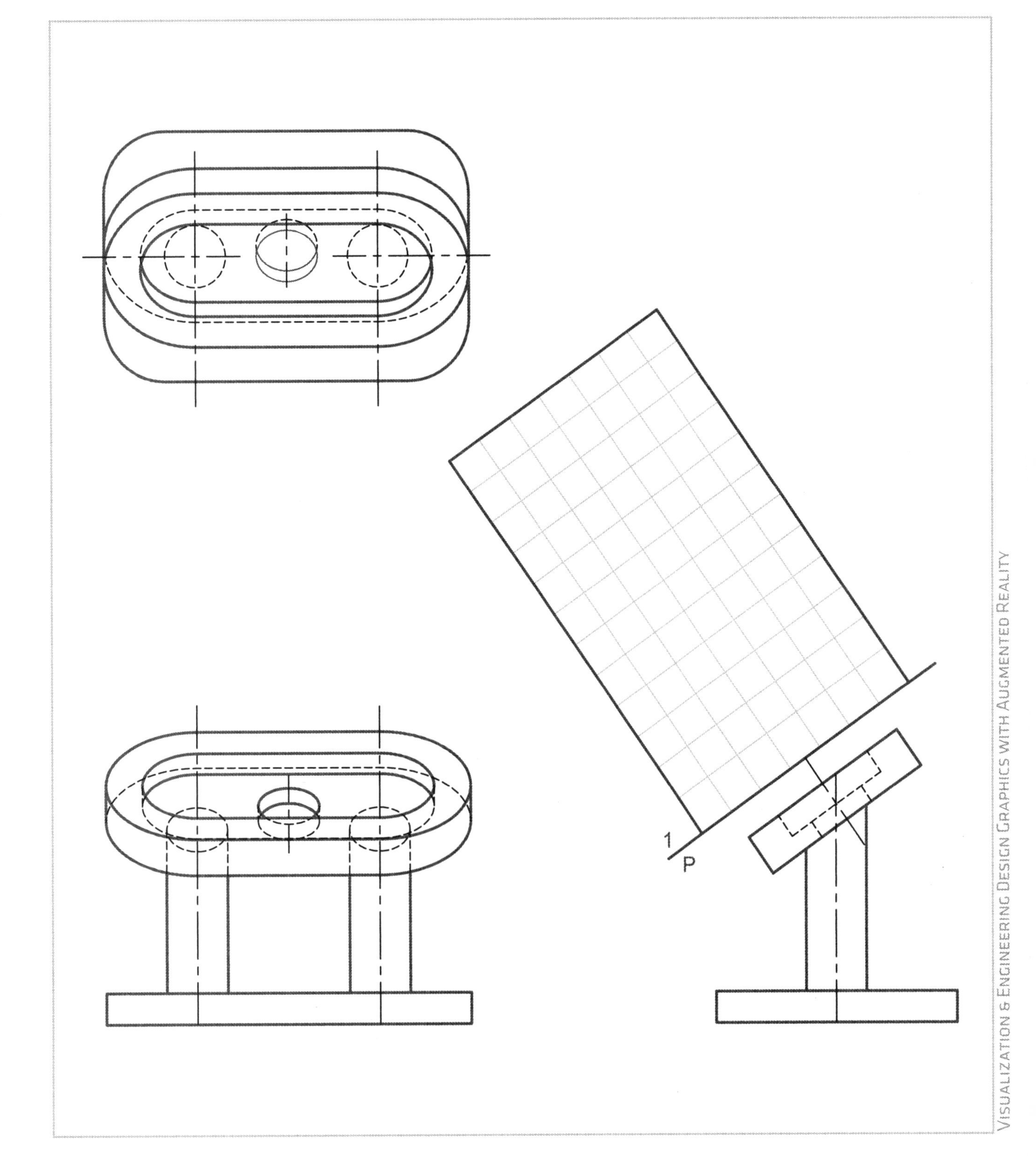

SKETCH THE APPROPRIATE AUXILIARY VIEW.

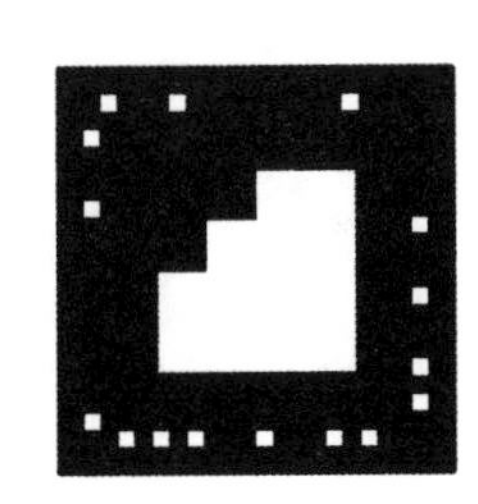

Auxiliary Views

Chapter 05
Exercise 06

Name:

Date:

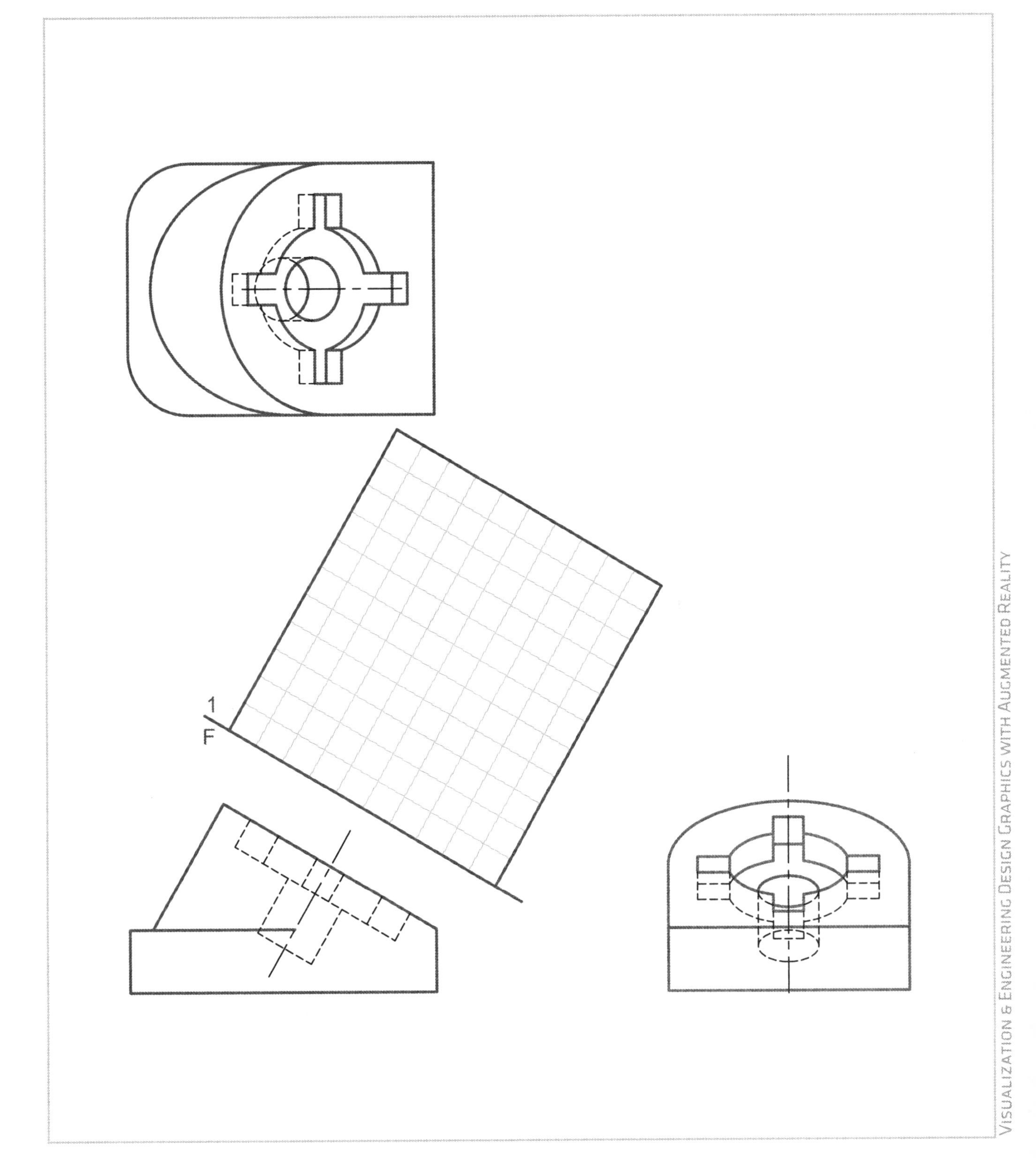

Sketch the appropriate auxiliary view.

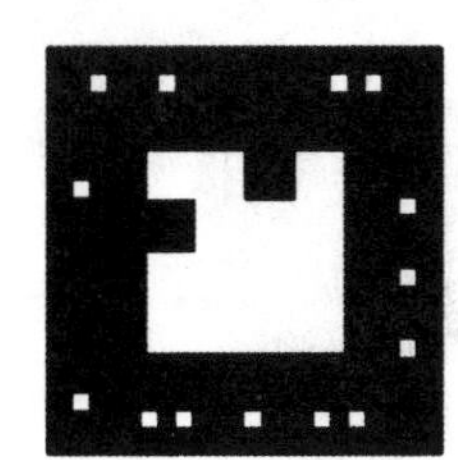

AUXILIARY VIEWS

CHAPTER 05

EXERCISE 07

NAME: S.V.

DATE: 5/2/18

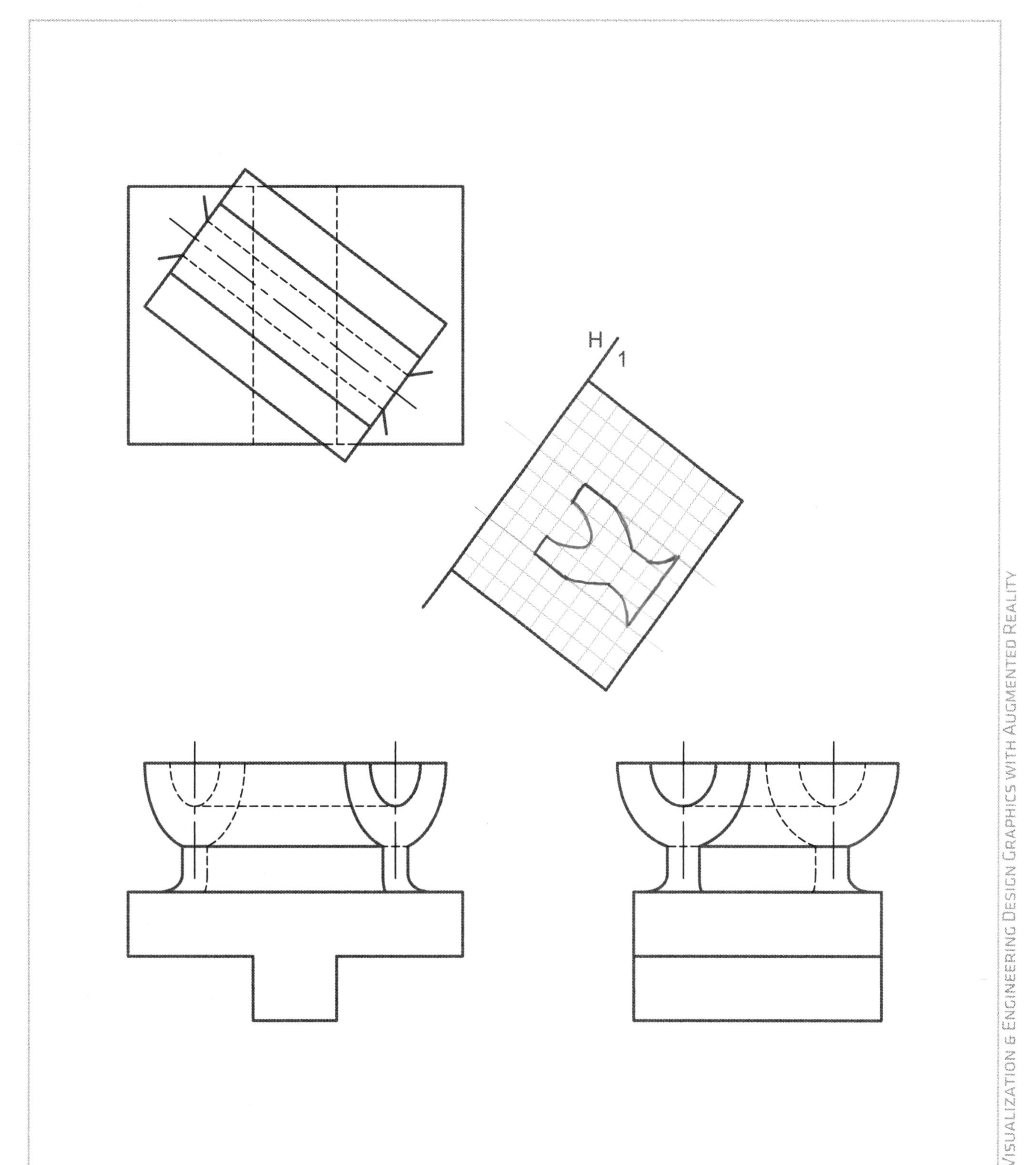

SKETCH THE APPROPRIATE AUXILIARY VIEW.

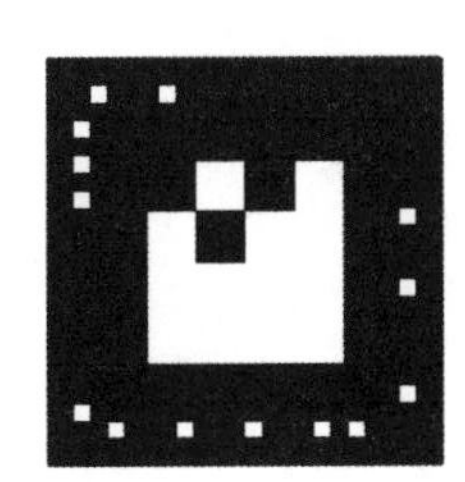

EXERCISE 08

NAME:

DATE:

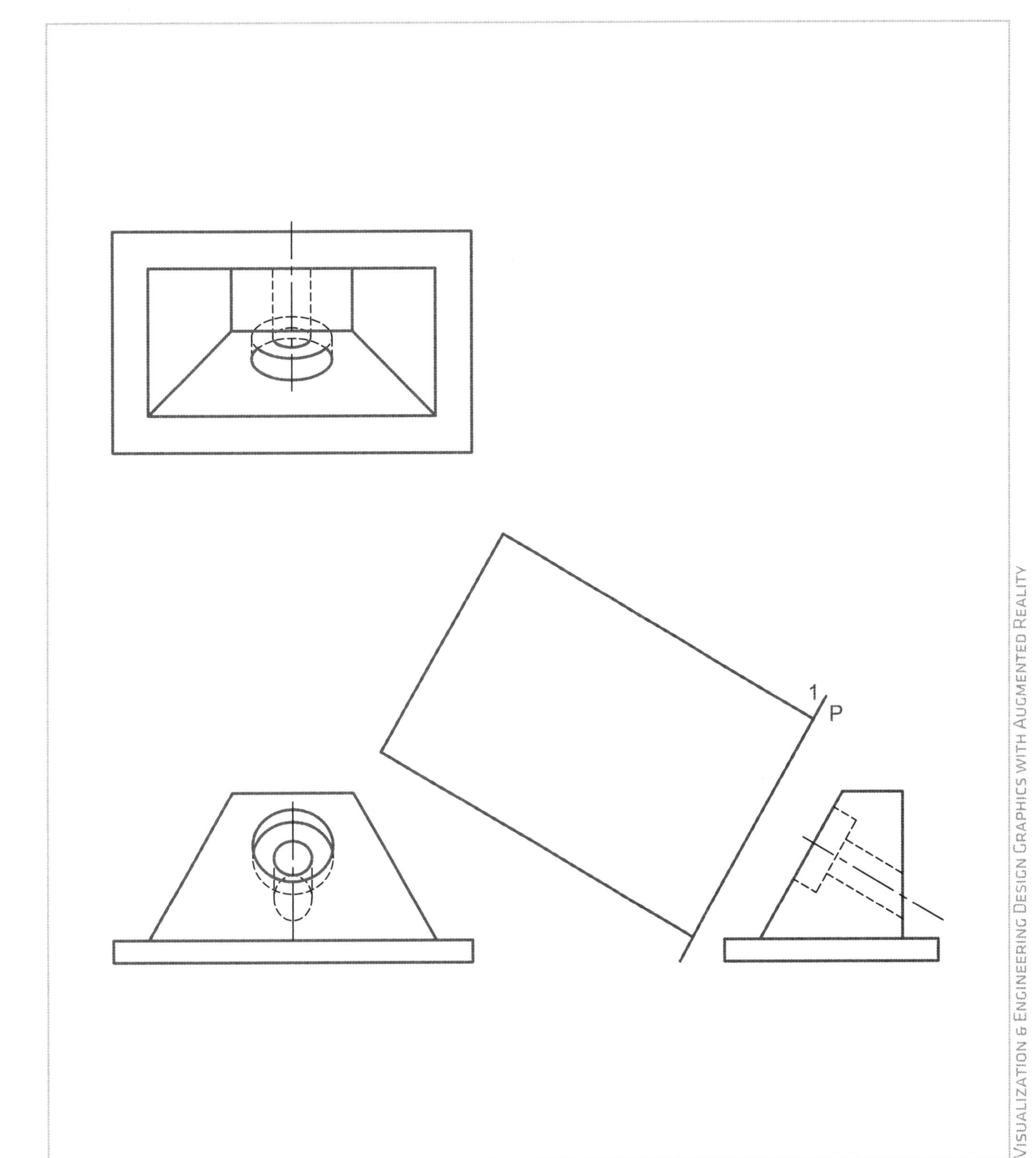

SKETCH THE APPROPRIATE AUXILIARY VIEW.

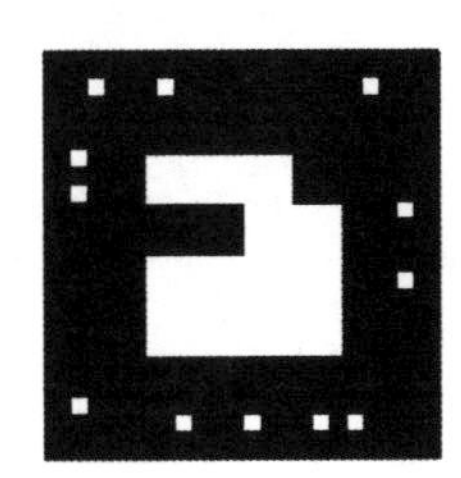

NAME:

EXERCISE 09

DATE:

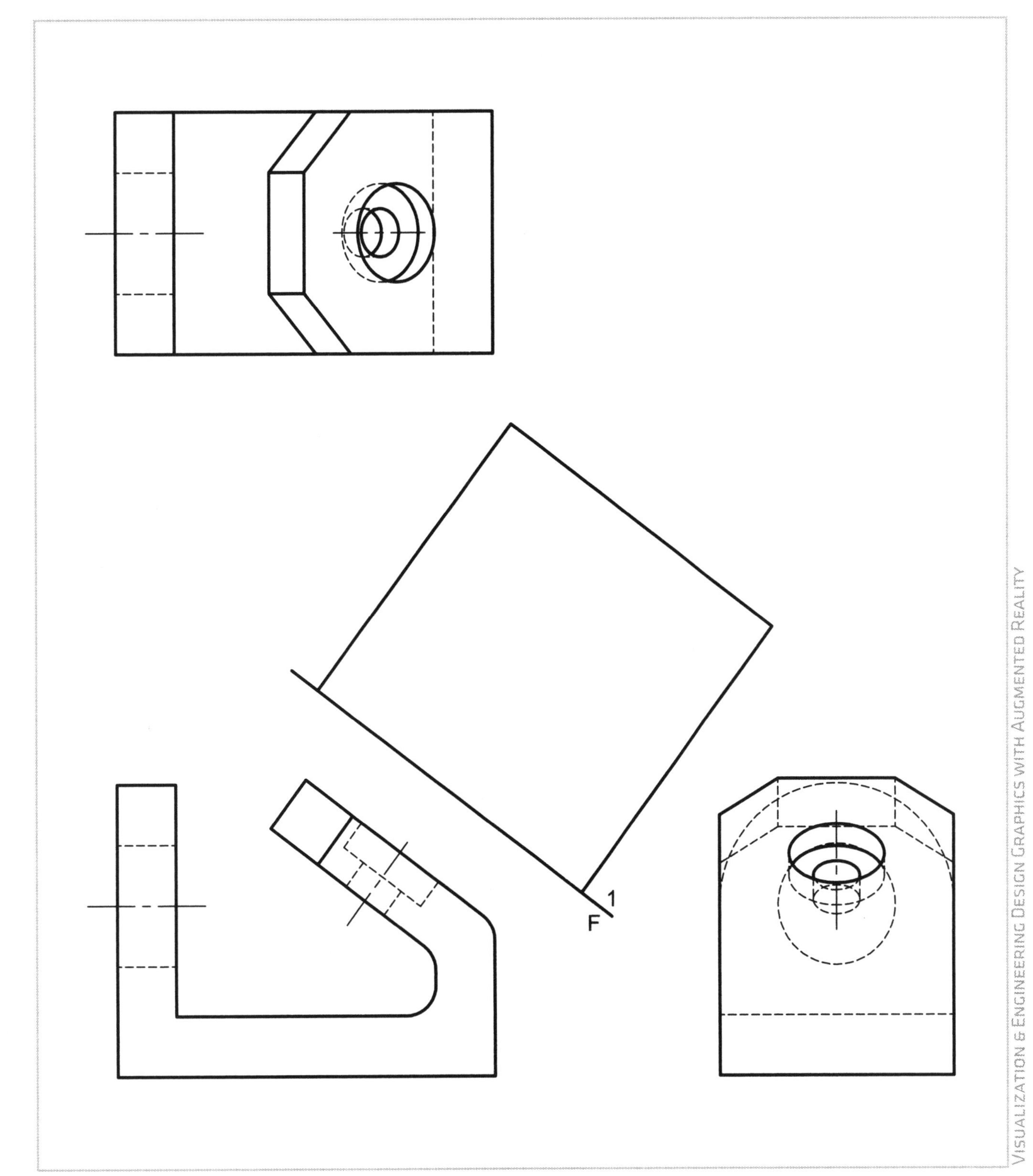

SKETCH THE APPROPRIATE AUXILIARY VIEW.

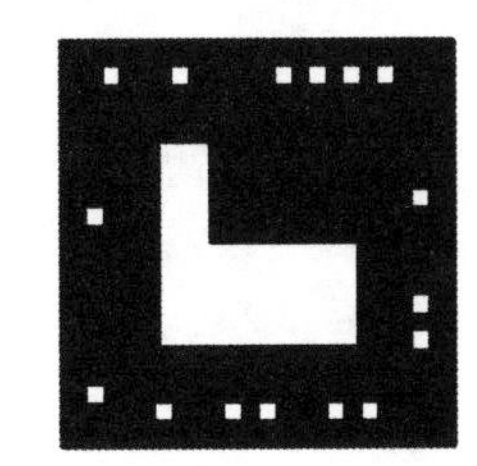
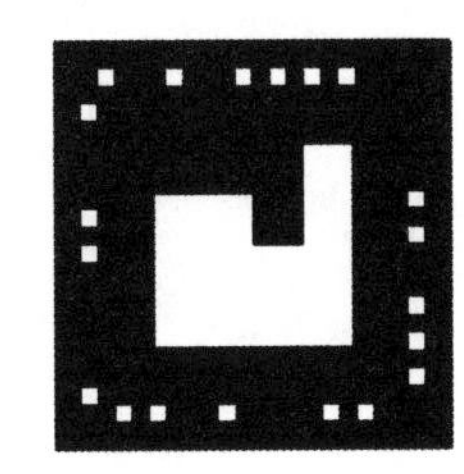

CHAPTER 05
EXERCISE 10

NAME:

DATE:

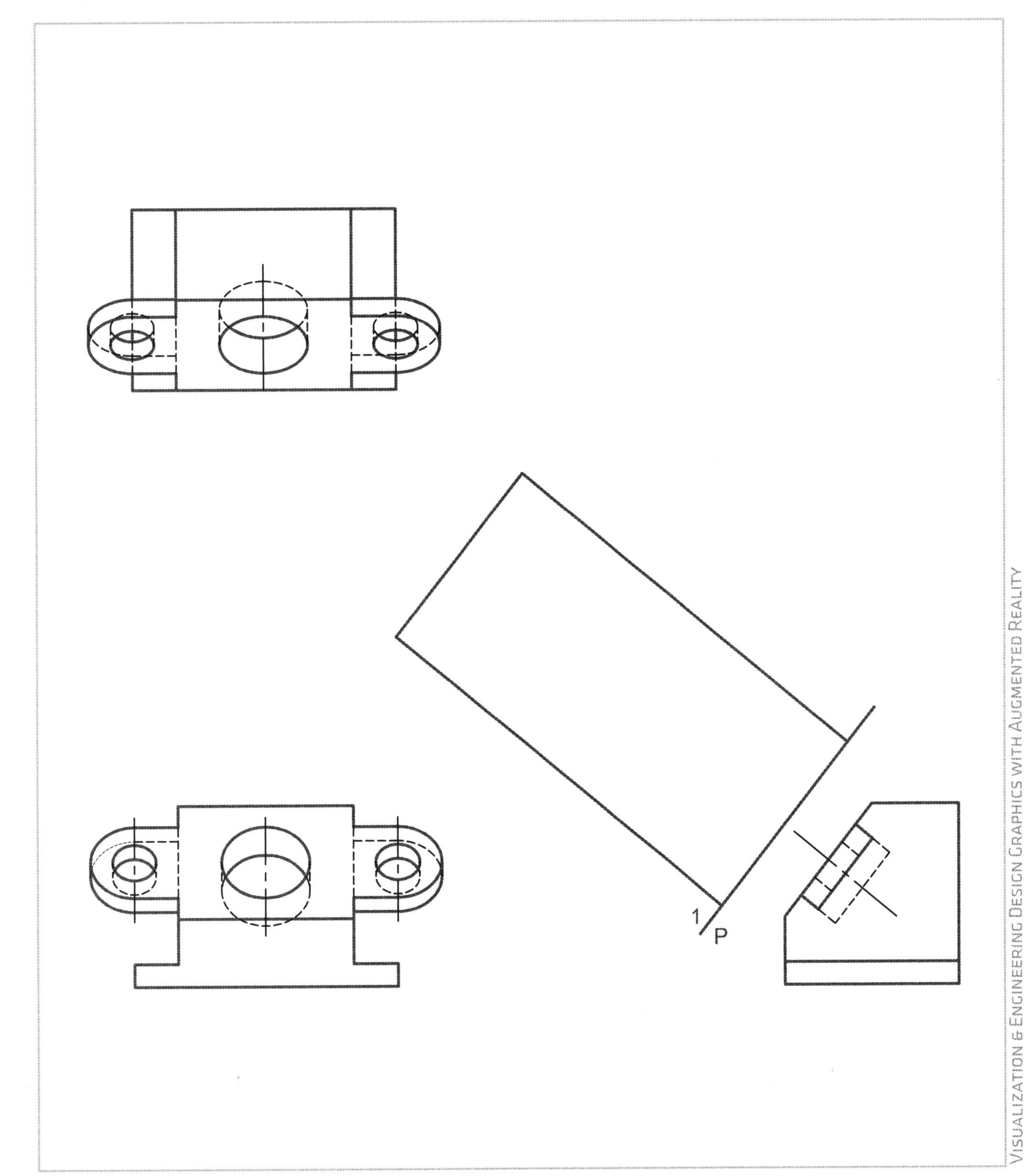

SKETCH THE APPROPRIATE AUXILIARY VIEW.

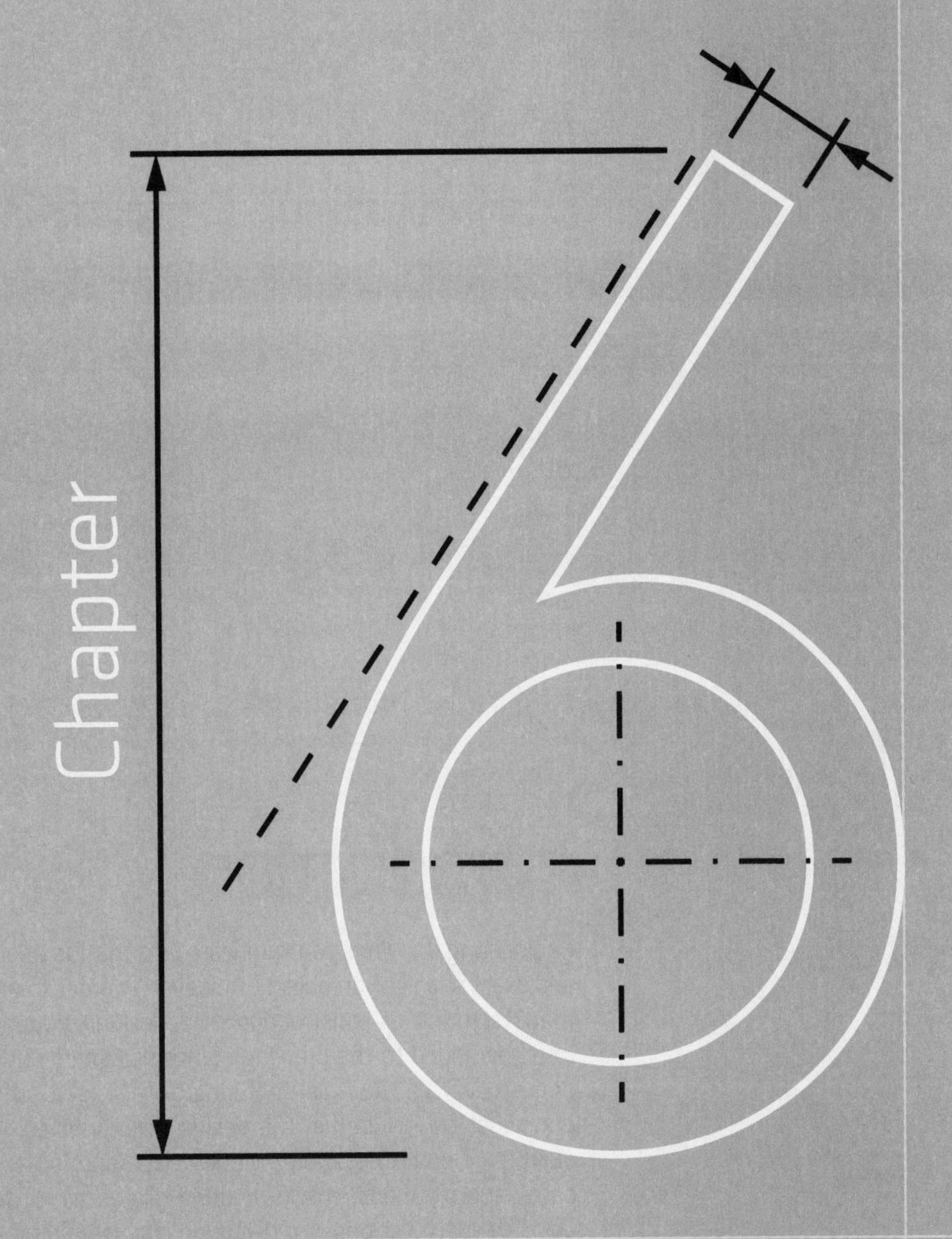

Dimensioning

Introduction

Engineering drawings communicate information about the geometry and exact shape of an object. However, in order to guarantee correct manufacturing or construction of a design, proper documentation must be added to the drawing. Since designers rarely manufacture, or even oversee the manufacturing of their idea, sufficient information must be included in the design document so a third party can build it. This information includes sizes and locations of features, beam specifications, manufacturing processes, or required materials. The specifications included in an engineering drawing need to be clear, concise, and provided in a standard manner to ensure that there are no mistakes or misinterpretations. While it is true that engineers may not complete the final manufacturing documents, they will affix their seal to the final drawings, and by doing so, will assume legal responsibility for the safety of the design.

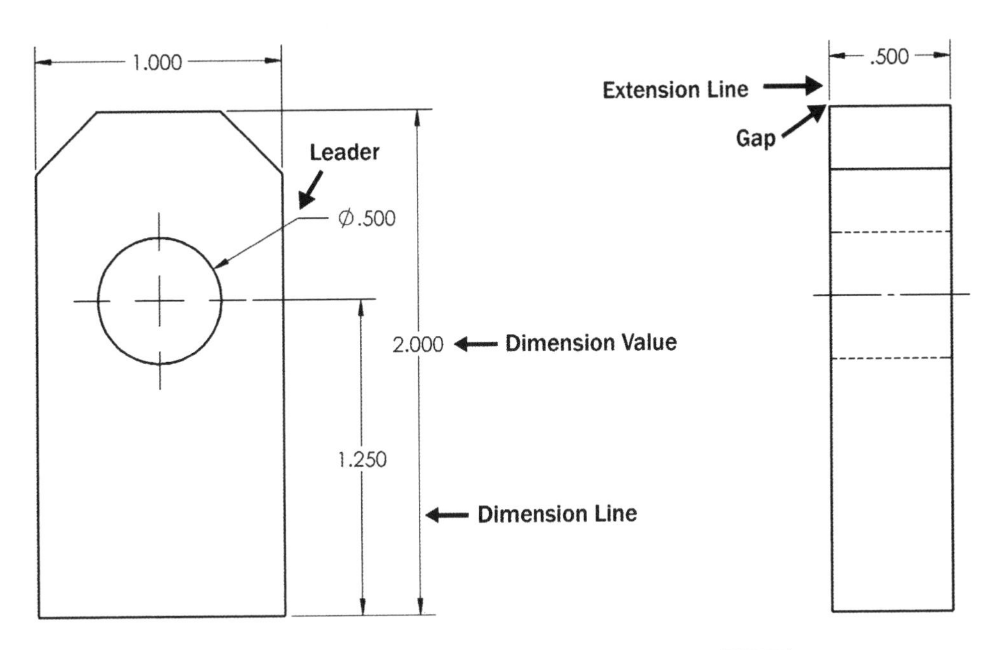

Dimension Terms FIG. 6.1

Dimension Terminology

Dimensioning is the process of adding size information to an engineering drawing. While different standards and industries require different dimensioning styles, the American standard ANSI Y14.5-2009, published by the American Society of Mechanical Engineers (ASME), provides some common practices to properly dimension designs.

Dimensions are comprised of extension lines, dimension lines, arrows, and leaders (see Figure 6.1). All dimension elements are drawn with thin lines (0.25 mm), although they are as dark as all other lines in the drawing. Extension lines are straight lines that extend from the feature being dimensioned, with a small gap (1/16") between the feature and the beginning of the extension line. This gap helps avoid confusion between the extension line and visible lines in the drawing. Dimension lines are straight lines with arrowheads at the ends that extend between two extension lines. The measured value is normally placed in the center of the dimension line. Arrows are usually drawn 1/8" long and 1/24" tall. Leader lines are typically used to dimension circular and curved features. They consist of a line with an arrow and an elbow connecting a specific feature of the drawing to a piece of textual information.

General Dimensioning Rules

The standard ANSI Y14.5M-2009 describes rules and practices that should be considered when dimensioning engineering drawings. Some of these rules are very general in scope and can be applied in many situations. Others are only used in specific domains and applications. In the following sections, you will study common dimensioning practices, starting with the more fundamental rules and finishing with particular cases of dimensioning.

- Both the drawing and the written information should be clear and easy to read; clarity is extremely important. Therefore, dimensions should be placed so that they do not interfere with the drawing and all information is easily understood.
- Drawings should always be fully dimensioned. However, only the minimum number of dimensions necessary should be provided. Do not over-dimension.
- Dimension units should be real-world and are implied. Measurements expressed in inches should not use the inch mark (") or "in" as an abbreviation. Likewise, metric dimensions should omit the "mm" abbreviation. Measurements less than one inch should not have a preceding zero. In metric drawings, measurements less than 1 mm are rare, except in the cases of very small assemblies, such as wrist watches. In these cases, the preceding zero should not be omitted.

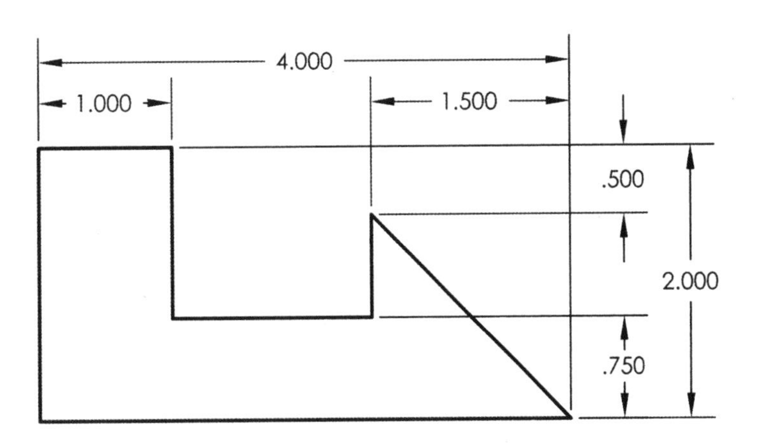

Unidirectional dimensions

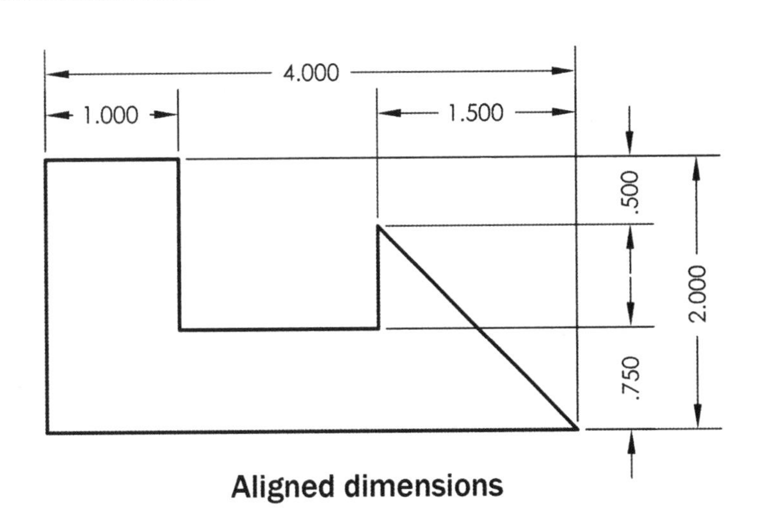

Aligned dimensions

Unidirectional dimensions vs. aligned dimensions FIG. 6.2

DIMENSIONING STYLES

Two dimensioning styles can be used based on the direction in which the text is oriented. Unidirectional dimensions appear in a horizontal position, with the text being read from right to left, even if the dimension lines are drawn top to bottom. Aligned dimensions are created with the text aligned with the direction of the dimension lines. Both dimensioning styles are correct. However, your drawings must be consistent. It is considered bad practice to use different dimensioning styles in the same drawing or set of drawings. Industry and company guidelines are generally the factors that will determine the style you will use. An example of unidirectional and aligned dimensions is shown in Figure 6.2

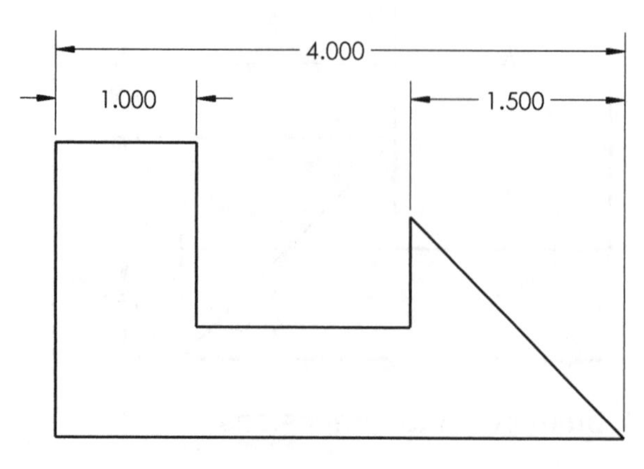

Correct Spacing

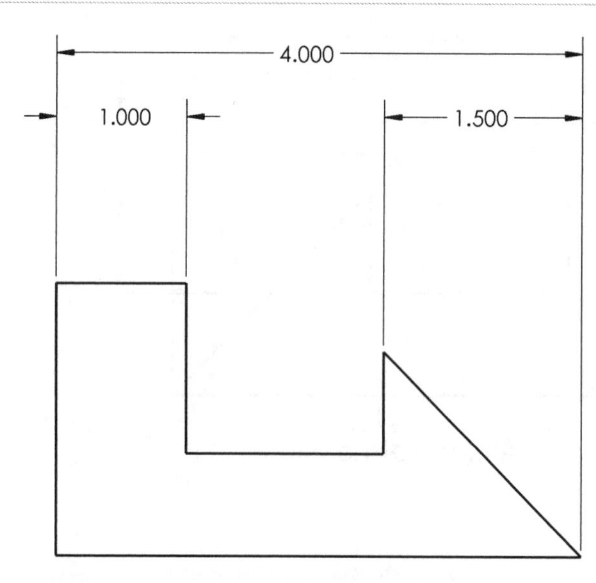

Incorrect Spacing

FIG. 6.3 Dimension spacing

DIMENSION SPACING

Dimensions need to be properly spaced in order to reduce confusion and increase readability. In general, the first row of dimensions should be located 3/8" away from the object being dimensioned, with each additional row being placed 1/4" away from the previous dimension. Placing dimensions at increased distances will also waste space, which is a primary concern when dimensioning (see Figure 6.3).

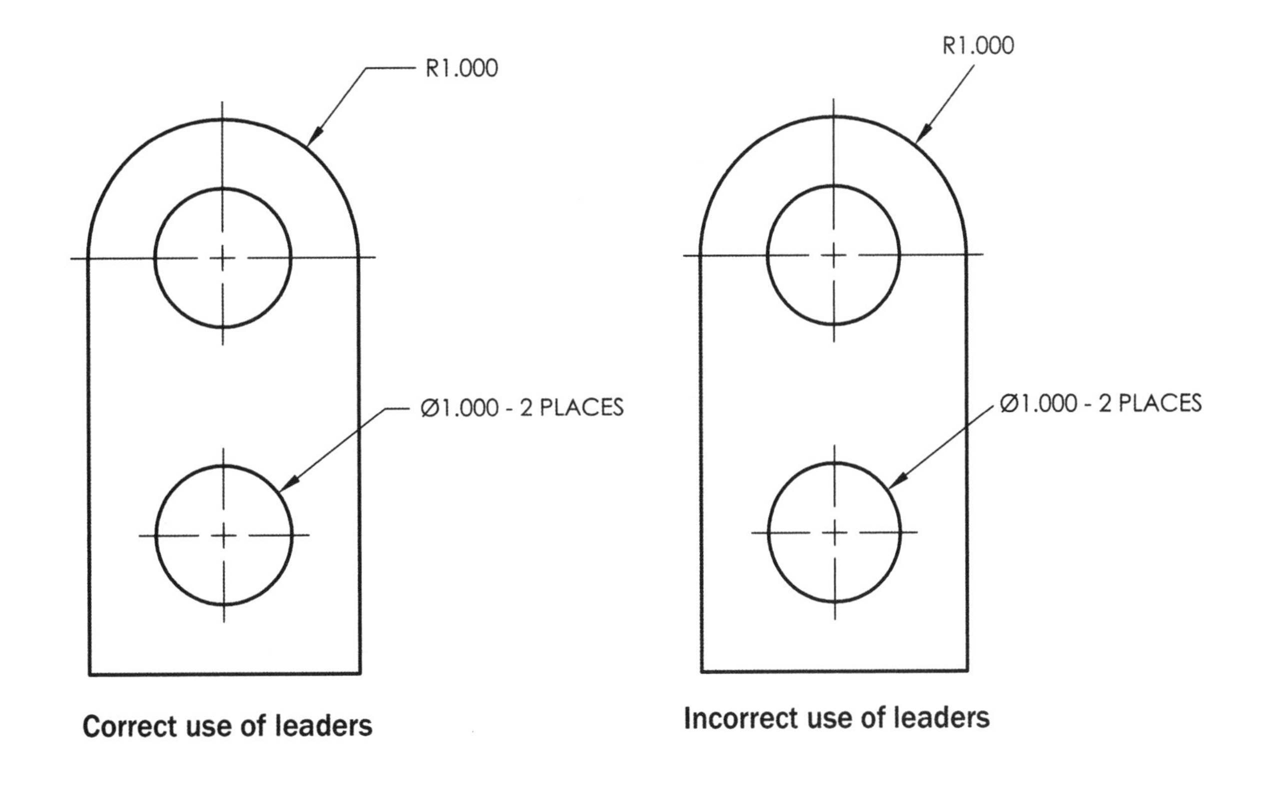

Use of leaders FIG. 6.4

USE OF LEADERS

Leaders are used to connect a feature of the drawing to specific information (in the form of a textual note) needed about that feature. Leaders originate from either the beginning or end of the note, with an elbow and arrow provided. Leaders can be used to dimension hole diameters, repetitive features (which will be discussed later), and thread notes. See Figure 6.4 for an example.

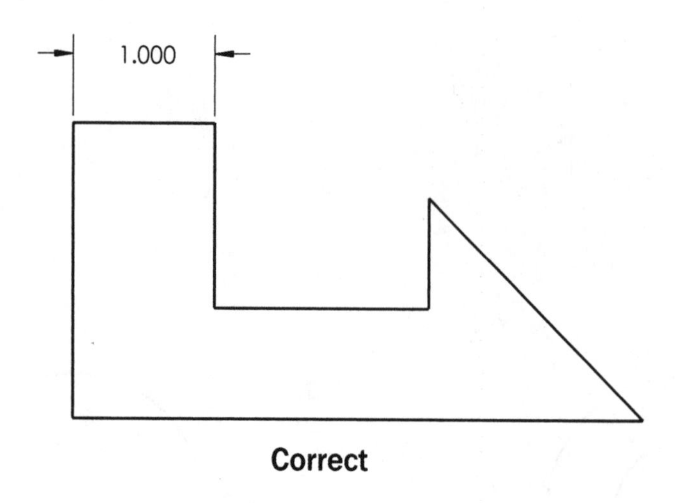

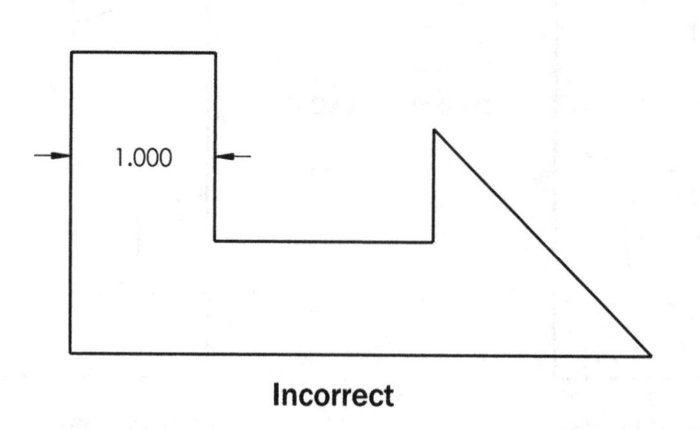

FIG. 6.5 Dimensions are placed outside the orthographic views

PLACE DIMENSIONS OUTSIDE VIEWS

Do not place any dimensions inside an orthographic view or use visible lines as extension lines, if possible. While dimensions inside (or on) pictorial views are common, dimensions located within standard orthographic views should be avoided. If more room is required to properly dimension the object, place the orthographic views further apart from one another to provide adequate room and spacing. See Figure 6.5 for an example. In complex drawings with many features, however, dimensions often have to be placed inside views.

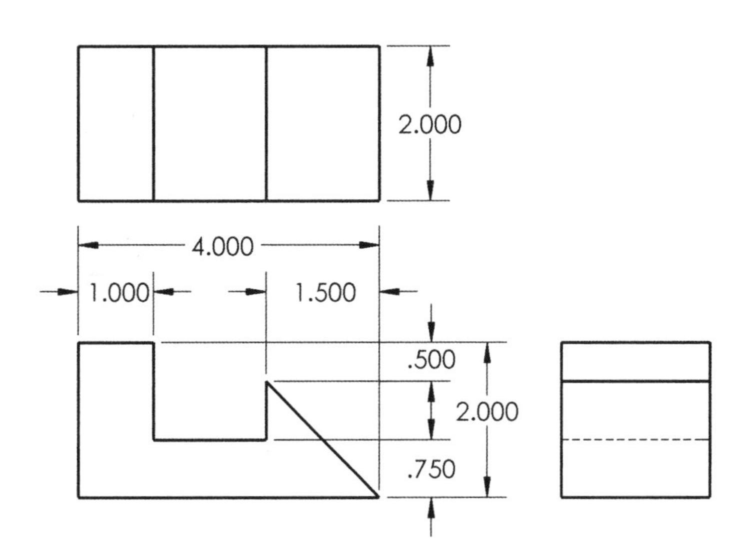

Correct

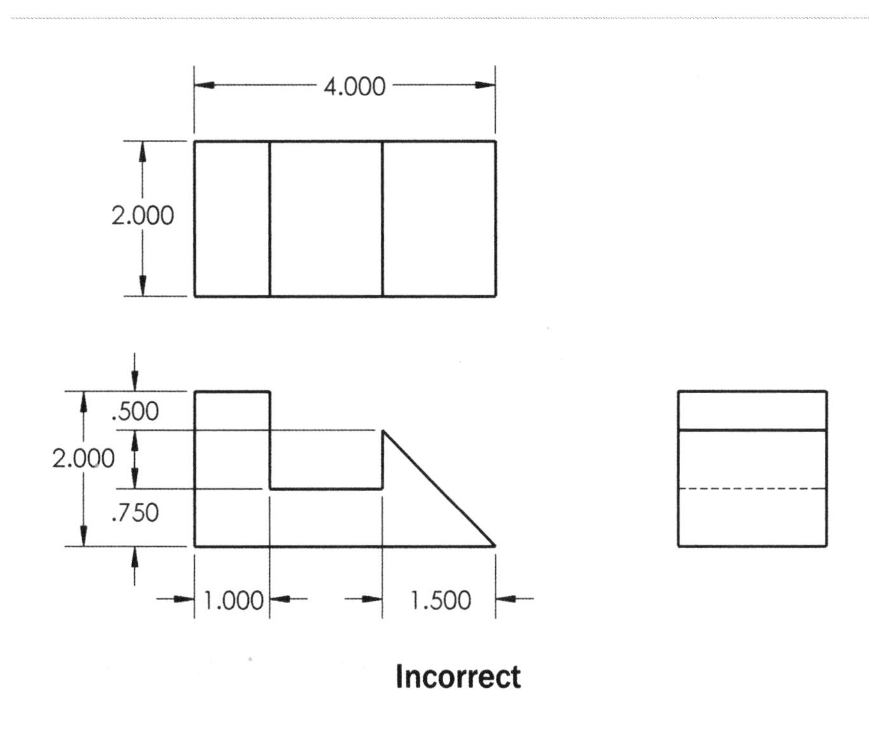

Incorrect

Dimensions are placed between orthographic views 

Place Dimensions Between Views

In order to save space, most dimensions should be placed between the orthographic views, if possible. Since it is possible (or even preferable) to place more than one object on a drawing, placing dimensions between views will reduce confusion. See Figure 6.6 for an example.

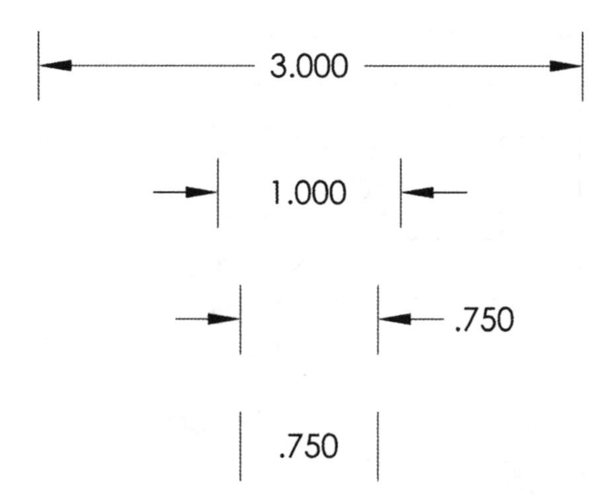

FIG. 6.7 Selected dimension features can be omitted for reasons of space

Omission of Dimension Features

There are instances in which there is not enough space in the drawing for all the elements of a linear dimension (two extension lines, a dimension line, two arrows, and the measured value). In these cases, it is appropriate to omit certain dimension features without decreasing clarity. It is acceptable to place the dimension value outside the extension lines, to omit arrows, or to even omit the dimension lines. The examples shown in Figure 6.7 illustrate some of these situations.

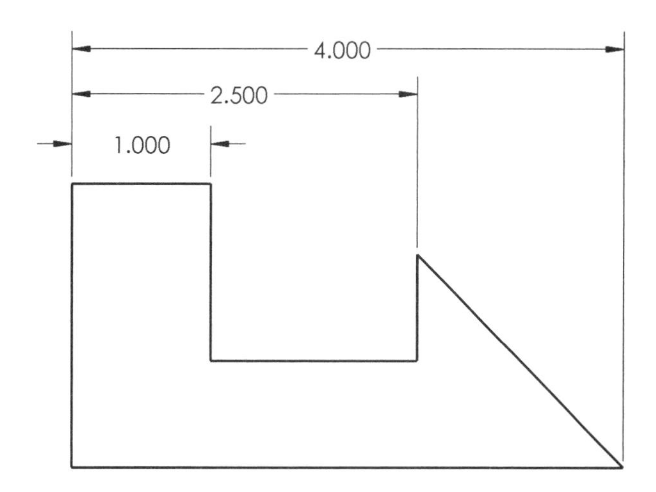

Baseline

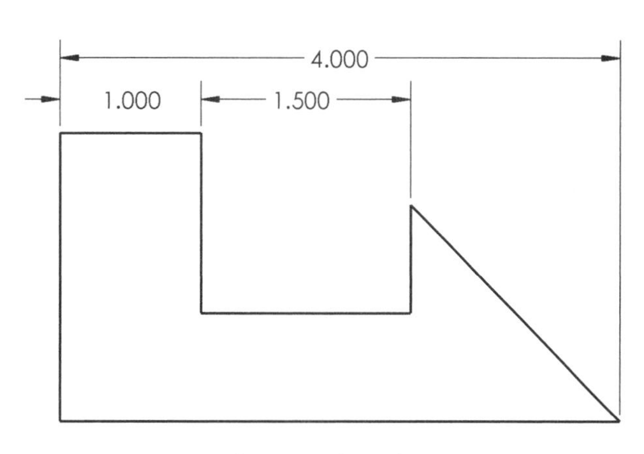

Conventional

Baseline vs. Conventional Dimensioning FIG. 6.8

Conventional Dimensions Vs. Baseline Dimensions

Two techniques are commonly used in dimensioning. Conventional dimensions provide an overall length dimension, located furthest away from the object, with intermediate dimensions place closer to the object. One intermediate dimension is omitted, because it can be calculated easily using the existing dimensions. Baseline dimensions originate from a single baseline, with each feature requiring a new row of dimensions. Baseline dimensions are more accurate and readable, but require more space than conventional dimensions. One advantage of using baseline dimensions is that if a mistake is made when manufacturing one feature, that mistake is not carried through to the subsequent features. See Figure 6.8 for an example.

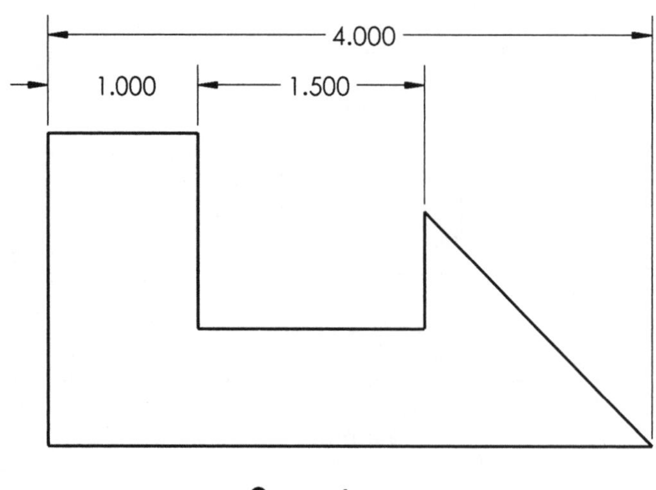

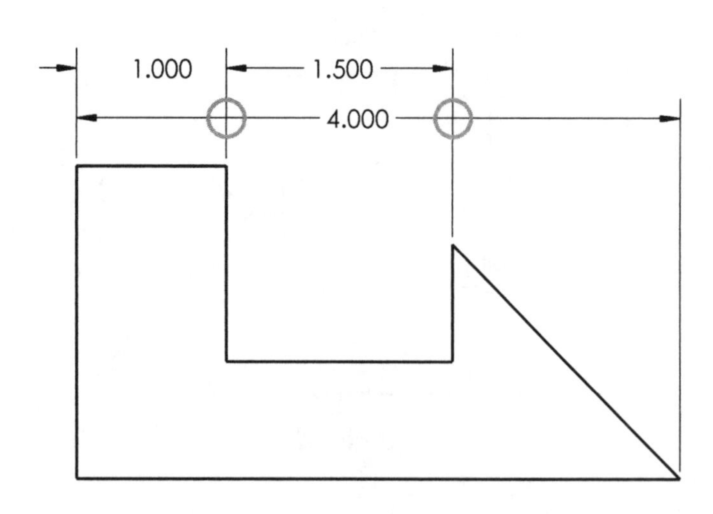

FIG. 6.9 Do not cross dimension lines

Do Not Cross Dimension Lines

While it is acceptable for visible lines in the drawing and extension lines in the dimension to intersect, it is considered bad practice to cross dimension lines. Also, extension lines should avoid crossing other extension lines whenever possible. This problem can be avoided if the largest dimension is always placed furthest away from the object. See Figure 6.9 for an example.

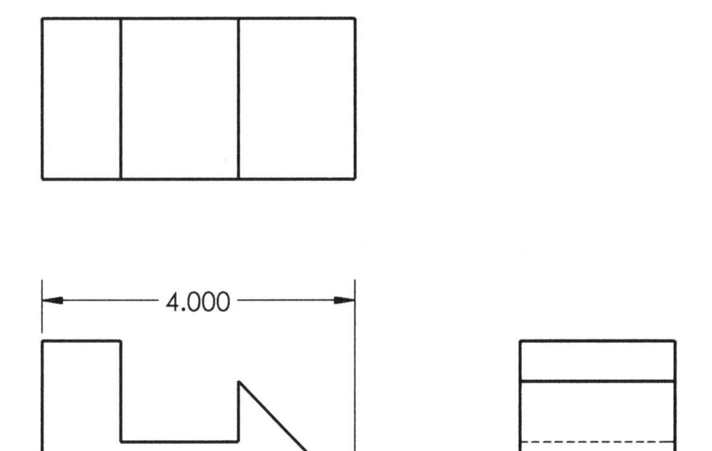

Correct dimension placement

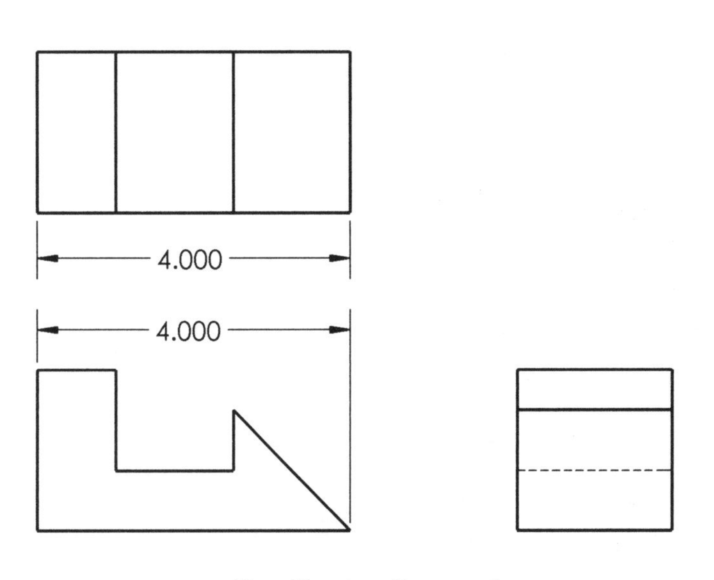

Duplicate dimension

Over-dimensioning FIG. 6.10

Do Not Over-Dimension

Use the minimum number of dimensions necessary to describe the object; do not duplicate dimensions. If a dimension can be calculated using other dimensions in the drawing, then such dimension can be implied and needs not to be provided explicitly in the drawing. See Figure 6.10 for an example.

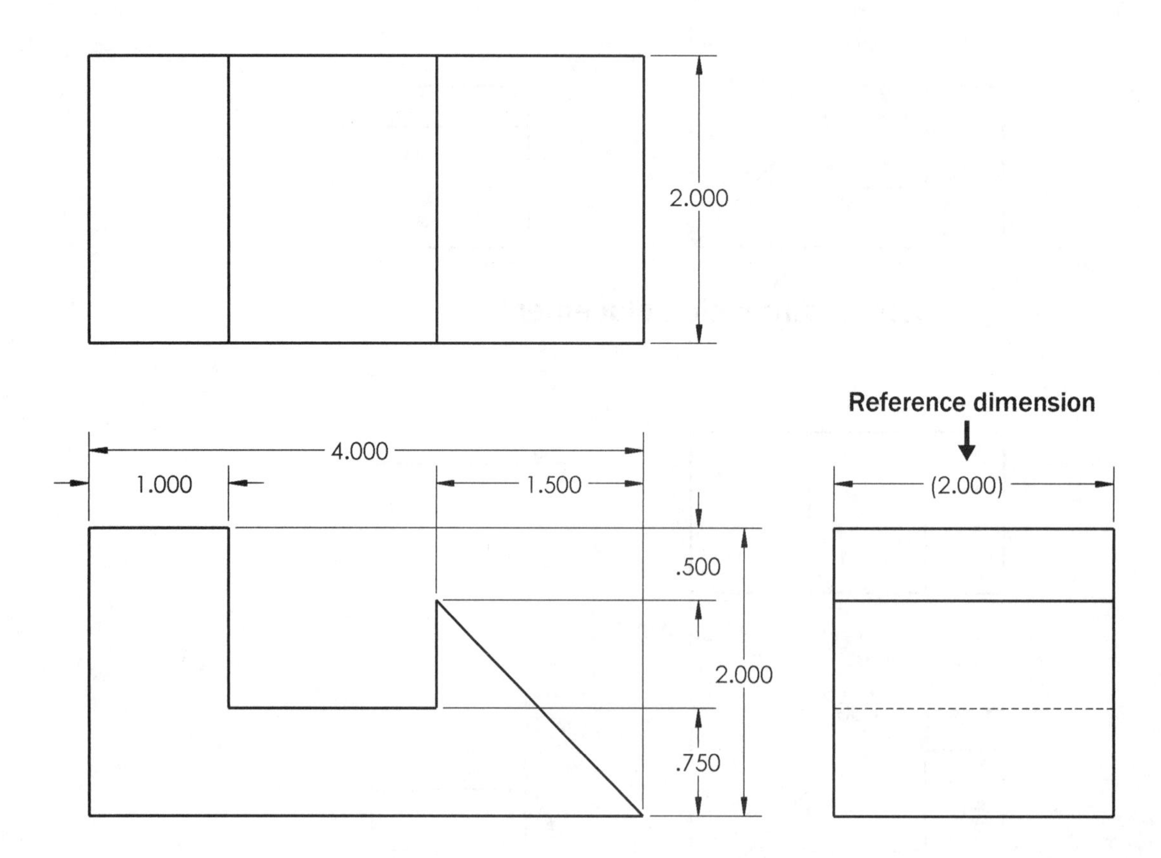

FIG. 6.11 Proper use of reference dimensions

USE OF REFERENCE DIMENSIONS

If there is a particular need to provide the same dimension twice (in different views) you can use reference dimensions. In certain situations, duplicating a dimension may eliminate the need to perform calculations and facilitate the understanding of the drawing. These duplicate dimensions are known as reference dimensions and must be either placed between parentheses of have the notation "REF" placed next to it. See Figure 6.11 for an example.

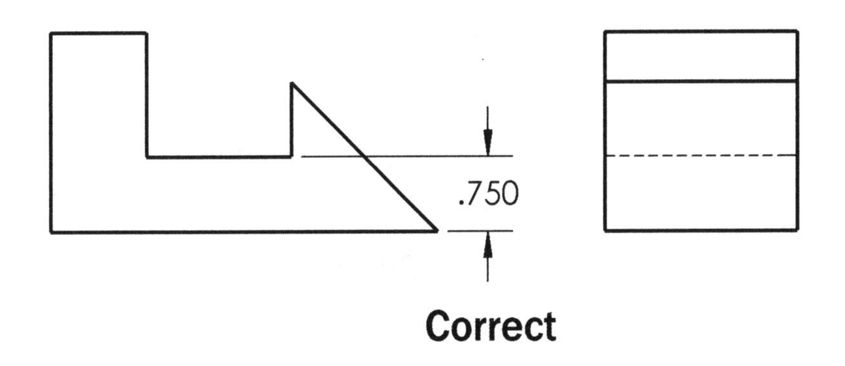

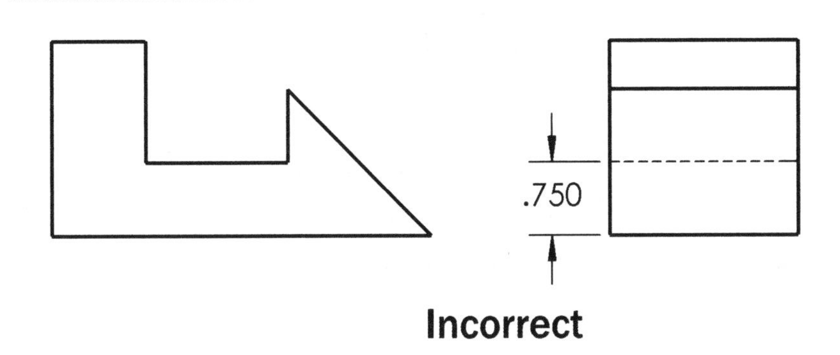

Do not dimension to hidden lines FIG. 6.12

Do Not Dimension to Hidden Lines

Always dimension to visible lines, if possible. If some feature cannot be seen as a visible line in any orthographic view, the solution is to create a sectioned orthographic view and dimension the feature in that view. Sectioned orthographic views will be discussed in later chapters. See Figure 6.12 for an example.

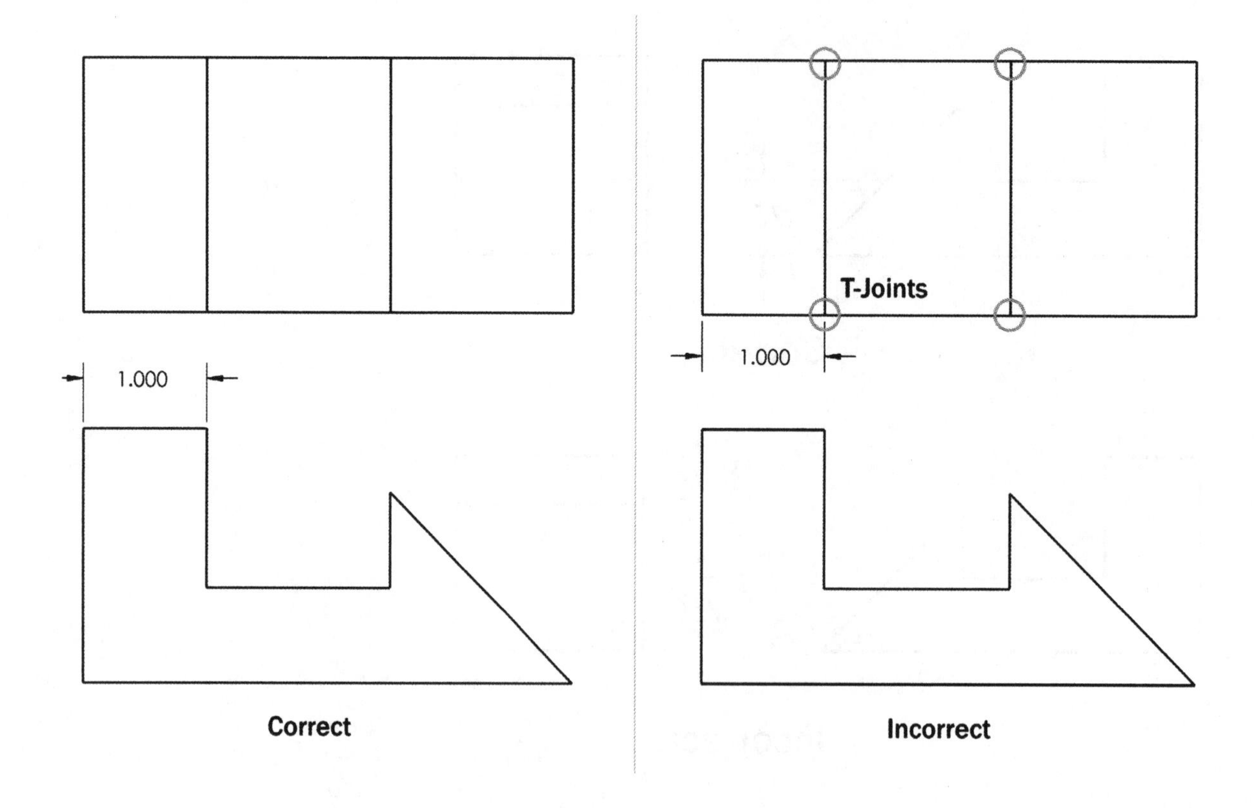

FIG. 6.13 Do not dimension to T-joints

Do Not Dimension To T-Joints

Apply as many dimensions as possible in the most descriptive view. Edge views will occasionally appear as right angle intersections in the form of the capital letter "T". These intersections are known as "T-Joints" and cannot be used for dimensioning. Edges appearing as T-Joints must be dimensioned in a view where they will appear as corners. See Figure 6.13 for an example.

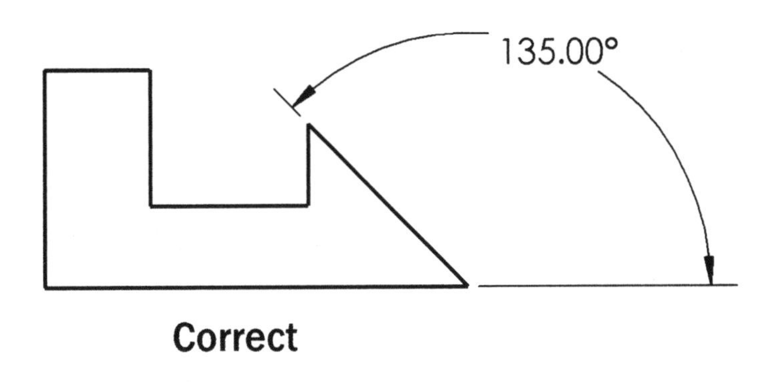

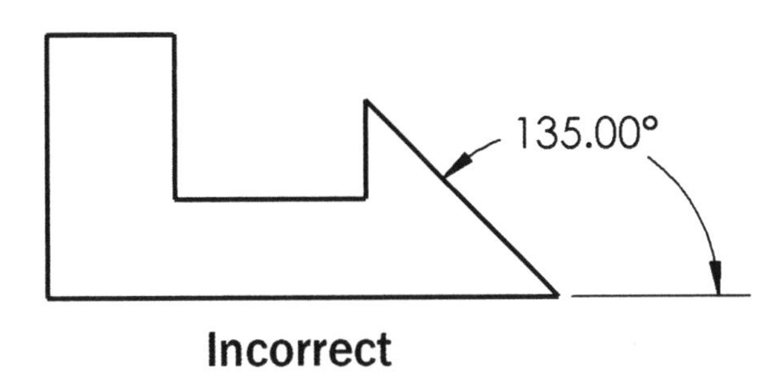

Correct placement of angular dimensions FIG. 6.14

DIMENSIONING ANGLED FEATURES

Angular features are dimensioned by constructing the extension lines a short distance past the visible lines denoting the feature. Objects with angled features can also be dimensioned by locating each vertex with linear dimensions, which oftentimes requires less space. See Figure 6.14 for an example.

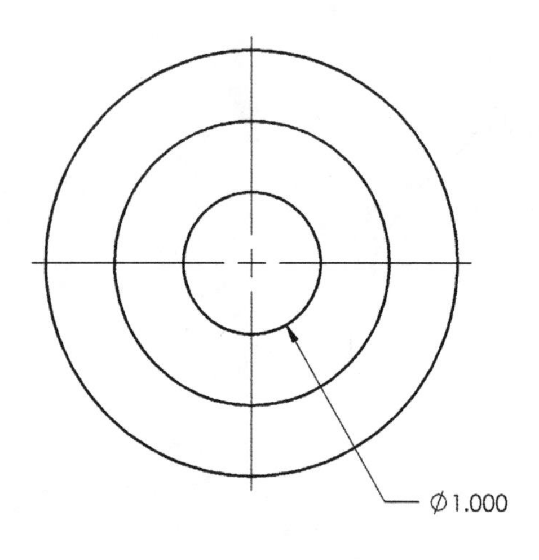

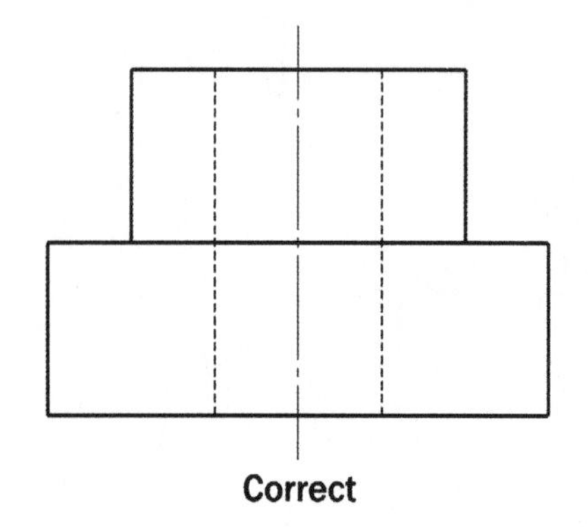

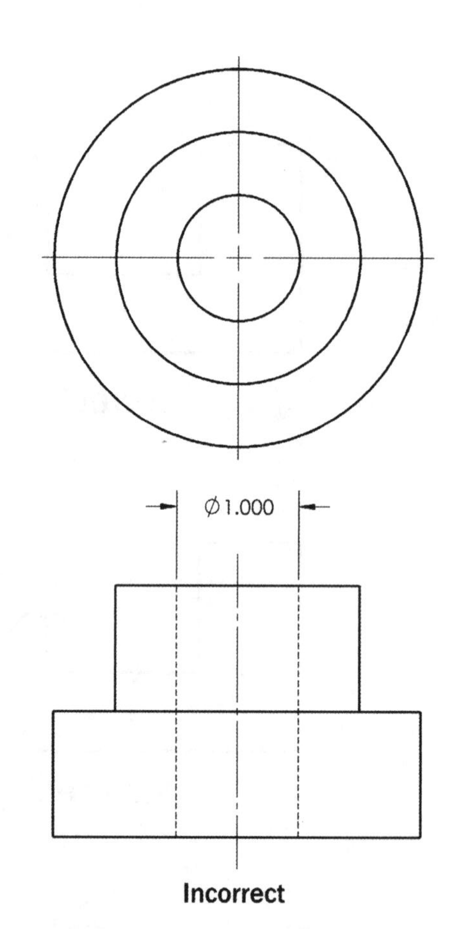

FIG. 6.16 Correct dimensioning of holes

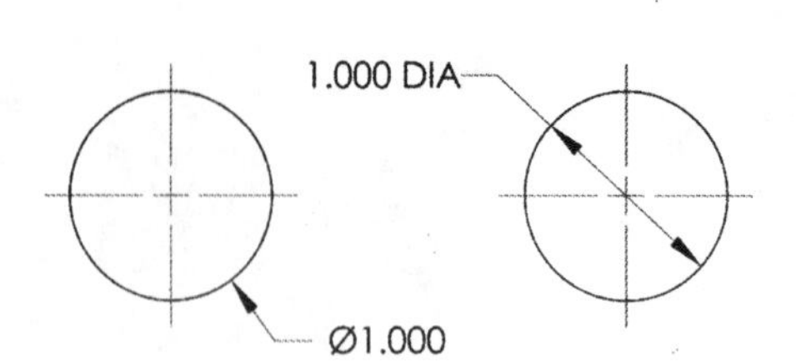

FIG. 6.15 Proper circle dimensioning

Dimensioning Circles

Circular features are dimensioned by constructing a leader, with an arrow pointing toward the center of the circle, or by drawing a chord the entire length of the diameter with arrows pointing diametrically outward. Circles are dimensioned with the diameter, either the ø symbol preceding the dimension or "DIA" placed after the dimension. See Figure 6.15 for examples.

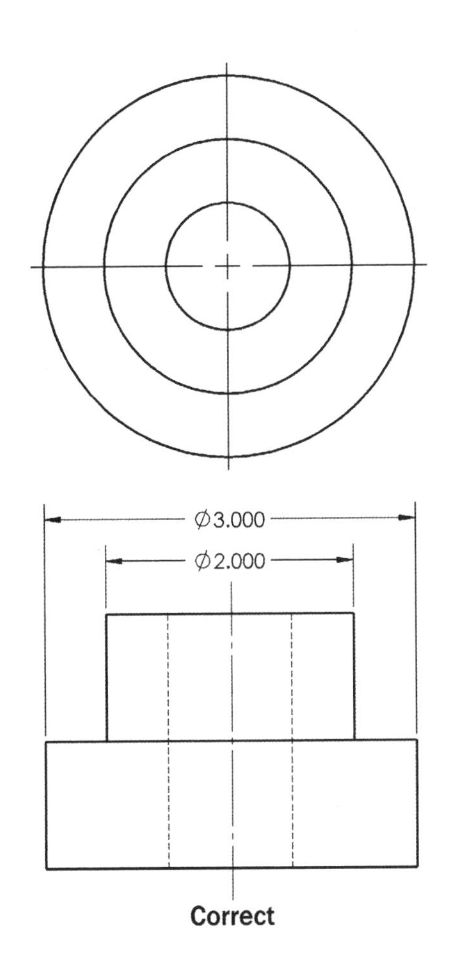

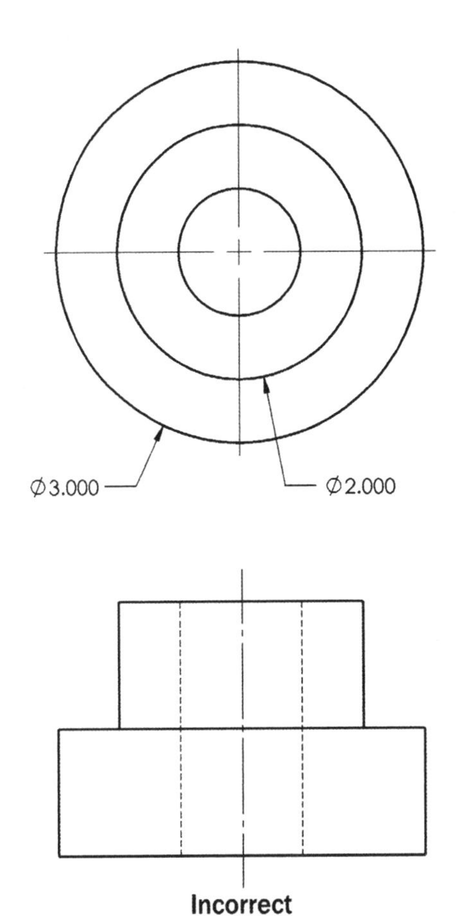

Correct dimensioning of cylinders FIG. 6.17

DIMENSIONING HOLES AND CYLINDERS

Holes should always be located and dimensioned in the view where they appear as circles. Cylinders, meanwhile, should always be located and dimensioned in the view where they appear as rectangles. See Figure 6.16 and Figure 6.17.

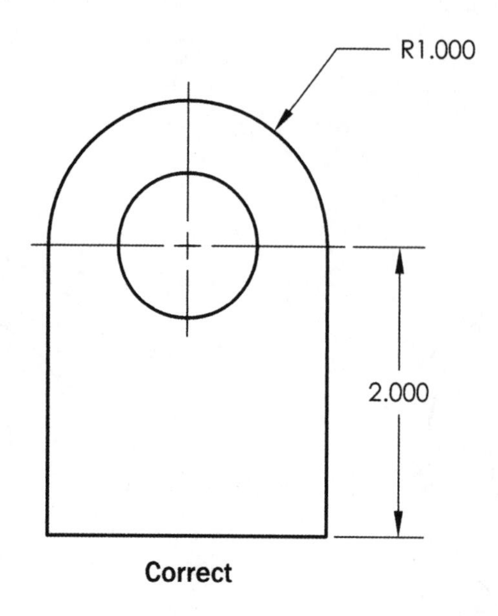

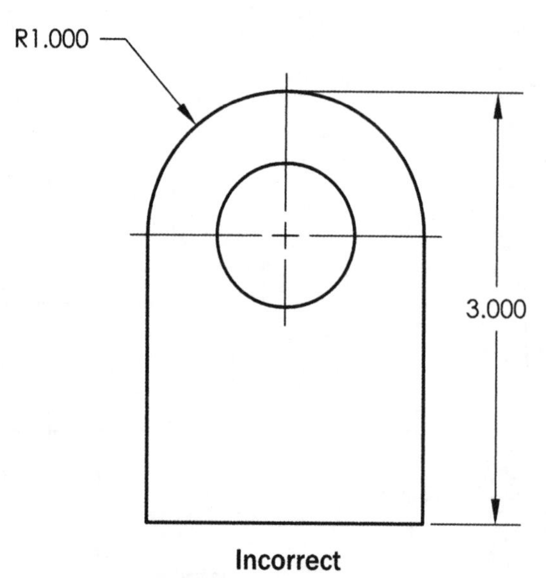

FIG. 6.18 Dimensioning of rounded corners

Dimensioning Objects with Rounded Ends

Objects with rounded ends should always be dimensioned with radii in their rounded views, using the center lines as extension lines. The abbreviation "R" will always precede such dimensions. As a general rule, arcs 180˚ or less are dimensioned with the radius, while arcs greater than 180˚ are dimensioned with the diameter. See Figure 6.18 for an example.

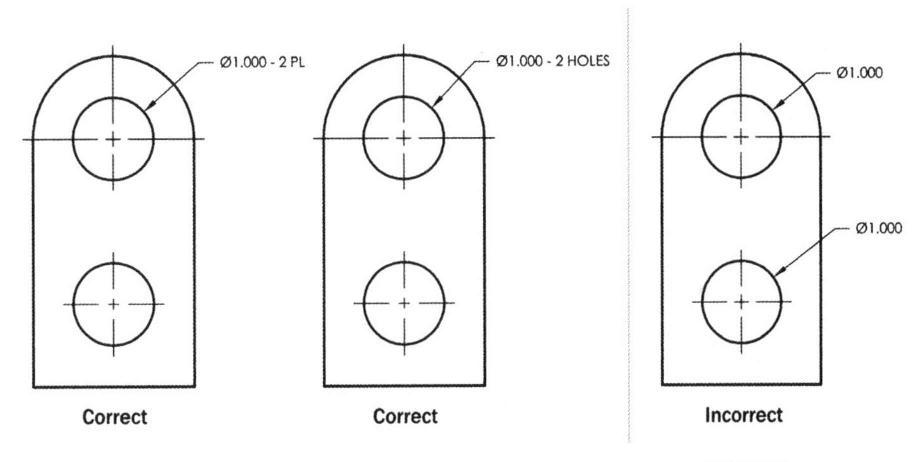

Dimensioning repetitive features FIG. 6.19

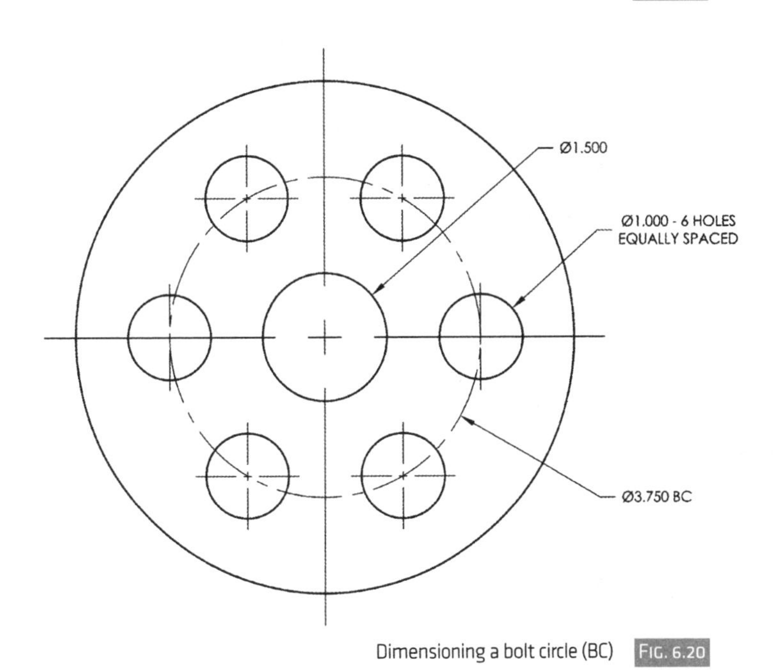

Dimensioning a bolt circle (BC) FIG. 6.20

Repetitive Features

Objects with repetitive features are oftentimes dimensioned with notes in order to conserve space. For instance, if an object has several holes of the same diameter, only one hole is dimensioned. This dimension is then edited to show the common information with the remaining holes. Common abbreviations include "PL" for places, "EA" for each, and "TYP" for typical, indicating that all features share the same characteristic. See Figure 6.19 for some examples.

Bolt circles are great examples of objects with repetitive features. Circular objects with equally spaced features, such as holes, can be easily dimensioned by applying notes. Bolt circles are constructed by drawing a centerline through the center of each hole in the pattern, and providing a note reflecting the similar diameter dimensions and spacing. See Figure 6.20 for an example.

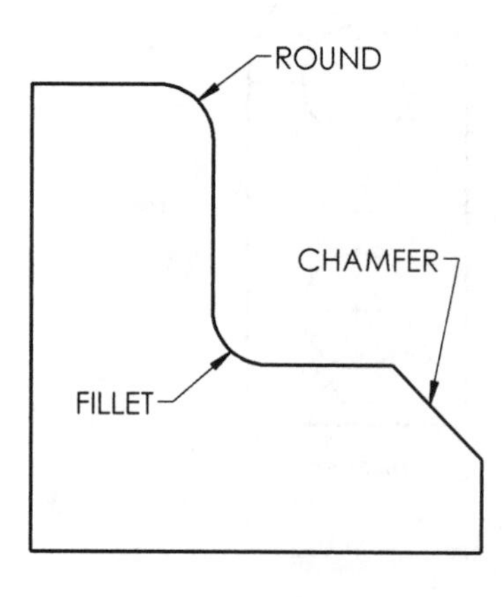

FIG. 6.21 Chamfers, fillets, and rounds

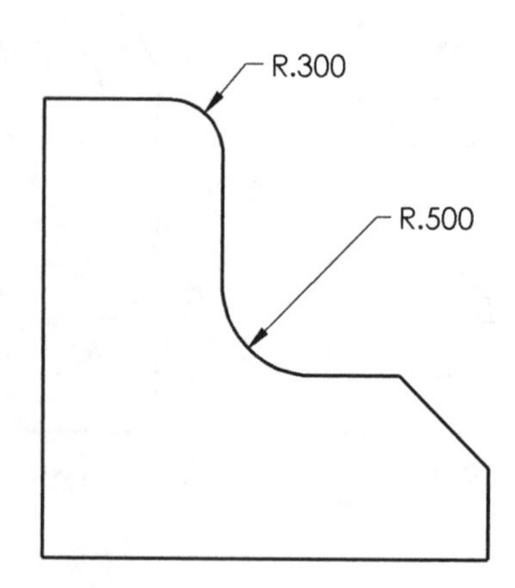

FIG. 6.23 Dimensioning fillets and rounds

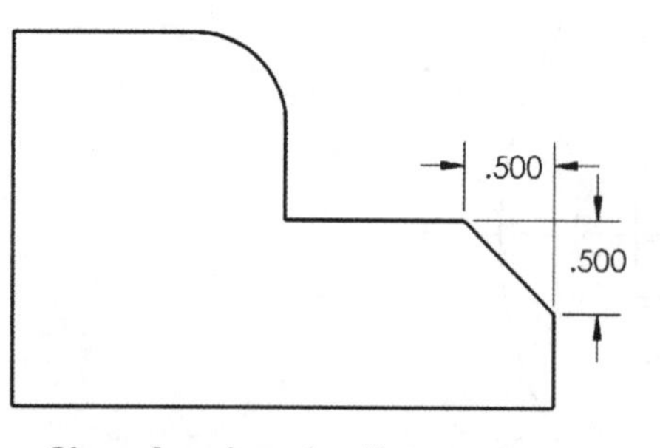

Chamfer given by distances

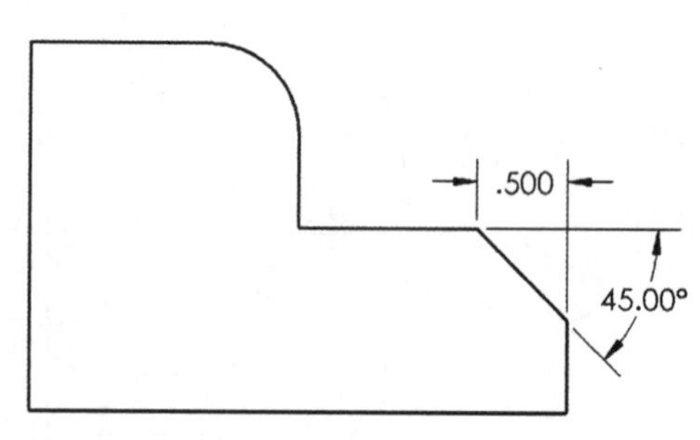

Chamfer given by distance and angle

FIG. 6.22 Dimensioning chamfers

Chamfers, Fillets, and Rounds

Chamfers are beveled edges that connect surfaces of an object in order to physically remove sharp edges encountered on machined parts. Fillets are rounded edges formed between the inside angle of two intersecting surfaces, while rounds are rounded edges formed between the outside angles of two intersecting surfaces (see Figure 6.21). Fillets and rounds help reduce stress and strengthen the connection between surfaces. Chamfers can be dimensioned by showing the horizontal and vertical distances of the feature or by providing the horizontal distance with the associated angle (see Figure 6.22). They can also be dimensioned by addition of a note. Both fillets and rounds are dimensioned with the radius, or with a note. See Figure 6.23.

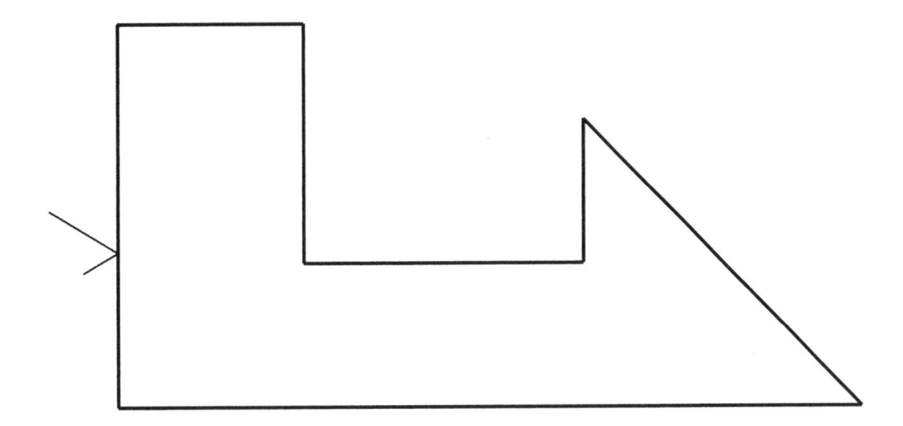

Finish mark FIG. 6.24

General Notes

Oftentimes, in order to adequately dimension an object or assembly, textual notes are required in addition to the standard dimensions already provided. Notes can be added to further specify manufacturing procedures, requirements for vendor items, or to reduce the amount of dimensions added to the orthographic views. As an example, if the radii of all fillets in an object are .500 inches, a note such as "ALL FILLETS R .500" can be included in the drawing, replacing multiple leader lines and dimensions.

Common examples of general notes include "FINISH ALL OVER (FAO)", or "BREAK SHARP EDGES TO R.50".

Finished Surfaces

Cast objects, by definition, have rough, pitted surfaces. Occasionally these surfaces need to be smoothed for better contact between mating parts or so that more accurate measurements can be made. This smoothing procedure is referred to as finishing. In engineering drawings, a finished surface is denoted by the addition of a "check mark" placed directly on the visible line representing the finished surface (see Figure 6.24).

Description	Abbreviation	Symbol
Diameter	DIA	Ø
Depth	DP	↧
Counter bored	CBORE or CB	⌴
Spot faced	SFACE or SF	⌴
Countersunk	CSINK or CSK	⌵
Counter drilled	CDRILL or CD	*No symbol*

FIG. 6.25 Standard hole callout symbols and abbreviations

Machined Holes

Holes are one of the most common features found in manufacturing. They are openings in an object that serve many purposes, such as providing an aperture to receive a fastener or reducing the amount of material used to construct a part. Machined holes are more precise than cast holes and are typically made with cutting devices, such as a counterbore tool. Machined holes have varying profiles, depending upon their intended purpose. Common machined holes include thru holes, drilled blind holes, counterbore, spot face, countersink, and counterdrilled holes.

Machined holes are generally dimensioned with notes that include special symbols, instead of dimensioning each specific feature of the hole profile. The hole's note is typically referred to as the "hole callout." Common dimension information provided in machined holes includes diameter, hole depth, a symbol indicating the hole type, and other information such as the angle of countersink. A hole is assumed to be a "THRU" hole (hole passes entirely through the object) unless the depth is specified. Common abbreviations and symbols are shown in Figure 6.25. In the following sections, the proper dimensioning techniques for different types of machined holes will be discussed.

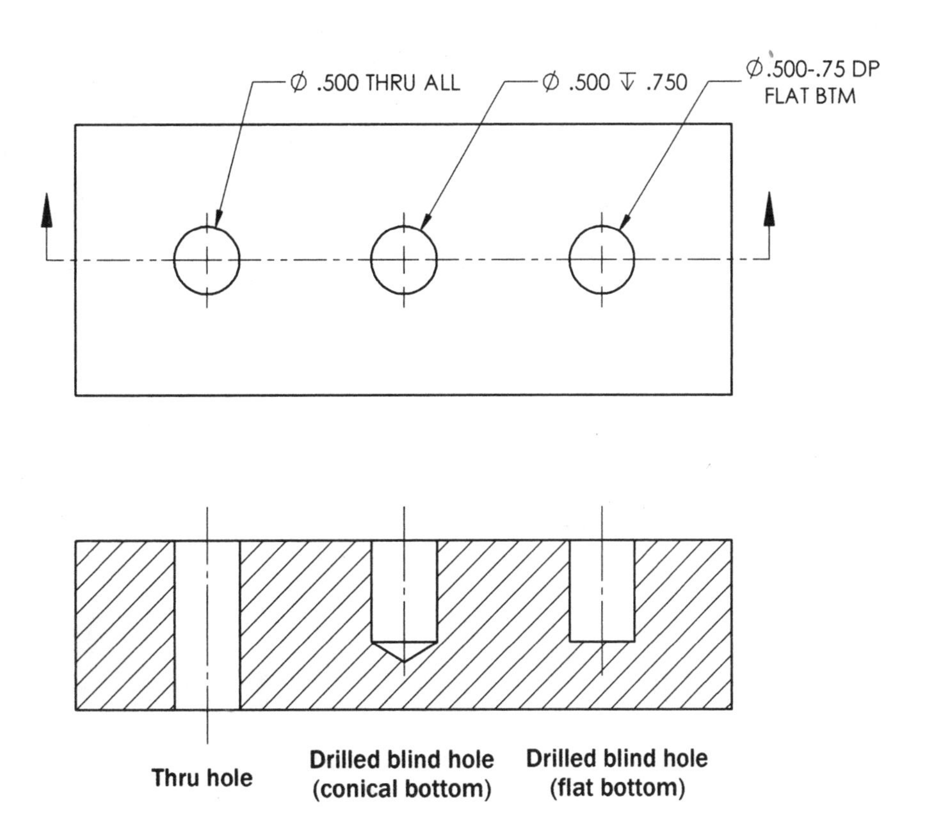

Proper dimensioning of simple hole profiles FIG. 6.26

HOLE TYPE

Thru holes are the simplest holes, pass entirely through the object, and are constructed with a drill bit. Drilled blind holes do not pass completely through the object and can have either flat or conically shaped bottoms, depending upon the application (see Figure 6.26). Drilled Blind holes must have the depth of the hole provided in the dimension.

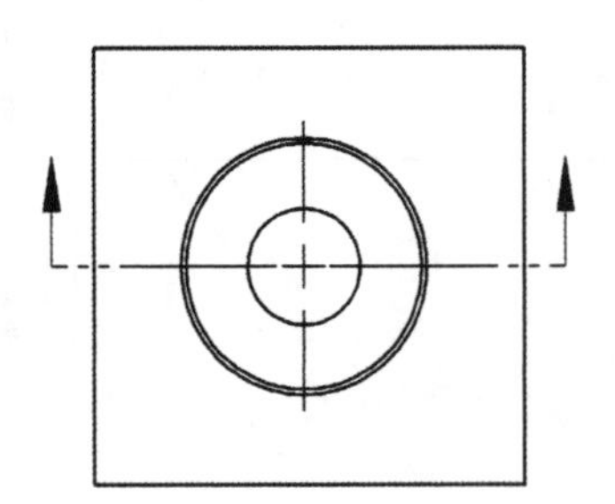

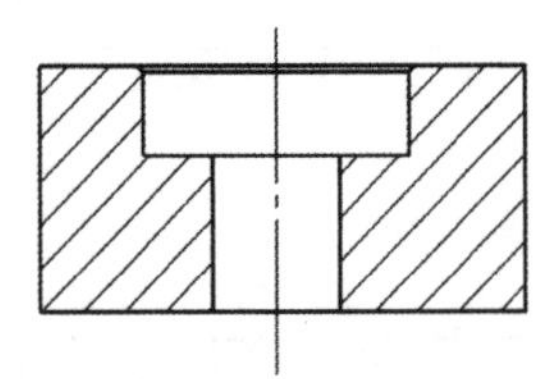

Fig. 6.27 Counterbored hole profile

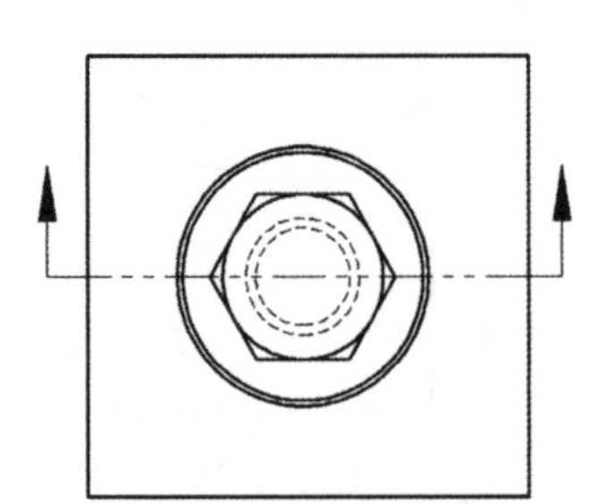

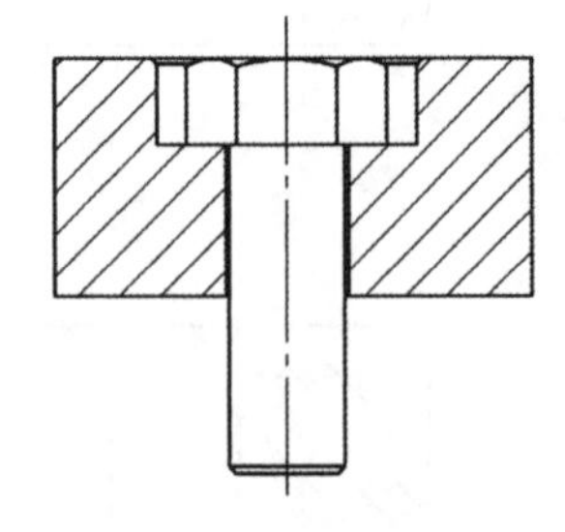

Fig. 6.28 Counterbored hole with fastener

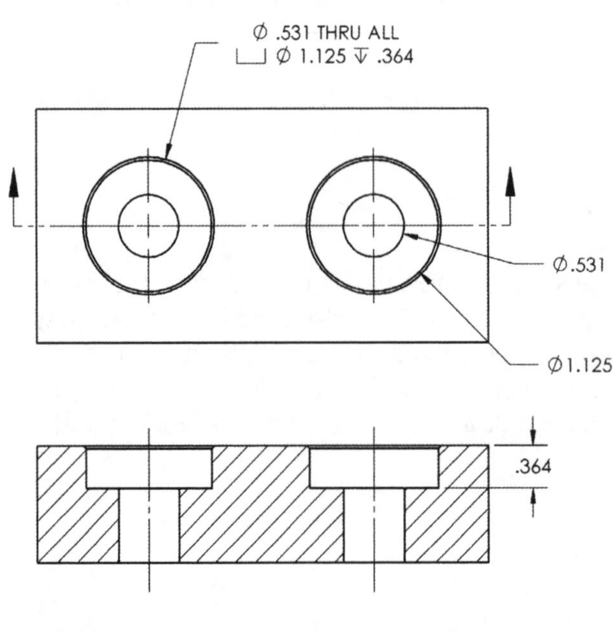

Fig. 6.29 Proper dimensioning of counterbored holes (left) and location of the dimensions (right)

Counterbore holes, shown in Figure 6.27, are used when hex head cap screws are required to sit level or below the surface of the part (see Figure 6.28).

The left hole shown in Figure 6.29 demonstrates the proper way to dimension a counterbored hole. The right hole is provided for illustration purposes only, so the student can identify the location of the dimensions given by the note.

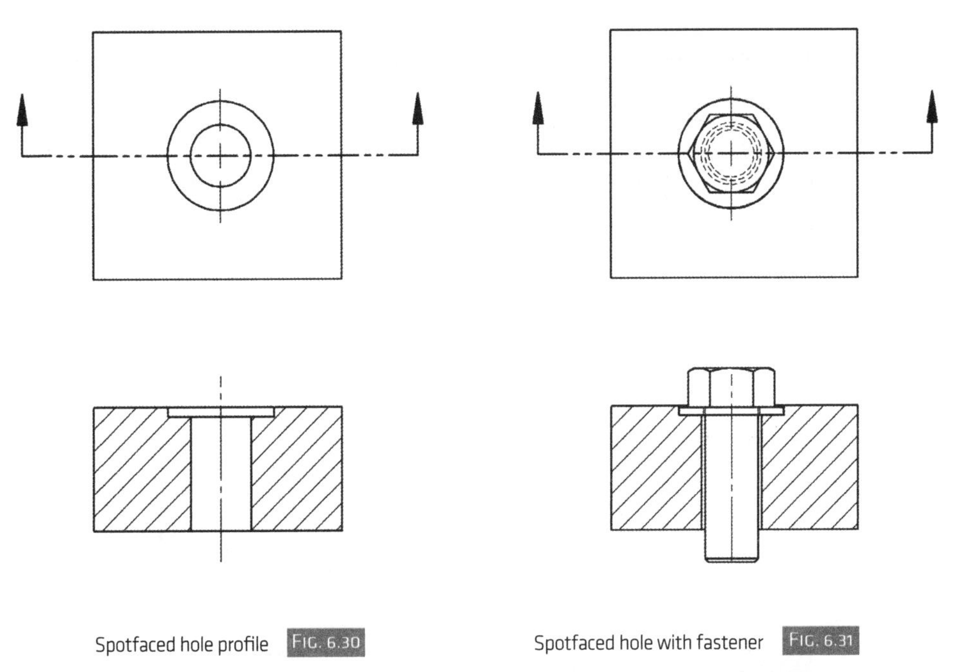

Spotfaced hole profile Fig. 6.30

Spotfaced hole with fastener Fig. 6.31

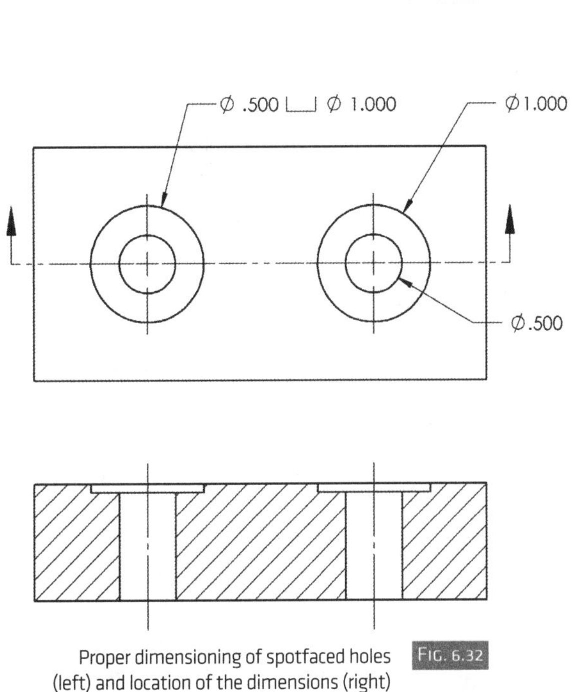

Proper dimensioning of spotfaced holes (left) and location of the dimensions (right) Fig. 6.32

Spot faced holes are counterbored holes, with a shallow counterbored used to smooth the surface of the part (see Figure 6.30). The depth of the counterbored feature is left to the judgment of the machinist and thus, not dimensioned in the drawing. This smoothing is required in cast or forged surfaces to provide better contact between the object and the fastener (see Figure 6.31).

The left hole shown in Figure 6.32 demonstrates the proper way to dimension a spotfaced hole. Notice that the depth of the counterbored feature is not dimensioned. The right hole is provided for illustration purposes only, so the student can identify the location of the dimensions given by the note.

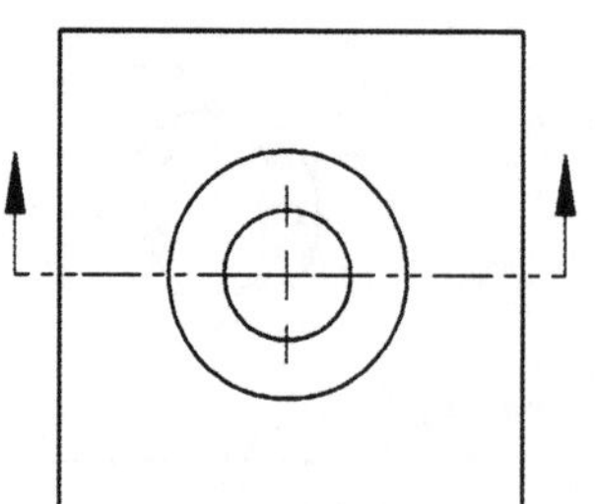

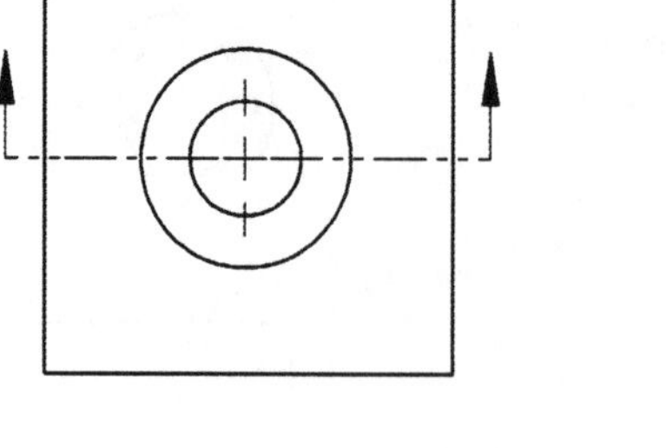

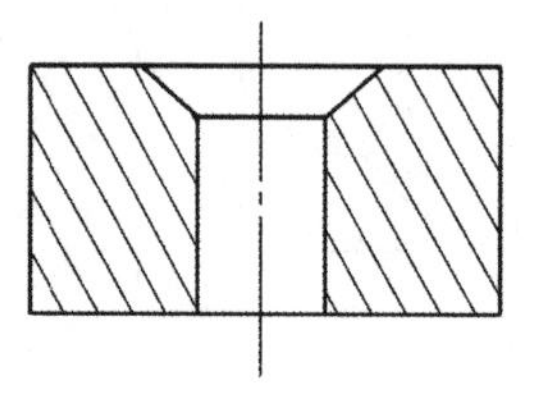

FIG. 6.33 Countersunk hole profile

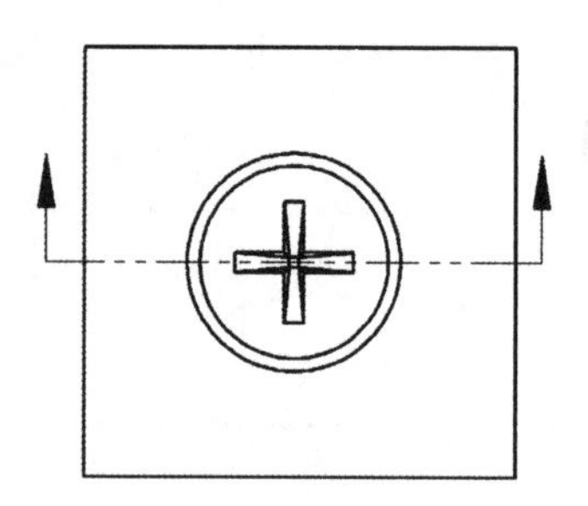

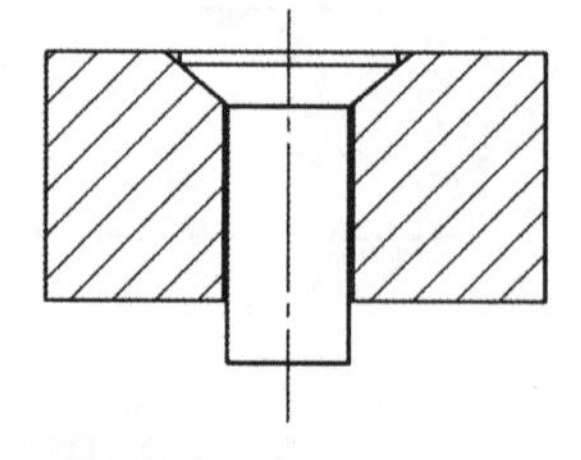

FIG. 6.34 Countersunk hole with fastener

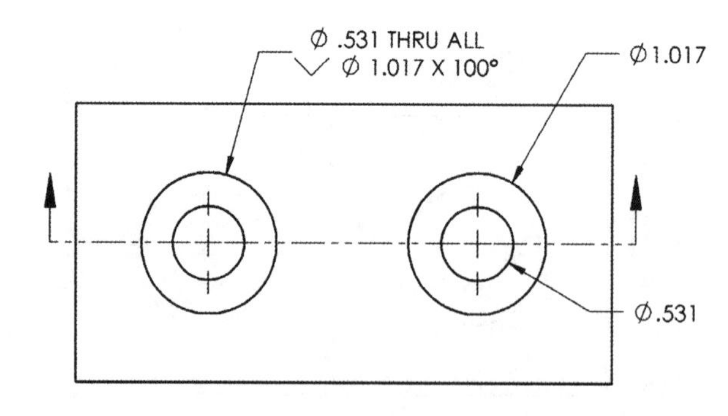

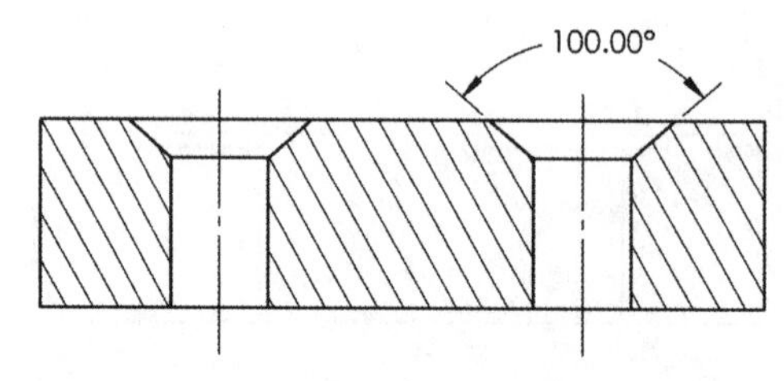

FIG. 6.35 Proper dimensioning of countersunk holes (left) and location of the dimensions (right)

Countersink holes are conically shaped holes (see Figure 6.33), usually constructed with angles of 60°, 82°, 90°, 100°, 110°, or 120°. Countersink holes are most often used in conjunction with flat head screws so the head of the fastener sits flush with the surface of the part (see Figure 6.34).

The left hole shown in Figure 6.35 demonstrates the proper way to dimension a countersunk hole. The right hole is provided for illustration purposes only, so the student can identify the location of the dimensions given by the note.

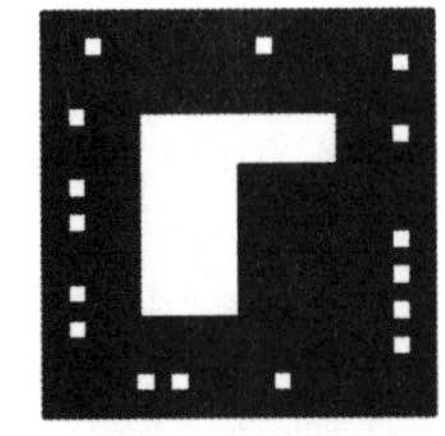

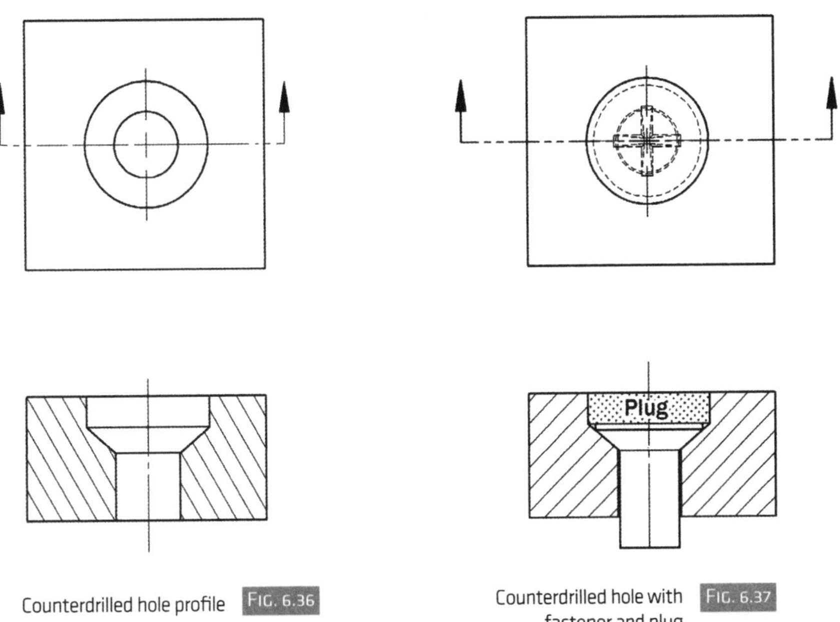

Counterdrilled hole profile FIG. 6.36

Counterdrilled hole with fastener and plug FIG. 6.37

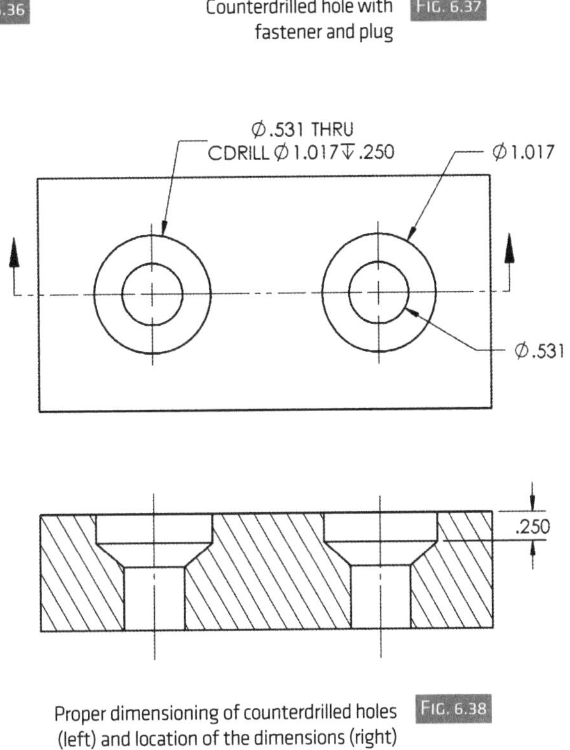

Proper dimensioning of counterdrilled holes (left) and location of the dimensions (right) FIG. 6.38

Counterdrilled holes are used when a fastener must seat below the object's surface (see Figure 6.36). The immediate volume above the screw head is often covered with a plug to ensure a smooth surface (see Figure 6.37).

The left hole shown in demonstrates the proper way to dimension a counterdrilled hole. The right hole is provided for illustration purposes only, so the student can identify the location of the dimensions given by the note.

DIMENSIONING

NAME:

CHAPTER 06
EXERCISE 01

DATE:

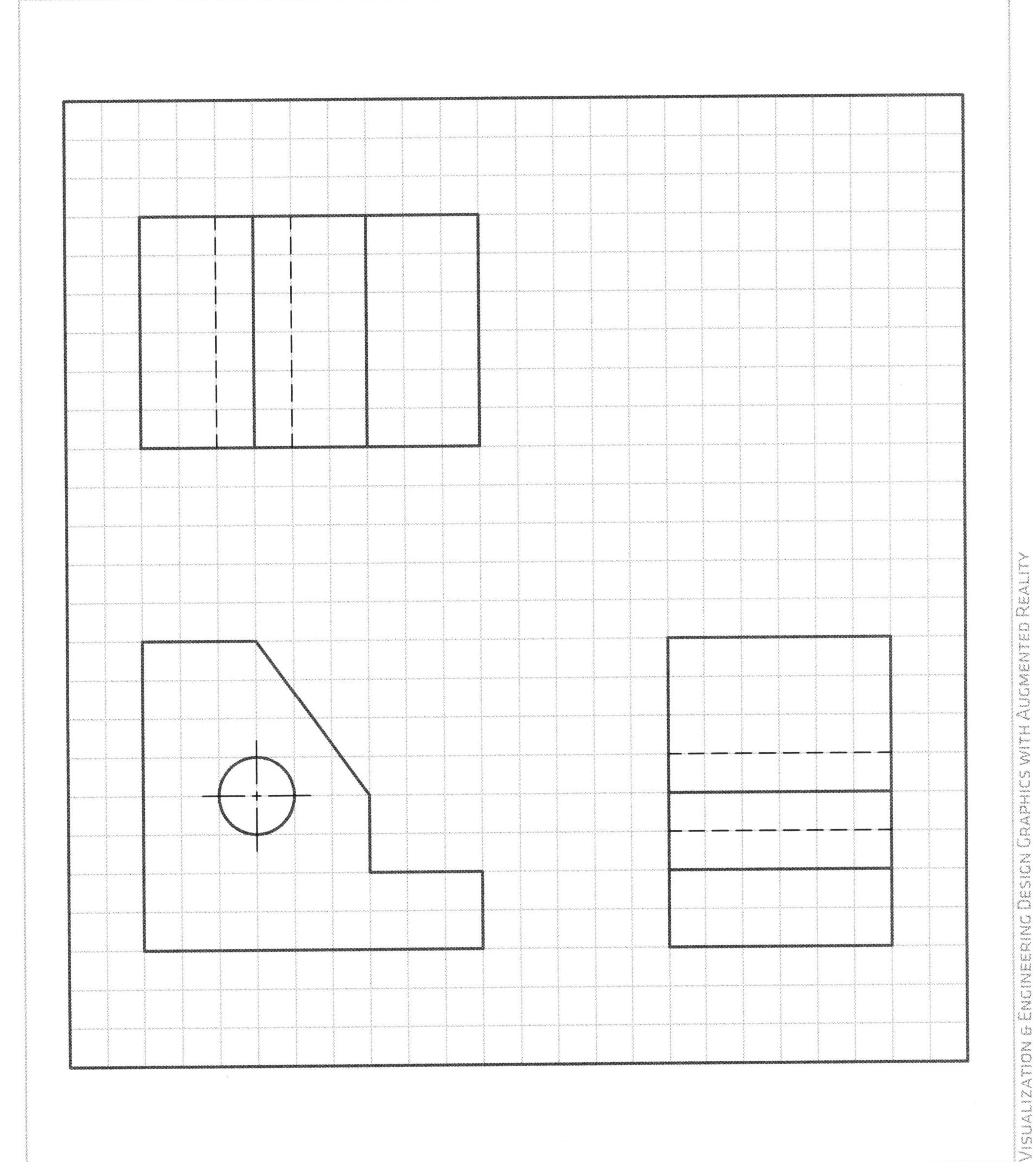

DIMENSION THE OBJECT SHOWN BELOW. NOTE THAT NOT ALL ORTHOGRAPHIC VIEWS WILL REQUIRE DIMENSIONS. DO NOT OVERDIMENSION. ASSUME GRID SPACING IS 0.2".

NAME:

EXERCISE 02

DATE:

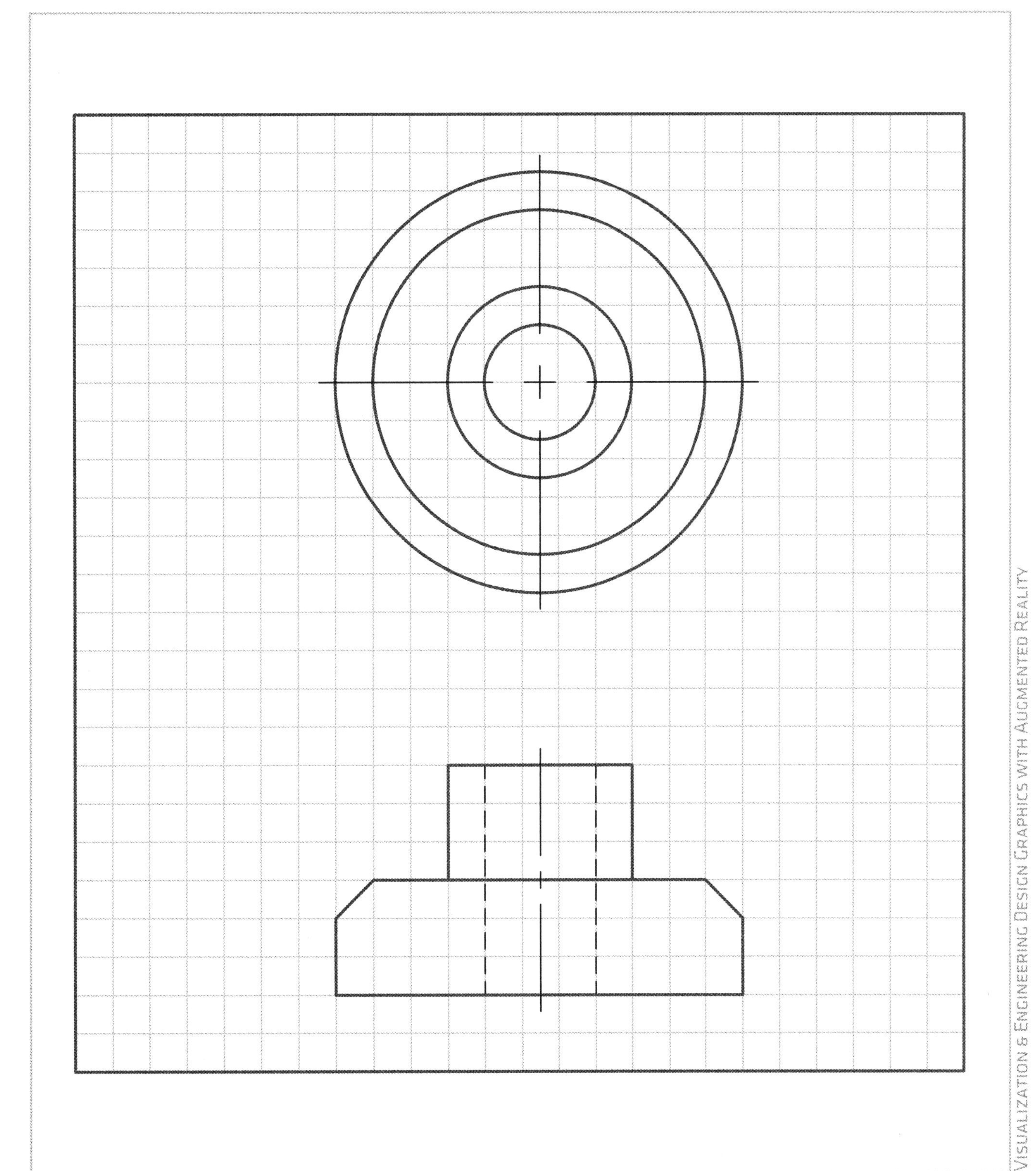

DIMENSION THE OBJECT SHOWN BELOW. NOTE THAT NOT ALL ORTHOGRAPHIC VIEWS WILL REQUIRE DIMENSIONS. DO NOT OVERDIMENSION. ASSUME GRID SPACING IS 0.2".

EXERCISE 03

NAME:

DATE:

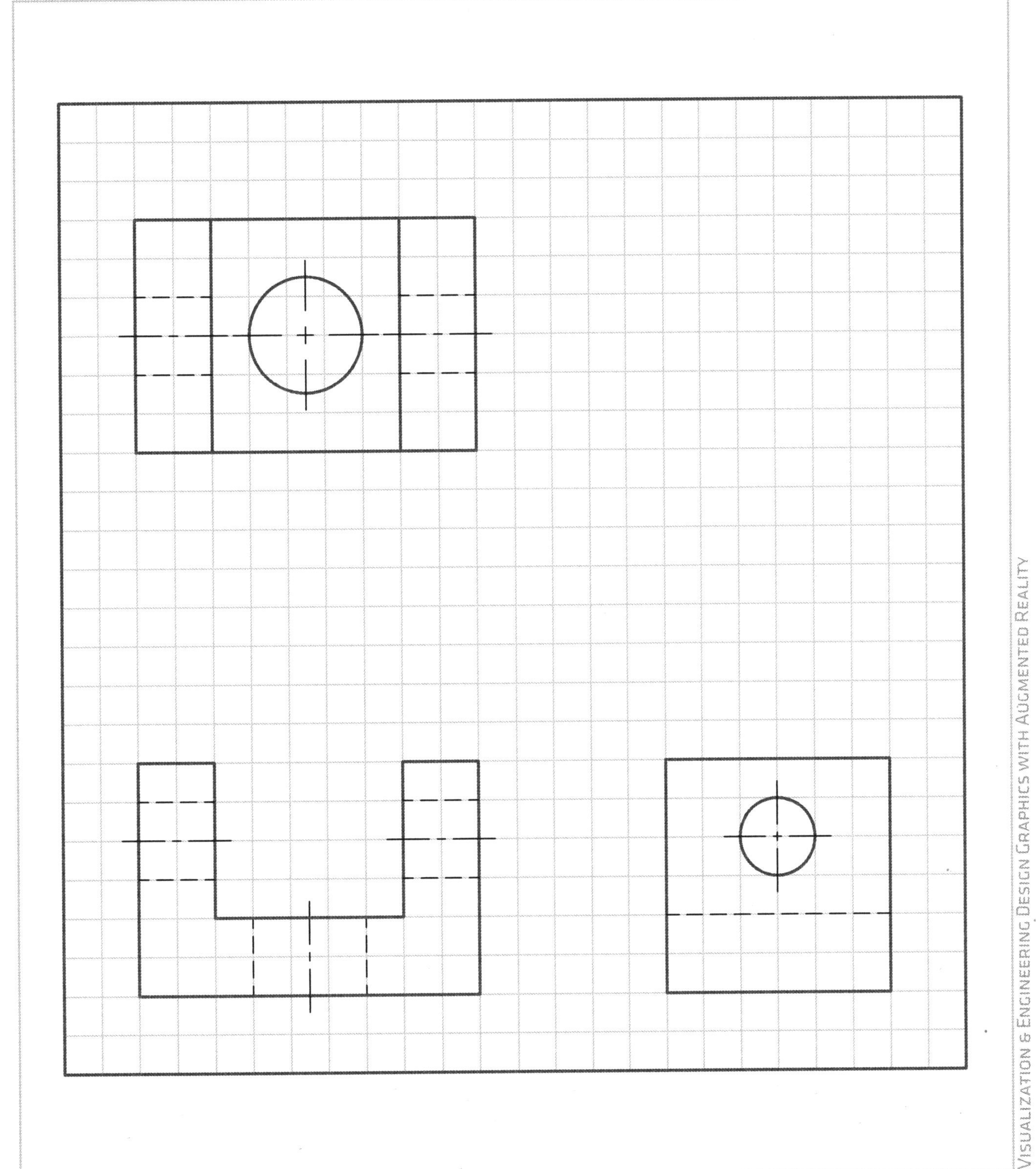

DIMENSION THE OBJECT SHOWN BELOW. NOTE THAT NOT ALL ORTHOGRAPHIC VIEWS WILL REQUIRE DIMENSIONS. DO NOT OVERDIMENSION. ASSUME GRID SPACING IS 0.2".

NAME:

DATE:

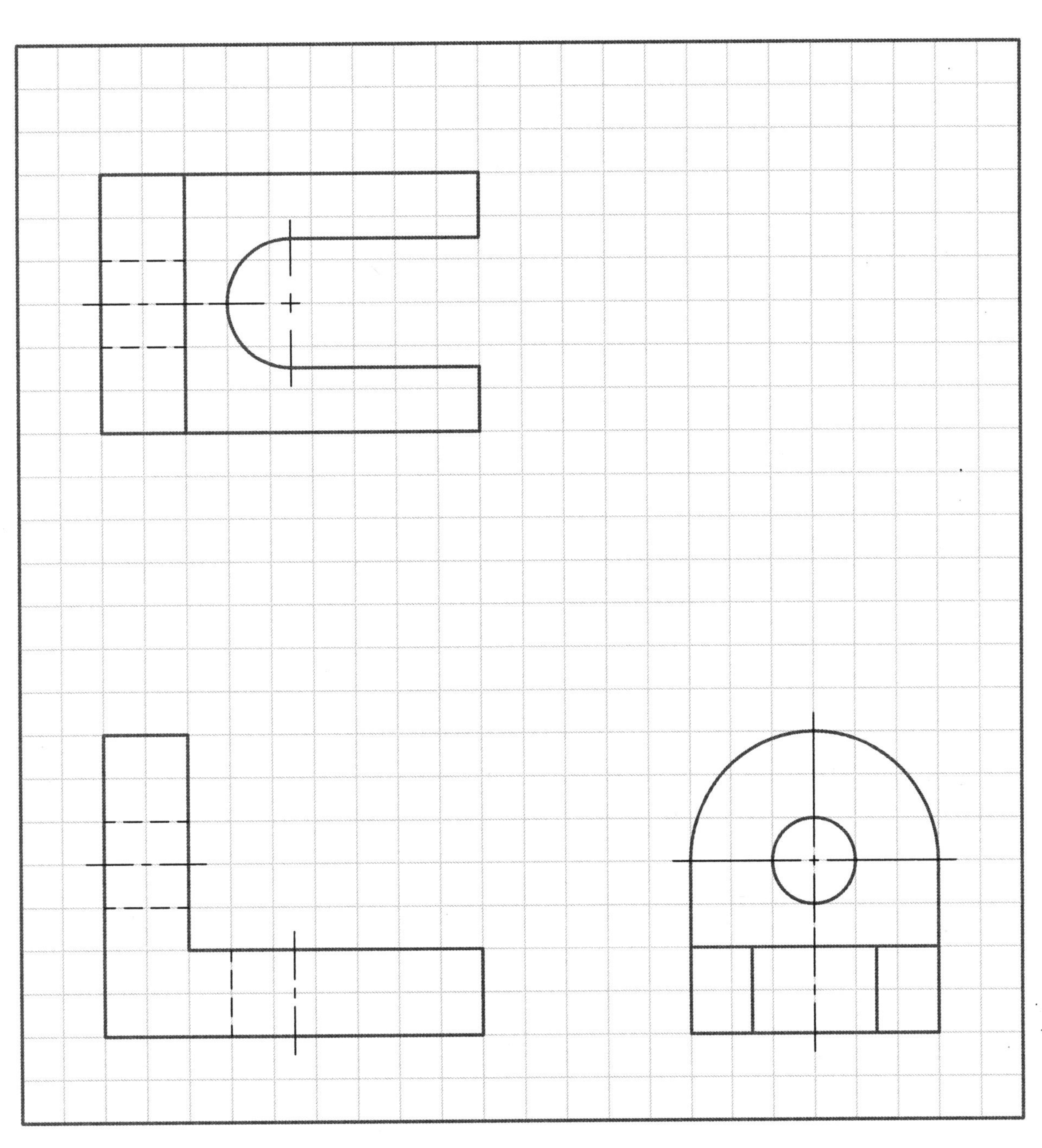

DIMENSION THE OBJECT SHOWN BELOW. NOTE THAT NOT ALL ORTHOGRAPHIC VIEWS WILL REQUIRE DIMENSIONS. DO NOT OVERDIMENSION. ASSUME GRID SPACING IS 0.2".

EXERCISE 05

NAME:

DATE:

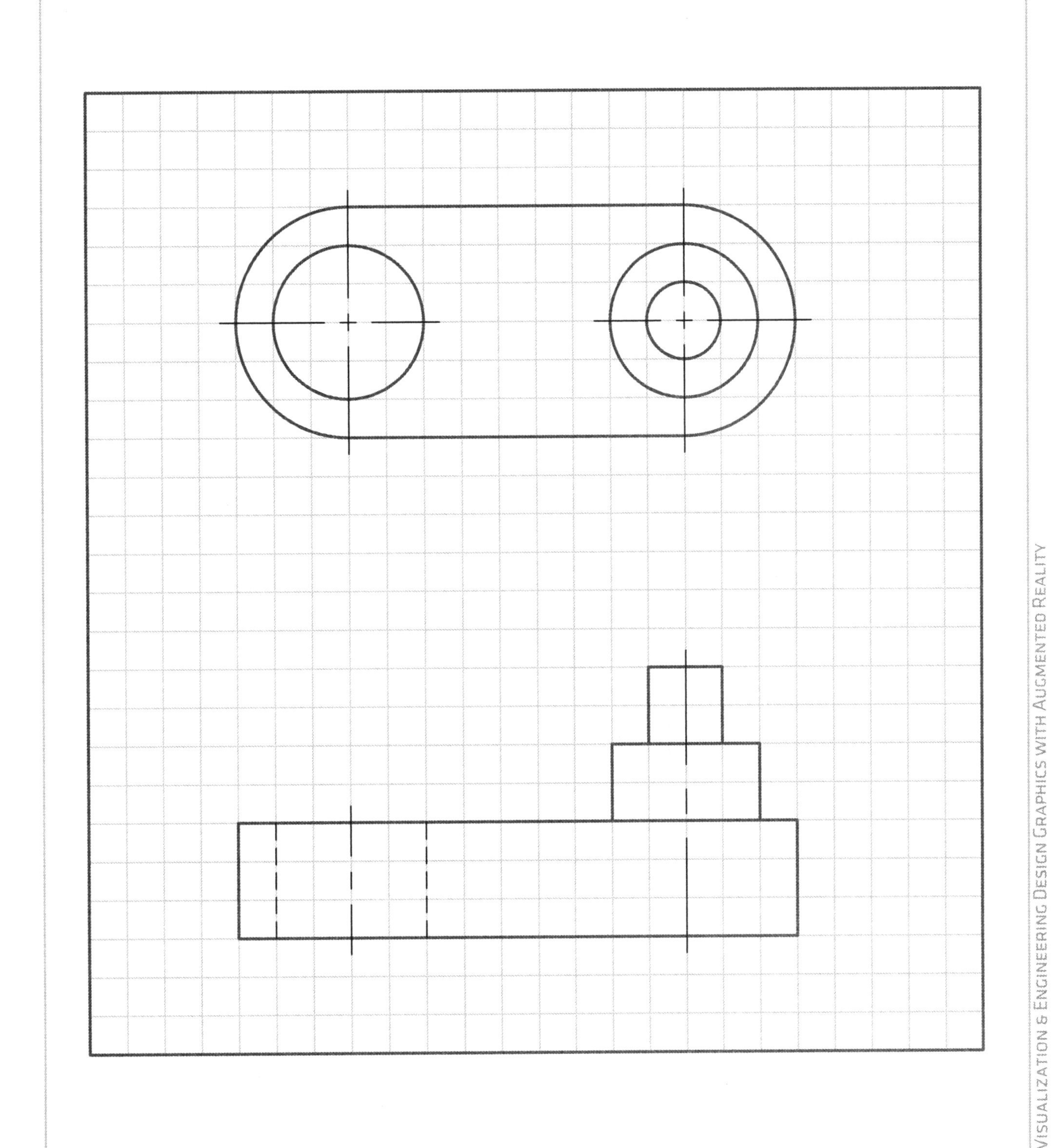

DIMENSION THE OBJECT SHOWN BELOW. NOTE THAT NOT ALL ORTHOGRAPHIC VIEWS WILL REQUIRE DIMENSIONS. DO NOT OVERDIMENSION. ASSUME GRID SPACING IS 0.2".

Dimensioning

Name:

Chapter 06
Exercise 06

Date:

Dimension the object shown below. Note that not all orthographic views will require dimensions. Do not overdimension. Assume grid spacing is 0.2".

EXERCISE 07

NAME:

DATE:

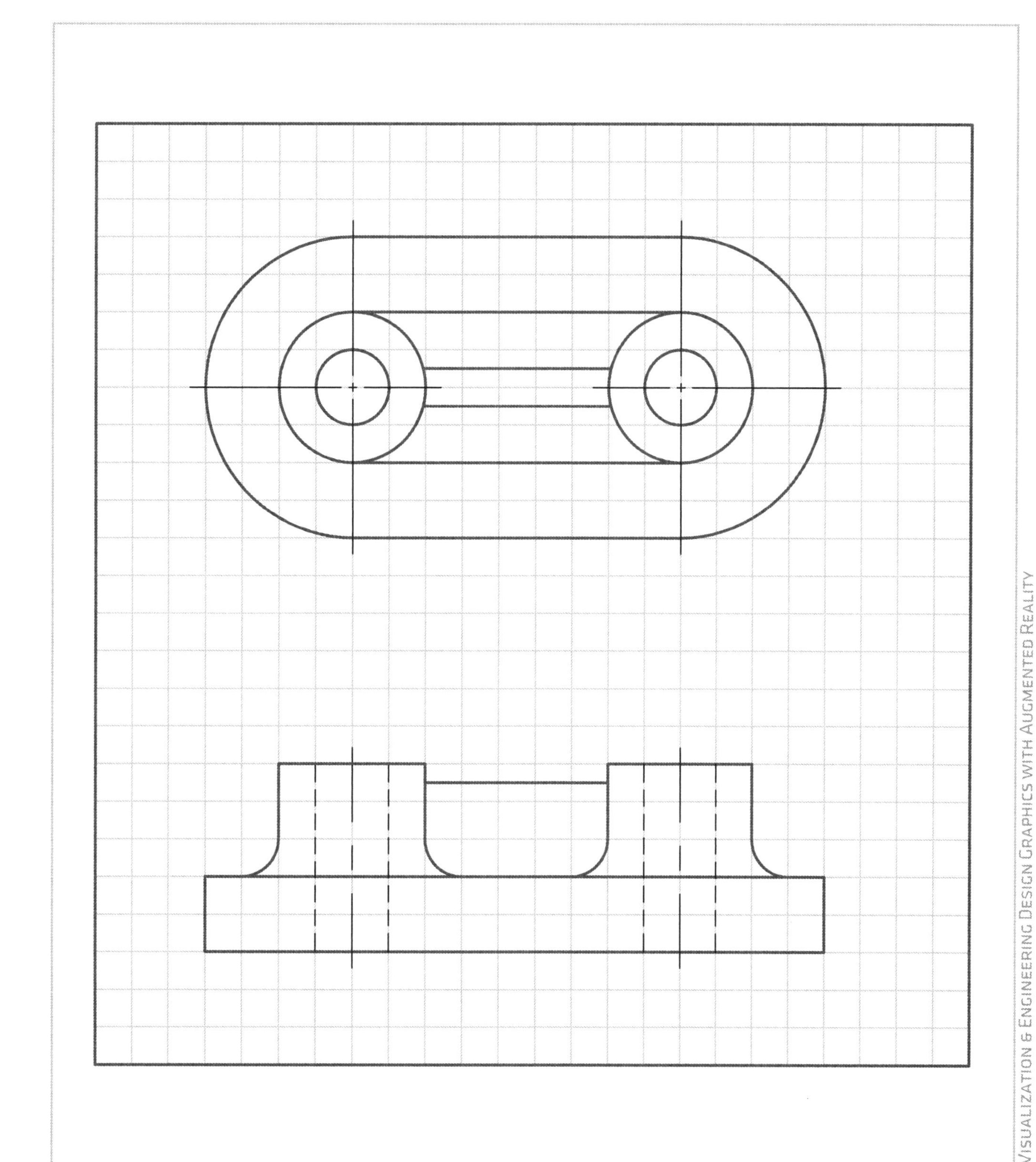

DIMENSION THE OBJECT SHOWN BELOW. NOTE THAT NOT ALL ORTHOGRAPHIC VIEWS WILL REQUIRE DIMENSIONS. DO NOT OVERDIMENSION. ASSUME GRID SPACING IS 0.2".

DIMENSIONING

NAME:

CHAPTER 06
EXERCISE 08

DATE:

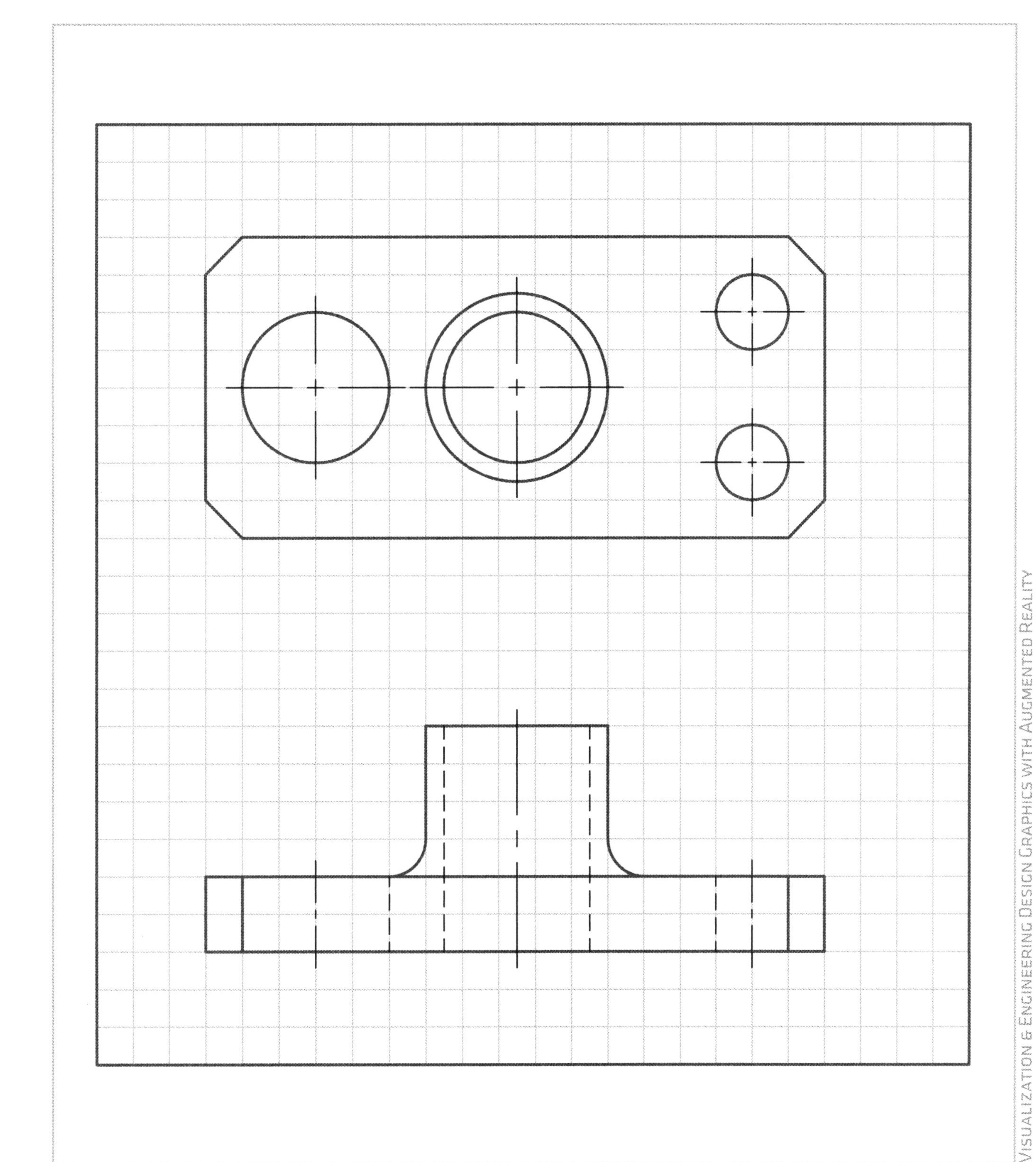

DIMENSION THE OBJECT SHOWN BELOW. NOTE THAT NOT ALL ORTHOGRAPHIC VIEWS WILL REQUIRE DIMENSIONS. DO NOT OVERDIMENSION. ASSUME GRID SPACING IS 0.2".

Dimensioning

Chapter 06
Exercise 09

Name:

Date:

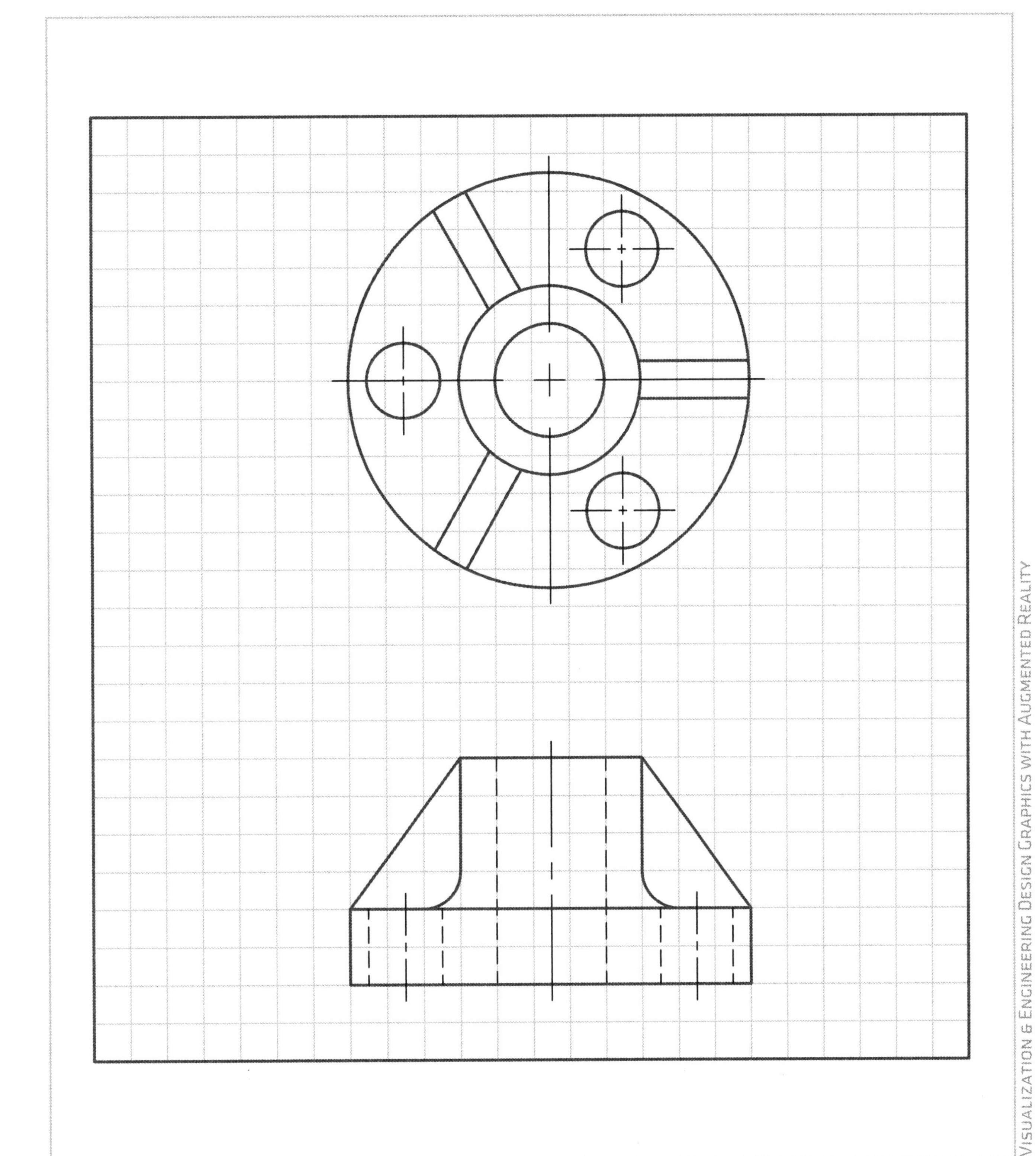

Dimension the object shown below. Note that not all orthographic views will require dimensions. Do not overdimension. Assume grid spacing is 0.2".

EXERCISE 10

NAME:

DATE:

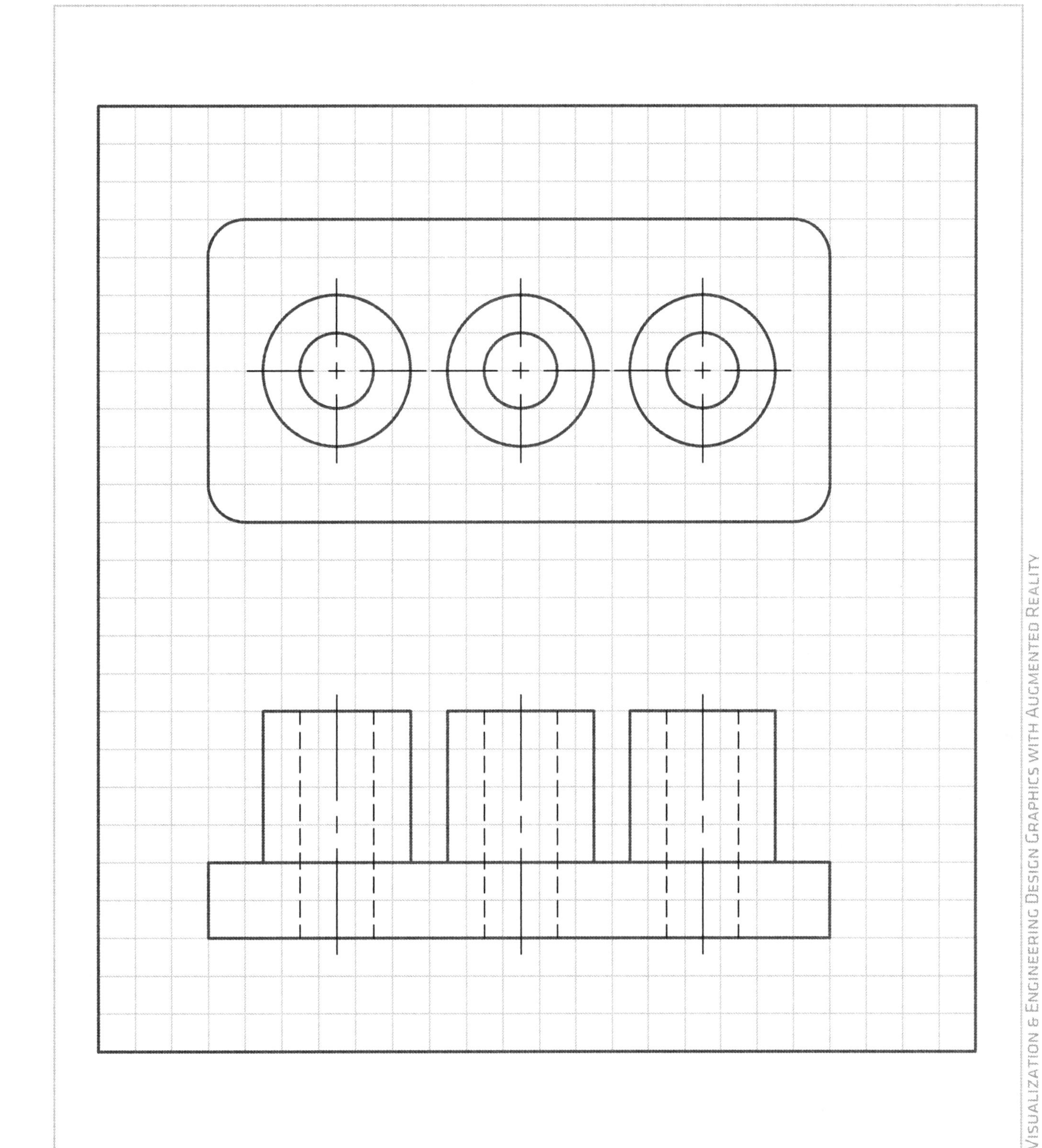

DIMENSION THE OBJECT SHOWN BELOW. NOTE THAT NOT ALL ORTHOGRAPHIC VIEWS WILL REQUIRE DIMENSIONS. DO NOT OVERDIMENSION. ASSUME GRID SPACING IS 0.2".

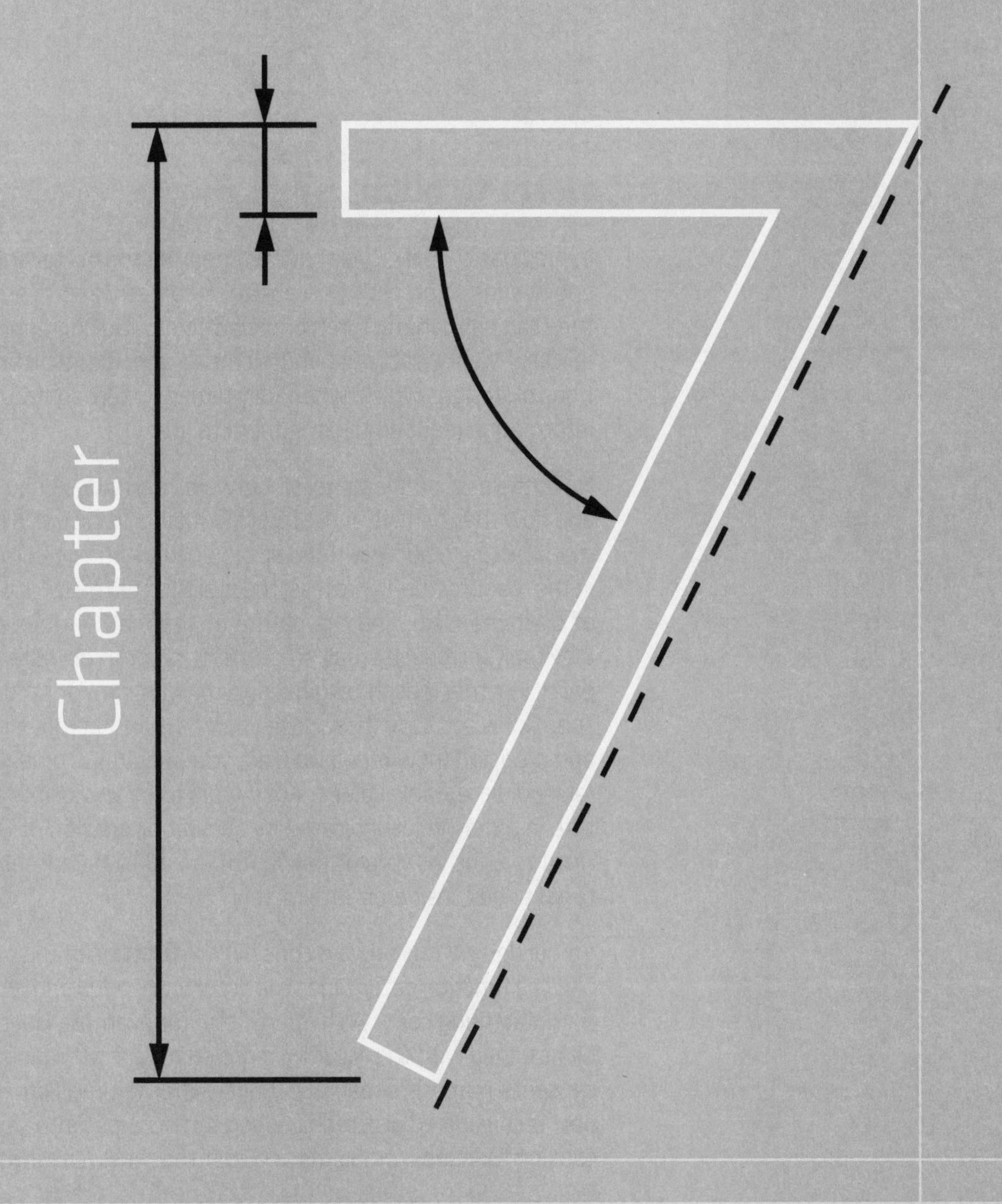

Tolerances

Introduction

In previous chapters, you have learned the formal techniques used in engineering to properly describe the geometry and sizes of objects so they can be manufactured or constructed. Orthographic projections, auxiliary views, sections, and pictorials provide realistic representations of designs which, when fully dimensioned, communicate all the information required to bring them to life.

Nevertheless, problems exist between parts designed theoretically and how they behave and interact in reality. In fact, it is impossible to manufacture objects with no error. The nature of the materials used in the manufacturing process, the precision of the tools used, the level of craftsmanship, and the nature of the machining operations may inevitably introduce small amounts of random or systemic error to a part. For this reason, engineering drawings must account for error; specifically accuracy (how close you can manufacture the true value), and precision (how repeatable are your results) in order to define the range of acceptable values. For instance, if the width of a certain feature in a drawing is indicated by a linear dimension of 6 inches, how close to 6 inches would that feature need to be once it is manufactured to be considered satisfactory?

Proper design must always consider the function of the part or assembly. The function determines the accuracy needed and, ultimately, the manufacturing cost. A children's toy, for example, does not need to be designed with the accuracy required for aircraft manufacturing because its purpose does not require extreme precision. In general, a part is considered acceptable when it can be put into service without causing functional problems at a cost that ensures profitability.

Accounting for error is not trivial and has a direct effect on cost. The smaller the error you allow in a design (or the greater the accuracy), the higher the cost of manufacturing. Greater accuracy often means using more expensive equipment or relying on more skillful craftsmen with higher labor and inspection rates. Defining acceptable parameters of accuracy and error also ensures interchangeability of parts in an assembly. All of these factors are essential in mass production, as all parts in an assembly need to fit and function together properly, even when parts or replacements are manufactured by different companies.

Tolerancing is a method that complements dimensioning by providing additional information about the amount of variation inherent in a manufactured part. In this chapter, standard tolerancing practices and applications are discussed.

$2.00^{+.005}_{-.000}$ $2.00\pm.003$ $\begin{matrix}2.004\\1.998\end{matrix}$

Unilateral form **Bilateral form** **Limit form**

Representation of tolerances 
FIG. 7.1

Tolerances

The term tolerance refers to the acceptable error allowed on a specific dimension. This error is specified as a range of values. For example, the diameter of a hole given as a dimension of ø2.00 inches with a tolerance of ±0.03, means that the hole is acceptable as long as it is drilled to a diameter between 1.97 inches and 2.03 inches.

Using proper tolerances, the functional requirements of a component can be achieved without manufacturing for unnecessary accuracy. Proper tolerancing reduces the cost of production and ensures the interchangeability of parts.

All dimensions in a drawing must have tolerances. Some dimensions will require smaller tolerances, as certain features require more accuracy, but every feature on every manufactured part is subject to variation. Tolerances are indicators that inform the machinist what type of tools and techniques are required in certain situations.

Tolerances can be expressed in three different forms: unilateral, bilateral, and limit. Unilateral tolerances, also known as asymmetrical tolerances, provide a range of acceptable values that deviate in only one direction, either plus or minus, from the specified dimension. A bilateral tolerance, also known as symmetric tolerance, provides equal plus and minus deviations from the specified dimension. Tolerances in limit form provide the maximum and minimum values, which determine the range of acceptable values. The examples shown in Figure 7.1 illustrate the different forms used to represent tolerances.

There are two types of tolerances: dimensional and geometric. Dimensional tolerances define the level accuracy required for features in terms of size and dimensions. Geometric tolerances are concerned with the geometric characteristics of shapes, locations, and profiles; not sizes or dimensions.

FORGED BRACKET			
AUTHOR:		TOLERANCES: 0.X ±.05 0.XX ±.005 ANG ±.5°	DRAWING NO: FY12-021
DATE:	SCALE: 1=1		SHEET: 1 OF 3

Fig. 7.2 General tolerance provided in title block

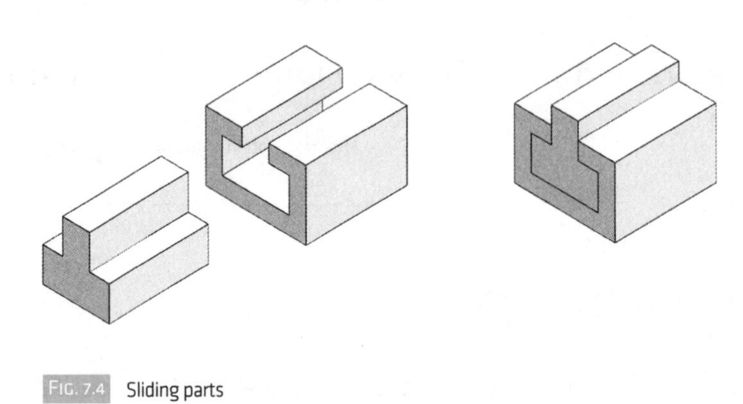

Fig. 7.4 Sliding parts

3.002
2.998

Fig. 7.3 Linear tolerance

Dimensional Tolerances

General Tolerances

General tolerances define the acceptable level of error for all dimensions in a drawing that are not individually identified. They are typically given in bilateral (symmetrical) form and found in the title block of the drawing, but are sometimes added to a drawing as a note. It is a common practice to provide tolerances based on the precision required for all dimensions on the drawing. See Figure 7.2 for an example.

Linear Tolerances

When a particular feature requires greater accuracy than expressed by the general tolerance, linear tolerances are used. A linear tolerance is an overriding value provided as part of a dimension, usually in limit form, to indicate a smaller allowable error on a specific feature (see Figure 7.3).

Mating or matching parts are components of a system or design that are made to fit with another part within a prescribed degree of accuracy. Some common examples found in mechanical designs include parts sliding against one another (see Figure 7.4), parts binding together in a single unit (see Figure 7.5), or a cylindrical shaft fitting inside a hole (see Figure 7.6).

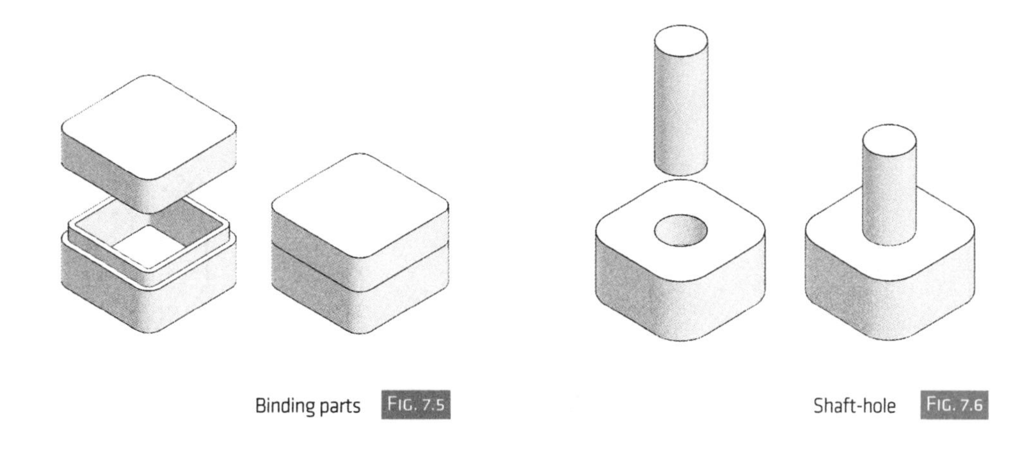

Binding parts FIG. 7.5

Shaft-hole FIG. 7.6

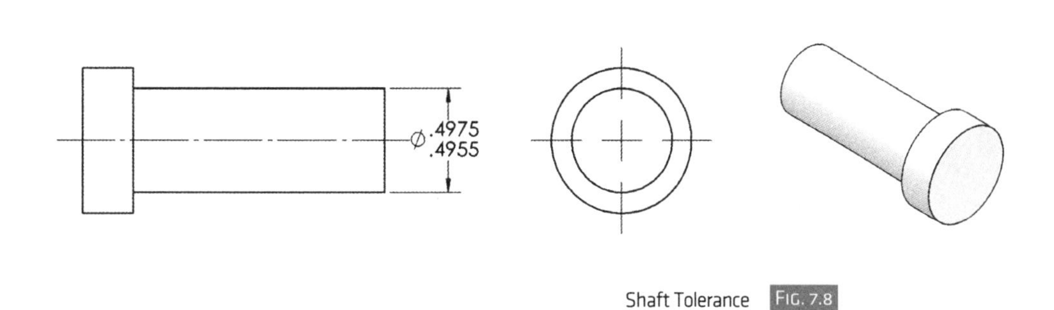

Shaft Tolerance FIG. 7.8

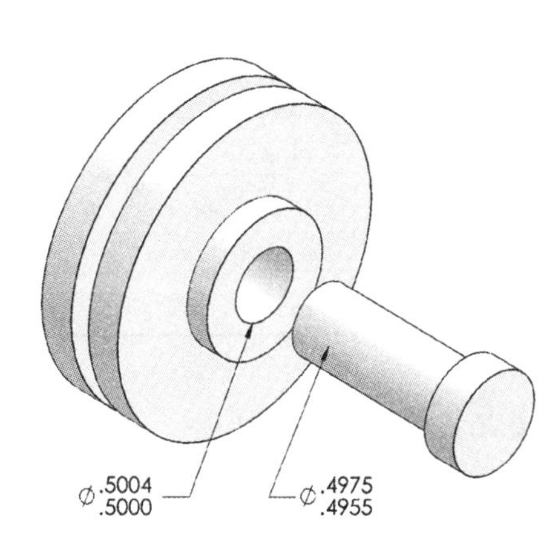

Pulley system with tolerances FIG. 7.7

The degree of tightness between mating parts is called the fit. Dimensioning mating parts requires special care in terms of tolerancing, as it is necessary to properly determine how tight or how loose the parts need to fit. Some situations require components that are held together tightly and securely, whereas other applications demand parts that can slide or rotate freely within an assembly.

Based on the relationship between two mating parts, four parameters can be defined: tolerance of the first mating part, tolerance of the second mating part, allowance, and maximum clearance. Although these concepts can be applied to any two mating parts, a fit consisting on a shaft and a hole, such as the pulley system shown in Figure 7.7, will be used for illustration purposes.

The tolerance of a feature can be defined as the range of permissible values, that is, the difference between the largest and the smallest acceptable deviation from the dimension. In the shaft shown in Figure 7.8, the upper limit is ø.4975 and the lower limit is ø.4955, therefore the shaft tolerance (ST) is ST = 0.4975 – 0.4955 = 0.0020.

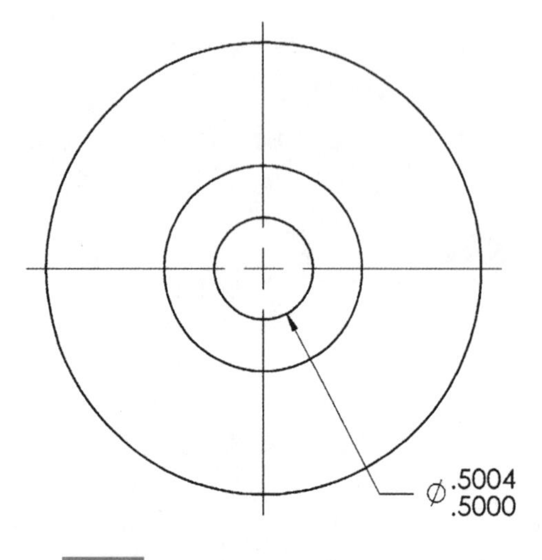

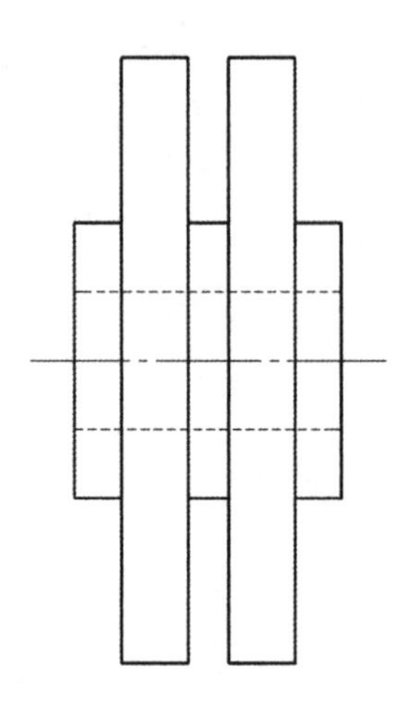

FIG. 7.9A Hole tolerance in pulley

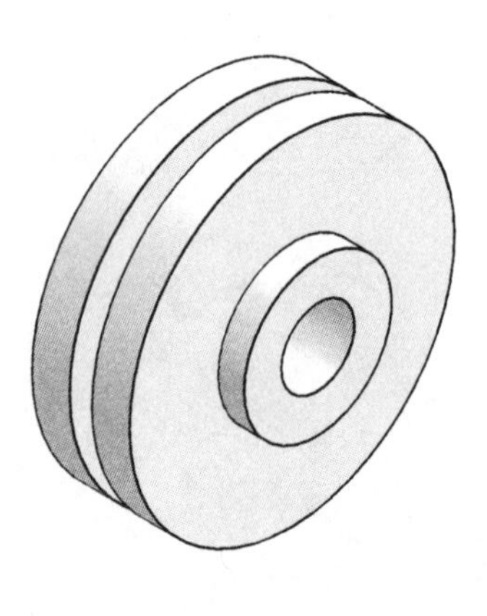

FIG. 7.9B Hole tolerance in pulley

For the hole in the pulley shown in Figure 7.9, the upper limit is ø.5004 and the lower limit is ø.5000, therefore the hole tolerance (HT) is HT = 0.5004 – 0.5000 = 0.0004.

Allowance determines the maximum amount of interference (the tightest fit) allowed for two mating parts. The tightest fit occurs when the hole is machined to its smallest allowable size and the mating part is machined to its largest allowable size. The difference between them is referred to as the allowance.

Allowance = Smallest Possible Hole (SH) – Largest Possible shaft (LS)

Maximum clearance can be defined as the maximum amount of space that is acceptable between two mating parts, determining the loosest possible fit.

Maximum Clearance = Largest Possible Hole (LH) – Smallest Possible Shaft (SS)

In the pulley system shown in the examples, the allowance and maximum clearance can be calculated as follows:

Allowance	=	0.5000 (SH)	–	0.4975 (LS)	=	0.0025
Maximum Clearance	=	0.5004 (LH)	–	0.4955 (SS)	=	0.0049

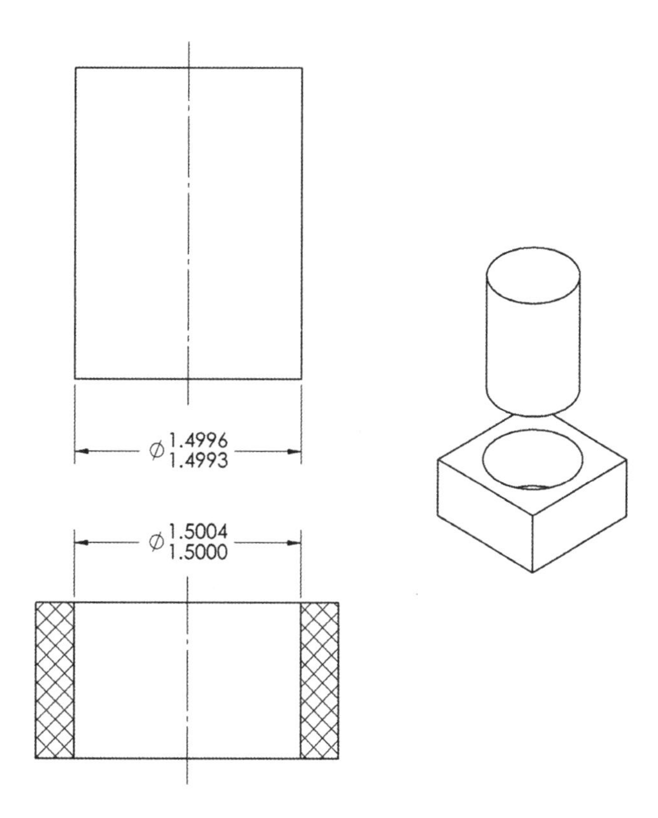

Clearance fit FIG. 7.10

Types of Fits

Design and functional requirements determine how tightly two parts are going to fit together. Some designs may require fits with large clearances, so parts do not interfere with each other, while other cases may need parts that fit tightly against one another. There are three major types of fits, which will be illustrated in the following sections using a basic cylindrical fit (hole and shaft system).

Clearance Fit

In a clearance fit, mating parts are designed to ensure that there is sufficient room (clearance) between them; the parts will never interfere. In a cylindrical clearance fit, the diameter of the internal part (shaft) will always be smaller than the diameter of the external part (hole), so relative motion between the two parts is always possible. See Figure 7.10 for an example of clearance fit.

Mating parts such as a door and a door frame, or a coin and a coin slot in a vending machine, are examples found in everyday life that are designed to not interfere with one another. In a more technical example, the pistons inside the cylinders in an internal combustion engine also require clearance fits.

Both allowance and maximum clearance are positive in assemblies with a clearance fit.

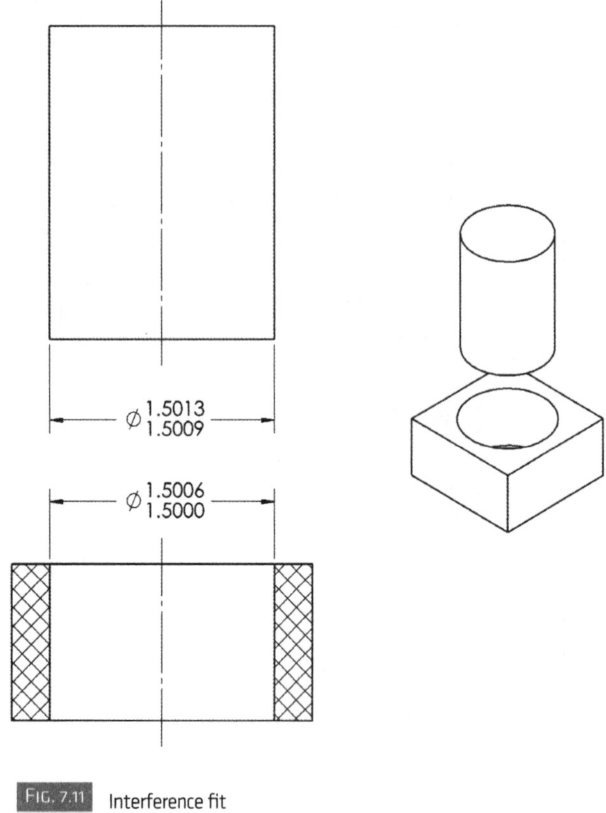

FIG. 7.11 Interference fit

Interference Fit

An interference fit, also called forced or press fit, is a type of fit where the mating parts always interfere with one another. The term interference refers to the fact that one part slightly intrudes with the other part's occupation of space, forcing both parts to slightly deform elastically to accommodate the fitting. In a cylindrical interference fit, the diameter of the internal part (shaft) will always be larger than the diameter of the external part (hole). See Figure 7.11 for an example of interference fit.

Assembling parts with an interference fit requires the use of force to press one part into the other. The binding is achieved by friction and the compression of one part against the other. With large parts and assemblies, interference fits are typically achieved by shrink fitting, a process in which the outside member is heated, causing the materials to expand, while keeping the inside member cool. When the outside part cools, it contracts, creating pressure against the inside component, thus tightening the fit. This type of fit is desirable for some designs that require holding parts together without fasteners or adhesive, such as a shaft in a bearing. Both allowance and maximum clearance are negative in assemblies with an interference fit.

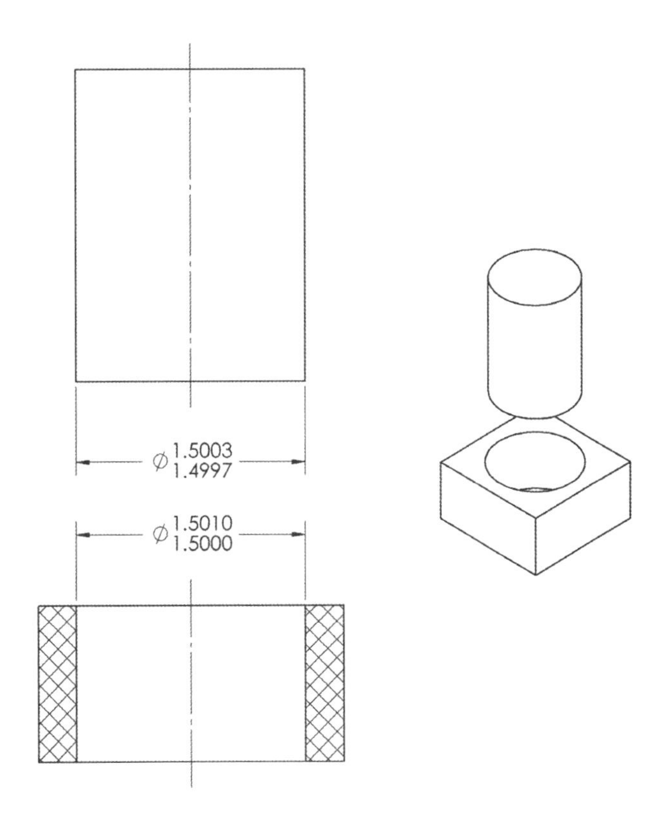

Transition fit FIG. 7.12

Transition Fit

In a transition fit, the two mating parts may either clear or interfere with each other. In a cylindrical transition fit, the diameter of the internal part (shaft) could be larger or smaller than the diameter of the external part (hole). See Figure 7.12 for an example of transition fit.

Transition fits are a compromise between clearance and interference fits, as they are the least expensive fit to manufacture. Transition fits are used in situations where accuracy is important but a small amount of clearance or interference is permissible. In a transition fit, the allowance is negative, and the maximum clearance is positive.

A particular type of transition fit results when the allowance equals zero. In this case, the mating parts may result in clearance between surfaces, or in surface contact, when the limits are reached. This type of fit is known as line fit. In a cylindrical line fit, the diameter of the internal part (shaft) could be smaller or equal to the diameter of the external part (hole).

Basic-Hole and Basic-Shaft Systems

Tolerances for mating parts can be calculated using two different systems: basic-hole and basic-shaft, depending on the component used as a reference to calculate the tolerances. This concept is an important factor in manufacturing, since it will determine the tools and processes required to machine the mating parts.

The basic-hole system uses the minimum hole size as a basic dimension. In this case, the minimum dimension of the hole remains constant, and the dimensions and tolerances for the parts are calculated based on this value. The size of the shaft is adjusted to obtain the various types of fits.

The basic-hole system is commonly used because of the manufacturing processes involved. Since the sizes of standard drills, reamers, and other tools available for producing holes are not adjustable, it is more convenient to machine holes of fixed sizes. On the other hand, shafts can be easily manufactured to any desired size to establish the correct fit between the mating parts, because of the processes involved (turning, grinding, etc) in machining a shaft.

The basic-shaft system is only used in specific areas, such as the textile industry. It is not as common as the basic-hole system. The basic-shaft system uses the maximum shaft size as the basic dimension. The maximum dimension of the shaft remains constant, and the dimensions and tolerances for the parts are calculated based on this value.

Type of Fit	Description	Classes
RC	Running or Sliding Fit	RC1 to RC9
LC	Locational Clearance Fit	LC1 to LC11
LT	Locational Transition Fit	LT1 to LT6
LN	Locational Interference Fit	LN1 to LN3
FN	Force and Shrink Fit	FN1 to FN5

ANSI English fits FIG. 7.13

Standard Fits

The three general types of fits listed previously can be further developed into several classes based on the tightness (allowance) and the clearance of the fit. The tolerances required in a force fit between two steel members, for example, are different from the tolerances used between a plastic box and a lid, even though both assemblies are force fits.

The tightness of a fit depends on multiple factors, including the material of the parts, the size, and the desired degree of tightness. For many applications, the tolerance values for the different types of fits have been standardized and recorded in tables that are widely available, for both English and metric systems. The use of standard tolerance tables simplifies the process of selecting specific tolerance values. Values can be found in the tables based on the fit needed for a particular application. Standard tolerance tables for both English and metric systems are provided in the appendix.

In the following sections, both English and metric fits are discussed.

English Fits

Five types of fits are defined in the ANSI English system, each with several classes, as shown in Figure 7.13.

Nominal Size Range (in)	Class RC 1			Class RC 2			Class RC 3		
	Clearance	Standard Limits		Clearance	Standard Limits		Clearance	Standard Limits	
		Hole H5	Shaft g4		Hole H6	Shaft g5		Hole H7	Shaft f6
Over To	*Values shown below are in thousandths of an inch*								
...	...	...	...	...	...	...	...	...	...
1.19 – 1.97	0.4 1.1	+0.4 0	-0.4 -0.7	0.4 1.4	+0.6 0	-0.4 -0.8	1.0 2.6	+1.0 0	-1.0 -1.6
1.97 – 3.15	0.4 1.2	+0.5 0	-0.4 -0.7	0.4 1.6	+0.7 0	-0.4 -0.9	1.2 3.1	+1.2 0	-1.2 -1.9
3.15 – 4.73	0.5 1.5	+0.6 0	-0.5 -0.9	0.5 2.0	+0.9 0	-0.5 -1.1	1.4 3.7	+1.4 0	-1.4 -2.3
4.73 – 7.09	0.6 1.8	+0.7 0	-0.6 -1.1	0.6 2.3	+1.0 0	-0.6 -1.3	1.6 4.2	+1.6 0	-1.6 -2.6
...	...	...	...	...	...	...	...	...	...

FIG. 7.14 Portion of ANSI Running and Sliding Fits (RC) tolerance table

A complete fit is provided by two letters that define the type of fit, plus a number, indicating the specific class. Therefore, an RC 3 fit indicates a class 3 running or sliding fit.

RC fits define tolerances for mating parts of multiple sizes that are intended to rotate or slide, with suitable lubrication at ambient temperature. LC, LT, and LN fits are locational fits used to determine only the location of the mating parts. Some classes, such as LN, provide accurate location, whereas others, such as LC, provide more freedom. FN fits provide tolerances for forced fits of various pressures.

Example

Given an RC 2 (Running and Sliding) cylindrical fit for a 3.00 inch diameter hole/shaft assembly, the tolerances of the two mating parts can be calculated using the corresponding RC 2 table, locating the diameter in the range shown in the first column (see Figure 7.14).

The tolerance values found on the table are +0.7 and 0, for the hole, and -0.4 and -0.9 for the shaft. Since the values shown in the table are expressed in thousands of an inch, the limits for the hole are 0.0007 and 0 inches, and for the shaft, -0.0004 and -0.0009 inches.

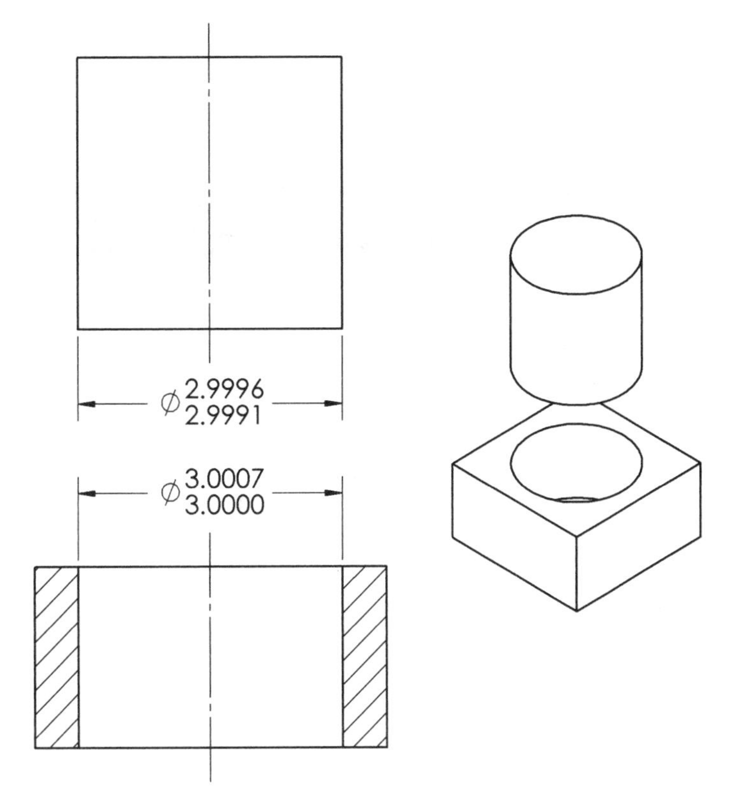

ANSI English fit example FIG. 7.15

These limits will be added to or subtracted from (depending on the sign) the base diameter of 3.00 inches to obtain the proper tolerances. Therefore:

- Largest Possible Hole (LH) = 3.00 + 0.0007 = 3.0007
- Smallest Possible Hole (SH) = 3.00 + 0 = 3.0000
- Largest Possible Shaft (LS) = 3.00 – 0.0004 = 2.9996
- Smallest Possible Shaft (SS) = 3.00 – 0.0009 = 2.9991

A representation of the two mating parts with the tolerances is shown in Figure 7.15.

Using the previous information, hole tolerance, shaft tolerance, allowance and maximum clearance for the fit can be calculated:

- Hole Tol. = Largest Possible Hole (LH) – Smallest Possible Hole (SH) ▸ Hole Tol. = 3.0007 – 3.0000 = 0.0007
- Shaft Tol. = Largest Possible Shaft (LS) – Smallest Possible Shaft (SS) ▸ Shaft Tol. = 2.9996 – 2.9991 = 0.0005
- Max. Clearance = Largest Possible Hole (LH) – Smallest Possible Shaft (SS) ▸ Max. Clearance = 3.0007 – 2.9991 = 0.0016
- Allowance = Smallest Possible Hole (SH) – Largest Possible shaft (LS) ▸ Allowance = 3.0000 – 2.9996 = 0.0004

Category	Type of Fit: Hole Basis	Type of Fit: Shaft Basis	Description
Clearance	H11/c11	C11/h11	Loose running fit
Clearance	H9/d9	D9/h9	Free running fit
Clearance	H8/f7	F8/h7	Close running fit
Clearance	H7/g6	G7/h6	Sliding fit
Clearance	H7/h6	H7/h6	Locational clearance fit
Transition	H7/k6	K7/h6	Locational transition fit
Transition	H7/n6	N7/h6	Locational transition fit (more accurate)
Interference	H7/p6	P7/h6	Locational interference fit
Interference	H7/s6	S7/h6	Medium drive
Interference	H7/u6	U7/h6	Force fit

FIG. 7.16 ISO preferred fits

Metric Fits

The International Organization for Standardization (ISO) defines a different series of preferred limits and tolerances for mating parts. The types of fits are divided into ten categories, as shown in Figure 7.16.

A complete fit is provided by two tolerance grades, the hole tolerance and the shaft tolerance, separated by a slash (/). Each tolerance grade is comprised of a letter, which indicates the fundamental deviation from the basic size, and a number, which indicates the international tolerance grade (IT).

The international tolerance grade (IT) is a standard reference number that relates a specific manufacturing process to a tolerance. It is used to determine what process is capable of producing a part to the required specification. There are 18 IT grades (IT01, IT0, and IT1 through IT16), but only grades IT5 through IT11 are used for fitting purposes.

For example, in a tolerance given as 20H7/g6:

- 20 indicates the basic diameter size (in mm).
- H7 indicates the hole tolerance. H determines the deviation from the basic size, and 7, the IT grade.
- g6 indicates the shaft tolerance. g determines the deviation from the basic size, and 6, the IT grade

Example

Given a H7/s6 (Medium drive) cylindrical fit for a 10 mm diameter hole/shaft assembly, the tolerances of the two mating parts can be calculated using the corresponding table, locating the exact diameter of the mating parts in the first column (see Figure 7.17). Unlike English tolerance tables, the values found on the table are the exact tolerances for the hole and the shaft.

Basic Size		Locational Interference			Medium Drive			Force		
		Hole H7	Shaft p6	Fit	Hole H7	Shaft s6	Fit	Hole H7	Shaft u6	Fit
...	...	...	...	...	...	...	...	...	...	...
6	Max	6.012	6.020	0.000	6.012	6.027	-0.007	6.012	6.031	-0.011
	Min	6.000	6.012	-0.020	6.000	6.019	-0.027	6.000	6.023	-0.031
8	Max	8.015	8.024	0.000	8.015	8.032	-0.008	8.015	8.037	-0.013
	Min	8.000	8.015	-0.024	8.000	8.023	-0.032	8.000	8.028	-0.037
10	Max	10.015	10.024	0.000	10.015	10.032	-0.008	10.015	10.037	-0.013
	Min	10.000	10.015	-0.024	10.000	10.023	-0.032	10.000	10.028	-0.037
12	Max	12.018	12.029	0.000	12.018	12.039	-0.010	12.018	12.044	-0.015
	Min	12.000	12.018	-0.029	12.000	12.028	-0.039	12.000	12.033	-0.044
...	...	...	...	...	...	...	...	...	...	...

Portion of ANSI Preferred Hole Basis Metric Transition and Interference Fits table FIG. 7.17

Therefore:

- Largest Possible Hole (LH) = 10.015
- Smallest Possible Hole (SH) = 10.000
- Largest Possible Shaft (LS) = 10.032
- Smallest Possible Shaft (SS) = 10.023

A representation of the two mating parts with the tolerances is shown in Figure 7.18.

Using the previous information, hole tolerance, shaft tolerance, allowance and maximum clearance for the fit can be calculated:

- Hole Tol. = Largest Possible Hole (LH) – Smallest Possible Hole (SH) ▸ Hole Tol. = 10.015 – 10.000 = 0.015
- Shaft Tol. = Largest Possible Shaft (LS) – Smallest Possible Shaft (SS) ▸ Shaft Tol. = 10.032 – 10.023 = 0.009
- Max. Clearance = Largest Possible Hole (LH) – Smallest Possible Shaft (SS) ▸ Max. Clearance = 10.015 – 10.023 = –0.008
- Allowance = Smallest Possible Hole (SH) – Largest Possible shaft (LS) ▸ Allowance = 10.000 – 10.032 = –0.032

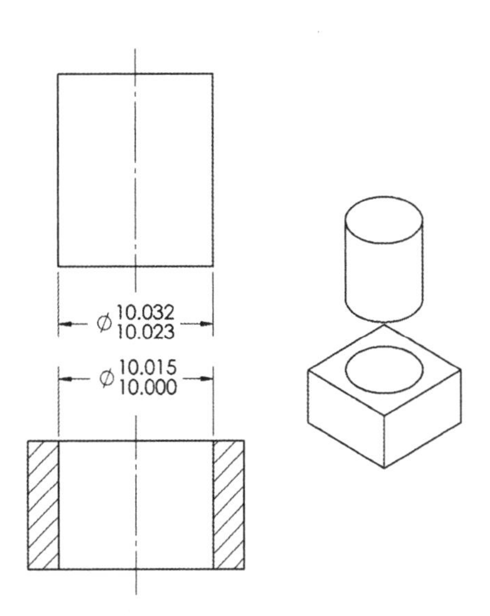

Metric fit example FIG. 7.18

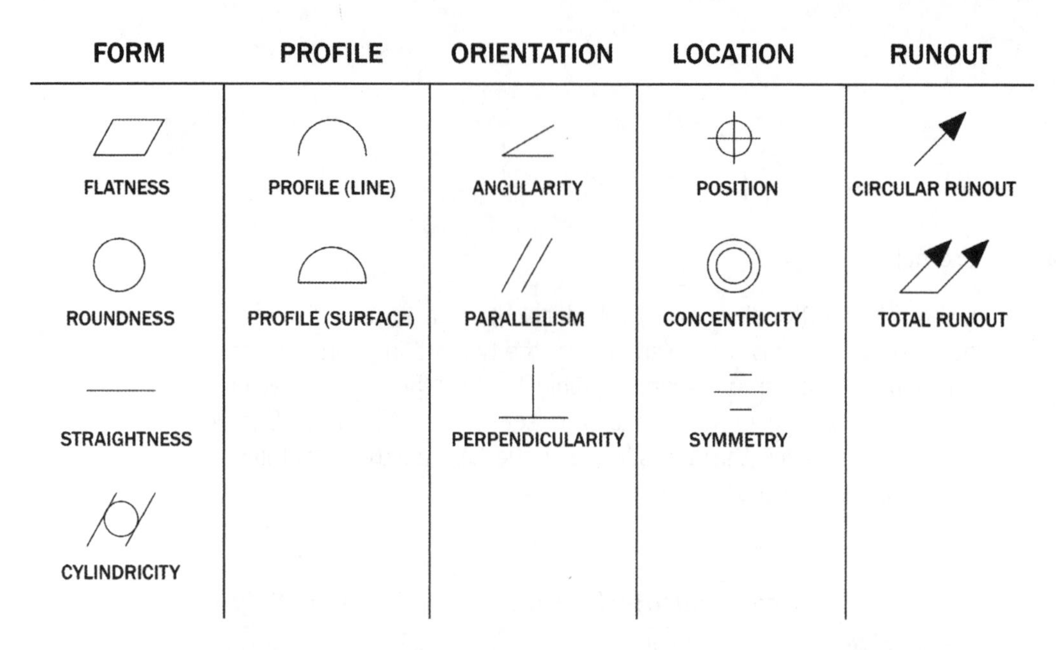

FIG. 7.19 Geometric characteristic symbols and categories

Geometric Tolerances

Geometric tolerances are used to define the allowable error of features in terms of shape, form, location and orientation. The proper application of geometric tolerances to a drawing may reduce the need for explanations and drawing notes when complex geometric conditions need to be communicated. In establishing geometric tolerances, designers must consider the manufacturing and inspection processes that will be used in producing the part and the part's relationship to other components in the assembly.

Geometric tolerancing is a broad and complex subject. Some authors have devoted entire books to geometric tolerancing practices; many consulting companies offer specialized GD&T (Geometric Dimensioning and Tolerancing) training to engineering firms; and some technical conferences and events are dedicated exclusively to this subject. Although certainly important and valuable, much of this information is out of the scope of this book. In the remaining pages of this chapter, geometric tolerancing is described from a purely descriptive standpoint, omitting details about specific design considerations and interpretations, and focusing on basic examples to provide an overall picture of the importance of geometric dimensioning and tolerancing.

A geometric tolerance is specified on a drawing by a feature control frame, a rectangular box with a leader line connected to the feature of interest. This box contains all the information required to accurately describe the geometric characteristics of a feature in a standard manner and a minimal use of space. The feature control frame is divided into different sections: the type of tolerance, tolerance value, and references (if necessary).

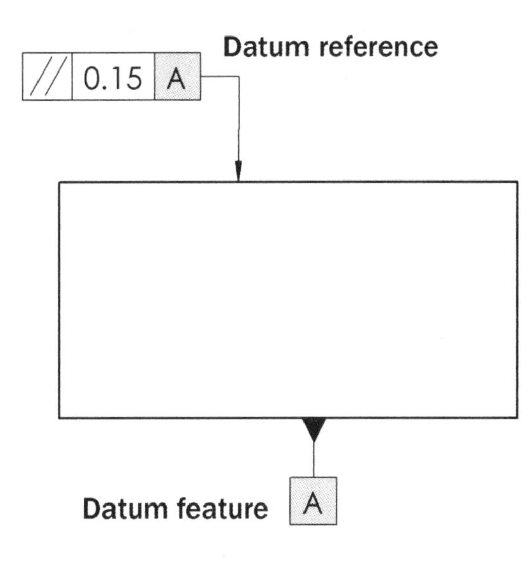

Use of datums FIG. 7.21

The first section of the feature control frame defines the type of tolerance, which is specified by a standard geometric characteristic symbol. Fourteen symbols, divided into five categories, are used, as shown in Figure 7.19.

The second section of the box is the tolerance value, which determines the allowable deviation of the feature from the perfect geometry implied on the drawing. The basic elements of a geometric tolerance are illustrated in Figure 7.20.

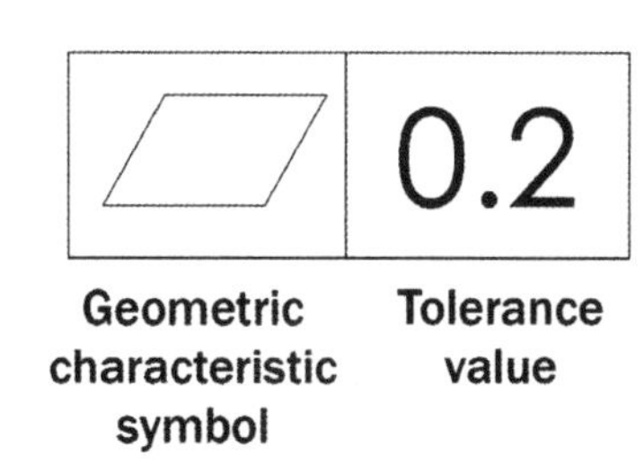

Feature Control Frame FIG. 7.20

Some geometric tolerances require the use of datum reference frames. These references specify the features (points, edges, or surfaces) from which the geometric relationship is established. For instance, the geometric tolerance used to indicate parallelism requires a datum reference, since it is necessary to indicate the plane in which the surface achieves the parallel relationship. Not providing a datum reference in this scenario will result in incomplete information. Datum reference frames are connected to datum features, which are symbols used to indicate references on the drawing. An example of a geometric tolerance with a datum feature is shown in Figure 7.21.

Feature modifiers can be used to alter the application or interpretation of certain sections of a geometric tolerance. They are specified by standard symbols that are attached to specific parts of the feature control frame. Common feature modifiers include Maximum Material Condition (MMC) and Least Material Condition (LMC). An example of a geometric tolerance with a feature modifier indicating Maximum Material Condition is shown in Figure 7.22. Maximum Material Condition and Least Material Condition are manufacturing concepts that involve using the larger or smaller end of the tolerance range in order to increase the strength or decrease the weight of a design, among other reasons.

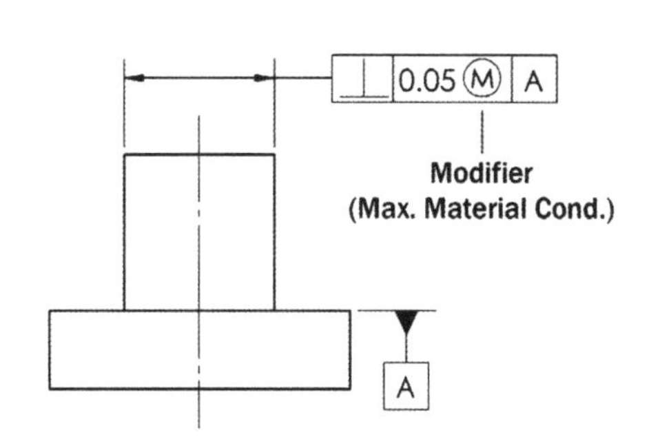

Feature Modifier FIG. 7.22

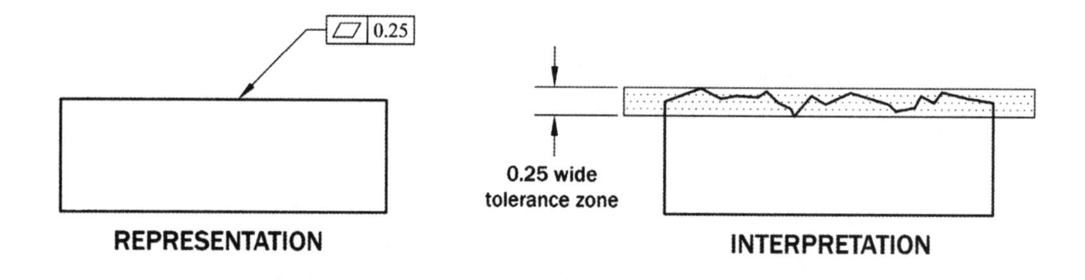

FIG. 7.23 Flatness geometric tolerance

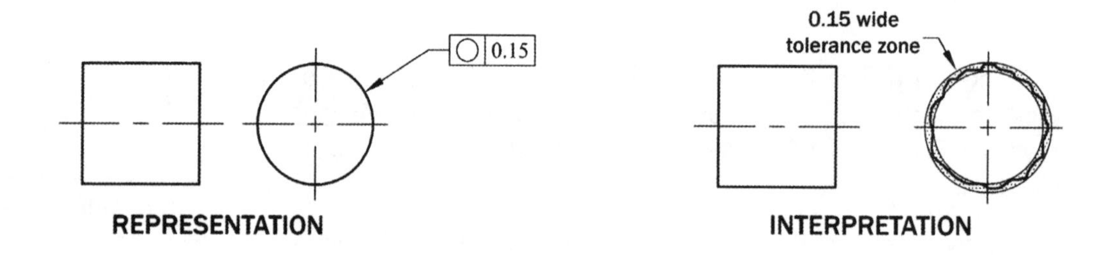

FIG. 7.24 Roundness geometric tolerance

TOLERANCES OF FORM

Flatness

A surface is flat when all its elements reside in one plane. A flatness tolerance specifies a tolerance zone between two parallel planes, separated by the value indicated in the tolerance, within which the surface must lie (see Figure 7.23). A flatness tolerance is never applied to a non-planar surface.

Roundness or Circularity

This tolerance is used to control the roundness along the length of a feature, such as a shaft or a hole. A roundness tolerance specifies a tolerance zone between two concentric circles, separated by the value indicated in the tolerance, within which the circular element must lie (see Figure 7.24). A roundness tolerance may be applied to any feature with a round cross-section.

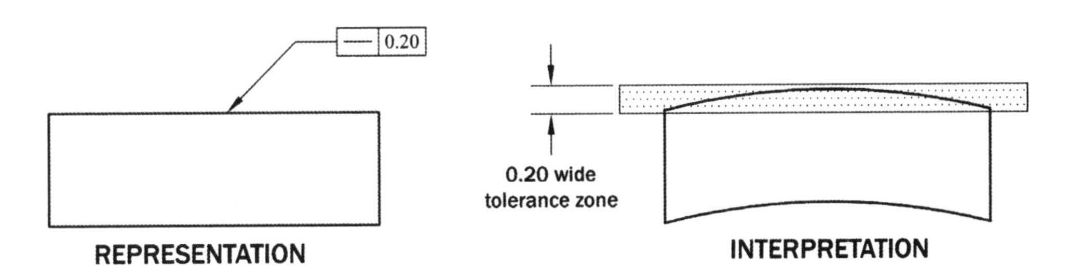

Straightness geometric tolerance FIG. 7.25

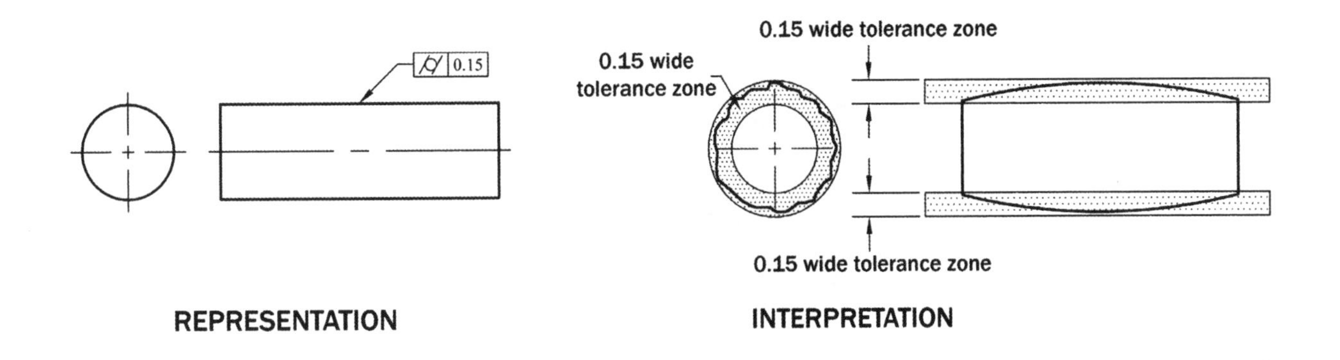

Cylindricity geometric tolerance FIG. 7.26

Straightness

The tolerance zone for a straightness control applies to an axis or to single elements on a surface. A straightness tolerance specifies a tolerance zone between two straight lines, separated by the value indicated in the tolerance, within which all points of the considered element must lie (see Figure 7.25).

Cylindricity

Cylindricity defines a tolerance zone between two concentric cylinders, separated by the value indicated in the tolerance, within which the cylindrical surface must lie (see Figure 7.26). This tolerance can be understood as a combination of roundness and straightness.

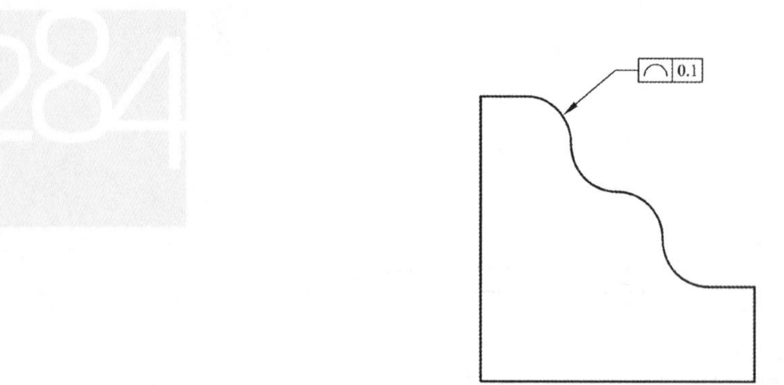

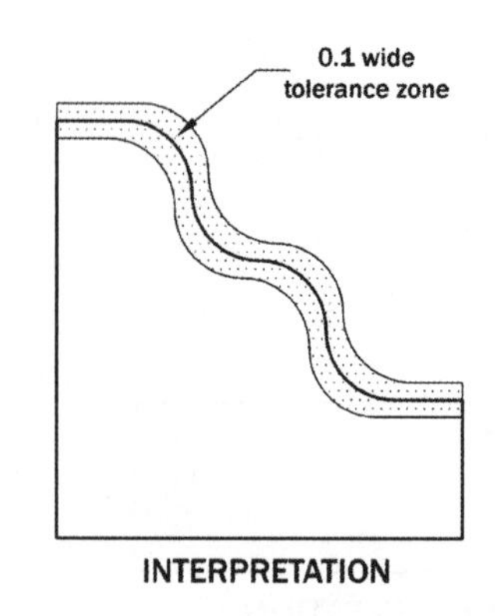

FIG. 7.27 Profile of line geometric tolerance

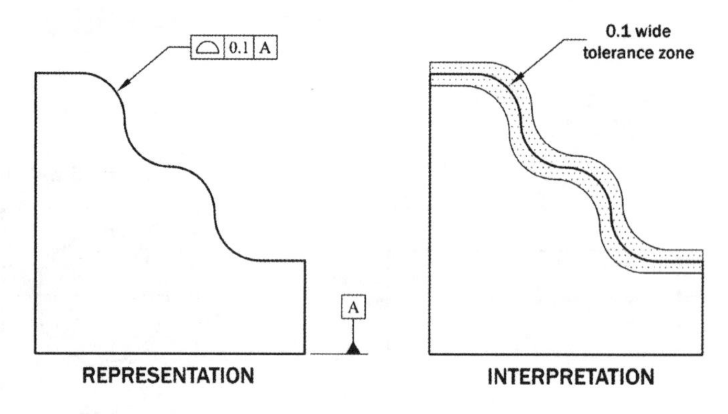

FIG. 7.28 Profile of surface geometric tolerance

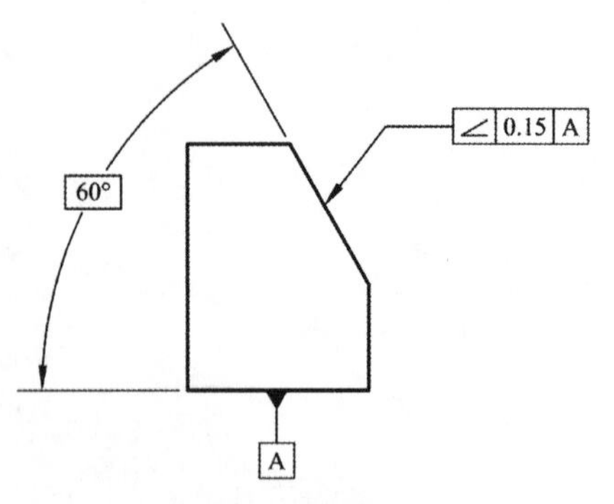

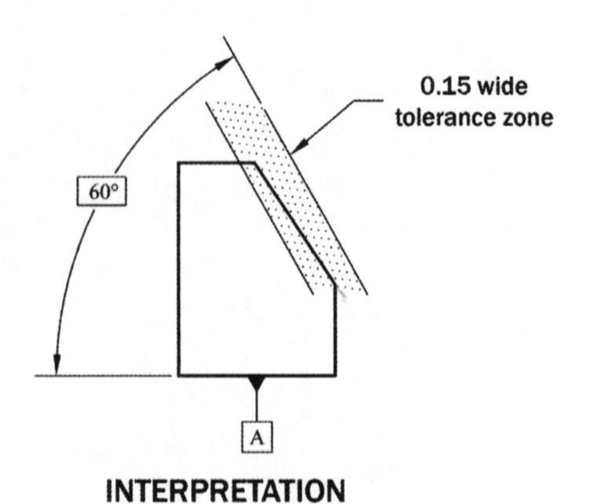

FIG. 7.29 Angularity geometric tolerance

Tolerances of Profile

The profile of a part is defined by the outline, as seen from a two dimensional view. Profile tolerances are typically used for controlling the allowable error in arcs, curves, and irregular profiles that cannot be defined by other geometric tolerances. The profile tolerance can be applied to lines or surfaces. Profile tolerances define tolerance zones between two boundaries, separated by the value indicated in the tolerance, within which the true profile of the line (see Figure 7.27) or surface (see Figure 7.28) must lie. Profile tolerances for surfaces are more common than profile tolerances for lines.

TOLERANCES OF ORIENTATION

Angularity

Angularity defines a tolerance zone between two parallel planes, separated by the value indicated in the tolerance and forming the specified angle with the datum, within which all points on the angular surface or axis must lie (see Figure 7.29). The angle may not be 90°, since such a case is covered by the perpendicularity control, which will be covered shortly.

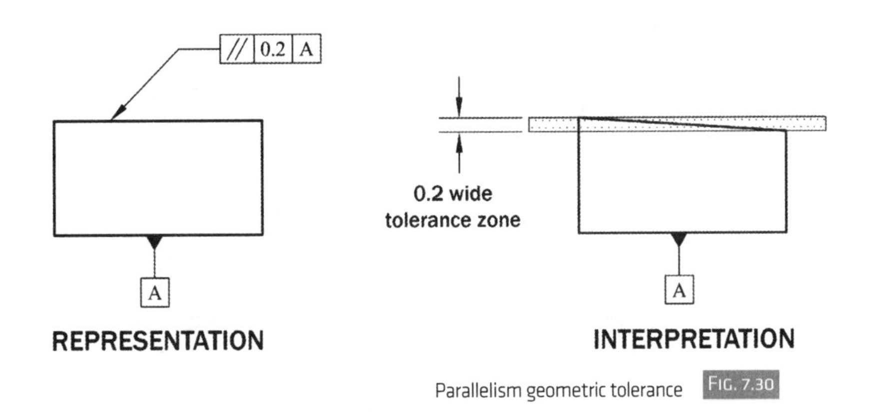

Parallelism geometric tolerance FIG. 7.30

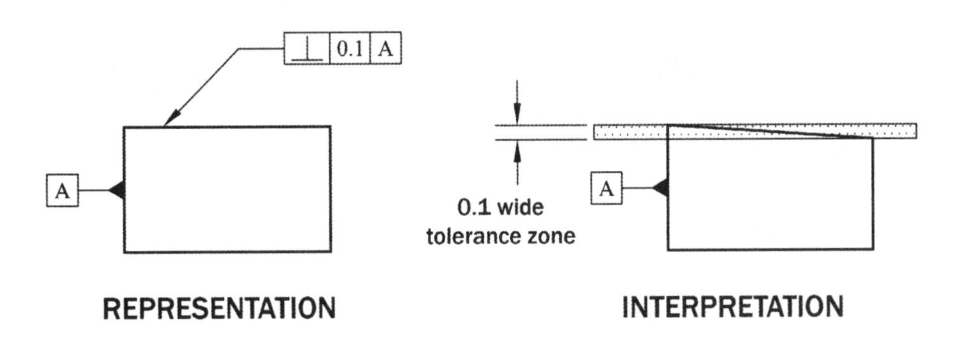

Perpendicularity geometric tolerance FIG. 7.31

Parallelism

Parallelism specifies that all points on a feature are at a constant distance from a datum. It defines a tolerance zone between two parallel planes, separated by the value indicated in the tolerance and parallel to a specified datum, within which all points on the angular surface or axis must lie (see Figure 7.30).

Perpendicularity

Perpendicularity specifies that all elements on a feature form a 90° angle with the specified datum. It defines a tolerance zone between two parallel planes, separated by the value indicated in the tolerance and perpendicular to a specified datum, within which all points on the angular surface or axis must lie (see Figure 7.31).

Tolerances of Location

True Position

True position is used to specify the location of holes, cylinders, or slots with respect to other surfaces. It defines a round tolerance zone within which the center point of the feature must lie (see Figure 7.32).

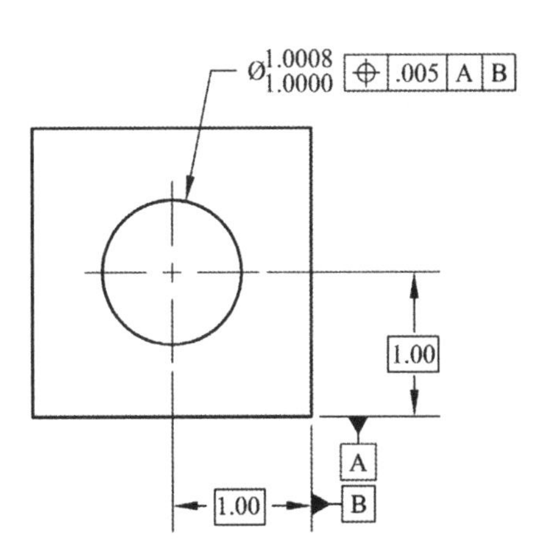

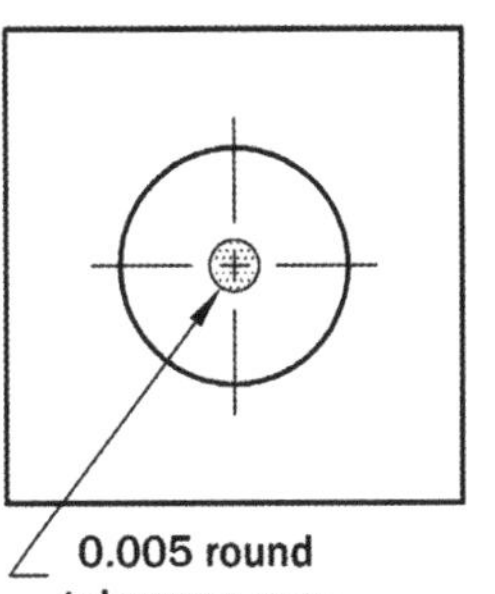

True position geometric tolerance FIG. 7.32

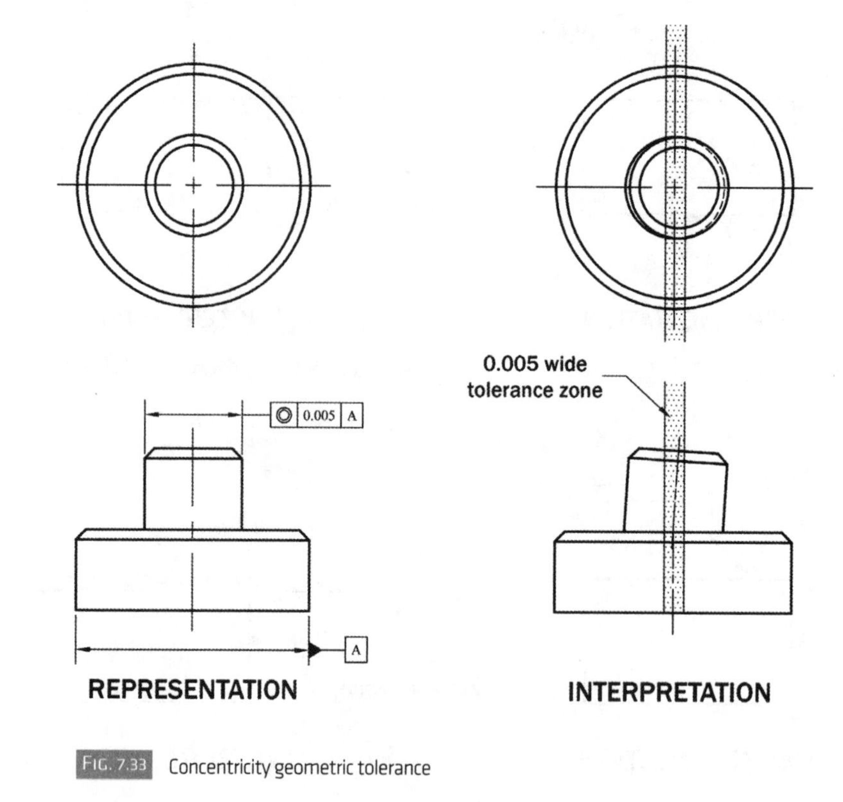

FIG. 7.33 Concentricity geometric tolerance

Although the use of linear tolerances in the horizontal and vertical dimensions to define true position is acceptable, the geometric tolerance is more accurate. The round tolerance zone defined by the true positioning geometric tolerance is more than 50% larger than the square tolerance zone defined by the linear dimensions. From a manufacturing perspective, this means that for the same tolerance, the machinist has more than 50% more margin of error without producing an unacceptable part.

Concentricity

The concentricity geometric tolerance defines the extent to which the axis or centerline of one cylindrical surface must be collinear with the axis or centerline of an adjacent cylindrical surface. It defines a cylindrical tolerance zone relative to the axis of a datum, within which all centerlines of the feature must lie (see Figure 7.33).

Symmetry

A part or a feature is said to be symmetrical when it has the same shape and size on opposite sides of a reference plane. A symmetry geometric tolerance defines a tolerance zone between two parallel planes, separated by the value indicated in the tolerance, within which the datum reference plane must lie (see Figure 7.34).

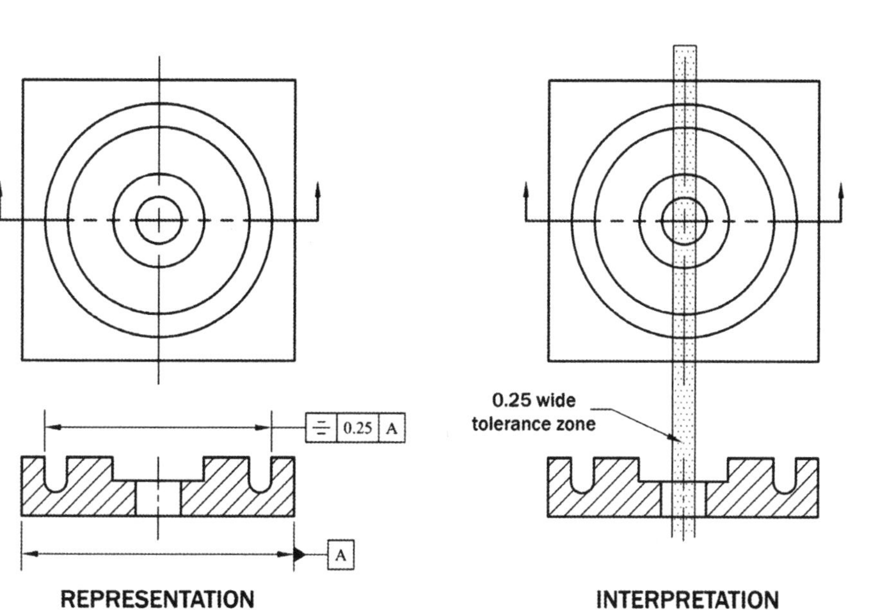

Symmetry geometric tolerance FIG. 7.34

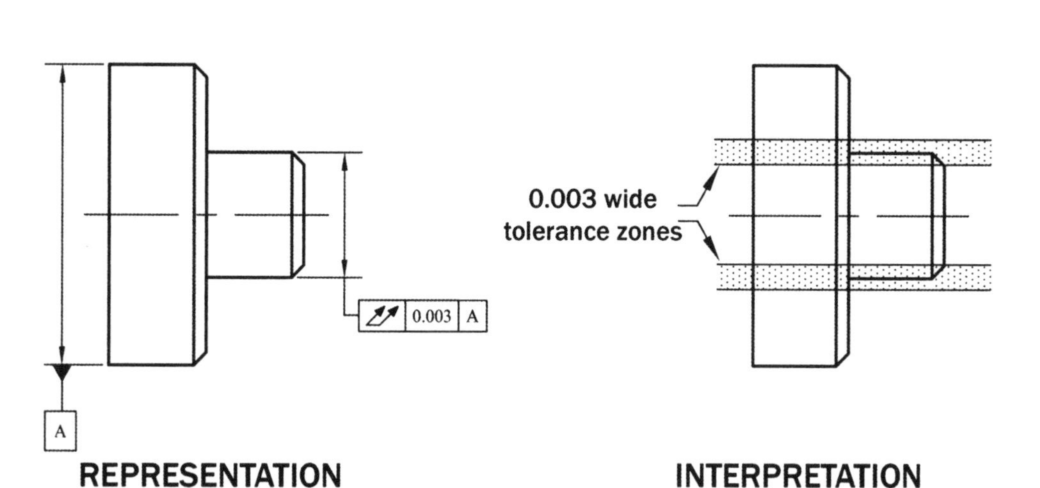

Total runout geometric tolerance FIG. 7.35

Tolerances of Runout

Runout is a geometric tolerance that defines the acceptable deviation from a perfect form on a surface or on a part revolved around its axis. It is a combined tolerance that incorporates variations of roundness, straightness, angularity, and profile. There are two types of runout: circular and total. The circular runout tolerance is used for single-line elements, defining a tolerance zone between two concentric circles, whereas total runout applies to an entire surface, defining a tolerance zone between two concentric cylinders. An example of total runout is shown in  Figure 7.35.

EXERCISE 01

NAME: SV

DATE:

DIAMETER: 2.00 INCHES
TYPE OF FIT: RC 3

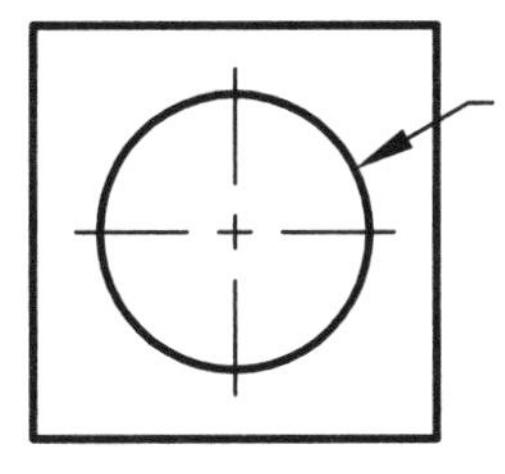

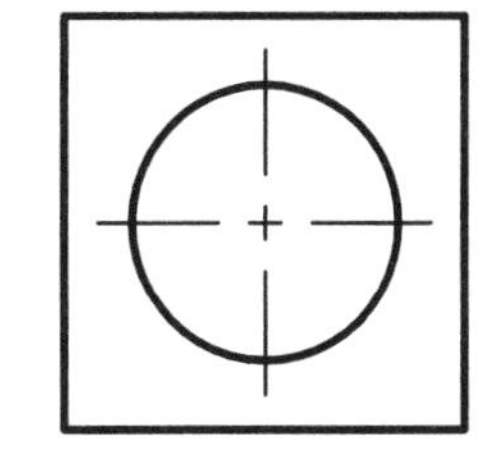

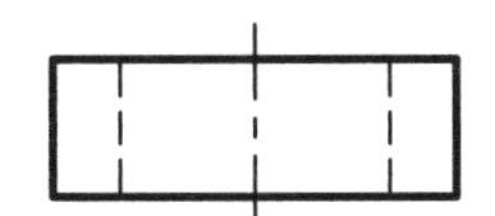

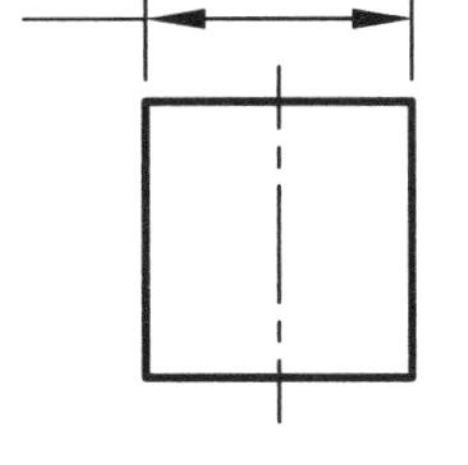

HOLE TOL: 0.0007

SHAFT TOL: 0.0005

MAX. CLEARANCE: 0.0016

ALLOWANCE: 0.0004

DIAMETER: 1.00 INCHES
TYPE OF FIT: LT 2

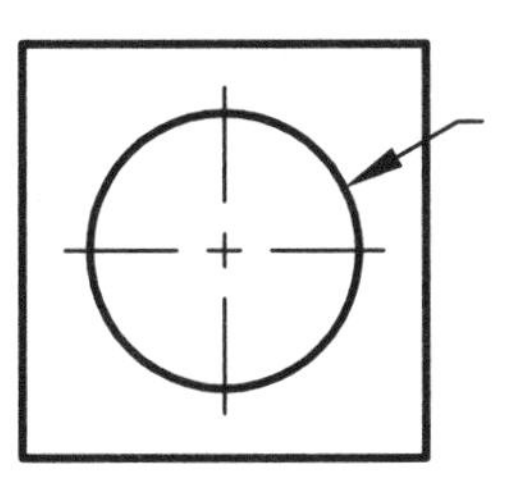

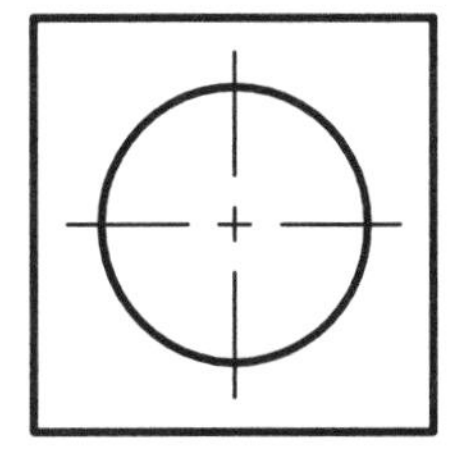

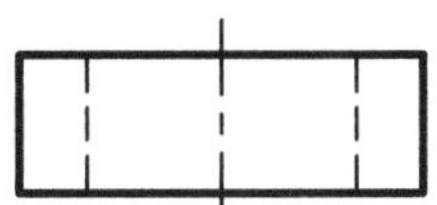

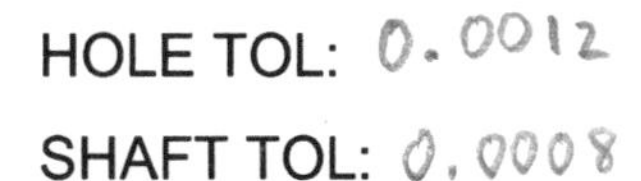

HOLE TOL: 0.0012

SHAFT TOL: 0.0008

MAX. CLEARANCE: 0.0016

ALLOWANCE: -0.0004

DIMENSION THE HOLES AND SHAFTS FOR THE REQUIRED LINEAR TOLERANCE. ALSO CALCULATE THE HOLE TOLERANCE, SHAFT TOLERANCE, MAXIMUM CLEARANCE, AND ALLOWANCE.

NAME:

DATE:

DIAMETER: 3.25 INCHES
TYPE OF FIT: FN 4

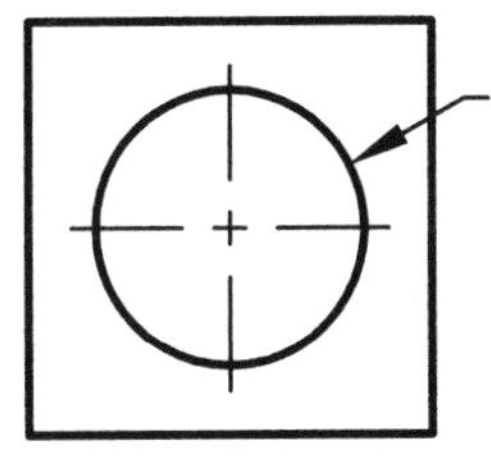
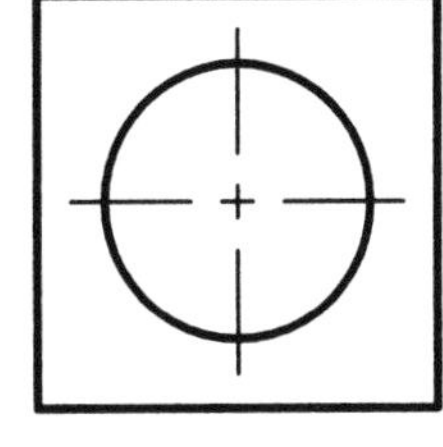
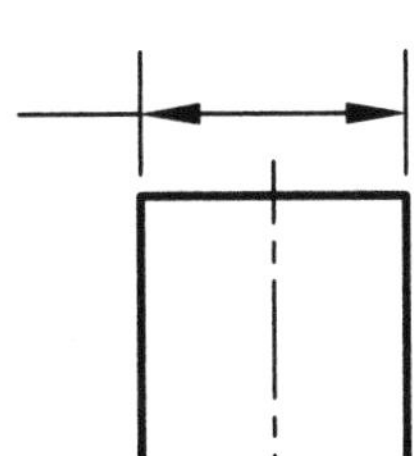
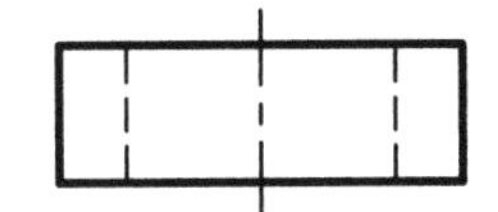

HOLE TOL:

SHAFT TOL:

MAX. CLEARANCE:

ALLOWANCE:

DIAMETER: 0.75 INCHES
TYPE OF FIT: LC 1

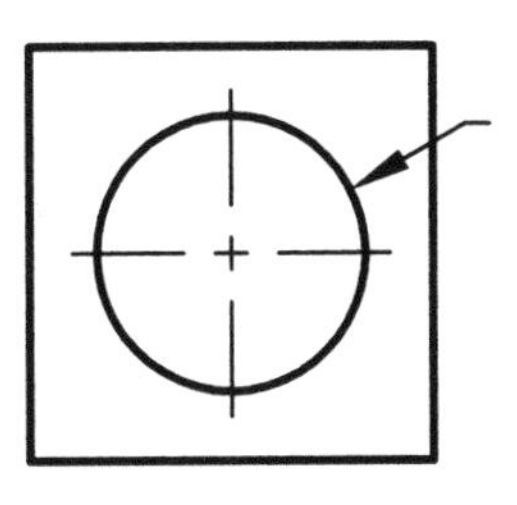
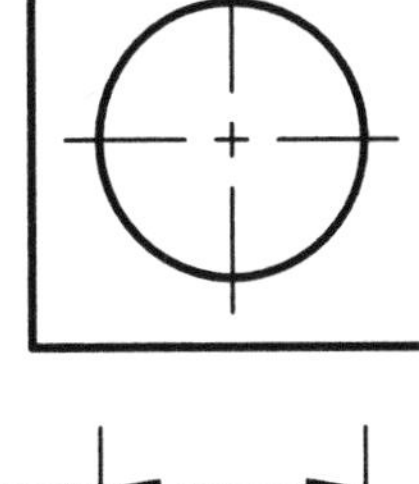
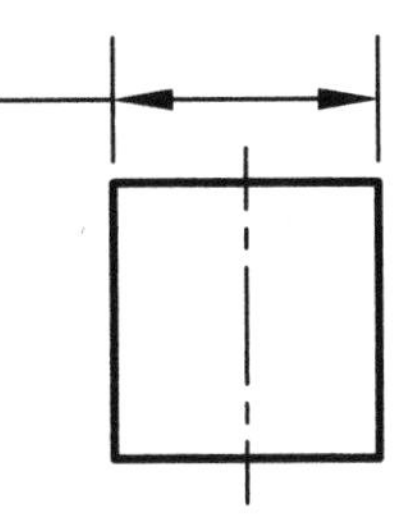
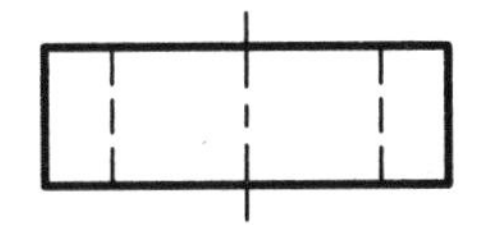

HOLE TOL:

SHAFT TOL:

MAX. CLEARANCE:

ALLOWANCE:

DIMENSION THE HOLES AND SHAFTS FOR THE REQUIRED LINEAR TOLERANCE. ALSO CALCULATE THE HOLE TOLERANCE, SHAFT TOLERANCE, MAXIMUM CLEARANCE, AND ALLOWANCE.

EXERCISE 03

NAME:

DATE:

DIAMETER: 4.50 INCHES
TYPE OF FIT: RC 8

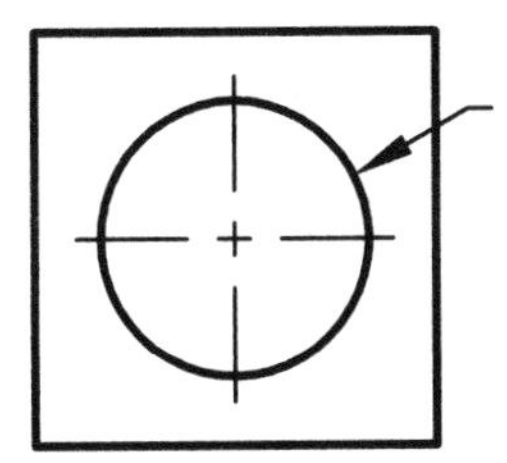

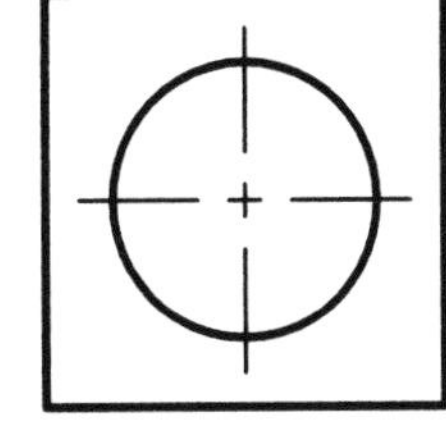

HOLE TOL:

SHAFT TOL:

MAX. CLEARANCE:

ALLOWANCE:

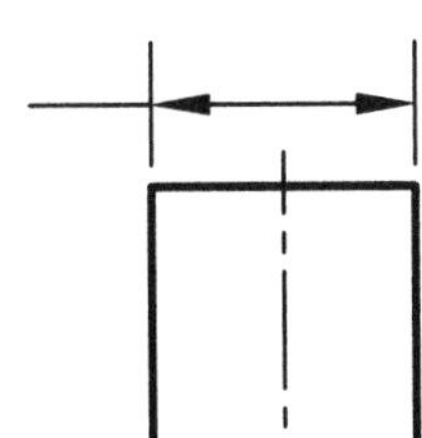

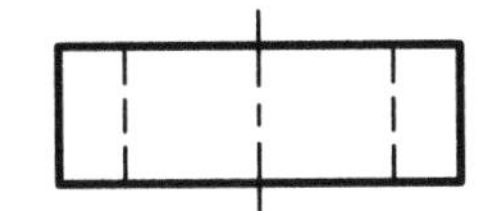

DIAMETER: 0.25 INCHES
TYPE OF FIT: LN 3

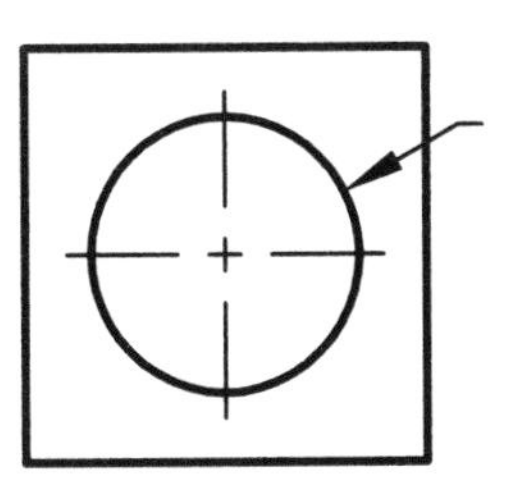

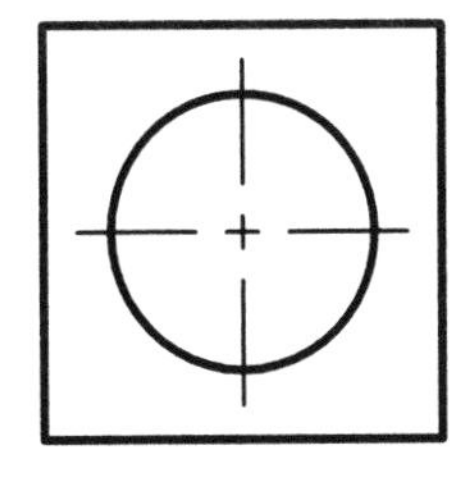

HOLE TOL:

SHAFT TOL:

MAX. CLEARANCE:

ALLOWANCE:

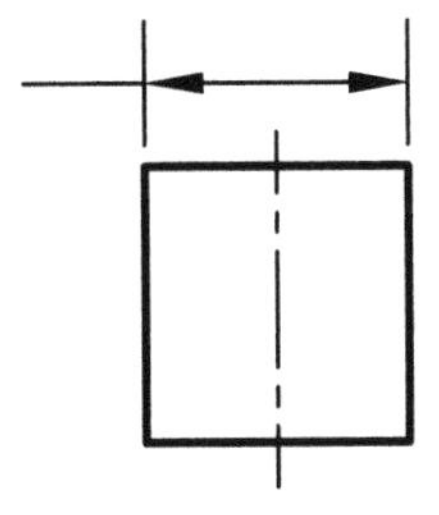

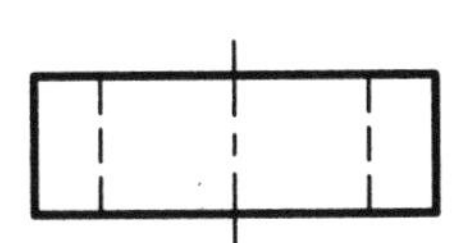

DIMENSION THE HOLES AND SHAFTS FOR THE REQUIRED LINEAR TOLERANCE. ALSO CALCULATE THE HOLE TOLERANCE, SHAFT TOLERANCE, MAXIMUM CLEARANCE, AND ALLOWANCE.

EXERCISE 04

NAME:

DATE:

DIAMETER: 2.75 INCHES
TYPE OF FIT: FN 4

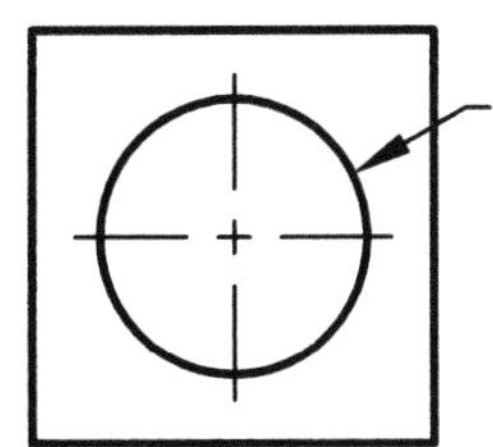
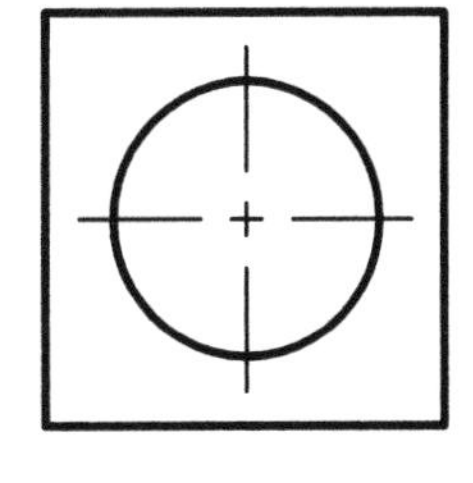
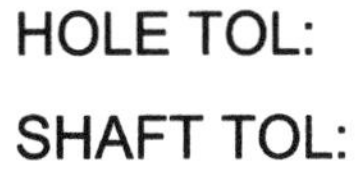
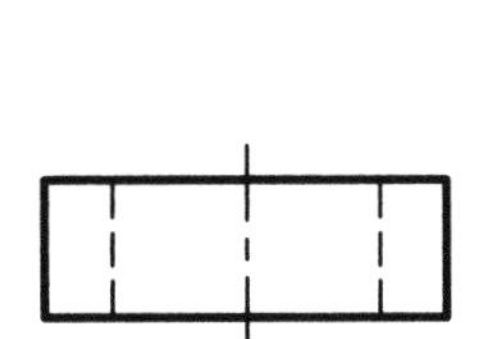
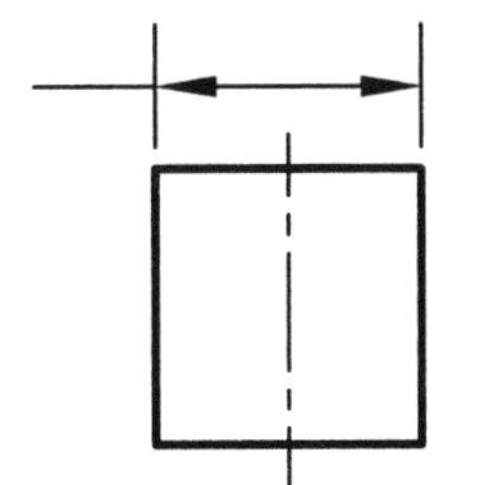

HOLE TOL:

SHAFT TOL:

MAX. CLEARANCE:

ALLOWANCE:

DIAMETER: 12.00 INCHES
TYPE OF FIT: RC 9

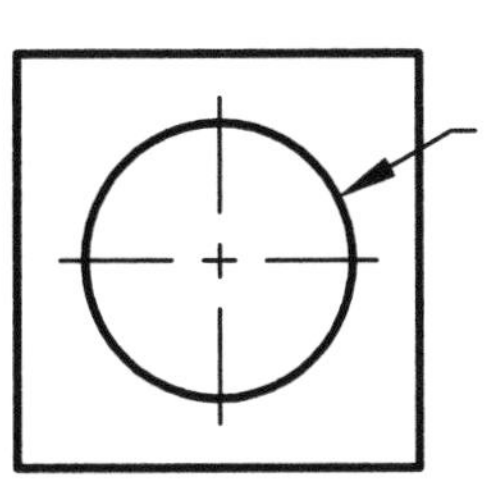
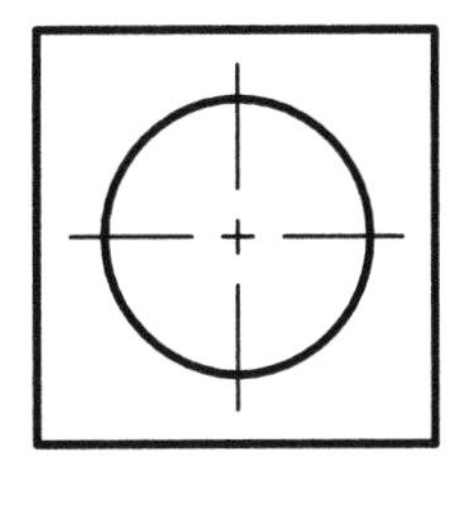

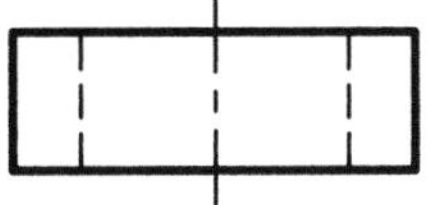
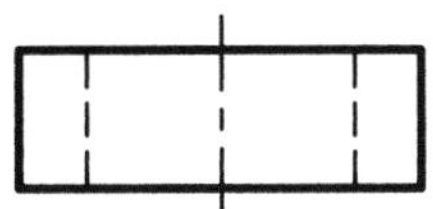
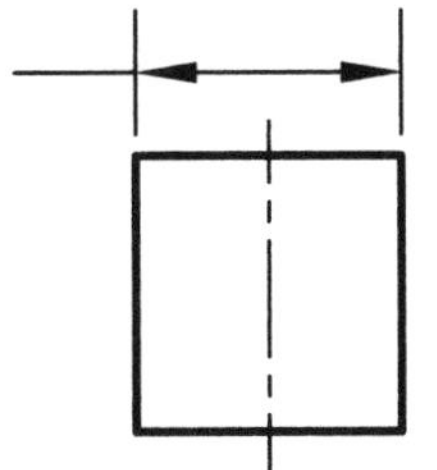

HOLE TOL:

SHAFT TOL:

MAX. CLEARANCE:

ALLOWANCE:

DIMENSION THE HOLES AND SHAFTS FOR THE REQUIRED LINEAR TOLERANCE. ALSO CALCULATE THE HOLE TOLERANCE, SHAFT TOLERANCE, MAXIMUM CLEARANCE, AND ALLOWANCE.

Tolerances

Chapter 07
Exercise 05

Name: SV

Date:

DIAMETER: 10 mm
TYPE OF FIT: H9/d9

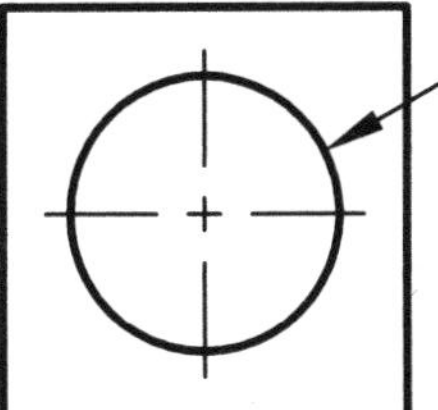
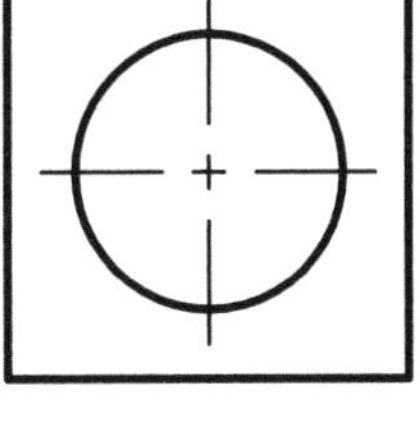
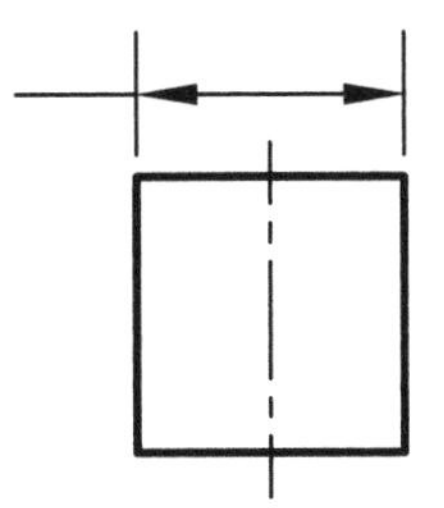

HOLE TOL: 36
SHAFT TOL: 36
MAX. CLEARANCE: 112
ALLOWANCE: 40

DIAMETER: 12 mm
TYPE OF FIT: H7/h6

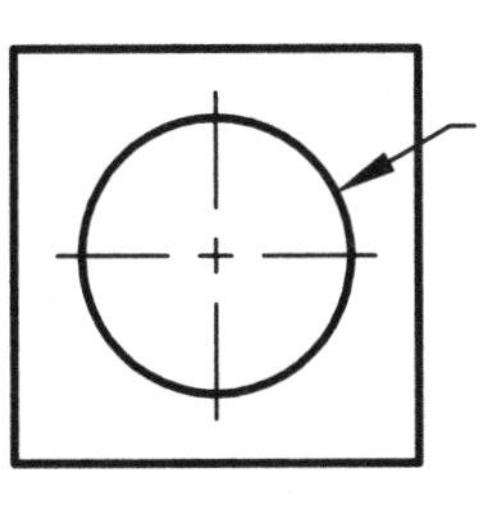
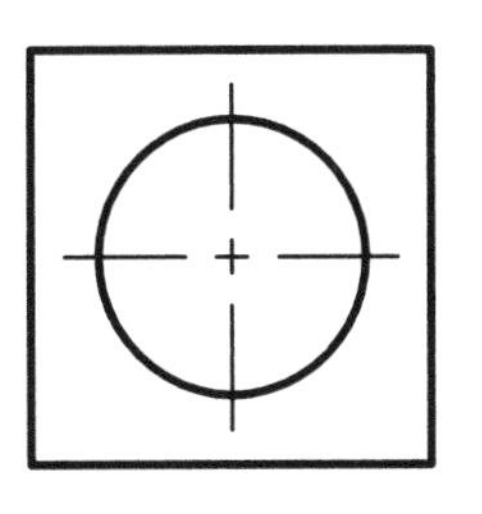
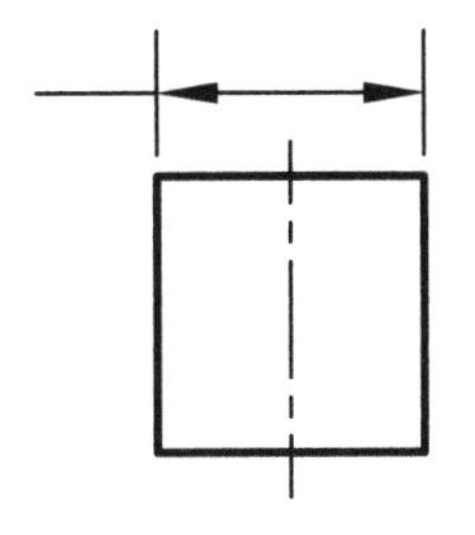
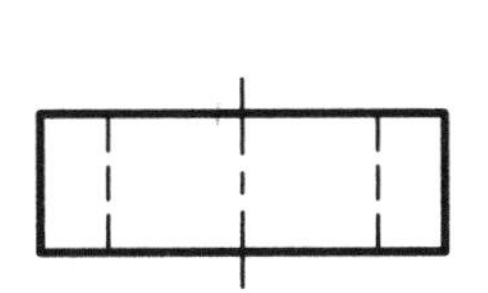

HOLE TOL: 18
SHAFT TOL: 11
MAX. CLEARANCE: 29
ALLOWANCE: 0

Dimension the holes and shafts for the required linear tolerance. Also calculate the hole tolerance, shaft tolerance, maximum clearance, and allowance.

EXERCISE 06

NAME:

DATE:

DIAMETER: 30 mm
TYPE OF FIT: H11/c11

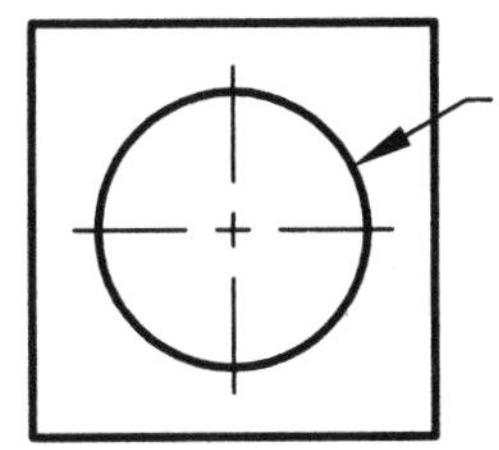

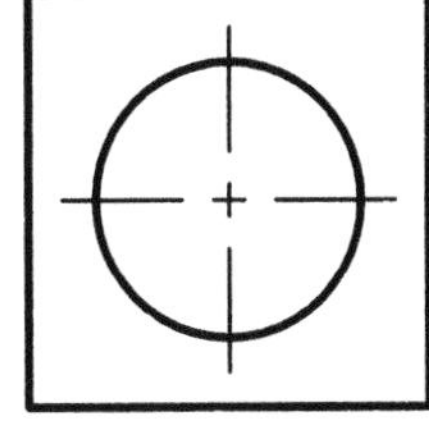

HOLE TOL:

SHAFT TOL:

MAX. CLEARANCE:

ALLOWANCE:

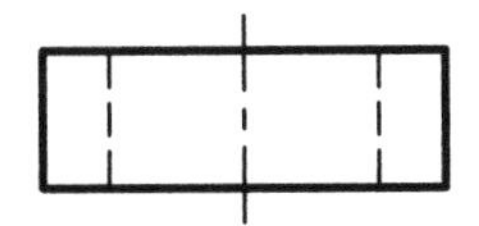

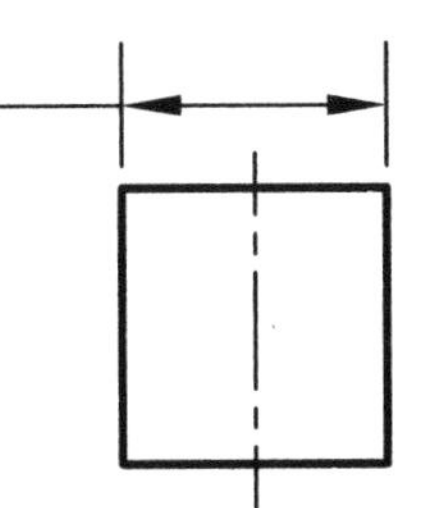

DIAMETER: 80 mm
TYPE OF FIT: H7/g6

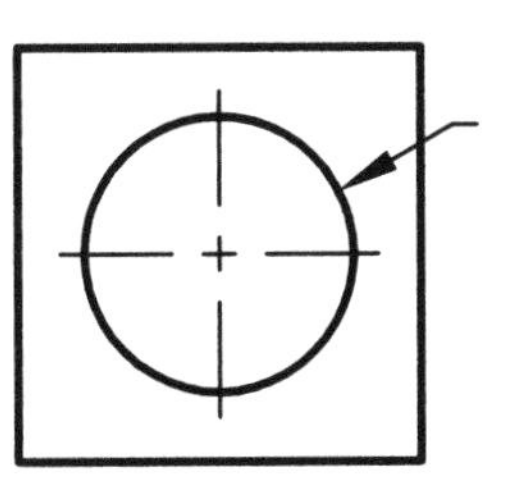

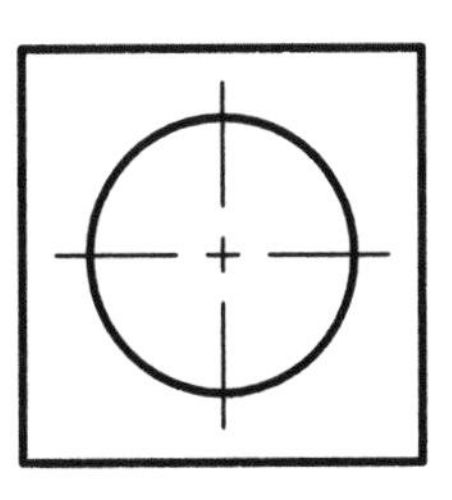

HOLE TOL:

SHAFT TOL:

MAX. CLEARANCE:

ALLOWANCE:

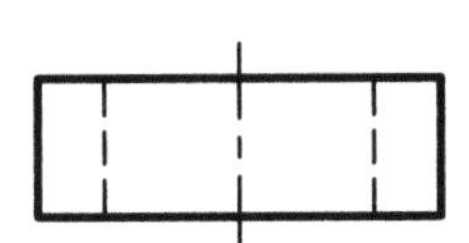

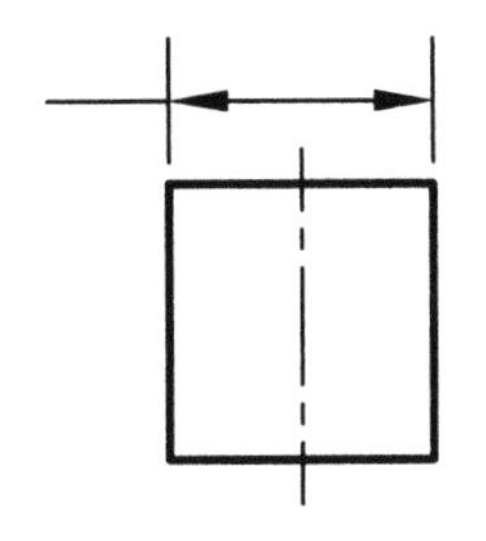

DIMENSION THE HOLES AND SHAFTS FOR THE REQUIRED LINEAR TOLERANCE. ALSO CALCULATE THE HOLE TOLERANCE, SHAFT TOLERANCE, MAXIMUM CLEARANCE, AND ALLOWANCE.

TOLERANCES

NAME:

CHAPTER 07
EXERCISE 07

DATE:

DIAMETER: 3 mm
TYPE OF FIT: H8/f7

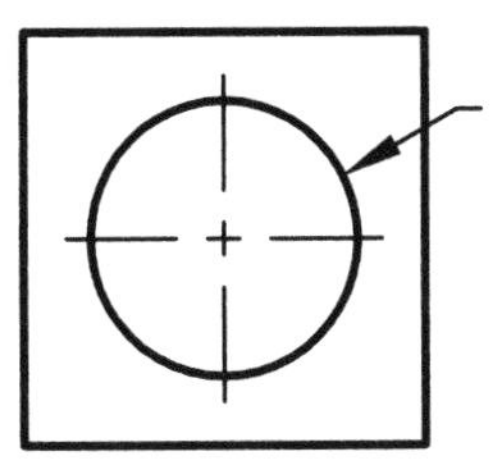

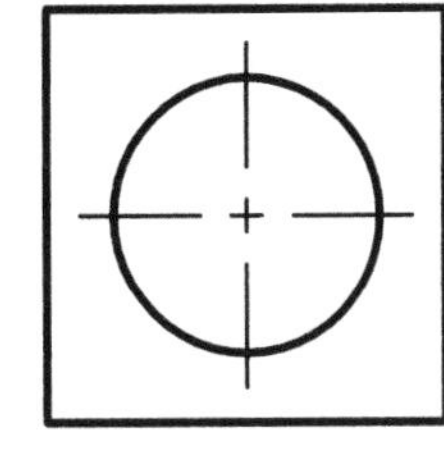

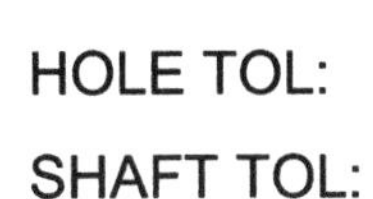

HOLE TOL:

SHAFT TOL:

MAX. CLEARANCE:

ALLOWANCE:

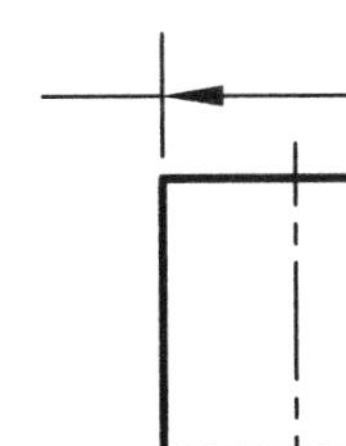

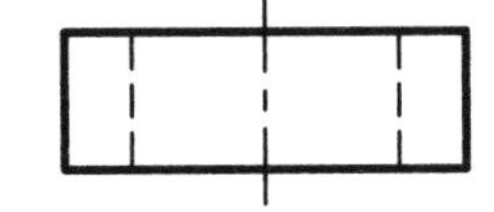

DIAMETER: 5 mm
TYPE OF FIT: H7/s6

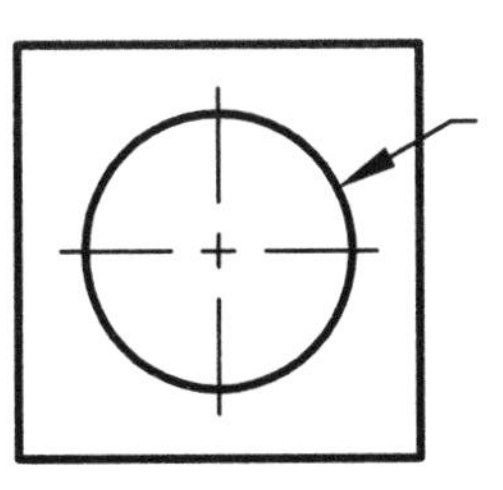

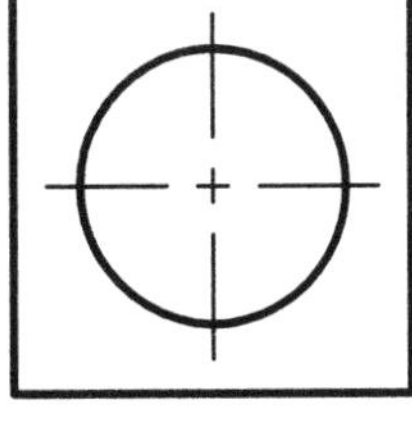

HOLE TOL:

SHAFT TOL:

MAX. CLEARANCE:

ALLOWANCE:

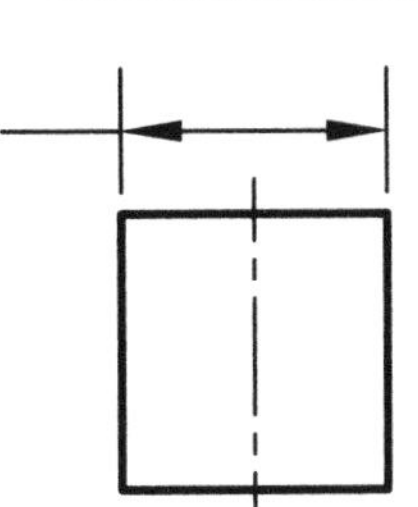

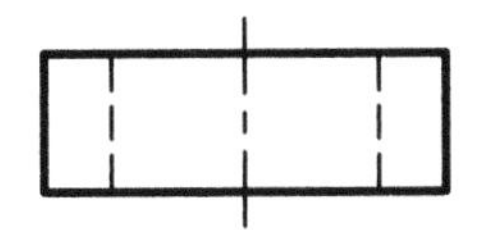

DIMENSION THE HOLES AND SHAFTS FOR THE REQUIRED LINEAR TOLERANCE. ALSO CALCULATE THE HOLE TOLERANCE, SHAFT TOLERANCE, MAXIMUM CLEARANCE, AND ALLOWANCE.

NAME:

DATE:

DIAMETER: 25 mm
TYPE OF FIT: H7/u6

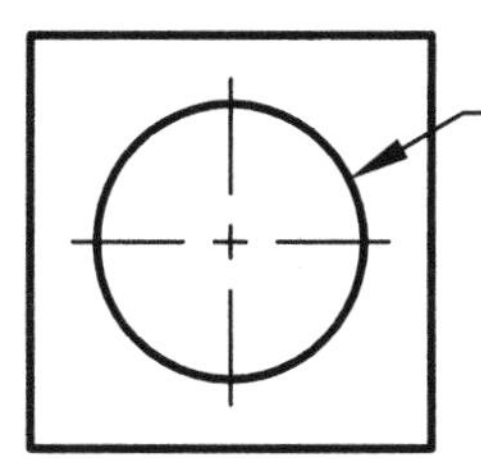

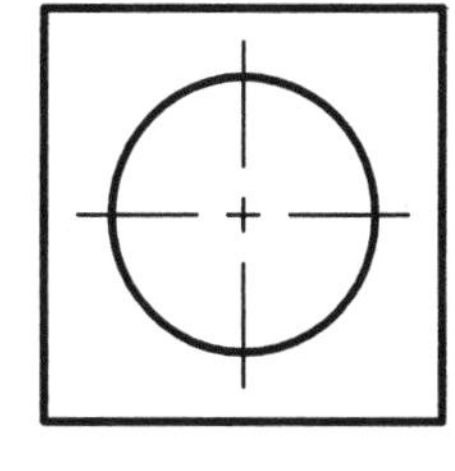

HOLE TOL:

SHAFT TOL:

MAX. CLEARANCE:

ALLOWANCE:

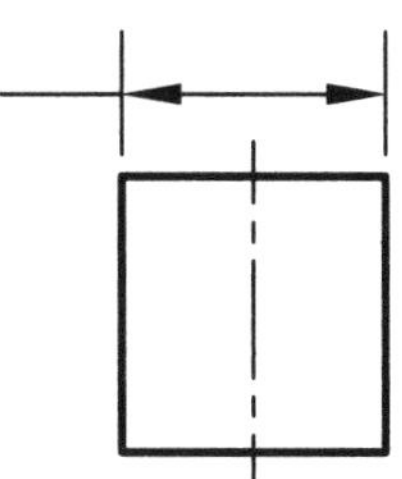

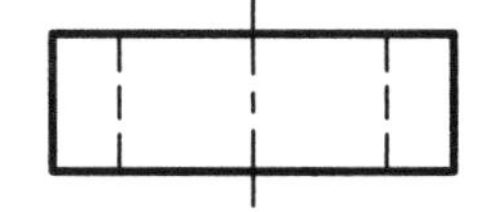

DIAMETER: 100 mm
TYPE OF FIT: H7/k6

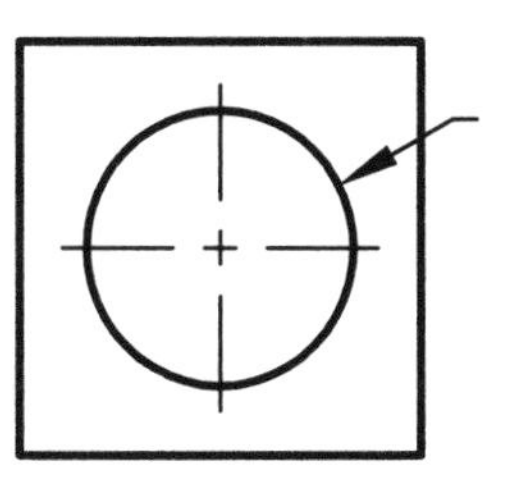

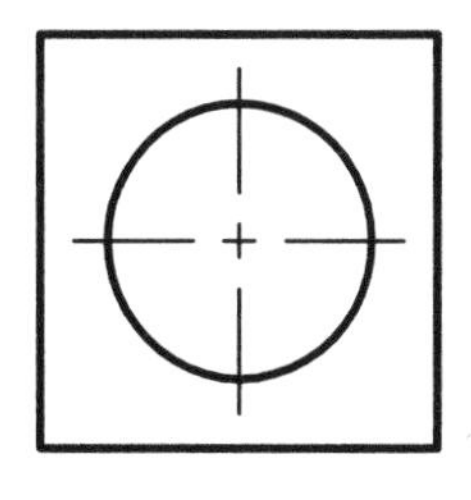

HOLE TOL:

SHAFT TOL:

MAX. CLEARANCE:

ALLOWANCE:

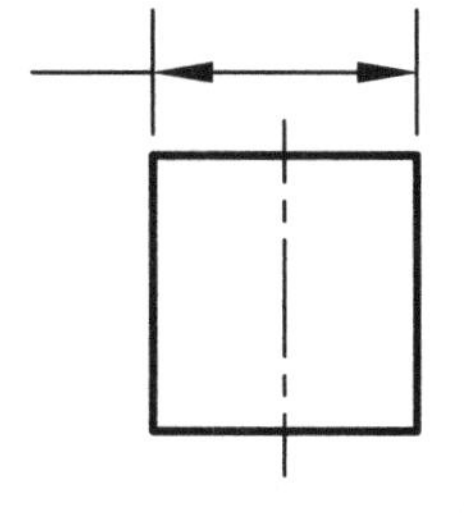

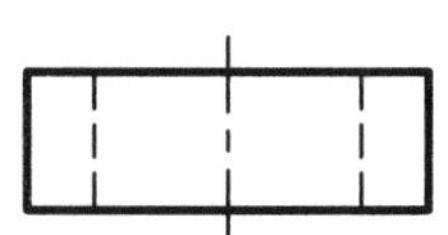

DIMENSION THE HOLES AND SHAFTS FOR THE REQUIRED LINEAR TOLERANCE. ALSO CALCULATE THE HOLE TOLERANCE, SHAFT TOLERANCE, MAXIMUM CLEARANCE, AND ALLOWANCE.

Tolerances

Name:

Chapter 07
Exercise 09

Date:

1. If the tolerance limits of a hole are Ø1.5004 and Ø1.5000, what do the shaft tolerance limits need to be if they are required allowance is .0007 and the shaft tolerance .0005? What type of fit is this?

2. If the tolerance limits of a shaft are Ø3.0019, what do the hole tolerance limits need to be if the required maximum clearance is -.0007 and the hole tolerance .0007? What type of fit is this?

3. If the tolerance limits of a hole are Ø8.001 and Ø8.000, what do the shaft tolerance limits need to be if the required maximum clearance is .002 and the allowance .005? What is the shaft tolerance? What type of fit is this?

Answer the following tolerancing questions for a cylindrical fit (hole/shaft). Show your work in the space provided.

TOLERANCES

CHAPTER 07
EXERCISE 10

NAME: SV

DATE:

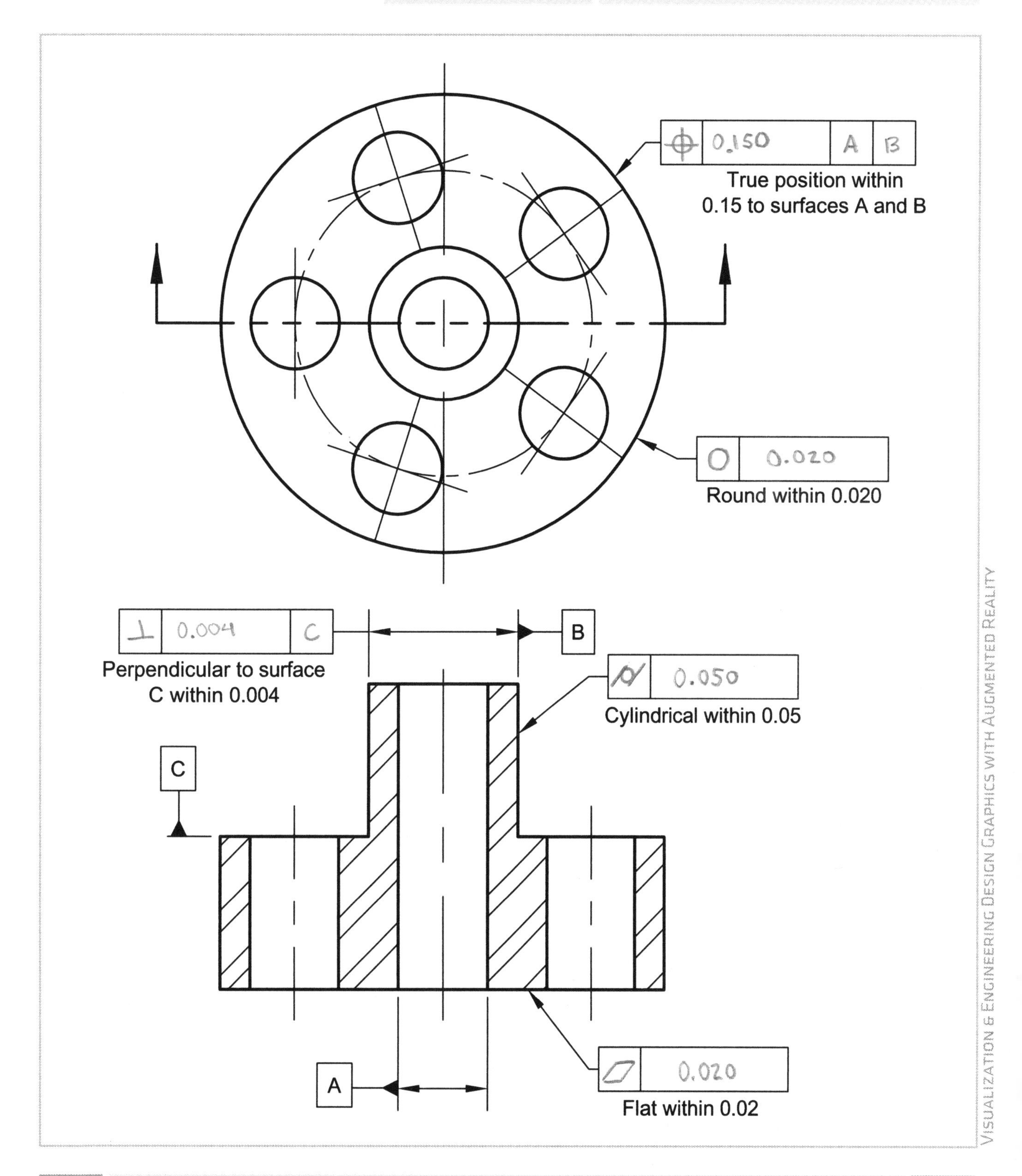

APPLY THE GEOMETRIC TOLERANCES TO THE DRAWING.

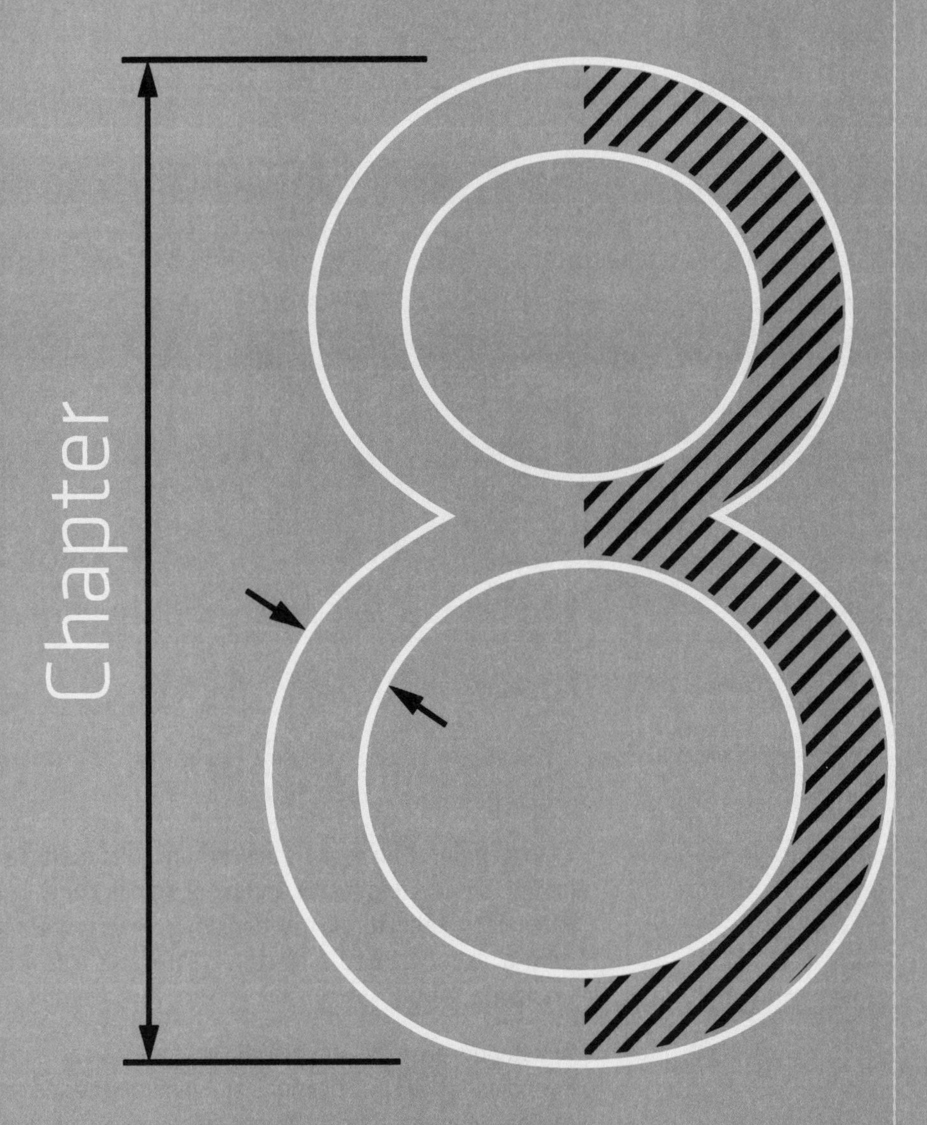

Chapter 8 Threaded Fasteners

Introduction

Most engineering designs are comprised of multiple components that need to be held together and fixed in their correct position. The term fastening refers to the mechanism by which two or more components are joined or secured in place. A fastener is a device designed for this purpose.

Fasteners are mass produced parts that can be easily purchased from vendors. Their specifications are generally defined by national and international standards. Proper selection of fasteners for a particular application is determined by many factors, including materials, loading capacity, environmental conditions, availability, and cost. The fasteners required to secure components in a highly corrosive environment, for example, will have different requirements than the fasteners used to hold together the different parts of an office chair.

Fastening is a broad and extensive field. In fact, entire books and reference manuals have been published devoted to this subject. This chapter is intended to provide a basic introduction to the field of joining and fastening systems from a purely descriptive standpoint. Design considerations, properties, and calculations for material, durability, strength, or weight are intentionally omitted. In this chapter, the basic fastening methods are discussed, with an emphasis on threaded fasteners.

Fasteners

Depending upon their function, fasteners can be classified as permanent or non-permanent. Permanent fastening methods are intended for parts that are not going to be disassembled. They create a stationary link between parts that cannot be separated without breaking the fastener or the components. Permanent fastening includes adhesives, welds, braces, solders, rivets, or nails. . Non-permanent fasteners are used for assemblies with a modular design, so they can be assembled and disassembled for maintenance, inspection, repair, or storage. Examples include screws, bolts, nuts, and pins. Many types of fasteners exist, each with different characteristics and design purposes. In production drawings, fasteners and other standard, mass produced components do not require orthographic views. Instead, only the specific information required to purchase the parts, in the form of regimented notation, needs to be provided.

FIG. 8.1 External threads on a bolt (left) and internal threads inside a nut (right)

Threaded Fasteners

Many non-permanent fasteners include threaded features. Threads are helical profiles, either cut (internal threads) or wrapped (external threads), along a cylindrical profile in order to transform rotational motion into linear motion, or to secure two or more parts together (see Figure 8.1).

Basic Definitions

Proper understanding of the basic terminology associated with threads is important. The terms defined in this section will be used throughout the entire chapter.

- Bolt: Cylindrical device with external helical profile designed for use with a hole and secured with a nut.
- Nut: Cylindrical device with internal threads used to mate with a bolt.
- Screw: Cylindrical device with external helical profile designed to be used in a threaded hole, sometimes along with a nut. In some cases, screws will cut corresponding internal threads on the part in the process of being seated.
- Head: The top portion of the screw or bolt, shaped so that it can easily interact with a driver (screwdriver or wrench) in order to mate with a hole.

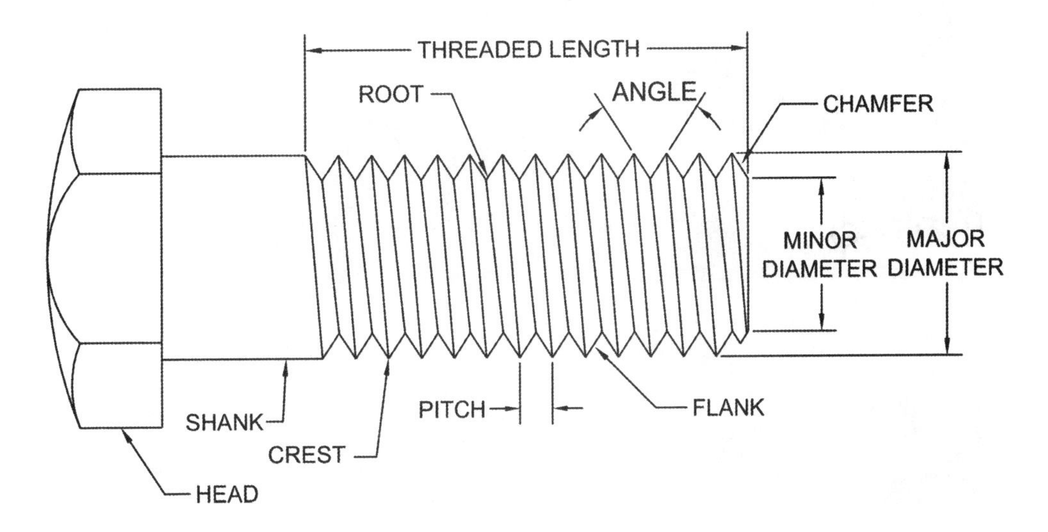

Thread terminology FIG. 8.2

- Shank: The cylindrical portion of the bolt between the head and the threaded portion.
- Root: The lowest point of the thread profile.
- Crest: The tallest point of the thread profile.
- Pitch: The longitudinal distance between two adjacent thread roots or crests.
- Flank: The surface of the thread that connects the root to the crest.
- Chamfer: The beveled edge of a bolt used in order to facilitate easier mating with the corresponding nut.

The previous terms are illustrated in Figure 8.2.

Thread Characteristics

The following characteristics are used to describe threads.

Direction

The majority of threads are constructed right-handed, so when the fastener is rotated clockwise around its longitudinal axis, the fastener advances forward. If rotated counter-clockwise, the fastener travels backwards. There are situations, however, where the opposite be-

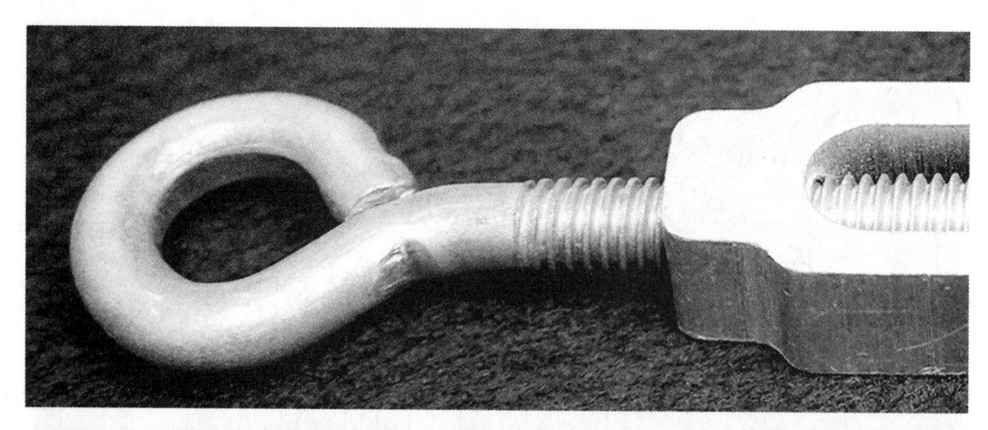

Fig. 8.3 Turnbuckle

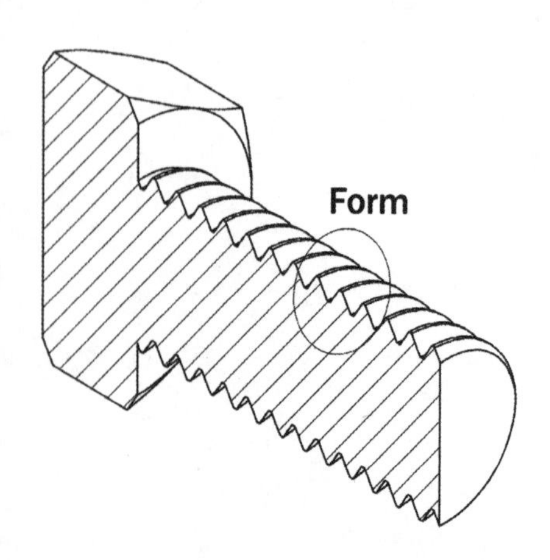

Fig. 8.4 Thread form

havior is required. A bolt with left-handed threads will travel forward when the thread is rotated counter-clockwise around its longitudinal axis. Left-handed threads are used to alleviate safety issues, such as with lawn mower blades, which are tightened opposite to the direction of blade rotation so they do not become loose when the mower is running. Supply links and certain gas regulators are situations where left-handed threads are used to ensure lines are not misconnected. Other devices, such as turnbuckles, utilize both left and right handed threads in order to increase tension in cables (see Figure 8.3).

Lead

The lead is the longitudinal distance traversed during one revolution of the fastener. For a single threaded object, the lead equals the pitch, which means that the fastener will travel forward or backward exactly one pitch distance when rotated one revolution. Some devices are created with double or triple threads, in which one revolution of the driver produces a longitudinal distance of either two or three times the pitch distance. Objects are double or triple threaded when rapid motion is preferred over holding power, or when greater distance per revolution is required while maintaining a larger thread surface area for strength.

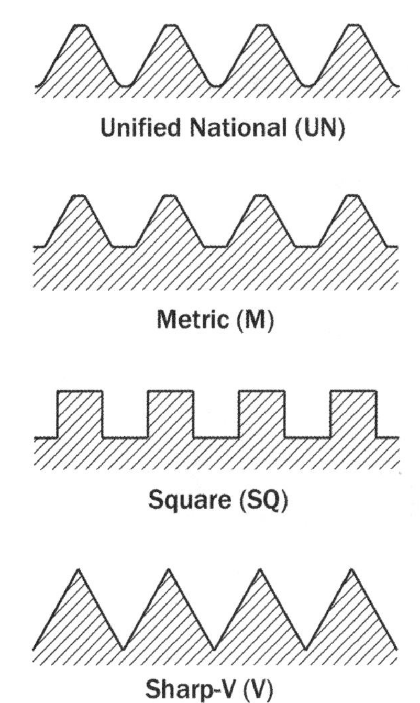

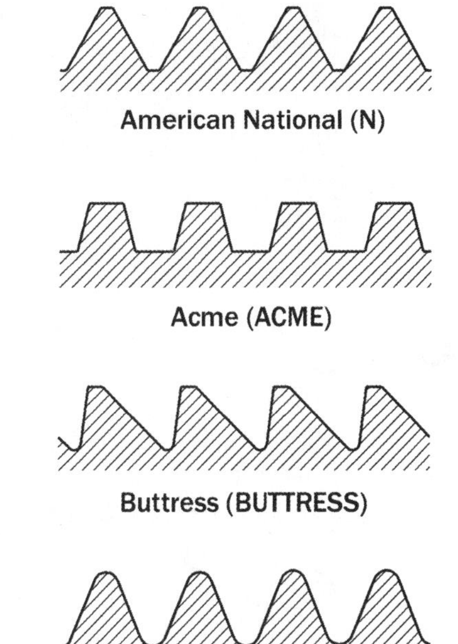

Common thread forms FIG. 8.5

Form

The form of a threaded fastener is defined as the cross-sectional shape of its profile, as shown in Figure 8.4. Different thread forms are defined by various standards organizations to ensure interchangeability between manufacturers, with each form's profile providing specific design capabilities. The most common thread forms are illustrated in Figure 8.5.

The most popular thread forms are Metric (defined in the ISO 261 standard) and Unified National (defined the ANSI Y14.6 standard).

The Sharp-V profile was the first thread standard in the United States. This form increased the friction of the thread, which creates tight seals, but was quickly replaced by the American National form because the sharp crests were easily damaged during manufacturing. The American National form flattened the sharp crests and roots of Sharp-V threads. The Unified National form is similar to the American National, except the roots are rounded instead of flattened, and is the current standard in the United States. The Metric form is the international standard.

Acme, Buttress, and Square thread forms are used quite extensively in industry. Acme threads are used when heavy loads and high accuracy are required. Buttress threads are useful when high axial loads

Fig. 8.6 Coarse (top) and fine threads (bottom)

are created in only one direction. Square threads are very efficient, but difficult to manufacture. Radial pressure is reduced because of the lack of thread angle.

Series

A thread's series is defined as the number of threads per inch for a specific diameter (for English threads only). Common series are designated coarse, fine, or extra fine, depending upon the diameter. For instance, 20 threads per inch can be defined as coarse (for ¼ inch bolts), fine (for ½ inch bolts), or extra fine (for 1 inch bolts). A coarse thread has a larger pitch (fewer threads per inch) than a fine thread (more threads per inch), as shown in Figure 8.6. Coarse threads are general-purpose threads used for holding. Fine threads are used when additional force is needed to hold components together. They are used extensively in the aircraft and automotive industries. Extra fine threads are used on short and small diameter fasteners.

Class of Fit

The fit of a thread defines how tightly the mating threaded fasteners fit together. Loose fits (assigned a value of 1) are used when a relative amount of looseness is desired. They are used in harsh environments, where corrosion may affect the thread. Regular or average fits (assigned a value of 2) are general-purpose threads used in normal ap-

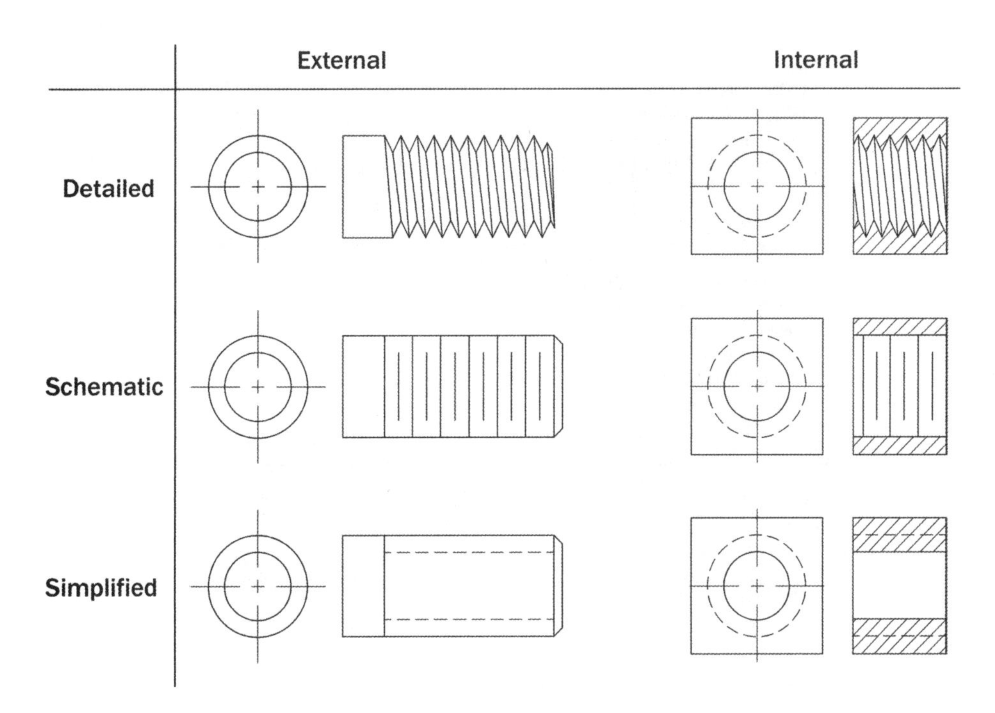

Thread symbols for external and internal threads shown orthographically and as sections FIG. 8.7

plications. Tight fits (assigned a value of 3) are used when fasteners need to resist the effects of vibration or support high pressures and stresses.

THREAD SPECIFICATION

Thread Symbols

Representing threaded fasteners on a drawing in a realistic manner oftentimes results in a lack of clarity, because of the inherent closeness of the lines (both visible and hidden). As an example, a thread with a large number of threads per inch may cause the printer toner to bleed together. To simplify drawings, three standard representations were developed: detailed, schematic, and simplified (see Figure 8.7). These thread symbols alert the machinist to search for a note indicating the specific information about the fastener.

Detailed thread symbols more closely resemble the actual threaded part but are time-consuming to create. Schematic thread symbols, using a combination of thicker root lines and thinner crest lines, approximate a threaded part and are easier to draw. Simplified threads use dashed lines to represent the minor diameter of the thread. To optimize performance, many parametric modeling applications make simplifications when representing threads since accurate threads would significantly increase the complexity of a part.

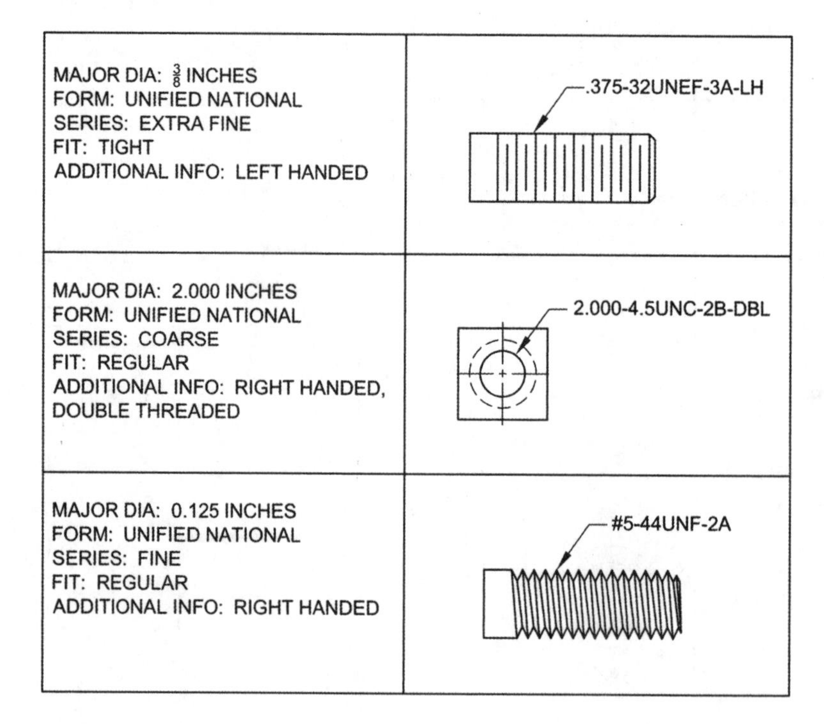

MAJOR DIA: 3/8 INCHES FORM: UNIFIED NATIONAL SERIES: EXTRA FINE FIT: TIGHT ADDITIONAL INFO: LEFT HANDED	.375-32UNEF-3A-LH
MAJOR DIA: 2.000 INCHES FORM: UNIFIED NATIONAL SERIES: COARSE FIT: REGULAR ADDITIONAL INFO: RIGHT HANDED, DOUBLE THREADED	2.000-4.5UNC-2B-DBL
MAJOR DIA: 0.125 INCHES FORM: UNIFIED NATIONAL SERIES: FINE FIT: REGULAR ADDITIONAL INFO: RIGHT HANDED	#5-44UNF-2A

FIG. 8.9 English thread note examples

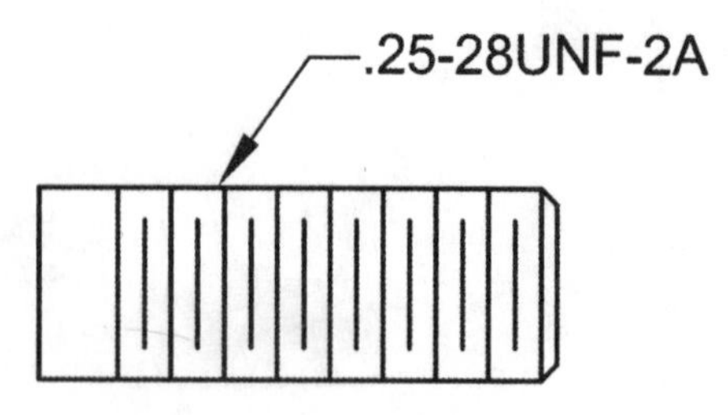

FIG. 8.8 English thread note

Thread Notes

Threads are identified on a drawing with notes that provide a complete specification about the thread. The thread note is connected to the thread symbol by the use of a leader. These notes take different forms, depending on whether they describe an English thread or a Metric thread.

English

Thread notes used for English threads must provide the following basic information in this sequence:

1. Thread diameter, shown as a fraction or decimal (1/4 or 0.25), followed by a hyphen. For small shanks, a standard number is assigned instead of the diameter.

2. Threads per inch. Form (specified with letter codes, such as "UN" for Unified National), and series ("C" for coarse, "F" for fine, and "EF" for extra fine), followed by a hyphen.

3. Class of fit ("1" for loose, "2" regular, and "3" for tight) and whether the thread is external, such as those found in bolts, screws, or threaded rods; or internal, such as those in nuts or threaded holes. External threads are represented with a capital letter "A". For internal threads, a capital "B" is used.

		Threads per Inch										
		Series with graded pitches			Series with constant pitches							
Sizes	Basic major diameter	Coarse UNC	Fine UNF	Extra Fine UNEF	4UN	6UN	8UN	12UN	16UN	20UN	28UN	32UN
...	...		...	...	...	...	...	...	...	...	...	...
1 - 1/8	1.125	7	12	18	-	-	8	UNF	16	20	28	-
1 - 3/16	1.188	-	-	18	-	-	8	12	16	20	28	-
1 – 1/4	1.25	7	12	18	-	-	8	UNF	16	20	28	-
1 – 5/16	1.313	-	-	18	-	-	8	12	16	20	28	-
1 – 3/8	1.375	6	12	18	-	UNC	8	UNF	16	20	28	-
...	...		...	...	...	...	...	...	...	...	...	...

English thread table FIG. 8.10

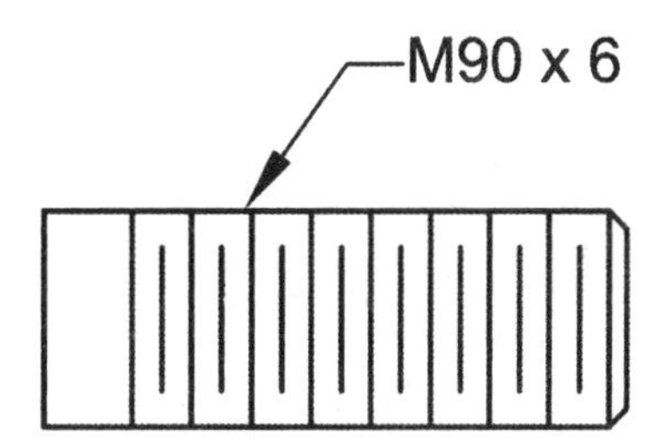

Metric thread note FIG. 8.11

As an example, the thread note shown in Figure 8.8 describes a thread with a .25 diameter, 28 threads per inch, "Unified National", fine series, average fit, external.

Additional information may be added to the thread note, such as whether the thread is double or triple. All threads are assumed to be right handed, unless "LH" follows the tail of the note. See Figure 8.9 for examples of various English thread notes.

For standard threads, the number of threads per inch can be found in standard thread tables, which are included in the Appendix Suppose you wish to find the threads per inch for a coarsely threaded 1.25" diameter bolt. The first column of the thread table provides diameters (in inches); locate the row corresponding to the 1.25"diameter. Next, look for the intersection between that row and the "Coarse" column. A coarsely threaded 1.25" diameter bolt has 7 threads per inch, as shown in Figure 8.10.

Metric

Standard metric fasteners are defined by ANSI in the standard B1.13, which is based on ISO references. Because of the smaller standard unit (mm), metric threads are only listed as coarse or fine. The capital letter "M" at the beginning of the note indicates metric form. Next, the thread diameter (in mm) is provided. An "x" (read as "by") is in-

MAJOR DIA: 4 mm FORM: ISO METRIC PITCH: 0.7 mm TOL CLASS: 6g (MED-REG. FIT) EXT OR INT: g (LOW CASE) (EXT) LENGTH: S (SHORT)	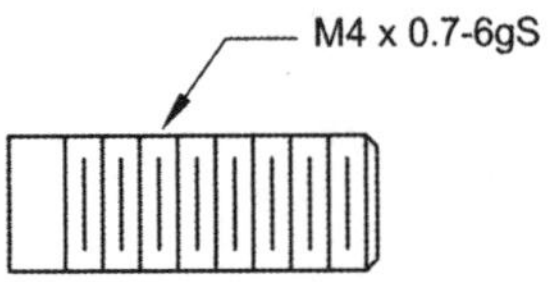 M4 x 0.7-6gS
MAJOR DIA: 10 mm FORM: ISO METRIC PITCH: 1.5 mm TOL CLASS: 4H (FINE-TIGHT FIT) EXT OR INT: H (UP CASE) (INT) LENGTH: 8 mm	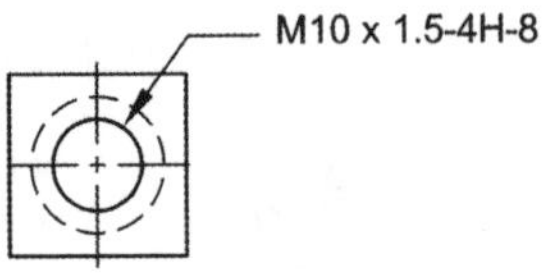 M10 x 1.5-4H-8
MAJOR DIA: 27 mm FORM: ISO METRIC PITCH: 3 mm TOL CLASS: 8g (COARSE-REG. FIT) EXT OR INT: g (LOW CASE) (EXT) LENGTH: 40 mm ADDITIONAL INFO: LEFT HANDED	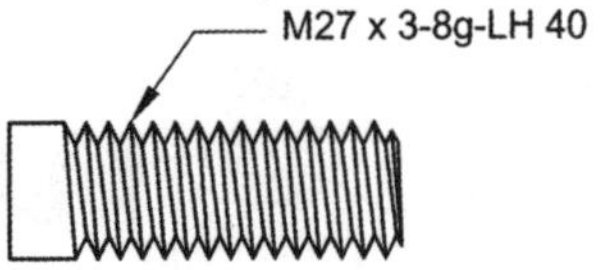 M27 x 3-8g-LH 40

FIG. 8.12 Metric thread note examples

Metric Threads

Major Diameter	Tap Drill	Pitch	
		Coarse	Fine
...	...	...	...
M16	14.00	2	1.5
M18	15.50	2.5	1.5
M20	17.50	**2.5**	1.5
M22	19.50	2.5	1.5
M24	21.00	3	2
...	...	...	...

FIG. 8.13 Metric thread table

cluded, followed by the pitch (in mm). An example of a basic metric thread note is shown in Figure 8.11.

For most applications, thread notes only listing diameter and pitch information is sufficient. Occasionally, further information may be required, such as tolerance class (fit) and thread length. As with English thread notes, if the fastener is left handed, "LH" must be added at the end of the note.

The tolerance class is represented by numbers from 3 to 9, followed by a letter (E, G, or H). The number correlates to the tolerance grade (a larger number indicates a larger tolerance), with 6 (medium) being most common. The letter represents the type of fit ("E" is loose, "G" is regular, and "H" is tight). Upper case letters are used for internal threads and lower case letters are used for external threads. Thread length can be indicated by numbers, or letters ("S" for short, "N" for normal, and "L" for long). See Figure 8.12 for examples of metric thread notes.

For standard metric threads, the pitch can be found in standard thread tables, which are included in the Appendix. Suppose you wish to find the pitch for a coarsely threaded 20 mm diameter bolt. The first column of the thread table provides diameters (in mm); locate the row corresponding to the M20 diameter. Next, look for the intersection between that row and the "Coarse" column. A coarsely threaded 20 mm diameter bolt has a pitch of 2.5 mm, as shown in Figure 8.13.

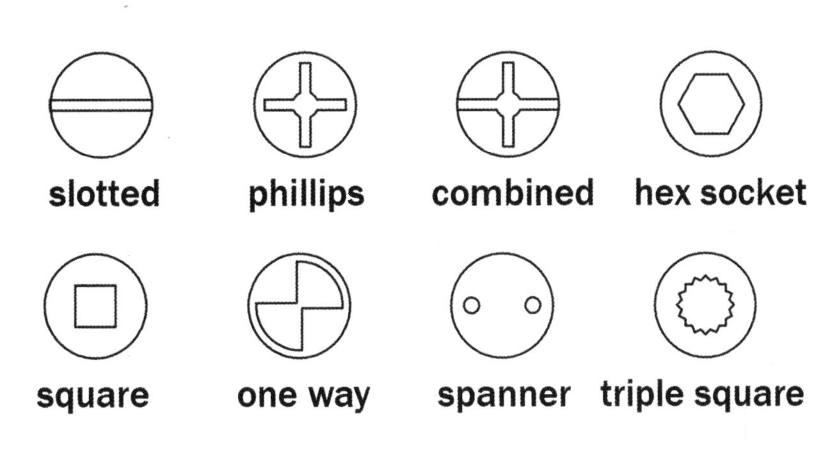

Common drive types FIG. 8.15

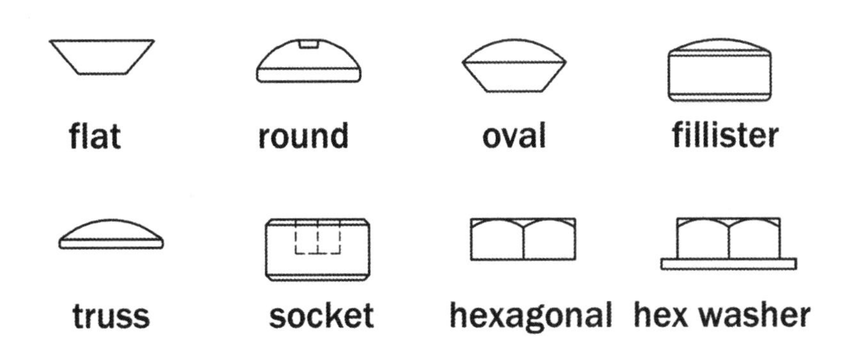

Common thread fasteners FIG. 8.14

HEAD AND DRIVE TYPES

The head is the top portion of a fastener. It is shaped so that a tool (of mating shape) can be used to seat it. Tools include sockets, screw drivers, Allen wrenches, etc. Most fasteners have a head, although some exceptions exist depending on the application. Common head types are shown in Figure 8.14.

The drive is a recessed profile, cut into the head of certain fasteners, to enable a driving tool to seat it. There are different types of drives, and numerous head-drive combinations. Oftentimes, when putting together a consumer product (such as a shelf, computer desk, or crib), the manufacturer will provide a special drive tool specifically designed for assembly. Common drive shapes are shown in Figure 8.15.

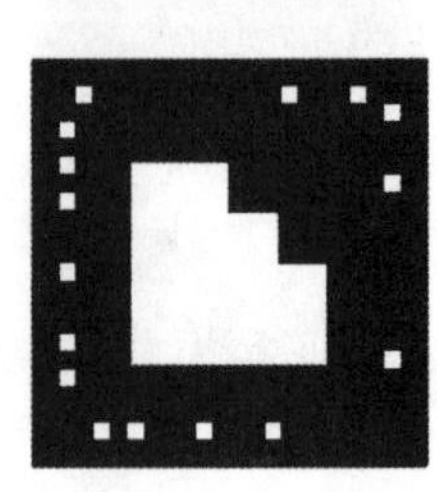

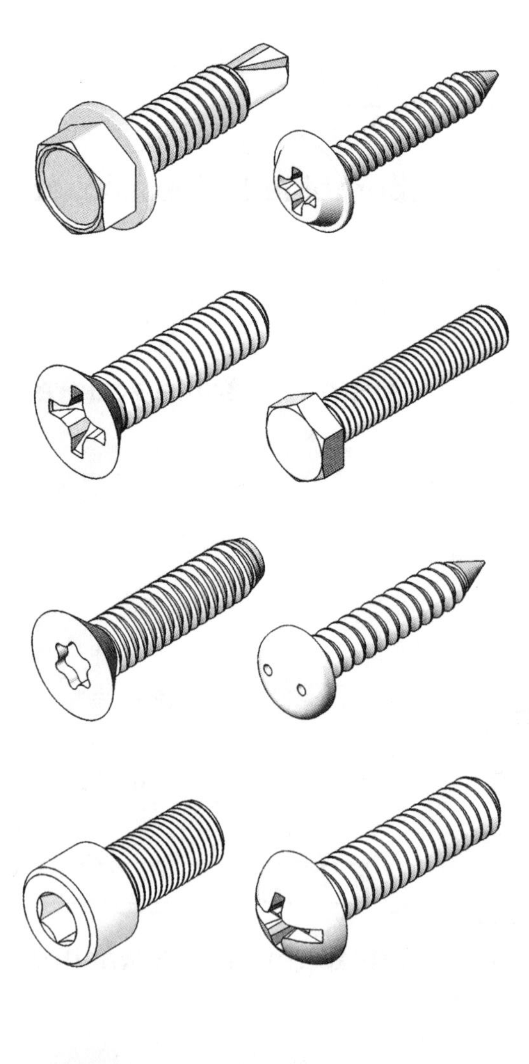

FIG. 8.16 Bolts and screws

BOLTS AND SCREWS

As stated earlier in the chapter, bolts are cylindrical fasteners with external threads designed to work in conjunction with nuts or holes. Screws are similar to bolts, typically cutting their internal threads on the mating part in the driving process. See Figure 8.16 for examples of bolts and screws.

Bolts and screws are rarely drawn and dimensioned, as they are standard parts. Usually, only notes are required (standard part notes, and their role in a set of working drawings, will be discussed in a later chapter). In addition to the thread note, when annotating bolts and screws, the length of the fastener (indicated with the letters "LG", for "long"), how much of the shank is threaded, and sometimes material, must be provided.

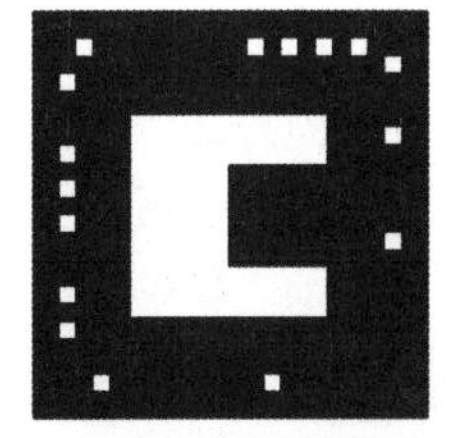

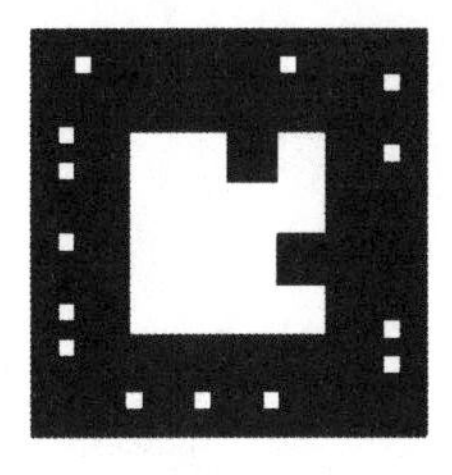

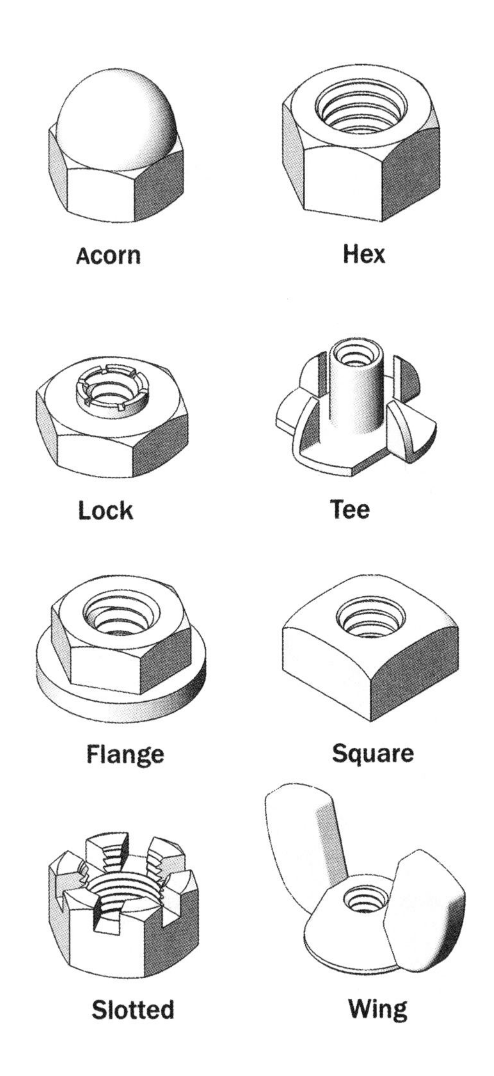

Common types of nuts FIG. 8.17

As an example, the following note can be used to describe a bolt: ½ - 13UNC-2A x 2.00 LG, REG HEX HD BOLT - SAE GRADE 7 STEEL. Likewise, the note: ½ - 13UNC-2A x 1.00 LG, FLAT HDCAP SCREW designates a screw.

Nuts

Nuts are fasteners with internal threads designed to be used in conjunction with bolts. Nuts can have a multitude of shapes and forms, depending on the application and the tool used to seat them (even your thumbs). Common nut types are illustrated in Figure 8.17.

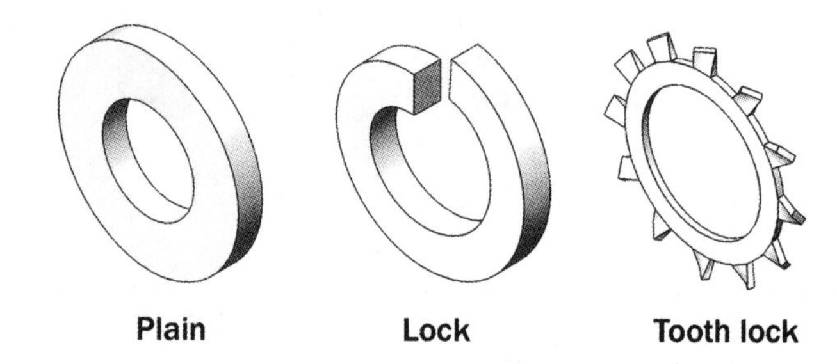

Fig. 8.18 Common types of washers

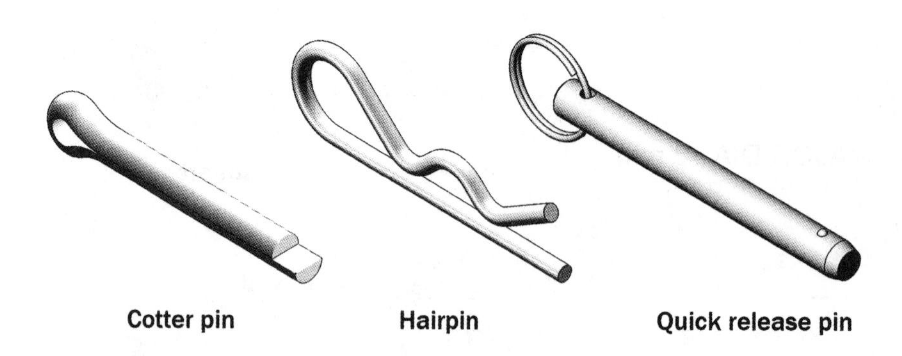

Fig. 8.19 Common types of pins

Unthreaded Fasteners

Some fasteners are unthreaded, such as washers and pins. Washers are small disk-shaped objects placed between a bolt and its mating component in order to provide a smooth contact surface and distribute pressure over the fastening area (see Figure 8.18). Some washers, such as lock washers, are used to prevent disassembly when subjected to vibration. Washers are annotated with the inside and outside diameters and their thickness. The following is an example of a typical plain washer annotation:

"1-1/16 x 2-1/2 x 0.2 TYPE A PLAIN WASHER"

(Inside diameter=1.0625", Outside diameter=2.5", and Thickness=0.2").

Pins are unthreaded devices used to lock components together. Pin selection depends upon the precision and strength needed in the assembly. Common types of pin include cotter pins, clevis pins, hitch pins, locking pins, and quick-release pins (see Figure 8.19).

THREADED FASTENERS

CHAPTER 08

EXERCISE 01

NAME:

DATE:

MAJOR DIA: 1.000 INCHES FORM: UNIFIED NATIONAL SERIES: COARSE FIT: TIGHT ADDITIONAL INFO: RIGHT HANDED	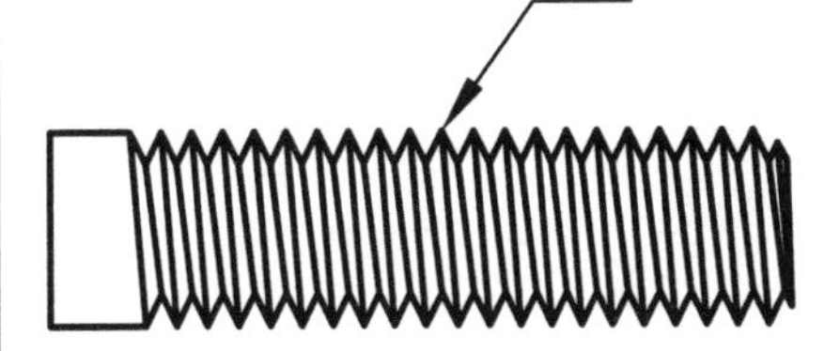 THREAD SYMBOL:
MAJOR DIA: 8 mm FORM: ISO METRIC SERIES: COARSE FIT: REGULAR ADDITIONAL INFO: RIGHT HANDED	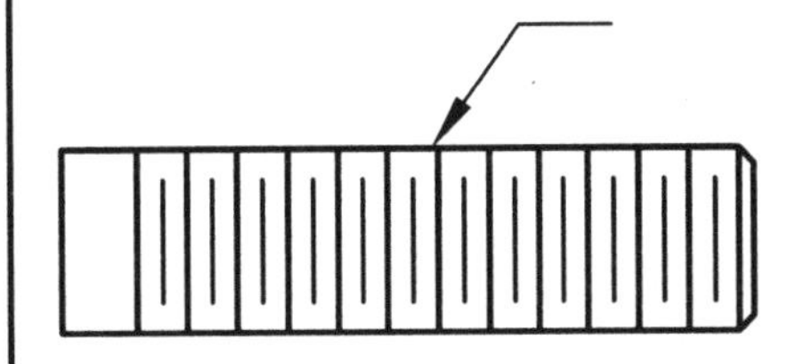 THREAD SYMBOL:
MAJOR DIA: 100 mm FORM: ISO METRIC SERIES: FINE FIT: REGULAR ADDITIONAL INFO: RIGHT HANDED	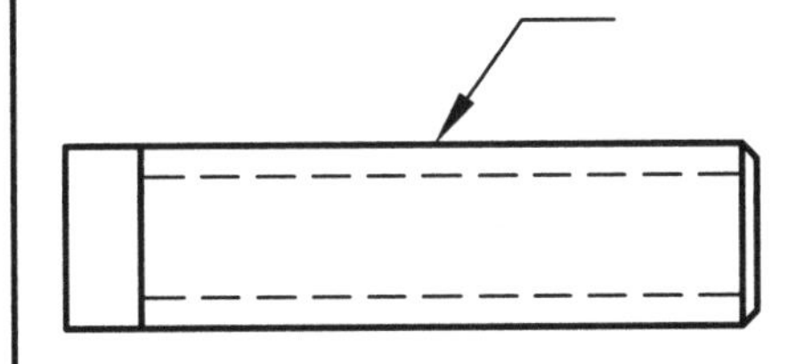 THREAD SYMBOL:
MAJOR DIA: 1.500 INCHES FORM: UNIFIED NATIONAL SERIES: EXTRA FINE FIT: LOOSE ADDITIONAL INFO: LEFT HANDED	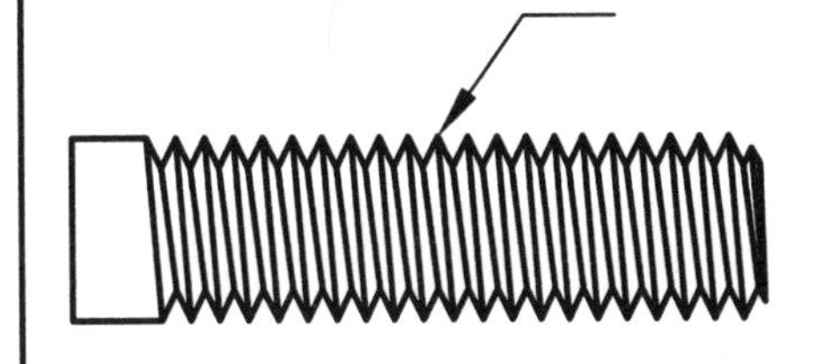 THREAD SYMBOL:

PROVIDE THE PROPER THREAD NOTES FOR THE FOLLOWING FASTENERS AND IDENTIFY THE THREAD SYMBOLS.

NAME: SV

DATE: 5/23/18

MAJOR DIA: 0.750 INCHES FORM: UNIFIED NATIONAL SERIES: EXTRA FINE FIT: REGULAR ADDITIONAL INFO: LEFT HANDED	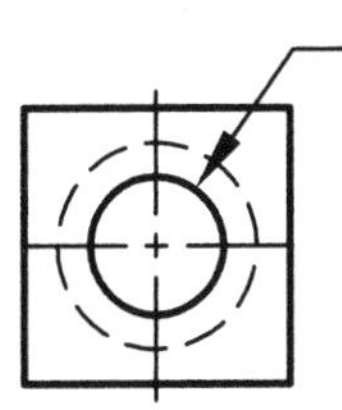 .75-UNEF-2B-LH
MAJOR DIA: 48 mm FORM: ISO METRIC SERIES: COARSE FIT: REGULAR ADDITIONAL INFO: RIGHT HANDED	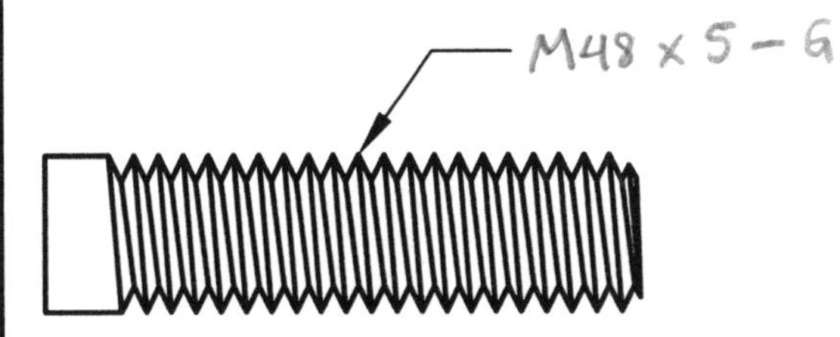 M48 x 5 - G
MAJOR DIA: 72 mm FORM: ISO METRIC SERIES: FINE FIT: REGULAR ADDITIONAL INFO: RIGHT HANDED	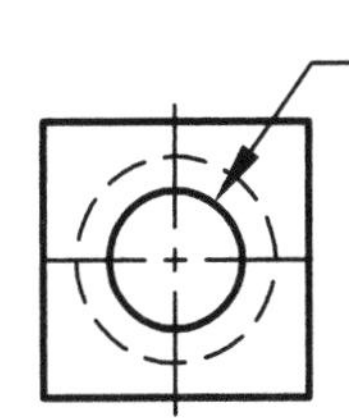 M72 x 4 - G
MAJOR DIA: 0.500 INCHES FORM: UNIFIED NATIONAL SERIES: COARSE FIT: TIGHT ADDITIONAL INFO: LEFT HANDED	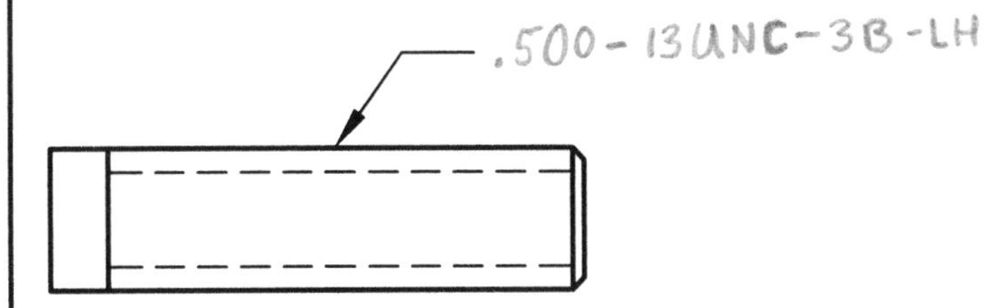 .500-13UNC-3B-LH

PROVIDE THE PROPER THREAD NOTES FOR THE FOLLOWING FASTENERS.

THREADED FASTENERS

CHAPTER 08
EXERCISE 03

NAME:

DATE:

MAJOR DIA: 0.250 INCHES FORM: UNIFIED NATIONAL SERIES: COARSE FIT: LOOSE ADDITIONAL INFO: RIGHT HANDED	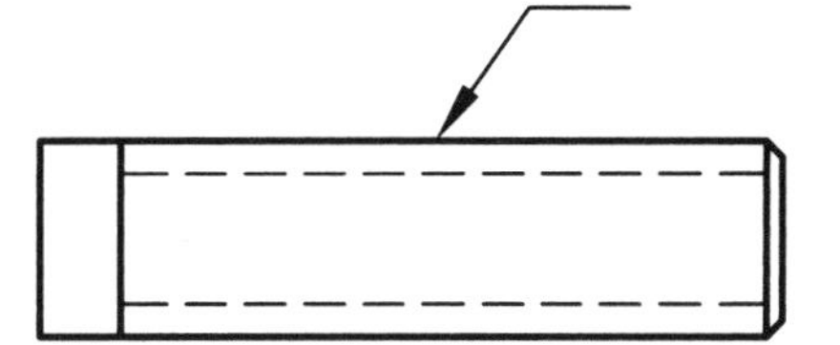
MAJOR DIA: 20 mm FORM: ISO METRIC SERIES: FINE FIT: REGULAR ADDITIONAL INFO: RIGHT HANDED	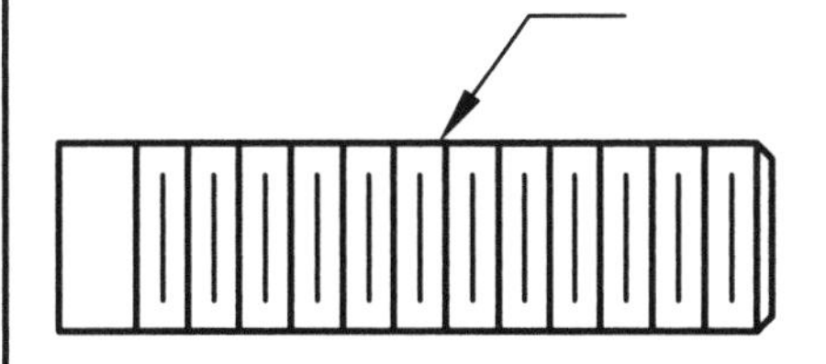
MAJOR DIA: 56 mm FORM: ISO METRIC SERIES: COARSE FIT: REGULAR ADDITIONAL INFO: LEFT HANDED	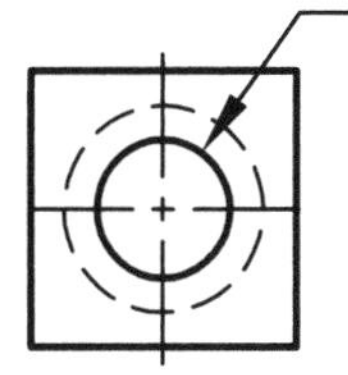
MAJOR DIA: 1.250 INCHES FORM: UNIFIED NATIONAL SERIES: EXTRA FINE FIT: REGULAR ADDITIONAL INFO: LEFT HANDED	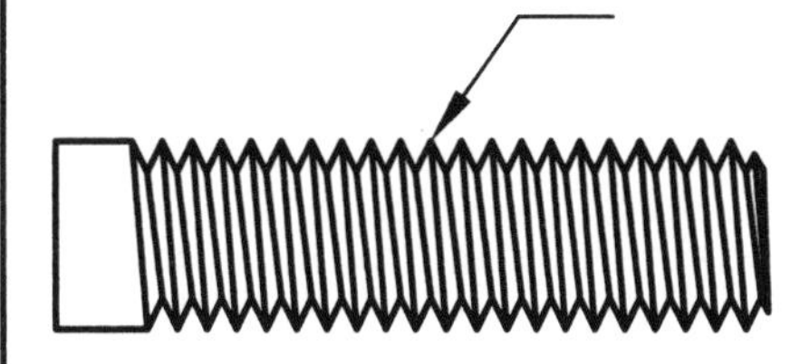

APPLY THE GEOMETRIC TOLERANCES TO THE DRAWING.

Threaded Fasteners

Chapter 08

Exercise 04

Name: SV

Date: 5/23/18

MAJOR DIA: 30 mm
FORM: ISO METRIC
SERIES: COARSE
FIT: REGULAR
ADDITIONAL INFO: LEFT HANDED

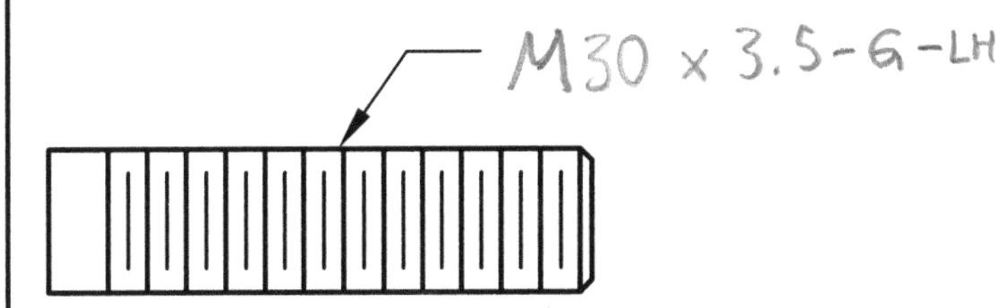

MAJOR DIA: 0.125 INCHES
FORM: UNIFIED NATIONAL
SERIES: COARSE
FIT: REGULAR
ADDITIONAL INFO: LEFT HANDED

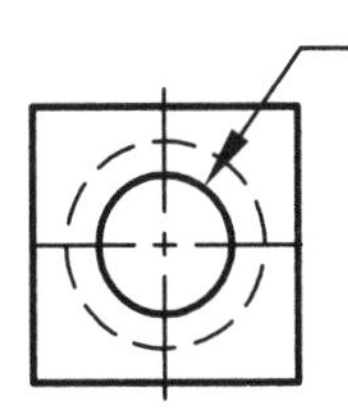

.125-UNC-2B-LH

MAJOR DIA: 80 mm
FORM: ISO METRIC
SERIES: FINE
FIT: REGULAR
ADDITIONAL INFO: RIGHT HANDED

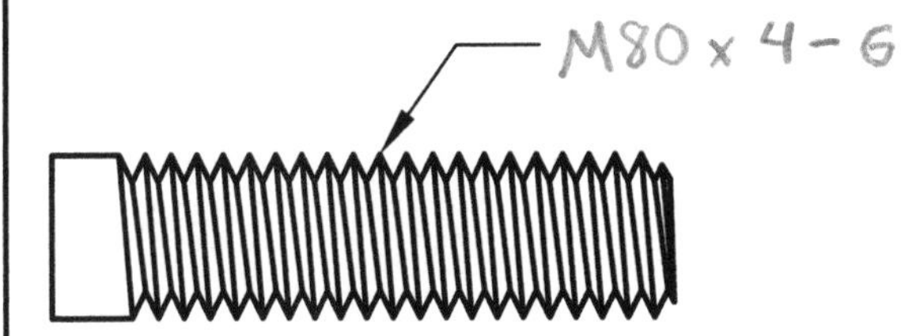

MAJOR DIA: 1.125 INCHES
FORM: UNIFIED NATIONAL
SERIES: EXTRA FINE
FIT: TIGHT
ADDITIONAL INFO: RIGHT HANDED, DOUBLE THREADED

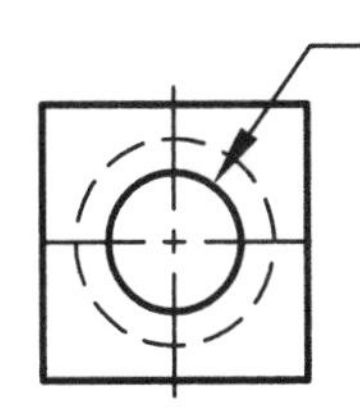

1.125-UNEF-3A-DBL

Provide the proper thread notes for the following fasteners.

THREADED FASTENERS

NAME: SV

CHAPTER 08
EXERCISE 05

DATE: 5/23/18

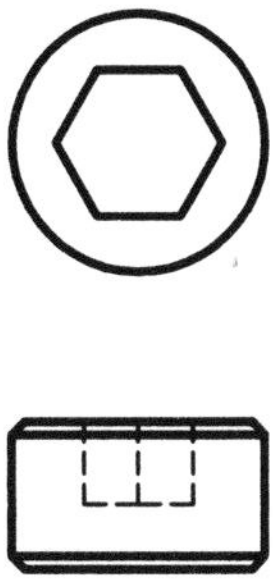

HEAD TYPE: Socket
DRIVE TYPE: Hex Socket

HEAD TYPE: Fillister
DRIVE TYPE: Triple Square

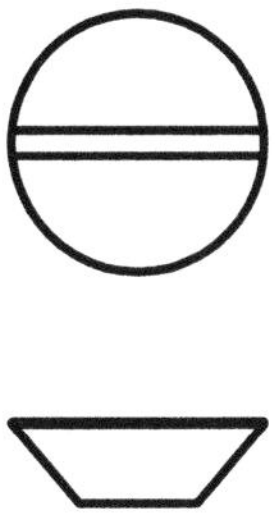

HEAD TYPE: Flat
DRIVE TYPE: Slotted

HEAD TYPE: Truss
DRIVE TYPE: Square

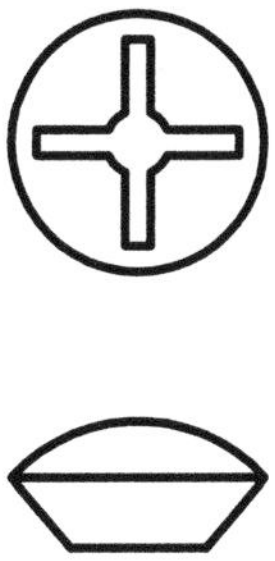

HEAD TYPE: Oval
DRIVE TYPE: Phillips

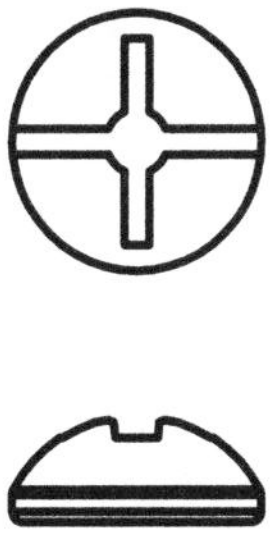

HEAD TYPE: Round
DRIVE TYPE: Combined

IDENTIFY THE HEAD AND DRIVE TYPES SHOWN BELOW.

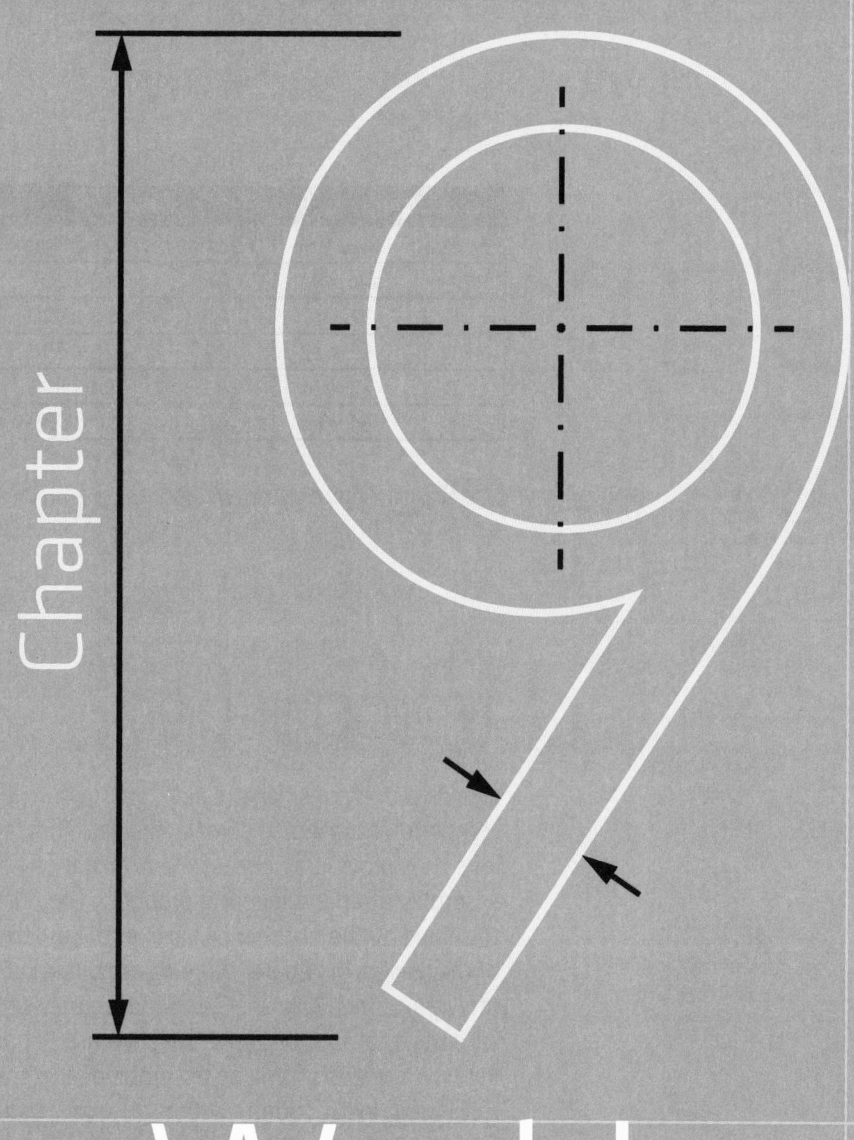

Chapter 9 Working Drawings

ANSI		ISO		Arch	
Format	Size (in)	Format	Size (mm)	Format	Size (in)
A	8.5 x 11	A4	210 x 297	Arch A	9 x 12
B	11 x 17	A3	297 x 420	Arch B	12 x 18
C	17 x 22	A2	420 x 594	Arch C	18 x 24
D	22 x 34	A1	594 x 841	Arch D	24 x 36
E	34 x 44	A0	841 x 1189	Arch E	36 x 48

FIG. 9.1 Standard ANSI, ISO, and Architectural paper sizes

Introduction

Working drawings, also called production drawings, are the final, complete documentation of a design. They are a collection of drawings that provide all necessary information for the construction and assembly of an engineering product. The number of drawings is determined by the number of parts in the assembly and the complexity of the design. In general, working drawings include orthographic views of all parts requiring special manufacture, detailed specifications for all parts that can be purchased from a vendor, a drawing illustrating how the design will be assembled, and specific manufacturing or machining instructions. Although many industries use customized formats and presentation styles, most aspects of working drawings have been standardized. In this chapter, an overview of the general and conventional practices used in creating a set of production drawings is discussed.

BLUEBIRD HOUSE LEFT PANEL		MATERIAL: UNTREATED CEDAR PLYWOOD	
DRAWN BY: JMO	CREATION DATE: 20 JAN 2013	COMMENTS:	
CHECKED BY: JDC	REVISION DATE: 14 FEB 2013		
SCALE: 1:3	TOLERANCES DEC ±.05 ANG ±.05		
DRAWING NO: 2013-01A			SHEET: 3 OF 4

Sample title block Fig. 9.2

Paper and Layout

The first step in creating a set of working drawings is deciding the appropriate paper size and drawing orientation (landscape vs. portrait). The selection of a specific paper size will be influenced by the availability of printers or plotters, the desired scale of the drawings to provide maximum clarity, and industry and company practices. For convenience, paper sizes have been standardized in many countries and industries. The most common standards for engineering are ANSI and ISO, although some countries and fields like architecture may prefer to use different paper sizes because of aspect ratios. The table shown in Figure 9.1 provides the standard ANSI, ISO, and architectural paper sizes.

All pages of a working drawing set need to have an adequate border and title block. The border outlines the drawing area and may have markings (numbers and letters) along the lines so that specific information can be quickly found by using an XY coordinate scheme. Although standard title blocks exist, it is more common to find company defined title block designs. Most title blocks will have space for drawing title, company name and logo, sheet number, drawing scale, tolerances, projection symbol, and names of CAD operator and supervisor. On large projects, where collaborative design is essential, there are places for revision dates and signatures. Title blocks are generally located in the lower right-hand corner of the drawing sheet so the information can be easily found without having to flip entire pages. Figure 9.2 illustrates a sample title block.

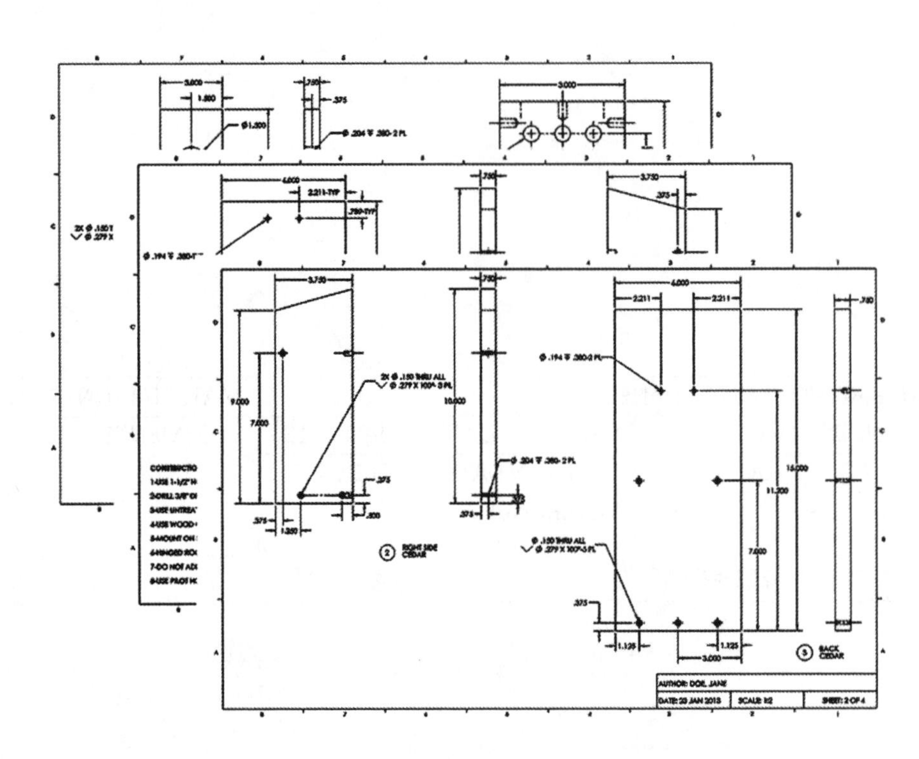

FIG. 9.3 Major components of a working drawing set
Above: Detail Drawings

Structure of a Set of Working Drawings

Working drawings are comprised of three major components: a drawing that shows how parts are assembled together, orthographic views of all parts that need special manufacturing, and textual notes for all standard parts (see Figure 9.3).

Assembly Drawings

Assembly drawings are used to illustrate how all the parts of a design fit together. They are typically shown in pictorial format (usually isometric or perspective), and either collapsed (parts assembled together) or exploded (the assembly pulled apart). Orthographic and section views can also be provided, if necessary. Assembly drawings are usually the first page in a set of working drawings but it is not uncommon to find them in the last page.

The complexity and number of parts will determine the most appropriate view for an assembly drawing. The assembly view should be oriented in order to best describe the geometry of the design and can be shown exploded or collapsed; whichever provides the most clarity. Route lines (lines connecting each component of the assembly to another) can be used to show order of assembly.

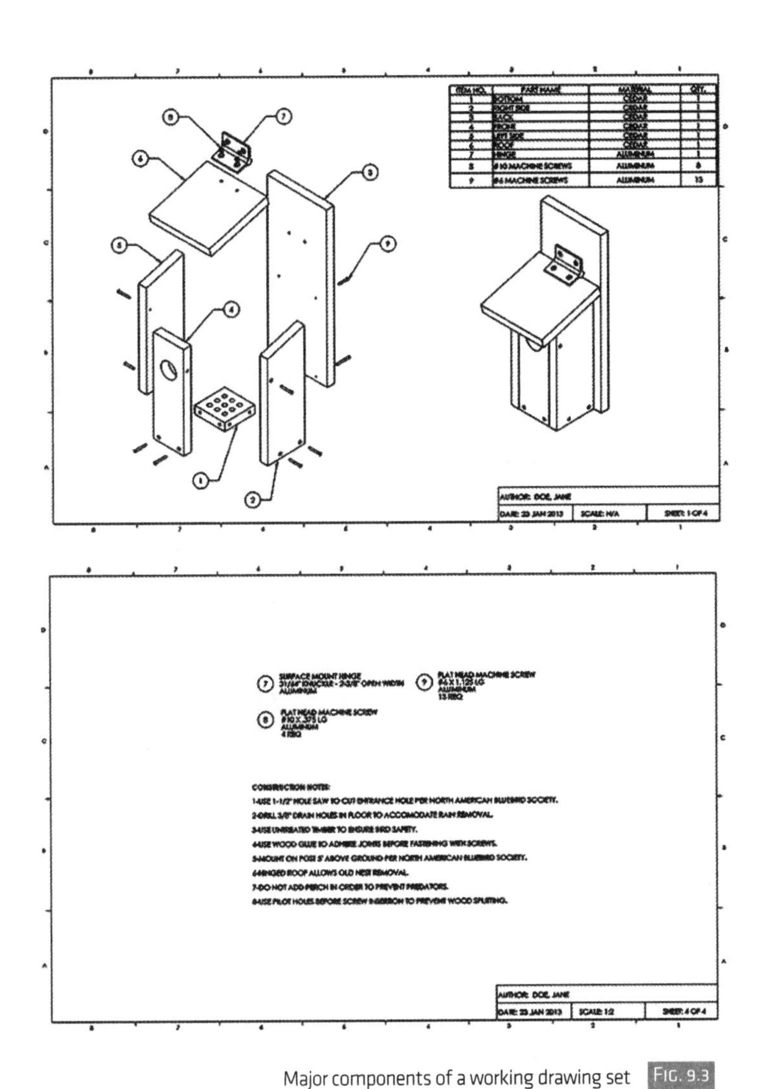

Major components of a working drawing set FIG. 9.3
Top: Assembly Drawing. Bottom: Standard Notes

Historically, some components could be simplified if the design presentation was not adversely affected, but this step is not as important today as parametric modelers dominate industry. Hidden lines, centerlines, and dimensions must be omitted, as they are with most pictorials, unless absolutely needed for clarity. If subassemblies are needed, multiple assembly drawings can be provided.

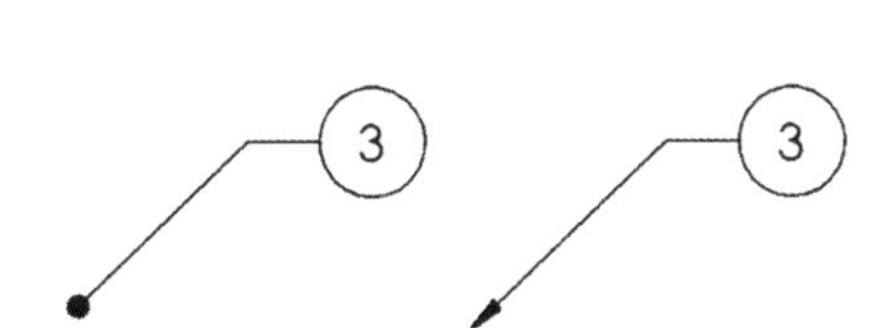

Balloons with leader lines FIG. 9.4

Each component in an assembly drawing must have a part number balloon that identifies it. The part number will be centered within a circle, known as balloon, with a size of three to four times the standard letter height, depending on the number of digits necessary. The balloon is connected to the assembly component with a leader line that usually terminates with an arrow or a dot (see Figure 9.4). Since part numbers will correspond with specific information about the components in the parts list and part detail drawings, it is essential that all numbers remain consistent throughout the drawing.

Balloons must be properly arranged within the assembly view ensuring they do not interfere with any lines in the drawing, if possible. This

ITEM NO.	PART NAME	MATERIAL	QTY.
1	BOTTOM	CEDAR	1
2	RIGHT SIDE	CEDAR	1
3	BACK	CEDAR	1
4	FRONT	CEDAR	1
5	LEFT SIDE	CEDAR	1
6	ROOF	CEDAR	1
7	HINGE	ALUMINUM	1
8	#10 MACHINE SCREWS	ALUMINUM	8
9	#6 MACHINE SCREWS	ALUMINUM	13

FIG. 9.5 Sample parts list

is particularly important in assemblies with large numbers of components. Additionally, if the same component is used more than once in the assembly, only one balloon is required.

The part numbers in the balloons shown in the assembly drawing must be linked to a row on a table known as bill of materials (BOM) or parts list. The bill of materials lists all components used in the assembly by part number in tabular format. Typically, the major components of the assembly are listed first and standard parts such as fasteners and other parts that will be purchased are listed last.

The bill of materials is usually displayed in the upper right-hand corner of the assembly drawing, with the components listed in ascending order (reading from top to bottom), or in the bottom right-hand corner, with the components listed in descending order (reading from bottom to top). Different industries and companies may require alternate placement.

The information provided in a typical parts list includes part number (which agrees with the corresponding balloon), part name, material used, and required quantity. Other information, such as part supplier or descriptions may be included, if necessary. A sample parts list is shown in Figure 9.5.

A sample assembly drawing with balloons and parts list is shown in Figure 9.6.

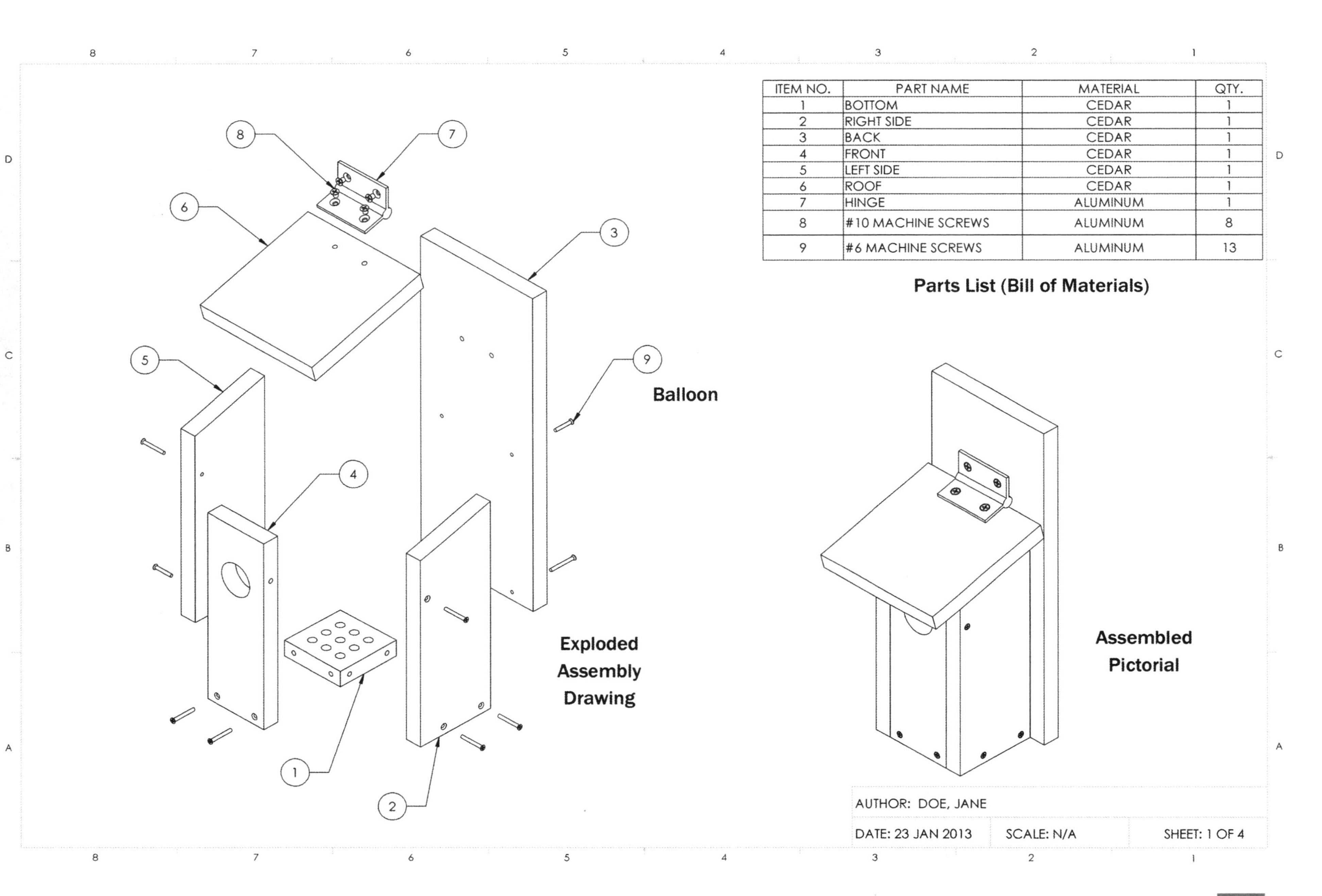

ITEM NO.	PART NAME	MATERIAL	QTY.
1	BOTTOM	CEDAR	1
2	RIGHT SIDE	CEDAR	1
3	BACK	CEDAR	1
4	FRONT	CEDAR	1
5	LEFT SIDE	CEDAR	1
6	ROOF	CEDAR	1
7	HINGE	ALUMINUM	1
8	#10 MACHINE SCREWS	ALUMINUM	8
9	#6 MACHINE SCREWS	ALUMINUM	13

Assembly drawing FIG. 9.6

Detail Drawings

Custom designed parts require detail drawings (fully dimensioned orthographic views) so that a third-party can manufacture them. Detail drawings can be displayed in any sequence throughout the working drawing set, but part numbers must be consistent with the parts list found on the assembly drawing. On larger sheets of paper, it is common to find multiple parts shown on the same page, in order to save space.

Detail drawings require a part name tag with part number balloon. The part number must be centered within the balloon, but without a leader connecting the balloon to the part. The part name tag includes part name, material, and required quantity, each on a different line. If all objects on a sheet are drawn at same scale, the scale is provided in the title block. If the scale differs between parts, the scale is provided with each part name tag; in the title block, the scale is indicated as "AS NOTED."

Detail drawings for the custom components of the birdhouse assembly are shown in Figure 9.7, Figure 9.8, and Figure 9.9.

Standard Part Notes

Vendor items do not require orthographic views, but notes that provide sufficient information so that they can be purchased. Standard part notes also require a part number balloon (without connecting leader) as discussed above, with part name, material, required quantity, and any specific information such as thread notes, screw lengths, or other identifying aspects.

Standard part notes are usually placed in unused space throughout the drawing (but not the assembly page) or can be reserved for the last sheet in the drawing set. Specific manufacturing instructions, such as required processes or order of operations, can also be placed on the working drawings.

Standard notes for parts 7, 8, and 9, as well as manufacturing instructions for the birdhouse assembly are shown in Figure 9.9.

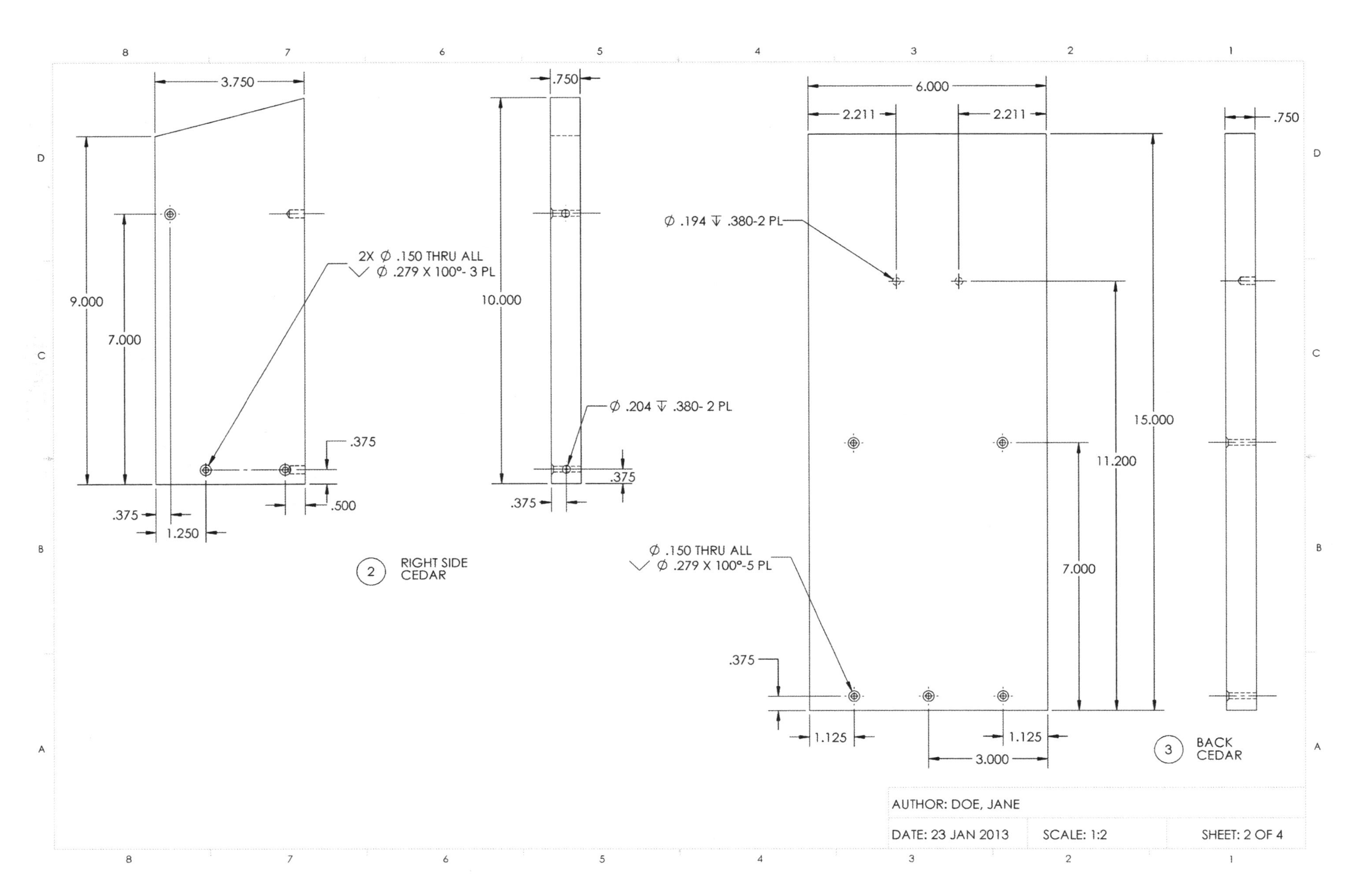

Detail drawing 1  FIG. 9.7

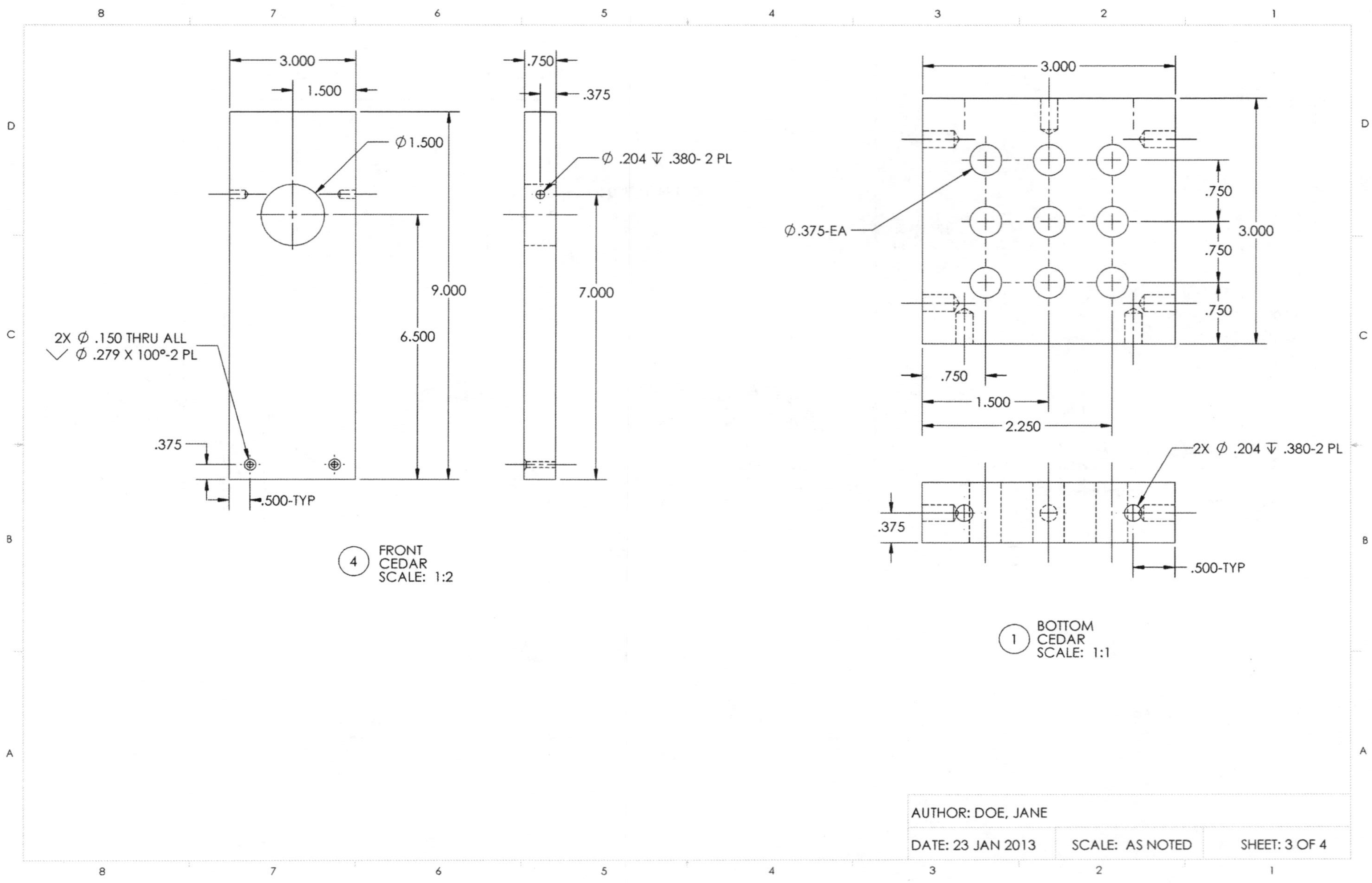

8 7 6 5 4 3 2 1

D

3.000
1.500
Ø1.500
9.000
6.500
2X Ø .150 THRU ALL
⌵ Ø .279 X 100°-2 PL
.375
.500-TYP

4 FRONT
CEDAR
SCALE: 1:2

.750
.375
Ø .204 ↧ .380- 2 PL
7.000

3.000
Ø.375-EA
.750
.750
.750
3.000
.750
1.500
2.250
2X Ø .204 ↧ .380-2 PL
.375
.500-TYP

1 BOTTOM
CEDAR
SCALE: 1:1

C

B

A

AUTHOR: DOE, JANE		
DATE: 23 JAN 2013	SCALE: AS NOTED	SHEET: 3 OF 4

8 7 6 5 4 3 2 1

Detail drawing 2 FIG. 9.8

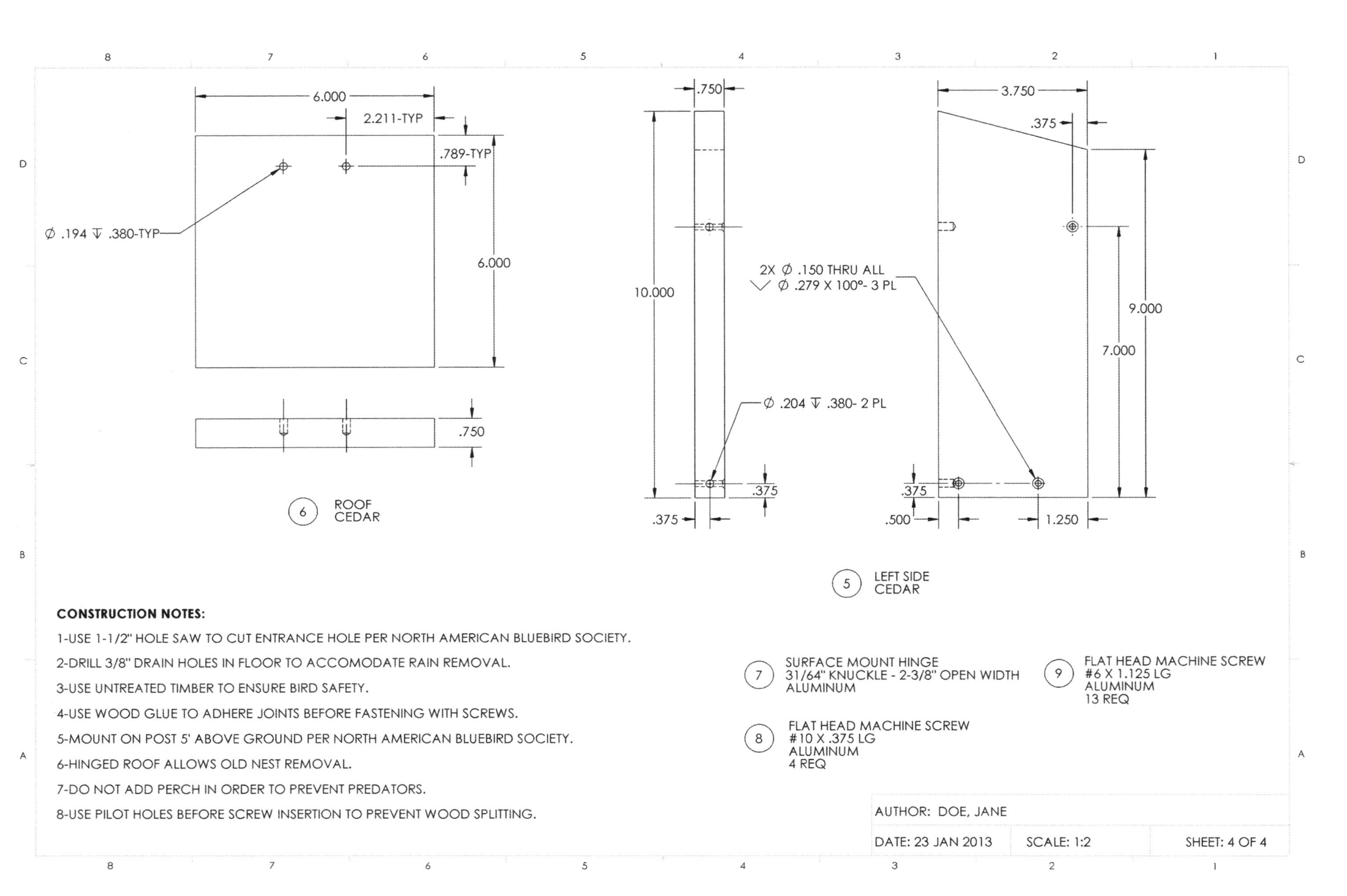

Detail drawing 3 with standard notes and instructions FIG. 9.9

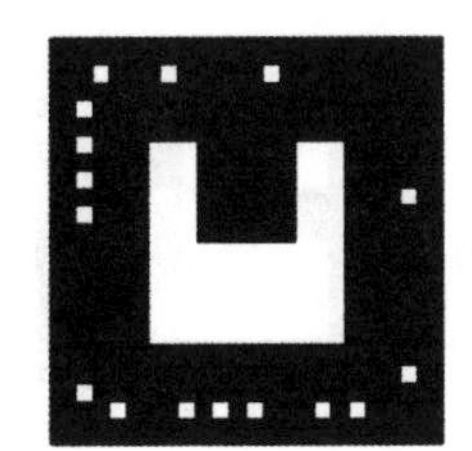

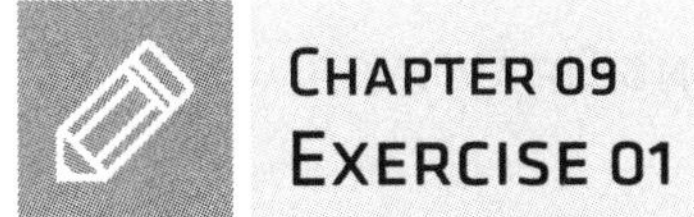

EXERCISE 01

CREATE A SET OF WORKING DRAWINGS FOR THE PLASTIC POWDER BOX ASSEMBLY SHOWN BELOW. SOME DIMENSIONS ARE INTENTIONALLY MISSING. ALL UNITS IN MM. THE TYPE OF FIT IS H7/K6.

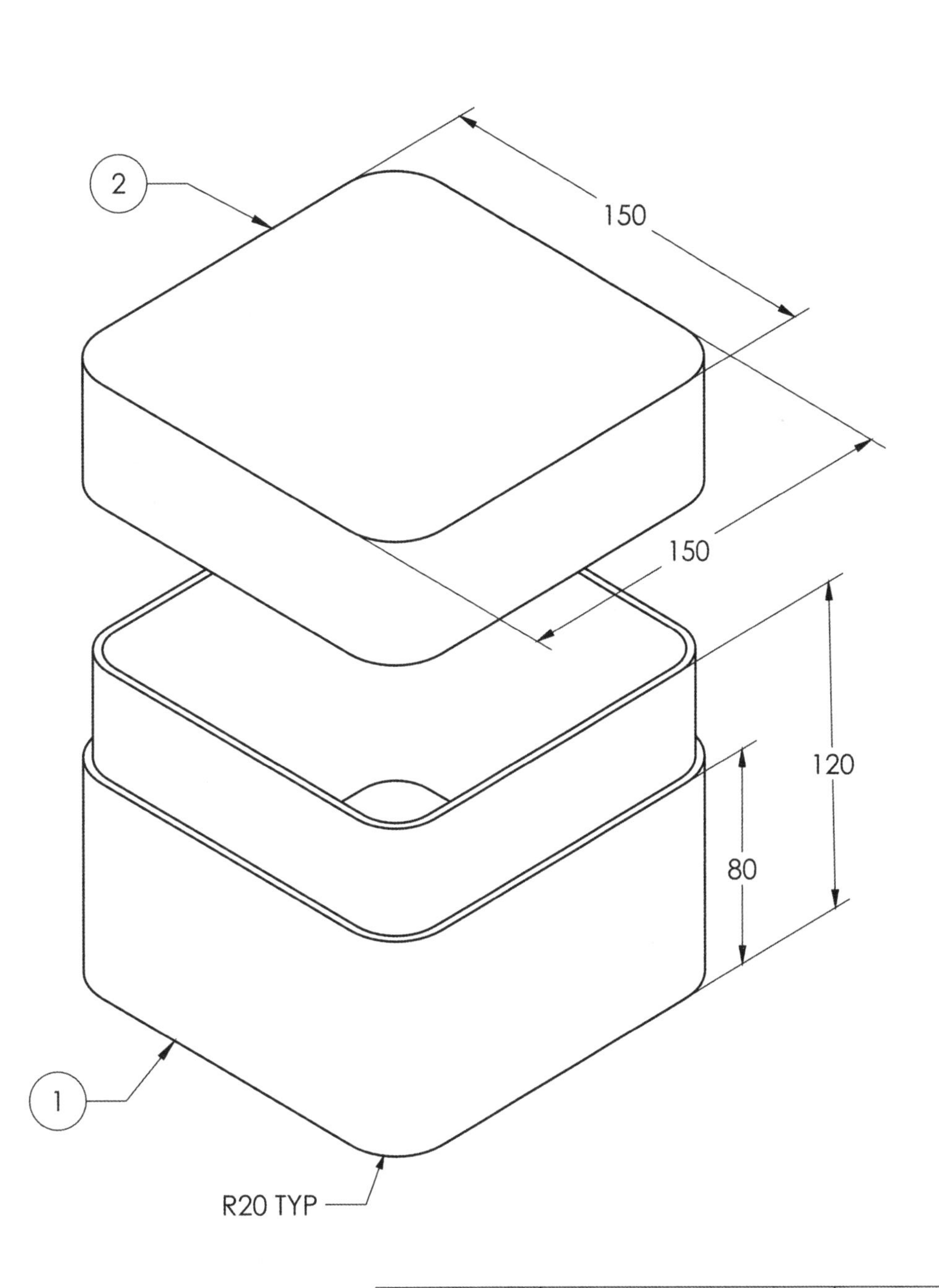

ITEM NO.	PART NAME	QTY.
1	BOX	1
2	LID	1

EXERCISE 02

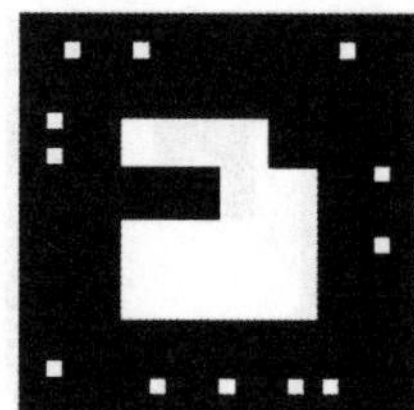

CREATE A SET OF WORKING DRAWINGS FOR THE BREAD COOLING RACK ASSEMBLY SHOWN BELOW. SOME DIMENSIONS ARE INTENTIONALLY MISSING. ALL UNITS IN MM. THE TYPE OF FIT IS H7/N6.

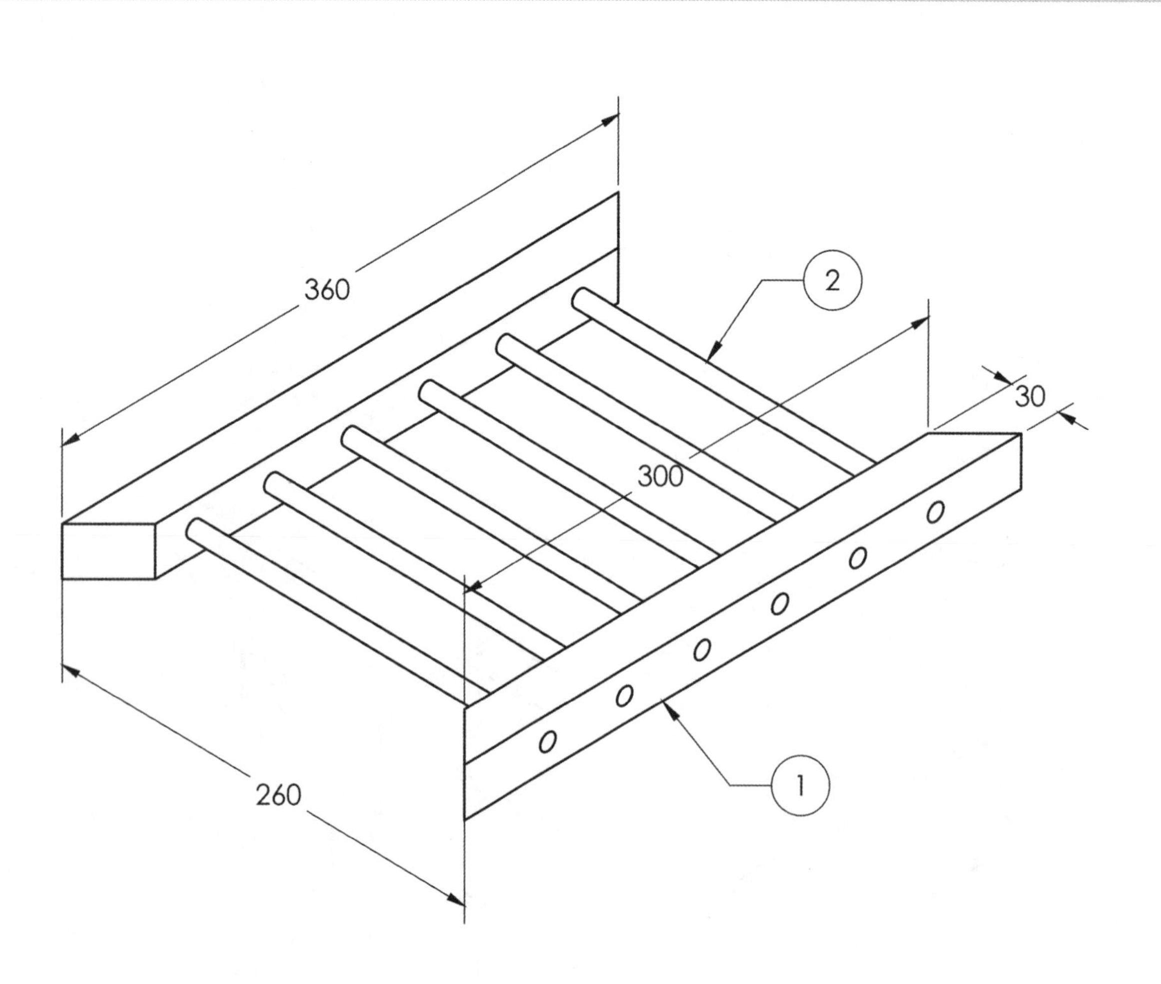

CONSTRUCTION NOTES:

1-USE MAPLE OR OTHER HARD WOOD.

2-10 mm DIA DOWELS.

3-SEAT DOWELS THEN GLUE IN PLACE.

4-CLEAN WITH VINEGAR AFTER EACH USE.

ITEM NO.	PART NAME	QTY.
1	SIDE SUPPORT	2
2	DOWEL	6

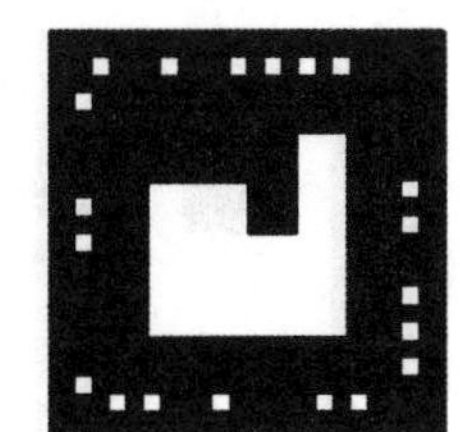

Complete a set of working drawings for the toy plane constructed of balsa wood shown below. Some dimensions are intentionally missing. All units in inches.

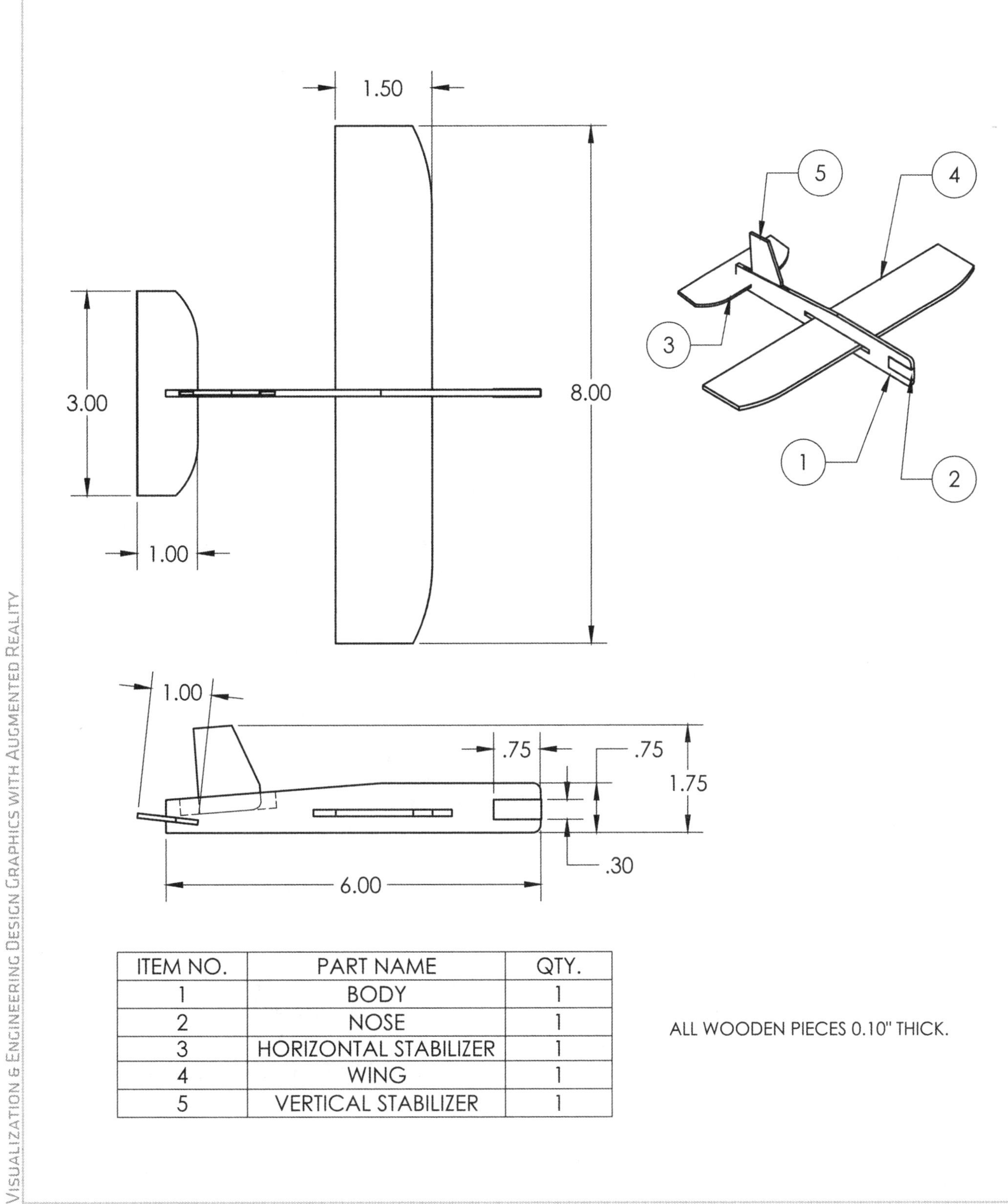

ITEM NO.	PART NAME	QTY.
1	BODY	1
2	NOSE	1
3	HORIZONTAL STABILIZER	1
4	WING	1
5	VERTICAL STABILIZER	1

ALL WOODEN PIECES 0.10" THICK.

Exercise 04-1

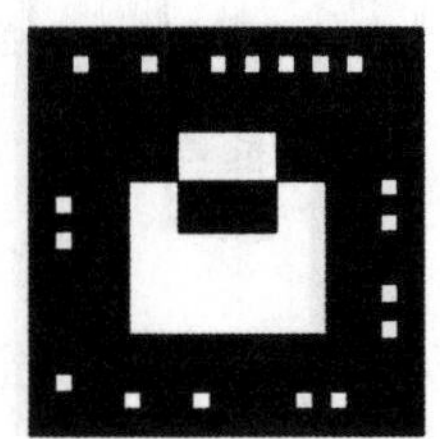

Create a set of working drawings for the mechanical base assembly shown below. Some dimensions are intentionally missing. All units in inches.

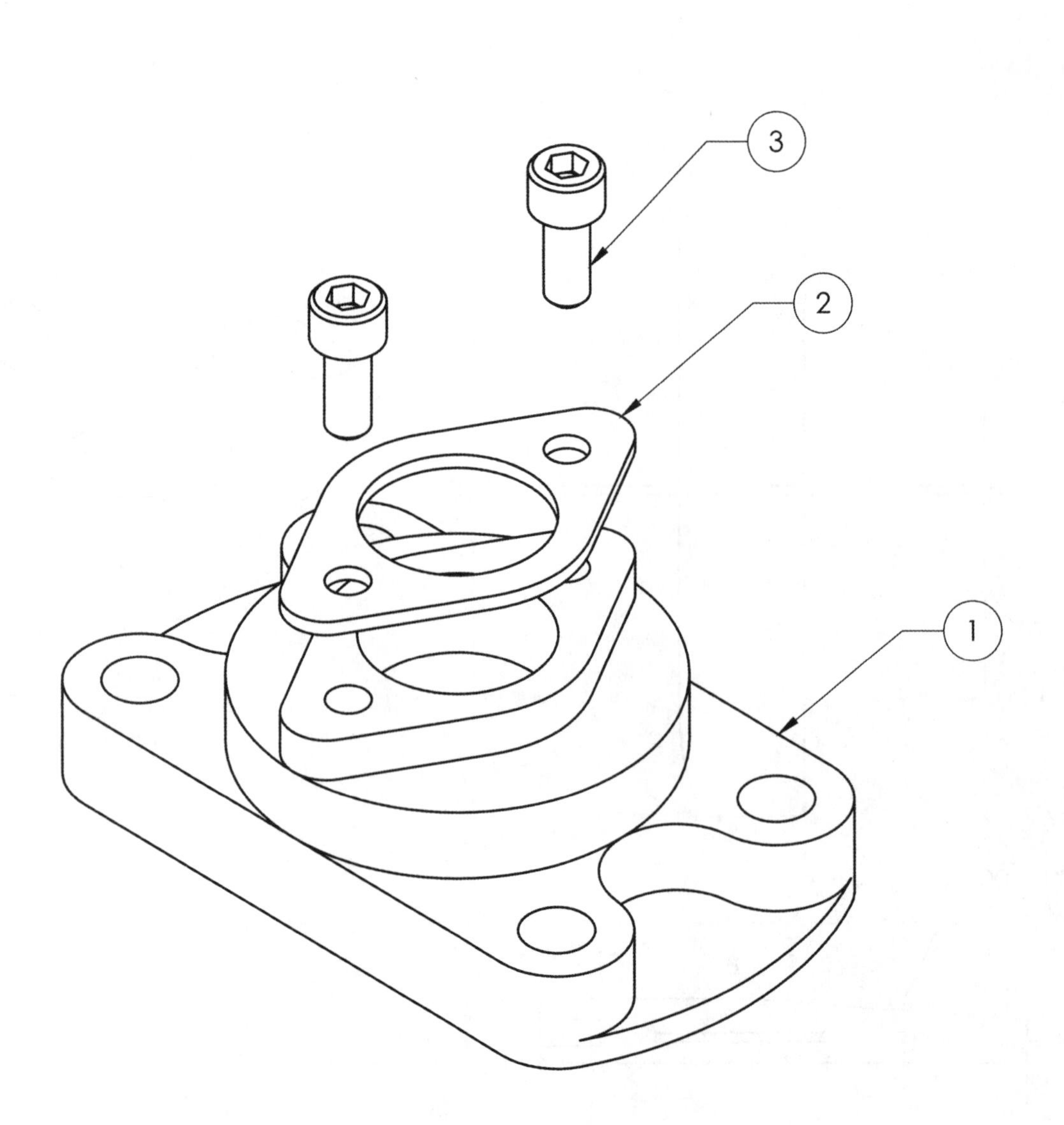

ITEM NO.	QTY.	PART NAME
11		MECHANICAL BASE
21		GASKET
32		SOCKET HD CAP SCREW

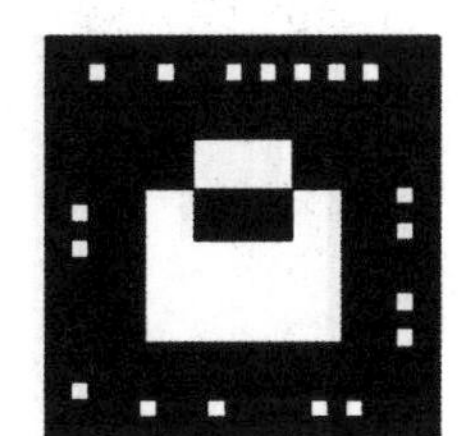
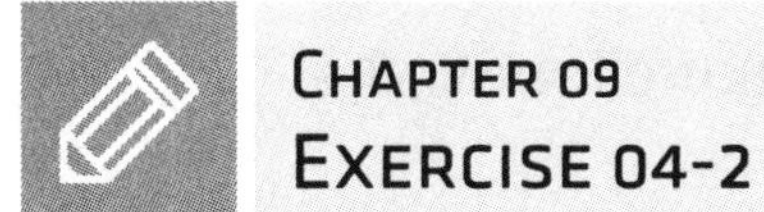

EXERCISE 04-2

CREATE A SET OF WORKING DRAWINGS FOR THE MECHANICAL BASE ASSEMBLY SHOWN BELOW. SOME DIMENSIONS ARE INTENTIONALLY MISSING. ALL UNITS IN INCHES.

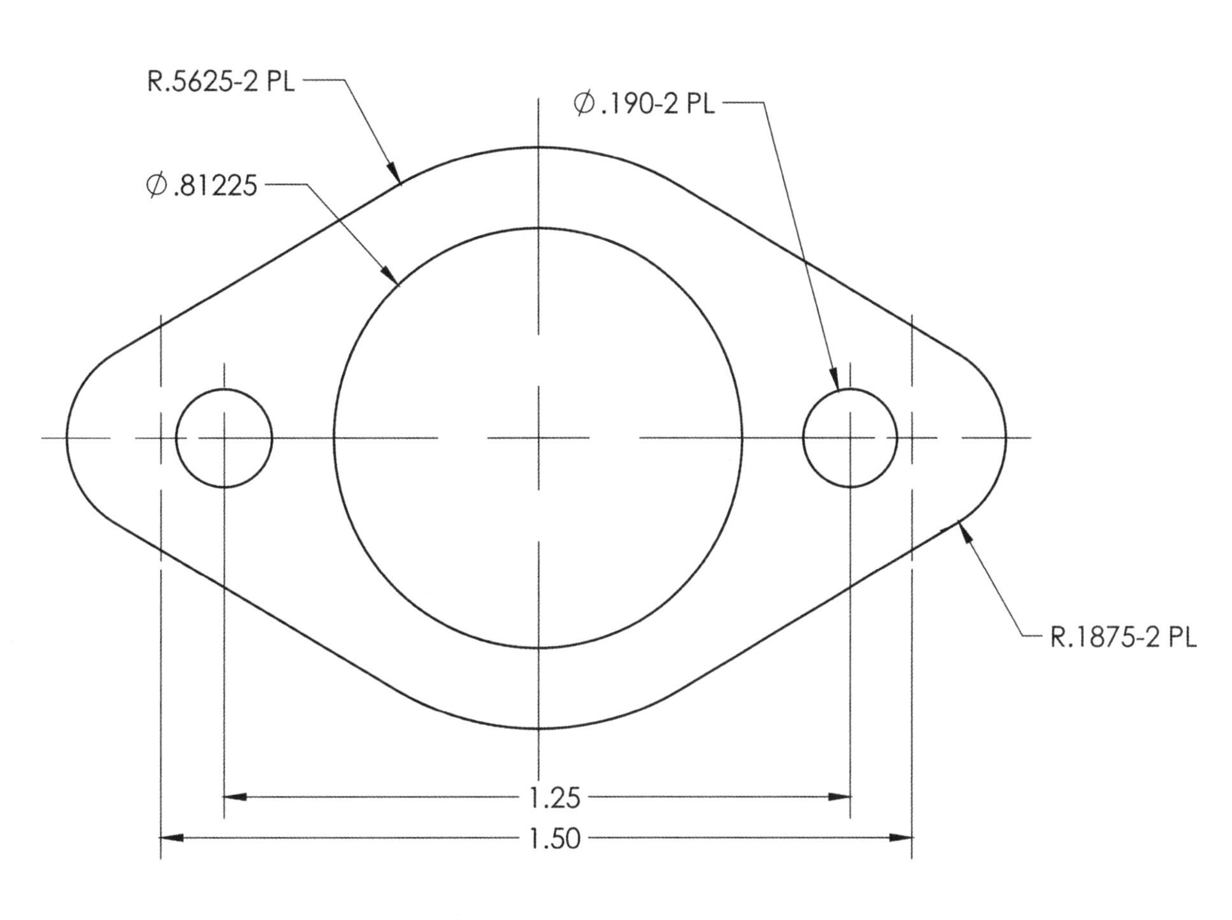

2 GASKET
0.0625 THICK
SILICON RUBBER

3 SOCKET HEAD CAP SCREW
STEEL
2 REQ

Exercise 04-3

Create a set of working drawings for the mechanical base assembly shown below. Some dimensions are intentionally missing. All units in inches.

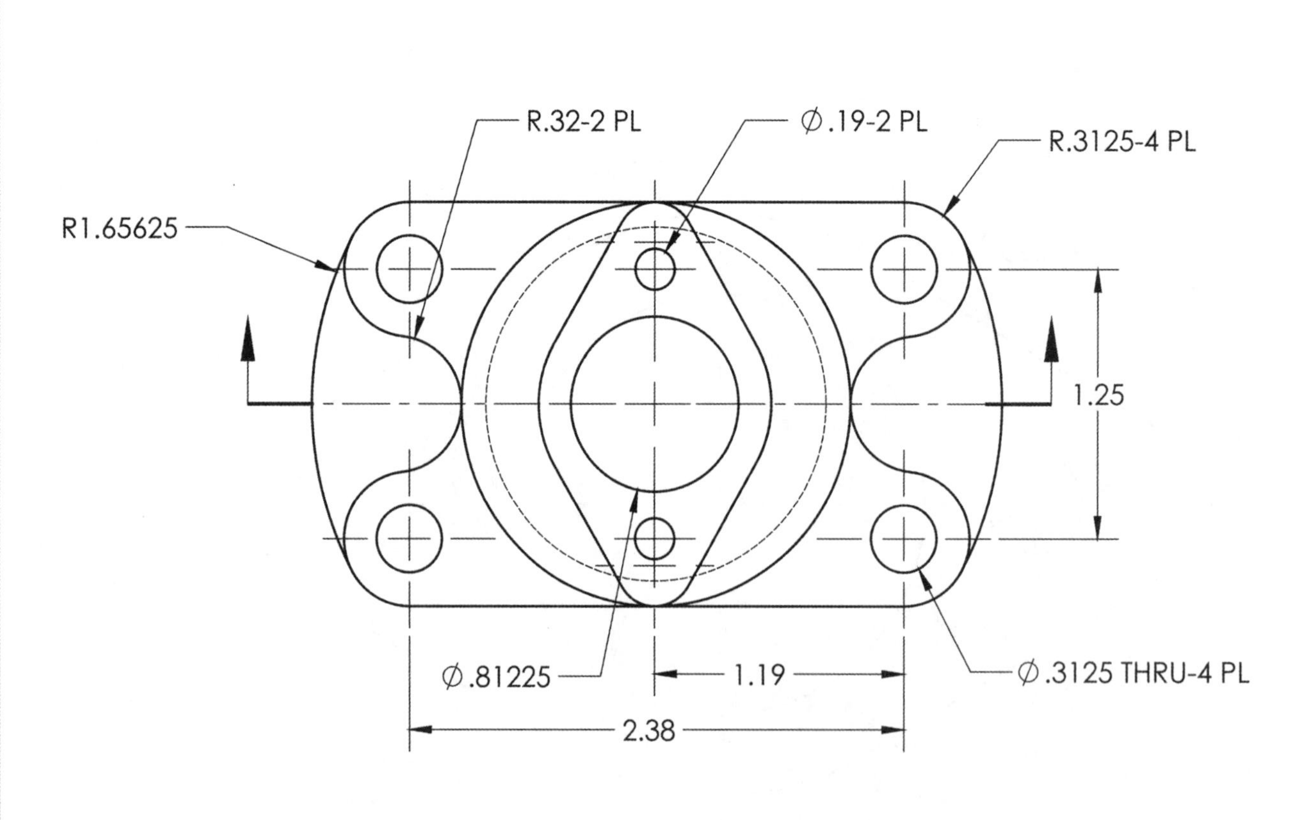

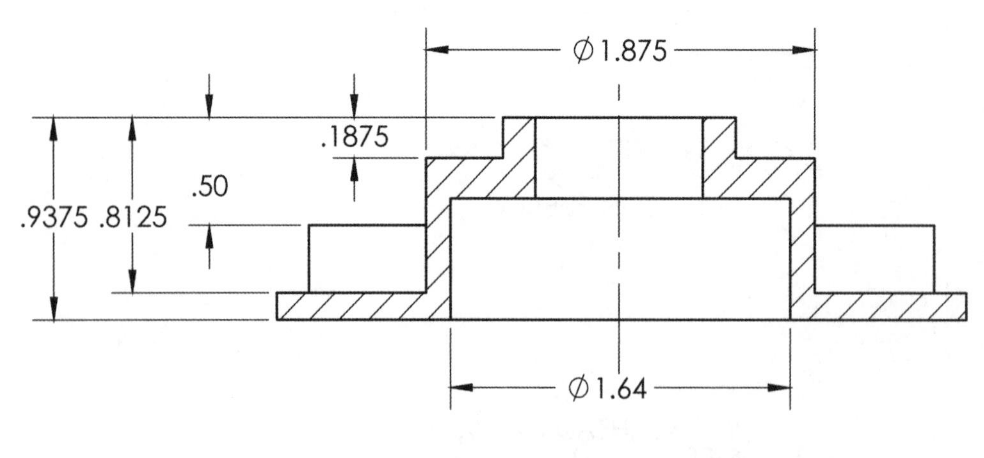

1 MECHANICAL BASE
STEEL

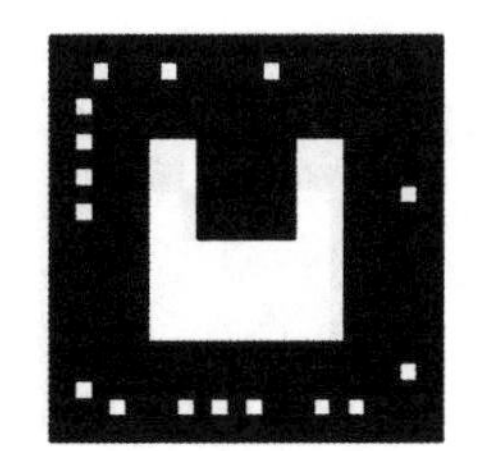
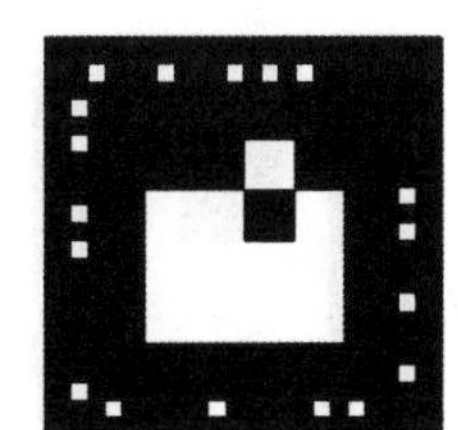
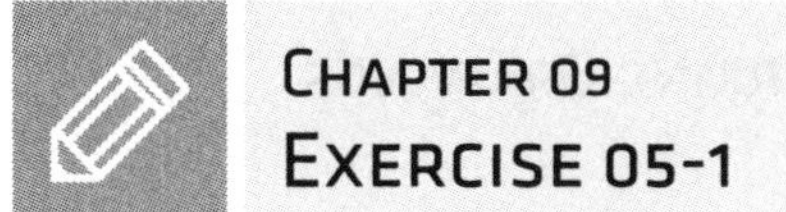

EXERCISE 05-1

CREATE A SET OF WORKING DRAWINGS FOR THE KNUCKLE JOINT ASSEMBLY SHOWN BELOW. SOME DIMENSIONS ARE INTENTIONALLY MISSING. ALL UNITS IN INCHES. ENSURE PROPER CLEARANCE BETWEEN PARTS.

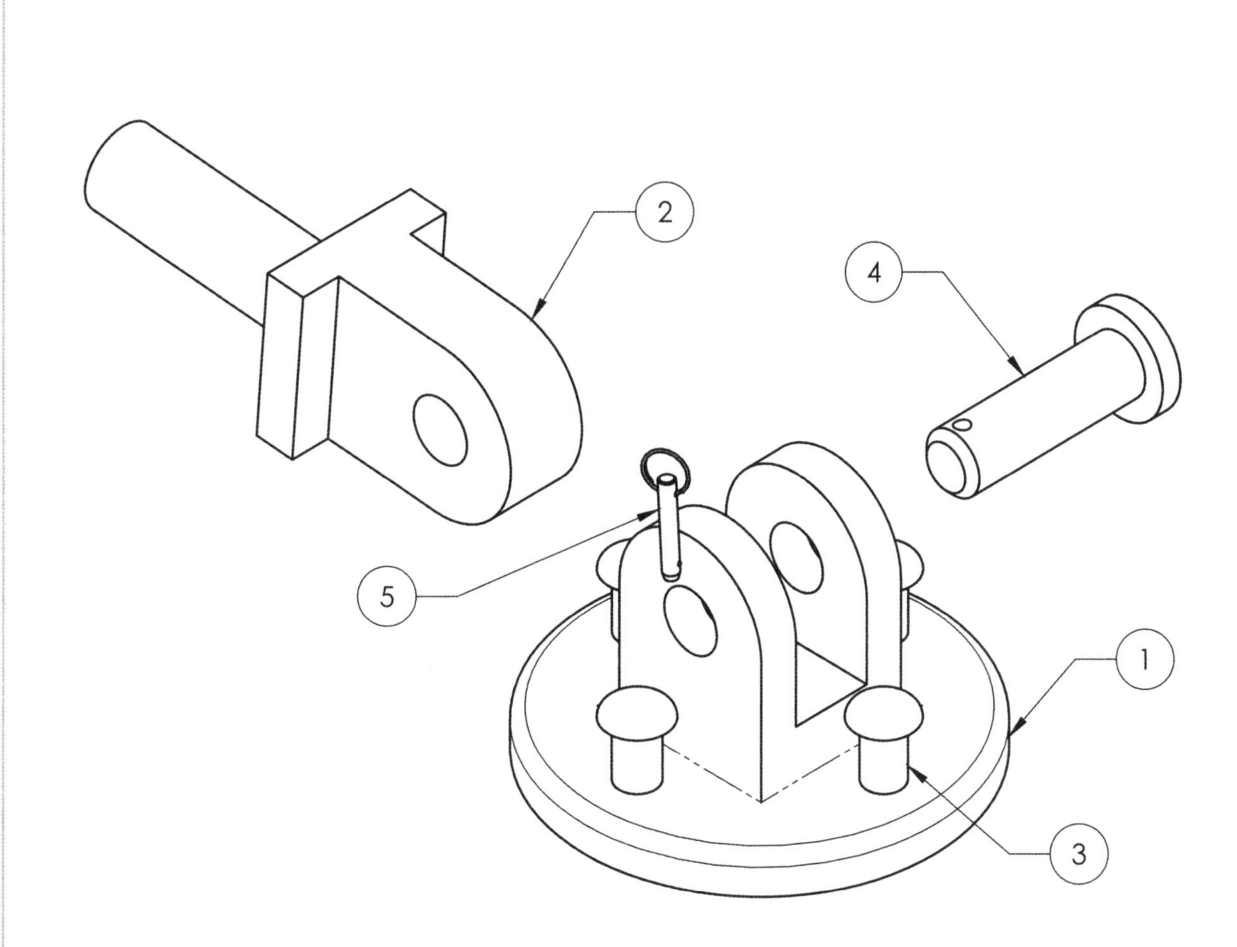

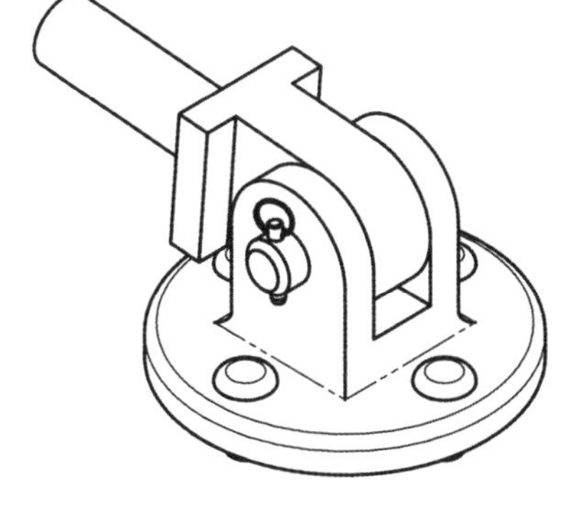

ITEM NO.	PART NAME	QTY.
1	MOUNTING BASE	1
2	EYE	1
3	$\varnothing$.50 TRUSS HD BOLT	4
4	PIN	1
5	LOCKING PIN	1

Exercise 05-2

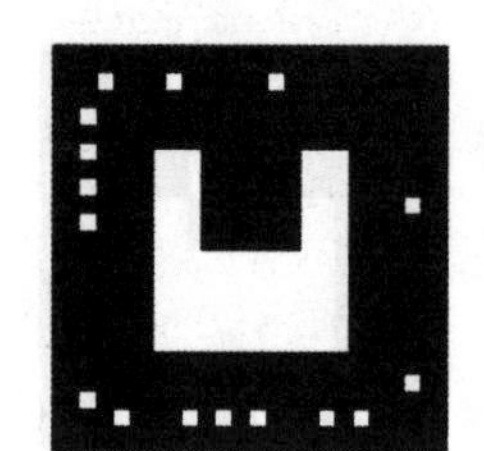

Create a set of working drawings for the knuckle joint assembly shown below. Some dimensions are intentionally missing. All units in inches. Ensure proper clearance between parts.

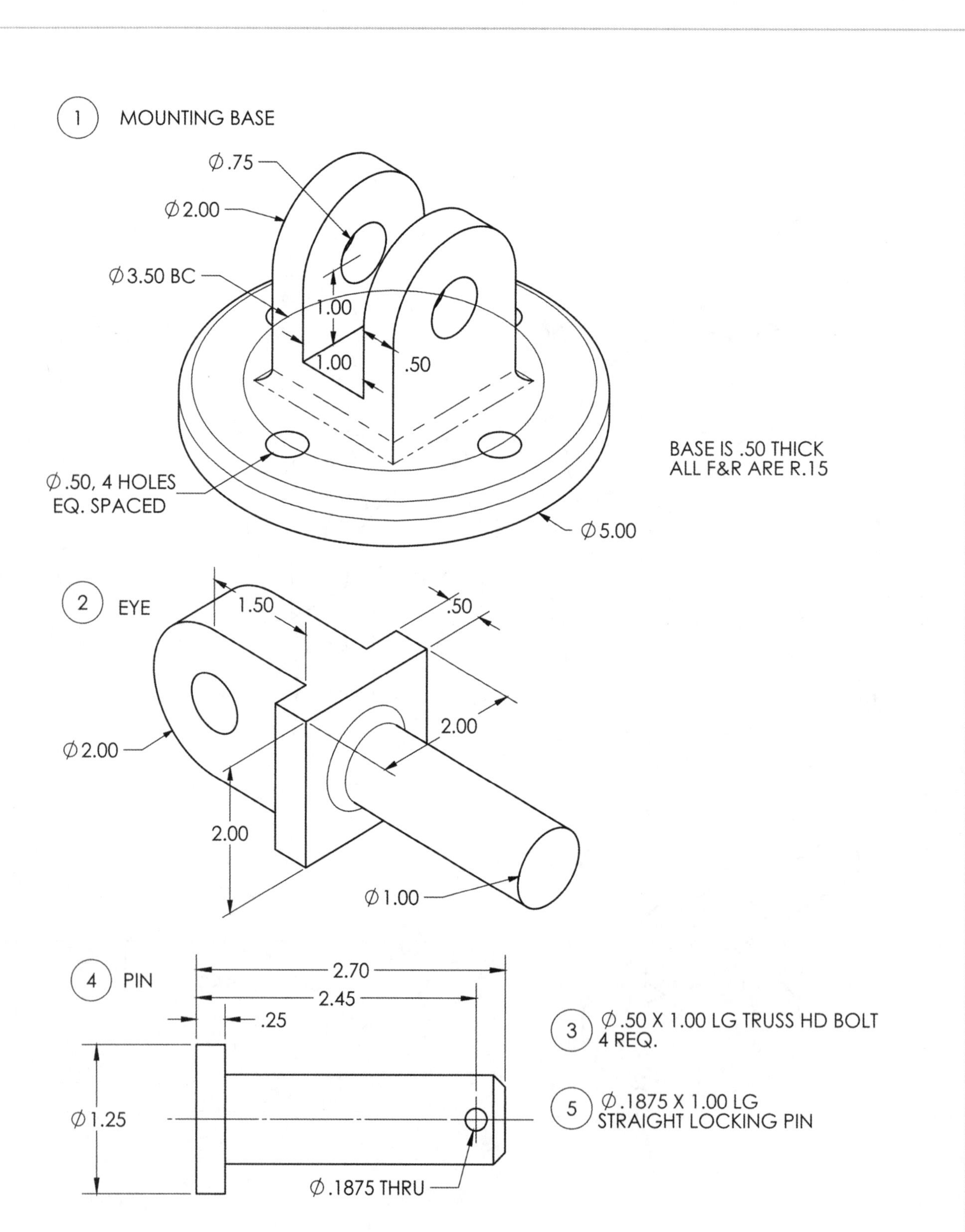

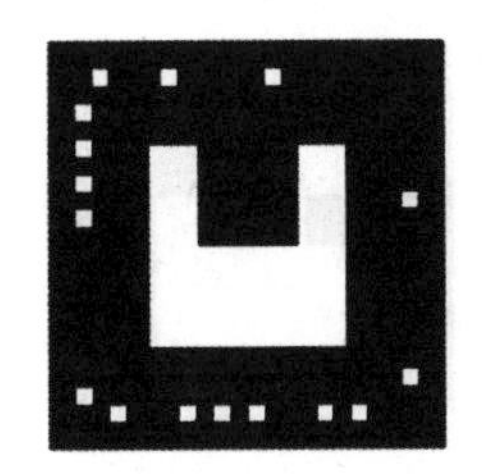

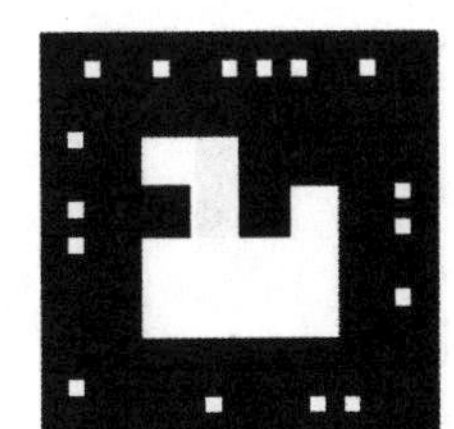

Exercise 06-1

Create a set of working drawings for the plastic spray bottle assembly shown below. Detail drawings follow.

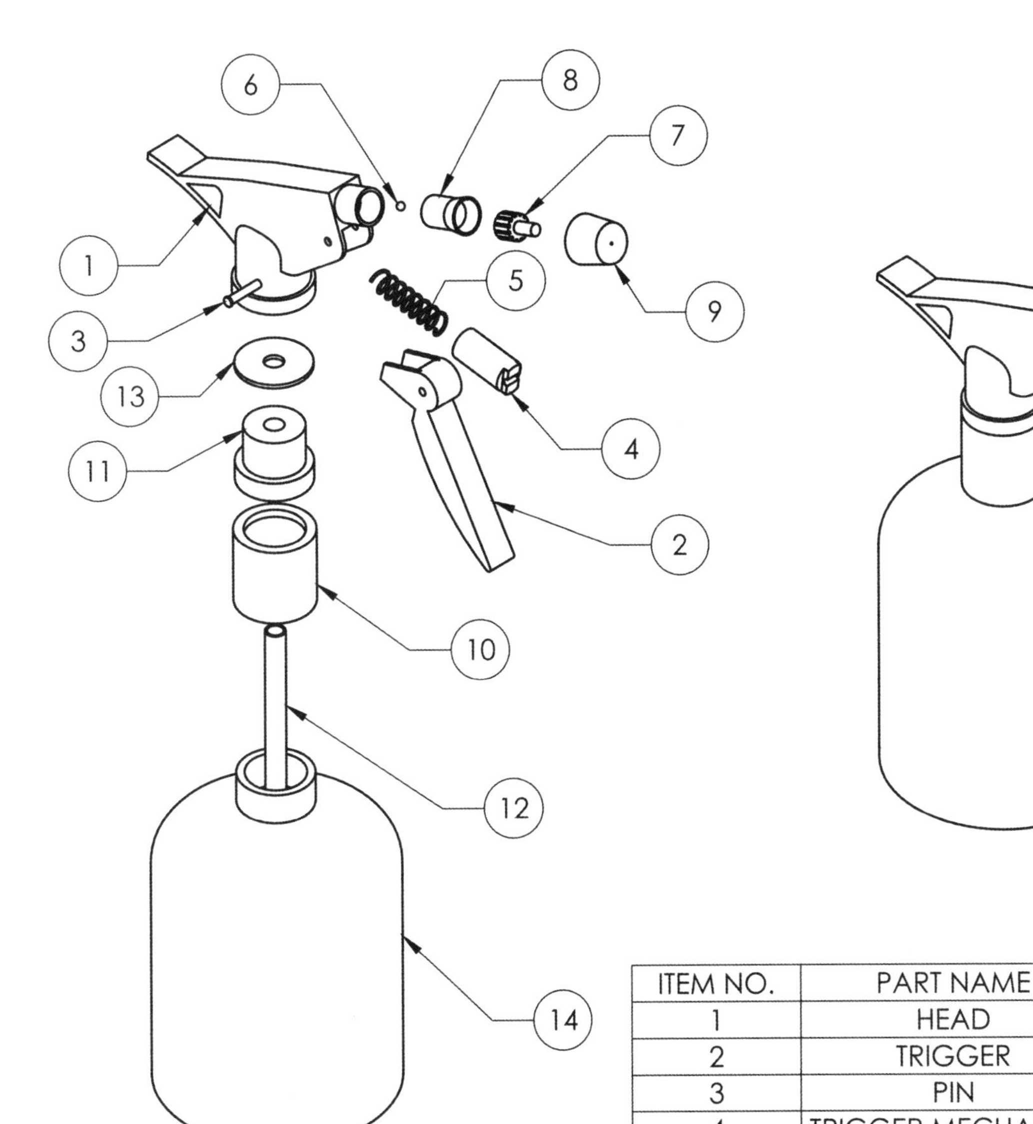

ITEM NO.	PART NAME	QTY.
1	HEAD	1
2	TRIGGER	1
3	PIN	1
4	TRIGGER MECHANISM	1
5	SPRING	1
6	BALL	2
7	NOZZLE	1
8	NOZZLE COVER	1
9	NOZZLE TIP	1
10	NECK	1
11	FITTING	1
12	TUBE	1
13	O-RING	1
14	BOTTLE	1

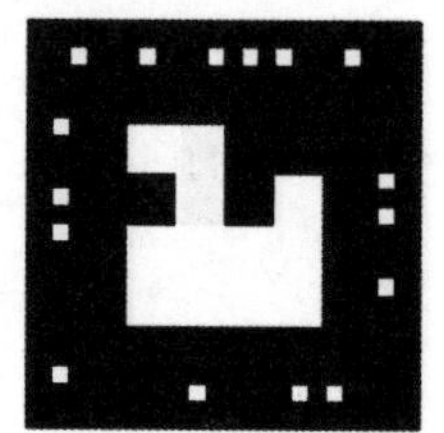

Create a set of working drawings for the plastic spray bottle assembly shown below. Detail drawings follow.

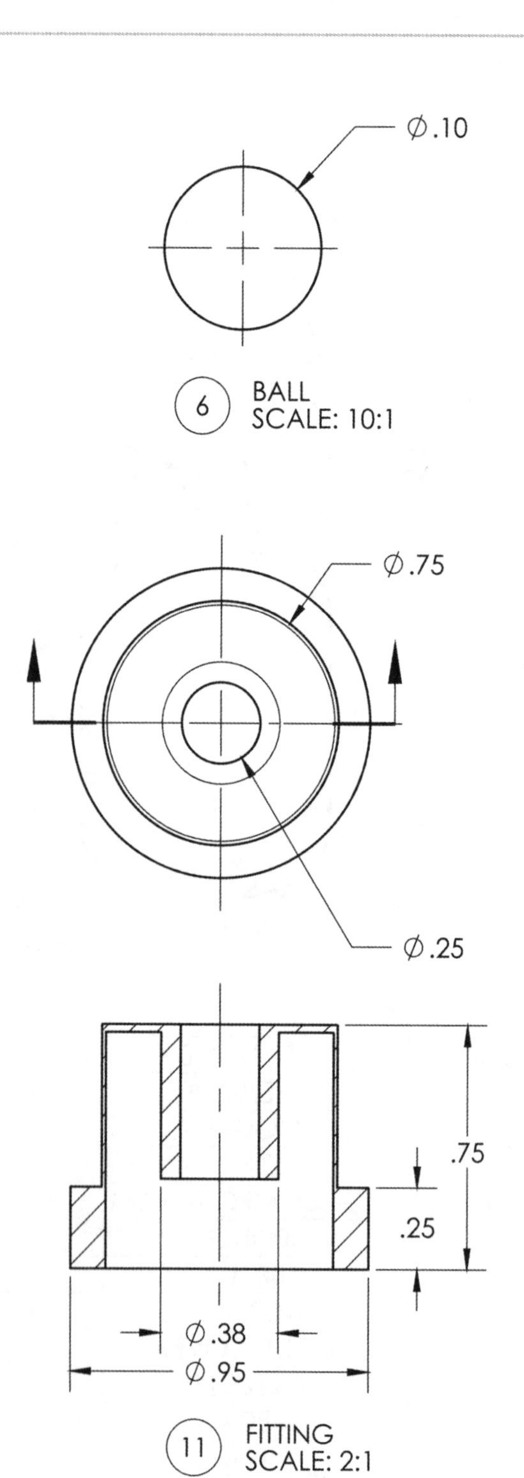

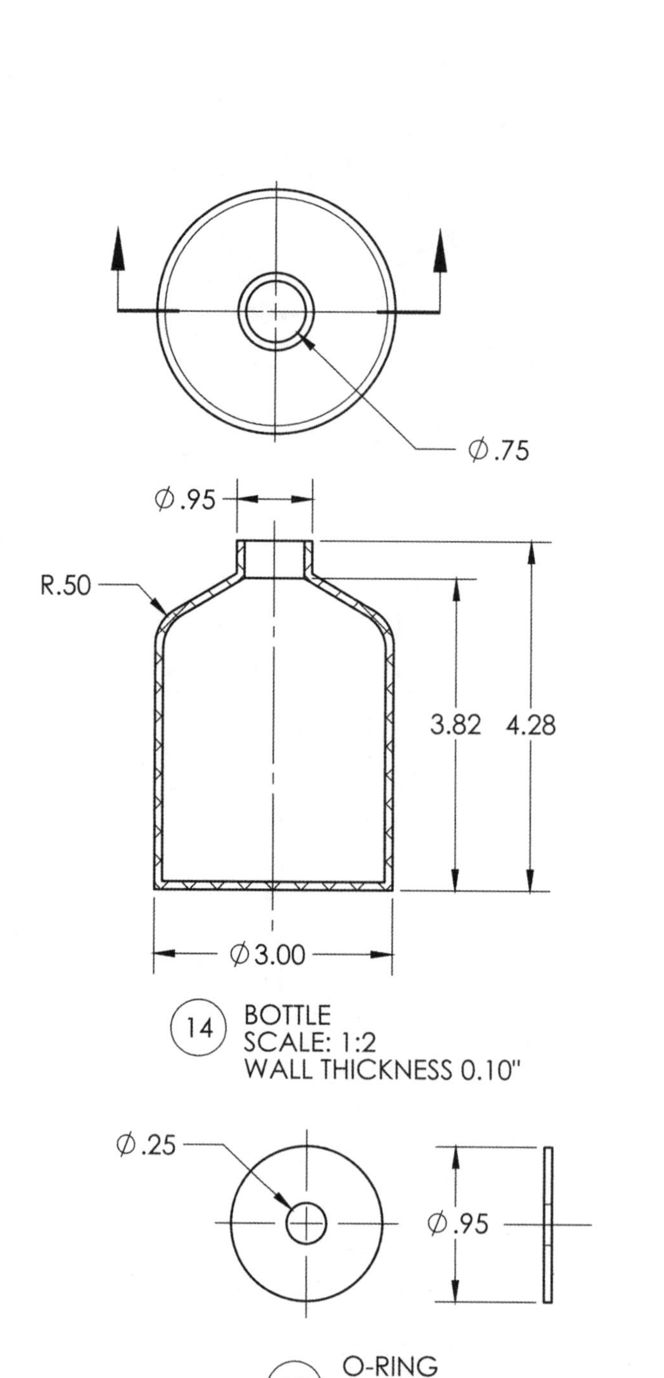

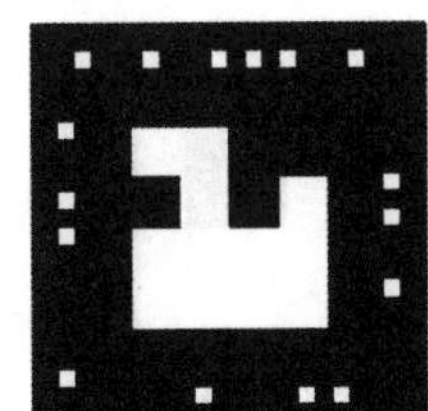

EXERCISE 06-3

CREATE A SET OF WORKING DRAWINGS FOR THE PLASTIC SPRAY BOTTLE ASSEMBLY SHOWN BELOW. DETAIL DRAWINGS FOLLOW.

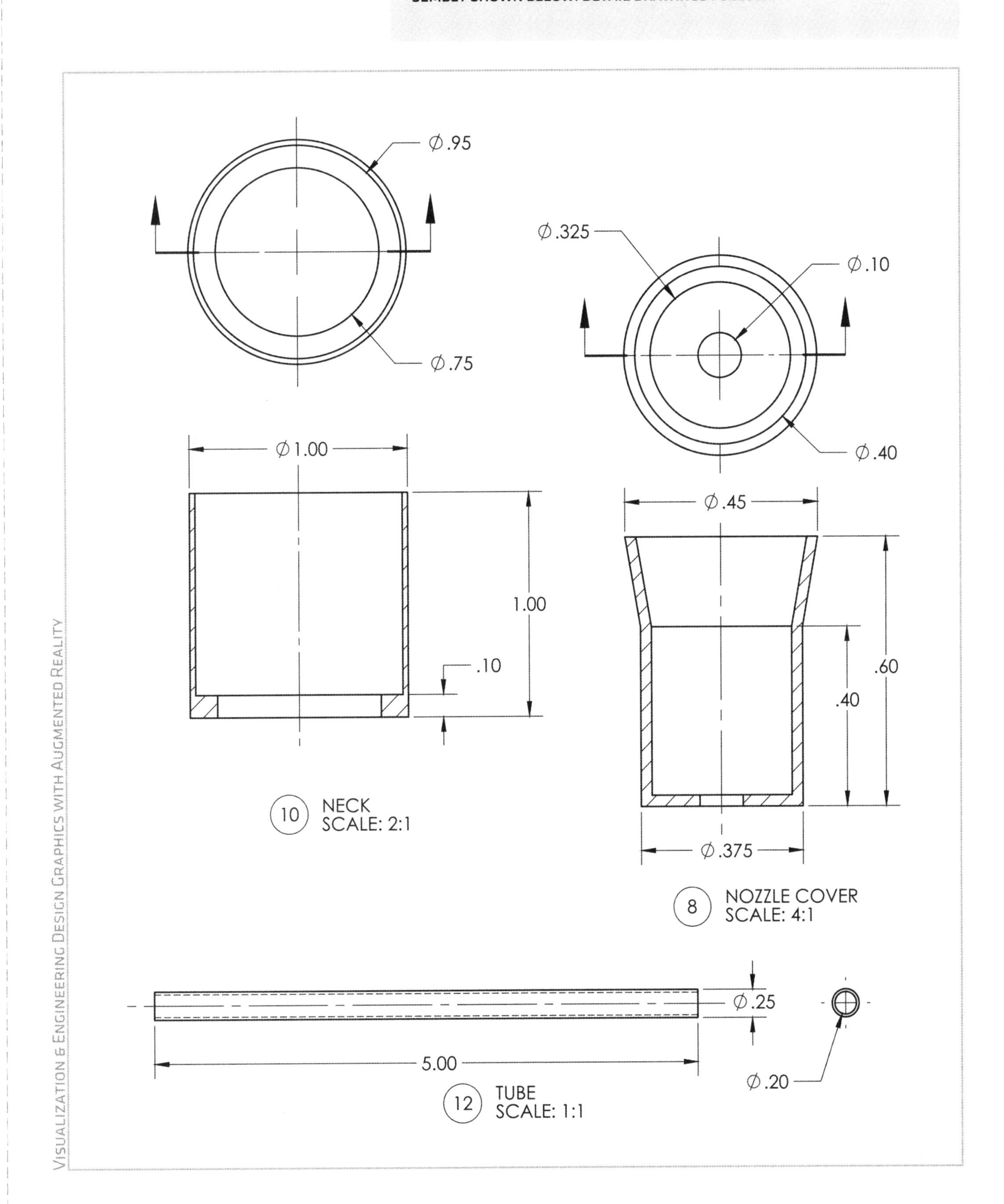

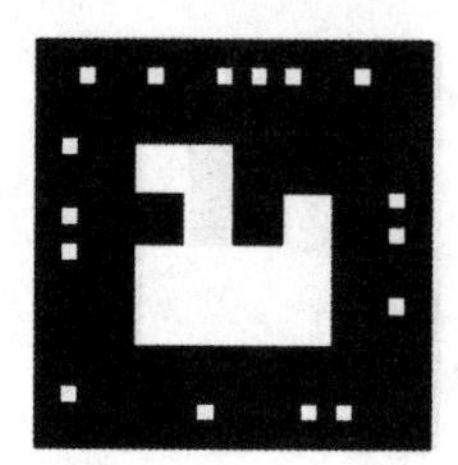

Create a set of working drawings for the plastic spray bottle assembly shown below. Detail drawings follow.

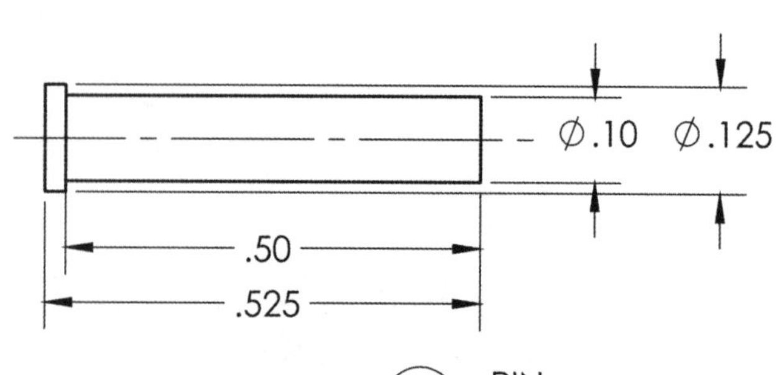

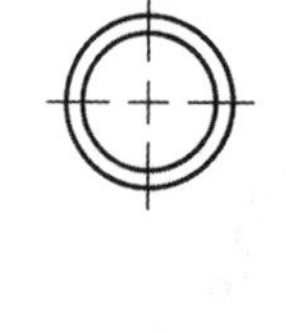

3 PIN
SCALE: 4:1

5 SPRING
O.D. - 0 .25"
WIRE DIA - 0.03'
1" LG

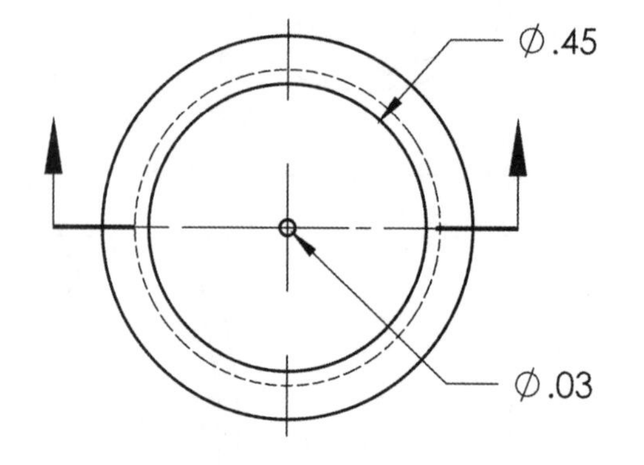

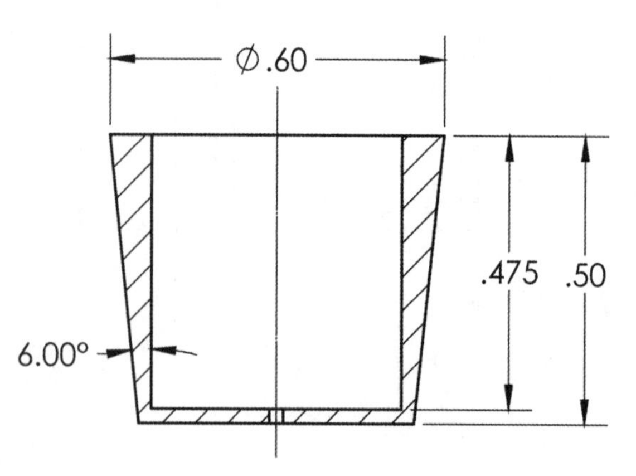

9 NOZZLE TIP
SCALE: 3:1

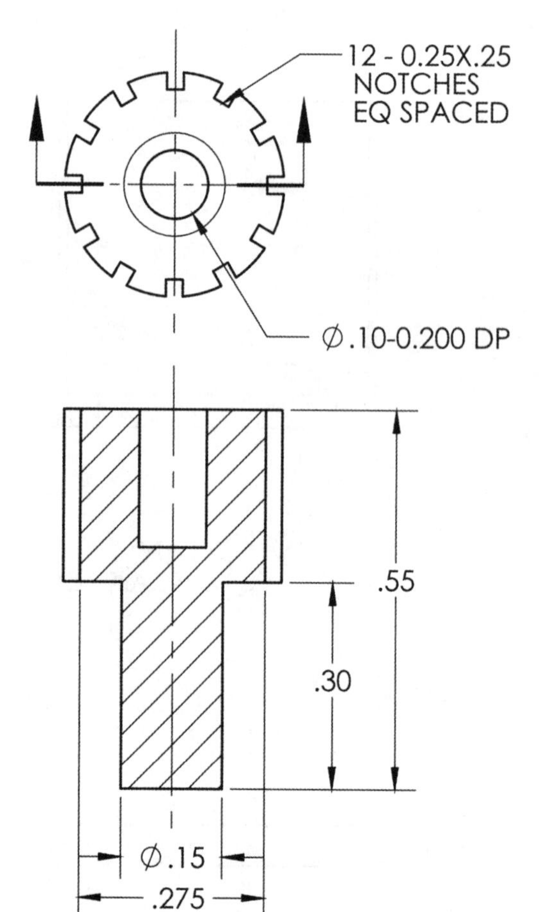

7 NOZZLE
SCALE: 4:1

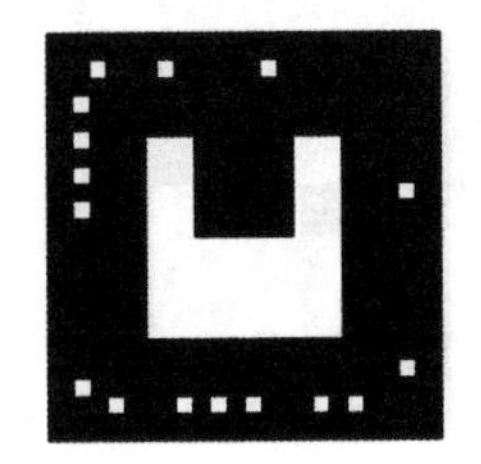

CREATE A SET OF WORKING DRAWINGS FOR THE PLASTIC SPRAY BOTTLE ASSEMBLY SHOWN BELOW. DETAIL DRAWINGS FOLLOW.

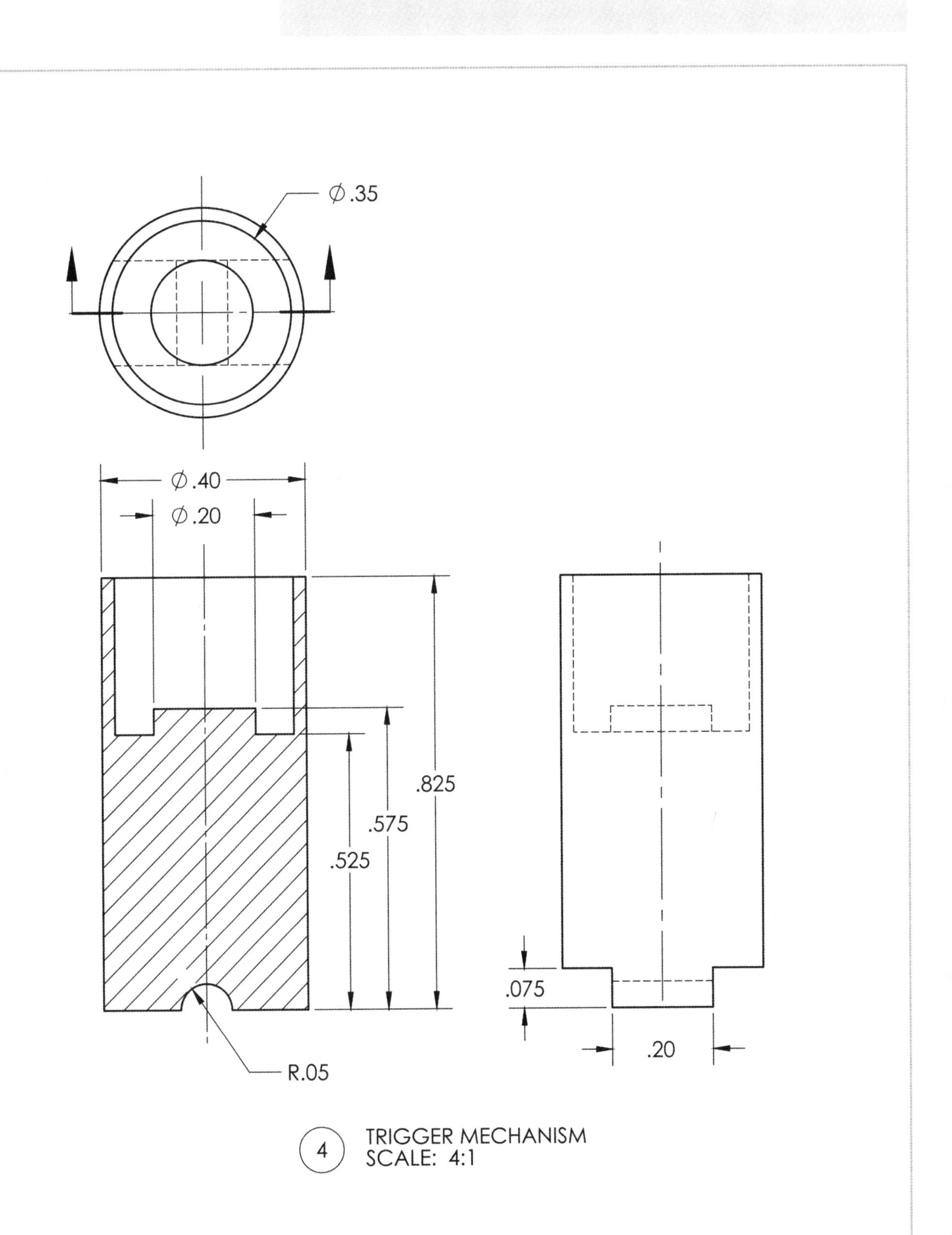

EXERCISE 06-6

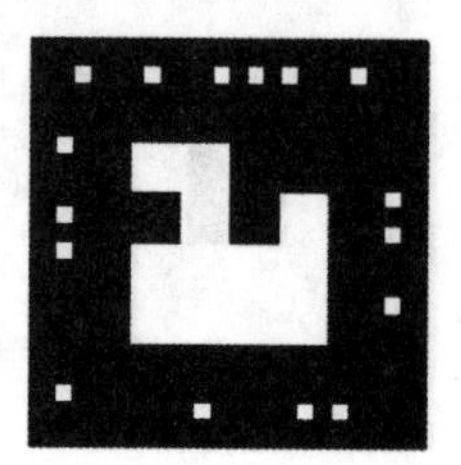

CREATE A SET OF WORKING DRAWINGS FOR THE PLASTIC SPRAY BOTTLE ASSEMBLY SHOWN BELOW. DETAIL DRAWINGS FOLLOW.

OBJECT IS SYMMETRICAL
HIDDEN LINES REMOVED FOR CLARITY

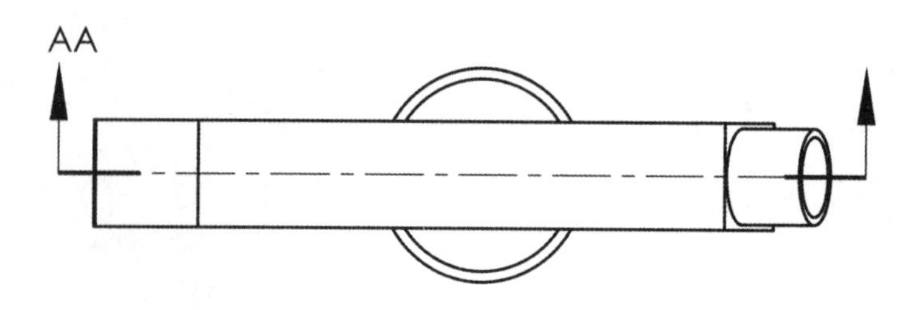

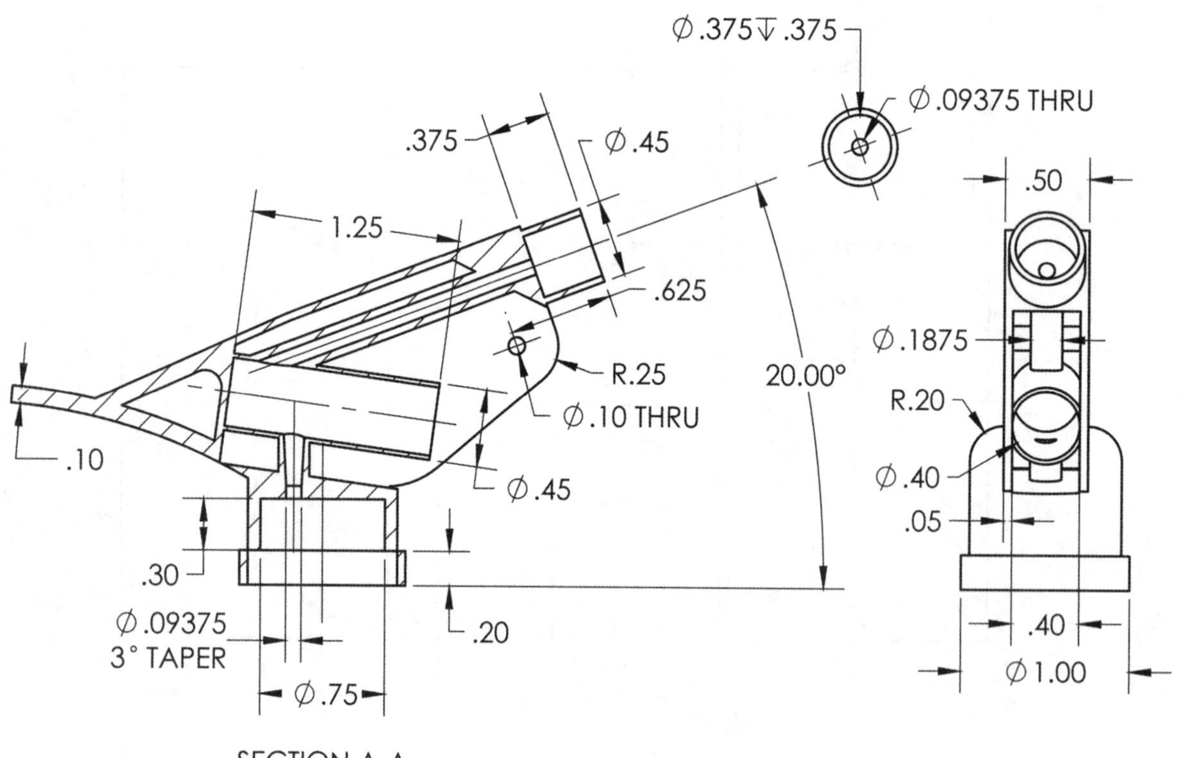

1 HEAD
SCALE: 1:1

Create a set of working drawings for the plastic spray bottle assembly shown below. Detail drawings follow.

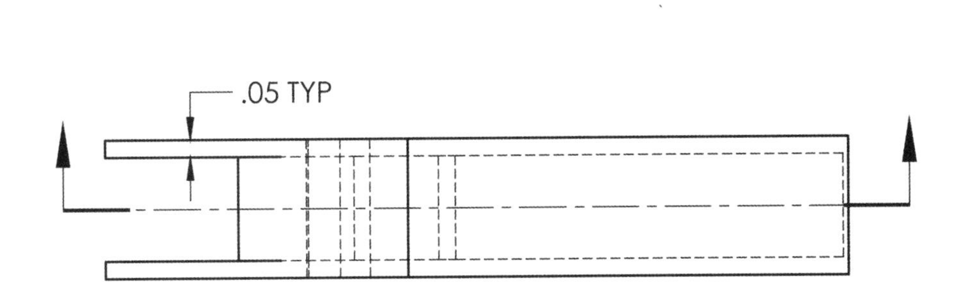

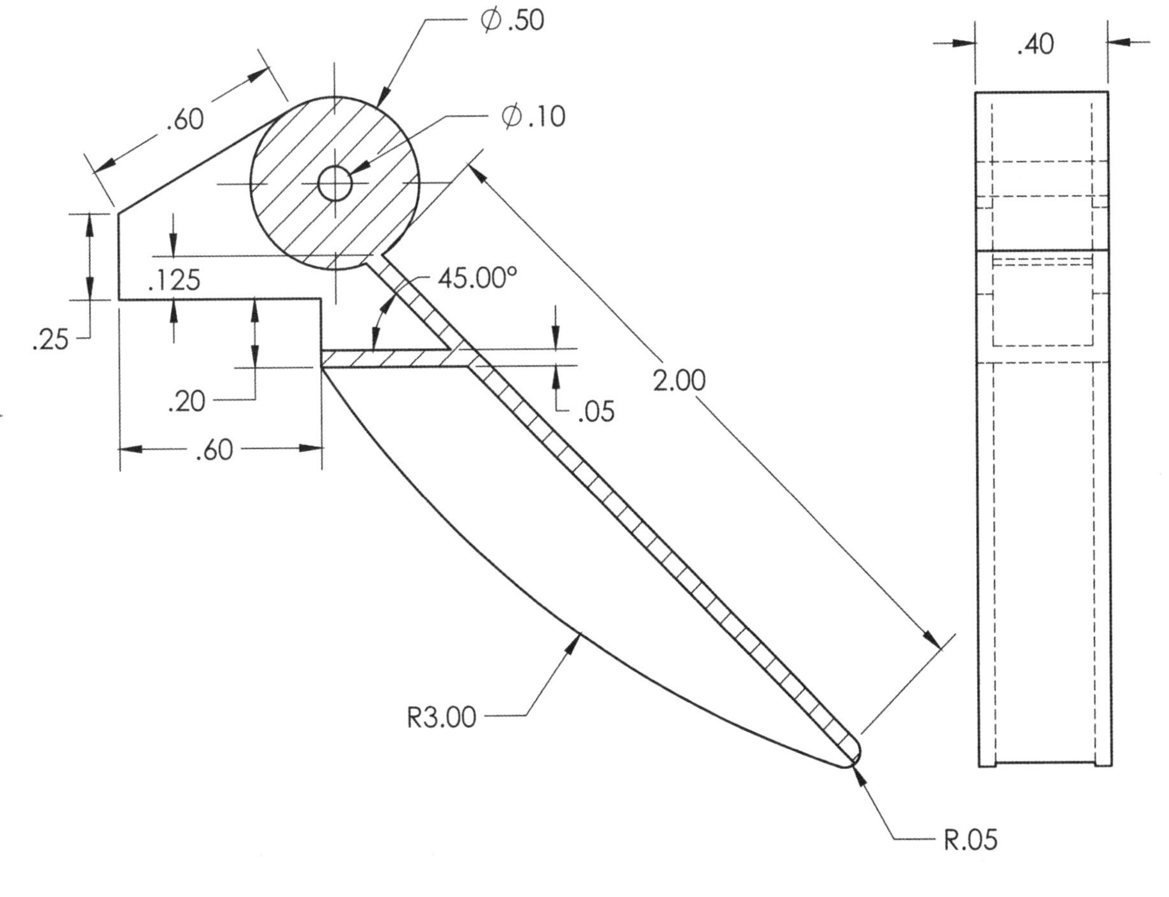

Exercise 07-1

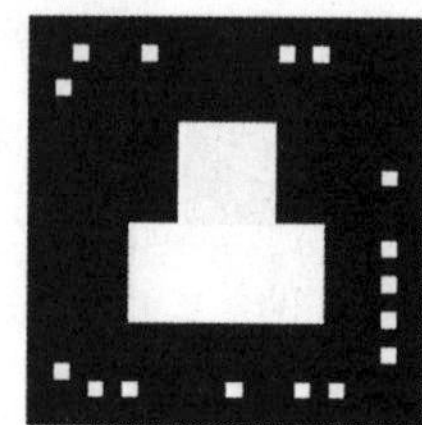

Create a set of working drawings for the tape dispenser assembly shown below. Detail drawings follow. Design your own base and body. Some dimensions are intentionally missing and others are provided for reference only. All units in inches.

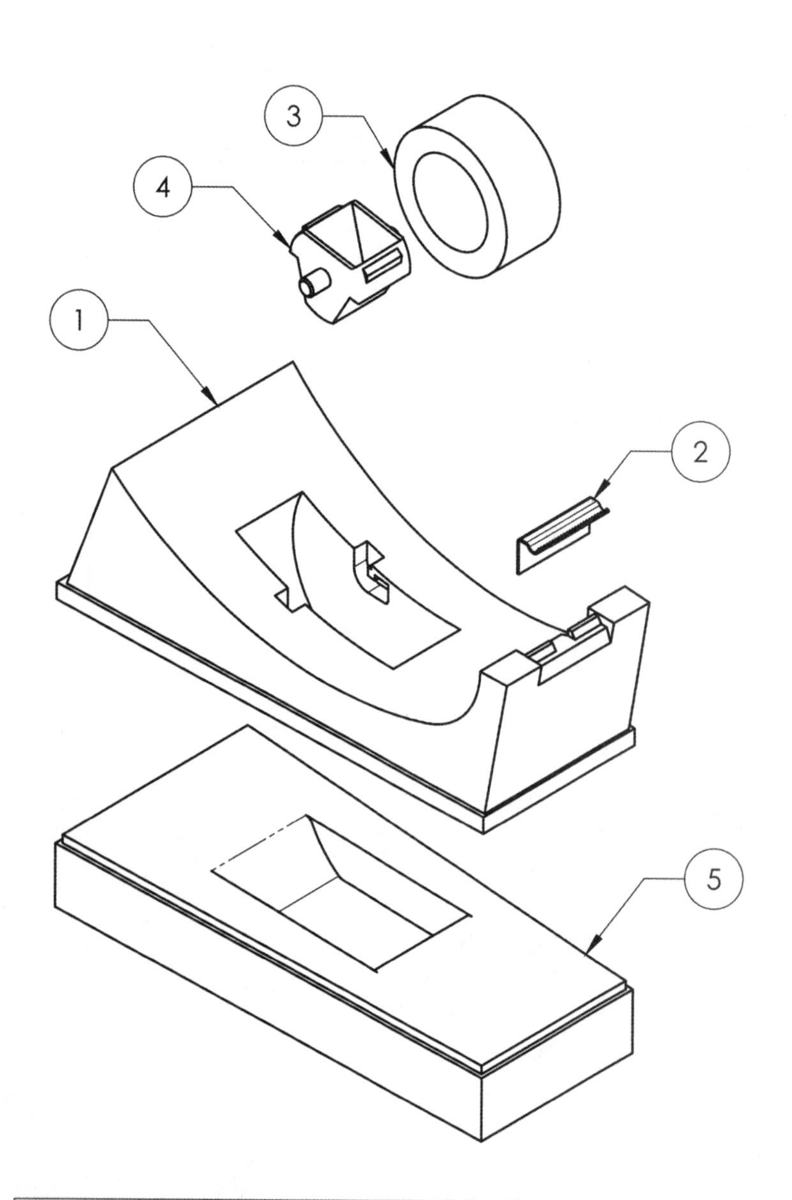

ITEM NO.	PART NAME	MATERIAL	FINISH	QTY.
1	BODY	ABS PLASTIC	GLOSS BLUE	1
2	CUTTERS	TEEL	N/A	1
3	ADHESIVE TAPE	CELLULOSE FILM	CLEAR	1
4	SPINDLE	ABS PLASTIC	DARK GREY	1
5	BASE	ABS PLASTIC	MATTE RUBBER COATING	1

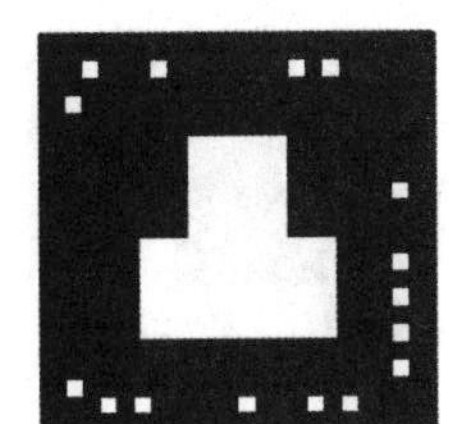

CREATE A SET OF WORKING DRAWINGS FOR THE TAPE DISPENSER ASSEMBLY SHOWN BELOW. DETAIL DRAWINGS FOLLOW. DESIGN YOUR OWN BASE AND BODY. SOME DIMENSIONS ARE INTENTIONALLY MISSING AND OTHERS ARE PROVIDED FOR REFERENCE ONLY. ALL UNITS IN INCHES.

1 BODY
ABS PLASTIC

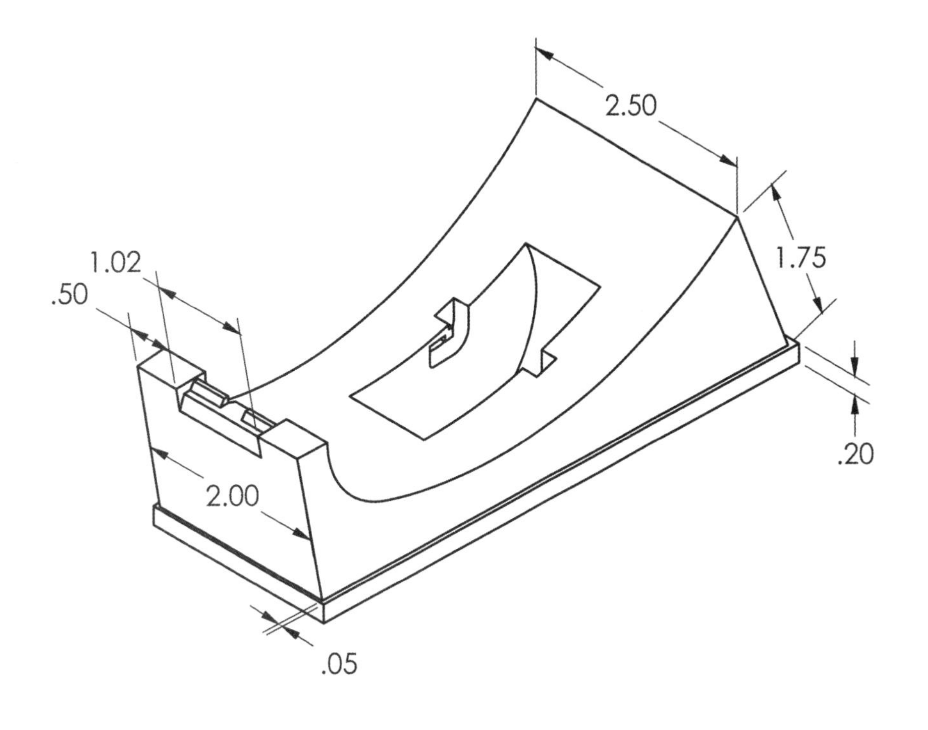

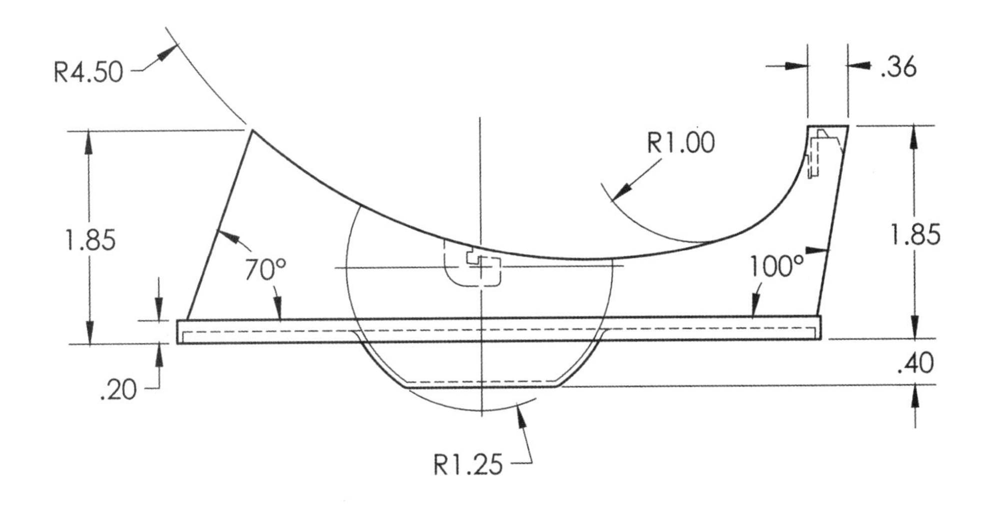

EXERCISE 07-3

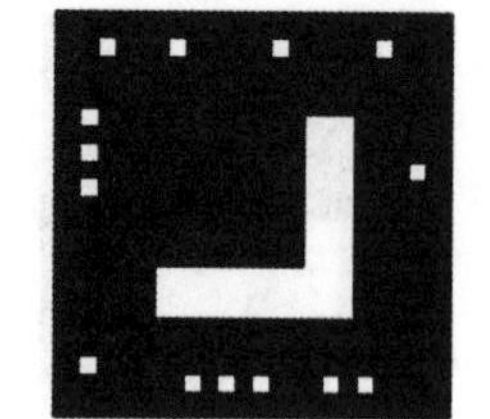

CREATE A SET OF WORKING DRAWINGS FOR THE TAPE DISPENSER ASSEMBLY SHOWN BELOW. DETAIL DRAWINGS FOLLOW. DESIGN YOUR OWN BASE AND BODY. SOME DIMENSIONS ARE INTENTIONALLY MISSING AND OTHERS ARE PROVIDED FOR REFERENCE ONLY. ALL UNITS IN INCHES.

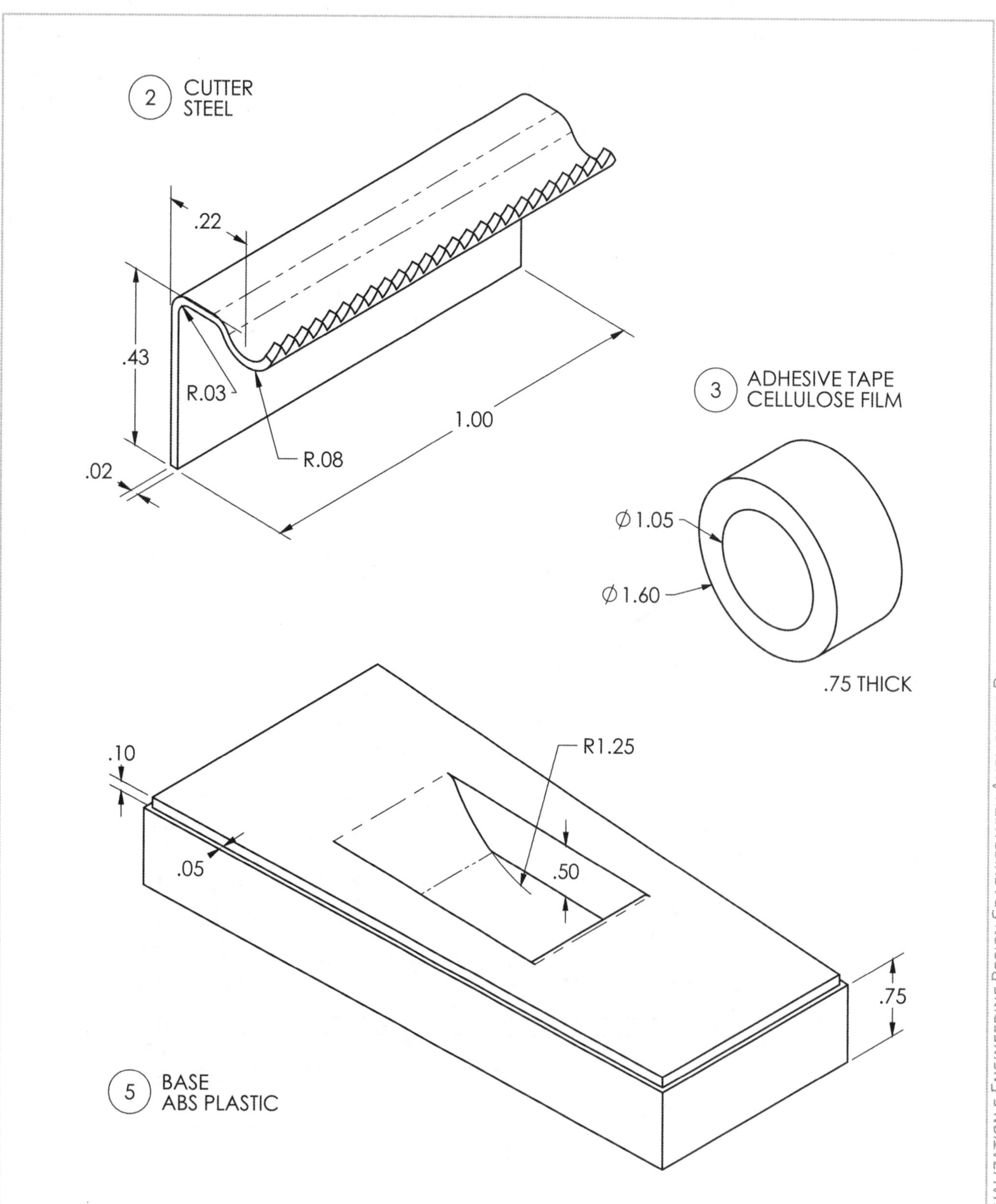

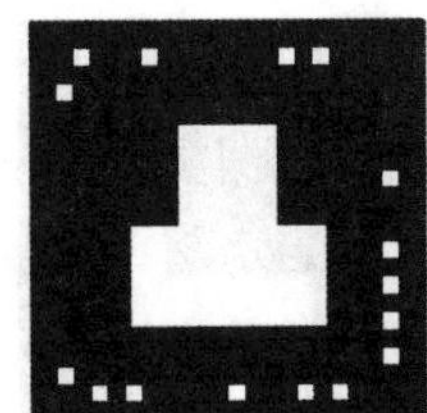
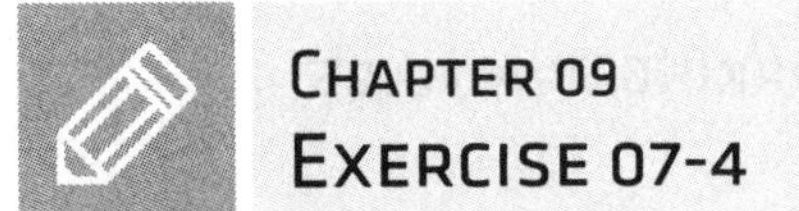

CREATE A SET OF WORKING DRAWINGS FOR THE TAPE DISPENSER ASSEMBLY SHOWN BELOW. DETAIL DRAWINGS FOLLOW. DESIGN YOUR OWN BASE AND BODY. SOME DIMENSIONS ARE INTENTIONALLY MISSING AND OTHERS ARE PROVIDED FOR REFERENCE ONLY. ALL UNITS IN INCHES.

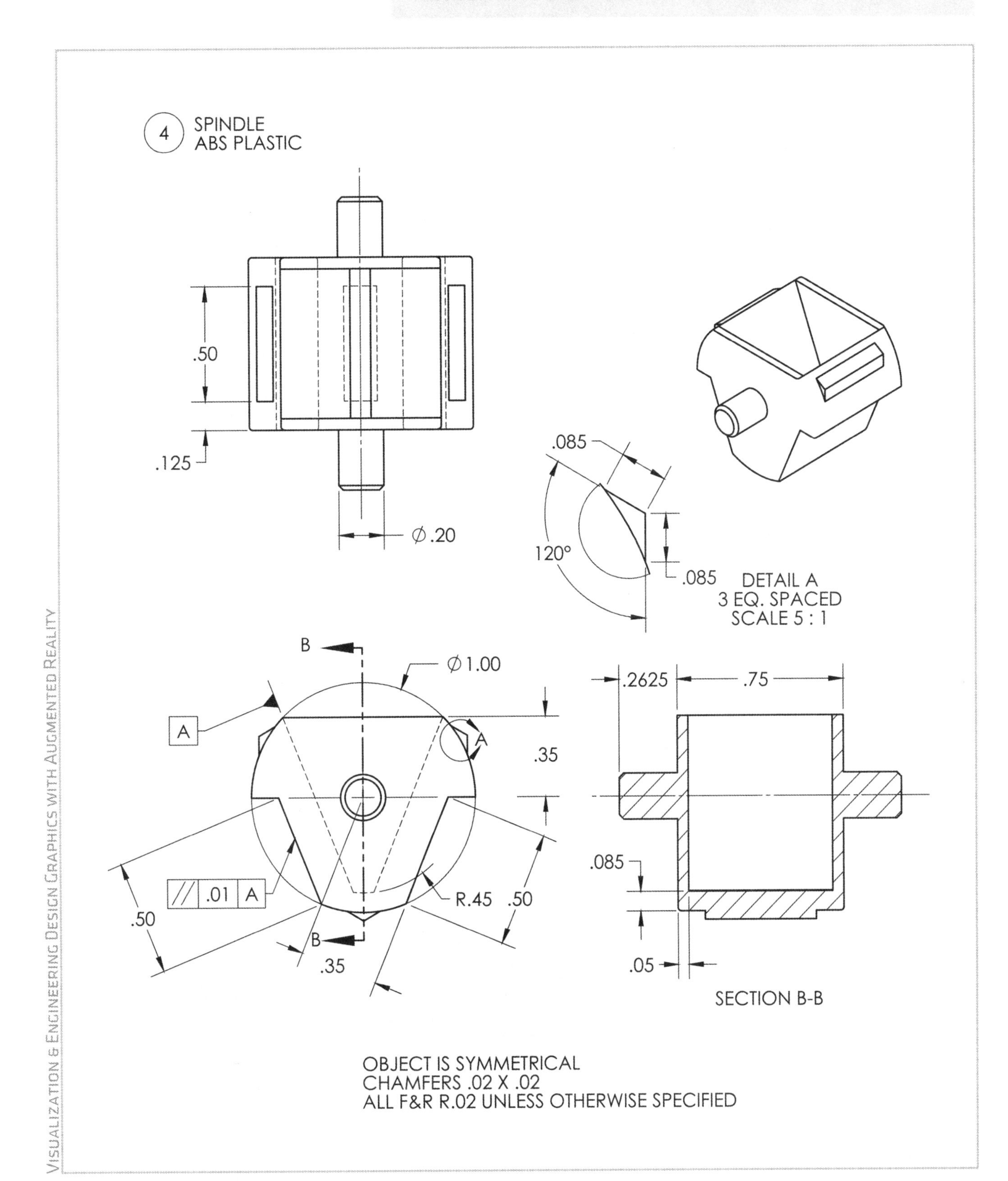

Exercise 08-1

Create a set of working drawings for the pillow block assembly shown below. Detail drawings follow. Some dimensions are intentionally missing. All units in inches.

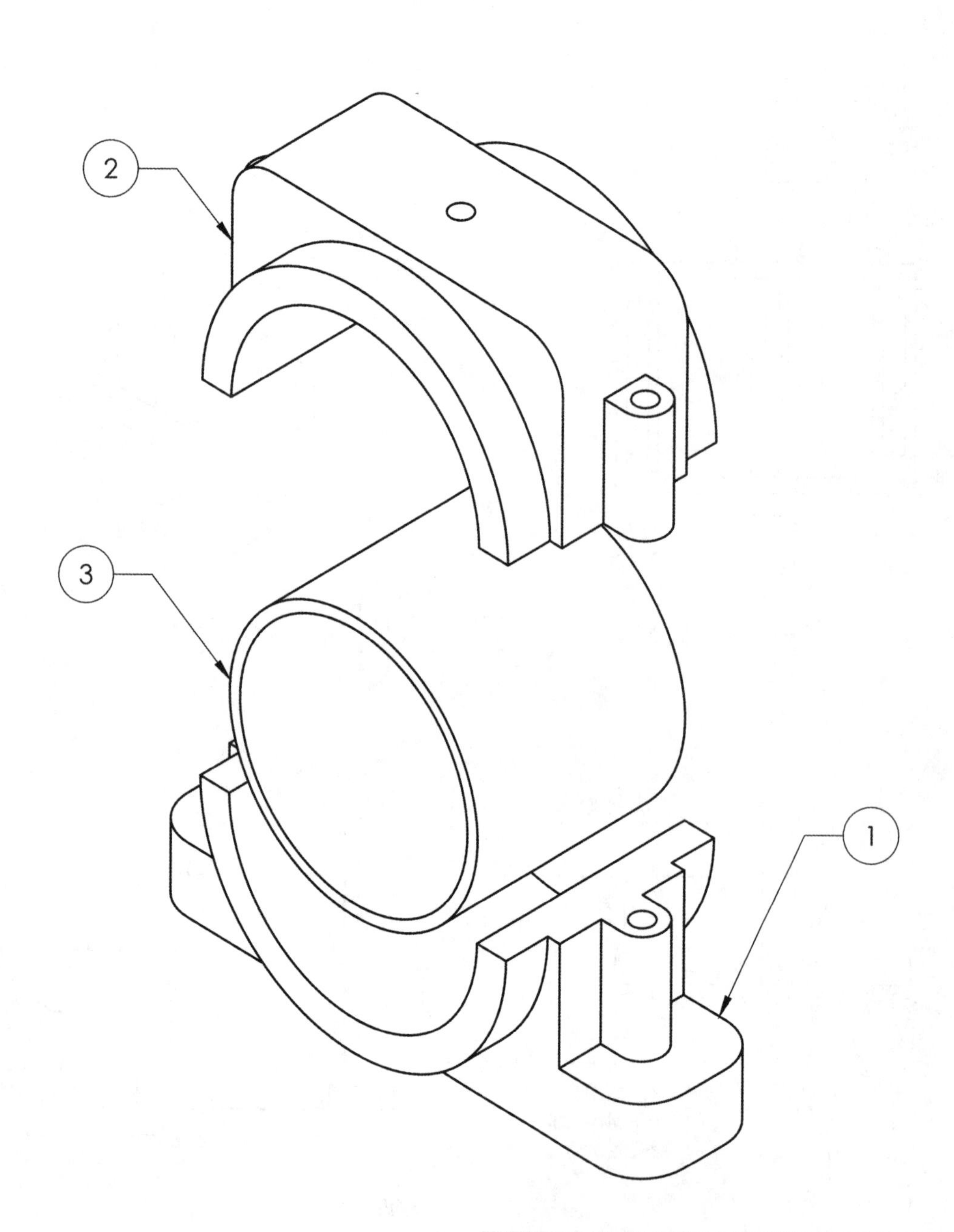

ITEM NO.	PART NAME	QTY.
1	PILLOW BASE	1
2	PILLOW CAP	1
3	BUSHING	1

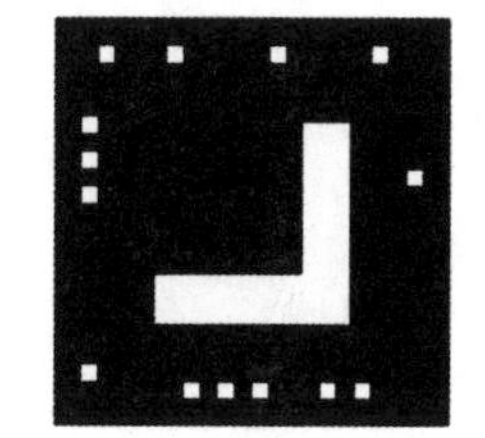

EXERCISE 08-2

CREATE A SET OF WORKING DRAWINGS FOR THE PILLOW BLOCK ASSEMBLY SHOWN BELOW. DETAIL DRAWINGS FOLLOW. SOME DIMENSIONS ARE INTENTIONALLY MISSING. ALL UNITS IN INCHES.

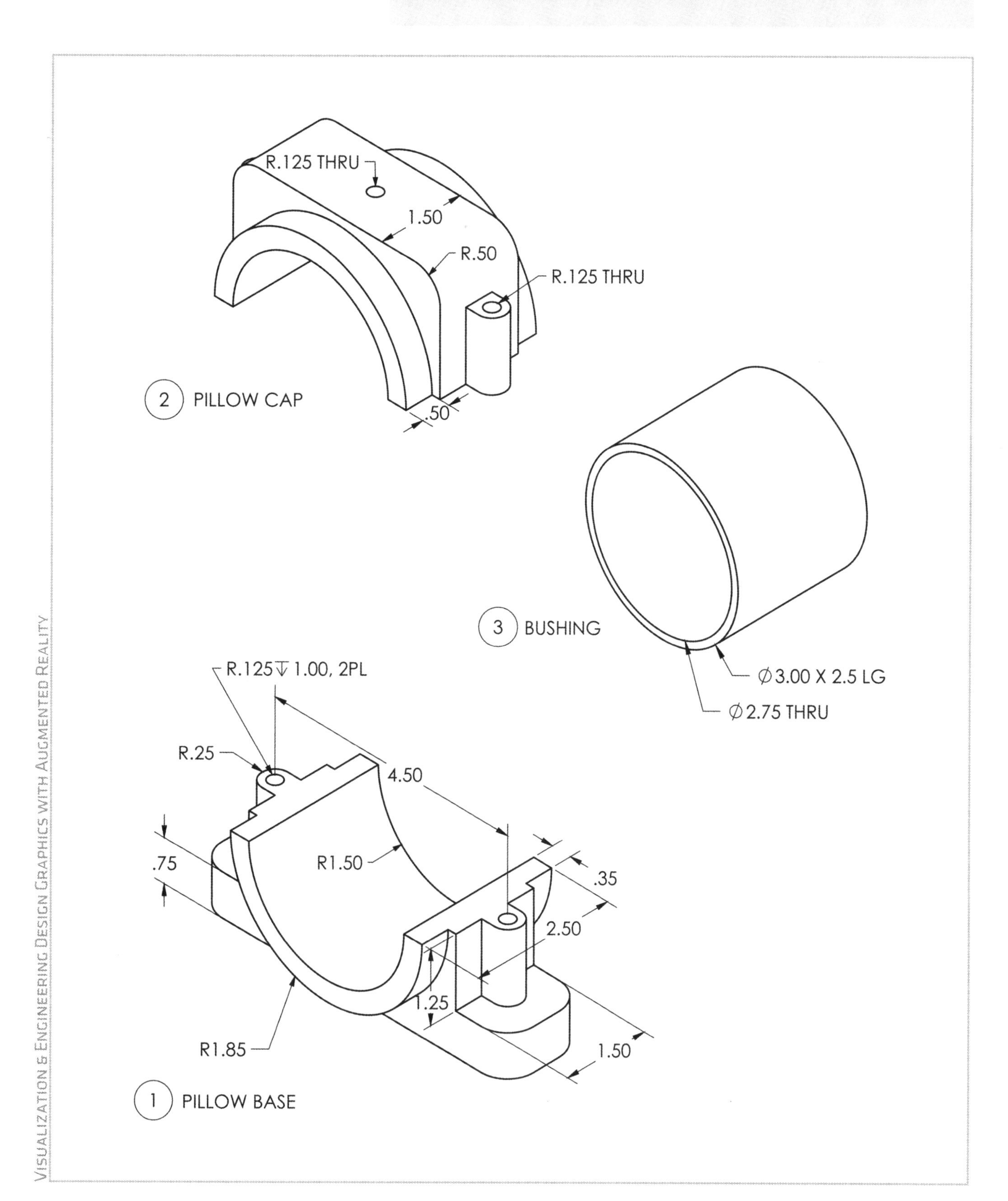

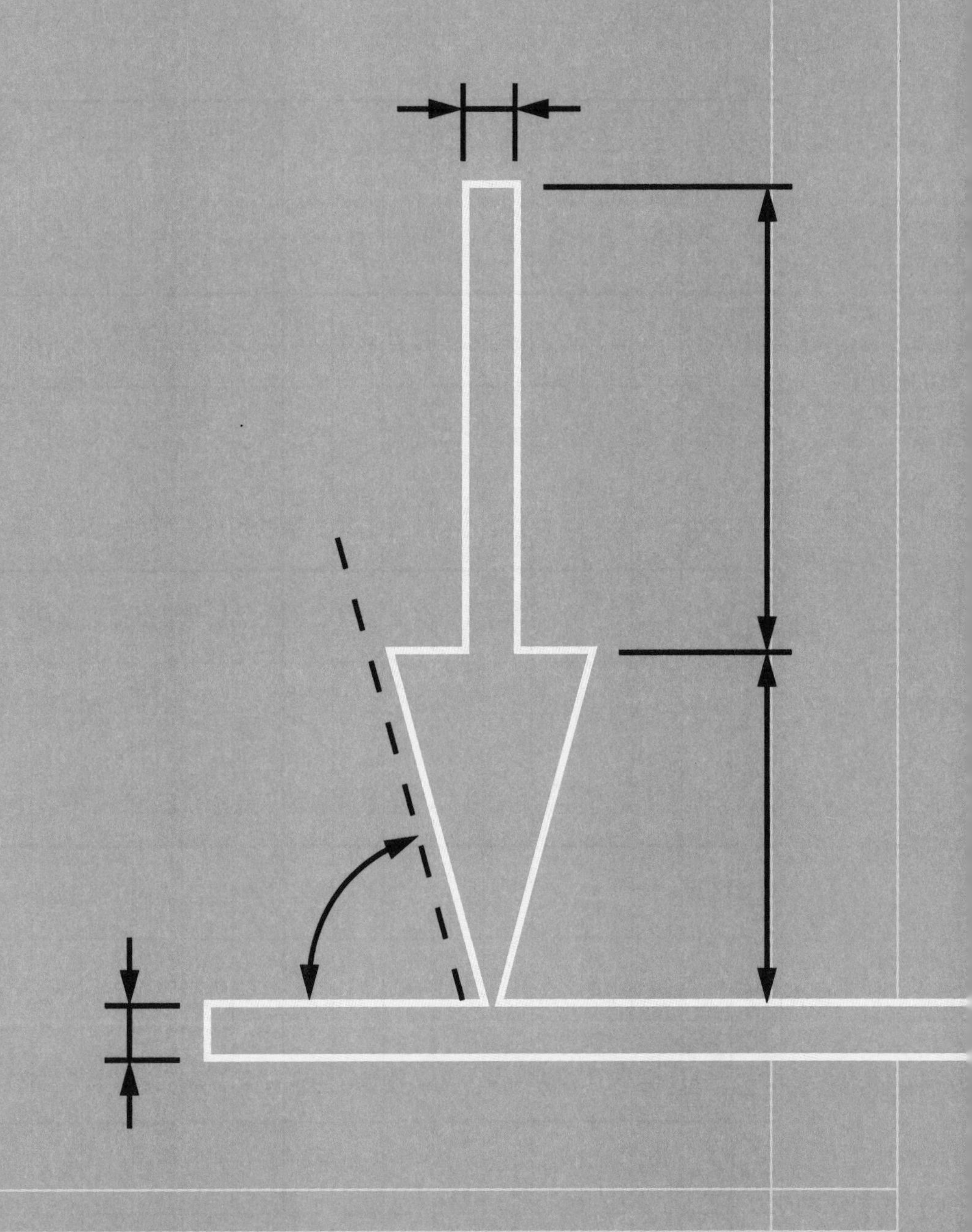

Appendix

ANSI RUNNING AND SLIDING FITS (Basic-Hole System)

Values shown below are in thousandths of an inch

Nominal Size Range (in)		Class RC1			Class RC2			Class RC3			Class RC4			Class RC5		
		Clearance	Standard Limits		Clearance	Standard Limits		Clearance	Standard Limits		Clearance	Standard Limits		Clearance	Standard Limits	
Over	To		Hole H5	Shaft g4		Hole H6	Shaft g5		Hole H7	Shaft f6		Hole H8	Shaft f7		Hole H8	Shaft e7
0	0,12	0,1	+0.2	-0.1	0,1	+0.25	-0.1	0,3	+0.4	-0.3	0,3	+0.6	-0.3	0.6	+0.6	-0.6
		0,45	0	-0.25	0,55	0	-0.3	0,95	0	-0.55	1,3	0	-0.7	1.6	-0	-1.0
0,12	0,24	0,15	+0.2	-0.15	0,15	+0.3	-0.15	0,4	+0.5	-0.4	0,4	+0.7	-0.4	0.8	+0.7	-0.8
		0,5	0	-0.3	0,65	0	-0.35	1,12	0	-0.7	1,6	0	-0.9	2.0	-0	-1.3
0,24	0,4	0,2	0.25	-0.2	0,2	+0.4	-0.2	0,5	+0.6	-0.5	0,5	+0.9	-0.5	1.0	+0.9	-1.0
		0,6	0	-0.35	0,85	0	-0.45	1,5	0	-0.9	2	0	-1.1	2.5	-0	-1.6
0,4	0,71	0,25	+0.3	-0.25	0,25	+0.4	-0.25	0,6	+0.7	-0.6	0,6	+1.0	-0.6	1.2	+1.0	-1.2
		0,75	0	-0.45	0,95	0	-0.55	1,7	0	-1.0	2,3	0	-1.3	2.9	-0	-1.9
0,71	1,19	0,3	+0.4	-0.3	0,3	+0.5	-0.3	0,8	+0.8	-0.8	0,8	+1.2	-0.8	1.6	+1.2	-1.6
		0,95	0	-0.55	1,2	0	-0.7	2,1	0	-1.3	2,8	0	-1.6	3.6	-0	-2.4
1,19	1,97	0,4	+0.4	-0.4	0,4	+0.6	-0.4	1	+1.0	-1.0	1.0	+1.6	-1.0	2.0	+1.6	-2.0
		1,1	0	-0.7	1,4	0	-0.8	2,6	0	-1.6	3,6	0	-2.0	4.6	-0	-3.0
1,97	3,15	0,4	+0.5	-0.4	0,4	+0.7	-0.4	1,2	+1.2	-1.2	1,2	+1.8	-1.2	2.5	+1.8	-2.5
		1,2	0	-0.7	1,6	0	-0.9	3,1	0	-1.9	4,2	0	-2.4	5.5	-0	-3.7
3,15	4,73	0,5	+0.6	-0.5	0,5	+0.9	-0.5	1,4	+1.4	-1.4	1,4	+2.2	-1.4	3.0	+2.2	-3.0
		1,5	0	-0.9	2.0	0	-1.1	3,7	0	-2.3	5	0	-2.8	6.6	-0	-4.4
4,73	7,09	0,6	+0.7	-0.6	0,6	+1.0	-0.6	1,6	+1.6	-1.6	1,6	+2.5	-1.6	3.5	+2.5	-3.5
		1,8	0	-1.1	2,3	0	-1.3	4,2	0	-2.6	5,7	0	-3.2	7.6	-0	-5.1
7,09	9,85	0,6	+0.8	-0.6	0,6	+1.2	-0.6	2	+1.8	-2.0	2	+2.8	-2.0	4.0	+2.8	-4.0
		2	0	-1.2	2,6	0	-1.4	5	0	-3.2	6,6	0	-3.8	8.6	-0	-5.8
9,85	12,41	0,8	+0.9	-0.8	0,8	+1.2	-0.8	2.5	+2.0	-2.5	2,5	+3.0	-2.5	5.0	+3.0	-5.0
		2,3	0	-1.4	2,9	0	-1.7	5,7	0	-3.7	7,5	0	-4.5	10.0	0	-7.0
12,41	15,75	1	+1.0	-1.0	1	+1.4	-1.0	3	+2.2	-3.0	3	+3.5	-3.0	6.0	+3.5	-6.0
		2,7	0	-1.7	3,4	0	-2.0	6,6	0	-4.4	8,7	0	-5.2	11.7	0	-8.2
15,75	19,69	1,2	+1.0	-1.2	1,2	+1.6	-1.2	4	+1.6	-4.0	4	+4.0	-4.0	8.0	+4.0	-8.0
		3	0	-2.0	3,8	0	-2.2	8,1	0	-5.6	10,5	0	-6.5	14.5	0	-10.5
19,69	30,09	1,6	+1.2	-1.6	1,6	+2.0	-1.6	5	+3.0	-5.0	5	+5.0	-5.0	10.0	+5.0	-10.0
		3,7	0	-2.5	4,8	0	-2.8	10	0	-7.0	13	0	-8.0	18.0	0	-13.0
30,09	41,49	2	+1.6	-2.0	2	+2.5	-2.0	6	+4.0	-6.0	6	+6.0	-6.0	12.0	+6.0	-12.0
		4,6	0	-3.0	6,1	0	-3.6	12,5	0	-8.5	16	0	-10.0	22.0	0	-16.0
41,49	56,19	2,5	+2.0	-2.5	2,5	+3.0	-2.5	8	+5.0	-8.0	8	+8.0	-8.0	16.0	+8.0	-16.0
		5,7	0	-3.7	7,5	0	-4.5	16	0	-11.0	21	0	-13.0	29.0	0	-21.0
56,19	76,39	3	+2.5	-3.0	3	+4.0	-3.0	10	+6.0	-10.0	10	+10.0	-10.0	20.0	+10.0	-20.0
		7,1	0	-4.6	9,5	0	-5.5	20	0	-14.0	26	0	-16.0	36.0	0	-26.0
76,39	100,9	4	+3.0	-4.0	4	+5.0	-4.0	12	+8.0	-12.0	12	+12.0	-12.0	25.0	+12.0	-25.0
		9	0	-6.0	12	0	-7.0	25	0	-17.0	32	0	-20.0	45.0	0	-33.0

ANSI RUNNING AND SLIDING FITS (Basic-Hole System) - continued

Values shown below are in thousandths of an inch

Nominal Size Range (in)		Class RC6			Class RC7			Class RC8			Class RC9		
		Clearance	Standard Limits		Clearance	Standard Limits		Clearance	Standard Limits		Clearance	Standard Limits	
Over	To		Hole H9	Shaft e8		Hole H9	Shaft d8		Hole H10	Shaft c9		Hole H11	Shaft
0	0,12	0.6 2.2	+1.0 -0	-0.6 -1.2	1.0 2.6	+1.0 0	-1.0 -1.6	2.5 5.1	+1.6 0	-2.5 -3.5	4.0 8.1	+2.5 0	-4.0 -5.6
0,12	0,24	0.8 2.7	+1.2 -0	-0.8 -1.5	1.2 3.1	+1.2 0	-1.2 -1.9	2.8 5.8	+1.8 0	-2.8 -4.0	4.5 9.0	+3.0 0	-4.5 -6.0
0,24	0,4	1.0 3.3	+1.4 -0	-1.0 -1.9	1.6 3.9	+1.4 0	-1.6 -2.5	3.0 6.6	+2.2 0	-3.0 -4.4	5.0 10.7	+3.5 0	-5.0 -7.2
0,4	0,71	1.2 3.8	+1.6 -0	-1.2 -2.2	2.0 4.6	+1.6 0	-2.0 -3.0	3.5 7.9	+2.8 0	-3.5 -5.1	6.0 12.8	+4.0 -0	-6.0 -8.8
0,71	1,19	1.6 4.8	+2.0 -0	-1.6 -2.8	2.5 5.7	+2.0 0	-2.5 -3.7	4.5 10.0	+3.5 0	-4.5 -6.5	7.0 15.5	+5.0 0	-7.0 -10.5
1,19	1,97	2.0 6.1	+2.5 -0	-2.0 -3.6	3.0 7.1	+2.5 0	-3.0 -4.6	5.0 11.5	+4.0 0	-5.0 -7.5	8.0 18.0	+6.0 0	-8.0 -12.0
1,97	3,15	2.5 7.3	+3.0 -0	-2.5 -4.3	4.0 8.8	+3.0 0	-4.0 -5.8	6.0 13.5	+4.5 0	-6.0 -9.0	9.0 20.5	+7.0 0	-9.0 -13.5
3,15	4,73	3.0 8.7	+3.5 -0	-3.0 -5.2	5.0 10.7	+3.5 0	-5.0 -7.2	7.0 15.5	+5.0 0	-7.0 -10.5	10.0 24.0	+9.0 0	-10.0 -15.0
4,73	7,09	3.5 10.0	+4.0 -0	-3.5 -6.0	6.0 12.5	+4.0 0	-6.0 -8.5	8.0 18.0	+6.0 0	-8.0 -12.0	12.0 28.0	+10.0 0	-12.0 -18.0
7,09	9,85	4.0 11.3	+4.5 0	-4.0 -6.8	7.0 14.3	+4.5 0	-7.0 -9.8	10.0 21.5	+7.0 0	-10.0 -14.5	15.0 34.0	+12.0 0	-15.0 -22.0
9,85	12,41	5.0 13.0	+5.0 0	-5.0 -8.0	8.0 16.0	+5.0 0	-8.0 -11.0	12.0 25.0	+8.0 0	-12.0 -17.0	18.0 38.0	+12.0 0	-18.0 -26.0
12,41	15,75	6.0 15.5	+6.0 0	-6.0 -9.5	10.0 19.5	+6.0 0	-10.0 -13.5	14.0 29.0	+9.0 0	-14.0 -20.0	22.0 45.0	+14.0 0	-22.0 -31.0
15,75	19,69	8.0 18.0	+6.0 0	-8.0 -12.0	12.0 22.0	+6.0 0	-12.0 -16.0	16.0 32.0	+10.0 0	-16.0 -22.0	25.0 51.0	+16.0 0	-25.0 -35.0
19,69	30,09	10.0 23.0	+8.0 0	-10.0 -15.0	16.0 29.0	+8.0 0	-16.0 -21.0	20.0 40.0	+12.0 0	-20.0 -28.0	30.0 62.0	+20.0 0	-30.0 -42.0
30,09	41,49	12.0 28.0	+10.0 0	-12.0 -18.0	20.0 36.0	+10.0 0	-20.0 -26.0	25.0 51.0	+16.0 0	-25.0 -35.0	40.0 81.0	+25.0 0	-40.0 -56.0
41,49	56,19	16.0 36.0	+12.0 0	-16.0 -24.0	25.0 45.0	+12.0 0	-25.0 -33.0	30.0 62.0	+20.0 0	-30.0 -42.0	50.0 100	+30.0 0	-50.0 -70.0
56,19	76,39	20.0 46.0	+16.0 0	-20.0 -30.0	30.0 56.0	+16.0 0	-30.0 -40.0	40.0 81.0	+25.0 0	-40.0 -56.0	60.0 125	+40.0 0	-60.0 -85.0
76,39	100,9	25.0 57.0	+20.0 0	-25.0 -37.0	40.0 72.0	+20.0 0	-40.0 -52.0	50.0 100	+30.0 0	-50.0 -70.0	80.0 160	+50.0 0	-80.0 -110

ANSI CLEARANCE LOCATIONAL FITS (Basic-Hole System)

Values shown below are in thousandths of an inch

Nominal Size Range (in)		Class LC1			Class LC2			Class LC3			Class LC4			Class LC5		
		Clearance	Standard Limits		Clearance	Standard Limits		Clearance	Standard Limits		Clearance	Standard Limits		Clearance	Standard Limits	
Over	To		Hole H6	Shaft h5		Hole H7	Shaft h6		Hole H8	Shaft h7		Hole H10	Shaft h9		Hole H7	Shaft g6
0	0,12	0 0,45	0,25 -0	+0 -0.2	0 0.65	+0.4 -0	+0 -0.25	0 1	+0.6 -0	+0 -0.4	0 2.6	+1.6 -0	+0 -1.0	0.1 0.75	+0.4 -0	-0.1 -0.35
0,12	0,24	0 0,5	+0.3 -0	+0 -0.2	0 0.8	+0.5 -0	+0 -0.3	0 1.2	+0.7 -0	+0 -0.5	0 3.0	+1.8 -0	+0 -1.2	0.15 0.95	+0.5 -0	-0.15 -0.45
0,24	0,4	0 0,65	+0.4 -0	+0 -0.25	0 1.0	+0.6 -0	+0 -0.4	0 1.5	+0.9 -0	+0 -0.6	0 3.6	+2.2 -0	+0 -1.4	0.2 1.2	+0.6 -0	-0.2 -0.6
0,4	0,71	0 0,7	+0.4 -0	+0 -0.3	0 1.1	+0.7 -0	+0 -0.4	0 1.7	+1.0 -0	+0 -0.7	0 4.4	+2.8 -0	+0 -1.6	0.25 1.35	+0.7 -0	-0.25 -0.65
0,71	1,19	0 0,9	+0.5 -0	+0 -0.4	0 1.3	+0.8 -0	+0 -0.5	0 2	+1.2 -0	+0 -0.8	0 5.5	+3.5 -0	+0 -2.0	0.3 1.6	+0.8 -0	-0.3 -0.8
1,19	1,97	0 1	+0.6 -0	+0 -0.4	0 1.6	+1.0 -0	+0 -0.6	0 2.6	+1.6 -0	+0 -1	0 6.5	+4.0 -0	+0 -2.5	0.4 2.0	+1.0 -0	-0.4 -1.0
1,97	3,15	0 1,2	+0.7 -0	+0 -0.5	0 1.9	+1.2 -0	+0 -0.7	0 3	+1.8 -0	+0 -1.2	0 7.5	+4.5 -0	+0 -3	0.4 2.3	+1.2 -0	-0.4 -1.1
3,15	4,73	0 1,5	+0.9 -0	+0 -0.6	0 2.3	+1.4 -0	+0 -0.9	0 3.6	+2.2 -0	+0 -1.4	0 8.5	+5.0 -0	+0 -3.5	0.5 2.8	+1.4 -0	-0.5 -1.4
4,73	7,09	0 1,7	+1.0 -0	+0 -0.7	0 2.6	+1.6 -0	+0 -1.0	0 4.1	+2.5 -0	+0 -1.6	0 10	+6.0 -0	+0 -4	0.6 3.2	+1.6 -0	-0.6 -1.6
7,09	9,85	0 2	+1.2 -0	+0 -0.8	0 3.0	+1.8 -0	+0 -1.2	0 4.6	+2.8 -0	+0 -1.8	0 11.5	+7.0 -0	+0 -4.5	0.6 3.6	+1.8 -0	-0.6 -1.8
9,85	12,41	0 2,1	+1.2 -0	+0 -0.9	0 3.2	+2.0 -0	+0 -1.2	0 5	+3.0 -0	+0 -2.0	0 13	+8.0 -0	+0 -5	0.7 3.9	+2.0 -0	-0.7 -1.9
12,41	15,75	0 2,4	+1.4 -0	+0 -1.0	0 3.6	+2.2 -0	+0 -1.4	0 5.7	+3.5 -0	+0 -2.2	0 15	+9.0 -0	+0 -6	0.7 4.3	+2.2 -0	-0.7 -2.1
15,75	19,69	0 2,6	+1.6 -0	+0 -1.0	0 4.1	+2.5 -0	+0 -1.6	0 6.5	+4 -0	+0 -2.5	0 16	+10.0 -0	+0 -6	0.8 4.9	+2.5 -0	-0.8 -2.4
19,69	30,09	0 3,2	+2.0 -0	+0 -1.2	0 5.0	+3 -0	+0 -2	0 8	+5 -0	+0 -3	0 20	+12.0 -0	+0 -8	0.9 5.9	+3.0 -0	-0.9 -2.9
30,09	41,49	0 4,1	+2.5 -0	+0 -1.6	0 6.5	+4 -0	+0 -2.5	0 10	+6 -0	+0 -4	0 26	+16.0 -0	+0 -10	1.0 7.5	+4.0 -0	-1.0 -3.5
41,49	56,19	0 5	+3.0 -0	+0 -2.0	0 8.0	+5 -0	+0 -3	0 13	+8 -0	+0 -5	0 32	+20.0 -0	+0 -12	1.2 9.2	+5.0 -0	-1.2 -4.2
56,19	76,39	0 6,5	+4.0 -0	+0 -2.5	0 10	+6 -0	+0 -4	0 16	+10 -0	+0 -6	0 41	+25.0 -0	+0 -16	1.2 11.2	+6.0 -0	-1.2 -5.2
76,39	100,9	0 8	+5.0 -0	+0 -3.0	0 13	+8 -0	+0 -5	0 20	+12 -0	+0 -8	0 50	+30.0 -0	+0 -20	1.4 14.4	+8.0 -0	-1.4 -6.4
100,9	131,9	0 10	+6.0 -0	+0 -4.0	0 16	+10 -0	+0 -6	0 26	+16 -0	+0 -10	0 65	+40.0 -0	+0 -25	1.6 17.6	+10.0 -0	-1.6 -7.6
131,9	171,9	0 13	+8.0 -0	+0 -5.0	0 20	+12 -0	+0 -8	0 32	+20 -0	+0 -12	0 8	+50.0 -0	+0 -30	1.8 21.8	+12.0 -0	-1.8 -9.8
171,90	200	0 16	+10.0 -0	+0 -6.0	0 26	+16 -0	+0 -10	0 41	+25 -0	+0 -16	0 100	+60.0 -0	+0 -40	1.8 27.8	+16.0 -0	-1.8 -11.8

ANSI CLEARANCE LOCATIONAL FITS (Basic-Hole System) - continued

Values shown below are in thousandths of an inch

Nominal Size Range (in)		Class LC6			Class LC7			Class LC8			Class LC9			Class LC10			Class LC11		
		Clearance	Standard Limits		Clearance	Standard Limits		Clearance	Standard Limits		Clearance	Standard Limits		Clearance	Standard Limits		Clearance	Standard Limits	
Over	To		Hole H9	Shaft f8		Hole H10	Shaft e9		Hole H10	Shaft c10		Hole H11	Shaft c10		Hole H12	Shaft		Hole H13	Shaft
0	0,12	0.3	+1.0	-0.3	0.6	+1.6	-0.6	1.0	+0.6	-1.0	2.5	+2.5	-2.5	4	+4	-4	5	+6	-5
		1.9	0	-0.9	3.2	0	-1.6	3.6	-0	-2.0	6.6	-0	-4.1	12	-0	-8	17	-0	-11
0,12	0,24	0.4	+1.2	-0.4	0.8	+1.8	-0.8	1.2	+1.8	-1.2	2.8	+3.0	-2.8	4.5	+5	-4.5	6	+7	-6
		2.3	0	-1.1	3.8	0	-2.0	4.2	-0	-2.4	7.6	-0	-4.6	14.5	-0	-9.5	20	-0	-13
0,24	0,4	0.5	+1.4	-0.5	1.0	+2.2	-1.0	1.6	+2.2	-1.6	3.0	+3.5	-3.0	5	+6	-5	7	+9	-7
		2.8	0	-1.4	4.6	0	-2.4	5.2	-0	-3.0	8.7	-0	-5.2	17	-0	-11	25	-0	-16
0,4	0,71	0.6	+1.6	-0.6	1.2	+2.8	-1.2	2.0	+2.8	-2.0	3.5	+4.0	-3.5	6	+7	-6	8	+0	-8
		3.2	0	-1.6	5.6	0	-2.8	6.4	-0	-3.6	10.3	-0	-6.3	20	-0	-13	28	-0	-18
0,71	1,19	0.8	+2.0	-0.8	1.6	+3.5	-1.6	2.5	+3.5	-2.5	4.5	+5.0	-4.5	7	+8	-7	10	+12	-10
		4.0	0	-2.0	7.1	0	-3.6	8.0	-0	-4.5	13.0	-0	-8.0	23	-0	-15	34	-0	-22
1,19	1,97	1.0	+2.5	-1.0	2.0	+4.0	-2.0	3.0	+4.0	-3.0	5	+6	-5	8	+10	-8	12	+16	-12
		5.1	0	-2.6	8.5	0	-4.5	9.5	-0	-5.5	15	-0	-9	28	-0	-18	44	-0	-28
1,97	3,15	1.2	+3.0	-1.2	2.5	+4.5	-2.5	4.0	+4.5	-4.0	6	+7	-6	10	+12	-10	14	+18	-14
		6.0	0	-3.0	10.0	0	-5.5	11.5	-0	-7.0	17.5	-0	-10.5	34	-0	-22	50	-0	-32
3,15	4,73	1.4	+3.5	-1.4	3.0	+5.0	-3.0	5.0	+5.0	-5.0	7	+9	-7	11	+14	-11	16	+22	-16
		7.1	0	-3.6	11.5	0	-6.5	13.5	-0	-8.5	21	-0	-12	39	-0	-25	60	-0	-38
4,73	7,09	1.6	+4.0	-1.6	3.5	+6.0	-3.5	6	+6	-6	8	+10	-8	12	+16	-12	18	+25	-18
		8.1	0	-4.1	13.5	0	-7.5	16	-0	-10	24	-0	-14	44	-0	-28	68	-0	-43
7,09	9,85	2.0	+4.5	-2.0	4.0	+7.0	-4.0	7	+7	-7	10	+12	-10	16	+18	-16	22	+28	-22
		9.3	0	-4.8	15.5	0	-8.5	18.5	-0	-11.5	29	-0	-17	52	-0	-34	78	-0	-50
9,85	12,41	2.2	+5.0	-2.2	4.5	+8.0	-4.5	7	+8	-7	12	+12	-12	20	+20	-20	28	+30	-28
		10.2	0	-5.2	17.5	0	-9.5	20	-0	-12	32	-0	-20	60	-0	-40	88	-0	-58
12,41	15,75	2.5	+6.0	-2.5	5.0	+9.0	-5	8	+9	-8	14	+14	-14	22	+22	-22	30	+35	-30
		12.0	0	-6.0	20.0	0	-11	23	-0	-14	37	-0	-23	66	-0	-44	100	-0	-65
15,75	19,69	2.8	+6.0	-2.8	5.0	+10.0	-5	9	+10	-9	16	+16	-16	25	+25	-25	35	+40	-35
		12.8	0	-6.8	21.0	0	-11	25	-0	-15	42	-0	-26	75	-0	-50	115	-0	-75
19,69	30,09	3.0	+8.0	-3.0	6.0	+12.0	-6	10	+12	-10	18	+20	-18	28	+30	-28	40	+50	-40
		16.0	0	-8.0	26.0	-0	-14	30	-0	-18	50	-0	-30	88	-0	-58	140	-0	-90
30,09	41,49	3.5	+10.0	-3.5	7.0	+16.0	-7	12	+16	-12	20	+25	-20	30	+40	-30	45	+60	-45
		19.5	0	-9.5	33.0	-0	-17	38	-0	-22	61	-0	-36	110	-0	-70	165	-0	-105
41,49	56,19	4.0	+12.0	-4.0	8.0	+20.0	-8	14	+20	-14	25	+30	-25	40	+50	-40	60	+80	-60
		24.0	0	-12.0	40.0	-0	-20	46	-0	-26	75	-0	-45	140	-0	-90	220	-0	-140
56,19	76,39	4.5	+16.0	-4.5	9.0	+25.0	-9	16	+25	-16	30	+40	-30	50	+60	-50	70	+100	-70
		30.5	0	-14.5	50.0	-0	-25	57	-0	-32	95	-0	-55	170	-0	-110	270	-0	-170
76,39	100,9	5.0	+20.0	-5	10.0	+30.0	-10	18	+30	-18	35	+50	-35	50	+80	-50	80	+125	-80
		37.0	0	-17	60.0	-0	-30	68	-0	-38	115	-0	-65	210	-0	-130	330	-0	-205
100,9	131,9	6.0	+25.0	-6	12.0	+40.0	-12	20	+40	-20	40	+60	-40	60	+100	-60	90	+160	-90
		47.0	0	-22	67.0	-0	-27	85	-0	-45	140	-0	-80	260	-0	-160	410	-0	-250
131,9	171,9	7.0	+30.0	-7	14.0	+50.0	-14	25	+50	-25	50	+80	-50	80	+125	-80	100	+200	-100
		57.0	0	-27	94.0	-0	-44	105	-0	-55	180	-0	-100	330	-0	-205	500	-0	-300
171,90	200	7.0	+40.0	-7	14.0	+60.0	-14	25	+60	-25	50	+100	-50	90	+160	-90	125	+250	-125
		72.0	0	-32	114.0	-0	-54	125	-0	-65	210	-0	-110	410	-0	-250	625	-0	-375

ANSI TRANSITION LOCATIONAL FITS (Basic-Hole System)

Values shown below are in thousandths of an inch

Nominal Size Range (in)		Class LT1			Class LT2			Class LT3			Class LT4			Class LT5			Class LT6		
		Fit	Standard Limits		Fit	Standard Limits		Fit	Standard Limits		Fit	Standard Limits		Fit	Standard Limits		Fit	Standard Limits	
Over	To		Hole H7	Shaft js6		Hole H8	Shaft js7		Hole H7	Shaft k6		Hole H8	Shaft k7		Hole H7	Shaft n6		Hole H7	Shaft n7
0	0,12	-0.10 +0.50	+0.4 -0	+0.10 -0.10	-0.2 +0.8	+0.6 -0	+0.2 -0.2							-0.5 +0.15	+0.4 -0	+0.5 +0.25	-0.65 +0.15	+0.4 -0	-0.65 +0.25
0,12	0,24	_0.15 +0.65	+0.5 -0	+0.15 -0.15	-0.25 +0.95	+0.7 -0	+0.25 -0.25							-0.6 +0.2	+0.5 -0	+0.6 +0.3	-0.8 +0.2	+0.5 -0	+0.8 +0.3
0,24	0,4	-0.2 +0.8	+0.6 -0	+0.2 -0.2	-0.3 +1.2	+0.9 -0	+0.3 -0.3	-0.5 +0.5	+0.6 -0	+0.5 +0.1	-0.7 +0.8	+0.9 -0	+0.7 +0.1	-0.8 +0.2	+0.6 -0	+0.8 +0.4	-1.0 +0.2	+0.6 -0	+1.0 +0.4
0,4	0,71	-0.2 +0.9	+0.7 -0	+0.2 -0.2	-0.35 +1.35	+1.0 -0	+0.35 -0.35	-0.5 +0.6	+0.7 -0	+0.5 +0.1	-0.8 +0.9	+1.0 -0	+0.8 +0.1	-0.9 +0.2	+0.7 -0	+0.9 +0.5	-1.2 +0.2	+0.7 -0	+1.2 +0.5
0,71	1,19	-0.25 +1.05	+0.8 -0	+0.25 -0.25	-0.4 +1.6	+1.2 -0	+0.4 -0.4	-0.6 +0.7	+0.8 -0	+0.6 +0.1	-0.9 +1.1	+1.2 -0	+0.9 +0.1	-1.1 +0.2	+0.8 -0	+1.1 +0.6	-1.4 +0.2	+0.8 -0	+1.4 +0.6
1,19	1,97	-0.3 +1.3	+1.0 -0	+0.3 -0.3	-0.5 +2.1	+1.6 -0	+0.5 -0.5	-0.7 +0.9	+1.0 -0	+0.7 +0.1	-1.1 +1.5	+1.6 -0	+1.1 +0.1	-1.3 +0.3	+1.0 -0	+1.3 +0.7	-1.7 +0.3	+1.0 -0	+1.7 +0.7
1,97	3,15	-0.3 +1.5	+1.2 -0	+0.3 -0.3	-0.6 +2.4	+1.8 -0	+0.6 -0.6	-0.8 +1.1	+1.2 -0	+0.8 +0.1	-1.3 +1.7	+1.8 -0	+1.3 +0.1	-1.5 +0.4	+1.2 -0	+1.5 +0.8	-2.0 +0.4	+1.2 -0	+2.0 +0.8
3,15	4,73	-0.4 +1.8	+1.4 -0	+0.4 -0.4	-0.7 +2.9	+2.2 -0	+0.7 -0.7	-1.0 +1.3	+1.4 -0	+1.0 +0.1	-1.5 +2.1	+2.2 -0	+1.5 +0.1	-1.9 +0.4	+1.4 -0	+1.9 +1.0	-2.4 +0.4	+1.4 -0	+2.4 +1.0
4,73	7,09	-0.5 +2.1	+1.6 -0	+0.5 -0.5	-0.8 +3.3	+2.5 -0	+0.8 -0.8	-1.1 +1.5	+1.6 -0	+1.1 +0.1	-1.7 +2.4	+2.5 -0	+1.7 +0.1	-2.2 +0.4	+1.6 -0	+2.2 +1.2	-2.8 +0.4	+1.6 -0	+2.8 +1.2
7,09	9,85	-0.6 +2.4	+1.8 -0	+0.6 -0.6	-0.9 +3.7	+2.8 -0	+0.9 -0.9	-1.4 +1.6	+1.8 -0	+1.4 +0.2	-2.0 +2.6	+2.8 -0	+2.0 +0.2	-2.6 +0.4	+1.8 -0	+2.6 +1.4	-3.2 +0.4	+1.8 -0	+3.2 +1.4
9,85	12,41	-0.6 +2.6	+2.0 -0	+0.6 -0.6	-1.0 +4.0	+3.0 -0	+1.0 -1.0	-1.4 +1.8	+2.0 -0	+1.4 +0.2	-2.2 +2.8	+3.0 -0	+2.2 +0.2	-2.6 +0.6	+2.0 -0	+2.6 +1.4	-3.4 +0.6	+2.0 -0	+3.4 +1.4
12,41	15,75	-0.7 +2.9	+2.2 -0	+0.7 -0.7	-1.0 +4.5	+3.5 -0	+1.0 -1.0	-1.6 +2.0	+2.2 -0	+1.6 +0.2	-2.4 +3.3	+3.5 -0	+2.4 +0.2	-3.0 +0.6	+2.2 -0	+3.0 +1.6	-3.8 +0.6	+2.2 -0	+3.8 +1.6
15,75	19,69	-0.8 +3.3	+2.5 -0	+0.8 -0.8	-1.2 +5.2	+4.0 -0	+1.2 -1.2	-1.8 +2.3	+2.5 -0	+1.8 +0.2	-2.7 +3.8	+4.0 -0	+2.7 +0.2	-3.4 +0.7	+2.5 -0	+3.4 +1.8	-4.3 +0.7	+2.5 -0	+4.3 +1.8

ANSI INTERFERENCE LOCATIONAL FITS (Basic-Hole System)

Values shown below are in thousandths of an inch

Nominal Size Range (in)		Class LN1			Class LN2			Class LN3		
		Limits of Interference	Standard Limits		Limits of Interference	Standard Limits		Limits of Interference	Standard Limits	
Over	To		Hole H6	Shaft n5		Hole H7	Shaft p6		Hole H7	Shaft r6
0	0,12	0	+0.25	+0.45	0	+0.4	+0.65	0.1	+0.4	+0.75
		0.45	-0	+0.25	0.65	-0	+0.4	0.75	-0	+0.5
0,12	0,24	0	+0.3	+0.5	0	+0.5	+0.8	0.1	+0.5	+0.9
		0.5	-0	+0.3	0.8	-0	+0.5	0.9	-0	+0.6
0,24	0,4	0	+0.4	+0.65	0	+0.6	+1.0	0.2	+0.6	+1.2
		0.65	-0	+0.4	1.0	-0	+0.6	1.2	-0	+0.8
0,4	0,71	0	+0.4	+-.8	0	+0.7	+1.1	0.3	+0.7	+1.4
		0.8	-0	+-.4	1.1	-0	+0.7	1.4	-0	+1.0
0,71	1,19	0	+0.5	+1.0	0	+0.8	+1.3	0.4	+0.8	+1.7
		1.0	-0	+0.5	1.3	-0	+0.8	1.7	-0	+1.2
1,19	1,97	0	+0.6	+1.1	0	+1.0	+1.6	0.4	+1.0	+2.0
		1.1	-0	+0.6	1.6	-0	+1.0	2.0	-0	+1.4
1,97	3,15	0.1	+0.7	+1.3	0.2	+1.2	+2.1	0.4	+1.2	+2.3
		1.3	-0	+0.7	2.1	-0	+1.4	2.3	-0	+1.6
3,15	4,73	0.1	+0.9	+1.6	0.2	+1.4	+2.5	0.6	+1.4	+2.9
		1.6	-0	+1.0	2.5	-0	+1.6	2.9	-0	+2.0
4,73	7,09	0.2	+1.0	+1.9	0.2	+1.6	+2.8	0.9	+1.6	+3.5
		1.9	-0	+1.2	2.8	-0	+1.8	3.5	-0	+2.5
7,09	9,85	0.2	+1.2	+2.2	0.2	+1.8	+3.2	1.2	+1.8	+4.2
		2.2	-0	+1.4	3.2	-0	+2.0	4.2	-0	+3.0
9,85	12,41	0.2	+1.2	+2.3	0.2	+2.0	+3.4	1.5	+2.0	+4.7
		2.3	-0	+1.4	3.4	-0	+2.2	4.7	-0	+3.5
12,41	15,75	0.2	+1.4	+2.6	0.3	+2.2	+3.9	2.3	+2.2	+5.9
		2.6	-0	+1.6	3.9	-0	+2.5	5.9	-0	+4.5
15,75	19,69	0.2	+1.6	+2.8	0.3	+2.5	+4.4	2.5	+2.5	+6.6
		2.8	-0	+1.8	4.4	-0	+2.8	6.6	-0	+5.0
19,69	30,09		+2.0		0.5	+3	+5.5	4	+3	+9
			-0		5.5	-0	+3.5	9	-0	+7
30,09	41,49		+2.5		0.5	+4	+7.0	5	+4	+11.5
			-0		7.0	-0	+4.5	11.5	-0	+9
41,49	56,19		+3.0		1	+5	+9	7	+5	+15
			-0		9	-0	+6	15	-0	+12
56,19	76,39		+4.0		1	+6	+11	10	+6	+20
			-0		11	-0	+7	20	-0	+16
76,39	100,9		+5.0		1	+8	+14	12	+8	+25
			-0		14	-0	+9	25	-0	+20
100,9	131,9		+6.0		2	+10	+18	15	+10	+31
			-0		18	-0	+12	31	-0	+25
131,9	171,9		+8.0		4	+12	+24	18	+12	+38
			-0		24	-0	+16	38	-0	+30
171,90	200		+10.0		4	+16	+30	24	+16	+50
			-0		30	-0	+20	50	-0	+40

ANSI FORCE AND SHRINK FITS (Basic-Hole System)

Values shown below are in thousandths of an inch

Nominal Size Range (in)		Class FN1			Class FN2			Class FN3			Class FN4			Class FN5		
		Limits of Interference	Standard Limits		Limits of Interference	Standard Limits		Limits of Interference	Standard Limits		Limits of Interference	Standard Limits		Limits of Interference	Standard Limits	
Over	To		Hole H6	Shaft		Hole H7	Shaft s6		Hole H7	Shaft t6		Hole H7	Shaft u6		Hole H8	Shaft x7
0	0,12	0,05	+0.25	+0.5	0,2	+0.4	+0.85				0.3	+0.4	+0.95	0.3	+0.6	+1.3
		0,5	-0	+0.3	0,85	-0	+0.6				0.95	-0	+0.7	1.3	-0	+0.9
0,12	0,24	0,1	+0.3	+0.6	0,2	+0.5	+1.0				0.4	+0.5	+1.2	0.5	+0.7	+1.7
		0,6	-0	+0.4	1	-0	+0.7				1.2	-0	-0.9	1.7	-0	+1.2
0,24	0,4	0.1	+0.4	+0.75	0.4	+0.6	+1.4				0.6	+0.6	+1.6	0.5	+0.9	+2.0
		0.75	-0	+0.5	1.4	-0	+1.0				1.6	-0	+1.2	2.0	-0	+1.4
0,4	0,56	0.1	-0.4	+0.8	0.5	+0.7	+1.6				0.7	+0.7	+1.8	0.6	+1.0	+2.3
		0.8	-0	+0.5	1.6	-0	+1.2				1.8	-0	+1.4	2.3	-0	+1.6
0,56	0,71	0.2	+0.4	+0.9	0.5	+0.7	+1.6				0.7	+0.7	+1.8	0.8	+1.0	+2.5
		0.9	-0	+0.6	1.6	-0	+1.2				1.8	-0	+1.4	2.5	-0	+1.8
0,71	0,95	0.2	+0.5	+1.1	0.6	+0.8	+1.9				0.8	+0.8	+2.1	1.0	+1.2	+3.0
		1.1	-0	+0.7	1.9	-0	+1.4				2.1	-0	+1.6	3.0	-0	+2.2
0,95	1,19	0.3	+0.5	+1.2	0.6	+0.8	+1.9	0.8	+0.8	+2.1	1.0	+0.8	+2.3	1.3	+1.2	+3.3
		1.2	-0	+0.8	1.9	-0	+1.4	2.1	-0	+1.6	2.3	-0	+1.8	3.3	-0	+2.5
1,19	1,58	0.3	+0.6	+1.3	0.8	+1.0	+2.4	1.0	+1.0	+2.6	1.5	+1.0	+3.1	1.4	+1.6	+4.0
		1.3	-0	+0.9	2.4	-0	+1.8	2.6	-0	+2.0	3.1	-0	+2.5	4.0	-0	+3.0
1,58	1,97	0.4	+0.6	+1.4	0.8	+1.0	+2.4	1.2	+1.0	+2.8	1.8	+1.0	+3.4	2.4	+1.6	+5.0
		1.4	-0	+1.0	2.4	-0	+1.8	2.8	-0	+2.2	3.4	-0	+2.8	5.0	-0	+4.0
1,97	2,56	0.6	+0.7	+1.8	0.8	+1.2	+2.7	1.3	+1.2	+3.2	2.3	+1.2	+4.2	3.2	+1.8	+6.2
		1.8	-0	+1.3	2.7	-0	+2.0	3.2	-0	+2.5	4.2	-0	+3.5	6.2	-0	+5.0
2,56	3,15	0.7	+0.7	+1.9	1.0	+1.2	+2.9	1.8	+1.2	+3.7	2.8	+1.2	+4.7	4.2	+1.8	+7.2
		1.9	-0	+1.4	2.9	-0	+2.2	3.7	-0	+3.0	4.7	-0	+4.0	7.2	-0	+6.0
3,15	3,94	0.9	+0.9	+2.4	1.4	+1.4	+3.7	2.1	+1.4	+4.4	3.6	+1.4	+5.9	4.8	+2.2	+8.4
		2.4	-0	+1.8	3.7	-0	+2.8	4.4	-0	+3.5	5.9	-0	+5.0	8.4	-0	+7.0
3,94	4,73	1.1	+0.9	+2.6	1.6	+1.4	+3.9	2.6	+1.4	+4.9	4.6	+1.4	+6.9	5.8	+2.2	+9.4
		2.6	-0	+2.0	3.9	-0	+3.0	4.9	-0	+4.0	6.9	-0	+6.0	9.4	-0	+8.0
4,73	5,52	1.2	+1.0	+2.9	1.9	+1.6	+4.5	3.4	+1.6	+6.0	5.4	+1.6	+8.0	7.5	+2.5	+11.6
		2.9	-0	+2.2	4.5	-0	+3.5	6.0	-0	+5.0	8.0	-0	+7.0	11.6	-0	+10.0
5,52	6,3	1.5	+1.0	+3.2	2.4	+1.6	+5.0	3.4	+1.6	+6.0	5.4	+1.6	+8.0	9.5	+2.5	+13.6
		3.2	-0	+2.5	5.0	-0	+4.0	6.0	-0	+5.0	8.0	-0	+7.0	13.6	-0	+12.0
6,3	7,09	1.8	+1.0	+3.5	2.9	+1.6	+5.5	4.4	+1.6	+7.0	6.4	+1.6	+9.0	9.5	+2.5	+13.6
		3.5	-0	+2.8	5.5	-0	+4.5	7.0	-0	+6.0	9.0	-0	+8.0	13.6	-0	+12.0
7,09	7,88	1.8	+1.2	+3.8	3.2	+1.8	+6.2	5.2	+1.8	+8.2	7.2	+1.8	+10.2	11.2	+2.8	+15.8
		3.8	-0	+3.0	6.2	-0	+5.0	8.2	-0	+7.0	10.2	-0	+9.0	15.8	-0	+14.0
7,88	8,86	2.3	+1.2	+4.3	3.2	+1.8	+6.2	5.2	+1.8	+8.2	8.2	+1.8	+11.2	13.2	+2.8	+17.8
		4.3	-0	+3.5	6.2	-0	+5.0	8.2	-0	+7.0	11.2	-0	+10.0	17.8	-0	+16.0
8,86	9,85	2.3	+1.2	+4.3	4.2	+1.8	+7.2	6.2	+1.8	+9.2	10.2	+1.8	+13.2	13.2	+2.8	+17.8
		4.3	-0	+3.5	7.2	-0	+6.0	9.2	-0	+8.0	13.2	-0	+12.0	17.8	-0	+16.0
9,85	11,03	2.8	+1.2	+4.9	4.0	+2.0	+7.2	7.0	+2.0	+10.2	10.0	+2.0	+13.2	15.0	+3.0	+20.0
		4.9	-0	+4.0	7.2	-0	+6.0	10.2	-0	+9.0	13.2	-0	+12.00	20.0	-0	+18.0
11,03	12,41	2.8	+1.2	+4.9	5.0	+2.0	+8.2	7.0	+2.0	+10.2	12.0	+2.0	+15.2	17.0	+3.0	+22.0
		4.9	-0	+4.0	8.2	-0	+7.0	10.2	-0	+9.0	15.2	-0	+14.0	22.0	-0	+20.0
12,41	13,98	3.1	+1.4	+5.5	5.8	+2.2	+9.4	7.8	+2.2	+11.4	13.8	+2.2	+17.4	18.5	+3.5	+24.2
		5.5	-0	+4.5	9.4	-0	+8.0	11.4	-0	+10.0	17.4	-0	+16.0	24.2	-0	+22.0
13,98	15,75	3.6	+1.4	+6.1	5.8	+2.2	+9.4	9.8	+2.2	+13.4	15.8	+2.2	+19.4	21.5	+3.5	+27.2
		6.1	-0	+5.0	9.4	-0	+8.0	13.4	-0	+12.0	19.4	-0	+18.0	27.2	-0	+25.0
15,75	17,72	4.4	+1.6	+7.0	6.5	+2.5	+10.6	9.5	+2.5	+13.6	17.5	+2.5	+21.6	24.0	+4.0	+30.5
		7.0	-0	+6.0	10.6	-0	+9.0	13.6	-0	+12.0	21.6	-0	+20.0	30.5	-0	+28.0
17,72	19,69	4.4	+1.6	+7.0	7.5	+2.5	+11.6	11.5	+2.5	+15.6	19.5	+2.5	+23.6	26.0	+4.0	+32.5
		7.0	-0	+6.0	11.6	-0	+10.0	15.6	-0	+14.0	23.6	-0	+22.0	32.5	-0	+30.0

ANSI PREFERRED METRIC HOLE BASIS CLEARANCE FITS

Basic Size (mm)		LOOSE RUNNING			FREE RUNNING			CLOSE RUNNING			SLIDING			LOCATIONAL CLEARANCE		
		Hole H11	Shaft c11	Fit	Hole H9	Shaft d9	Fit	Hole H8	Shaft f7	Fit	Hole H7	Shaft g6	Fit	Hole H7	Shaft h6	Fit
1	Max	1,060	0,940	0,180	1,025	0,980	0,070	1,014	0,994	0,030	1,010	0,998	0,018	1,010	1,000	0,016
	Min	1,000	0,880	0,060	1,000	0,955	0,020	1,000	0,984	0,006	1,000	0,992	0,002	1,000	0,994	0,000
1,2	Max	1,260	1,140	0,180	1,225	1,180	0,070	1,214	1,194	0,030	1,210	1,198	0,018	1,210	1,200	0,016
	Min	1,200	1,080	0,060	1,200	1,155	0,020	1,200	1,184	0,006	1,200	1,192	0,002	1,200	1,194	0,000
1,6	Max	1,660	1,540	0,180	1,625	1,580	0,070	1,614	1,594	0,030	1,610	1,598	0,018	1,610	1,600	0,016
	Min	1,600	1,480	0,060	1,600	1,555	0,020	1,600	1,584	0,006	1,600	1,592	0,002	1,600	1,594	0,000
2	Max	2,060	1,940	0,180	2,025	1,980	0,070	2,014	1,994	0,030	2,010	1,998	0,018	2,010	2,000	0,016
	Min	2,000	1,880	0,060	2,000	1,955	0,020	2,000	1,984	0,006	2,000	1,992	0,002	2,000	1,994	0,000
2,5	Max	2,560	2,440	0,180	2,525	2,480	0,070	2,514	2,494	0,030	2,510	2,498	0,018	2,510	2,500	0,016
	Min	2,500	2,380	0,060	2,500	2,455	0,020	2,500	2,484	0,006	2,500	2,492	0,002	2,500	2,494	0,000
3	Max	3,060	2,940	0,180	3,025	2,980	0,070	3,014	2,994	0,030	3,010	2,998	0,018	3,010	3,000	0,016
	Min	3,000	2,880	0,060	3,000	2,955	0,020	3,000	2,984	0,006	3,000	2,992	0,002	3,000	2,994	0,000
4	Max	4,075	3,930	0,220	4,030	3,970	0,090	4,018	3,990	0,040	4,012	3,996	0,024	4,012	4,000	0,020
	Min	4,000	3,855	0,070	4,000	3,940	0,030	4,000	3,978	0,010	4,000	3,988	0,004	4,000	3,992	0,000
5	Max	5,075	4,930	0,220	5,030	4,970	0,090	5,018	4,990	0,040	5,012	4,996	0,024	5,012	5,000	0,020
	Min	5,000	4,855	0,070	5,000	4,940	0,030	5,000	4,978	0,010	5,000	4,988	0,004	5,000	4,992	0,000
6	Max	6,075	5,930	0,220	6,030	5,970	0,090	6,018	5,990	0,040	6,012	5,996	0,024	6,012	6,000	0,020
	Min	6,000	5,855	0,070	6,000	5,940	0,030	6,000	5,978	0,010	6,000	5,988	0,004	6,000	5,992	0,000
8	Max	8,090	7,920	0,260	8,036	7,960	0,112	8,022	7,987	0,050	8,015	7,995	0,029	8,015	8,000	0,024
	Min	8,000	7,830	0,080	8,000	7,924	0,040	8,000	7,972	0,013	8,000	7,986	0,005	8,000	7,991	0,000
10	Max	10,090	9,920	0,260	10,036	9,960	0,112	10,022	9,987	0,050	10,015	9,995	0,029	10,015	10,000	0,024
	Min	10,000	9,830	0,080	10,000	9,924	0,040	10,000	9,972	0,013	10,000	9,986	0,005	10,000	9,991	0,000
12	Max	12,110	11,905	0,315	12,043	11,950	0,136	12,027	11,984	0,061	12,018	11,994	0,035	12,018	12,000	0,029
	Min	12,000	11,795	0,095	12,000	11,907	0,050	12,000	11,966	0,016	12,000	11,983	0,006	12,000	11,989	0,000
16	Max	16,110	15,905	0,315	16,043	15,950	0,136	16,027	15,984	0,061	16,018	15,994	0,035	16,018	16,000	0,029
	Min	16,000	15,795	0,095	16,000	15,907	0,050	16,000	15,966	0,016	16,000	15,983	0,006	16,000	15,989	0,000
20	Max	20,130	19,890	0,370	20,052	19,935	0,169	20,033	19,980	0,074	20,021	19,993	0,041	20,021	20,000	0,034
	Min	20,000	19,760	0,110	20,000	19,883	0,065	20,000	19,959	0,020	20,000	19,980	0,007	20,000	19,987	0,000
25	Max	25,130	24,890	0,370	25,052	24,935	0,169	25,033	24,980	0,074	25,021	24,993	0,041	25,021	25,000	0,034
	Min	25,000	24,760	0,110	25,000	24,883	0,065	25,000	24,959	0,020	25,000	24,980	0,007	25,000	24,987	0,000
30	Max	30,130	29,890	0,370	30,052	29,935	0,169	30,033	29,980	0,074	30,021	29,993	0,041	30,021	30,000	0,034
	Min	30,000	29,760	0,110	30,000	29,883	0,065	30,000	29,959	0,020	30,000	29,980	0,007	30,000	29,987	0,000
40	Max	40,160	39,880	0,440	40,062	39,920	0,204	40,039	39,975	0,089	40,025	39,991	0,050	40,025	40,000	0,041
	Min	40,000	39,720	0,120	40,000	39,858	0,080	40,000	39,950	0,025	40,000	39,975	0,009	40,000	39,984	0,000
50	Max	50,160	49,870	0,450	50,062	49,920	0,204	50,039	49,975	0,089	50,025	49,991	0,050	50,025	50,000	0,041
	Min	50,000	49,710	0,130	50,000	49,858	0,080	50,000	49,950	0,025	50,000	49,975	0,009	50,000	49,984	0,000
60	Max	60,190	59,860	0,520	60,074	59,900	0,248	60,046	59,970	0,106	60,030	59,990	0,059	60,030	60,000	0,049
	Min	60,000	59,670	0,140	60,000	59,826	0,100	60,000	59,940	0,030	60,000	59,971	0,010	60,000	59,981	0,000
80	Max	80,190	79,850	0,530	80,074	79,900	0,248	80,046	79,970	0,106	80,030	79,990	0,059	80,030	80,000	0,049
	Min	80,000	79,660	0,150	80,000	79,826	0,100	80,000	79,940	0,030	80,000	79,971	0,010	80,000	79,981	0,000
100	Max	100,200	99,830	0,610	100,087	99,880	0,294	100,054	99,964	0,125	100,035	99,988	0,069	100,035	100,000	0,057
	Min	100,000	99,610	0,170	100,000	99,793	0,120	100,000	99,929	0,036	100,000	99,966	0,012	100,000	99,978	0,000
120	Max	120,220	119,820	0,620	120,087	119,880	0,294	120,054	119,964	0,125	120,035	119,988	0,069	120,035	120,000	0,057
	Min	120,000	119,600	0,180	120,000	119,793	0,120	120,000	119,929	0,036	120,000	119,966	0,012	120,000	119,978	0,000
160	Max	160,250	159,790	0,710	160,100	159,855	0,345	160,063	159,957	0,146	160,040	159,986	0,079	160,040	160,000	0,065
	Min	160,000	159,540	0,210	160,000	159,755	0,145	160,000	159,917	0,043	160,000	159,961	0,014	160,000	159,975	0,000
200	Max	200,290	199,760	0,820	200,115	199,830	0,400	200,072	199,950	0,168	200,046	199,985	0,090	200,046	200,000	0,075
	Min	200,000	199,470	0,240	200,000	199,715	0,170	200,000	199,904	0,050	200,000	199,956	0,015	200,000	199,971	0,000
250	Max	250,290	249,720	0,860	250,115	249,830	0,400	250,072	249,950	0,168	250,046	249,985	0,090	250,046	250,000	0,075
	Min	250,000	249,430	0,280	250,000	249,715	0,170	250,000	249,904	0,050	250,000	249,956	0,015	250,000	249,971	0,000
300	Max	300,320	299,670	0,970	300,130	299,810	0,450	300,081	299,944	0,189	300,052	299,983	0,101	300,052	300,000	0,084
	Min	300,000	299,350	0,330	300,000	299,680	0,190	300,000	299,892	0,056	300,000	299,951	0,017	300,000	299,968	0,000
400	Max	400,360	399,600	1,120	400,140	399,790	0,490	400,089	399,938	0,208	400,057	399,982	0,111	400,057	400,000	0,093
	Min	400,000	399,240	0,400	400,000	399,650	0,210	400,000	399,881	0,062	400,000	399,946	0,018	400,000	399,964	0,000
500	Max	500,400	499,520	1,280	500,155	499,770	0,540	500,097	499,932	0,228	500,063	499,980	0,123	500,063	500,000	0,103
	Min	500,000	499,120	0,480	500,000	499,615	0,230	500,000	499,869	0,068	500,000	499,940	0,020	500,000	499,960	0,000

ANSI PREFERRED METRIC SHAFT BASIS TRANSITION AND INTERFERENCE FITS

Basic Size (mm)		LOCATIONAL TRANSTION			LOCATIONAL TRANSITION			LOCATIONAL INTERFERENCE			MEDIUM DRIVE			FORCE		
		Hole K7	Shaft h6	Fit	Hole N7	Shaft h6	Fit	Hole P7	Shaft h6	Fit	Hole S7	Shaft h6	Fit	Hole U7	Shaft h6	Fit
1	Max	1,000	1,000	0,006	0,996	1,000	0,002	0,994	1,000	0,000	0,986	1,000	-0,008	0,982	1,000	-0,012
	Min	0,990	0,994	-0,010	0,986	0,994	-0,014	0,984	0,994	-0,016	0,976	0,994	-0,024	0,972	0,994	-0,028
1,2	Max	1,200	1,200	0,006	1,196	1,200	0,002	1,194	1,200	0,000	1,186	1,200	-0,008	1,182	1,200	-0,012
	Min	1,190	1,194	-0,010	1,186	1,194	-0,014	1,184	1,194	-0,016	1,176	1,194	-0,024	1,172	1,194	-0,028
1,6	Max	1,600	1,600	0,006	1,596	1,600	0,002	1,594	1,600	0,000	1,586	1,600	-0,008	1,582	1,600	-0,012
	Min	1,590	1,594	-0,010	1,586	1,594	-0,014	1,584	1,594	-0,016	1,576	1,594	-0,024	1,572	1,594	-0,028
2	Max	2,000	2,000	0,006	1,996	2,000	0,002	1,994	2,000	0,000	1,986	2,000	-0,008	1,982	2,000	-0,012
	Min	1,990	1,994	-0,010	1,986	1,994	-0,014	1,984	1,994	-0,016	1,976	1,994	-0,024	1,972	1,994	-0,028
2,5	Max	2,500	2,500	0,006	2,496	2,500	0,002	2,494	2,500	0,000	2,486	2,500	0,000	2,482	2,500	-0,012
	Min	2,490	2,494	-0,010	2,486	2,494	-0,014	2,484	2,494	-0,016	2,476	2,494	-0,024	2,472	2,494	-0,028
3	Max	3,000	3,000	0,006	2,996	3,000	0,002	2,994	3,000	0,000	2,986	3,000	-0,008	2,982	3,000	-0,012
	Min	2,990	2,994	-0,010	2,986	2,994	-0,014	2,984	2,994	-0,016	2,976	2,994	-0,024	2,972	2,994	-0,028
4	Max	4,003	4,000	0,011	3,996	4,000	0,004	3,992	4,000	0,000	3,985	4,000	-0,007	3,981	4,000	-0,011
	Min	3,991	3,992	-0,009	3,984	3,992	-0,016	3,980	3,992	-0,020	3,973	3,992	-0,027	3,969	3,992	-0,031
5	Max	5,003	5,000	0,011	4,996	5,000	0,004	4,992	5,000	0,000	4,985	5,000	-0,007	4,981	5,000	-0,011
	Min	4,991	4,992	-0,009	4,984	4,992	-0,016	4,980	4,992	-0,020	4,973	4,992	-0,027	4,969	4,992	-0,031
6	Max	6,003	6,000	0,011	5,996	6,000	0,004	5,992	6,000	0,000	5,985	6,000	-0,007	5,981	6,000	-0,011
	Min	5,991	5,992	-0,009	5,984	5,992	-0,016	5,980	5,992	-0,020	5,973	5,992	-0,027	5,969	5,992	-0,031
8	Max	8,005	8,000	0,014	7,996	8,000	0,005	7,991	8,000	0,000	7,983	8,000	-0,008	7,978	8,000	-0,013
	Min	7,990	7,991	-0,010	7,981	7,991	-0,019	7,976	7,991	-0,024	7,968	7,991	-0,032	7,963	7,991	-0,037
10	Max	10,005	10,000	0,014	9,996	10,000	0,005	9,991	10,000	0,000	9,983	10,000	-0,008	9,978	10,000	-0,013
	Min	9,990	9,991	-0,010	9,981	9,991	-0,019	9,976	9,991	-0,024	9,968	9,991	-0,032	9,963	9,991	-0,037
12	Max	12,006	12,000	0,017	11,995	12,000	0,006	11,989	12,000	0,000	11,979	12,000	-0,010	11,974	12,000	-0,015
	Min	11,988	11,989	-0,012	11,977	11,989	-0,023	11,971	11,989	-0,029	11,961	11,989	-0,039	11,956	11,989	-0,044
16	Max	16,006	16,000	0,017	15,995	16,000	0,006	15,989	16,000	0,000	15,979	16,000	-0,010	15,974	16,000	-0,015
	Min	15,988	15,989	-0,012	15,977	15,989	-0,023	15,971	15,989	-0,029	15,961	15,989	-0,039	15,956	15,989	-0,044
20	Max	20,006	20,000	0,019	19,993	20,000	0,006	19,986	20,000	-0,001	19,973	20,000	-0,014	19,967	20,000	-0,020
	Min	19,985	19,987	-0,015	19,972	19,987	-0,028	19,965	19,987	-0,035	19,952	19,987	-0,048	19,946	19,987	-0,054
25	Max	25,006	25,000	0,019	24,993	25,000	0,006	24,986	25,000	-0,001	24,973	25,000	-0,014	24,960	25,000	-0,027
	Min	24,985	24,987	-0,015	24,972	24,987	-0,028	24,965	24,987	-0,035	24,592	24,987	-0,048	24,939	24,987	-0,061
30	Max	30,006	30,000	0,019	29,993	30,000	0,006	29,986	30,000	-0,001	29,973	30,000	-0,014	29,960	30,000	-0,027
	Min	29,985	29,987	-0,015	29,972	29,987	-0,028	29,965	29,987	-0,035	29,952	29,987	-0,048	29,939	29,987	-0,061
40	Max	40,007	40,000	0,023	39,992	40,000	0,008	39,983	40,000	-0,001	39,966	40,000	-0,018	39,949	40,000	-0,035
	Min	39,982	39,984	-0,018	39,967	39,984	-0,033	39,958	39,984	-0,042	39,941	39,984	-0,059	39,924	39,984	-0,076
50	Max	50,007	50,000	0,023	49,992	50,000	0,008	49,983	50,000	-0,001	49,966	50,000	-0,018	49,939	50,000	-0,045
	Min	49,982	49,984	-0,018	49,967	49,984	-0,033	49,958	49,984	-0,042	49,941	49,984	-0,059	49,914	49,984	-0,086
60	Max	60,009	60,000	0,028	59,991	60,000	0,010	59,979	60,000	-0,002	59,958	60,000	-0,023	59,924	60,000	-0,057
	Min	59,979	59,981	-0,021	59,961	59,981	-0,039	59,949	59,981	-0,051	59,928	59,981	-0,072	59,894	59,981	-0,106
80	Max	80,009	80,000	0,028	79,991	80,000	0,010	79,979	80,000	-0,002	79,952	80,000	-0,029	79,909	80,000	-0,072
	Min	79,979	79,981	-0,021	79,961	79,981	-0,039	79,949	79,981	-0,051	79,922	79,981	-0,078	79,879	79,981	-0,121
100	Max	100,010	100,000	0,032	99,990	100,000	0,012	99,976	100,000	-0,002	99,942	100,000	-0,036	99,889	100,000	-0,089
	Min	99,975	99,978	-0,025	99,955	99,978	-0,045	99,941	99,978	-0,059	99,907	99,978	-0,093	99,854	99,978	-0,146
120	Max	120,010	120,000	0,032	119,990	120,000	0,012	119,976	120,000	-0,002	119,934	120,000	-0,044	119,869	120,000	-0,109
	Min	119,975	119,978	-0,025	119,955	119,978	-0,045	119,941	119,978	-0,059	119,899	119,978	-0,101	119,834	119,978	-0,166
160	Max	160,012	160,000	0,037	159,988	160,000	0,013	159,972	160,000	-0,003	159,915	160,000	-0,060	159,825	160,000	-0,150
	Min	159,972	159,975	-0,028	159,948	159,975	-0,052	159,932	159,975	-0,068	159,875	159,975	-0,125	159,785	159,975	-0,215
200	Max	200,013	200,000	0,042	199,986	200,000	0,015	199,967	200,000	-0,004	199,895	200,000	-0,076	199,781	200,000	-0,190
	Min	199,967	199,971	-0,033	199,940	199,971	-0,060	199,921	199,971	-0,079	199,849	199,971	-0,151	199,735	199,971	-0,265
250	Max	250,013	250,000	0,042	249,986	250,000	0,015	249,967	250,000	-0,004	249,877	250,000	-0,094	249,733	250,000	-0,238
	Min	249,967	249,971	-0,033	249,940	249,971	-0,060	249,921	249,971	-0,079	249,831	249,971	-0,169	249,687	249,971	-0,313
300	Max	300,016	300,000	0,048	299,986	300,000	0,018	299,964	300,000	-0,004	299,850	300,000	-0,118	299,670	300,000	-0,298
	Min	299,964	299,968	-0,036	299,934	299,968	-0,066	299,912	299,968	-0,088	299,798	299,968	-0,202	299,618	299,968	-0,382
400	Max	400,017	400,000	0,053	399,984	400,000	0,020	399,959	400,000	-0,005	399,813	400,000	-0,151	399,586	400,000	-0,378
	Min	399,960	399,964	-0,040	399,927	399,964	-0,073	399,902	399,964	-0,098	399,756	399,964	-0,244	399,529	399,964	-0,471
500	Max	500,018	500,000	0,058	499,983	500,000	0,023	499,955	500,000	-0,005	499,771	500,000	-0,189	499,483	500,000	-0,477
	Min	499,955	499,960	-0,045	499,920	499,960	-0,080	499,892	499,960	-0,108	499,708	499,960	-0,292	499,420	499,960	-0,580

ANSI PREFERRED METRIC HOLE BASIS TRANSITION AND INTERFERENCE FITS

Basic Size (mm)		LOCATIONAL TRANSTION			LOCATIONAL TRANSITION			LOCATIONAL INTERFERENCE			MEDIUM DRIVE			FORCE		
		Hole H7	Shaft k6	Fit	Hole H7	Shaft n6	Fit	Hole H7	Shaft p6	Fit	Hole H7	Shaft s6	Fit	Hole H7	Shaft u6	Fit
1	Max	1,010	1,006	0,010	1,010	1,010	0,006	1,010	1,012	0,004	1,010	1,020	-0,004	1,010	1,024	-0,008
	Min	1,000	1,000	-0,006	1,000	1,004	-0,010	1,000	1,014	-0,012	1,000	1,014	-0,020	1,000	1,018	-0,024
1,2	Max	1,210	1,206	0,010	1,210	1,210	0,006	1,210	1,212	0,004	1,210	1,220	-0,004	1,210	1,224	-0,008
	Min	1,200	1,200	-0,006	1,200	1,204	-0,010	1,200	1,206	-0,012	1,200	1,214	-0,020	1,200	1,218	-0,024
1,6	Max	1,610	1,606	0,010	1,610	1,610	0,006	1,610	1,612	0,004	1,610	1,620	-0,004	1,610	1,624	-0,008
	Min	1,600	1,600	-0,006	1,600	1,604	-0,010	1,600	1,606	-0,012	1,600	1,614	-0,020	1,600	1,618	-0,024
2	Max	2,010	2,006	0,010	2,010	2,010	0,006	2,010	2,010	0,004	2,101	2,020	-0,004	2,010	2,024	-0,008
	Min	2,000	2,000	-0,006	2,000	2,004	-0,010	2,000	2,006	-0,012	2,000	2,014	-0,020	2,000	2,018	-0,024
2,5	Max	2,510	2,506	0,010	2,510	2,510	0,006	2,510	2,512	0,004	2,510	2,520	-0,004	2,510	2,524	-0,008
	Min	2,500	2,500	-0,006	2,500	2,504	-0,010	2,500	2,506	-0,012	2,500	2,514	-0,020	2,500	2,518	-0,024
3	Max	3,010	3,006	0,010	3,010	3,010	0,006	3,010	3,012	0,004	3,010	3,020	-0,004	3,010	3,024	-0,008
	Min	3,000	3,000	-0,006	3,000	3,004	-0,010	3,000	3,006	-0,020	3,000	3,014	-0,020	3,000	3,018	-0,024
4	Max	4,012	4,009	0,011	4,012	4,016	0,004	4,012	4,020	0,000	4,012	4,027	-0,007	4,012	4,031	-0,011
	Min	4,000	4,001	-0,009	4,000	4,008	-0,016	4,000	4,012	-0,020	4,000	4,019	-0,027	4,000	4,023	-0,031
5	Max	5,012	5,009	0,011	5,012	5,016	0,004	5,012	5,020	0,000	5,012	5,027	-0,007	5,012	5,031	-0,011
	Min	5,000	5,001	-0,009	5,000	5,008	-0,016	5,000	5,012	-0,020	5,000	5,019	-0,027	5,000	5,023	-0,031
6	Max	6,012	6,009	0,011	6,012	6,016	0,004	6,012	6,020	0,000	6,012	6,027	-0,007	6,012	6,031	-0,011
	Min	6,000	6,001	-0,009	6,000	6,008	-0,016	6,000	6,012	-0,020	6,000	6,019	-0,027	6,000	6,023	-0,031
8	Max	8,015	8,010	0,014	8,015	8,019	0,005	8,015	8,024	0,000	8,015	8,032	-0,008	8,015	8,037	-0,013
	Min	8,000	8,001	-0,010	8,000	8,010	-0,019	8,000	8,015	-0,024	8,000	8,023	-0,032	8,000	8,028	-0,037
10	Max	10,015	10,010	0,014	10,015	10,019	0,005	10,015	10,024	0,000	10,015	10,032	-0,008	10,015	10,037	-0,013
	Min	10,000	10,001	-0,010	10,000	10,010	-0,019	10,000	10,015	-0,024	10,000	10,023	-0,032	10,000	10,028	-0,037
12	Max	12,018	12,012	0,017	12,018	12,023	0,006	12,018	12,029	0,000	12,018	12,039	-0,010	12,018	12,044	-0,015
	Min	12,000	12,001	-0,012	12,000	12,012	-0,023	12,000	12,018	-0,029	12,000	12,028	-0,039	12,000	12,033	-0,044
16	Max	16,018	16,012	0,017	16,018	16,023	0,006	16,018	16,029	0,000	16,018	16,039	-0,010	16,018	16,044	-0,015
	Min	16,000	16,001	-0,012	16,000	16,012	-0,023	16,000	16,018	-0,029	16,000	16,028	-0,039	16,000	16,033	-0,044
20	Max	20,021	20,015	0,019	20,021	20,028	0,006	20,021	20,035	-0,001	20,021	20,048	-0,014	20,021	20,054	-0,020
	Min	20,000	20,002	-0,015	20,000	20,015	-0,028	20,000	20,022	-0,035	20,000	20,035	-0,048	20,000	20,041	-0,054
25	Max	25,021	25,015	0,019	25,021	25,028	0,006	25,021	25,035	-0,001	25,021	25,048	-0,014	25,021	25,061	-0,027
	Min	25,000	25,002	-0,015	25,000	25,015	-0,028	25,000	25,022	-0,035	25,000	25,035	-0,048	25,000	25,048	-0,061
30	Max	30,021	30,015	0,019	30,021	30,028	0,006	30,021	30,035	-0,001	30,021	30,048	-0,014	30,021	30,061	-0,027
	Min	30,000	30,002	-0,015	30,000	30,015	-0,028	30,000	30,022	-0,035	30,000	30,035	-0,048	30,000	30,048	-0,061
40	Max	40,025	40,018	0,023	40,025	40,033	0,008	40,025	40,042	-0,001	40,025	40,059	-0,018	40,025	40,076	-0,035
	Min	40,000	40,002	-0,018	40,000	40,017	-0,033	40,000	40,026	-0,042	40,000	40,043	-0,059	40,000	40,060	-0,076
50	Max	50,025	50,018	0,023	50,025	50,033	0,008	50,025	50,042	-0,001	50,025	50,059	-0,018	50,025	50,086	-0,045
	Min	50,000	50,002	-0,018	50,000	50,017	-0,033	50,000	50,026	-0,042	50,000	50,043	-0,059	50,000	50,070	-0,086
60	Max	60,030	60,021	0,028	60,030	60,039	0,010	60,030	60,051	-0,002	60,030	60,072	-0,023	60,030	60,106	-0,057
	Min	60,000	60,002	-0,021	60,000	60,020	-0,039	60,000	60,032	-0,051	60,000	60,053	-0,072	60,000	60,087	-0,106
80	Max	80,030	80,021	0,028	80,030	80,039	0,010	80,030	80,051	-0,002	80,030	80,078	-0,029	80,030	80,121	-0,072
	Min	80,000	80,002	-0,021	80,000	80,020	-0,039	80,000	80,032	-0,051	80,000	80,059	-0,078	80,000	80,102	-0,121
100	Max	100,035	100,025	0,032	100,035	100,045	0,012	100,035	100,059	-0,002	100,035	100,093	-0,036	100,035	100,146	-0,089
	Min	100,000	100,003	-0,025	100,000	100,023	-0,045	100,000	100,037	-0,059	100,000	100,071	-0,093	100,000	100,124	-0,146
120	Max	120,035	120,025	0,032	120,035	120,045	0,012	120,035	120,059	-0,002	120,035	120,010	-0,044	120,035	120,166	-0,109
	Min	120,000	120,003	-0,025	120,000	120,023	-0,045	120,000	120,037	-0,059	120,000	120,079	-0,101	120,000	120,144	-0,166
160	Max	160,040	160,028	0,037	160,040	160,052	0,013	160,040	160,068	-0,003	160,040	160,125	-0,060	160,040	160,215	-0,150
	Min	160,000	160,003	-0,028	160,000	160,027	-0,052	160,000	160,043	-0,068	160,000	160,100	-0,125	160,000	160,190	-0,215
200	Max	200,046	200,033	0,042	200,046	200,060	0,015	200,046	200,079	-0,004	200,046	200,151	-0,076	200,046	200,265	-0,190
	Min	200,000	200,004	-0,033	200,000	200,031	-0,060	200,000	200,050	-0,079	200,000	200,122	-0,151	200,000	200,236	-0,265
250	Max	250,046	250,033	0,042	250,046	250,060	0,015	250,046	250,079	-0,004	250,046	250,169	-0,094	250,046	250,313	-0,238
	Min	250,000	250,004	-0,033	250,000	250,031	-0,060	250,000	250,050	-0,079	250,000	250,140	-0,169	250,000	250,284	-0,313
300	Max	300,052	300,036	0,048	300,052	300,066	0,018	300,052	300,088	-0,004	300,052	300,202	-0,118	300,052	300,382	-0,298
	Min	300,000	300,004	-0,036	300,000	300,034	-0,066	300,000	300,056	-0,088	300,000	300,170	-0,202	300,000	300,350	-0,382
400	Max	400,057	400,040	0,053	400,057	400,073	0,020	400,057	400,098	-0,005	400,057	400,244	-0,151	400,057	400,471	-0,378
	Min	400,000	400,004	-0,040	400,000	400,037	-0,073	400,000	400,062	-0,098	400,000	400,208	-0,244	400,000	400,435	-0,471
500	Max	500,063	500,045	0,058	500,063	500,080	0,023	500,063	500,108	-0,005	500,063	500,292	-0,189	500,063	500,580	-0,477
	Min	500,000	500,005	-0,045	500,000	500,040	-0,080	500,000	500,068	-0,108	500,000	500,252	-0,292	500,000	500,540	-0,580

ANSI PREFERRED METRIC SHAFT BASIS CLEARANCE FITS

Basic Size (mm)		LOOSE RUNNING			FREE RUNNING			CLOSE RUNNING			SLIDING			LOCATIONAL CLEARANCE		
		Hole C11	Shaft h11	Fit	Hole D9	Shaft h9	Fit	Hole F8	Shaft h7	Fit	Hole G7	Shaft h6	Fit	Hole H7	Shaft h6	Fit
1	Max	1,120	1,000	0,180	1,045	1,000	0,070	1,020	1,000	0,030	1,012	1,000	0,018	1,010	1,000	0,016
	Min	1,060	0,940	0,060	1,020	0,975	0,020	1,006	0,990	0,006	1,002	0,994	0,002	1,000	0,994	0,000
1,2	Max	1,320	1,200	0,180	1,245	1,200	0,070	1,220	1,200	0,030	1,212	1,200	0,018	1,210	1,200	0,016
	Min	1,260	1,140	0,060	1,220	1,175	0,020	1,206	1,190	0,006	1,202	1,194	0,002	1,200	1,194	0,000
1,6	Max	1,720	1,600	0,180	1,645	1,600	0,070	1,620	1,600	0,030	1,612	1,600	0,018	1,610	1,600	0,016
	Min	1,660	1,540	0,060	1,620	1,575	0,020	1,606	1,590	0,006	1,602	1,594	0,002	1,600	1,594	0,000
2	Max	2,120	2,000	0,180	2,045	2,000	0,070	2,020	2,000	0,030	2,012	2,000	0,018	2,010	2,000	0,016
	Min	2,060	1,940	0,060	2,020	1,975	0,020	2,006	1,990	0,006	2,002	1,994	0,002	2,000	1,994	0,000
2,5	Max	2,620	2,500	0,180	2,545	2,500	0,070	2,520	2,500	0,030	2,512	2,500	0,018	2,510	2,500	0,016
	Min	2,560	2,440	0,060	2,520	2,475	0,020	2,506	2,490	0,006	2,502	2,494	0,002	2,500	2,494	0,000
3	Max	3,120	3,000	0,180	3,045	3,000	0,070	3,020	3,000	0,030	3,012	3,000	0,080	3,010	3,000	0,016
	Min	3,060	2,940	0,060	3,020	2,975	0,020	3,006	2,990	0,006	3,002	2,994	0,002	3,000	2,994	0,000
4	Max	4,145	4,000	0,220	4,060	4,000	0,090	4,028	4,000	0,040	4,016	4,000	0,024	4,012	4,000	0,020
	Min	4,070	3,925	0,070	4,030	3,970	0,030	4,010	3,988	0,010	4,004	3,992	0,004	4,000	3,992	0,000
5	Max	5,145	5,000	0,220	5,060	5,000	0,090	5,028	5,000	0,040	5,016	5,000	0,024	5,012	5,000	0,020
	Min	5,070	4,925	0,070	5,030	4,970	0,030	5,010	4,988	0,010	5,004	4,992	0,004	5,000	4,992	0,000
6	Max	6,145	6,000	0,220	6,060	6,000	0,090	6,028	6,000	0,040	6,016	6,000	0,024	6,012	6,000	0,020
	Min	6,070	5,925	0,070	6,030	5,970	0,030	6,010	5,988	0,010	6,004	5,992	0,004	6,000	5,992	0,000
8	Max	8,170	8,000	0,260	8,076	8,000	0,112	8,035	8,000	0,050	8,020	8,000	0,029	8,015	8,000	0,024
	Min	8,080	7,910	0,080	8,040	7,964	0,040	8,013	7,985	0,013	8,005	7,991	0,005	8,000	7,991	0,000
10	Max	10,170	10,000	0,260	10,076	10,000	0,112	10,035	10,000	0,050	10,020	10,000	0,029	10,015	10,000	0,024
	Min	10,080	9,910	0,080	10,040	9,964	0,040	10,013	9,985	0,013	10,005	9,991	0,005	10,000	9,991	0,000
12	Max	12,205	12,000	0,315	12,093	12,000	0,136	12,043	12,000	0,061	12,024	12,000	0,035	12,018	12,000	0,029
	Min	12,095	11,890	0,095	12,050	11,957	0,050	12,016	11,982	0,016	12,006	11,989	0,006	12,000	11,989	0,000
16	Max	16,205	16,000	0,315	16,093	16,000	0,136	16,043	16,000	0,061	16,024	16,000	0,035	16,018	16,000	0,029
	Min	16,095	15,890	0,095	16,050	15,957	0,050	16,016	15,982	0,016	16,006	15,989	0,006	16,000	15,989	0,000
20	Max	20,240	20,000	0,370	20,117	20,000	0,169	20,053	20,000	0,074	20,028	20,000	0,041	20,021	20,000	0,034
	Min	20,110	19,870	0,110	20,065	19,948	0,065	20,020	19,979	0,020	20,007	19,987	0,007	20,000	19,987	0,000
25	Max	25,240	25,000	0,370	25,117	25,000	0,169	25,053	25,000	0,074	25,028	25,000	0,041	25,021	25,000	0,034
	Min	25,110	24,870	0,110	25,065	24,948	0,065	25,020	24,979	0,020	25,007	24,987	0,007	25,000	24,987	0,000
30	Max	30,240	30,000	0,370	30,117	30,000	0,169	30,053	30,000	0,074	30,028	30,000	0,041	30,021	30,000	0,034
	Min	30,110	29,870	0,110	30,065	29,948	0,065	30,020	29,979	0,020	30,007	29,987	0,007	30,000	29,987	0,000
40	Max	40,280	40,000	0,440	40,142	40,000	0,204	40,064	40,000	0,089	40,034	40,000	0,050	40,025	40,000	0,041
	Min	40,120	39,840	0,120	40,080	39,938	0,080	40,025	39,975	0,025	40,009	39,984	0,009	40,000	39,984	0,000
50	Max	50,290	50,000	0,450	50,142	50,000	0,204	50,064	50,000	0,089	50,034	50,000	0,050	50,025	50,000	0,041
	Min	50,130	49,840	0,130	50,080	49,938	0,080	50,025	49,975	0,025	50,009	49,984	0,009	50,000	49,984	0,000
60	Max	60,330	60,000	0,520	60,174	60,000	0,248	60,076	60,000	0,106	60,040	60,000	0,059	60,030	60,000	0,049
	Min	60,140	59,810	0,140	60,100	59,926	0,100	60,030	59,970	0,030	60,010	59,981	0,010	60,000	59,981	0,000
80	Max	80,340	80,000	0,530	80,174	80,000	0,248	80,076	80,000	0,106	80,040	80,000	0,059	80,030	80,000	0,049
	Min	80,150	79,810	0,150	80,100	79,926	0,100	80,030	79,970	0,030	80,010	79,981	0,010	80,000	79,981	0,000
100	Max	100,390	100,000	0,610	100,207	100,000	0,294	100,090	100,000	0,125	100,047	100,000	0,069	100,035	100,000	0,057
	Min	100,170	99,780	0,170	100,120	99,913	0,120	100,036	99,965	0,036	100,012	99,978	0,012	100,000	99,978	0,000
120	Max	120,400	120,000	0,620	120,207	120,000	0,294	120,090	120,000	0,125	120,047	120,000	0,069	120,035	120,000	0,057
	Min	120,180	119,780	0,180	120,120	119,913	0,120	120,036	119,965	0,036	120,012	119,978	0,012	120,000	119,978	0,000
160	Max	160,460	160,000	0,710	160,245	160,000	0,345	160,106	160,000	0,146	160,054	160,000	0,079	160,040	160,000	0,065
	Min	160,210	159,750	0,210	160,145	159,900	0,145	160,043	159,960	0,043	160,014	159,975	0,014	160,000	159,975	0,000
200	Max	200,530	200,000	0,820	200,285	200,000	0,400	200,122	200,000	0,168	200,061	200,000	0,090	200,046	200,000	0,075
	Min	200,240	199,710	0,240	200,170	199,885	0,170	200,050	199,954	0,050	200,015	199,971	0,015	200,000	199,971	0,000
250	Max	250,570	250,000	0,860	250,285	250,000	0,400	250,122	250,000	0,168	250,061	250,000	0,090	250,046	250,000	0,075
	Min	250,280	249,710	0,280	250,170	249,885	0,170	250,050	249,954	0,050	250,015	249,971	0,015	250,000	249,971	0,000
300	Max	300,650	300,000	0,970	300,320	300,000	0,450	300,137	300,000	0,189	300,069	300,000	0,101	300,052	300,000	0,084
	Min	300,330	299,680	0,330	300,190	299,870	0,190	300,056	299,948	0,056	300,017	299,968	0,017	300,000	299,968	0,000
400	Max	400,760	400,000	1,120	400,350	400,000	0,490	400,151	400,000	0,208	400,075	400,000	0,111	400,057	400,000	0,093
	Min	400,400	399,640	0,400	400,210	399,860	0,210	400,062	399,943	0,062	400,018	399,964	0,018	400,000	399,964	0,000
500	Max	500,880	500,000	1,280	500,385	500,000	0,540	500,165	500,000	0,228	500,083	500,000	0,123	500,063	500,000	0,103
	Min	500,480	499,600	0,480	500,230	499,845	0,230	500,068	499,937	0,068	500,020	499,960	0,020	500,000	499,960	0,000

ANSI UNIFIED AND AMERICAN NATIONAL THREADS

Sizes	Basic Major Diameter	THREADS PER INCH										
		Series with graded pitches			Series with constant pitches							
		Coarse UNC	Fine UNF	Extra Fine UNEF	4UN	6UN	8UN	12UN	16UN	20UN	28UN	32UN
0	0,060	-	80	-	-	-	-	-	-	-	-	-
1	0,073	64	72	-	-	-	-	-	-	-	-	-
2	0,086	56	64	-	-	-	-	-	-	-	-	-
3	0,099	48	56	-	-	-	-	-	-	-	-	-
4	0,112	40	48	-	-	-	-	-	-	-	-	-
5	0,125	40	44	-	-	-	-	-	-	-	-	-
6	0,138	32	40	-	-	-	-	-	-	-	-	UNC
8	0,164	32	36	-	-	-	-	-	-	-	-	UNC
10	0,190	24	32	-	-	-	-	-	-	-	-	UNF
12	0,216	24	28	32	-	-	-	-	-	-	UNF	UNEF
1/4	0,250	20	28	32	-	-	-	-	-	UNC	UNF	UNEF
5/16	0,3125	18	24	32	-	-	-	-	-	20	28	UNEF
3/8	0,375	16	24	32	-	-	-	-	UNC	20	28	UNEF
7/16	0,4375	14	20	28	-	-	-	-	16	UNF	UNEF	32
1/2	0,500	13	20	28	-	-	-	-	16	UNF	UNEF	32
9/16	0,5625	12	18	24	-	-	-	UNC	16	20	28	32
5/8	0,625	11	18	24	-	-	-	12	16	20	28	32
11/16	0,6875	-	-	24	-	-	-	12	16	20	28	32
3/4	0,750	10	16	20	-	-	-	12	UNF	UNEF	28	32
13/16	0,8125	-	-	20	-	-	-	12	16	UNEF	28	32
7/8	0,875	9	14	20	-	-	-	12	16	UNEF	28	32
15/16	0,9375	-	-	20	-	-	-	12	16	UNEF	28	32
1	1,000	8	12	20	-	-	UNC	UNF	16	UNEF	28	32
1 - 1/16	1,063	-	-	18	-	-	8	12	16	20	28	-
1 - 1/8	1,125	7	12	18	-	-	8	UNF	16	20	28	-
1 - 3/16	1,188	-	-	18	-	-	8	12	16	20	28	-
1 - 1/4	1,250	7	12	18	-	-	8	UNF	16	20	28	-
1 - 5/16	1,313	-	-	18	-	-	8	12	16	20	28	-
1 - 3/8	1,375	6	12	18	-	UNC	8	UNF	16	20	28	-
1 - 7/16	1,438	-	-	18	-	6	8	12	16	20	28	-
1 - 1/2	1,500	6	12	18	-	UNC	8	UNF	16	20	28	-
1 - 9/16	1,563	-	-	18	-	6	8	12	16	20	-	-
1 - 5/8	1,625	-	-	18	-	6	8	12	16	20	-	-
1 - 11/16	1,688	-	-	18	-	6	8	12	16	20	-	-
1 - 3/4	1,750	5	-	-	-	6	8	12	16	20	-	-
1 - 13/16	1,8125	-	-	-	-	6	8	12	16	20	-	-
1 - 7/8	1,875	-	-	-	-	6	8	12	16	20	-	-
1 - 15/16	1,9375	-	-	-	-	6	8	12	16	20	-	-
2	2,000	4,5	-	-	-	6	8	12	16	20	-	-
2 - 1/8	2,125	-	-	-	-	6	8	12	16	20	-	-
2 - 1/4	2,225	4,5	-	-	-	6	8	12	16	20	-	-
2 - 3/8	2,375	-	-	-	-	6	8	12	16	20	-	-
2 - 1/2	2,500	4	-	-	UNC	6	8	12	16	20	-	-
2 - 5/8	2,625	-	-	-	4	6	8	12	16	20	-	-
2 - 3/4	2,750	4	-	-	UNC	6	8	12	16	20	-	-
2 - 7/8	2,875	-	-	-	4	6	8	12	16	20	-	-
3	3,000	4	-	-	UNC	6	8	12	16	20	-	-
3 - 1/8	3,125	-	-	-	4	6	8	12	16	-	-	-
3 - 1/4	3,250	4	-	-	UNC	6	8	12	16	-	-	-
3 - 3/8	3,375	-	-	-	4	6	8	12	16	-	-	-
3 - 1/2	3,500	4	-	-	UNC	6	8	12	16	-	-	-
3 - 5/8	3,625	-	-	-	4	6	8	12	16	-	-	-
3 - 3/4	3,750	4	-	-	UNC	6	8	12	16	-	-	-
3 - 7/8	3,875	-	-	-	4	6	8	12	16	-	-	-
4	4,000	4	-	-	UNC	6	8	12	16	-	-	-
4 - 1/8	4,125	-	-	-	4	6	8	12	16	-	-	-
4 - 1/4	4,250	-	-	-	4	6	8	12	16	-	-	-
4 - 3/8	4,375	-	-	-	4	6	8	12	16	-	-	-
4 - 1/2	4,500	-	-	-	4	6	8	12	16	-	-	-
4 - 5/8	4,625	-	-	-	4	6	8	12	16	-	-	-
4 - 3/4	4,750	-	-	-	4	6	8	12	16	-	-	-
4 - 7/8	4,875	-	-	-	4	6	8	12	16	-	-	-
5	5,000	-	-	-	4	6	8	12	16	-	-	-
5 - 1/8	5,125	-	-	-	4	6	8	12	16	-	-	-
5 - 1/4	5,250	-	-	-	4	6	8	12	16	-	-	-
5 - 3/8	5,375	-	-	-	4	6	8	12	16	-	-	-
5 - 1/2	5,500	-	-	-	4	6	8	12	16	-	-	-
5 - 5/8	5,625	-	-	-	4	6	8	12	16	-	-	-
5 - 3/4	5,750	-	-	-	4	6	8	12	16	-	-	-
5 - 7/8	5,875	-	-	-	4	6	8	12	16	-	-	-
6	6,000	-	-	-	4	6	8	12	16	-	-	-

ANSI METRIC THREADS

Major Diameter	Tap Drill	Pitch	
		Coarse	Fine
M1.6	1,25	0,35	-
M1.8	1,45	0,35	-
M2	1,60	0,4	-
M2.2	1,75	0,45	-
M2.5	2,05	0,45	-
M3	2,50	0,5	-
M3.5	2,90	0,6	-
M4	3,30	0,7	-
M4.5	3,75	0,75	-
M5	4,20	0,8	-
M6	5,00	1	-
M7	6,00	1	-
M8	6,80	1,25	1
M9	7,75	1,25	-
M10	8,50	1,5	1,25
M12	10,30	1,75	1,25
M14	12,00	2	1,5
M16	14,00	2	1,5
M18	15,50	2,5	1,5
M20	17,50	2,5	1,5
M22	19,50	2,5	1,5
M24	21,00	3	2
M27	24,00	3	2
M30	26,50	3,5	2
M33	29,50	3,5	2
M36	32,00	4	3
M39	35,00	4	3
M42	37,50	4,5	3
M45	40,50	4,5	3
M48	43,50	5	3
M56	50,50	5,5	4
M64	58,00	6	4
M72	66,00	6	4
M80	74,00	6	4
M90	84,00	6	4
M100	94,00	6	4